THE HANDBOOK ON THE ECONOMY OF WAR

The Handbook on the Political Economy of War

Edited by

Christopher J. Coyne

Mercatus Center and Department of Economics, George Mason University, USA

Rachel L. Mathers

Department of Accounting, Economics, and Finance, Delaware State University, USA

Edward Elgar
Cheltenham, UK • Northampton, MA, USA

Published by
Edward Elgar Publishing Limited
The Lypiatts
15 Lansdown Road
Cheltenham
Glos GL50 2JA
UK

Edward Elgar Publishing, Inc.
William Pratt House
9 Dewey Court
Northampton
Massachusetts 01060
USA

A catalogue record for this book
is available from the British Library

Library of Congress Control Number: 2010929030

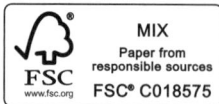

MIX
Paper from
responsible sources

FSC
www.fsc.org   FSC® C018575

ISBN 978 1 84844 248 1 (cased)

Typeset by Servis Filmsetting Ltd, Stockport, Cheshire
Printed and bound by MPG Books Group, UK

Contents

List of contributors   viii
Acknowledgements   xii

1   Introduction   1
    Christopher J. Coyne and Rachel L. Mathers

PART I   WHY WARS ARE WAGED

2   Theories and causes of war   13
    Jack S. Levy
3   The reasons for wars: an updated survey   34
    Matthew O. Jackson and Massimo Morelli
4   Can't we all just get along? Fractionalization, institutions and
    economic consequences   58
    Peter T. Leeson and Claudia R. Williamson
5   Psychological aspects of war   72
    Iain Hardie, Dominic Johnson and Dominic Tierney

PART II   WAYS OF WAGING WAR

6   What is guerrilla warfare?   95
    Anthony James Joes
7   The economics of torture   109
    Pavel Yakovlev
8   Terrorism in rational choice perspective   126
    William F. Shughart II
9   The political economy of conscription   154
    Panu Poutvaara and Andreas Wagener

PART III   CIVIL WAR AND REVOLUTION

10   Economic perspectives on civil wars   177
    Nathan Fiala and Stergios Skaperdas
11   Political economy of Third World revolutions   195
    Misagh Parsa

PART IV   THE ARMS TRADE

12   The arms trade   217
     David Kinsella
13   Arms trade offsets: what do we know?   243
     Jurgen Brauer and John Paul Dunne

PART V   POLITICAL AND ECONOMIC SYSTEMS

14   The capitalist peace   269
     Erich Weede
15   On the democratic peace   281
     Sebastian Rosato
16   International conflict and leadership tenure   315
     Randall J. Blimes
17   A public choice perspective on defense and alliance policy   335
     Bernhard Klingen
18   International regimes and war   356
     James Ashley Morrison and Avery F. White

PART VI   POST-CONFLICT RECONSTRUCTION AND
          NATION BUILDING

19   Fixing failed states: a dissenting view   379
     Justin Logan and Christopher Preble
20   Choice and consequence in strategies of transitional justice   397
     Geoff Dancy
21   Dynamics of military occupation   432
     Michael Hechter and Oriol Vidal-Aparicio
22   Three's company? Towards an understanding of third-party
     intervention effectiveness   453
     David Carment and Martin Fischer
23   Credible commitment in post-conflict recovery   474
     Thomas Edward Flores and Irfan Nooruddin
24   Conflict, credibility and asset prices   498
     Gregory M. Dempster and Justin P. Isaacs

PART VII   ALTERNATIVES TO WAR

25   Disaggregated trade flows and international conflict   515
     Han Dorussen and Hugh Ward

26 Sanctions as alternatives to war   534
     David Cortright and George A. Lopez
27 International negotiation and conflict prevention   571
     I. William Zartman
28 The economics of peacekeeping   589
     Lloyd J. Dumas

Index   607

Contributors

Editors

Christopher J. Coyne is F.A. Harper Professor of Economics at the Mercatus Center, and a member of the Department of Economics at George Mason University, Fairfax, VA, USA.

Rachel L. Mathers is Assistant Professor of Economics in the Department of Accounting, Economics, and Finance at Delaware State University, Dover, DE, USA.

Contributors

Randall J. Blimes is Assistant Professor of Political Science at Brigham Young University–Hawaii, Laie, HI, USA.

Jurgen Brauer is Professor of Economics at James M. Hull College of Business, Augusta State University, Augusta, GA, USA.

David Carment is Professor of International Affairs at Carleton University, Ottawa, ON, Canada.

David Cortright is Director of Policy Studies at the Kroc Institute for International Peace Studies at the University of Notre Dame Notre Dame, IN, USA.

Geoff Dancy is a Ph.D. candidate in political science at the University of Minnesota, Minneapolis, MN, USA.

Gregory M. Dempster is Elliott Associate Professor of Economics at Hampden-Sydney College, Hampden-Sydney, VA, USA.

Han Dorussen is professor of Government, University of Essex, Colchester, UK.

Lloyd J. Dumas is Professor of Political Economy, Economics and Public Policy at the University of Texas at Dallas, Richardson, TX, USA.

John Paul Dunne is Professor of Economics at the University of the West of England, Bristol, UK.

Nathan Fiala is a consultant for the World Bank Human Development Unit, Washington DC, USA.

Martin Fischer is a doctoral candidate at the Norman Paterson School of International Affairs at Carleton University, Ottawa, ON, Canada.

Thomas Edward Flores is an assistant professor at the Institute for Conflict Analysis and Resolution at George Mason University, Arlington, VA, USA.

Iain Hardie is Lecturer in International Relations at the University of Edinburgh, Edinburgh, UK.

Michael Hechter is Foundation Professor of Global Studies at Arizona State University, Tempe, AZ, USA.

Justin P. Isaacs is Associate Professor of Economics and Director of the BB&T Program on Capitalism at Hampden-Sydney College, Hampden-Sydney, VA, USA.

Matthew O. Jackson is William D. Eberle Professor of Economics at Stanford University, Stanford, CA, USA, an external faculty member of the Santa Fe institute, Santa Fe, NM, USA, and a fellow at the Canadian Institute for Advanced Research, Toronto, ON, Canada.

Anthony James Joes is Professor of Political Science at Saint Joseph's University, Philadelphia, PA, USA.

Dominic Johnson is Reader in Politics and International Relations at the University of Edinburgh, Edinburgh, UK.

David Kinsella is Professor of Political Science and International Studies at the Mark O. Hatfield School of Government at Portland State University, Portland, OR, USA.

Bernhard Klingen is a research associate at the Department of Economics, University of Mannheim, Mannheim, Germany.

Peter T. Leeson is BB&T Professor for the Study of Capitalism at George Mason University, Fairfax, VA, USA.

Jack S. Levy is Board of Governors' Professor of Political Science at Rutgers University, New Brunswick, NJ, USA.

Justin Logan is Associate Director of Foreign Policy Studies at the Cato Institute, Washington DC, USA.

George A. Lopez is the Rev. Theodore M. Hesburgh, C.S.C., Chair in Peace Studies at the Kroc Institute for International Peace Studies at the University of Notre Dame, Notre Dame, IN, USA.

Massimo Morelli is Professor of Economics and Political Science at Columbia University, New York, NY, USA, and Professor of Economics at the European University Institute, Florence, Italy.

James Ashley Morrison is Assistant Professor of Political Science at Middlebury College, Middlebury, VT, USA.

Irfan Nooruddin is an associate professor of political science at The Ohio State University, Columbus, OH, USA.

Misagh Parsa is Professor of Sociology at Dartmouth College, Hanover, NH, USA.

Panu Poutvaara is Professor of Economics at the University of Munich and Department Head at the Ifo Institute for Economic Research, Munich, Germany.

Christopher Preble is Director of Foreign Policy Studies at the Cato Institute, Washington DC, USA.

Sebastian Rosato is Assistant Professor of Political Science at the University of Notre Dame, Notre Dame, IN, USA.

William F. Shughart II is the Frederick A. P. Barnard Distinguished Professor of Economics at the University of Mississippi, University, MS, USA.

Stergios Skaperdas is Professor of Economics at the University of California, Irvine, CA, USA.

Dominic Tierney is Assistant Professor of Political Science at Swarthmore College, Swarthmore, PA, USA.

Oriol Vidal-Aparicio is a doctoral student at the School of Politics and Global Studies of Arizona State University, Tempe, AZ, USA.

Andreas Wagener is Professor of Economics in the Department of Economics and Management at the University of Hannover, Germany.

Hugh Ward is a professor in the Department of Government, University of Essex, Colchester, UK.

Erich Weede taught sociology at the University of Bonn, Bonn, Germany, until his retirement in fall 2004.

Avery F. White is a student at Middlebury College, Middlebury, VT, USA.

Claudia R. Williamson is a post-doctoral fellow at the Development Research Institute at New York University, New York, NY, USA.

Pavel Yakovlev is Assistant Professor of Economics at Duquesne University, Pittsburgh, PA, USA.

I. William Zartman is Professor Emeritus at The School of Advanced International Studies, The Johns Hopkins University, Washington DC, USA.

Acknowledgements

This project is several years in the making and would not be possible without the generous support of several individuals and organizations. We would like to jointly thank the West Virginia University College of Business and Economics Kendrick Fund for Free Market Research and the Charles G. Koch Charitable Foundation for financial support. Christopher Coyne acknowledges the support of the Social Philosophy and Policy Center at Bowling Green State University, where he was a Visiting Scholar during the summer of 2010 when the final editing of the *Handbook* was completed.

Christopher Coyne and Rachel Mathers

1 Introduction
Christopher J. Coyne and Rachel L. Mathers

1.1 INTRODUCTION

Political economy is an interdisciplinary approach that draws on concepts from economics, law, political science and sociology to understand how economic, legal, political and social systems influence each other and outcomes. In the broadest sense, the concept of war refers to organized violence between distinct social entities. The entities involved in war may refer to nation-states (inter-state war), distinct social groups within a given state (civil war or revolution) or third parties representing states or groups who choose not to engage in war directly (proxy war). *The Handbook on the Political Economy of War* applies the political economy approach to explore the various aspects of war. Our focus is broad and considers such issues as the causes of war, revolutions, post-war occupation and ways of avoiding war.

By defining political economy and war in the broadest sense, the *Handbook* brings together a broad range of scholars with different backgrounds and expertise to address a wide range of topics. Scholars included in the *Handbook* come from a variety of disciplines, including economics, political science, sociology and policy studies, to name a few. The topics addressed by these scholars include, but are not limited to, an analysis of why wars begin, how wars are waged, what happens after war has ceased, and various alternatives to war, among other topics.

In the chapters that follow, some of the leading researchers working on issues related to war and conflict have contributed an overview of the fundamental concepts in their area of expertise, both providing a useful reference for those unfamiliar with these topics and a vision of future research endeavors for those already working in these areas. The chapters included in the *Handbook* are intended to serve as a guide to important research questions in the political economy of war. The chapters are written in an accessible manner, with the intent of providing the core elements of the political economy of war such that scholars in a variety of fields will find this compendium useful. Likewise, given its accessibility, practitioners and policymakers should also find the *Handbook* useful in contributing to a greater understanding of the political economy of war. The chapters communicate both past and current research in several important areas of war and conflict. Most contributors also discuss future areas of research.

This introduction is intended to provide a brief background on the political economy of war, followed by a discussion of the current importance of this area of research. It concludes with an overview of the organization of the chapters in this *Handbook*, which represent some of the main subfields of the study of the political economy of war.

1.2   BACKGROUND ON THE POLITICAL ECONOMY OF WAR

Interest in the political economy of war is as old as the economics discipline itself, as evidenced by Adam Smith's ([1776] 1977) writings in *An Inquiry into the Nature and Causes of the Wealth of Nations,* where he discusses some aspects of war. For example, in Book V, Smith ([1776] 1977, p. 455–6) discusses how war leads to increases in the public debt, as those in government seek to cover the expenses of war without increasing taxes for fear of repercussion by citizens:

> The ordinary expence of the greater part of modern governments in time of peace being equal or nearly equal to their ordinary revenue, when war comes they are both unwilling and unable to increase their revenue in proportion to the increase of their expence. They are unwilling for fear of offending the people, who, by so great and so sudden an increase of taxes, would soon be disgusted with the war; and they are unable from not well knowing what taxes would be sufficient to produce the revenue wanted. The facility of borrowing delivers them from the embarrassment which this fear and inability would otherwise occasion. By means of borrowing they are enabled, with a very moderate increase of taxes, to raise, from year to year, money sufficient for carrying on the war, and by the practice of perpetually funding they are enabled, with the smallest possible increase of taxes, to raise annually the largest possible sum of money.

According to Smith, increases in public debt could have long-term negative consequences on the financial health of the country carrying out the war. At the extreme, excessive debt could result in bankruptcy and economic collapse. Although Smith did not offer a complete theory of the political economy of war, he clearly recognized the importance of the political and economic aspects of the use of military.

The analysis of war in modern political economy can be traced back to the 1960s. Several prominent works during this period include Schelling's (1960) use of game theory to analyse conflict, Peck and Scherer's (1962) study of defense contract competition and the nonmarket accoutrement of procuring weapons in *The Weapons Acquisition Process*, and Olson and Zeckhauser's (1966) study of military alliances in a public goods framework (see Hartley and Sandler 1995). Another notable development in the literature of the 1960s and 1970s is the study of agrarian revolutions and the role of inequality grievances in sparking conflict (see Blattman and Miguel 2010). From these pieces, emerged a strand of literature including a combination of game theory, analytic narratives and statistical techniques to analyse the various aspects of war.

Theoretical contributions to the analysis of war have been numerous. During the 1980s, models of armed conflict, based on Haavelmo's (1954) contest model, offered new insight into the theoretical explanations for war and the role of resource competition in this framework (see Hirshleifer 1988, 1989). For example, Garfinkel (1990) and Skaperdas (1992) use this framework to explain the probability of success in armed conflict, based on the allocation of resources to production and appropriation. Further, Jean and Rufin's (1996) *Economie des Guerres Civiles* provides an analysis of the economic factors involved in war. The importance of the interaction between political and economic factors in determining war outcomes has been widely acknowledged; for example, Berdal and Keen's (1997) work derived policy implications from their analysis of economic and political agendas. These models are unique in their assumptions, as property rights and contracts cannot be guaranteed, which further exhibits the complexities of modeling war using the standard economic tools.

Though the contest models of armed conflict provided a theory of success or failure, war was the equilibrium and new theoretical insights were necessary to explain why compromise either works or fails to prevent or cease armed conflict. Among the work in this area are Fearon's (1995) explanation of the potential shortcomings of bargaining efforts, Anderson's (1999) examination of the effects of aid on markets and war and Acemoglu and Robinson's (2001, 2006) bargaining models of elites and the poor. Among Fearon's (1995) list of bargaining's shortcomings, there has been continued theoretical work to shed light on the cases in which war is rational. In particular, Powell (2002) analyses the role of asymmetric information, where one side either overestimates its own strength or underestimates the opposing side. Garfinkel and Skaperdas (2000), Powell (2006) and McBride and Skaperdas (2007) analyse the role of commitment problems in bargaining breakdowns, where the future balance of power can lead a group to war in the present.

In addition to contest models and theoretical explanations for rational warfare, micro-level theories focusing on individual behavior have contributed to the understanding of the formation and function of groups embroiled in conflict. For example, some work in this area has focused on the efficiency gains of group action versus individual action, the size and property rights of groups, and the management of inter- and intra-group conflict (Blattman and Miguel 2010). The role of ethnicity in war has also been a topic of analysis, as studied by Horowitz (1985) and Easterly and Levine (1997). Post-conflict reconstruction is a continuing debate in the literature, as evidenced by the large number of articles and books written on the subject (see Carbonnier 1998; Duffield 1998; Coyne 2008).

Though the theoretical work in the political economy of war began more than half a century ago, the empirical tests of these theories are relatively new, having emerged in the last 10 to 15 years. Most empirical studies on the political economy of war are cross-country analyses, and some of the most notable of these include Collier and Hoeffler's (1998, 2004) claim that economic incentives, not grievances, spur conflict and Fearon and Laitin's (2003) logit specification of cross-country regressions for the onset of war. While the application of regression analysis to the political economy of war yielded additional insight into the key theoretical claims in the literature, issues of data limitations and endogeneity led to concerns regarding the reliability of these results. To address these issues, recent research efforts have focused on developing improved datasets and strategies to determine causality with more accuracy. For example, the use of exogenous variables as instruments, the construction of new, more descriptive, datasets, regression analysis with clearer ties to theory and the use of case studies to provide a more in-depth analysis of war in conjunction with empirical regressions are several advances witnessed in the literature (Blattman and Miguel 2010). Stewart and Fitzgerald's (2000) analysis of the costs of war, both economic and social, is one example of the use of both case studies and standard statistical techniques to add to our understanding of the political economy of war.

The importance of both theoretical and empirical studies on the political economy of war is evidenced by the number of books and articles published on the subject. Some of the main journals featuring articles on the political economy of war are *Conflict Management and Peace Science*, the *International Journal of Conflict and Violence*, *International Organization*, the *Journal of Peace Research*, the *Journal of Conflict Resolution*, the *Journal of International Affairs* and *Public Choice*, among many others. Most indicative of the impact of studies on the political economy of war is the presence of such articles in some of the leading general-interest journals across a variety of disciplines, such as the *American Economic Review*, the *American Journal of Political Science*, the *American Journal of Sociology*, the *American Political Science Review*, the *Journal of Political Economy* and the *Quarterly Journal of Economics*.

Though the study of the political economy of war has advanced greatly since its inception, there still remain many questions to be answered and areas where methodological improvements are necessary. As mentioned earlier, there have been substantial improvements in measurement and regression analysis over the past several decades. Further investigation into potential measurement errors or specification errors is important, as well as ensuring that sound theory underlies empirical attempts to explain the nuances of war. Also relevant is the question of the applicability of one result to all cases; given the intricacies of each conflict, these studies may not be appropriate for general applicability in future conflict situations. Future research into the short-term and lasting effects of war leaves room for many inquiries, especially in the areas of institutional analysis at both the formal and informal levels. Cultural factors have only recently been introduced into institutional studies and economic growth studies, thus there remains fertile ground for new research. Cultural inputs in the form of belief systems, norms, ideology and identity clearly play a role in the prevention or onset of war, and therefore require deeper study.

1.3 IMPORTANCE OF THE POLITICAL ECONOMY OF WAR

The study of the political economy of war will continue to be of great importance in the foreseeable future for several reasons. Though warfare has morphed in form throughout history, it is as relevant a problem now as it was in earlier times and, some would argue, perhaps more so. Large sums of funding – in the form of aid and military efforts – and the potential for extensive loss of human lives are at stake, placing the analysis of the various aspects of warfare – the causes of war, war prevention, alternatives to war, reconstruction and so forth – at center stage and of critical import to policy-makers and individual citizens, whose lives and livelihoods are at risk. With the modern threats of terrorism, ongoing civil warfare and post-conflict reconstruction efforts as daily reminders of the costs of war, the necessity for research in this area is evident. Specifically, we identify three key reasons why the political economy of war will continue to be of importance.

First, the political economy of war is an essential element of the study of economic development. Internal violence is a central cause of continued economic stagnation in many of the world's poorest countries. As Collier (2007, p. 18) notes, many of these countries "are stuck in a pattern of violent internal challenges to government," which contributes to continued poverty. Understanding the causes of this conflict trap and potential solutions is a central policy issue. Given this, social scientists are paying increasing attention to how war and conflict impact economic development for the worse. The causality of the empirical relationship between these two variables is still debated, though there is consensus that the two are intertwined. There is merit in developing clearer models of how conflict and economic development are interrelated, an effort that will require a deep appreciation of the various aspects of the political economy of war discussed in this volume. Understanding how conflict can be avoided or resolved is a critical aspect of understanding the broader process of economic development.

Second, the study of the political economy of war is critical given ongoing concerns over weak and failed states. These states have the potential to create significant decreases in the well-being of their own citizens and those of other nations due to their dysfunction in providing basic services to their citizens, their detrimental policy decisions and their predatory actions. Continued conflict limits the emergence of sustainable economic, legal, social and political institutions which can overcome many of the problems created by weak and failed states. Research in the area of the political economy of war is critical to understanding the various dynamics of weak and failed states, as well as feasible policies toward these states.

Third, understanding the political economy of war is vital to gauging the feasibility of reconstruction efforts in post-conflict societies. To determine which strategies have the greatest potential for success, one must understand the incentives and constraints existing in post-conflict situations. To this end, the study of the political economy of war offers the wisdom of historical analyses of past efforts and educated hypotheses applicable to current or future reconstruction efforts based on the incentives and constraints at play. Of particular importance is the thorough analysis of the various institutions involved in reconstruction including both formal institutions – for example, written laws and regulations – and informal institutions – for example, norms and beliefs. Comprehending the complex interplay between economic, legal, political and social institutions is at the heart of political economy and central for understanding the viability of current and future reconstruction efforts.

These three reasons for the continued importance of the political economy of war may explain why there has been growing attention given to this topic by scholars from across the social sciences. In spite of continued research in these areas, much work remains in understanding the various aspects of the political economy of war. It is our hope that this volume will serve as a bridge between existing research and future research in this area.

1.4   ORGANIZATION OF THE BOOK

The Handbook on the Political Economy of War is organized into seven broad parts based on the prominence of these topics in the political economy of war literature. Each part consists of multiple chapters exploring key concepts and issues relevant to the broader category. As mentioned previously, this *Handbook* is intended as a compendium and reference for the study of the political economy of war, providing an exploration into the major topics in the related literature. As such, the *Handbook* chapters include both theoretical and empirical aspects, both of which lend expertise to an examination of relevant policy implications and avenues for future research in the field.

The *Handbook* begins with four chapters detailing various aspects of the rationale for waging war, including a variety of theories explicating the causal mechanisms involved in spurring or evading conflict. The first two chapters provide comprehensive surveys of the causes and reasons of war. The remaining chapters explore specific causal mechanisms in greater detail including ethnic fractionalization and psychological contributors to war. This analysis is followed by four chapters exploring the ways of waging war, covering a range of tactics including guerilla warfare, torture, terrorism and conscription. Recognized scholars in these areas have been tasked with providing a thorough analysis of each of these methods for waging war.

The third part of the *Handbook* focuses on civil war and revolution. It includes two chapters exploring the economics of civil wars and the political economy of revolutions in developing countries. The contributors write from a variety of different academic backgrounds, facilitating the cross-discipline exchange of knowledge and providing a full and in-depth spectrum of analysis of this topic. Continuing in this vein, the fourth part includes two additional chapters with contributions specifically examining the arms trade.

The next part (Part V) consists of five chapters concerning the interrelation between economic and political systems and war and peace. The first two chapters explore the capitalist peace thesis and the democratic peace thesis, respectively. The authors provide a detailed survey of the literature on each topic and discuss the empirical support for and against each thesis. This part also includes chapters explaining international regimes and war, defense and alliance policy and an analysis of how leadership tenure influences international conflicts.

A reference for the political economy of war would be incomplete without a foray into post-conflict reconstruction, the focus of the six chapters included in the sixth part of the *Handbook*. With contributions from a host of different perspectives and disciplines, this part details many of the complications associated with transition and reconstruction after war, such as transitional justice, military occupation and third-party intervention. Two chapters focus on the issue of credible commitment in reconstruction. One chapter explores the importance of credibility for reform and provides potential solutions to the problem of credible commitment in the context of reconstruction. Another chapter explains how asset values can be used as indicators of credibility.

Finally, Part VII concludes the *Handbook* with four chapters offering analysis of some alternatives to war, including sanctions, negotiations and other strategies of peacekeeping. We view the contributions in this part as essential to a comprehensive understanding of the political economy of war because any process or outcome cannot be fully understood without also appreciating alternative courses of action. Though this part concludes the *Handbook*, it by no means closes the book on research in this field of study, as there are numerous avenues for future research on the political economy of war, both theoretical and empirical.

REFERENCES

Acemoglu, D. and J. Robinson (2001), "A theory of political transitions", *The American Economic Review*, **91** (4), 938–63.

Acemoglu, D. and J. Robinson (2006), *Economic Origins of Democracy and Dictatorship*, Cambridge, MA: Cambridge University Press.

Anderson, M.B. (1999), *Do No Harm: How Aid Can Support Peace – or War*, Boulder, CO: Lynne Rienner.

Berdal, M. and D. Keen (1997), "Violence and economic agendas in civil wars: some policy implications", *Millennium: Journal of International Studies*, **26** (3), 795–818.

Blattman, C. and E. Miguel (2010), "Civil war," *Journal of Economic Literature*, **48** (1), 3–57.

Carbonnier, G. (1998), "Conflict, postwar rebuilding, and the economy: a critical review of the literature," UNRISD and War-Torn Societies Project, Geneva, Occasional Paper No.2.

Collier, P. (2007), The *Bottom Billion: Why the Poorest Countries are Failing and What Can Be Done About It*, New York, NY: Oxford University Press.

Collier, P. and A. Hoeffler (1998), "On economic causes of civil war", *Oxford Economic Papers*, **50** (4), 563–73.

Collier, P. and A. Hoeffler (2004), "Greed and grievance in civil war", *Oxford Economic Papers*, **56** (4), 563–95.

Coyne, C.J. (2008), *After War: The Political Economy of Exporting Democracy*, Stanford, CA: Stanford University Press.

Duffield, M. (1998), "Post-Modern Conflict: Warlords, Post-adjustment States and Private Protection", *Civil Wars*, **1** (1), 66–102.

Easterly, B. and R. Levine (1997), "Africa's growth tragedy: policies and ethnic divisions", *Quarterly Journal of Economics*, **112** (4), 1203–50.

Fearon, J. (1995), "Rationalist explanations for war", *International Organization*, **49** (3), 379–414.

Fearon, J. and D. Laitin (2003), "Ethnicity, insurgency and civil war", *American Political Science Review*, **97** (1), 75–90.

Garfinkel, M.R. (1990), "Arming as a strategic investment in a cooperative equilibrium", *American Economic Review*, **80** (1), 50–68.

Garfinkel, M.R. and S. Skaperdas (2000), "Conflict without misperceptions or incomplete information: how the future matters", *Journal of Conflict Resolution*, **44** (6), 793–807.

Haavelmo, T. (1954), *A Study in the Theory of Economic Evolution*, Amsterdam: North Holland.

Hartley, K. and T. Sandler (1995), "Introduction", in K. Hartley and T. Sandler (eds), *Handbook of Defense Economics*, Vol. 1, Amsterdam: Elsevier, pp. 1–12.

Hirshleifer, J. (1988), "The analytics of continuing conflict", *Synthese*, **76** (2), 201–233.

Hirshleifer, J. (1989), "Conflict and rent-seeking functions: ratio versus difference models of relative success", *Public Choice*, **63** (2), 101–112.

Horowitz, D.L. (1985), *Ethnic Groups in Conflict*, Berkeley, CA: University of California Press.

Jean, F. and J.-C. Rufin (eds) (1996), *Economie des Guerres Civiles*, Paris: Hachette.

McBride, M. and S. Skaperdas (2007), "Explaining conflict in low-income countries: incomplete contracting in the shadow of the future," in K.A. Konrad and M. Gradstein (eds), *Institutions and Norms in Economic Development*, Cambridge, MA: MIT Press, pp. 141–62.

Olson, M. and R. Zeckhauser (1966), "An economic theory of alliances", *Review of Economics and Statistics*, **48** (3), 266–79.

Peck, M.J. and F.M. Scherer (1962), *The Weapons Acquisition Process*, Cambridge, MA: Harvard University Press.

Powell, R. (2002), "Bargaining theory and international conflict", *Annual Review of Political Science*, **5** (1), 1–30.

Powell, R. (2006), "War as a commitment problem", *International Organization*, **60** (1), 169–203.

Schelling, T.C. (1960), *The Strategy of Conflict*, Cambridge, MA: Harvard University Press.

Skaperdas, S. (1992), "Cooperation, conflict, and power in the absence of property rights", *American Economic Review*, **82** (4), 720–39.

Smith, A. ([1776] 1977), *An Inquiry into the Nature and Causes of the Wealth of Nations*, Edwin M. Cannan (ed.), Chicago, IL: University Of Chicago Press.

Stewart, F. and V. Fitzgerald (eds) (2000), *War and Underdevelopment: The Economic and Social Consequences of Conflict*, Oxford, UK: Oxford University Press.

PART I

WHY WARS ARE WAGED

2 Theories and causes of war
Jack S. Levy

2.1 INTRODUCTION

The question of what causes war has engaged scholars, journalists, public intellectuals and others for thousands of years. We have a variety of theories but no consensus as to what the causes of war are or how best to study them. There are enormous differences across different disciplines – philosophy, theology, literature, history, economics, political science, anthropology, sociology, psychology, mathematics, biology and primatology, to name a few – but substantial differences within disciplines as well, driven by different ontological and epistemological perspectives, theoretical preconceptions and methodological preferences.[1]

Both the complexity of war and of the study of war complicates the task of writing a relatively short essay on the causes of war. I use this essay to place the chapters in this volume on the political economy of war and peace in the broader context of some of the leading theories in political science on the causes of war. Although it is clear that a complete understanding of the causes of war needs to draw on work in many disciplines, it is also clear that political science has a special place in the study of war. Leading scholars in several disciplines define war as large-scale organized violence between political organizations (Malinowski 1941; Vasquez 2009). Many also accept Clausewitz' ([1832] 1976) argument that war is fundamentally political, a "continuation of politics by other means." If war is an instrument of policy to advance the interests of a political organization, then an explanation of war requires an understanding of why the authorized decision-makers of political organizations choose to resort to military force rather than adopt another strategy for advancing their interests and resolving differences with their adversaries. It also requires an understanding of how the perceptions and behavior of adversarial political units interact to result in war. That is, war involves both decision-making by a political organization and strategic interaction between adversarial political organizations.

The primary focus of this essay is on the causes of interstate war, which has dominated the attention of most scholarship on war for hundreds of years. Although the frequency of interstate war, and particularly of great power war, has declined over time (Levy 1983), and although civil wars have increased in frequency in the last half century (Hewitt, Wilkenfeld and Gurr 2010) and are likely to be the most frequent form of warfare for years to come, interstate war remains the most consequential form of warfare, both in terms of its human and economic destructiveness and its political impact on the international system.

I organize this review of the causes of war around a modified version of the "levels of analysis" framework, which has been quite influential in the study of international relations and foreign policy. After briefly summarizing the framework I turn to some conceptual issues. I then summarize some of the leading theories of war, classifying them in terms of the level of their primary causal variables.[2]

2.2   PRELIMINARY CONCEPTUAL ISSUES

Waltz (1959) suggested three "images" of war – the individual, the nation-state and the international system – and used these to categorize the causes of war. Singer (1961) referred to these as "levels of analysis." The individual level focuses primarily on human nature and on individual political leaders and their belief systems, psychological processes, emotional states and personalities. The nation-state (or national) level includes factors such as the type of political system (authoritarian or democratic, and variations of each), the structure of the economy, the nature of the policymaking process, the role of public opinion and interest groups, ethnicity and nationalism, and political culture and ideology. The system level includes the anarchic structure of the international system, the distribution of military and economic power among the leading states in the system, patterns of military alliances and international trade, and other factors that constitute the external environment common to all states.

I modify this standard typology slightly by introducing a separate decision-making level (Jervis 1976, Chapter 1), which can be further decomposed into distinct individual and organizational levels. The former incorporates Waltz' individual-level variables and the latter incorporates state-level factors like bureaucratic politics and organizational processes. At the system level, one could also distinguish between the global system, regional systems and the international environment of a particular state. The global system is the same for all states, but the regional system and particular external environment is not. I also add a distinct "dyadic" or "interactional" level, which reflects the influence of variables characterizing the relationship between two particular adversaries, including their history, their bargaining relationship and other factors.

Although the levels-of-analysis framework is commonly used to cat-egorize the causal variables contributing to war (or to other foreign policy outcomes), it is sometimes used in a different way, to refer to the level of the dependent variable rather to the level of the independent variable.[3] In this usage, we might want to explain the policy preferences of an indi-vidual decision-maker or of an organization, the foreign policy behavior of a state, or patterns of interactions within a pair of states or within the international system as a whole. That is, we might want to explain pref-erences, behavior or outcomes at the individual, organizational, state, dyadic or system level.

These distinctions among different levels of the dependent variable are important, because war-related patterns validated at one level may not necessarily hold for other levels. A more conciliatory foreign policy at the nation-state level does not necessarily result in a lower probability of war at the dyadic level, as Britain and France discovered in the aftermath of the 1938 Munich Conference. Similarly, a strong preponderance of power at the dyadic level may contribute to peace because the strong do not need to fight and the weak are unable to fight (Tammen et al. 2000), but a strong preponderance of power at the system level (at least in con-tinental systems like Europe), where alliances are relevant, is likely to lead to a counterbalancing coalition and war, as balance of power theory suggests. To take a different example, the evidence is overwhelming that democratic states rarely if ever go to war with each other (a dyadic-level outcome), but most research suggests that democracies are just as warlike as are non-democracies in terms of how frequently they fight (Russett and Oneal 2001). In addition, since democratic–democratic dyads are the most peaceful but democratic–authoritarian dyads are the most warlike, the conversion of a state from an autocracy to a democracy will increase the probability of war in a system of few democracies but decrease the proba-bility of war in a system of many democracies. Actions that might increase the probability of war at one "level" might not increase the probability of war at another level.

We can use causal variables at one level to explain outcomes at another level, but we have to be careful to specify the precise theoretical connec-tions between variables at different levels, since there is no *logical* connec-tion between relationships at different levels. An individual level theory focusing on a leader's beliefs, personality and policy preferences is logi-cally insufficient to explain a state's decision to use military force, which is a state-level outcome. We would need to explain how the leader's prefer-ences, along with the preferences of other decision-makers, are translated into a foreign policy decision for the state. Similarly, a national-level explanation of a state's decision to use force does not constitute a logically complete explanation for war defined as violence between political organizations. A monadic-level theory cannot explain a dyadic-level outcome. Dyadic and perhaps systemic variables must be included. This does not necessarily mean that dyadic- and system-level variables have a greater causal influence on war than do individual or domestic variables, only that the former cannot be logically excluded from the analysis. Similarly, state-level variables are necessary to explain foreign policy decisions, but that does not necessarily mean they carry greater causal weight than individual-level variables.[4]

2.3   SYSTEM-LEVEL THEORIES

The study of the causes of war in political science has traditionally been dominated by "realist" theories, a family of theories that assume that sovereign states (or other territorially defined groups) act rationally to advance their security, power and wealth in an anarchic international system defined by the absence of a legitimate authority to regulate disputes and enforce agreements.[5] Anarchy, in conjunction with uncertainties about the intentions of the adversary, creates a system of insecurity and competition that leads political leaders to focus on short-term security needs, worst-case outcomes and on their relative position in the system. They build up their military strength and use coercive threats to influence the adversary, maintain their reputations and advance their interests. Realists argue that the primary determinant of international outcomes is the distribution of power at the dyadic or systemic levels. As Thucydides' (1996, p. 352) argued in the Melian Dialogue, "the strong do what they can and the weak suffer what they must."

Most realists recognize that war can arise through both deliberate and inadvertent processes, though they disagree about which of these processes occurs most often. A state that perceives a direct conflict of interest with an adversary and is dissatisfied with the status quo may conclude that its interests would be best served by resorting to military force. Alternatively, two states that are each content with the status quo and more interested in maintaining their current position than in extending their influence may still end up in war as the result of a conflict spiral driven by fear and uncertainty. Uncertainty about the adversary's intentions may lead a "security-seeking" (as opposed to predatory) state to increase its military power for purely defensive purposes, but these actions are often perceived as threatening by their adversary, which responds with defensive actions that are similarly perceived as threatening by the other. This can generate an action–reaction cycle and a conflict spiral that leaves all states worse off, that is difficult to reverse and that can sometimes escalate to war. This is the core of the security dilemma: actions that states take to increase their security often induce a response by adversaries that results in a decrease in their security (Jervis 1978).[6] In the realist view, wars can arise either through predatory aggression or through a conflict spiral leading to an inadvertent war.[7]

Realist theories give primary emphasis to the distribution of power. This is prominent in balance of power theories, which come in many variations but which generally posit the avoidance of hegemony as the primary goal of states and the maintenance of an equilibrium of power in the system as the primary instrumental goal (Morgenthau 1948; Waltz 1979). The theory predicts that states, and particularly great powers, will build up their arms and form alliances to balance against those who constitute the primary threats to their interests and particularly against any state that threatens to secure a hegemonic position over the system. Balance of power theorists argue that the balancing mechanism almost always works successfully to avoid hegemony, either because potential hegemons are deterred by their anticipation of a military coalition forming against them or because they are defeated in war after deterrence fails. Classic examples of high concentrations of power leading to counter-hegemonic coalitions and "hegemonic wars" are the two World Wars of the twentieth century against Germany and the French Revolutionary and Napoleonic Wars (1792–1815).

Although balance of power theorists agree that threats of hegemony generate counterbalancing coalitions that frequently lead to general wars, they disagree about the consequences of less extreme concentrations of power in the system, where a traditional rival or neighboring state rather than the strongest power in the system may constitute the greatest security threat to a state. There are long-standing debates about the relative war-proneness of "bipolar" systems characterized by the approximate parity of two great powers that stand far above the rest (like the Cold War system) and "multipolar" systems characterized by the dispersion of power among several great powers (nineteenth-century Europe, for example), but the arguments advanced in support of each are theoretically underspecified and the evidence is inconclusive (Levy and Thompson 2010, Chapter 2).

Balance of power propositions about counter-hegemonic balancing naturally lead to the "puzzle" of why no balancing coalition has formed against the United States after the end of the Cold War, given the historically unprecedented power of the US. Although some realists argue that it is just a matter of time before such a coalition arises, others argue that a balancing coalition will not arise, for several reasons: (1) the United States is a benign hegemon that does not threaten most other states (Walt 2005); (2) offshore balancers like the US do not provoke balancing coalitions (Mearsheimer 2001); (3) the US is too strong and balancing is too risky (Brooks and Wohlforth 2008); and (4) states balance against threats of land-based hegemonies in continental systems like Europe but not against threats of hegemony in the global maritime system (Levy and Thompson 2010: Chapter 2).

In contrast to balance of power theory, which predicts that high concentrations of power in the international system generate counterbalancing coalitions so that hegemonies never arise, power transition theory (Organski 1958; Tammen et al. 2000) posits that hegemony is common and that it is conducive to peace.[8] The theory stipulates that differential rates of growth driven largely by industrialization lead to the rise and fall of dominant states. The probability of war peaks at the point at which the declining leader is overtaken by a rising challenger that is dissatisfied with the status quo.[9] Power transition theorists argue that unipolarity under US leadership helps maintain the peace, but that the inevitable decline of US dominance and the rise of China or other great powers creates an increasing risk of great power war. The point of a Sino-American power transition, estimated to occur within a few decades, will be the point of maximum danger. Power transition theorists minimize the deterrent effects of nuclear weapons and argue that the key to peace will be whether or not China is satisfied with the existing status quo and with the global political economy, in particular.

Power transition theorists generally argue that a dissatisfied rising power is likely to initiate a war prior to the point of power transition with the dominant power in order to accelerate the transition and then reconstruct the international economic, political and legal system in a way that serves its own interests. This is a puzzling argument, because the rising state is likely to lose any war that occurs prior to the point of transition. The rising state's incentives are to delay, wait until it is stronger and exploit its greater strength to extract concessions from the former leader under the threat of war. Recognizing this danger, the declining leader may have an incentive to initiate or provoke a "preventive war" to defeat its rising adversary while the opportunity is still available (Levy 2008).[10] Preventive logic, which is also invoked by balance of power theorists, applies not only to complete power transitions but also to situations in which a rising adversary threatens to cross a critical threshold of military capabilities. Preventive logic motivated the Israeli strike against the Iraqi nuclear reactor in 1981, and it was the public rationale for the US war against Iraq in 2003.

Most statistical studies have shown that balance of power theories and power transition theories, along with realist theories more generally, can explain only a limited amount of the variance of war and peace in the international system. These empirical limitations, along with questions about the logical coherence of each of these theories, have led international relations theorists to shift to the level of the dyadic interactions between states as the dependent variable or unit of analysis, in an attempt to provide a more complete explanation for war and peace.

2.4   DYADIC-LEVEL THEORIES

Quantitative researchers have been able to explain more of the variation in war and peace between states at the dyadic level than at the system level (of the dependent variable). The best known finding is that democratic states rarely if ever go to war with each other, which we discuss in the next section on state and societal level causal variables. Researchers have also demonstrated that most wars are between contiguous states (Bremer 1992), that territorial disputes are far more likely to escalate to war than are disputes over other issues (Senese and Vasquez 2008), and that preponderance of power at the dyadic level (but not at the system level) is a strong predictor of peace (Tammen et al. 2000). A new line of research on international rivalries has demonstrated that the history of the interactions between pairs of states have an enormous impact on their behavior and on the likelihood of war between them (Diehl and Goertz 2000; Colaresi, Rasler and Thompson 2007).[11] Combining dyadic-level rivalries and territorial disputes with variables traditionally associated with the realist paradigm (arms races, system-level alliances and crises), and conceiving of the later as the product of a realist culture, Senese and Vasquez (2008) have developed and tested a "steps to war" model that nicely captures conflict spiral dynamics. Scholars have also begun to conceptualize and model war as a bargaining breakdown between states. This "bargaining model of war" has been one of the most influential research programs in the international relations field during the last 15 years, and it deserves particular attention here.

2.4.1   The Bargaining Model of War

Economists are familiar with the logic underlying the bargaining model of war, an early form of which was introduced to the international relations field by Blainey (1988, Chapter 8), an economic historian. The model was then formalized by Fearon (1995) and further developed by others (Wagner 2000). The basic argument is that war is an inefficient means of resolving conflicts of interests because it destroys resources that might otherwise be distributed among adversaries. There should in principle be some negotiated settlement that is mutually preferred to war. Any theory of war must be able to explain why states or other actors end up in war rather than with a negotiated settlement.

Fearon (1995) recognized that psychological variables might provide one answer to this question, and that the domestic political interests of political leaders might provide another. He narrowed the question and asked how rational unitary actors might end up in war despite the costs and inefficiency of war.[12] He demonstrated that there are only three sets of conditions under which two rational unitary actors could end up in war with each other: private information and incentives to misrepresent that information, commitment problems and indivisible issues.

The *private information* path to war refines and formalizes Blainey's (1988) argument that wars arise when (and only when) there are disagreements about relative power and hence about the likely outcome of war. If actors share similar expectations as to how war is likely to end, they should be able to reach a settlement based on those shared expectations, one that gives each party the same payoff that it expects to receive from war but without the economic and human costs of war. The presence of private information, however, can lead to different expectations about the likely outcome of war and consequently to different assessments of whether one can do better by fighting than by negotiating. If one (or both) actor(s) believes that its interests will be better served by war than by a negotiated settlement, taking into account the costs of war, then it will presumably demand more concessions and a better settlement, and it will fight if its demands are not met. Sharing information might narrow or eliminate the gap in expectations, but in the process it might alert the adversary to its weaknesses (or to its strengths) and give the adversary the opportunity to compensate for its weaknesses by building new weapons, securing allies, changing its strategy or initiating a preemptive strike. Thus sharing information is often not a viable strategy, so private information combined with incentives to misrepresent that information constitutes a path to war for rational unitary actors.

Scholars have applied the private information argument to the conduct and termination of war as well as to the outbreak of war, and in doing so develop Blainey's (1988) argument that the conduct of war reveals information about relative military capabilities and about mutual resolve and hence the likely outcome of war. This contributes to a convergence of expectations about the consequences of future fighting, which increases the likelihood of the termination of war based on a negotiated settlement (Goemans 2000; Wagner 2000; Slantchev 2003).

The *commitment problem* is the source of a second rationalist path to war (Fearon 1995; Wagner 2000; Powell 2006). If the relative distribution of power between two states is shifting (more accurately, if one or both states perceive that it is likely to shift in the future), it may be difficult for actors to reach a settlement that is mutually preferred to war, even if actors have shared information and therefore shared expectations of the likely outcome of war. If the weaker actor is increasing in strength, and especially if it is expected to surpass the power of its adversary, it has incentives to reach a settlement – both because it is likely to lose any war fought now and also because it will have a stronger negotiating position later. The state in relative decline presumably would like to reach a settlement that freezes the status quo, but it is likely to be skeptical about whether any such settlement would last. It understands that the adversary would have incentives to initiate a new set of demands once power has shifted in its favor in the future, and to resort to force if those concessions are not granted.

The rising state might prefer to settle now, and might promise to honor the present settlement, but how credible is that promise once underlying conditions have changed and once the adversary has the coercive power to extract greater concessions and the military power to enforce those concessions? This is the commitment problem. The only concessions that would work to satisfy the declining power are those that would restrict the growth of the rising state and hence its future bargaining advantages, but the rising state is unlikely to accept such restrictions. This narrows the bargaining space and increases the probability of war.[13]

The third path to war among rational unitary actors involves *indivisible issues* (Fearon 1995). Any mutually acceptable settlement requires a division of goods that is proportionate to the likely outcome of the war, which requires in principle that the issues in dispute be infinitely divisible. If issues are not divisible, it may not be possible to construct a settlement that each adversary prefers to war. Although material goods are often divisible, issues of principle, including many religious issues and some territorial issues, are often not divisible.

It might be possible to construct a mutually agreeable settlement if the difficult issue is linked to another issue (Morgan 1994) or if one side makes side payments to another. Moreover, the source of indivisibility is often a domestic pressure group with strong political influence, which means that we are no longer dealing with a unitary actor. These considerations lead Fearon (1995) to downplay the importance of the indivisibility of issues and emphasize the role of private information (and incentives to misrepresent that information) and commitment problems as the two primary rationalist paths to war.

2.5   STATE AND SOCIETAL-LEVEL THEORIES

Efforts to explain war as the product of causal factors internal to states has a long history in the study of international relations, going back to Kant's ([1795] 1949) arguments about the pacifying role of republican regimes, economic interdependence and international law and institutions. Marxist–Leninist theories (Lenin [1916] 1939) have had some influence in the international relations field (but probably more in revisionist history), with their more plausible elements being incorporated into liberal pressure-group explanations but without the philosophical foundations of Marxist theory. Given the declining influence of Marxist–Leninist theories since the early 1990s, however, I do not cover them here. It was about that time that scholars became convinced of the near absence of wars between democracies, launching the study of the democratic peace as a leading research program in international politics. We now turn to the democratic peace and its close cousin, the capitalist peace.[14]

2.5.1   The Democratic Peace

A substantial amount of empirical research demonstrates that democracies rarely if ever go to war with each other (Ray 1995; Doyle 1997). This argument is quite robust with respect to a wide range of definitions of democracy and of war, suggesting that even imperfect democracies almost never fight with each other. Scholars then demonstrated that this strong empirical regularity was not spurious – it could not be explained by the geographic separation of democratic states, by alliance patterns, by the suppression of potential conflicts between democracies in the period since World War II by American hegemonic power, or by other economic or geopolitical factors correlated with democracy (Maoz 1997; Russett and Oneal 2001).

The strong consensus that democracies rarely if ever fight each other is not matched by comparable agreement as to how to best explain this pattern, and the democratic peace remains a law-like empirical regularity in search of a theoretical explanation. One explanation is the "democratic culture and norms" model (Owen 1997; Russett and Oneal 2001), which emphasizes that democratic societies are inherently averse to war because of the nature of democratic political cultures and because (as Kant argued) citizens will not vote to send themselves off to war. Another line of argument is that the norms of political competition and peaceful resolution of disputes within democracies are extended to interactions with other democracies but not with non-democracies, in part because of democracies' fears of being exploited by the latter.

A closely related explanation for the dyadic democratic peace is the "institutional constraints model," which emphasizes the electoral accountability to the public through regular elections and the dispersion of power within the government and checks and balances among governmental institutions. Political leaders are institutionally constrained from undertaking unilateral military action and are required to secure support from the public before authorizing the use of military force. In addition, the press in democratic states ensures a relatively open political debate (compared to that in authoritarian regimes) on issues of war and peace (Russett and Oneal 2001).

Both the democratic norms model and the institutional constraints model have problems explaining the fact that democratic states have frequently fought imperial wars and initiated wars against autocracies who do not pose imminent security threats (Reiter and Stam 2002). Some respond by emphasizing a shared identity among democratic states (Risse-Kappen 1995). Although this argument accounts for democratic hostility against non-democratic states, it fails to explain the fact that democracies occasionally engage in covert action and even low-level wars against each other (James and Mitchell 1995). Another limitation of the institutional model is that it generally assumes that leaders have more hawkish policy preferences than do their publics.

The relative inclination of leaders and publics to advocate the use of military force is an interesting empirical question. That issue has not been resolved, but it is easy to identify a number of cases in which political leaders are pushed into wars they would prefer to avoid by xenophobic publics (American behavior in the Spanish–American War, for example). More frequently, political leaders are tempted to use military force externally for the primary purpose of generating a "rally 'round the flag" effect that increases their domestic political support. This "diversionary theory of war" (Levy 1989) has led to a long line of empirical studies, which have generated mixed results. The gap between the mixed results of quantitative studies and the extensive evidence from historical case studies that the diversionary motivation has been quite important in a limited number of cases is a puzzle that researchers are currently attempting to answer.

Logical and empirical limitations of the democratic norms and institutional models led Bueno de Mesquita et al. (2003) to construct an alternative institutional explanation of the democratic peace that is more consistent with other dimensions of the war behavior of democracies. The model posits that the primary goal of political leaders is their own political survival. They theorize that political leaders with larger winning coalitions (usually characteristic of democracies) require successful public policies to retain office, whereas political leaders with smaller winning coalitions (authoritarian states) require the satisfaction of key supporters through the distribution of private goods. The prediction is that democratic leaders' tenure in office is more dependent upon the outcome of wars than is that of authoritarian leaders. In fact, unsuccessful wars (for the state) are more likely to lead to the removal from power of democratic leaders than of authoritarian leaders (Bueno de Mesquita et al. 2003). Consequently, democratic leaders initiate war only if they are confident of winning. In addition, in the wars that they do fight democratic leaders have political incentives to devote enormous resources to ensure a successful outcome. Autocratic leaders, whose political futures are less sensitive to the outcome of war and who need to conserve resources to distribute to their key supporters at home, devote fewer resources to the conduct of the war.

The model provides a nice explanation for the near absence of war between democracies. In any such war each side, understanding the stakes, would invest enormous resources, which would substantially increase the costs of war for both sides. Anticipating this outcome, democratic leaders try particularly hard to find a negotiated settlement that will avoid the costs of fighting. The model also accounts for the frequent war involvement of democratic states and other aspects of their war behavior that standard institutional and cultural models cannot explain.

Schultz (2001) provides still another institutional explanation of the democratic peace, one based on information, signaling, transparency and the office-seeking priorities of partisan political oppositions. Schultz argues that because the organized political opposition does not share the government's incentives to bluff about the state's military capabilities and resolve in a crisis, and because of the transparency of the democratic process reinforced by a free press, the behavior of the opposition sends a credible signal to the adversary of the government's likely resolve in a crisis.

If the opposition does not support the government – either because it believes that the government is bluffing and lacks the capabilities or resolve to implement the threat, or because it believes that the war will be unpopular (or both) – then the government cannot stand firm in a crisis. Observing the opposition's behavior and understanding its logic, the adversary adopts a harder line in crisis bargaining. Democratic leaders anticipate the adversary's behavior and avoid getting involved in crises to begin with. If the domestic opposition supports the government, however, leaders are freer to initiate an interstate dispute, knowing that it will be able to stand firm in the face of adversary resistance. The adversary anticipates this and behaves more cautiously.

This logic suggests that democratic states and their adversaries are each less likely to misperceive each other's resolve in a crisis, and so crises involving democratic states are less likely to escalate to war. Misperceptions are further reduced in crises involving two democracies, though it is not clear whether this reduction is substantial enough to account for the democratic peace. The importance of this argument is enhanced by the fact that misperceptions based on private information and incentives to misrepresent that information play a key role in the processes leading to war.

2.5.2   The Capitalist Peace

A second component of Kant's "eternal peace" was economic interdependence, and the proposition that trade promotes peace became the cornerstone of nineteenth-century liberal international theory (Silberner ([1946] 1972). Liberal theorists propose several interrelated theoretical mechanisms through which trade – or economic interdependence more generally – advances peace, but the primary argument emphasizes the economic opportunity costs of war. Trade generates economic benefits for both parties. The expectation that war will interfere with trade and consequently diminish or eliminate the gains from trade helps to deter political leaders from behavior that might risk war with important trading partners (Polachek 1980; Russett and Oneal 2001).[15]

Causal factors at the domestic level reinforce the trade-promotes-peace proposition. Liberals argue that trade enhances prosperity and that prosperity removes domestic conditions conducive to war. Economic stagnation can lead political elites to engage in the diversionary use of force to solidify their domestic political support, and it can also lead to pressures for protectionism that can lead to retaliatory actions that increase hostilities and possibly generate conflict spirals. In addition, prosperity helps to promote a culture of acquisitiveness. As Blainey (1988, p. 10) summarized nineteenth-century liberal attitudes, "Men were too busy growing rich to have time for war." Others argue that trade promotes prosperity, prosperity promotes democracy and democracy promotes peace (Weede 1995), a theme that has been developed further by those arguing that the capitalist peace trumps the democratic peace (Gartzke 2007).[16] In addition, trade increases the influence of groups that benefit from trade and who consequently have an interest in maintaining a peaceful environment for trade (Rogowski 1989).

Some have questioned the theoretical logic underlying these arguments for the trade-promotes-peace proposition, and others question their empirical validity. Some realists minimize the causal weight of the deterrent effects of the economic opportunity costs of war, arguing that they are small relative to the national security interests at stake.[17] Others argue that economic interdependence, especially if it is asymmetrical, creates conditions that tempt one side to exploit its dominant position and coerce the other on security as well as economic issues, increasing the probability of militarized conflict (Hirschman [1945] 1980; Gowa 1994).

Many rationalists emphasize that state-level preferences for peace cannot explain war or peace as a dyadic outcome and criticize the economic opportunity cost model's neglect of a theory of bargaining. They argue that in the absence of more information about expectations regarding the economic benefits of trade, the impact of war on trade, and each side's risk orientation and domestic sensitivity to those costs, the impact of economic interdependence on peace within a dyad is theoretically indeterminate. This has led some to construct a signaling game model of economic interdependence and peace. Trade provides states with additional instruments that they can use to credibly signal commitment during a crisis (by threatening to cut off trade) and do so with less risk of escalation inherent in the use of military threats to signal resolve (Morrow 2003).

Another critique is that liberal scholars have misspecified the relationship between trade and peace. Some argue that the causal arrow is reversed and that it is peace that creates the conditions under which trade can flourish (Blainey 1988). Others claim that the inference that trade promotes peace is spurious, because states with common interests have tendencies to trade with each other and not to fight each other. In this model the commonality of interests is the key causal variable (Gartzke 2007).

The question of the relationship between economic interdependence and peace has also generated a sizeable empirical literature during the last 15 years. The majority view now holds that trade is associated with peace (Russett and Oneal 2001), but some find a positive correlation between trade and war (Barbieri 2002). Others are more cautious and argue that confidence in the capitalist peace needs to be tempered by a recognition that difficult endogeneity problems have yet to be solved, that analyses are sensitive to exactly how interdependence is operationally defined, that some evidence suggests that trade might be associated with a reduction in the frequency of militarized interstate disputes but with an increase in the frequency of war, and that some prominent historical cases (most notably World War I) appear to contradict the trade promotes peace proposition (Schneider, Barbieri and Gleditsch, 2003). For these reasons, current empirical support for the link between economic interdependence must be regarded as provisional, and research needs to focus not only on the aggregate relationship but also on the conditions under which economic interdependence promotes peace.

2.6 INDIVIDUAL-LEVEL THEORIES

Many attempts to explain the initiation of the American war against Iraq in 2003 give considerable weight to the role of US President George W. Bush. This is consistent with a long line of research that traces decisions for war or peace to the belief systems of key decision-makers, the psychological processes through which they acquire information and make decisions, and their personalities and emotional states. Political leaders vary along these dimensions because of political socialization, personality, education, formative experiences, and a range of other factors. These differences lead to variations across leaders in their conceptions of the national interest, the strategies best suited to advancing those interests, the time frame within which goals and threats are evaluated, the nature of the adversary, and other key elements of the state's decision-making calculus.[18] As a result, different political leaders in the same situation will make different decisions. This has led a number of international relations scholars to develop individual-level explanations for foreign policy behavior (George 1969; Holsti and George 1975; Jervis 1976). These explanations are easier to apply to decision-making in individual wars than to generalize about all wars, but the implication is that attempts to construct a general theory of war are limited by the role of individual-level variables that are often difficult to operationalize across cases.

Covering the full range of individual-level theories relevant to war is impossible here, and I restrict my attention to the efforts of some international relations scholars to apply prospect theory to questions of war and peace.

2.6.1 Applications of Prospect Theory

Some international relations theorists, skeptical of the descriptive accuracy of expected utility theory, have explored the capacity of prospect theory to help explain foreign policy decisions on war and peace and other issues. Prospect theory, developed by Kahneman and Tversky (1979) to account for growing evidence that people systematically depart from the predictions of expected utility theory, posits that people are more sensitive to changes in assets than to levels of assets and that they "frame" choice problems around a reference point. People give more weight to losses from that reference point than to comparable gains beyond it (loss aversion). They are risk-averse in choices among gains and risk-acceptant in choices among losses. Individuals' strong aversion to losses, particularly "dead" (or certain) losses, leads them to accept significant risks in the hope of avoiding loss, even though the expected value of the gamble may be lower than the value of the certain loss. In addition, people value what they have more than comparable things not in their possession (the endowment effect), and as a result actual losses hurt more than foregone gains.

Reference dependence, loss aversion and variable risk propensities have important consequences, so how an individual identifies a reference point for a particular choice problem is critical. A change in reference point can lead to a change in preference (preference reversal) even if the values and probabilities associated with possible outcomes remain unchanged. Individuals who must make a decision about alternative medical treatments, for example, respond differently if they are informed that the survival rate of a particular treatment is 90 percent than if they are informed that the mortality rate is 10 percent, although the two are logically equivalent.

Although how individuals identify a reference point is critical, the process is subjective. Most experimental studies of framing, and almost all applications of the theory to international relations, focus on the effects of framing on choice rather than on the sources of framing. As a result, prospect theory remains "a reference-dependent theory without a theory of the reference point" (Levy 1997). Still, we can say a few things. People often (but not always) frame choice problems around the status quo. Sometimes, however, framing is influenced by expectation levels, aspiration levels and social comparisons. In addition, there is evidence that people "renormalize" their reference points after making gains much more quickly than they do after incurring losses. As a result, sunk costs often affect choice.[19]

These basic prospect theory propositions lead to a number of predictions about state behavior on issues of war and peace. (1) States take far more risks to defend territory that they would to acquire that territory in the first place. More generally, state leaders take more risks to maintain their international positions, reputations, and domestic political support against potential losses than they do to enhance their positions. (2) Political leaders are punished more by domestic publics for incurring losses than for failing to make gains. (3) After suffering losses, political leaders, rather than adjusting to their losses, tend to take substantial risks to recover those losses.[20] The adversary, after making gains, renormalizes its reference point and then takes substantial risks to defend the new status quo. As a result, both parties will take disproportionate risks in future bargaining over the disputed territory. (4) Political leaders are more likely to respond to failing military interventions by upping the ante in an attempt to recover their losses than by withdrawing in an attempt to cut their losses. (5) Attempts to deter an adversary from making gains tend to be more successful than attempts to deter an adversary from recovering losses or to compel him/her to accept losses.[21] (6) States can more easily cooperate over the distribution of gains than over the distribution of losses. They will take more risks and bargain harder to minimize their share of the costs than to maximize their share of the gains (Levy 1997; McDermott 1998).

Many of these hypotheses come across as intuitively quite plausible. Validating them empirically in the ill-structured world of international relations, however, is far more difficult than in highly controlled laboratory conditions (Levy 1997). Since important variables like power, reputation, security and identity cannot easily be measured on an interval-level scale, it is often quite difficult to test a prospect theory explanation against an expected utility explanation. In addition, nearly all interesting problems in international relations involve choices under uncertainty, where probabilities are unknown, rather than choices under risk, where probabilities are known and where theory is less developed.[22] A major task for international relations researchers is to construct research designs that facilitate the effective testing of prospect theoretic propositions about war and peace.

2.7   CONCLUSION

This admittedly brief survey of some of the leading theories of the causes of interstate war, while reinforcing the view that international relations theorists are as divided as ever as to what the causes of war are and how best to study those causes, suggests some points of convergence. Scholars have moved further away from the view that a single monocausal theory can provide an adequate explanation for war, and toward a growing acceptance of the belief that an adequate understanding of war must incorporate variables at several levels of analysis. They have begun to acknowledge that there may be multiple paths to war, though they have yet to define what that concept means or fully accept its methodological implications. There is also growing agreement that our confidence in theoretical propositions is enhanced if those propositions are subject to tests utilizing several different methodologies, and, in fact, the combination of formal, statistical and historical case study approaches is becoming increasingly common in the field. This is particularly evident in the study of the democratic peace, but it is true in studies of the capitalist peace, the diversionary theory of war and other theories as well. This growing acceptance of methodological pluralism is one reason for optimism about the feasibility of continued progress in our efforts to understand the causes of war and the conditions for peace.

NOTES

1. These within-discipline differences may be least pronounced for those like economics that share a common theoretical and methodological paradigm, but much greater for disciplines characterized by ongoing theoretical and particularly meta-theoretical debates.
2. For more detailed reviews of the causes of war see Vasquez (2009) and Levy and Thompson (2010), which also include useful bibliographies. For a good review of the statistical evidence see Bennett and Stam (2004).
3. The dual use of the levels of analysis concept makes it necessary for scholars to be clear about their own usage, and the common failure to do so is a source of confusion in the literature. For further discussion of levels of analysis see Jervis (1976, Chapter 1) and Levy and Thompson (2010, Chapter 1). The level of the dependent variable is sometimes referred to as the "unit" of analysis.
4. On the role of necessary conditions in causal analysis see Goertz and Levy (2007).
5. For an overview of different realist theories of war see Doyle (1997) and Walt (2002).
6. Conflict spirals are often exacerbated by non-rational psychological processes (Jervis 1976).
7. "Inadvertent wars" are inadvertent only in the sense that neither side wants or expects war in the early stage of a crisis. Inadvertent wars almost always begin with a calculated decision for war.
8. Power transition theorists share most realist assumptions but emphasize hierarchy and order rather than anarchy, and they generally do not self-identify as realists. Gilpin (1981) declares himself a realist and advances "hegemonic transition theory," which is very similar.
9. The apparent contradiction between balance of power theory's emphasis on the destabilizing effects of hegemonic concentrations of power and power transition theory's emphasis on their stabilizing effects is only apparent, given the implicit scope conditions of the two theories. Balance of power theories implicitly focus on the historical European system, and power transition theory focuses on power and wealth in the global system (Levy and Thompson 2010). The most war-prone situation is one in which the concentration of power is increasing in the European system and decreasing in the global system (Rasler and Thompson 1994). The periods before the French Revolutionary Wars and World War I are good examples.
10. Scholars and statesmen often confuse a preventive strike, which aims to block a rising adversary from posing a future threat, from a preemptive strike, which anticipates an imminent attack by the adversary and which aims to gain a first-mover advantage.
11. Depending on one's precise definition of rivalry, 50–75 percent of the interstate wars of the last two centuries have been between rivals.
12. A rational unitary actor is a value-maximizing actor with a consistent and transitive set of preferences.
13. The commitment problem is especially relevant to theories of power transition and preventive war. It has also been applied extensively to ethnic conflicts (Fearon, 1998).
14. Space limitations preclude coverage of an interesting line of work on the influence of economic-based domestic coalitions on the grand strategies of states (Snyder 1991; Lobell 2003; Narizny 2007). On cultural explanations see Huntington (1996) and Lebow (2008).
15. The nature of this proposition might suggest that theories of economic interdependence and peace are best classified at the dyadic level. We treat these theories at the state-societal level because many variations have a strong domestic component and because they are closely linked to democratic peace theories.
16. Blainey (1988) argues that prosperity enlarges the size of "war chests" and removes constraints on decisions for war.
17. On the empirical level, it is not clear how much war inhibits trade. Barbieri and Levy (1999) find that trade often continues between wartime adversaries, though the frequency, magnitude and political and economic consequences of trading with the enemy remains to be established.

18. On time horizons, inter-temporal tradeoffs, and behavioral deviations from standard exponential discounting models, see Streich and Levy (2007).
19. Prospect theory also posits that people generally underweight probabilities (relative to utilities) but overweight small probabilities, generating a non-linear probability weighting function. Behavioral economists have given some attention to the implications probability weighting function but most political scientists have not.
20. By substantial (or disproportionate or excessive) risks, I mean relative to the predictions of an expected value calculus.
21. This is a slight reformation of Schelling's (1966) observation that deterrence is easier than compellence.
22. One thing we do know, however, is that people are more averse to uncertainty than to risk. They prefer a choice involving a known probability p than one involving a probability distribution with a mean of p (Camerer 1995, p. 646). In terms of Donald Rumsfeld's famous distinction, people are more risk averse in response to "unknown unknowns" than they are to "known unknowns."

REFERENCES

Barbieri, K. (2002), *The Liberal Illusion: Does Trade Promote Peace?* Ann Arbor, MI: University of Michigan Press.
Barbieri, K. and J.S. Levy (1999), "Sleeping with the enemy: the impact of war on trade", *Journal of Peace Research,* **36** (4), 463–79.
Bennett, D.S., and A.C. Stam III (2004), *The Behavioral Origins of War*, Ann Arbor, MI: University of Michigan Press.
Blainey, Geoffrey (1988), *The Causes of War*, 3rd edn., New York: Free Press.
Bremer, S.A. (1992), "Dangerous dyads: conditions affecting the likelihood of interstate war, 1816–1965", *Journal of Conflict Resolution*, **36** (2), 309–41.
Brooks, S.G., and W.C. Wohlforth (2008), *World Out of Balance: International Relations and the Challenge of American Primacy*, Princeton, NJ: Princeton University Press.
Bueno de Mesquita, B., J.D. Morrow, R.M. Siverson, and A. Smith (2003), *The Logic of Political Survival.* Cambridge, MA: MIT Press.
Camerer, C. (1995), "Individual decision-making", in J.H. Kagel and A.E. Roth (eds.), *The Handbook of Experimental Economics*, Princeton, NJ: Princeton University Press, pp. 587–703.
Clausewitz, C. von ([1832] 1976), *On War*, by M. Howard and P. Paret (eds and trans), Princeton, NJ: Princeton University Press.
Colaresi, M., K. Rasler and W.R. Thompson (2007), *Strategic Rivalry: Space, Position and Conflict Escalation in World Politics*, Cambridge, UK: Cambridge University Press.
Diehl, P.F. and G. Goertz (2000), *War and Peace in International Rivalry*, Ann Arbor, MI: University of Michigan Press.
Doyle, M.W. (1997), *Ways of War and Peace.* New York, NY: W.W. Norton.
Fearon, J. (1995), "Rationalist explanations for war", *International Organization*, **49** (3), 379–414.
Fearon, J.D. (1998), "Commitment problems and the spread of ethnic conflict", in D.A. Lake and D. Rothchild (eds), *The International Spread of Ethnic Conflict*, Princeton, NJ: Princeton University Press, pp. 107–26.
Gartzke, E. (2007), "The capitalist peace", *American Journal of Political Science*, **51** (1), 161–91.
George, A.L. (1969), "The 'operational code': a neglected approach to the study of political leaders and decisionmaking", *International Studies Quarterly*, **13** (2), 190–222.
Gilpin, R. (1981), *War and Change in World Politics*, New York, NY: Cambridge University Press.

Goemans, H.E. (2000), *War and Punishment: The Causes of War Termination and the First World War*, Princeton, NJ: Princeton University Press.

Goertz, G. and J.S. Levy (2007), "Causal explanation, necessary conditions, and case studies", in G. Goertz and J.S. Levy (eds), *Explaining War and Peace: Case Studies and Necessary Condition Counterfactuals*, New York, NY: Routledge, pp. 9–45.

Gowa, J. (1994), *Allies, Adversaries, and International Trade*, Princeton, NJ: Princeton University Press.

Hewitt, J.J., J. Wilkenfeld and T.R. Gurr (2008), *Peace and Conflict 2010*. Boulder, CO: Paradigm.

Hirschman, A.O. ([1945] 1980), *National Power and the Structure of Foreign Trade*, Berkeley, CA: University of California Press.

Holsti, O.R., and A.L. George (1975), "The effects of stress on the performance of foreign policy-makers", in C.P. Cotter, *Political Science Annual*, Indianapolis, IN: Bobbs-Merrill, pp. 255–319.

Huntington, S.P. (1996), *The Clash of Civilizations and the Remaking of World Order*, New York, NY: Simon and Schuster.

James, P. and G.E. Mitchell II (1995), "Targets of covert pressure: the hidden victims of the democratic peace", *International Interactions*, **21** (1), 85–107.

Jervis, R. (1976), *Perception and Misperception in International Politics*, Princeton, NJ: Princeton University Press.

Jervis, R. (1978), "Cooperation under the Security Dilemma", *World Politics*, **30** (2), 186–213.

Kahneman, D. and A. Tversky (1979), "Prospect theory: an analysis of decision under risk", *Econometrica*, **47** (2), 263–91.

Kant, I. ([1795] 1949), "Eternal peace", in C.J. Frederich (ed.) *The Philosophy of Kant*, New York, NY: Modern Library, pp. 430–76.

Lebow, R.N. (2008), *A Cultural Theory of International Relations*, New York, NY: Cambridge University Press.

Lenin, V.I. ([1916] 1939), *Imperialism*. New York, NY: International Publishers.

Levy, J.S. (1983), *War in the Modern Great Power System, 1495–1975*, Lexington, KY: University Press of Kentucky.

Levy, J.S. (1989), "The diversionary theory of war: a critique", in M.I. Midlarsky (ed.) *Handbook of War Studies*, Boston, MA: Unwin Hyman, pp. 259–88.

Levy, J.S. (1997), "Prospect theory, rational choice, and international relations", *International Studies Quarterly*, **41** (1), 87–112.

Levy, J.S. (2008), "Preventive war and democratic politics", *International Studies Quarterly*, **52** (1), 1–24.

Levy, J.S. and W.R. Thompson (2010), *Causes of War*, Oxford, UK: Wiley-Blackwell.

Lobell, S.E. (2003), *The Challenge of Hegemony: Grand Strategy, Trade, and Domestic Politics*, Ann Arbor, MI: The University of Michigan Press.

McDermott, R. (1998), *Risk-Taking in International Politics: Prospect Theory in American Foreign Policy*, Ann Arbor, MI: University of Michigan Press.

Malinowski, B. ([1941] 1968), "An anthropological analysis of war", *American Journal of Sociology*, **46** (4), 521–50.

Maoz, Z. (1997), "The debate over the democratic peace: rearguard action or cracks in the wall?", *International Security*, **32**, 162–98.

Mearsheimer, J.J. (2001), *The Tragedy of Great Power Politics*. New York, NY: Norton.

Morgan, T.C. (1994), *Untying the Knot of War: A Bargaining Theory of International Crises*, Ann Arbor, MI: University of Michigan Press.

Morgenthau, H.J. (1948), *Politics Among Nations*, New York, NY: Knopf.

Morrow, J.D. (2003), "Assessing the role of trade as a source of costly signals", in E.D. Mansfield and B. Pollins (eds) *Economic Interdependence and International Conflict*, Ann Arbor, MI: University of Michigan Press, pp. 89–95.

Narizny, K. (2007), *The Political Economy of Grand Strategy*, Ithaca, NY: Cornell University Press.

Organski, A.F.K. (1958), *World Politics*, New York, NY: Knopf.

Owen, J. IV (1997), *Liberal Peace Liberal War: American Politics and International Security*, Ithaca, NY: Cornell University Press.

Polachek, S.W. (1980). "Conflict and Trade", *Journal of Conflict Resolution*, **24** (1), 55–78.

Powell, R. (2006), "War as a commitment problem", *International Organization*, **60** (1), 169–204.

Rasler, K.A. and W.R. Thompson (1994), *The Great Powers and Global Struggle, 1490–1990*, Lexington, KY: University Press of Kentucky.

Ray, J.L. (1995), *Democracy and International Conflict*, Columbia, SC: University of South Carolina Press.

Reiter, D. and A.C. Stam III (2002), *Democracies at War*, Princeton, NJ: Princeton University Press.

Risse-Kappen, T. (1995), "Democratic peace – warlike democracies? A social constructivist interpretation of the liberal argument", *European Journal of International Relations*, **1** (4), 491–517.

Rogowski, R. (1989), *Commerce and Coalitions: How Trade Affects Domestic Political Alignments*, Princeton, NJ: Princeton University Press.

Russett, B. and J.R. Oneal (2001), *Triangulating Peace: Democracy, Interdependence, and International Organization*. New York: W.W. Norton.

Schelling, T.C. (1966), *Arms and Influence*, New Haven, CT: Yale University Press.

Schneider, G., K. Barbieri and N.P. Gleditsch, eds. (2003), *Globalisation and Armed Conflict*, Lanham, MD: Rowman & Littlefield.

Schultz, K.A. (2001), *Democracy and Coercive Diplomacy*, Princeton, NJ: Princeton University Press.

Senese, P.D. and J.A. Vasquez (2008), *The Steps to War: An Empirical Study*, Princeton, NJ: Princeton University Press.

Silberner, E. ([1946] 1972), *The Problem of War in Nineteenth Century Economic Thought*, A.H. Krappe (trans), Princeton, NJ: Princeton University Press.

Singer, J.D. (1961), "The levels of analysis problem in international relations", *World Politics*, **14** (1), 77–92.

Slantchev, B.L. (2003), "The principle of convergence in wartime negotiations", *American Political Science Review*, **97** (4), 621–32.

Snyder, J. (1991), *Myths of Empire: Domestic Politics and International Ambition*, Ithaca, NY: Cornell University Press.

Streich, P. and J.S. Levy (2007), "Time horizons, discounting, and intertemporal choice", *Journal of Conflict Resolution*, **51** (2), 199–226.

Tammen, R.L., J. Kugler, D. Lemke, C. Alsharabati, B. Efird and A.F.K. Organski (2000), *Power Transitions: Strategies for the 21st Century*, New York, NY: Chatham House Publishers.

Thucydides (1996), "History of the Peloponnesian War", in R.B. Strassler (ed.), *The Landmark Thucydides,* New York, NY: Free Press.

Vasquez, J.A. (2009), *The War Puzzle Revisited*, New York, NY: Cambridge University Press.

Wagner, R.H. (2000), "Bargaining and war", *American Journal of Political Science*, **44** (3), 469–84.

Walt, S.M. (2002), "The enduring relevance of the realist tradition", in I. Katznelson and H.V. Milner (eds), *Political Science: State of the Discipline*, New York, NY: W.W. Norton, pp. 197–230.

Walt, S.M. (2005), *Taming American Power: The Global Response to US Primacy*, New York, NY: W.W. Norton.

Waltz, K.N. (1959), *Man, the State, and War*, New York, NY: Columbia University Press.

Waltz, K.N. (1979) *Theory of International Politics*, Reading, MA: Addison-Wessley.

Weede, E. (1995), "Economic policy and international security: rent-seeking, free trade and democratic peace", *European Journal of International Relations*, **1** (4), 519–37.

3 The reasons for wars: an updated survey
Matthew O. Jackson and Massimo Morelli

3.1 INTRODUCTION

Why do wars occur and recur, especially in cases when the decisions involved are made by careful and rational actors? There are many answers to this question. Given the importance of the question, and the wide range of answers, it is essential to have a perspective on the various sources of conflict. In this chapter we provide a critical overview of the theory of war. In particular, we provide not just a taxonomy of causes of conflict, but also some insight into the necessity of and interrelation between different factors that lead to war.

Let us offer a brief preview of the way in which we categorize causes of war. There are two prerequisites for a war between (rational) actors. One is that the costs of war cannot be overwhelmingly high. By that we mean that there must be some plausible situations in the eyes of the decision-makers such that the anticipated gains from a war in terms of resources, power, glory, territory and so forth exceed the expected costs of conflict, including expected damages to property and life. Thus, for war to occur with rational actors, at least one of the sides involved has to expect that the gains from the conflict will outweigh the costs incurred. Without this prerequisite there can be lasting peace.[1] Second, as cogently argued by Fearon (1995), there has to be a failure in bargaining, so that for some reason there is an inability to reach a mutually advantageous and enforceable agreement. The main tasks in understanding war between rational actors are thus to see why bargaining fails and what incentives or circumstances might lead countries to arm in ways such that the expected benefits from war outweigh the costs for at least one of the sides.

A good portion of our overview of the causes of war is thus spent discussing a framework of different bargaining failures. We emphasize that understanding sources of bargaining failure is not only useful as a categorization, but also because different types of failures lead to different conclusions about the types of wars that emerge, and particularly about things like the duration of war. We return to comment on this after discussing various reasons for bargaining failure. Below, we talk in detail about the following five reasons for bargaining failure:[2]

1. Asymmetric information about the potential costs and benefits of war.
2. A lack of ability to enforce a bargaining agreement and/or a lack of the ability to credibly commit to abide by an agreement.
3. Indivisibilities of resources that might change hands in a war, so that not all potentially mutually beneficial bargaining agreements are feasible.
4. Agency problems, where the incentives of leaders differ from those of the populations that they represent.
5. Multilateral interactions where every potential agreement is blocked by some coalition of states or constituencies who can derail it.

To illustrate the importance of understanding which reason lies behind a conflict, note that if there is a lack of ability to enforce or commit to an agreement, then a war may last a long time. It will last until either one side has emerged victorious or the situation has changed so that the costs of continued conflict have become overwhelmingly high for all sides. Such a lack of enforceable agreements is often one of the main ingredients leading to protracted wars. In contrast, suppose that enforceable and credible agreements are possible, but that the states start with asymmetric information, for instance, about the relative strength of one of the two countries. In such a case, there can be a bargaining failure which leads to war. However, in such a setting once war really begins the relative strengths of the countries can become clearer, and given that credible bargaining is possible and can avoid further costs of war the states could then reach an agreement to end the war. So, different durations of wars can correspond to different sources of bargaining failures. We expand on this below.

The chapter is organized as follows. For a clearer understanding of the boundaries of rationalist versus non-rationalist explanations, we start by briefly discussing non-rationalist explanations in Section 3.2. Section 3.3 provides a taxonomy of bargaining failures and how these relate to conflict; Section 3.4 contains a discussion of which theories described in Section 3.3 shed light on the observations of the democratic peace. In Section 3.5 we report on the state of the literature on endogenous armaments and power and the implications for conflict and war.

3.2   THE REALM OF RATIONALITY

Before proceeding to discuss various bargaining failures as causes of war, we discuss some of the alternative sources of conflict that are sometimes thought to fall into the realm of irrationality. We argue that many of these are more usefully viewed as being rational in nature, and hence the bargaining failure categorization still applies to many conflicts that are sometimes thought to be irrational. In order for our discussion to be as unambiguous as possible, we begin by clarifying what we mean when we dichotomize between rational and irrational actors. When we refer to a rational action by an agent we require that action to maximize the expected payoff to that agent out of the available actions and relative to the agent's beliefs about the potential consequences of the actions. This does not necessarily require that the beliefs be accurate, nor that the payoffs of the individual agent correspond to what is best for the state or country that he or she might represent.[3] This is a broader definition of a rationalist explanation than is usually understood in international relations, where it is common to associate a rationalist approach to realist and neo-realist theories of conflict with unitary actors that are exclusively interested in material costs and benefits. Our broader definition should make it clear that what matters is that players, given the payoffs that they face from different outcomes, choose their actions to maximize it given their beliefs about the opponents' actions, hence the qualification "material costs and benefits" is not necessary, nor is it necessary to confine the use of the rationalist approach to the world of unitary actors.

With this viewpoint in mind, let us discuss some causes of war that are often thought of as relying on some level of "irrationality." As we shall see, with our broad definition of rationality, even many of these may be interpreted as rational causes of war. This is not simply an issue of semantics, since the distinction has fundamental implications for how wars might be initiated, and if and how they can be avoided or terminated.

3.2.1 Religion

In principle, a war between two theocracies, or two states led by people of different religions, can be thought of as having rational explanations. It is a question of defining the objectives of the agents. For example, the goal might not be materially based, but might be based on increasing the size of the population of one religion or eradicating another. In such situations, even with full commitment and bargaining opportunities, there might be no agreement that appeases an aggressor. One reason that one might place such motivations outside of the realm of "rationality," is that such objectives are often not put forth by leaders as if they are acting by choice, but instead leaders claim to be acting on behalf or under the direction of a higher being or religious code. Thus, the leaders in such settings do not necessarily view themselves as "optimizing" or "choosing" between paths but instead as following ordained directions. Perhaps even more importantly, from our perspective, such agents cannot be bargained with. That is, even if agreements are available and fully enforceable, such agents are driven by a specific goal that may be incompatible with the well-being or autonomy of another population. Thus, there is a critical distinction between a leader who is choosing and optimizing, even though his or her rhetoric may be religious in nature, and a leader who believes that he or she acts simply as a channel for a higher being.

In this light, many wars that are thought of as being religious in nature can still be well-understood from a rational perspective. To make this point clear, let us discuss two prominent examples that are often considered to be at least partly religious wars: the Crusades and the Thirty Years' War.

Although the Crusades were complicated by the fact that the aggressor was a coalition of national and sub-national armies, they fell under a common religious flag. Beyond the rhetoric, the commonality of interests within the Christian coalition can be doubted. As Fisher (1992) remarks about the interests of crusaders:

> Undoubtedly, many of the Crusaders were inspired by a genuine religious motive next to their mundane concern for a share in the spoils. However, the idea of Christian unity failed again to achieve political reality. The Crusaders not only carved up the newly won territories in the East into petty principalities but also continued to struggle against each other in Europe. And they ultimately failed to hold the East precisely because they could not square their particular interests with the universal idea that had inspired them (Fisher 1992, p. 438).

"Thus, the politics of the Crusades, while showing that religious ideas can have some political effect, remained alliances circumscribed by the exigencies of power" (1992, p. 443). Effectively, the crusades involved many factions and took place over many fronts and to a large extent involved attempts to gain or regain control of various territories, ranging from the Iberian peninsula, to Constantinople, to parts of the middle east including Jerusalem. The important aspect of this from our perspective is that the Crusades took place at least partly due to a lack of ability to credibly commit to abide by agreements, to the multiplicity of factions involved on multiple fronts and due to situations with great frictions in communication and in gaining information (for example, see Runciman (1951, 1954)). Thus, the Crusades can be partly understood from a combination of the rationalist perspectives that we discuss below.

Regarding the Thirty Years' War, even though before 1618 there was an eruption of religious divisions within Europe emanating from multiple protestant reforms and movements, and religious motivation was used by some leaders to justify actions and to mobilize people, again part of the instability derived from a multi-lateral power struggle and a lack of enforceable agreements. As argued by Gutmann (1988), a central reason for the failure of many settlement attempts was the difficulty of enforcing a new distribution of power that was so different from the official distribution of power defended by the papacy and imperial power. The Westphalia Agreements that ended the war in 1648 cut the connections between some of the territorial and religious disputes, and the principles of autonomy and territory that were embodied in the agreement laid a foundation for modern states.[4] To establish religious tolerance Catholics and Protestants were co-mingled within some of the same territories, and religious leaders were prohibited from having authority over people in separate territories. Thus, although the Thirty Years' War involved religious motivations, the various factions were also motivated by territory, peace and autonomy, and were eventually able to find a rather complicated agreement that was self-sustaining.

The long-standing conflict between Israel and the Palestinians could be viewed as another instance of a religious conflict that is often given non-rationalist explanations. However, it may more usefully be viewed through a rationalist lens. One of the central difficulties in resolving this Middle-Eastern conflict is in finding a stable agreement that is credible in the long run on behalf of the many different factions that comprise the two sides of the conflict. Even though the Oslo Peace Accords followed land for peace principles as one would expect in a rationalist dispute, when violence resumed the blame was given to "fundamentalism" on various sides (a typical non-rationalist explanation). The rationalist explanation for conflict based on multilateral bargaining, which we discuss below, is a more useful lens with which to view this conflict. In this case, both the Israelis and the Palestinians consist of many different constituencies and so although it appears to be a bilateral conflict it is in fact multilateral. In such settings, it can be that even with fully rational individual actors, agreements are not possible since the states end up being inconsistent in their decision-making as they are collectively aggregating the preferences of many different actors. This rationalist explanation is one that we discuss in more detail below.

3.2.2   Revenge

Revenge is another reason for war that one would instinctively place within the set of non-rationalist explanations of war. It is important, however, to distinguish an emotional version of revenge from a version of what someone might call revenge in the context of a repeated game: the punishment phase involved in trigger strategies of one kind or another. It is the emotional version that falls within the non-rationalist explanations.[5] Revenge in emotional terms involves actions motivated exclusively by anger for a past action, and not motivated by the potential incentive consequences, nor decided ex ante as part of an optimal strategy. Wars driven by revenge are also rare, although famous examples include the motivation of the Achaeans' in the Trojan war, at least according to the description in the Iliad.[6]

3.2.3 Ethnic Cleansing and Other Mass Killings

As in our discussion of religion, one could in principle rationalize the incentives to eliminate another ethnic group or minority group by a desire to obtain a larger share of the social cake, in the present and/or in the future (see Esteban and Ray 2008 and Esteban, Morelli and Rohner 2010). Sometimes ideologies are generally uncompromising and not justified by reasoned choice but by appealing to other principles.

Hitler had the affirmation of the dominance of his race as a primary objective. However, as much as ethnic domination and apparent insanity were part of Hitler's motivations, part of the understanding of the Second World War involves seeing why conflict was not avoided through concessions, and there, rationalist explanations can help. As we mention below, for example, the failure of the Munich Agreement was due to credible commitment problems, and would have failed even if ethnicity and apparent insanity were not in the picture.

A final caveat should be made about the possibility of wars caused by insanity of one or more leaders. As we shall see below when we discuss the "spiral" theory of war by Schelling and others, the fear of the insanity of an opponent may also cause a rational motivation for attacking, so even here the boundary between rational and non-rational is fuzzy. We place such explanations within the rationalist explanations because it can be that fully rational agents end up in war because of their uncertainty about the rationality of others.

3.3 BARGAINING FAILURES AND WAR

As mentioned in the introduction, we see two necessary ingredients for a war between rational agents. First, the costs of war cannot be overwhelmingly high. That is, for war to occur, at least one of the two parties must see a net potential gain from war under some circumstances.[7] Second, there must be some impediment to bargaining, so that an enforceable and credible agreement cannot be reached. Effectively, rational decision-makers weigh gains and losses from war given their objectives, beliefs, environment and constraints, and so if a mutually advantageous agreement is possible they should reach it. In an important paper, Fearon (1995) points out the criticality of bargaining failure for war. Basically, if rational agents come to the table with mutually consistent beliefs about the potential outcome of a costly war, then they should be able to reach a bargain to avoid it. In such a situation states can agree to split resources as they are expected to be split by a war, and then gain the extra surplus of the avoided destruction and costs of war.

Thus, to really understand the multitude of ways that wars may occur, it is illuminating to provide a taxonomy of bargaining failures and their roles in wars. As pointed out in Fearon (1995), there are various ways in which such bargaining might fail. It might be that the agents do not have the same beliefs or expectations about the potential outcome of a war. It could also be that they cannot commit to abide by an agreement and that there are no external means of enforcing an agreement. It might be that resources are indivisible and so there is no way to realize the split of resources that are expected as an outcome of a war. Beyond these three ways that are central to Fearon's analysis, we add another two. It might also be that the agents who bargain or make decisions do not have the same payoffs as the states at large, so that their incentives are distorted from what might be mutually beneficial to the populations. Finally, when considering multilateral bargaining, it might be that there is no outcome that is stable against coalitional deviations from groups of countries. In this section we elaborate on these five sources of bargaining failure, and we integrate this picture with some of the recent advancements in the theory of war.

3.3.1   Asymmetric Information and Bargaining Failures

Asymmetries of information can arise from a variety of sources. It could be an asymmetry of information about the relative strengths of the countries either because of differences in what they know about each other's armaments, quality of military personnel and tactics, determination, geography, political climate or even about the relative probability of different outcomes.

The possibility of a bargaining failure due to asymmetric information has a solid foundation in economics, and was made very clear in work by Myerson and Satterthwaite (1983). To see the basic insights in the context of war, suppose that there are two countries and one of them, referred to as country A, has unknown strength. In particular, suppose that country A can either be strong or weak with equal probability in the eyes of the other country. Imagine that war involves a relatively small cost, that the victor in a war gains control of all resources, and that war results in one of the two countries conquering the other. Suppose that if country A is strong then it wins a war with probability 3/4 and if it is weak it wins with probability 1/4. So, in order to always avoid a war, an agreement must provide the strong version of country A with at least 3/4 of all resources less the cost of war (in expectation, presuming it maximizes expected payoff). Now the asymmetry of information enters: a weak version of country A cannot be distinguished from a strong one by country B. Thus if the strong version of country A always gets at least 3/4 of the resources less the cost of war, then since a weak version of the country cannot be distinguished from a strong version by country B, a weak version of country A must also expect at least 3/4 of the total resources less the cost of war from an agreement, as it can mimic a strong version of the country and get a high payoff without risk of war. This means that country B must get at most 1/4 of all resources plus the cost of war. If the cost of war is low enough, then country B is better off simply going to war and taking its chances rather than reaching such an unfavorable bargain. This is obviously a highly stylized example, but it encapsulates the difficulties with bargaining in the face of asymmetric information. Generally, it may be difficult for a weak country to pretend to be a strong one, but there can still be some degree of asymmetric information across countries and even lesser asymmetries can make it impossible to find agreements that all parties will agree to in all circumstances.

It is important to note that imperfect information about the opponent's resolve or strength is a source of conflict that does not require any violation of common knowledge of rationality. The above reasoning is such that all the actors are fully rational, understand the setting, and fully comprehend all of its implications. It is also clear that the countries would like to avoid the difficulty. In particular, a strong version of country A would like to be able to distinguish itself from the weak version. If it could credibly demonstrate its strength, that would solve the problem. That is, if strength can be revealed peacefully and credibly (even at some minor cost), then there is a bargain which works as follows: if country A reveals strength, then it gets 3/4 of all resources and if it does not reveal its strength then it is presumed to be weak and only gets 1/4 of all resources. This solves the incentive problem as the weak version of country A can no longer pretend to be strong. Weakness is presumed unless evidence is presented to the contrary. This provides some insight into why countries might be willing to demonstrate arms (for instance, publicly testing nuclear devices, holding military parades and exercises in observable settings and so forth). There might be other settings where hiding strength is advantageous because bargaining is precluded,[8] but in settings where binding agreements can be reached there are powerful incentives for the strongest types to reveal their strength to distinguish themselves from weaker types and to cement their bargaining position. Moreover, this is not limited to settings with just two potential strengths. Even with many different gradations of strength, the strongest wants to reveal itself, and then the next strongest will want to reveal itself and so forth, and this then unravels so all but the weakest types want to distinguish themselves. So this is robust to much richer information environments than the example above.

With such asymmetries of information, whether war will occur will depend on the extent to which the private information of individuals can be credibly revealed or not as well as how relevant the private information is to forecasting the outcome of a war. If it is really impossible to fully and credibly reveal information and such information is critical to predicting the outcome of a potential war, it can be that bargaining will fail and war must be expected with at least some probability. An early paper providing a model of war decisions with asymmetrically informed countries, and pointing out that an uninformed country may sometimes have to go to war to avoid bluffing behavior by an informed country, is Brito and Intriligator (1985).

The form of information asymmetry discussed above concerns potential outcomes of a war. A second information-based reason for a bargaining failure is that agents have inconsistent beliefs. For example, it could be that two states each are optimistic and are convinced that they will benefit from a war. In these cases war can erupt, as long as the inconsistency of beliefs is large enough to compensate for the cost of war. For instance, if both parties expect to win a war with a high enough probability, then there would not exist any agreement that avoids war.[9] The possibility and examples of wars that are attributed to such miscalculations or errors due to lack of information or to different priors about relative power have been discussed by Blainey (1973), Gartzke (1999), Wagner (2000) and Smith and Stam (2003), among others.

A third form of information asymmetry concerns incomplete information about the motivations of other agents. Here it is believed that there is some probability that the other actor might be irrational.[10] This includes spiraling models such as those discussed in Waltz (1959) and Schelling (1963), and more recently Kydd (1997). These ideas have been elaborated and extended upon by Baliga and Sjöström (2004) and subsequent works. The idea common to these works is that even a small probability of being faced by an armed irrational foe can lead a rational country to arm to some level. In turn, this now means that either a foe who is irrational, or a foe who thinks that I might be irrational will be arming, and this then leads me to arm even more, and this feedback continues to build. Depending on the specifics of the payoffs to arming and potential conflict, it can be that the rational countries each arm to very high levels and are ready to attack first because of the fear that the other side may attack first. In some cases, communication can help overcome this problem, since it can be in both countries' interests to be known to be rational, but this depends on the specifics of the setting and the type of communication available, as Baliga and Sjöström (2009) show.

3.3.2 Commitment Problems

Commitment problems are possibly the single most pervasive reason for bargaining failure. This applies to many aspects of agreements that might avoid conflict, including promises to make future transfers and/or not to attack in the future. The implications of the inability to guarantee an agreement have been understood for centuries and, for instance, under-lie the basic anarchic state of nature described by Hobbes (1651) in the *Leviathan*. As Hobbes states (1651, Chapter 13), "Because of this distrust amongst men, the most reasonable way for any man to make himself safe is to strike first, that is, by force or cunning subdue other men – as many of them as he can, until he sees no other power great enough to endanger him. This is no more than what he needs for his own survival, and is generally allowed." Effectively there is nothing stopping someone from grabbing resources except fear of retaliation. Hobbes goes on to suggest that reason-able people can come to realize the inherent difficulties with anarchy and cede their rights to a Leviathan in order to live in peace. However, such social contracts do not generally appear in the international arena, and hence for an agreement to endure it has to be balanced in such a way as to be self-enforcing. In some cases, an outside authority, for instance, an international organization such as the UN, can serve as an enforcer of an agreement, but the role of that international organization and its members' incentives to really enforce the agreement are then part of a bigger picture where things need to be self-enforcing. Powell (2006) provides a rich set of illustrations of the pervasiveness of commitment problems.[11]

What does self-enforcement entail? Effectively it must be that, in terms of our earlier discussion, the costs of war subsequent to whatever trans-fers of wealth or territory become overwhelmingly high. That is, for an agreement to be self-sustaining the states need to be sufficiently balanced in terms of strength and the allocation of resources, so that a war would not benefit any of the states in expectation. It can also be that even if one does not start at such a situation, then by giving up some resources one of the states becomes a less attractive target or a less threatening adversary and one reaches a situation where the costs of war outweigh the potential gains and so peace is self-enforcing (see Bevia and Corchon 2010 for some discussion). Another way in which things might be made self-enforcing involves reputation. If a country faces potential conflicts with many other countries, then abiding by an agreement with one country can make it possible to credibly abide by agreements in other cases. Thus, it may be in a country's interest to abide by a collection of many agreements even when it might prefer to breach any single one of the agreements in isolation. Such self-enforcement involves embedding in a rich context and will depend on a variety of factors.

Let us also comment on some of the ways that a lack of commitment in agreements might lead to war.[12]

Commitment not to attack after a received transfer or to deliver intertemporal transfers

The most basic difficulty with a lack of commitment is the obvious one. A country delivering resources cannot trust that the other will not demand more or attack after receiving the resources. A notable example of such a failure of appeasement due to a lack of commitment is the Munich Agreement of 1938, after which Hitler invaded Czechoslovakia despite the agreement.

One idea that has been explored in terms of avoiding such difficulties is to make a series of transfers at a carefully determined rate over time that balances the incentives for conflict against anticipated future transfers. It is not always possible for such an approach to work, but it can in some circumstances, depending on which transfers are possible, how patient the countries are, how imbalanced they are and how attractive or costly conflict is.[13]

First strike advantages and preemptive war

As the quote of Hobbes makes clear, one difficulty in attaining peace is that the natural anarchy in which international relations reside often leads to a first-strike advantage (preemption). That is, an element of stealth or surprise provides a significant advantage. If there were no first-strike advantage, and countries could have a well-founded expectation of the expected outcome of war, then there would be some mutual allocation of resources leading to a better outcome for all countries than war (presuming that the allocation does not further alter the expected outcome of war). That agreement becomes self-enforcing since it provides countries each with more than their expected resources after a war, and so war is worse for all involved in expectations. However, this presumes that the expected outcome of a war is the same independently of how the war starts. In many cases, the outcome depends on who initiates a war. A significant offensive advantage to war can lead war to be inevitable. As a simple illustration, imagine two evenly matched countries with an even split of resources and a cost to war. If war leads to an evenly matched outcome regardless of who attacks first or under what circumstances, then peace is self-enforcing. In contrast, if a country that strikes first gains a large advantage by doing so, and expects to gain resources with a high enough probability, then peace is destabilized. Each country would like to strike before the other, and also understands that the other also has an incentive to attack first, and so must react by expecting a war, and so war becomes inevitable. Various models of this appear in Powell (1993), Fearon (1995), Chassang and Padro i Miquel (2008) and Esteban, Morelli and Rohner (2010).

Preventive war
Even in situations where countries are balanced in the short run, a country may fear that an opponent will become stronger over time and that the balance will be destabilized over time, and may therefore wish to attack today to prevent being attacked by a stronger opponent in the future. Taylor (1954) is an early reference for this perspective, arguing that wars among great powers between 1848 and 1918 can be explained as preventive wars.

Interestingly, preventive incentives are not just an issue when countries are evenly matched and anticipate becoming unevenly matched in the future, but also when one country has a current arms advantage and worries that the other will catch up in the future and that the future situation will be unstable (possibly due to first-strike advantages, or some other considerations), and so wishes to attack while the balance is in their favor. This was an important concern during the early period of the Cold War when the United States had nuclear weapon capabilities and the Soviet Union did not. There were debates about whether or not the United States should fight a preventative war during both the Truman and Eisenhower administrations. The fact that this did not happen has been argued to be due to a feeling that this was inconsistent with democratic principles (for example, see the discussion in Silverstone 2007 and Levy 2008), but from a purely rationalist perspective it might be that the fear of the future instability was insufficient to engage in a war at that time.

War as part of a dynamic bargaining process
Leventoglu and Slantchev (2007) report that almost 70 percent of conflicts end with a negotiated settlement, and almost no conflict ends with the complete elimination of one side, and hence the theory should explain

why in many cases a commitment/self-enforcement problem disappears over time and a negotiated settlement eventually becomes feasible. They provide conditions, viewing war as part of a dynamic bargaining process, for a limited war to happen in equilibrium, and commitment to a negotiated settlement to appear after a period of war.[14]

In summary, the pervasiveness of commitment problems comes from the lack of any external enforcement device in an international setting, and so any agreement is really only lasting if it is in the interest of all parties to continue to abide by it. A simple transfer of resources will not suffice unless it aligns incentives, or there are larger reputational concerns involved, or transfers are delicately arranged inter-temporally. There are many factors in such anarchic settings that naturally lead to instability such as preemptive and preventive motives, as well as the earlier mentioned asymmetries of information.

3.3.3   Indivisibilities and Other Physical Impediments

Consider a situation where a fairly precisely balanced agreement needs to be reached in order to avoid conflict. If it is difficult to finely divide territory, or other natural resources in ways that strike the exact balance needed, that could lead to an inability to reach an agreement in the face of war. While indivisibilities are a seemingly important impediment to bargaining, Fearon (1995) dismisses them as a significant explanation for war. Even if some resources are indivisible, it must be that there are no other resources that could be used to compensate.[15] Agreements involving trade of large sections of land and money (for example, the Louisiana Purchase), are plentiful, and the many dimensions through which wealth can be transferred from one state to another make it rare that a war occurs as a result from an inability to divide resources.

In terms of other impediments, delays in communication can make basic forms of bargaining difficult or impossible. While that is less of an issue in modern times, it was a substantial hurdle in times where armies might end up weeks or months in distance away from the leaders that commissioned them (as in the Crusades). This leads to substantial delays in communication between the main parties involved in a potential conflict, and in such settings reaching an agreement that avoids conflict may be precluded even if such an agreement exists.

3.3.4   Agency Problems

Even when decision-makers are fully informed and have perfectly consistent beliefs, conflict may still be rationally chosen when there are differences in preferences between decision-makers and the rest of their country (a principal-agent problem). As explained in Jackson and Morelli (2007), when the decision-makers are biased relative to their countries war can occur, regardless of the availability of enforceable or binding agreements.[16] The leader of a country might not face the same risks as the country's citizens, or it might be that the leader expects greater gains or glory from a war than the citizens.[17]

Furthermore, as Jackson and Morelli (2007) point out, it can even be that a country would like to choose leaders that have different preferences from that of the country to improve their bargaining position. Overall the risk of war that this implies ex ante can be compensated by the ability of a hawkishly-biased leader to obtain better deals at bargaining tables.[18] This means that even though democracies might be expected to have unbiased leaders who represent the preferences of the average citizen, unbiasedness cannot be guaranteed in democracies either.

Clearly, the ways in which leaders come to power differ across political regimes and this can affect the type of leader that emerges and the extent to which they represent the population as a whole. According to the selectorate theory in Bueno de Mesquita et al. (2003), democratic leaders need a larger coalition to support them relative to non-democratic leaders. Keeping a larger coalition satisfied is more costly and hence losing a war is relatively more costly for democratic leaders, and generally makes them less prone to war.

3.3.5   Multilateral Bargaining Failures

As an illustration of the potential bargaining failures that arise in a multilateral setting, let us consider a simple three-state conflict. Suppose that there are three equally powerful countries with equal resources. Also suppose that if two countries cooperate, they can easily defeat the third with relatively low costs of war. In such a situation any pair of countries can expect to get almost all of the resources in the world by ganging up on the third. There is no bargain that is stable here.[19] If the countries are about to sign an agreement, it must be that at least one of the countries gets at least a third of the total resources. The other two countries could gain by not signing the agreement, cooperating to defeat this third country and then afterwards splitting the resources evenly (and reaching a balanced and self-enforcing agreement once the world is reduced to two countries).[20]

What happens in settings with multilateral interactions will depend on the specifics of the bargaining process, the relative powers of different coalitions and many other factors. What is clear, however, is that with three or more countries the fact that there is complete information, divisible outcomes and an enforceable bargaining technology does not preclude war. This is an important and relatively unexplored territory in the theory of war, and given the innumerable wars that involve more than two states, understanding multilateral bargaining and war is an important area for future research.

Let us add a remark to this. Even when there are just two countries involved in a war, it might be multilateral considerations that derail peace. Although countries are sometimes discussed as if they are unitary actors, it is clear that they are composed of many actors with different objectives. As we know from the basics of collective decision-making, an organization that is comprised of many actors does not necessarily act as if it were maximizing some objective function. Basic voting cycles can emerge and so a country composed of individually rational actors can exhibit intransitivities and other inconsistencies in its decision-making that make the country difficult or impossible to bargain with.

3.4   DEMOCRATIC PEACE

As an example of how the various theories interact, let us consider a well-studied empirical regularity in international relations, namely the "democratic peace"; that is, the observation that democracies rarely go to war with one another (for example, see Doyle 1986 and Russett 1993). The idea that incentives of aristocrats to go to war differ from that of democratic leaders is not new, and is well articulated by Kant ([1795] 1991).

An important explanation of democratic peace is an agency one. As discussed above, Jackson and Morelli (2007) point out, when a leader has a disproportionately high share of benefits relative to costs from war when compared to the average citizen, then war can occur, but such a war will not occur if self-enforcing agreements are feasible and leaders are unbiased representatives. This "unbiased peace" result can be viewed as an explanation of democratic peace, since the checks and balances of a democracy can help reduce the chance of having a biased leader.

Conconi, Sahuguet and Zanardi (2009) extend this argument from Jackson and Morelli (2007), introducing an explicit election and reelection mechanism to control the bias of leaders. They show, theoretically and empirically, that the incentives of reelection can lead leaders to be unbiased in their decision-making, but that democratically elected leaders who do not face reelection can act similarly to autocratic leaders. Thus, the democratic peace observations are refined, and it is democratically elected leaders who face reelection who do not go to war with other democratically elected leaders also facing reelection. But autocrats or democratically elected leaders under the last term of a term-limit can diverge from the population's interests and go to war. So it seems that a driving force behind the democratic peace is how a leader's incentives are kept in line with the population through potential reelection.[21]

It is worth noting that the interactions between an executive's behavior and election prospects can be quite complicated. For example, going counter to the incentives to avoid conflict when facing reelection, there are also "wag the dog" sorts of situations, such as that described by Hess and Orphanides (1995, 2001a), where an incumbent leader facing poor reelection prospects has greater incentives to initiate a war. The Hess and Orphanides (1995) explanation is that a conflict might reveal information about the leader's abilities to the electorate that increases the probability of reelection. As Hess and Orphanides (2001b) suggest, such behavior can be correlated with recessions where an incumbent may be at a disadvantage.

Moving to the role of asymmetric information for the explanation of democratic peace, Fearon (1997) emphasized that so called "audience costs" (the cost of misrepresentations) are much higher in a democracy, and substantial audience costs can make signaling of information more effective in democracies, which in turn reduces asymmetries in information, and thus reduces the probability of war.

Fearon (2008) emphasizes another channel to rationalize democratic peace that involves commitment issues. The stronger country between two potential contenders usually has a higher GDP per capita. If it is democratic, then, even if the leader promises to a set of supporters some benefits from the war, the possibility cannot be avoided that eventually, once democratic rules apply to the unified country in case of victory, the GDP per capita of the winning country will go down. Hence voters of a richer democracy who believe that the unified country will lead to wealth redistribution should be against the war, and hence only weak contenders should remain interested in wars. However, weaker countries will generally have less interest in entering a conflict to begin with due to a low probability of success.

3.5 ENDOGENOUS POWER

So far we have not talked much about the incentives of countries to arm. It is important to recognize that the probability of war depends on prior investments in arms, and that, in turn, the incentives to arm depend on how arms affect future incentives to go to war or to bargain. Thus, to fully understand decisions to go to war, such decisions cannot be divorced from the broader endogenous armament environment in which they reside.

There are studies of armament decisions in the case where conflict is inevitable (or bargaining is inevitable), such as that of Hirshleifer (1989, 1995) and Skaperdas (1992). The case where both decisions, whether to arm and whether to attack, are present is analysed in Powell (1993) and Jackson and Morelli (2009). The key difference in the analyses is the timing of the arming decisions. Powell's model leads to peace, and is one where countries move in alternating time periods and have their armament levels fixed for the intermediate periods. In such a setting, country 1 will set its arms at a level that it knows will be sufficient to deter the other country. The other country when called upon to move must then set its arms at a similar level, to deter future attacks when the first country can readjust its arms. This results in constant positive armaments and perpetual peace. In Jackson and Morelli (2009), the armament decisions are simultaneous, so that there is a sense in which countries cannot fully react to each other's armament levels but must anticipate them. In that setting, for a range of scenarios, countries randomize[22] between a variety of strategies that must include hawkish, dovish and deterrence armament levels. Of course, this is in the absence of commitment, as otherwise countries would sign binding agreements not to attack each other and the question of armament would become moot. The intuition behind why war is inevitable and some variation in arms levels necessarily result is fairly straightforward. A complete lack of arms on the part of both countries is not a stable outcome, since a country that anticipates that the other will be completely unprotected, would prefer to arm and attack (presuming that the costs of war are not overwhelmingly high, in which case perpetual peace and no arms are an equilibrium). Let us then consider the other extreme, where both countries arm to a high level and mutually deter attacks. This also fails to be an equilibrium point. Given that there is a positive cost of war, it is true that if the countries are both heavily armed, then neither wants to attack the other. However, given the costs of war, deterrence is still assured if one country slightly reduces its arms. Given the savings of arms costs, then there is no equilibrium with mutually high levels, as one country should lower its arms level to a slightly lower deterrence level. This incentive then ends up ratcheting down the arms levels, as it is always better to have slightly lower arms than the other country given that war will not occur if arms levels are close enough to each other. However, if we keep ratcheting arms levels down so that the countries are not arming very much, then we return to the first reasoning that one of the countries should deviate to arm heavily and go to war. So, there is no stable pair of arms levels, and the equilibrium must involve some randomization, and over at least several types of arms levels. Jackson and Morelli also investigate comparative statics when there is a probability that the countries will have an opportunity to bargain (in a credible way) to avoid a war. Increasing the probability of a bargaining opportunity leads countries to make less use of deterrence armament strategies and more use of hawkish and dovish strategies, so the possibility of potential conflict increases. The idea is that as bargaining becomes more likely, deterrence strategies become less valuable, all else held equal, as do hawkisk strategies, while dovish strategies become more valuable. To ensure stability, one needs to increase the use of dovish strategies, which then reestablishes value to the hawkish strategies and increases their use, which then also maintains a reason to have at least some deterrence activity. The overall comparative statics that come out of this are that there is a lower probability of war due to the increased bargaining opportunities; however, there is a higher probability of war conditional on bargaining not being feasible.

Interestingly, peaceful outcomes are not necessarily the efficient ones in such endogenous-arms settings. Arms are wasteful, and so having many periods of peace but with costly armament levels can be worse than simply having an early conflict and then thereafter living in a unified country with peace without the need for arms.[23]

Another interesting case is the one in which arms remain unobservable even after the investment phase has ended and war is about to start. Meirowitz and Sartori (2008) analyse this case, and they also show that war cannot be avoided even if bargaining technologies exist. In their case, the source of the positive probability of war is asymmetric information, whereas in Jackson and Morelli's observable case the bargaining failures fall under the category of commitment and enforcement frictions.

Beyond these models of endogenous power, there are also models such as that of Chassang and Padro i Miquel (2008). They consider comparative statics in weapons stocks, which sheds light on the incentives to arm and which sorts of arms and levels of arms countries might seek. They note that the advantage to a first strike affects the perceived value to the attacker, while the incentive to preemptively attack rather than risk being attacked is something that comes out of the payoffs of the potential target. Increasing the arms of just one country increases the advantage over an opponent in terms of striking first, which can increase preemption tensions. However, mutual increases in arms can lower the risk of suffering an attack and lower preemption tensions. They use this to note that extremely destructive weapons such as nuclear weapons can produce a more even balance and result in mutual deterrence, while arming with less destructive weapons might provide enough of an asymmetry that it results in incentives to strike first, and thus also an incentive to preemptively attack.

3.6   THE DURATION OF WARS

As mentioned briefly in the introduction, part of the importance of under-standing the various reasons for war is that different scenarios lead to different sorts of outcomes. To see this most starkly, consider a situation where a war starts due to a lack of commitment. In such a case a war can be protracted. A peace agreement only becomes attainable after the balance of power has shifted so that it becomes in both sides' interest to agree to peace. This can take a long time. In contrast, if bargaining is possible, but fails due to asymmetric information about the relative strengths of coun-tries, then a bargain should be reached as soon as the relative strengths of the countries becomes clear. This may take some time, but might happen much more quickly, and with lower costs, than it would take for the balance of power to shift significantly enough to lead to self-enforcement.

Exactly how long the war might last when there is no ability to commit can depend on many factors. In the case of asymmetric information, a model that offers predictions in this regard, where a country learns about another country's strength or resolve over time, is often referred to as a war of attrition (for example, see Smith 1974 and Bishop and Cannings 1978). The time at which a war of attrition ends depends on the specifics of the gain from winning, the costs of staying in the conflict, the patience of the actors and the level of uncertainty. The basic structure is one where two opponents incur costs at some rate per unit of time as long as they stay in conflict. The first one to give up loses and the other one wins. The uncertainty can be about the value to the other from winning, or the cost of conflict, or the patience. As the conflict goes on, it reveals that the other has not yet given up indicating a higher patience, lower cost or greater patience. Eventually one of the two sides gives up.

It should be clear that our discussion applies to many sorts of conflicts and not just to inter-state wars. For example, it applies to things like civil wars, coups and revolutions, and even strikes and other social and economic conflicts. Indeed, even some of the literature that is specifically aimed at understanding conflict in one arena can shed light on others. As an example, Acemoglu, Ticchi and Vindigni (2009) provide an explana-tion for the long duration of some civil wars.[24] They explain that a gov-ernment can fear having too strong a military, as a strong military can initiate coups especially in contexts where a government cannot commit to maintaining the resources directed to the military once a conflict ends. Understanding this interaction between a government and a military thus provides an additional lens into arming decisions, which then not only affects the number of conflicts that take place internally and their duration (as for instance a weaker military may take a long time to eradicate a rebel group), but then also has implications for the likelihood and potential duration of external conflicts.

3.7   CONCLUDING REMARKS

We have presented a rich framework within which we can understand the prerequisites for war. Although our discussion has drawn mainly from the large literature on inter-state war, many of the same issues are at play in civil wars and other forms of conflict. Again, there must exist incentives for conflict and some barriers to the ability to reach an enforceable bargain. Some revolutions and coups arise from an agency problem either on the part of the current ruler or the leader of the attack. Some civil wars erupt because of ethnic or religious diversities manifesting themselves in the form of multilateral bargaining failures.

Although the theoretical understanding of the various causes of wars is developing well, and there are innumerable case studies of war and analyses of particular conflicts, systematic empirical work that analyses the origins of wars across many cases is still relatively lacking. A richer understanding of the origins of wars would help further advance the theory, and would help in sorting more frequent and important causes from those which are less so; and ultimately would help in developing policies aimed at avoiding the costs of conflict.

ACKNOWLEDGEMENTS

We thank CEPR for allowing us to organize a workshop on conflict in Switzerland in the months before the deadline for this chapter. We also thank Bob Powell and Stergios Skaperdas for helpful comments on earlier drafts.

NOTES

1. See Meirowitz and Sartori (2008) and Jackson and Morelli (2009) for the point that this is true even when armament decisions are endogenous, a subject that we discuss below.
2. This expands on the list of Fearon (1995), which included the first three elements.
3. In order for this not to become a tautology, one has to be careful. An "irrational" act can always be rationalized simply by saying that it gave the agent taking it a high payoff for some intrinsic reason. Thus in order to have bite, the payoffs to agents for various actions have to have some natural specification. Although the distinction is thus partly semantic, or reliant on some idea of what natural payoffs should be, we still find it to be a useful dichotomy.

4. See Krasner (1995) for an account of the role of territory and autonomy principles.
5. Nonetheless, emotional responses can still be understood from an evolutionary perspective as providing the ability to commit to certain actions in particular circumstances. Such commitment can be welfare improving in certain circumstances. For example, in a simple bargaining game, it can be advantageous to have the other side know that a player will become angry and refuse further negotiations if not given an adequate share of the pie.
6. Interestingly, the Iliad also contains numerous discussions of ransoms, slaves, territories and various other prizes and glories as motivations. However, repeated references are made to revenge for the stealing of Helen as well as the defense of honor and anger as the primary impetus for various actions of Agamemnon, Menelaus and Achilles at different points in the war (not to mention Fate and the play of the gods).
7. As we shall discuss below, there is a subtlety here. In cases where an actor is uncertain about the rationality of another, it could be that they attack preemptively even when sure that the outcome will be worse than avoiding war. They could wish to attack because they fear the other will attack, and because attacking first is preferable to being attacked. Thus, the costs not being overwhelmingly high should be restricted to cases where rationality is common knowledge or where there are no preemptive advantages.
8. For example, see Slantchev (2007).
9. At some level to have a war and such inconsistent beliefs when bargaining is possible, it is critical that the information structure and the rationality of the agents not be common knowledge, as defined in the seminal paper by Aumann (1976).
10. This is effectively a "rationalist" explanation, since there is no need for the other actor to be irrational, just that rational actors allow for this possibility and react to it.
11. Powell also shows that even some cases in which conflict seems to be due to indivisibilities (Kirshner 2000) can be viewed as due to commitment problems.
12. There is a strand of the bargaining literature which points out that in some contexts ability to "commit" can lead to conflict. The idea there, following Nash (1953), Schelling (1966), Crawford (1982) and see also Ellingsen and Miettinen (2008) and Querou (2009a), is that players can commit to accepting no less than a certain fraction of the pie. If players can make simultaneous commitments, it is possible for them to reach incompatible demands in settings with uncertainty about whether commitments are binding.
13. Schwarz and Sonin (2008) show that war can be avoided with a continuous stream of transfers that comes at a fast enough rate to always have the aggressor wish to delay rather than attack.
14. Yared (2009) extends this analysis to incorporate commitment problems and asymmetric information as potential combined causes of limited wars during the bargaining process. For other perspectives on war as part of a bargaining process, see Bloch, Sanchez-Pages and Soubeyran (2006), Sanchez-Pages (2005) and Chassang and Padro i Miquel (2010).
15. As Powell (2006) points out, there is another way to avoid indivisibilities. Even if there are no other resources to transfer, the two sides could always resort to a lottery that has the same odds as the war but without the cost. The answer as to why such a lottery might not work then relates back to an inability to commit to abide by the agreement ex post.
16. See Lake (1992) for an alternative notion of bias and Bevia and Corchon (2010) for an extension of the Jackson and Morelli (2007) theory and for some related predictions on the role of inequality.
17. Implicitly, there is a sort of contracting failure here in aligning the leader's preferences with that of the citizenship. This might be due to an inability to contract with the leader and so represent some sort of commitment problem or other bargaining failure. Or, as we discuss below, it might even be that the citizens gain by having a leader whose bargaining position is more hawkish than they would have if they were bargaining on their own behalf.

18. Freshtman and Judd (1987) and Jones (1989) develop a similar delegation logic in different contexts. Querou (2009b) examines agency issues in collective bargaining settings.
19. Stability has many meanings in international relations, as can be seen in Niou, Ordeshook and Rose (1989). In this example, any basic notion of multilateral stability fails.
20. This is what is known as an empty core in the cooperative game theory literature. See Ray (2007) for a recent discussion of multilateral interactions and the possibility of reaching binding agreements and how that depends on the presence of local public goods.
21. For an analysis of the political costs of war for different regimes, see Bueno de Mesquita and Siverson (1995) and Chiozza and Goemans (2004) . See Downs and Rocke (1994) and Tarar (2006) for different discussions of the incentives of an executive to engage in war relative to the electorate's incentives to retain the executive.
22. It is a bit strange to think of countries randomizing in armament decisions. In fact, it is not at all necessary that the country randomize, but just that its decision-making process not be fully predictable to the other country. What is critical is that the other country be unsure of the precise armament level that its opponent will take.
23. For this last observation, see also Garfinkel and Skaperdas (2000).
24. See also Powell (2009) for a view on how power distributional issues can lead to specific patterns in the persistence, duration, and recurrence of conflict.

REFERENCES

Acemoglu, D., D. Ticchi and A. Vindigni (2009), 'Persistence of Civil Wars", unpublished manuscript MIT.
Aumann, R.J. (1976), "Agreeing to Disagree", *The Annals of Statistics*, **4** (6), 1236–9.
Baliga, S. and T. Sjöström (2004), "Arms Races and Negotiations", *Review of Economic Studies*, **71** (2), 351–69.
Baliga, S. and T. Sjöström (2009), "The strategy of manipulating conflict", unpublished manuscript, Northwestern University.
Bevia, C. and L. Corchon (2010), "Peace Agreements without commitment", Games and Economic Behavior, **68** (2), 469–87.
Bishop, D.T. and Cannings, C. (1978), "A generalized war of attrition", *Journal of Theoretical Biology*, **70**, 85–124
Blainey, G. (1973), *The Causes of War*, New York, NY: the Free Press.
Bloch, F., S. Sanchez-Pages and R. Soubeyran (2006), "When does universal peace prevail? Secession and group formation in conflict", *Economics of Governance*, **7**, 3–29.
Brito, D.L. and M.D. Intriligator (1985), "Conflict, war, and redistribution", *The American Political Science Review*, **79** (4), 943–57.
Bueno de Mesquita, B., J.D. Morrow, R.M. Siverson and A. Smith (2003), *Logic of Political Survival*, Cambridge, MA: MIT Press.
Bueno de Mesquita, B. and R.M. Siverson (1995), "War and the survival of political leaders: a comparative study of regime types and political accountability", *American Political Science Review*, **89** (4), 841–55.
Chassang, S. and G. Padró i Miquel (2008), "Conflict and deterrence under strategic risk", NBER Working Paper # 13964.
Chassang, S. and G. Padró i Miquel (2010), "Economic shocks and civil war", *Quarterly Journal of Political Science*, in press.
Chiozza, G. and H.E. Goemans (2004), "International conflict and the tenure of leaders: is war still ex post costly?", *American Journal of Political Science*, **48** (3), 604–19.
Conconi, P., N. Sahuguet and M. Zanardi (2009), "Democratic peace and electoral accountability", unpublished manuscript, ECARES and CEPR.

Crawford, V. (1982), "A theory of disagreement in bargaining", *Econometrica*, **50**, 607–37.

Downs, G.W. and D.M. Rocke (1994), "Conflict, agency, and gambling for resurrection: the principal-agent problem goes to war", *American Journal of Political Science*, **38** (2), 362–80.

Doyle, M.W. (1986), "Liberalism and world politics", The American Political Science Review, **80**, 1151–69.

Ellingsen, T. and T. Miettinen (2008), "Commitment and conflict in bilateral bargaining", *American Economic Review*, **98**, 1629–35.

Esteban, J., M. Morelli and D. Rohner (2010), "Strategic mass killings", unpublished manuscript, Columbia University.

Esteban, J. and D. Ray (2008), "On the salience of ethnic conflict", *American Economic Review*, **98**, 2185–202.

Fearon, J.D. (1995), "Rationalist explanations for war", *International Organization*, **49** (3), 379–414.

Fearon, J.D. (1997), "Signaling foreign policy interests: tying hands versus sinking costs", *Journal of Conflict Resolution*, **41** (1), 68–90.

Fearon, J.D. (2008), "A simple political economy of relations among democracies and autocracies", unpublished manuscript, Stanford University.

Fisher, M. (1992), "Feudal Europe, 800–1300: communal discourse and conflictual practices", *International Organization*, **46**, 427–66.

Freshtman, C. and K.L. Judd (1987), "Equilibrium incentives in oligopoly", The American Economic Review, **77** (5), 927–40.

Garfinkel, M.R. and S. Skaperdas (2000), "Conflict without misperceptions or incomplete information: how the future matters", *Journal of Conflict Resolution*, **44–6**, 793–807.

Gartzke, E.A. (1999), "War is in the error term", *International Organization*, **53** (3), 567–87.

Gutmann, M.P. (1988), "The Origins of the Thirty Years' War", *Journal of Interdisciplinary History*, **18** (4), 749–70.

Hess, G. and A. Orphanides (1995), "War politics: an economic rational-voter framework", *American Economic Review*, **85** (4), 828–46.

Hess, G. and A. Orphanides (2001a) "War and democracy", *Journal of Political Economy*, **109** (4), 776–810.

Hess, G. and A. Orphanides (2001b), "Economic conditions, elections, and the magnitude of foreign conflicts", *Journal of Public Economics*, **80** (1), 121–40.

Hirshleifer, J. (1989), "Conflict and rent-seeking success functions: ratio vs. difference models of relative success", *Public Choice*, **63**, 101–12.

Hirshleifer, J. (1995), "Anarchy and its breakdown", *Journal of Political Economy*, **103** (1), 26–52.

Hobbes, T. (1651) *Leviathan, or the Matter, Forme, and Power of a Commonwealth, Ecclesiasticall and Civil*, available at http://www.earlymoderntexts.com/f_hobbes.html [Focus on Chapters 13, 14, 15, 17–24, 26, 29, (they are short)].

Jackson, M.O. and M. Morelli (2007), "Political bias and war", *American Economic Review*, **97** (4), 1353–73.

Jackson, M.O. and M. Morelli (2009), "Strategic militarization, deterrence and war between nations", *Quarterly Journal of Political Science*, **4** (3), 279–313.

Jones, S. (1989), "Have your lawyer call my lawyer: bilateral delegation in bargaining situations", *Journal of Economic Behavior and Organization*, **11**, 159–74.

Kant, I. ([1795] 1991), "Toward perpetual peace: a philosophical sketch", in H.S. Reiss and H.B. Nisbet (eds), *Kant's Political Writings*, Cambridge, UK: Cambridge University Press, pp. 93–130.

Kirshner, J. (2000), "Rationalist explanations for war?" *Security Studies*, **10** (1), 143–50.

Krasner, S.D. (1995), "Compromising Westphalia", *International Security*, **20** (3), 115–51.

Kydd, A.H. (1997), "Game theory and the spiral model", *World Politics*, **49** (3), 371–400.

Lake, D.A. (1992), "Powerful pacifists: democratic states and war", *American Political Science Review*, **86** (1), 24–37.

Leventoglu, B. and B. Slantchev (2007), "The armed peace: a punctuated equilibrium theory of war", *American Journal of Political Science*, vol. **51** (4), 755–71.

Levy, J. (2008), "Preventive war and democratic politics", *International Studies Quarterly*, **52**, 1.

Meirowitz, A.H. and A.E. Satori (2008), "Strategic uncertainty as a cause of war", *Quarterly Journal of Political Science*, **3** (4), 327–52.

Morelli, M. and D. Rohner (2009), "Natural Resource Distribution and. Multiple Forms of Civil War", unpublished manuscript, Columbia University.

Myerson, R.B. and M.A. Satterthwaite (1983), "Efficient mechanisms for bilateral trading", *Journal of Economic Theory*, **29** (2), 265–81.

Nash, J. (1953), "Two-person cooperative games", *Econometrica*, **21**, 1.

Niou, E.M.S., P.C. Ordeshook and G.F. Rose (1989), *The Balance of Power: Stability in International Systems*. Cambridge, UK: Cambridge University Press.

Powell, R. (1993), "Guns, butter and anarchy", *American Political Science Review*, **87**, 115–32.

Powell, R. (2006), "War as a commitment problem", *International Organization*, **60**, 169–203.

Powell, R. (2009), "Persistent fighting to forestall adverse shifts in the distribution of power", unpublished manuscript, UC Berkeley.

Querou, N. (2009a), "Commitment and the optimality of negotiation or conflict", unpublished manuscript, Queens University, Belfast.

Querou, N. (2009b), "Group bargaining and conflict", unpublished manuscript, Queens University, Belfast.

Ray, D. (2007), *A Game-Theoretic Perspective on Coalition Formation*, Oxford, UK: Oxford University Press.

Runciman, S. (1951–1954), *A History of the Crusades*, 3 vols., Cambridge, UK: Cambridge Press.

Russett, B. (1993), *Grasping the Democratic Peace: Principles for a Post-Cold War World*, Princeton, NJ: Princeton University Press.

Sanchez-Pages, S. (2005), "Conflict as a part of the bargaining process", unpublished manuscript.

Schelling, T.C. (1963), *The Strategy of Conflict*, London and New York: Oxford University Press.

Schelling, T.C. (1966), *Arms and Influence*, New Haven and London: Yale University Press.

Schwarz, M. and K. Sonin (2008), "A theory of brinkmanship, conflicts, and commitments", *Journal of Law, Economics, and Organization*, **24** (1), 161–83.

Silverstone, S.A. (2007), *Preventive War and American Democracy*, New York, NY: Routledge.

Slantchev, B. (2007), "Feigning weakness", unpublished manuscript, University of California at San Diego.

Skaperdas S. (1992), "Cooperation, conflict, and power in the absence of property rights", *American Economic Review*, **82** (4), 720–39.

Smith, A. (1998), "Fighting battles, winning wars; opening up the black box of war: politics and the conduct of war", *Journal of Conflict Resolution*, **42**, 301–20.

Smith, A. and A. Stam (2003), "Bargaining and the nature of war", *Journal of Conflict Resolution*, **20** (10), 1–30.

Smith, J.M. (1974), "Theory of games and the evolution of animal contests", *Journal of Theoretical Biology*, **47**, 209–21.

Tarar, A. (2006), "Diversionary incentives and the bargaining approach to war", *International Studies Quarterly*, **50** (1), 169–88.

Taylor, A.J.P. (1954), *The Struggle for Mastery in Europe, 1848 to 1918*, Oxford: Clarendon Press.

Wagner, R.H. (2000), "Bargaining and war", *American Journal of Political Science*, **44** (3), 469–84.

Waltz, K. (1959), *Man, the State, and War*, New York, NY: Columbia University Press.

Yared, P. (2009), "A dynamic theory of concessions and war", unpublished manuscript, Columbia University.

4 Can't we all just get along? Fractionalization, institutions and economic consequences
Peter T. Leeson and Claudia R. Williamson

4.1 INTRODUCTION

It's often said that "variety is the spice of life." When it comes to kinds of people, variety can be a spice; but it can also be poison. On the one hand, the gains from specialization and exchange under the division of labor are potentially larger when individuals are diverse. On the other hand, the differences between individuals can be a divisive force that catalyzes destructive conflict. This chapter considers social differences, how institutions affect them and their relationship to economic outcomes. Broadly speaking, consideration of such questions falls under the rubric of studies examining what the social science literature calls "fractionalization."

A fractionalized society is one with numerous, socially distant groups. The social distance in question, or what is the same, the relevant lines of demarcation distinguishing different social groups, can have many sources. In principle, any cause for notable difference between the members of various groups may be a source of social distance. In practice, social scientists have focused their attention on several common sources of such distance: ethnicity, language and religion. This makes sense since important social cleavages often fall along ethno-linguistic and/or religious lines.

Social scientists have attempted to measure fractionalization in several ways. In the early 1960s a team of Soviet researchers constructed the first such measure, which reflects the probability that two randomly selected individuals belong to different ethnolinguistic groups. Using this measure, fractionalization increases when there are many small social groups and reaches its theoretical maximum when each member of society constitutes his or her own group. The first attempts to examine the relationship between ethnolinguistic fractionalization and economic growth relied on this variable (see Canning and Fay 1993; Mauro 1995; Easterly and Levine 1997).

Gunnemark (1991) provides two additional measures of fractionalization based on language differences. The first measures the share of the population in each country in 1990 where the official language is not the language spoken at home. The second measures the percentage of the population that does not speak the most widely used language in the country. Roberts (1962) and Muller (1964) offer two other, and closely related, measures of linguistic fractionalization. Roberts' measure considers the probability that two randomly selected individuals do not speak the same language. Muller's measure considers the probability that two randomly selected individuals speak different languages.

La Porta et al. (1999) create an index of ethnolinguistic fractionalization based on an average value of the five fractionalization measures described above. Alesina et al. (2003) separate social distance into ethnic, religious and linguistic components relying on data from *Encyclopedia Britannica* (2001) and the *CIA World Factbook* (2000). Annett (2001), Fearon (2003) and Bossert, D'Ambrosio and La Ferrara (2006) have also created alternative fractionalization indices. There are other measures of social diversity besides these. But the measures discussed above are among the most important and commonly used in empirical analyses that address the relationship between social diversity and various political-economic outcomes. This is useful to bear in mind when considering the empirical results of such studies. When a study finds, for instance, that greater "fractionalization" leads to Y, it is typically a greater probability that two individuals are from different ethnic groups, speak different languages, subscribe to different religions or some combination of these things that allegedly leads to Y.

4.2 FRACTIONALIZATION AND ECONOMIC OUTCOMES: PREDICTIONS AND RESULTS

The literature that addresses fractionalization develops several theoretical predictions about how social diversity might affect economic outcomes. In general these predictions are not happy ones. With few exceptions, political economists tend to see fractionalized populations faring considerably worse than more socially homogenous populations and, in several cases, researchers have found evidence suggesting that such pessimism is justified. Empirically, fractionalization has been associated with more civil conflict, fewer public goods, lower levels of trust, lower quality governments, poor public polices and ultimately worse economic performance.

For example, in their influential study, Easterly and Levine (1997) find that ethnolinguistic fractionalization is associated with high black market premia, poor financial development, low provision of infrastructure, low levels of education and has a large negative impact on economic growth.

Going from complete ethnolinguistic homogeneity to complete heterogeneity reduces a country's economic growth rate by 2.3 percentage points. Posner (2004a, 2004b), who revisits this finding using a different measure of fractionalization, finds even stronger results. Alesina et al. (2003) find that if a completely ethnically homogeneous country were to become completely heterogeneous that annual growth would fall by 1.9 percentage points. This same relationship holds for linguistic fractionalization but not for religious fractionalization.

The basic intuition behind fractionalization's deleterious economic effects is straightforward: people who are different from one another have difficulty getting along and are more likely to conflict (through bullets or ballots) than people who are more similar to one another.

One potential channel of social diversity's negative influence on economic performance is through public goods (see, for instance, Alesina and Spolaore 1997; Alesina and Tabellini 1989; Alesina and Rodrik 1994). According to this reasoning, socially homogenous citizens have homogenous needs. They desire the same kinds and level of education, view the tradeoff between more hospitals and more prisons similarly and so on. Their optimal public good mixes and quantities are similar.

In contrast, socially heterogeneous citizens have much more heterogeneous needs. Members of one social group may want educational facilities that emphasize one subject, while members of another social group may benefit more from educational facilities that emphasize something else. Members of one group may desire more police protection, while members of another, because of different circumstances, may desire that additional money be spent on roads instead. Diversity of preferences can be problematic because if citizens cannot reach consensus about the appropriate mix of public goods and levels of their provision, their disagreement may lead public goods to be underprovided. Since, in such cases, money appropriated for public expenditures goes toward the production of public goods that benefit another social group rather than one's own, the members of each social group vote for lower appropriations than they would if they expected to realize the full benefits of appropriations for public goods.

Even if their preferences over public goods are similar, the presence of multiple social groups may lead public goods to be underprovided. Voters may choose lower levels of public goods when a large percentage of tax revenue is collected from one social group and spent on providing public goods to be shared with other social groups. For example, Alesina, Baquir and Easterly (1999) find that in more ethnically fragmented US cities, public spending on education, roads, sewers and trash pickup is lower.

Collier and Garg (1998) provide additional evidence in support of the hypothesis that social diversity may reduce public sector efficiency, though through a different channel. They find that in Ghana's public sector, strong local kin groups are able to secure a 25 percent higher wage over members from minority groups. Barr and Oduro (2002) find a significant earning differential between ethnic groups in Ghana's manufacturing sector, suggesting that diversity may not only lower government efficiency but that it may lower private sector efficiency as well.

There are other potential channels through which fractionalization may cause economic harm. Alesina and Drazen (1991) develop a model in which the presence of different social groups delays macroeconomic stabilization. In an attempt to shift the costs of stabilization to the members of another group, a "war of attrition" emerges whereby stabilization is delayed until one group concedes to the other, allowing their rivals to determine how the burden of stabilizing the economy will be distributed.

Fractionalization may also undermine economic progress by encouraging and exacerbating the negative effects of corruption and rent-seeking. As Shleifer and Vishny (1993) point out, when multiple agents must be bribed to get something done, corruption's effect is especially destructive. Since such agents supra-optimally extort their victims, victims reduce their output, leading to less for victims and bribe takers. Fractionalized societies are more likely to produce this outcome because each social group may be assigned its own area of bureaucratic control (Easterly and Levine 1997, p. 1214). Closely related, the presence of numerous social groups can create common pool problems in government whereby no group takes into account the full costs of its behavior, since these costs are borne partly by the members of other groups (Easterly and Levine 1997, p. 1215; see also, Persson, Roland and Tabellini 1997). Mauro (1995) and Dincer (2008), for example, find a positive relationship between fractionalization and government corruption. La Porta et al. (1999) find that fractionalization is associated with lower quality government overall, including not only higher corruption but also less secure property rights, more regulation and intervention, lower government efficiency, inferior public goods provision and less political freedom.

The foregoing channels of fractionalization's harmful effect on economic outcomes are essentially peaceful. They involve conflict; but conflict takes place through political battles, disagreement over policies and so on. However, fractionalization may also harm economic outcomes by leading to violent conflicts, such as ethnic- or religious-based wars. Such wars may result as the members of different social groups seek vengeance against others for perceived, or real, past aggressions. For example, Gurr and Moore (1997) develop a theory of ethnic conflict in which historical suppression and grievances tie ethnic groups together, making it easier for them to overcome collective action problems. This, in turn, leads to increased mobilization and increased conflict.

Simple opportunism by one group seeking to empower itself and disempower others for its groups' profit may also contribute to civil war. For instance, Collier and Hoeffler (2004) persuasively argue that civil war is better thought of as a criminal activity in which ethnic groups attempt to seize control of power to maximize income to the group than as the result of one group trying to "right the wrongs" that other groups' have done them.

If social diversity is accompanied by an expectation that when the members of one social group are in power they will use their political control to benefit themselves at other groups' expense, the benefit of being a part of the group with political power and cost of being a part of the social group without such power rise. This encourages social groups to go to war with one another so that they can secure political authority. Once a group has secured such authority, it's interested in preserving its power and so has incentives to centralize political institutions. In this way, fractionalization can also contribute to more centralized political regimes. For example, Aghion, Alesina and Trebbi (2004) find a positive relationship between ethnic fractionalization and autocratic government.

The evidence on fractionalization's relationship to civil war is mixed but not especially comforting for more diverse societies. Ellingsen (2000) finds that fractionalization is positively related to the probability of civil war. Collier and Hoeffler (1998) find a non-monotonic relationship between the two. Blimes (2006) finds that although ethnic fractionalization does not have a direct effect on the onset of war, it does have an indirect effect by increasing the other variables that do directly affect the onset of war, such levels of income. Fearon and Laitin (2003) find that neither ethnic nor religious characteristics appear to be important determinants of civil war, but that conditions favoring insurgency, such as poverty, political instability, rough terrain and large populations, are. Montalvo and Reynal-Querol (2005a, 2005b) find that ethnic polarization – a related but different kind of social heterogeneity that is maximized where there are two groups of equal size – is a good predictor of civil war but that ethnic fractionalization is a poor predictor.[1]

4.3   FRACTIONALIZATION AND INSTITUTIONS

A small but growing sub-literature that examines the relationship between fractionalization and economic outcomes emphasizes that social diversity's effects on economic outcomes are brokered through the channel of institutions. According to this research, institutions largely determine the nature of diversity's impact on economic performance. Some kinds of institutions, such as autocracy and government ownership, can exacerbate fractionalization's potentially harmful effects for economic progress. Other institutions, such as democracy and private property rights, can attenuate fractionalization's potentially nefarious impacts – perhaps neutralizing diversity's ability to undermine progress entirely.

Paul Collier (1998, 2001), for example, argues that democracy can largely offset the negative consequences typically associated with ethnic fractionalization. According to Collier (1998, p. 3), "democracy has the potential both to discipline governments into delivering reasonable economic policies and to provide a framework in which groups can negotiate mutually beneficial outcomes." Cooperation may be easier to secure in socially homogenous societies, making the presence of democratic political institutions unimportant for effective social decision-making in this environment. In contrast, in diverse societies, democracy may be indispensible for social cooperation because it provides a peaceful mechanism for mediating disputes between the members of diverse social groups. This logic turns the reasoning of Alesina, Baqir and Easterly (1999) discussed above, which sees voting as an important means through which fractionalization undermines public policy, on its head. Collier empirically examines his argument and finds strong support for it. Under a fully democratic system, a maximally fractionalized population performs only modestly worse in terms of economic growth than a completely homogeneous one. This finding suggests that having the "right" political institutions, alone, is enough to nearly fully offset social diversity's negative effect on economic performance.

William Easterly (2001) – one of the authors of the influential study that initiated the literature on fractionalization's negative effect on economic performance – has made a similar argument and finds even more reassuring results. According to Easterly, (2001a, p. 690) "institutions that give legal protection to minorities, guarantee freedom from expropriation, grant freedom from repudiation of contracts, and facilitate cooperation for public services" can significantly "constrain the amount of damage that one ethnic group could do to another." The institutions that he appeals to here are wide ranging, but in general are those associated with well-protected private property rights.

The reason why private property rights may have a helpful effect on neutralizing fractionalization's potentially harmful effect on economic outcomes is straightforward. On the one hand, in societies with well-protected private property rights the payoffs of cooperating with the members of other social groups for economic purposes are larger because the rewards of successful cooperation are enjoyed more fully by those who create them.

And on the other hand, because governments in such societies have less power to intervene in the economy and bestow privileges on some parts of the population at other citizens' expense, the payoffs from rent-seeking, warring for control of government and other manifestations of destructive competition for political influence and authority are smaller. Because of these factors, the energies of diverse citizens in societies with well-protected private property rights are channeled toward wealth-creating production and cooperation and away from wealth-destroying conflict over political power. In contrast, in societies without well-protected private property rights, precisely the reverse incentives exist. Individuals earn less by cooperating with one another and more by fighting for political power to wield over others. In these ways "bad" institutions catalyze the potentially wealth-destroying features of fractionalization by facilitating social groups' ability to pillage and plunder one another.

Easterly empirically investigates the hypothesis that "good" institutions can ameliorate fractionalization's negative economic effects. He finds that sufficiently high quality institutions do so *completely*. Stated differently, the influential result from his previous paper disappears when the institutional quality is maximized. While fractionalization does indeed undermine economic performance in the presence of poor quality institutions, in the presence of high quality institutions, fractionalization has no effect on economic performance at all.

Another approach in the literature that considers the interaction between institutions and social diversity suggests that what matters for economic progress is individuals' ability to realize the gains from widespread exchange. This ability is a function of institutions, not social diversity per se (Leeson 2005). According to this view, what should concern social scientists is not the probability that two randomly selected agents who interact will be from different groups, but rather *whether or not two agents from different groups can peacefully exchange*. It may make more sense, then, to define fractionalization in these terms rather than as it has traditionally been defined. Non-fractionalized agents are able to reap the benefits from trade regardless, despite being from different groups. Fractionalized agents, on the other hand, are unable to do so and instead interact predominantly inside their small in-groups.

Fearon and Laitin (1996) point out that interethnic cooperation is more common than interethnic conflict. This is counterintuitive from the perspective of much of the literature that discusses social diversity. Leeson (2008) presents a theoretical model in which socially distant individuals leverage their social differences to facilitate cooperation and exchange, especially in environments in which government is not present to provide the security they require to produce and trade.[2] At the root of this model is simple signaling. Because adopting the practices, customs and behaviors of outsiders is costly, only individuals who plan to cooperate with outsiders will adopt them. Critical to this logic is the idea that social homogeneity/heterogeneity is a variable of choice rather than fixed and exogenously given, as much of the literature treats it. By manipulating their social distance from others, heterogeneous agents are able to capture the gains from inter-group trade.

If an individual who is part of social group A wants to trade with the members of social group B but the members of B are not sure they can trust him, a member of A can invest in reducing the social distance between himself and the members of B, signaling his cooperative intentions. Uncooperative members of A have high discount rates. This is why they behave uncooperatively. Cooperative members of A have lower discount rates, which is why they behave cooperatively. Because they discount the gains from future exchange more heavily than cooperators, uncooperative members of A find it relatively more costly to invest in creating some degree of homogeneity with the members of B, the value of which will only be recouped sometime down the road. Because cooperative and uncooperative types have different costs of shrinking the social distance between themselves and outsiders, if the social distance-reducing investment cost is set high enough, only the cooperative members of A will undertake it enabling the members of B to identify through this signal who they can profitably trade with and who they cannot. In this way the members of B are able to eliminate the uncertainty of trading with unknown members of A, enabling inter-group exchange.

Long before Europeans appeared on the scene, for example, the members of diverse social groups in precolonial Africa were engaged in extensive trade, which they facilitated through social-distance reducing signaling along the lines described above (Leeson 2005, 2006, 2008). Three customs/practices in particular served as the basis for these signals: individuals' relationship to authority, land practices and rituals and religious association. By voluntarily agreeing to follow the directions and decisions of an outsiders' tribal leader, voluntarily agreeing to follow the land-use mandates of an outsiders' "Earth Priest," and voluntarily converting to an outsiders' religion, including joining an outsider's "secret society," socially diverse individuals facilitated inter-group exchange.

Each of these signals was costly. A group's leader could render a decision that ran against an outsider's interest, making it costly for him to agree to be bound by such decision-making. A group's Earth Priest could direct an outsider to work the least productive plot of land in the community, imposing a large cost on the outsider. And in some cases joining a group's secret society required payment, making religious conversion costly for outsiders. The costliness of attempting to reduce social distance through such activities enabled them to act as effective signals of trustworthiness that facilitated exchange.

Precolonial Africa is not the only example of socially diverse agents leveraging their differences to promote inter-group cooperation. Medieval international traders provide another case (Leeson 2006). Such traders faced the same basic problem as precolonial Africans. To realize the significant benefits of widespread exchange they needed to trade with outsiders, in this case literal foreigners. But to do so they had to put themselves at risk by interacting with people who they were very different from and about whom they knew little. To help overcome this difficulty, international traders invested in learning the languages of those they wanted to trade with, married outsiders, adopted outsiders' style of dress and so on. These social distance-reducing signals communicated trustworthiness, which in turn facilitated trade between heterogeneous individuals.

By interfering with the signaling mechanism that socially diverse individuals use to help overcome the obstacles that stand in the way of their ability to capture the gains from inter-group trade, governments can "fractionalize" societies in the sense of the meaning given to this term above, in other words, government can prevent socially diverse individuals from cooperating and facilitate inter-group conflict of the sort associated with poor economic performance discussed earlier. For this reason, although most of the literature on fractionalization is interested in focusing on the arrow of causation running from social diversity to poor institutions to economic decay, if we want to better understand the nature of the relationship between diversity, institutions and economic outcomes, it may make more sense to focus on the arrow of causation running from poor institutions, to problematic diversity, to economic decay.

For example, Leeson (2005, 2007) and Carilli, Coyne and Leeson (2008) argue that by introducing "noise" into the social distance-reducing signals that socially heterogeneous individuals send to one another to facilitate cooperation, government attempts to promote social homogenization can lead to balkanization and inter-group conflict. Consider, for instance, the members of two different social groups who adopt of one another's languages as a social distance-reducing signal to promote inter-group cooperation. If, in an attempt to promote "national unity," their government mandates the use of one of the group's languages, outsiders can no longer use language to communicate their credibility to the members of the other group. It is precisely the voluntary nature of adopting an outsider's language that makes the adoption, and thus the signal, costly and consequently effective. When government mandates the use of one group's language, the members of this group can no longer tell if outsiders who use their language invested in learning their language because they would have done so anyway to facilitate inter-group cooperation, of if they have done so because the government requires them to. If language is an important social distance-reducing signal, this signal "noise" can curtail inter-group interaction and promote a reversion to in-group interactions. Less interaction with the members of other groups can break down amicable relations and foster feelings of suspicion and hostility, sowing seeds that eventually lead to inter-group conflict.

Deliberate government 'homogenization policies,' such as mandating a uniform language, are not needed to incapacitate social distance-reducing signaling, however. *Any* government mandate that requires citizens' uniform compliance, or prescribes uniform behavior – even very the establishment of state-created laws – has the potential to have this effect. If the members of one social group's voluntary adherence to rule Z, which has been traditionally adhered to by the members of some other social group, is an important social distance-reducing signal, and government legislates adherence to rule Z, rule Z ceases to function as an effective social distance-reducing signal. In principle, the resulting signal "noise" can lead to the breakdown of inter-group cooperation and generate the potential problems of fractionalization discussed earlier in this chapter.

The colonization of Africa provides some evidence of this effect. In many cases colonizers replaced indigenous institutions, such as traditional trial authorities and traditional land-use arrangements, with other institutions of their own creation, and abolished other indigenous institutions, such as secret societies, altogether.[3]

Most colonial powers created the institution of the Native Authority or Native Administration under the auspices of "indirect" rule to govern Africans through native rulers in each community. To do so they often appointed and installed previously informal leaders or community elders as formal rulers in a region. In contrast to precolonial arrangements, the Native Authority required community members to follow the dictates of the ruler imposed over them, endowed rulers with formal powers of adjudication and so on. Under these conditions, an individual's allegiance to the community leader could not effectively signal information regarding his credibility. The Native Authority, which made leader allegiance mandatory, had the effect of making submission to leaders ambiguous in terms of its ability to signal an agent's credibility to others. Conflict between individuals as a result of this colonial-created signal noise began to manifest itself during the colonial period, often taking the form of legal battles. For example, colonization gave rise to "escalating numbers of civil conflicts over marriage, divorce, inheritance, and succession initiated by litigants professing different customs" (Roberts and Mann 1991, p. 21).

Similarly, colonial administrations vested the formal right to allocate land in Earth Priests where they could find them, and failing this they gave these powers to colonial-installed chiefs. Under a land policy that empowered rulers to allocate land usage, an outsider's use of the same area of land need not reflect the fact that the land-using community had admitted him under the belief that he was credible. It might only reflect the ruler's command. This created uncertainty in exchanging with outsiders and promoted in-group interactions.

Likewise, colonial policy restricting migration inhibited individuals' ability to signal credibility to members of other communities, diminishing their ability to interact peacefully. In precolonial Africa, where individuals could come and go between areas as these pleased, it was possible for them to be "members" of multiple communities, and, as such, to exchange with the members of multiple groups. Furthermore, agents' ability to voluntarily exit social groups strongly signaled their credibility to group members where they stayed. By legally requiring individuals to remain attached to their ruler-allocated areas of land, colonial land policy created noise in the signals used to convey credibility to outsiders. In some cases colonial policy explicitly prohibited rulers from allocating land to outsiders or restricted the kind of land access that outsiders could have, further undermining inter-group exchange. This result contributed to the sharp rise in property disputes between Africans under colonialism. Instead of property usage creating membership in a group and cooperation, it became a primary point of conflict.

Colonial policy regarding native religious practice and organizations also incapacitated the signals sent between diverse individuals to make possible widespread exchange. Colonial powers in most places worked closely with Christian missionaries to curtail what they considered offensive native religious practices. Elsewhere, colonial law explicitly prohibited certain religious practices and associations, in particular those associated with secret societies. Colonial criminalization of many religious practices and certain quasi-religious associations like cults and secret societies effectively eliminated these practices and organizations as potential signals of credibility to outsiders, further undermining socially diverse individuals' ability to cooperate.

4.4 CONCLUDING REMARKS

The social science literature generally sees social diversity as a significant negative when it comes to economic performance. While, theoretically, there are reasons fractionalization may lead to problems that thwart economic progress, there are also reasons – virtually undiscussed in this literature – for why diversity might actually benefit economic progress. The literature tends to find unhappy effects of diversity on economic outcomes. But it also finds that when institutions are high quality that they go away. It is therefore somewhat strange that diversity continues to be seen as an important reason for economic decay in many parts of the developing world.

It seems quite straightforward that these parts of the world are not suffering because there is a great deal of diversity in them. Rather, they are suffering because they have poor institutions. These institutional failures – namely the absence of property protection and unconstrained government – would encourage conflict and decline even in the most homogeneous of societies. Compared to the issue of institutional failure itself, whether or not social heterogeneity exacerbates the negative effects of institutional failure is quite unimportant. To use a bad analogy, having one's arm chopped off may be especially life-threatening for people with thin blood. But the main problem is to avoid having one's arm chopped off. Focusing on the "problems of thin blood" is bizarre and misplaces the point of concern. The same is true with respect of focusing on the problems of social diversity, when attention should be focused on the problems of institutional failure instead.

It's true that social diversity may influence what institutions are adopted, and thus indirectly contribute to this larger problem. But it seems that the larger problem runs in the other direction. That is, far more damage is done by "bad" institutions that undermine socially diverse individuals' realize the gains from widespread, inter-group cooperation. We are likely to learn more of value about fractionalization's relationship to economic outcomes by focusing our energies on exploring this issue, which we hope future research will consider in greater depth.

NOTES

1. On polarization, see Esteban and Ray (1994, 2008).
2. Leeson (2009) discusses some private institutions that the members of warring social groups developed to reduce and control inter-group conflict in the sixteenth-century Anglo-Scottish borderlands.
3. The following discussion draws extensively on Leeson (2005).

REFERENCES

Aghion, P., A. Alesina and F. Trebbi (2004), "Endogenous political institutions", *Quarterly Journal of Economics*, **119** (2), 565–611.

Alesina, A., R. Baqir and W. Easterly (1999), "Public goods and ethnic divisions", *Quarterly Journal of Economics*, **114** (4), 1243–84.

Alesina, A., A. Devleeschauwer, W. Easterly, S. Kurlat and R. Wacziarg (2003), "Fractionalization", *Journal of Economic Growth*, **8** (2), 155–94.

Alesina, A. and A. Drazen (1991), "Why are stabilizations delayed?" *American Economic Review*, **81** (5), 1170–88.

Alesina, A. and D. Rodrik (1994), "Distributive politics and economic growth", *The Quarterly Journal of Economics*, **109** (2), 465–90.

Alesina, A. and E. Spolaore (1997), "On the number and size of nations", *QuarterlyJournal of Economics*, **112** (4), 1027–56.

Alesina, A. and G. Tabellini (1989), "External debt, capital flight and political risk", *Journal of International Economics*, **27** (3–4), 199–220.

Annett, A. (2001), "Social fractionalization, political instability, and the size of government," *IMF Staff Papers*, **48** (3), 561–92.

Barr, A. and A. Oduro (2002), "Ethnic fractionalization in African labour markets," *Journal of Development Economics*, **68** (2), 355–79.

Blimes, R.J. (2006), "The indirect effect of ethnic heterogeneity on the likelihood of civil war onset," *Journal of Conflict Resolution*, **50** (4), 536–47.

Bossert, W., C. D'Ambrosio and E. La Ferrara (2006), "A generalized index of fractionalization", Innocenzo Gasparini Institute for Economic Research Working Paper No. 313.

Carilli, A.M., C.J. Coyne and P.T. Leeson (2008), "Government intervention and the structure of social capital", *Review of Austrian Economics*, **21** (2–3), 209–218.

Canning, D. and M. Fay (1993), "The effect of transportation networks on economic growth", Discussion Paper Series, Columbia University, Department of Economics.

Central Intelligence Agency (2000), *CIA World Factbook*, Washington DC: CIA Office of Public Affairs.

Collier, P. (1998), "The political economy of ethnicity", The Centre for the Study of African Economies Working Paper Series, Paper 72.

Collier, P. (2001), "Ethnic diversity: an economic analysis", *Economic Policy*, **32**, 128–66.

Collier, P. and A. Garg (1998), "On kin groups and wages in Africa", *Oxford Bulletin of Economics and Statistics*, **61** (2), 133–51.

Collier, P. and A. Hoeffler (1998), "On economic causes of civil war", *Oxford Economic Papers*, **50** (4), 563–73.

Collier, P. and A. Hoeffler (2004), "Greed and grievance in civil war", *Oxford Economic Papers*, **56** (4), 563–95.

Dincer, O.C. (2008), "Ethnic and religious diversity and corruption", *Economic Letters*, **99** (1), 98–102.

Easterly, W. (2001a), "Can institutions resolve ethnic conflict", *Economic Development and Cultural Change*, **49** (4), 687–706.

Easterly, W. and R. Levine (1997), "Africa's growth tragedy: policies and ethnic divisions", The Quaterly Journal of Economics, **112** (4), 1203–1250.

Ellingsen, T. (2000), "Colorful community or ethnic witches' brew? Multiethnicity and domestic conflict during and after the Cold War", *Journal of Conflict resolution*, **44** (2), 228–49.

Encyclopedia Britannica (2001), Chicago, IL: Encyclopedia Britannica.

Esteban, J. and D. Ray (1994), "On the measurement of polarization", *Econometrica*, **62** (4), 819–51.

Esteban, J. and D. Ray (2008), "On the salience of ethnic conflict", *American Economic Review*, **98** (5), 2185–202.

Fearon, J.D. (2003), "Ethnic structure and cultural diversity by country", *Journal of Economic Growth*, **8** (2), 195–222.

Fearon, J.D. and D.D. Laitin (1996), "Explaining interethnic cooperation", *American Political Science Review*, **90** (4), 715–35.

Fearon, J.D. and D.D. Laitin (2003), "Ethnicity, insurgency, and civil war", *American Political Science Review*, **97** (1), 75–90.

Gunnemark, E.V. (1991), *Countries, Peoples, and their Languages: The LinguisticHandbook*, Gothenburg, Sweden: Lanstryckeriet.

Gurr, T.R. and W.H. Moore (1997), "Ethnopolitical rebellion: a cross sectional analysis of the 1980s with risk assessments for the 1990s", *American Journal of Political Science*, **41** (4), 1079–103.

La Porta, R., F. Lopez de Silanes, A. Shleifer and R.W. Vishny (1999), "The quality of Government", *Journal of Law, Economics, and Organization*, **15** (1), 222–79.

Leeson, P.T. (2005), "Endogenizing fractionalization", *Journal of Institutional Economics*, **1** (1), 75–98.

Leeson, P.T. (2006), "Cooperation and conflict: evidence on self-enforcing arrangements and heterogeneous groups", *American Journal of Economics and Sociology*, **65** (4), 891–907.

Leeson, P.T. (2007), "Balkanization and assimilation: examining the effects of state-created homogeneity", *Review of Social Economy*, **65** (2), 141–64.

Leeson, P.T. (2008), "Social distance and self-enforcing exchange", *Journal of Legal Studies*, **37** (1), 161–88.

Leeson, P.T. (2009), "The laws of lawlessness", *Journal of Legal Studies*, **38** (2), 471–503.

Mauro, P. (1995), "Corruption and growth", *Quarterly Journal of Economics*, **110** (3), 681–712.

Montalvo, J.G. and M. Reynal-Querol (2005a), "Ethnic diversity and economic development", *Journal of Development Economics*, **76** (2), 293–323.

Montalvo, J.G. and M. Reynal-Querol (2005b), "Ethnic polarization, potential conflict, and civil wars", *American Economic Review*, **95** (3), 796–816.

Muller, S.H. (1964), *The World's Living Languages: Basic Facts of Their Structure, Kinship, Location, and Number of Speakers*, New York, NY: Ungar.

Persson, T., G. Roland and G.Tabellini (1997), "Separation of powers and political accountability", *Quarterly Journal of Economics*, **112** (4), 1163–202.

Posner, D.N. (2004a), "Measuring ethnic fractionalization in Africa", *American Journal of Political Science*, **48** (4), 849–63.

Posner, D.N. (2004b), "The political salience of cultural difference: why Chewas and Tumbukas are allies in Zambia and adversaries in Malawi", *American Political Science Review*, **98** (4), 529–45.

Roberts, J. (1962), "Sociocultural change and communication problems", *Study of the Role of Second Languages in Asia, Africa, and Latin America*, Frank A. Rice (ed).,Washington DC: Center for Applied Linguistics of the Modern Language Association of America, pp. 105–23.

Roberts, R. and K. Mann (1991), "Law in Colonial Africa", in K. Mann and R. Roberts (eds), *Law in Colonial Africa*, Portsmouth, NH: Heinmann.

Shleifer, A. and R. Vishny (1993), "Corruption", The Quarterly Journal of Economics, **108** (3), 599–617.

5 Psychological aspects of war
Iain Hardie, Dominic Johnson and Dominic Tierney

5.1 INTRODUCTION

Large segments of the social sciences remain dominated by the idea that humans are "rational" beings, whose decisions and behavior can be understood and predicted by analysing the costs, benefits and risks at stake. Decades of research in experimental psychology have cast doubt on this model (Gilovich, Griffin and Kahneman 2002; Sears, Huddy and Jervis 2003; Fiske and Taylor 2007), and the recent financial crisis has driven the point home to economists and political economists alike (Akerlof and Shiller 2009). In many situations, humans are not rational decision-makers. Instead, our judgments and decisions are dramatically influenced by a variety of psychological biases, and by physiological states of emotion, stress and other biochemical phenomena (such as hormones). Models that rely on rational choice are thus intrinsically built on flawed assumptions, even if they sometimes approximate observed behavior. Nowhere are these assumptions more important than understanding the causes and consequences of war, where the costs of poor decisions – and even of poor theoretical models underlying them – can be measured in blood and treasure.

Rejecting or revising rational choice models does not mean the end of useful models or predictions. Deviations from the expectations of rational choice theory are not random or unpredictable. On the contrary, the findings of experimental psychology suggest that people have *systematic, predictable* judgment and decision-making biases in given contexts. If you know the context, you can predict (on average) how people will respond as well as the direction of bias. For example, people become more risk-acceptant when they are facing losses rather than gains. Thus, although the "cognitive revolution" may lead to the rejection or modification of cherished models, it also (in principle) produces more accurate predictions about real people in the real world.

In the following, we introduce the concept of psychological biases. We then outline some of the biases most important to war. This is followed by an examination of some broad "independent variables" – *when* should we expect psychological biases to contribute more or less to policy outcomes?

Finally, we present some conclusions about the status and future of psychological biases in the political economy of war.

5.1.1   What are Psychological Biases?

In this chapter we are not concerned with psychological *pathologies* – dysfunctions of the human brain arising from physiological or neurological disorders or damage that lead to clinical psychiatric conditions. Such conditions may be very important for international relations where they occur among key decision-makers (Ludwig 2002; Post 2003; Post and George 2004; McDermott 2007). However, our quarry is something less blatant but no less important: psychological phenomena that potentially influence judgment and decision-making among *normal mentally healthy adults*. These phenomena arise from the normal biological structure and functioning of the human brain.

Experimental research in cognitive and motivational psychology and behavioral economics reveal a vast array of biases in judgment and decision-making (for some major reviews, see Kagel and Roth 1995; Tetlock 1998; Gilovich et al. 2002; Sears et al. 2003; Fiske and Taylor 2007). There are dozens of named biases, including such phenomena as: the "availability heuristic" (a tendency to make predictions that are biased by recent experience); the "bandwagon effect" (a tendency to do or believe the same as others); the "projection bias" (a tendency to assume that others share similar beliefs to oneself); the "false consensus effect" (a tendency to expect others to agree with oneself); and "discounting bias" (to prefer immediate over long-term rewards). Some of the best known biases have entire research programs centered around them, such as prospect theory, cognitive dissonance, overconfidence, in-group/out-group bias, and the fundamental attribution error – important phenomena that we will discuss in more detail later.

Despite this long research tradition, a classically trained economist or political economist might well remain skeptical of the importance of psychological biases. The implication is that humans are constantly making errors and mistakes, which would incur considerable costs over time. Therefore, psychological biases may seem both descriptively and normatively suspect. Do people really make such costly mistakes in real life? Don't people learn from their errors and improve? From an evolutionary standpoint, shouldn't millions of years of natural selection have eradicated such costly traits? One might therefore suspect that many such results stem from psychologists "setting people up" in odd or unusual settings, or even a publishing bias in which quirky results are preferentially published over completely unsurprising ones.

However, there is a growing mountain of literature demonstrating that psychological biases are widespread, pervasive and powerful among diverse subject groups, across cultures and across a range of contexts and settings. Results are robust and replicable, and there is no longer any doubt that they describe real phenomena in the population at large.

A further criticism is that psychological biases are typically discovered and studied using student subjects. How do we know whether such findings apply to real-world decision-makers? Surely professional decision-makers are *less* likely to exhibit such biases because they are more intelligent or experienced? There is some evidence that IQ correlates with rationality in economic games (Burnham 2009), that expert financial decision-makers may be less likely to fall prey to certain biases (Fenton-O'Creevy 2005) and that students and military personnel differ in their responses to experimental scenarios (Redd, Mintz and Vedlitz 2006).

However, there is plenty of theory and evidence to suggest that, on the whole, expert decision-makers are just as likely to exhibit psychological biases as anyone else (Tetlock 2005; Hermann and Choi 2007). An important distinction here is that expert decision-makers may (or may not) be better at avoiding *errors* or *mistakes* (that is, poor judgment which can be improved on with experience), but there is no reason to suspect that they are immune from *psychological biases*, which are the result of brain structure and function – and thus common to all people (we all have human brains). Experience and intelligence can add cautious thought processes, but they do not necessarily eliminate underlying biases.

If anything, elite decision-makers may be *more* likely to exhibit psychological biases than the average person. First, they usually have limited time, which decreases the effort available for weighing up alternative options and their costs, benefits, and risks. Second, they are likely to be under great stress (at least with respect to the events at hand), which is exactly the kind of state in which the brain will revert to subconscious decision-making heuristics (Rosen 2004; Wilson 2004). Third, the stakes are high in politics (especially in times of crisis or war), which may increase the activation or influence of some psychological biases. For example, cognitive dissonance may not really come into play over trivial issues about which you do not care, but becomes extremely powerful precisely when core beliefs are being challenged or cherished desires are under threat.

5.2   PSYCHOLOGICAL BIASES AND WAR

An initial null hypothesis might be that wars are fought over material interests, begun and won by the materially stronger side, while victors gain and losers suffer. A rational approach to the political economy of war would likely start with these assumptions. In practice, there are radical deviations even from these simple notions. Wars are often motivated (at least partly) by non-material factors such as glory, pride, honor, reputation, revenge, justice, fear, hatred and overconfidence (Tuchman 1984; Welch 1993; Mercer 1996; Toft 2003; Johnson 2004). Even wars over territory, which might appear to come closest to the kind of conflicts that would be fought over solid material gains and losses, appear to contain a large psychological element. A recent review found that, if there is any consensus about territoriality and war, it is that symbolic, not material, interests drive war over territory (Kahler and Walter 2006). Other trends are also surprising. Often the weaker side initiates and even wins wars (Mack 1975; Paul 1994; Wang and Ray 1994; Arreguín-Toft 2005), and many wars are followed by widely differing perceptions of the winners and losers (Johnson and Tierney 2006; Mandel 2006; Martel 2006).

The key underlying cause of such puzzling behavior is human psychology. A number of psychological phenomena affecting decision-making elites, the media, soldiers and the public are powerful enough to help initiate wars, to support and fight them in widely differing ways, and in extreme cases, to turn victories into defeats. Although by no means exhaustive (for other reviews, see Jervis 1976; Sears et al. 2003; McDermott 2004a), in the following section we outline several biases that are potentially important for the political economy of war.

5.2.1   Threat Assessment

Wars (and international relations in general, via the Security Dilemma) typically centre around some kind of threat. But what matters most in terms of explaining and predicting war is the *perception* of threat – real or imagined. Psychological biases play a huge role in the assessment of and response to threat. A major phenomenon revealed by experimental psychology is the "Fundamental Attribution Error" (FAE), in which people tend to attribute the behavior of others to "dispositional" causes (their characteristics, personality, or intentions), while one's own behavior is attributed to "situational" causes (such as limited choices, environmental constraints, necessity, or competing concerns, Jones and Harris 1967; Darley and Cooper 1998). In international relations, this means that people are likely to perceive the actions of foreign states (for example, military deployments, territorial claims, alliances or economic budgets) as representing deliberate belligerence while one's own military deployments, territorial claims, alliances or economic budgets are perceived as being defensive or a response to circumstance. It is also assumed that this defensive motivation will be obvious to the adversary, but, of course, they see the situation with a similar set of biases from the other side.

The effect of the FAE is just as important (and dangerous) in international trade and cooperation as it is in conflict. Members of one nation are likely to perceive their own painstaking efforts at, say, environmental policy or the supply of energy resources to other countries as necessarily slow or limited because they are working against numerous difficult constraints, whereas they will perceive the same actions by other nations as a deliberate attempt to make relative gains, oblivious or dismissive of those other countries' own unique or similar constraints. China, for example, gets heavy attention in the US news media for its burgeoning consumption rates, which is hardly surprising for a rapidly developing nation of a billion people, but less attention on positive aspects such as its environmental protection schemes (Diamond 2008). Similarly, interruptions in gas supplies to Europe as a result of a dispute between Russia and the Ukraine can be seen as primarily a legitimate commercial dispute about under-priced gas, but there is no shortage of theories that it is geopolitically inspired. Whatever the reality, the Fundamental Attribution Error predicts that people will be biased in a conspiratorial direction.

5.2.2 Risk-taking: Rolling the Dice of War

Another key psychological phenomenon affecting people's perceptions of threat is prospect theory. In decisions involving uncertain outcomes, people are risk-averse when choosing among potential gains (the "domain of gains"), but risk-prone when choosing among potential losses (the "domain of losses"). In particular, people tend to gamble more when facing definite losses (Kahneman and Tversky 1979; McDermott 1997). Various authors have successfully used prospect theory to explain otherwise puzzling decisions in key events such as the Cuban Missile Crisis and Japan's decision for war in 1941 (for reviews, see McDermott 1997; Levy 2000, 2003). The bias is also likely to be important for the political economy of war, offering an explanation for why states escalate wars rather than accept small losses, despite mounting human and material costs (Taliaferro 2004).

The predictions of prospect theory depend on the decision-maker's *perception* of the relevant costs and risks. One study of US climate change policy argued that President Bill Clinton saw himself in a domain of losses (because of impending environmental costs) while George W. Bush saw himself in a domain of gains (because of impending economic growth). Consequently, Clinton was considered to be risk-*prone* in pursuing the Kyoto protocol, given the inherent uncertainties and costs of the treaty for the US economy (Nelson 2005). Perceptions thus play a role in whether, when and how prospect theory influences policy preferences across different people and circumstances.

5.2.3 Enemies

Of the long list of psychological biases in human judgment and decision-making, one of the most widespread and powerful is the "in-group/out-group" bias – a pervasive feature of normal, mentally healthy adults that forms the backbone of a now dominant paradigm of social psychology known as "Social Identity Theory" (Tajfel 1974; Turner 1987). A mass of empirical evidence demonstrates that people: (1) rapidly identify with their in-groups (even strangers assigned into arbitrary groups); (2) systematically overvalue their own group's performance and qualities; and (3) systematically devalue the performance and qualities of other groups (Fiske 2002; Hewstone, Rubin and Willis 2002; Fiske and Taylor 2007). To put it bluntly, humans are nepotistic and prejudiced. Decades of research have replicated and confirmed the basic finding, and experiments have revealed a number of related effects, for example, that people over-estimate the ideological difference between their own and opposing groups, and see their opponents' viewpoints as more extreme than they in fact are (Robinson and Keltner 1997).

The in-group/out-group bias is seen as a key cause of conflict, because it contributes to prejudice, racism, xenophobia, violence and war. Psychologist Susan Fiske called it nothing less than the "problem of the century" (Fiske 2002). Out-groups are not necessarily "enemies" of course, but this is testament to the power of the bias – it occurs even in so called "minimal group paradigms", that is, groups which are created entirely artificially in experimental labs (for instance, according to whether people guess the number of dots on a picture to be more or less than a given number, or whether they prefer paintings by Klimt or Klee). The bias is of course hugely magnified in real life groups in direct, high stakes (supposed or actual) competition with each other – Manchester United versus Chelsea, Republican versus Democrat, "West" versus "terrorists", Nazi versus Red Army.

The in-group/out-group bias is important for our analysis of war for a very simple reason. If people engage in aggression (at least partly) on the basis of expected costs and benefits and their probability of winning, then anything that increases their expected gains and reduces the expected costs (via the perception of their side's superiority and the other sides' inferiority) will increase the perceived utility, and thus the probability of inter-group violence.

The in-group/out-group bias also makes the group more likely to become offended by the adversary in the first place – cocooned as they are in a bubble of self-reinforcing superiority – again increasing the probability of conflict. A review of human aggression studies showed that "groups whose members demonstrate higher levels of self-esteem also demonstrate higher levels of hostility and violence," and "collective violence tends to be linked to explicit beliefs in the superiority of the violent group" (Rabbie 1989; Baumeister and Boden 1998, pp. 115, 116). This finding concurs with studies on the Mafia and youth gangs, in which lethal violence tends to follow specific insults to a group's status (Wrangham and Wilson 2004). As we saw with the Fundamental Attribution Error, even behavior that would seem innocuous to a third party may come to be seen as an imminent threat that demands a response.

The in-group/out-group bias is important for political economy because, beyond any direct contribution to causing or exacerbating expensive wars, the mere *perception* of adversaries as an alien out-group can lead to significant peacetime expenses including arms races and economic competition. One could argue that the USSR, for example, bankrupted itself for fear of destruction by its enemies.

5.2.4   Causes of War

The literature on the causes of war is enormous (for reviews, see Singer and Small 1972; Blainey 1973; Vasquez 1993, 2000; Fearon 1995; Brown 1998; Van Evera 1999; Bennett and Stam 2004; Levy, this volume; Jackson and Morelli, this volume). Violent conflict has been traced to a wide range of causes including conquest, territory, balance of power, arms races, political power, democratization, preemptive wars to counter imminent threats, preventive wars to thwart rising powers and so on.

For our purposes, much more interesting than the various purported causes of war are the common themes cutting across many such explanations. Irrespective of the underlying causes of war (whether political, economic, social and so forth), decision-making about if, when and how to fight often appears to be affected by common psychological biases. Perhaps the most commonly cited psychological factor across history, even championed by scholars otherwise promoting alternative theories, is overconfidence.

Overconfidence has long been identified as a cause of war, because it encourages over-ambition, poor planning, reckless diplomacy, overestimation of one's strength, underestimation of the enemy and a resultant underestimation of the costs of war (which can include a staggering economic cost). Overconfidence thus provokes conflicts that would otherwise be avoided, and risks battlefield defeat against superior opponents. Two landmark books on the causes of war – despite being separated by 25 years of work on the subject – both pointed to overconfidence (or "false optimism") as a recurrent and powerful phenomenon on the eve of war (Blainey 1973; Van Evera 1999).

A number of additional studies of the causes of war found over-confidence to be a critical factor (White 1968; Lebow 1981; Howard 1983; Tuchman 1984; Stoessinger 1998; Ganguly 2001; Johnson 2004; Kahneman and Renshon 2006). For example, many have argued that biases towards overconfidence contributed to European states' belief that they could all win a quick victory in 1914 (Van Evera 1999), US expectations in Vietnam (Tuchman 1984), and the Bush administrations' discounting of the challenges of post-war reconstruction in Iraq (Fallows 2004; Woodward 2005). Jack Levy concluded that: "Of all forms of mis-perceptions, the one most likely to play a critical role in the processes leading to war is the underestimation of the adversary's capabilities" (Levy 1983, p. 83).

Psychologist Irving Janis argued that decision-making within groups is especially likely to exacerbate optimistic biases because a process of "groupthink" creates and reinforces perceptions of superiority. Groups tend toward: a shared illusion of invulnerability; collective attempts to maintain shaky but cherished assumptions; an unquestioned belief in the group's inherent morality; stereotyping the enemy as too evil for nego-tiation, or too weak to be a threat; a collective illusion of unanimity in a majority viewpoint (based on the faulty assumption that silence means consent); and self-appointed "mind guards" to protect the group from information that might weaken resolve (Janis 1972; t'Hart 1990; Kowert 2002).

Although overconfidence may seem strange to rational choice theorists, it is no surprise to psychologists or behavioural economists. A long stand-ing research program has documented how normal, mentally healthy people tend to have "positive illusions" about their abilities, their control over events, and their vulnerability to risk (Taylor and Brown 1988, 1994; Taylor 1989; Nettle 2004). Positive illusions have long been cited as a cause of policy failure and disasters in political science but also in a wide range of other domains, from sports, to business, to climate change, to finance and banking (Tuchman 1984; Goleman 1989; Camerer and Lovallo 1999; Wrangham 1999; Barber and Odean 2001; Griffin and Tversky 2002; Johnson 2004; Van den Steen 2004; Fenton-O'Creevy 2005; Malmendier and Tate 2005; Johnson et al. 2006; Gladwell 2009).

5.2.5 Fighting Wars

The prosecution of war requires continued assessment of resources, successes, failures and alternative strategies. One significant psychological phenomenon that affects such assessments is "cognitive dissonance." Contradictory information generates psychological discomfort, and as a result people subconsciously: (1) try to make dissonant information fit their existing beliefs; and (2) actively avoid situations that increase dissonance. The phenomenon of cognitive dissonance therefore tends to select, organize or distort conflicting information so that it matches preferred or pre-existing beliefs (Festinger 1957; Cooper 2007). Cognitive dissonance appears to be subtle yet powerful – we are often blissfully unaware that we are passively excluding or discounting important information from our thoughts.

For example, in the lead up to the 2003 Iraq War, the Bush administration downplayed information suggesting that war with Iraq was unnecessary or would go badly. Major assessments of the likely challenges of post-war reconstruction – carried out by the US Army War College and the US State Department – went unheeded. There appears to have been little useful consideration of the likely financial cost of the war, estimated subsequently at US$3 trillion (Stiglitz and Bilmes 2008). One insider, the White House economic advisor Lawrence Lindsay, suggested to the *Wall Street Journal* a figure of $100–200 billion, and was forced to resign soon afterward (Fallows 2004).

In contrast, dubious and unsubstantiated evidence that Iraq had, or was developing, weapons of mass destruction (WMD) was treated to a much lower level of critical scrutiny (Fallows 2004; Woodward 2004, 2005). Even pieces of raw intelligence were discussed by top administration officials (most famously by Colin Powell at the UN), which, in normal times, would never have occurred without rigorous processing by intelligence analysts. This was of course partly for political reasons (generating or protecting the information that would support their favored policy), but there is good evidence that, when decision-makers decided on their preferred course of action (war), cognitive dissonance played its part by generating the image of Iraq they wanted to see.

5.2.6 Types of Wars

Scholars have categorized wars in many ways, but one important distinction relevant to today's conflicts is the difference between conventional wars between states (such as the 1991 Persian Gulf War) and nation-building missions (such as the current operations in Iraq and Afghanistan).

Here, psychological factors may lead people to support the former more than the latter (Johnson and Tierney 2006; Tierney 2010).

Polls suggest that Americans are quite favorable to the use of force to restrain the aggressive foreign policies of other states. They are also sympathetic to the use of force for strictly humanitarian operations. However, the US public has little stomach for nation-building missions that aim to engender internal political change (Russett and Nincic 1976; Jentleson and Britton 1998).

Conventional wars include clear markers of success such as shifting front lines and casualties. By contrast, nation-building missions are a complex mix of political, economic, social and military goals, none of which have clear metrics of success. Here, people can supply their own, often unattainable, metrics based on Western standards of democracy and stability, or the idealist rhetoric of presidents. Media presentation is also crucial. In nation-building missions, the fact that electricity production is up or unemployment is down is rarely reported, but dramatic events like bombings are front-page news. Progress may be genuine and impressive, but it seldom excites people who can more easily see the costs in lives and dollars.

Opposition to nation-building is also influenced by historical perceptions, in particular in the United States by memories of Vietnam. Such memories revive buried fears about getting bogged down in an unwinnable war against an amorphous enemy in civilian clothes (the analogy is often drawn with Iraq and Afghanistan). In Somalia, polling questions that evoked Vietnam by using the phrase "bogged down" produced more critical responses than similar questions without the evocative phrase (Johnson and Tierney 2006, p. 228). Irrespective of the actual gains and losses on the ground, nation-building missions can *look* like another Vietnam, and this belief can have powerful consequences whether the analogy is a good one or not.

Perhaps most significantly for political economy, nation-building missions involve massive infrastructure investment and multi-year financial commitments, and the public is likely to conclude that such expenditure is wasted in a quagmire. The initial US intervention in Somalia in 1992 helped to avert a humanitarian crisis, and cost the US about $700 million. The political scientist John Mueller concluded: "Never before, perhaps, has so much been done for so many at such little cost" (Mueller 2004, p. 127). Unfortunately, Americans forgot all of this, as they quickly perceived the mission as a debacle.

5.3   SOURCES OF VARIATION: WHEN DO PSYCHOLOGICAL BIASES MATTER?

Psychological biases vary widely along at least three dimensions: (1) they vary among individuals (different individuals will do different things); (2) they vary with contextual factors (the same individual will do different things in different contexts); (3) they vary with the degree to which they are expressed in different decision-making environments (the same individual in the same context will lead to different policy outcomes in different regimes). So in terms of their impact on international relations, human traits are not fixed at all. Their many sources of variation can in principle explain large amounts of variation in political outcomes such as war and peace.

A given psychological bias (such as prospect theory or cognitive dissonance) often has its own *specific* sources of variation. However, there are also some *general* factors (independent variables), which alter the potential influence of a wide variety of different psychological biases for similar reasons. Here, we consider three: regime type, decision-making process and urgency.

5.3.1   Regime Type

Psychological biases may be equally likely to *occur* in any state. However, they are more likely to *influence policy outcomes* in non-democratic states (Janis 1972; t'Hart 1990; Tetlock 1998; Kowert 2002). An autocrat's beliefs and wishes can be translated into policy directly and largely unopposed, and there are no rival parties or free media to challenge the government line. In democracies, by contrast, constitutional checks and balances, as well as public and media scrutiny, tend to detect, oppose, impede or prevent faulty assessment by the leadership. If and when psychological biases are at work, such protocols make individuals less able to shape policy by personal whim. Any psychological biases experienced by, say, Alexander the Great could directly affect policy outcomes, but modern leaders must navigate their preferences through a web of institutional constraints.

Beyond formal arrangements, the freewheeling "marketplace of ideas" in democracies helps to uncover self-serving arguments or unfounded assumptions, and protect democratic states from "myths of empire" that produce risky foreign adventures (Snyder 1991; Kaufmann 2004). Leaders in democracies are also more sensitive to domestic costs, and therefore initiate wars with greater care, only starting conflicts they are certain they can win (Reiter and Stam 2002).

Predictions about the effect of regime type on biases are corroborated by case studies. For example, Sumit Ganguly (2001) found that military over-optimism was evident in all of the wars between India and Pakistan, but it was much reduced on the Indian side because its more democratic institutions served to check unwarranted overconfidence.

Democracies, however, remain vulnerable to certain pathologies that promote psychological biases, such as the tendency to rally around the leader during the early stages of crises and wars. For example, Franklin D. Roosevelt received an enormous approval jump after Pearl Harbor, which was hardly a triumph for the United States (if anything, it exposed grave errors in foreign policy and intelligence, Kahn 1999). Similarly, the terrorist attacks of 9/11 and the US invasion of Iraq both had a major positive effect on Bush's presidential approval ratings. Furthermore, even apparently open decision-making groups may suffer from "groupthink" which subtly corroborates certain views and stifles others (Janis 1972; Mueller 1973; t'Hart 1990).

The marketplace of ideas may break down because certain actors control the flow of information, an administration's decision-making becomes closed and efficient, or institutional checks and balances are circumvented (Kaufmann 2004; Desch 2008). Louis Fisher (2003) argues that the democratic process failed to exert the normal checks and balances on presidential power prior to the 2003 Iraq War. Congress handed authorization for war to President George W. Bush, according to Fisher, in the belief that there was a significant WMD threat from Iraq, and that giving war powers to the president would help to *decrease* the chance of war (since it might act as a deterrent against Saddam Hussein).[1] However, Congress approved the resolution several months *before* the decision to invade, not by consensus following a rigorous debate, nor even by making a firm decision.[2] In the end, "the legislation would decide neither for nor against war. That judgment, which the Constitution places in Congress, would now be left in the hands of the President" (Fisher 2003, p. 404). This process may have allowed psychological biases, such as overconfidence, groupthink and cognitive dissonance, to emerge unchecked, and contributed to poor planning for the war (Alter 2002; Jervis 2003; Fallows 2004; Woodward 2004). In effect, the democratic model shifted closer to an autocratic model.

In summary, the extent of psychological biases may differ between individuals and between contexts. But none of this variation matters if psychological biases are blocked from affecting policy outcomes. Thus, variation in our main dependent variable of interest – war and peace – can be explained by the effectiveness of institutional checks and balances in preventing psychological biases creeping into policy decisions. Managing psychological biases is in part about managing the environments in which they thrive or die.

5.3.2   Decision-making Process

The decision-making *process* can also promote or reduce psychological biases, over and above differences in regime type. The more diverse the decision-making group, the more likely it is that biases will be averted by countervailing voices, differing experiences, mindsets, backgrounds, non-partisan opinions and devil's advocates. By comparison, a closed debate results in more limited options being raised or evaluated, a narrower range of voices being heard and an absence of challenges to assumptions.

The decision-making process may of course often be *correlated* with regime type. For example, autocratic leaders tend toward a closed model of decision-making. Cocooned in a world of "yes men," at the center of a system that glorifies them, autocrats are rarely challenged about their judgments and decisions, which often leaves their decision-making seriously compromised. In 2003, for example, Saddam Hussein remained apparently confident even as US tanks entered Baghdad (Woods, Lacey and Murray 2006).

However, there is also considerable variation in the decision-making process *within* regime types. Hitler's foreign policy decision-making, for example, was relatively open to begin with, and became closed after the Munich crisis, a change that affected the decision for war in 1939 (Johnson 2004; Roberts 2009). Such variation is evident within democracies as well. Certain American presidents such as Dwight Eisenhower favored a "collegial" style of decision-making with a major role for the Cabinet, while other presidents such as Richard Nixon supported a "centralized" decision-making structure in which real power rested in the hands of Nixon and Henry Kissinger (George 1980; George and George 1998).

Compare, for example, Kennedy's decision-making during the Cuban missile crisis, which promoted an intensive and expansive debate on US options, with Johnson's more closed decision-making environment over Vietnam. Johnson believed, as James Nathan noted in 1975, that "success in international crises was largely a matter of national guts; that the opponent would yield to superior force; that presidential control of force can be 'suitable,' 'selective,' 'swift,' 'effective,' and 'responsive' to civilian authority; and that crisis management and execution are too dangerous and events move too rapidly for anything but the tightest secrecy" (Nathan 1975, pp. 280–1). In Paul Kowert's view, Johnson "suffered a great deal politically from pursuing policies endorsed by ideologically unified top advisors but not subjected to wider scrutiny" (Kowert 2002, p. 164).

The decision-making process can be compromised at the wider government level as well. Especially early in the war, opposition to the prevailing policy of escalation was politically challenging, being interpreted as a lack of support for American soldiers fighting overseas, and an implicit admission of American failure. When new members of Congress convened in 1965, Vice President Hubert Humphrey told them, "If you feel an urge to stand up and make a speech attacking Vietnamese policy, don't make it" (Tuchman 1984, p. 334). He was not asking them to cover up governmental mistakes, but rather offering them professional advice about how to ensure reelection.

5.3.3   Urgency

The rational model of decision-making is most likely to approximate reality when one has plenty of time to think through and debate hypothetical problems. By contrast, psychological biases are likely to be important precisely when we do *not* have so much time or opportunity to think, such as in a rapidly escalating crisis or war. Experiments with students demonstrate, of course, that many psychological biases occur even when the stakes are low (for example, a few dollars), there is little or no stress (anonymous games) and subjects have no personal vested interest in the game (often the tasks are boring or deliberately abstract). However, there is little doubt that psychological biases are also evident or actually exaggerated among leaders embroiled in high stakes crises.

In urgent situations, psychological biases are likely to be more common and more severe because: (1) decisions must be made quickly (so not all options, costs, benefits and risks can be considered carefully); (2) there is no time to gather or debate information (making it less likely that faulty judgments will be corrected); (3) policy options are limited (because an urgent situation precludes preventive measures and demands action); (4) decision-makers are under stress (which can impair judgment, Nicholson 1992; Rosen 2004); (5) there are strong emotions (which directly alter perceptions, judgments and decisions, McDermott 2004b); and (6) the stakes are high (which makes many psychological biases, such as cognitive dissonance, more powerful).

5.4   CONCLUSIONS

We can explain a lot about war without ever thinking about psychology. However, wars are launched and fought by human beings, and it is valuable to explore the role of human psychology. Decisions to fight come down to strategic choices, and the game theory literature not surprisingly focuses our attention on the role of human judgments and decision-making (Powell 1991; Stein 1990; Allan and Schmidt 1994), which often violate the expectations of rational choice theory (Kahneman, Slovic and Tversky 1982; Gilovich et al. 2002).

Psychological explanations of war are already a core part of political science (Jervis 1976; Tetlock 1998; Sears et al. 2003; McDermott 2004a; Rosen 2004), not to mention underlying (in the guise of assumptions about human nature) major theories of international relations (Waltz 1959; Brown 1998). But this has evidently not filtered through into political economy (Elms 2008). Recent world events – especially the financial crisis – and other emerging literature suggest that psychology is a major and underappreciated factor in international political economy (Akerlof and Shiller 2009).

There is no reason to expect that psychological biases will disappear with time, irrespective of education, training or experience. They are consequences of how the brain evolved to function in the Pleistocene environment of the last 2 million years of human history, and cannot be changed (Pinker 2002; Barkow 2006). What we *can* change, however, is the environment and contexts in which these brains operate. If we identify and put people in conducive circumstances, we can avoid the emergence of detrimental biases and even exploit them to our advantage. One key example here is globalization. Our perceived social world is – in many ways – getting smaller as we are increasingly able to interact with other people and ideas globally and instantaneously. We are therefore less likely to lack information about other nations, more likely to gain feedback about our pre-existing beliefs and less likely to perceive ourselves as within a well-defined in-group and other nations as out-groups. Globalization, in theory, can limit the emergence and effect of certain psychological biases.

But other factors may increase the "mismatch" between our evolved psychology and effective decision-making. New technologies increasingly *distance* us from personal contact and the consequences of our actions, freeing us to act without the feedback and adjustment that governs behavior in normal face-to-face circumstances. The point was bluntly made by Nobel Laureate Niko Tinbergen, who argued that modern technology was a key promoter of aggression: "Very few aircrews who are willing, indeed eager, to drop their bombs 'on target' would be willing to strangle, stab, or burn children (or, for that matter, adults) with their own hands; they would stop short of killing, in response to the appeasement and distress signals of their opponents" (Tinbergen 1968, p. 1415). The rise of smart weapons, targeting on computer screens, pilotless drones and other forms of warfare means killing is easier. This may increase combat effectiveness, but it also may make the option of war more attractive.

The role of psychology may be increasingly important given the types of wars that we face in the twenty-first century. Modern conflicts increasingly tend to be small wars of intervention, nation-building and counter-insurgency (Mandel 2006; Kilcullen 2009) – precisely the kinds of wars that may appear compelling on humanitarian or security grounds but which end up being prone to considerable misperception (Johnson and Tierney 2006). With no clear front lines or material gains, ambiguity and prolonged operations leave goals and successes open to interpretation and bias, and psychological factors among elites, the media and voters take on a special importance.

There is great scope for more research. First, although there is a large literature applying *ideas* from psychology to political science, there are fewer that perform rigorous tests of predictions in comparison to alternative competing models (such as rational choice or socialization or political incentives). In many cases psychological phenomena are merely proposed as potentially important to a given political domain, with various predictions approximately fulfilled, but they have not always been subjected to high levels of scientific scrutiny. The acid test is whether psychological theories are stronger – in terms of explaining more variation in the dependent variable – than existing theories.

Second, political science and political economy do not have any tradition of experimentation. Instead, we often rely on case studies, or correlational studies with real-world empirical data. As a result, predictions about psychological phenomena tend to be transplanted directly from the psychology literature, and then used to explain behavior in very different political contexts. It would benefit the field to examine psychological phenomena in controlled laboratory manipulations that not only address causation rather than correlation, but which can be designed to better match our political contexts and research questions of interest. Recent work using wargames to study psychological phenomena in politically relevant settings is a step in this direction, albeit with their own complications and limitations that have to be addressed (Johnson et al. 2006; McDermott and Cowden 2008). Behavioral economics and neuroeconomics also offer growing experimental subfields that offer insights of direct importance for political economy (Elms 2008; Akerlof and Shiller 2009).

Third, we need to tackle several big underlying questions. Are psychological phenomena destined to offer small alterations to otherwise more general theories? Or can they do more? For instance, given the strong historical assumptions about human nature that underlie many dominant theories in international relations (stemming from Kant, Rousseau,

Hobbes, Waltz and so forth), anything that changes our underlying assumptions (and knowledge) about human nature offers the potential for novel theory building. As we accumulate a science of human nature, will psychology offer a new model of international relations?

To sum up, psychology has a long history and an increasing prominence in our understanding of war. The rise of ambiguous wars against non-state actors (as well as additional factors like partisan divergence and technological change) create fertile ground for psychological factors to wreak havoc in the future. Perhaps the one positive side is the rich potential for future studies across political science. These are vital to improving our theoretical models – and ultimately to effective decision-making in practice. At the least, the field would benefit immensely by bringing brains to debates over the political economy of war.

NOTES

1. This last factor was not only a belief among hawks – even French President Jacques Chirac held this view, and used it to convince the Syrians to vote in favor of the original UN resolution (Jervis 2003).
2. "Joint Resolution to Authorize the use of United States Armed Forces against Iraq." 107th Congress, 2nd Session, Resolution 114, 10 October 2002.

REFERENCES

Akerlof, G.A. and R.J. Shiller (2009), *Animal Spirits: How Human Psychology Drives the Economy, and Why it Matters for Global Capitalism*, Princeton, NJ: Princeton University Press.

Allan, P. and C. Schmidt (eds), (1994), *Game Theory and International Relations: Preferences, Information and Empirical Evidence*, Cheltenham, UK: Edward Elgar.

Alter, K.J. (2002), "Is 'groupthink' driving us to war?", *The Boston Globe*, 21 September 2002.

Arreguín-Toft, I. (2005), *How the Weak Win Wars: A Theory of Asymmetric Conflict*, Cambridge, UK: Cambridge University Press.

Barber, B.M. and T. Odean (2001), "Boys will be boys: gender, overconfidence, and common stock investment", *Quarterly Journal of Economics,* **116**, 261–92.

Barkow, J.H. (2006), *Missing the Revolution: Darwinism for Social Scientists*, Oxford, UK: Oxford University Press.

Baumeister, R.F. and J.M. Boden (1998), "Aggression and the self: high self-esteem, low selfcontrol, and ego threat", in R.G. Geen and E. Donnerstein (eds), *Human Aggression: Theories, Research, and Implications for Social Policy*, San Diego, CA: Academic Press, pp. 111–37.

Bennett, D.S. and A.C. Stam (2004), *The Behavioral Origins of War*, Ann Arbor, MI: University of Michigan Press.

Blainey, G.A. (1973), *The Causes of War*, New York, NY: Free Press.

Brown, M.E. (ed), (1998), *Theories of War and Peace*, Cambridge, MA: MIT Press.

Burnham, T. (2009), "Higher cognitive ability is associated with lower entries in a p-beauty contest", *Journal of Economic Behavior and Organization*, **72** (1), 171–5.

Camerer, C. and D. Lovallo (1999), "Overconfidence and excess entry: an experimental approach", *The American Economic Review*, **89** (1), 306–18.

Cooper, J. (2007), *Cognitive Dissonance: 50 Years of a Classic Theory*, New York, NY: Sage.

Darley, J.M. and J. Cooper (1998), *Attribution and Social Interaction: The Legacy of Edward E. Jones*, Washington DC: American Psychological Association Press.

Desch, M.C. (2008), *Power and Military Effectiveness: The Fallacy of Democratic Triumphalism*, Baltimore, MD: The Johns Hopkins University Press.

Diamond, J. (2008), "What's your consumption factor?", *New York Times*, 2 January 2008, p. A19.

Elms, D.K. (2008), "New directions for IPE: drawing from behavioral economics", *International Studies Review*, **10** (2), 239–65.

Fallows, J. (2004), "Blind into Baghdad", *The Atlantic Monthly* (January/February), 53–74.

Fearon, J.D. (1995), "Rationalist explanations for war", *International Organization*, **49** (3), 379–414.

Fenton-O'Creevy, M. (2005), *Traders: Risks, Decisions and Management in Financial Markets*, Oxford, UK: Oxford University Press.

Festinger, L. (1957), *A Theory of Cognitive Dissonance*, Stanford, CA: Stanford University Press.

Fisher, L. (2003), "Deciding on war against Iraq: institutional failures", *Political Science Quarterly*, **118** (3), 389–410.

Fiske, S.T. (2002), "What we know about bias and intergroup conflict, problem of the century", *Current Directions in Psychological Science*, **11**, 123–8.

Fiske, S.T. and S.E. Taylor (2007), *Social Cognition: From Brains to Culture*, New York, NY: McGraw-Hill.

Ganguly, S. (2001), *Conflict Unending: India-Pakistan Tensions Since 1947*, New Delhi: Oxford University Press.

George, A.L. (1980), *Presidential Decisionmaking in Foreign Policy: The Effective Use of Information and Advice*, Boulder, CO: Westview Press.

George, A.L. and J.L. George (1998), *Presidential Personality and Performance*, Boulder, CO: Westview Press.

Gilovich, T., D. Griffin and D. Kahneman (eds), (2002), *Heuristics and Biases: The Psychology of Intuitive Judgment*, Cambridge, UK: Cambridge University Press.

Gladwell, M. (2009), "Cocksure: banks, battles, and the psychology of overconfidence", *New Yorker*, 27 July 2009.

Goleman, D.J. (1989), "What is negative about positive illusions? When benefits for the individual harm the collective", *Journal of Social and Clinical Psychology*, **8** (2), 190–7.

Griffin, D.W. and A. Tversky (2002), "The weighing of evidence and the determinants of confidence", in T. Gilovich, D. Griffin and D. Kahneman (eds), *Heuristics and Biases: The Psychology of Intuitive Judgment*, Cambridge, UK: Cambridge University Press, pp. 230–49.

Hermann, R.K. and J.K. Choi (2007), "From prediction to learning: opening expert's minds to unfolding history", *International Security*, **31** (4), 132–61.

Hewstone, M., M. Rubin and H. Willis (2002), "Intergroup bias", *Annual Review of Psychology*, **53**, 575–604.

Howard, M. (1983), *The Causes of War and Other Essays*, Cambridge, MA: Harvard University Press.

Janis, I.L. (1972), *Victims of Groupthink: Psychological Studies of Policy Decisions and Fiascoes*, Boston, MA: Houghton Mifflin.

Jentleson, B.W. and R.L. Britton (1998), "Still pretty prudent: post-cold war American public opinion on the use of military force", *Journal of Conflict Resolution*, **42** (4), 395–417.

Jervis, R. (1976), *Perception and Misperception in International Politics*, Princeton, NJ: Princeton University Press.

Jervis, R. (2003), "The confrontation between Iraq and US: implications for the theory and practice of deterrence", *European Journal of International Relations*, **9** (2), 315–37.

Johnson, D.D.P. (2004), *Overconfidence and War: The Havoc and Glory of Positive Illusions*, Cambridge, MA: Harvard University Press.

Johnson, D.D.P., R. McDermott E. Barrett, et al. (2006), "Overconfidence in wargames: experimental evidence on expectations, aggression, gender and testosterone", *Proceedings of the Royal Society of London, Series B*, **273** (1600), 2513–20.

Johnson, D.D.P. and D.R. Tierney (2006), *Failing to Win: Perceptions of Victory and Defeat in International Politics*, Cambridge, MA: Harvard University Press.

Jones, E.E. and V.A. Harris (1967), "The attribution of attitudes", *Journal of Experimental Social Psychology*, **3**, 1–24.

Kagel, J.H. and A.E. Roth (eds), (1995), *The Handbook of Experimental Economics*, Princeton, NJ: Princeton University Press.

Kahler, M. and B.F. Walter (2006), *Territoriality and Conflict in an Era of Globalization*, Cambridge, UK: Cambridge University Press.

Kahn, D. (1999), "Pearl Harbor as an intelligence failure", in A. Iriye (ed.), *Pearl Harbor and the Coming of the Pacific War: A Brief History with Documents and Essays*, Boston, MA: Bedford/St. Martin's, pp. 158–69.

Kahneman, D. and J. Renshon (2006), "Why hawks win", *Foreign Policy* (158 January/ February), 34–38.

Kahneman, D., P. Slovic and A. Tversky (1982), *Judgment Under Uncertainty: Heuristics and Biases*, Cambridge, UK: Cambridge University Press.

Kahneman, D. and A. Tversky (1979), "Prospect theory: an analysis of decisions under risk", *Econometrica*, **47**, 263–91.

Kaufmann, C. (2004), "Threat inflation and the failure of the marketplace of ideas: the selling of the Iraq War", *International Security*, **29** (1), 5–48.

Kilcullen, D. (2009), *The Accidental Guerrilla: Fighting Small Wars in the Midst of a Big One*, Oxford, UK: Oxford University Press.

Kowert, P.A. (2002), *Groupthink or Deadlock: When Do Leaders Learn from Their Advisors?* Albany, NY: State University of Albany Press.

Lebow, R.N. (1981), *Between Peace and War: The Nature of International Crisis*, Baltimore, MD: John Hopkins.

Levy, J.S. (1983), "Misperception and the causes of war: theoretical linkages and analytical problems", *World Politics*, **36**, 76–99.

Levy, J.S. (2000), "Loss aversion, framing effects and international conflict", in M.I. Midlarsky (ed.), *Handbook of War Studies 2*, Michigan, MI: University of Michigan Press, pp. 193–221.

Levy, J.S. (2003), "Applications of Prospect Theory to political science", *Synthese*, **135** (2), 215–41.

Ludwig, A.M. (2002), *King of the Mountain: The Nature of Political Leadership*, Lexington, KY: University Press of Kentucky.

McDermott, R. (1997), *Risk-taking in International Politics: Prospect Theory in American Foreign Policy*, Ann Arbor, MI: University of Michigan Press.

McDermott, R. (2004a), *Political Psychology in International Relations*, Ann Arbor, MI: The University of Michigan Press.

McDermott, R. (2004b), "The feeling of rationality: the meaning of neuroscientific advances for political science", *Perspectives on Politics*, **2** (4), 691–706.

McDermott, R. (2007), *Presidential Leadership, Illness, and Decision Making*, Cambridge, UK: Cambridge University Press.

McDermott, R. and J. Cowden (2008), "The role of hostile communications in a crisis simulation game", *Peace and Conflict*, **14**, 151–67.

Mack, A.J.R. (1975), "Why big nations lose small wars: the politics of asymmetric conflict", *World Politics*, **27** (2), 175–200.

Malmendier, U. and G. Tate (2005), "C.E.O. overconfidence and corporate investment", *The Journal of Finance*, **60** (6), 2661–700.

Mandel, R. (2006), *The Meaning of Military Victory*, Boulder, CO: Lynne Rienner Publishers.

Martel, W.C. (2006), *Victory in War: Foundations of Modern Military Policy*, Cambridge, UK: Cambridge University Press.

Mercer, J. (1996), *Reputation and International Politics*, Ithaca, NY: Cornell University Press.

Mueller, J.E. (1973), *War, Presidents and Public Opinion*, New York, NY: John Wiley & Sons, Inc.

Mueller, J.E. (2004), *The Remnants of War*, Ithaca, NY: Cornell University Press.

Nathan, J.A. (1975), "The Missile Crisis: his finest hour now", *World Politics*, **27**, 256–81.

Nelson, H.T. (2005), "Presidential Leadership: A Prospect Theory Analysis of US Climate Policy under Presidents Clinton and GW Bush", Paper presented at the International Studies Association, Hilton Hawaiian Village, Honolulu, Hawaii, 5 March 2005.

Nettle, D. (2004), "Adaptive illusions: optimism, control and human rationality", in D. Evans and P. Cruse (eds), *Emotion, Evolution and Rationality* (Oxford, UK: Oxford University Press, pp. 193–208.

Nicholson, M. (1992), *Rationality and the Analysis of International Conflict*, Cambridge, UK: Cambridge University Press.

Paul, T.V. (1994), *Asymmetric Conflicts: War Initiation by Weaker Powers*, Cambridge, UK: Cambridge University Press.

Pinker, S. (2002), *The Blank Slate: The Modern Denial of Human Nature*, New York, UK: Penguin Putnam.

Post, J.M. (2003), *The Psychological Assessment of Political Leaders: With Profiles of Saddam Hussein and Bill Clinton*, Ann Arbor, MI: University of Michigan Press.

Post, J.M. and A. George (2004), *Leaders and their Followers in a Dangerous World: The Psychology of Political Behavior*, Ithaca, NY: Cornell University Press.

Powell, R. (1991), "Absolute and relative gains in international relations theory", *American Political Science Review*, **85** (4), 1303–20.

Rabbie, J.M. (1989), "Group processes as stimulants of aggression", in J. Groebel and R.A. Hinde (eds), *Aggression and War*, Cambridge, UK: Cambridge University Press, pp. 141–55.

Redd, S.B., A. Mintz and A. Vedlitz (2006), "Can we generalize from student experiments to the real world in political science, military affairs and international relations?", *Journal of Conflict Resolution*, **50**, 757–76.

Reiter, D. and A.C. Stam (2002), *Democracies at War*, Princeton, NJ: Princeton University Press.

Roberts, A. (2009), *The Storm of War: A New History of the Second World War*, London: Allen Lane.

Robinson, R.J. and D. Keltner (1997), "Defending the status quo: power and bias in social conflict", *Personality and Social Psychology Bulletin*, **23**, 1066–77.

Rosen, S.P. (2004), *War and Human Nature*, Princeton, NJ: Princeton University Press.

Russett, B. and M. Nincic (1976), "American public opinion on the use of military force abroad", *Political Science Quarterly*, **91** (3), 411–23.

Sears, D.O., L. Huddy and R. Jervis (2003), *Oxford Handbook of Political Psychology*, Oxford, UK: Oxford University Press.

Singer, J.D. and M. Small (1972), *The Wages of War 1816–1965: A Statistical Handbook*, New York, NY: John Wiley & Sons.

Snyder, J. (1991), *Myths of Empire: Domestic Politics and Political Ambition*, Ithaca, NY: Cornell University Press.

Stein, A. (1990), *Why Nations Cooperate: Circumstance and Choice in International Relations*, Ithaca, NY: Cornell University Press.

Stiglitz, J.E. and L. Bilmes (2008), *The Three Trillion Dollar War: The True Cost of the Iraq Conflict*, New York, NY: W.W. Norton.

Stoessinger, J.G. (1998), *Why Nations Go To War*, New York, NY: St. Martin's.

t'Hart, P. (1990), *Groupthink in Government: A Study of Small Groups and Policy Failure*, Amsterdam: Swets and Zeitlinger.

Tajfel, H. (1974), "Social identity and intergroup behaviour", *Social Science Information*, **13** (2), 65–93.

Taliaferro, J.W. (2004), *Balancing Risks: Great Power Intervention in the Periphery*, Ithaca, NY: Cornell University Press.

Taylor, S.E. (1989), *Positive Illusions: Creative Self-Deception and the Healthy Mind*, New York, NY: Basic Books.

Taylor, S.E. and J.D. Brown (1988), "Illusion and well-being: a social psychological perspective on mental health", *Psychological Bulletin*, **103**, 193–210.

Taylor, S.E. and J.D. Brown (1994), "Positive illusions and well-being revisited: separating fact from fiction", *Psychological Bulletin*, **116** (1), 21–7.

Tetlock, P.E. (1998), "Social psychology and world politics", in D. Gilbert, S. Fiske and G. Lindzey (eds), *Handbook of Social Psychology*, New York, NY: McGraw Hill, pp. 868–912.

Tetlock, P.E. (2005), *Expert Political Judgment: How Good Is It? How Can We Know?* Princeton, NJ: Princeton University Press.

Tierney, D. (2010), *How We Fight: Crusades, Quagmires, and the American Way of War*, New York, NY: Little Brown.

Tinbergen, N. (1968), "On war and peace in animals and man: an ethologist's approach to the biology of aggression", *Science*, **160**, 1411–18.

Toft, M.D. (2003), *The Geography of Ethnic Conflict: Identity, Interests, and the Indivisibility of Territory*, Princeton, NJ: Princeton University Press.

Tuchman, B. (1984), *The March of Folly: From Troy to Vietnam*, New York, NY: Alfred A. Knopf.

Turner, J.C. (1987), "A self-categorization theory", in J.C. Turner, M.A. Hogg, P.J. Oakes, S.D. Reicher and M.S. Wetherell (eds), *Rediscovering the Social Group: A Self-Categorization Theory*, Oxford, UK: Basil Blackwell, pp. 42–67.

Van den Steen, E. (2004), "Rational overoptimism (and other biases)", *American Economic Review*, **94**, 1141–51.

Van Evera, S. (1999), *Causes of War*, Ithaca, NY: Cornell University Press.

Vasquez, J.A. (1993), *The War Puzzle*, Cambridge, UK: Cambridge University Press.

Vasquez, J.A. (ed), (2000), *What Do We Know About War?* Lanham, MD: Rowan & Littlefield.

Waltz, K.N. (1959), *Man, the State and War: A Theoretical Analysis*, New York, NY: Columbia University Press.

Wang, K. and Ray, J.L. (1994), "Beginners and winners: the fate of initiators of interstate wars involving great powers since 1495", *International Studies Quarterly*, **38**, 139–54.

Welch, D.A. (1993), *Justice and the Genesis of War*, Cambridge, UK: Cambridge University Press.

White, R.K. (1968), *Nobody Wanted War: Misperception in Vietnam and Other Wars*, New York, NY: Doubleday.

Wilson, T.D. (2004), *Strangers to Ourselves: Discovering the Adaptive Unconscious*, Cambridge, MA: Belknap Press.

Woods, K., J. Lacey and W. Murray (2006), "Saddam's delusions: the view from the inside", *Foreign Affairs*, **85** (3 May/June), 2–26.

Woodward, B. (2004), *Plan of Attack*, New York, NY: Simon & Schuster.

Woodward, B. (2005), *State of Denial*, New York, NY: Simon & Schuster.

Wrangham, R.W. (1999), "Is military incompetence adaptive?", *Evolution and Human Behaviour*, **20**, 3–17.

Wrangham, R.W. & Wilson M.L. (2004), "Collective violence: comparisons between youths and chimpanzees", *Annals of the New York Academy of Sciences*, **1036**, 233–56.

PART II

WAYS OF WAGING WAR

6 What is guerrilla warfare?
Anthony James Joes

6.1 GUERRILLAS VERSUS TERRORISTS

Because the terms "guerrilla" and "terrorist" are often, and incorrectly, used interchangeably, it will be useful to distinguish those terms. It is true enough that elements of most, if not all, present and past guerrilla movements have engaged in what many observers would label terrorist acts at one time or another. But the essential difference between the two types of activity is crucial. No definition of terrorism would come close to satisfying everyone, or even most people, but in this context we will employ the usage of Bard O'Neill (2005, p.33): terrorism means "the threat or use of physical coercion against noncombatants, especially civilians." Guerrillas, on the other hand, are those who, whatever else they may do, deliberately fight against ostensibly more powerful armed forces by making unexpected attacks against vulnerable military targets and who are sustained, in the ideal, by good intelligence, secure bases, popular support and high morale (Joes 2004, p.10). Guerrillas can do anything that terrorists can, but the reverse is definitely not true. The crucial differentiation lies in the approach to fighting: the main and sometimes exclusive target of guerrillas (from the Spanish for "small war") is the security forces of the opponent. Thus, the fundamental distinction between the two types is the role that deliberately sought armed combat plays in their method of operation.

6.2 SOME WELLSPRINGS OF GUERRILLA CONFLICTS

An older generation of Americans associates the term "guerrilla" with the term "Communist," for reasons easy to understand. While most guerrilla insurgencies from the 1940s through the 1960s were or claimed to be Communist-directed or inspired (in China, Malaya, the Philippines, Greece, French Vietnam and South Vietnam), no necessary relationship exists between guerrilla war per se and any particular ideology. Instances of guerrilla conflict have been recorded as far back as the time of the Hittites in the fifteen century BC; guerrillas have in fact most often been the instrument of nationalist, monarchist and/or conservative groups. The rolls of famous guerrilla chieftains include several Americans (Francis Marion the "Swamp Fox" and the Confederate John Mosby, for example); the United States has aided guerrilla movements in Angola, Nicaragua, Tibet and most spectacularly in Afghanistan.

Primary causes of guerrilla outbreaks have included a desire for independence (as in the Thirteen Colonies) or to escape colonialism (as in French Algeria), a reaction against genocide (Poland in World War Il, Chechnya in the 1990s) or a combination of these and other motives. In the Vendée and other provinces of France during the Revolutionary Terror, in Napoleonic Spain, Tibet and Sudan, and from the Mexican *Cristeros* of the 1920s to the Afghan *mujahideen* of the 1980s, the principal motive among guerrilla insurgents is the defense of religion.

6.3   GUERRILLA WARFARE AS A MAJOR CHALLENGE

Guerrillas have often presented serious problems to great military powers. In the early years of the twentieth century C.E. Callwell ([1906] 1976, p. 126) warned that "Guerrilla warfare is what regular armies always have most to dread, and when this is directed by a leader with a genius for war, an effective campaign becomes well-nigh impossible." Because of their ability to protract the fighting, the strategic situation favors well-led guerrillas. The guerrilla conflict that most Americans probably have some awareness of is that of South Vietnam, but other examples of militarily formidable states encountering serious problems with guerrillas abound. These include the British in the American War of Independence, in Cyprus and in Northern Ireland; the French against domestic guerrillas during the Revolutionary and Napoleonic periods, in Spain (where the term "guerrilla" originated) and in Vietnam; the Japanese in China; the Germans in Yugoslavia; the Soviets in Afghanistan; the Russians in Chechnya; and the (Communist) Vietnamese in Cambodia. Everybody used to know that General Cornwallis surrendered to the French and the Americans at Yorktown in 1781, but few have ever been aware that Cornwallis had gone to Yorktown to escape the constant harassment by American guerrillas in the Carolinas. And at the battle of Waterloo, Napoleon fatefully lacked the 30 000 troops which he had had to dispatch to combat an uprising by pro-monarchist guerrillas in the Vendée.

In spite of their ability to present the most powerful countries with serious challenges, the great majority of guerrilla insurgencies have in fact been defeated. Nevertheless, in the relatively rare instances where guerrillas have achieved success, the results have radically altered the shape of world politics: consider the cases of Mao Tse-tung's China, French Vietnam, Castro's Cuba and Soviet Afghanistan.

6.4 THE RELEVANCE OF EARLIER GUERRILLA CONFLICTS

The notorious present-mindedness of many Americans and their obsession with technology have led to suggestions that insurgency in the twenty-first century is an almost entirely new phenomenon, requiring radically different methods and strategies to combat it. Nevertheless, the continuities of guerrilla warfare are striking, and warn against any tendency to treat the analysis of previous insurgencies as mere library exercises.

In their Iberian provinces, the Romans confronted guerrilla tactics hard to distinguish from those used in the same country against the forces of Napoleon 19 centuries later. And consider the following scenario: a superpower, self-conscious carrier of a universalistic ideology, invades a backward country directly across its border. Gravely underestimating the difficulty of this operation, the superpower commits forces inadequate to their task. To this key error, the invaders add widespread looting, sacrilege, rape and casual murder. This behavior provokes a determined popular resistance, sustained by xenophobia, religious fervor and outside aid. This unexpectedly fierce and protracted struggle severely undermines the reputation of the superpower, and plays a major role in its ultimate collapse a few years later.

Is the foregoing a serviceable summary of the Soviet experience in Afghanistan in the 1980s? Yes, indeed; but it also summarizes the consequences of Napoleon's invasion of Spain in 1808. Spain was Napoleon's Afghanistan.

And while no one denies the "globalization" of terrorist organizations in the present day, consider that in the latter half of the 1940s, Communist insurgencies blazed concurrently in, among other places, China, Malaya, the Philippines, Greece and Vietnam – a global phenomenon indeed. Years ago, the distinguished strategist Bernard Brodie (1976, p. 54) wrote that "the only empirical data we have about how people conduct war and behave under its stresses is our experience with it in the past, however much we have to make adjustments for subsequent changes in conditions." Contemporary RAND researchers uphold this view: "Iraq and Afghanistan are consonant with some general characteristics of insurgency and counterinsurgency, and are more similar to than different from many previous insurgencies" (Long 2006, p.15), and in an age when insurgencies have worldwide reach, counterinsurgents can ill-afford not to examine the complexities of past cases and the continuities among them, *especially since the complexities of the insurgency that the counterinsurgents are facing may not be elucidated until much later* . . . counterinsurgents should continue to learn from the successes and mistakes of other counterinsurgencies to avoid the repetition of mistakes (Warner 2007, p. 69, italics added).

And the recent Army/Marine Corps counterinsurgency manual states that "knowledge of the history and principles of insurgency and COIN provides a solid foundation that informed readers can use to assess insurgencies . . . All insurgencies are different; however, broad historical trends underlie the factors motivating insurgencies" (US Army- Marine Corps Counterinsurgency Field Manual 2006, p. li-liii).[1]

6.5   TACTICS, NOT IDEOLOGY

Guerrilla tactics are the method of warfare adopted by those who wish to wage war but are manifestly inferior to their enemies (normally a government or an occupation army) in numbers, training, equipment and international recognition. Guerrilla war is the war of the weak. Nevertheless, recall that even the strongest powers have experienced great difficulties trying to defeat or even merely contain a guerrilla movement. The objective of guerrillas is a protracted war of attrition against superior enemy military forces, and especially their logistical system. The principal guerrilla tactic is surprise, made possible by mobility and intelligence. Guerrillas adopt this form of warfare because of, among other weaknesses, their overall numerical inferiority; but well-led guerrillas will always have numerical superiority *at the point of contact* with the enemy. This is what Mao meant when he said that the strategy of the guerrillas is to pit one man against ten (strategic inferiority) but their tactics are to pit ten men against one (tactical superiority.)

6.6   CLAUSEWITZ'S ADVICE

What, then, are the fundamentals of these guerrilla tactics? Two centuries ago, Carl von Clausewitz, arguably the greatest Western theorist of war, identified what he believed to be "the only conditions under which a [guerrilla outbreak] can be effective" ([1832] 1976, p. 480). The most important of those conditions are that guerrillas should: (1) operate over a wide area, so that their movements do not become stereotyped and they cannot be surrounded easily; (2) stay away from the seacoast, so that the government cannot make use of amphibious movements against them; (3) choose as the center of their activity an area of rough terrain, thus impeding the movements of heavily armed and well-equipped hostile troops while rewarding the lightly armed guerrillas with relative mobility (the revealing Roman word for the baggage a regular army carried around with it was *impedimenta*); and (4) have by definition the support of most of the population of the affected region.

In Latin America, guerrillas have sometimes flourished in areas where the presence of the state was tenuous or nonexistent; this is the case of the FARC in Colombia and formerly of the Sendero Luminoso in Peru.

6.7   MAO TSE-TUNG AND GUERRILLA WAR

Probably the most famous practitioner and theorist of guerrilla warfare is Mao Tse-tung. Mao developed his ideas about guerrilla conflict against the Japanese invaders after 1937 and against Chiang Kai-shek's nationalist government before 1937 and after 1945. Mao's writings on this subject, and commentaries on those writings by others, are voluminous. Nevertheless, Mao always taught that guerrilla warfare was a necessary but temporary stage of China's Communist revolution. The true destiny of guerrillas was to evolve into regular, conventionally armed and trained military forces. How were guerrillas to contribute to Mao's overall strategy?

> The principal object of the action of a guerrilla unit lies in dealing the enemy the strongest possible blows to his morale, and in creating disorder and agitation in his rear, in drawing off his principal forces to the flanks or to the rear, in stopping or slowing down his operations, and ultimately in dissipating his fighting strength so that the enemy's units are crushed one by one [by conventional forces] and he is precipitated into a situation where, even by rapid and deceptive actions, he can neither advance nor retreat (Mao 1966, p. 81).

Furthermore, "many minor victories [make] a major victory. Herein lies the great strategic role of guerrilla warfare in the war of resistance [against Japan]" (Mao 1967, p, 85). To this end, "if we [guerrillas] do not have a 100 percent guarantee of victory, we should not fight a battle" (Mao 1966, p. 56).[2]

For Mao, the "peculiar quality of the operations of a guerrilla unit lies in taking the enemy by surprise" (1966, p. 86). The "great superiority of a small guerrilla unit lies in its mobility," (1966, p. 73) and "the sole habitual tactic of a guerrilla unit is the ambush" (1966, p. 102). Clearly, the mobility of the guerrillas, and hence their ability to achieve surprise

– the master key in all warfare – is a paradoxical consequence of their inferiority vis-à-vis conventional forces: the relative poverty of guerrilla units lets them move quickly and quietly. But in Mao's thinking, even the best tactics were subordinate in importance to political aims: he therefore stressed the vital necessity of political indoctrination of his armed followers. As Cromwell's army was a church in arms, so Mao's army was a party in arms. Another important ingredient of the Maoist approach was that prisoners must be well treated, and even released, in order to undermine the enemy's willingness to fight to the death – or to fight at all.

Mao also insisted repeatedly on the need for guerrillas to have a base area, a secure refuge where they could stockpile food and weapons, train recruits, indoctrinate prisoners and nurse the wounded. Clearly the best location for such a base is in an inaccessible area. It was relatively easy for Mao to establish secure bases because of the great expanse of China, the country's utterly inadequate transportation network and the quite limited numbers and technology of the Japanese. The emphasis Mao placed on secure base areas led him to conclude logically that successful guerrilla warfare would not be possible in a small country.[3] This may well be true as a general principle. But in fact lengthy guerrilla conflicts have occurred in Cyprus, Northern Ireland and Chechnya, among other places (all three considerably smaller in area than the State of New Jersey, USA).

Another notable student of guerrilla warfare was the Argentine Ernesto "Che" Guevara. He warned that a guerrilla insurgency cannot achieve success against a democratic government, or even against one that pretends to be democratic, because in such a situation the possibilities of non-violent change have not been exhausted (Guevara 1960). A contemporary way of expressing this idea is that "the ballot box is the coffin of insurgency." Guevara unaccountably ignored his own analysis, consequently losing his life in an ill-conceived and incompetently executed effort to overthrow the popular government of Bolivia.

6.8   OUTSIDE AID TO GUERRILLAS

Outside assistance has been invaluable, and arguably decisive, to guerrilla insurgencies. "Unless governments are utterly incompetent, devoid of political will, and lacking resources, insurgent organizations normally must obtain outside assistance if they are to succeed" (O'Neill 2005, p. 111) and "external assistance appears to be the most common enabler of insurgent success" (Record 2007, p. xii).[4] From the American War of Independence and Napoleonic Spain to Tito's Yugoslavia, French Vietnam, South Vietnam and Soviet Afghanistan, outside assistance to the insurgent side has proven crucial.[5] Where such assistance did not reach the guerrillas, as in the cases of the Boers, the Mexican Cristeros, British Malaya, French Algeria, Tibet and the Philippines (twice: after the Spanish American War and World War II), the insurgency was unsuccessful.[6]

Assistance to guerrillas from outside the combat area can also assume an indirect form. This type of assistance can be crucial even when the aid is coming from a source that does not intend to help the guerrillas, or actually fears them. Two examples of such indirect aid stand out. The first stemmed from the Japanese invasion of China, which very badly damaged both Chiang Kai-shek's army and his prestige, and allowed the Communists the time and space to recruit large numbers of guerrillas. Without this Japanese assistance, however much unintended, it is very difficult to perceive how Mao could have escaped annihilation by Chiang, not to speak of how he might have eventually defeated him.

The other instance of indirect aid to guerrillas involved Castro's insurgency against the regime of President Batista. The Eisenhower Administration declared an embargo on arms sent to Cuba to either side. Within Cuba many interpreted this move as expressing Washington's belief, or even hope, that Batista's days were numbered, and led to a collapse of morale within the regime's armed forces (which were not very good to begin with).

Colombia offers an ominous variation on the theme of outside aid to guerrillas. In that country, for many years now the FARC guerrillas have enjoyed an income of close to US$1 billion from the drug trade. In Colombia, the guerrillas are rich.

6.9   GETTING THE PARADIGM WRONG

The victories of Mao Tse-tung and Fidel Castro produced many would-be imitators, especially during the '60s and '70s. They all failed, and their failures resulted primarily from a misunderstanding of the revolutionary guerrilla paradigm they thought they were following.

Arguably the largest guerrilla movement of the twentieth century was that organized by Mao Tse-tung in China in the period 1937–1945. Eventually several hundred thousand Chinese participated in that conflict as guerrillas, operating mainly under the Japanese occupation of eastern and southern China. Mao wrote a great deal about the correct conduct of guerrilla warfare, and most of it was and continues to be quite sound. But the idea, widespread in the 1960s, that would-be guerrilla leaders needed only to familiarize themselves with Mao's tactical writings and then apply them in virtually any context led to repeated disasters. The failure of

Maoist imitators is rooted not in the inadequacy of Maoist tactics, but in the particularity of the Chinese context in which they were first developed and applied. Chiang Kai-shek had driven Mao's Chinese Communist party and army to the edge of extinction by 1936; that was the origin of the famous Long March, actually a Long Retreat. It was the Japanese invasion that saved the Chinese Communist movement and provided Mao with the opportunity to revitalize his forces so badly mauled by Chiang's nationalists. Japanese numbers were quite inadequate for the task of maintaining control of all or even most of China, especially in light of that vast country's primitive transportation system.[7] The weapons and equipment of Japanese forces in China were superior to those of Chiang, but unimpressive by Western standards. Thus the armies of Imperial Japan were powerful enough to inflict massive damage on Chiang's forces and to force him to retreat deep into remote southwestern China, but never strong enough to cause him either to surrender or to negotiate. Worse, Japanese forces in China pursued policies that can only be labeled barbarous, steeling the determination of most Chinese to resist them to the end. Finally, it is too often forgotten that Mao's eventual triumph over Chiang's nationalists was won not by guerrilla forces but by massive conventional armies, to a large degree equipped with Japanese and Soviet weapons. In a word: no Japanese invasion, no Maoist victory.

Clouds of romantic myths, propaganda and ignorance continue to surround the Castro victory in Cuba. The simple truth, however, is that the growing repression and corruption of the Batista regime had antagonized key elements of Cuban society, including the business sectors and the Church, and earned the increasingly open distaste of the US administration. By 1956 the Batista regime, identified with no particular class, region or group, was politically quite isolated. At the head of a few hundred guerrillas in the eastern mountains, Fidel Castro promised free elections and a return to democratic freedoms, *not* the Leninist dictatorship and prolonged confrontation with the United States that he eventually delivered.

The Batista army was led by "corrupt, cruel and lazy officers without combat experience" (Thomas 1977, p. 215). During the desultory 2-year contest with the guerrillas, many units in Batista's 15 000-man army never fired a single shot, and in all suffered about 300 casualties – less than three a week. The Eisenhower administration eventually imposed an arms embargo on the regime. Clearly, the Castro revolution was in actuality a Batista collapse. When Castro's admirers attempted guerrilla insurgencies against Venezuela or Bolivia, for example, countries with real armed forces, democratic procedures and the backing of the US, they suffered quick, ignominious and total defeat.

6.10 URBAN GUERRILLA WARFARE

The phenomenon called urban guerilla warfare violates the fundamental precepts of Clausewitz and Mao Tse-tung, among others. It is close to impossible for a specific group inside a city to receive delivery of foreign aid. Of course, for urban guerrillas to possess an inaccessible base area is quite impossible. In cities the guerrillas must operate in secret, thus being unable to recruit significant numbers. Perhaps worst of all, urban guerrillas are subject to encirclement, the fatal situation that almost all of Clausewitz's and Mao's advice is aimed against.

Now, if what has been said so far is mainly true, then it is reasonable, almost mandatory, to expect that attempts to wage protracted guerrilla warfare in urban areas should fail. And that is precisely what we find. All the famous urban guerrilla insurgencies of the past six decades (at least) – no matter how much popular support they may have enjoyed, no matter how much one may sympathize with their cause – have suffered defeat. In Warsaw against the Nazis in 1944, Budapest against the Soviets in 1956, Algiers against the French in the 1950s, Sao Paulo and Montevideo against the Uruguayan and Brazilian governments in the 1960s, Saigon against the South Vietnamese and the Americans in 1968 (the famous Tet Offensive), Northern Ireland against the British in the 1990s, in Chechnya against the Russians in 1994–1996 – all these urban uprisings failed completely.

6.11 ELEMENTS OF SUCCESSFUL COUNTERINSURGENCY

Most guerrilla insurgencies in history have failed. Their failure has sometimes occurred simply because the counterinsurgent forces had overwhelming superiority and/or engaged in genocidal practices. For this discussion, however, we will identify actual techniques of counterinsurgency that demonstrate the intelligent and effective employment of resources aimed at the restoration of peace and order. We have abstracted these techniques primarily, but not exclusively, from the counterinsurgencies of the Americans in the Philippines after the Spanish–American War, the British in Malaya after World War II and the French in Algeria during 1956–1962. A successful counterinsurgency will be rooted in an intelligent analysis of the nature of guerrilla warfare in general, and of the particular conflict in question.

From the strategic viewpoint – meaning the creation or shaping of an environment that will ensure the eventual defeat of the guerrillas – the counterinsurgents' effort must absolutely consist of three elements. First, they need to close off the theater of conflict, isolating the guerrillas as completely as possible from outside assistance. If this cannot be accomplished, the counterinsurgency will almost certainly be long and costly, and quite possibly unsuccessful. Second, they must commit sufficient forces to the conflict (a number that of course will vary depending on time and place and the strength of the guerrillas). There is no "cheap" counterinsurgency. Third, the counterinsurgent side must offer the population, including the guerrillas, a peaceful path to the redress of grievances, real or imagined. This path does not necessarily have to mean democratic elections; different cultures have different methods for the resolution of conflict.

If these strategic elements are in place, then proven counterinsurgent tactics can begin to have their effect. The most essential weapon in the hands of the counterinsurgents is *good intelligence*: who are the guerrillas, how many, what do they want, who are their sympathizers, and what actual or potential divisions exist among them. (The best sources of intelligence are defectors, captured enemy personnel, amnesty-takers, intercepted messages and local civilians hostile to the guerrillas.)

Amnesty is calculated to take advantage of the fact that in almost all insurgencies certain persons will wish to give up the guerrilla life, either because they were initially coerced into it (as in Greece in the 1940s or in South Vietnam in the late 1960s) or because they have become disenchanted with the difficulties of guerrilla existence, especially if the prospects of victory are fading. Well-timed amnesties to guerrillas can have profound effects. President Magsaysay's offer of amnesty to the Filipino Huks induced many of them to lay down their arms; in South Vietnam approximately 194 000 Viet Cong and North Vietnamese regulars took advantage of the government's amnesty programs.

If the counterinsurgents have fairly well isolated the theater of conflict from outside aid, then *draining firearms* from guerrilla-affected areas can be an important counterinsurgent device. House-to-house searches for weapons are disruptive and can turn civilians into enemies of the government. The American army in the Philippines employed a more fruitful method for reducing the firearms available to guerrillas: anyone who turned in a firearm to the American army could obtain either a cash payment or the release of a guerrilla prisoner of choice – no questions asked.

Guerrillas are normally quite dependent on the civilian economy for food. In British Malaya, the authorities evolved the policy of strictly *controlling food supplies*; thus, for example, storekeepers were permitted to sell only limited amounts of rice at any one time, and were forbidden to sell anyone cans of food that they had not first punctured. One of the consequences of food control was that the guerrillas had to spend a great deal of time cultivating fields, which were often discovered by security forces. Similar methods had worked effectively for the Americans in the Philippines after 1898 (O'Ballance 1966; Short 1975; Joes 2000).

Many students of insurgency maintain that the heart of an effective counterinsurgency must be the *separation of the civilian population from guerrillas*. This can be accomplished in several ways: (1) massive influxes of security forces into a particular district or sector that drive the guerrillas into marginal areas; (2) the identification and apprehension of non-combatant collaborators of the guerrillas; (3) local self-defense militias capable of resisting guerrilla attempts to enter their area; and (4) resettlement of civilian populations to relatively safe areas. Local self-defense seems to be the best course, because it involves the mobilization of the civilian population against the guerrillas; this method had great effect in Peru, for example, against the Shining Path (*Sendero Luminoso*). Of course, if the guerrilla movement is widely popular, arming the civilian population will mean arming the guerrillas. Resettlement – removing civilians from an area controlled or frequented by guerrillas – is the most controversial method; resettlement seems to have badly hurt the guerrillas in Malaya, but critics see removal in most instances as an admission by the authorities that they cannot provide security. In any case, resettlement is disruptive and expensive.

In addition to village militias, the counterinsurgents can mobilize the local population by incorporating elements of it into regular military units, with the authorities providing pay, weapons and sometimes uniforms. Such programs were very extensive in South Vietnam, in French Algeria, Portuguese Africa and elsewhere. Perhaps counterintuitively, creating local militias and enrolling indigenous personnel in the regular armed units of the counterinsurgent forces is very often not difficult at all. This is because, in many instances, a guerrilla insurgency is really a form of civil war, with the guerrillas representing not only opposition to the regime that holds or claims power, but also one element or group of elements in an ethnically or religiously divided society. Thus the counterinsurgent side, with a modicum of dexterity, can recruit supporters from those social elements who fear and oppose the ethnic and/or religious groups from which the guerrillas are largely drawn. The majority of soldiers in the Portuguese forces in Africa during the 1960s were indigenous. In Malaya, the British automatically received the support of the Malays, who viewed the guerrilla movement (with good reason) as Chinese. In Algeria more Arabs wore the French colors than served with the guerrillas. In French Indochina the Vietnamese who served in French or pro-French military units were at least equal in number to those who fought for the Viet Minh.

Dividing the guerrillas from the civil population is one side of the coin;

the other is dividing insurgent leaders from their followers. In most cases, the leaders of a guerrilla insurgency have open-ended aspirations that cannot be satisfied short of a complete surrender by the authorities. On the other hand, many have joined the ranks of a guerrilla movement because of quite specific grievances (ruinous taxes and rents, mistreatment by officials, land disputes and so on). Any competent government can redress such grievances to at least some extent and thus provide reasons why rank and file guerrillas should give up the difficult and dangerous life of the insurgent. This approach can be especially effective if a peaceful road to change exists, or is created.

But arguably the most necessary weapon in the counterinsurgent arsenal is *rectitude*, especially toward civilians and prisoners. Perhaps the easiest way to prove this proposition is to consider what happens when counterinsurgents have systematically violated right conduct. None dispute that German barbarism in Russia during World War II contributed mightily toward Nazism's final collapse. The same applies to the Japanese in China; indeed, Mao Tse-tung predicted early on the eventual defeat of the Japanese precisely because of their atrocious conduct. From Napoleonic Spain to Soviet Afghanistan, the road of warfare is littered with the wreckage of counterinsurgencies that forgot, or disdained, rectitude. Bad conduct creates guerrillas; right conduct saves counterinsurgent lives.

Preventing outside aid from reaching guerrillas, closing cross-border sanctuaries through diplomatic or other means, collecting good intelligence, establishing a peaceful path to change, controlling food supplies, offering huge rewards for the capture of insurgent leaders, exchanging prisoners for firearms, recruiting indigenous personnel, constructing roads to facilitate the movement of security forces, enacting appropriate administrative and socioeconomic reforms, granting amnesty and practicing rectitude – all these together constitute an impressive repertoire of *nonlethal yet effective* tactics available to counterinsurgents. They can constitute an essentially political approach to insurgency, of which Clausewitz would have heartily approved.

NOTES

1. See also Beckett (2005), and Gray (2006). Certainly, insurgents learn, or try to learn, from past insurgencies; see Harmon (1992).
2. Confer: "We should resolutely fight a decisive engagement in every campaign or battle in which we are sure of victory; we should avoid a decisive engagement in every campaign or battle in which we are not sure of victory; and we should absolutely avoid a strategically decisive engagement on which the fate of the whole nation is staked" because "we are not gamblers who risk everything on a single throw" (Mao 1963, p. 254, 257).

3. "Small countries like Belgium which lack this [territorial] condition have little or no probability" of waging a successful guerrilla campaign (Mao 1963, p. 171) Of course, Belgium's advanced transportation system would also gravely menace any guerrilla effort.
4. See also Record 2007, Chapter 2, and Record 2006.
5. Machiavelli wrote: "When once the people have taken up arms against you, there will never be lacking foreigners to assist them." *The Prince* (1940), Chapter XX.
6. Geography helped isolate the combat area in the Philippines and Malaya; in Algeria, the French constructed sophisticated and effective systems of electrified fences along its borders.
7. Most estimates of the number of Japanese troops in China proper (excluding the puppet state of Manchukuo) during 1941–1945 hover around 1 million, to subdue and occupy a country of close to 480 million. This is the equivalent of President Lincoln attempting to subdue the Confederacy with an army of 19 000. Regarding this crucial point of Japanese manpower, see Mao (1967, p. 23, 86).

REFERENCES

Beckett, I.F.W. (2005), *Insurgency in Iraq: An Historical Perspective*, Carlisle, PA: Strategic Studies Institute.
Brodie, Bernard (1976), "The continuing relevance of *On War*", in M. Howard and P. Paret (eds), Carl von Clausewitz, *On War*, Princeton, NJ: Princeton University Press, pp. 263–306.
Callwell, C.E. ([1906] 1976), *Small Wars: Their Principles and Practices*, Wakefield, UK: EP Publishing.
Clausewitz, C. von ([1832] 1976), *On War*, M. Howard and P. Paret (trans. and eds), Princeton, NJ: Princeton University Press.
Gray, C.S. (2006), *Irregular Enemies and the Essence of Strategy: Can the American Way of War Adapt?* Carlisle, PA: Strategic Studies Institute.
Guevara, E. (1960), *Guerrilla Warfare*, New York, NY: Vintage.
Harmon, C.C. (1992), "Illustration of 'learning' in Counterinsurgency", *Comparative Strategy*, **11**, 29–48.
Joes, A.J. (2000), *America and Guerrilla Warfare*, Lexington, KY: University Press of Kentucky.
Joes, A.J. (2004), *Resisting Rebellion: The History and Politics of Counterinsurgency*, Lexington, KY: University Press of Kentucky.
Long, A. (2006), *The "Other War": Lessons from Five Decades of RAND Counterinsurgent Research*, Santa Monica, CA: RAND.
Machiavelli, N. (1940), *The Prince and the Discources*, New York, NY: Modern library.
Mao Tse-tung (1966), *Basic Tactics*, Stuart Schram (trans.), New York, NY: Praeger.
Mao Tse-tung (1967), *Problems of Strategy in Guerrilla War against Japan*, in *Selected Works of Mao-Tse-tung*, Peking: Foreign Languages Press.
Mao Tse-tung (1963), *Selected Military Writings*, Peking: Foreign Languages Press.
O'Ballance, E. (1966), *Malaya: The Communist Insurgent War*, Hamden, CT: Archon.
O'Neill, B. (2005), *Insurgency and Terrorism: Inside Modern Revolutionary Warfare*, Washington, DC: Potomac.
Record, J. (2007), *Beating Goliath: Why Insurgencies Win*, Washington, DC: Potomac.
Record, J. (2006), "External assistance: enabler of insurgent success", *Parameters*, **36**, 36–49.
Short, Anthony (1975), *The Communist Insurrection in Malaya, 1948–1960*, New York: Crane, Russak.
Thomas, Hugh (1977), *The Cuban Revolution*, New York: Harper and Row.

Warner, Leslie Ann (2007), "Conclusions: Lessons Learned for Future Counterinsurgencies", in *Money in the Bank: Lessons Learned from Past Counterinsurgencies*, Santa Monica, CA: RAND, pp. 67–76.
US Army-Marine Corps Counterinsurgency Field Manual (2006), Chicago, IL: University of Chicago.

7 The economics of torture
Pavel Yakovlev

7.1 INTRODUCTION

Torture is an act by which severe pain (mental or physical) is intentionally inflicted on a person.[1] Although torture is officially acknowledged by virtually all countries to be an extreme violation of human rights, two-thirds of all countries, according to Amnesty International, do not consistently abide by anti-torture treaties.[2] Despite being condemned by law and several international treaties, torture is still widely used today by many governments, many of which claim to be democratic (Shue 1978; Neumayer 2005; McCoy 2005; Rejali 2007).

Existing research on torture and other human rights abuses is dominated by conflict scholars, political scientists, human rights scholars and sociologists. While their scholarly contributions are very valuable, an economic analysis of torture would be highly complementary, but it is largely absent from the literature. This chapter offers a multidisciplinary literature review on this topic. The review begins with a historical perspective on torture followed by a discussion on anti-torture treaties, some empirical evidence on the determinants of torture, and positive arguments for or against torture. In addition, the chapter develops a simple model that examines the optimal level of torture that will be chosen when the costs of torture are widespread and the benefits are concentrated. The model shows that the optimal level of torture depends on the probability of retaliation from the opposing side in a conflict.

7.2 A HISTORICAL PRIMER TO TORTURE

For much of human history, torture has been a legitimate method of coercion, intimidation or information gathering. Torture has been used in all societies in the ancient world with the possible exception of the Hebrew people (Evans and Morgan 1998). Often, prisoners of war were either killed or taken into slavery, which usually meant facing inhumane treatment and torture in ancient Egypt, Greece and Rome, for example. During the Middle Ages, the incidence and severity of torture expanded beyond what Roman law would have sanctioned (Evans and Morgan 1998). Only when the movement for the abolition of torture and for the establishment of penal reform swept throughout Europe in the eighteenth century did torture begin to be widely regarded as an unacceptable and barbaric practice (Evans and Morgan 1998). However, the moral triumph over torture did not lead to a complete elimination of torture as it re-emerged in the nineteenth and twentieth century in Austria, Italy and Russia and later in the twentieth century in Algeria (1954–62), Northern Ireland (1963–94), Israel and the Soviet Union (Evans and Morgan 1998).

The Eastern Front of World War II was the largest single front in the history of warfare and was unparalleled in the mistreatment of war prisoners. Soviet prisoners of war, or POWs, died in large numbers in German prison camps from brutal treatment, starvation and overall neglect. In contrast, the treatment of US and other Western POWs in Nazi Germany was relatively decent and largely in accordance with the Geneva Conventions.[3] Allegedly, some German prison camps even offered the Western POWs of lower rank financial compensation for their labor, while officers of higher rank were excused from work altogether (Reid 1953). However, Nazi Germany refused to extend the same treatment to the Soviet POWs, supposedly because the Soviet Union did not sign the 1929 Geneva Convention (Rolf 1998; North 2006). The Japanese empire did not treat prisoners of war in accordance with the Geneva Conventions either. In fact, Emperor Hirohito issued a directive that removed the constraints of the Hague Convention in order to worsen the treatment of Chinese POWs (Fujiwara 1995). More recently, *The Economist* (May 17 2008, p. 102) reported that the US guards at the Abu Ghraib prison in Iraq were allegedly told by their superiors that the protections afforded by the Geneva Conventions did not apply to the detainees they were holding (Gourevitch and Morris 2008).

Although torture has been used for a variety of purposes since its inception, its application has gone through changes in recent times. In contrast to modern judicial practices, torture and punishment were often one and the same. However, the emergence of the modern state was characterized by the creation of doctrines of human rights and social contract, which made torture unacceptable (Evans and Morgan 1998). In the past, the use of torture was more likely to be linked to the status of the victim such as in the case of mistreatment of African-American slaves in the Southern States or those considered to be "racially impure" in Hitler's Germany and Mussolini's Italy, and under *apartheid* in South Africa. Based on this evidence, Evans and Morgan (1998) argue that the use of torture seems to be inseparably linked to the changing nature of the state and its relationship with its citizens. In totalitarian states, for instance, torture is likely to be used more for intimidation purposes rather than information gathering.

7.3 TO TORTURE, OR NOT TO TORTURE: WHAT'S TREATY GOT TO DO WITH IT?

The aforementioned differences in treatment of Soviet and American POWs by Nazi Germany in World War II might suggest that the incidence and severity of torture might depend on whether a country has signed the appropriate convention. This is not necessarily so. For instance, Germany's official justification for the poor treatment of the Soviet POWs was that the Soviet Union had not signed the Geneva Conventions. However, under article 82 of the Geneva Convention (1929), signatory countries had to give POWs of all countries, signatory or not, the same rights. Furthermore, a month after the German invasion of the Soviet Union in 1941, the USSR offered Nazi Germany the opportunity to sign a reciprocal adherence to the Hague Convention. The offer was left unanswered (Beevor 2001).

There is a growing body of evidence showing that signing various human rights conventions does not guarantee actual compliance with these treaties. On the contrary, dictatorships with higher levels of torture might be more inclined to join the UN Convention Against Torture or CAT (Hathaway 2003, 2007; Vreeland 2008). Some of the most repressive governments have ratified various human rights treaties, but appear to have a questionable desire to comply with these treaties in reality (Hafner-Burton and Tsutsui 2007). Surprisingly, treaty ratification might be followed by even higher levels of torture and inhumane treatment (Hathaway 2002, 2003). There is evidence suggesting that compliance with human rights treaties and avoidance of torture are more effective in established democracies with strong civil institutions and activism (Hafner-Burton and Tsutsui 2007). So, why do repressive governments voluntarily sign human rights treaties, such as CAT, that prohibit torture and other inhumane acts? Perhaps, signing human rights treaties allows the totalitarian regimes to create an appearance of civil rights in order to reduce the probability of conflict with powerful democratic countries and continue to receive more international aid. In the absence of credible enforcement mechanisms to ensure that these nations actually comply with the human rights treaties, signing the treaty is a low cost option for dictators to maintain the status quo. Alternatively, by signing CAT, oppressive governments make a small concession to internal political opposition, while they are still able to rely on torture and other oppressive strategies to maintain their grip on power. Hence the paradox: dictatorships sign international human rights agreements that go against their ability to maintain internal control.

Neumayer (2005) conducts a quantitative analysis of whether international human rights treaties actually increase respect for human rights and finds that human rights treaties might be able to improve respect for human rights, conditional on the extent of democracy and the strength of civil society. However, somewhat disheartening evidence comes from McCoy (2005), who investigates whether or not the exposure to School of the Americas (SOA) professional military training instills a greater respect for human rights in SOA graduates. McCoy finds that, while the overall number of abusers is small among SOA graduates, the abusers themselves are disproportionately represented by officers and students who took multiple SOA courses as opposed to their counterparts who took only one course. McCoy's findings imply that repeated exposure to SOA training is associated with increased human rights violations. One of the possible explanations for this puzzling result is that officers, who often become convenient "scapegoat" targets for their superiors, tend to take more SOA courses than regular soldiers. In light of this rather ironic evidence, one may wonder about the effectiveness of anti-torture treaties in general and the SOA program in particular.

7.4   POSITIVE ARGUMENTS ON TORTURE

In many present day countries, torture is explicitly outlawed by the constitution and is subject to criminal punishment. Moreover, courts almost everywhere are required to exclude evidence obtained through torture. Nonetheless, official intolerance of torture seems to diverge from practice even in countries that are often perceived as the champions of democratic values and human rights. While there are many moral arguments for and against torture, this chapter avoids normative discussions on torture in favor of the objective (positive) analysis of torture.

Although generally objecting to torture, a few scholars argue that torture should be allowed under extreme or dire circumstances. They typical cite the "ticking time bomb" argument in defense of torture which refers to situations where the timely access to information obtained through torture is justified by the many lives that could be saved. In other words, their implicit cost–benefit analysis justifies torture when the value of lives saved vastly outweighs the moral cost of torture. However, Alex Tabarrok argues that the ticking time bomb argument can allow the government to abuse its torture powers.[4] Tabarrok proposes making torture illegal, without exceptions, in order to raise the cost of torture sufficiently high so as to prevent a government from using torture unless it is absolutely imperative. In this case, the government officials should violate the law and hope for a pardon based on the merits of their decision. Similarly, Shue (1978) argues that even if torture might be necessary for national security purposes, it ought to remain illegal as to make this option least feasible by requiring one to defend his or her choice to torture legally and ex post. On the other had, economist James Miller makes another interesting argument for legalizing torture on convicted criminals on the grounds that torture, however unpopular, can be a more cost effective and no less immoral method of criminal punishment than imprisonment.[5] Miller argues that torture may not necessarily be any less immoral or criminal than prison rape and other abuses that many prisoners are subjected to as the result of their imprisonment.

7.5   TORTURE THROUGH THE LENS OF THE CONFLICT LITERATURE

Since torture is strongly linked to other types of human rights abuses, perhaps it should be examined in the broader context of violence and coercion. Torture appears to be highly correlated with extrajudicial killings, disappearance of political opponents and political imprisonment, as well as restrictions of basic civil freedoms such as freedom of speech, freedom of religion, freedom of movement, freedom of assembly and association, free and fair elections, and workers' and women's rights. Hence, a review of the conflict literature might be helpful in understanding why torture is so prevalent.

Most of the economic analysis of conflict is based on the rational economic framework, which postulates that warfare becomes an attractive dispute resolution method when property rights or contract agreements are poorly defined and enforced because warfare becomes the enforcement mechanism in its own right. In his pioneering work, Schelling (1960) argues that nations with complete information should never go to war because a peaceful settlement is less costly than a conflict. However, the inability to enforce that peaceful settlement is what creates the need for war as a costly enforcement mechanism. By the same logic, torture is inferior to peaceful dispute resolution (that is, interrogation) and should not occur unless its function is to be the enforcement mechanism.

However, even if torture is the necessary enforcement mechanism, its effectiveness in obtaining the desired level and accuracy of information shall not remain undisputed. According to Rejali (2004, 2007) and Koppl (2005), torture may not be any more effective in obtaining secret information than traditional human intelligence because of the fundamental problem of asymmetric information (Akerlof 1970). For example, torture that yields inaccurate information may set anti-terrorist efforts on a wrong path and divert valuable resources away from preventing a massive terrorist attack as in the case of the ticking time bomb scenario. Koppl (2005) reasons that if the torturer knows nothing about the secret information set he is trying to extract, he is not able to verify whether the tortured subject is telling the truth or a lie. Without knowing the relevant information set, the torturer cannot vouch for the accuracy of the received information, but learning about this information set through torture is the objective in the first place. The torturer is trapped in a vicious circle due to the asymmetric information problem. Then, why are acts of torture so prevalent?

Several attempts to reconcile these puzzles have been made. Perhaps, torture is not only used as a means of obtaining information but also as a means of maintaining social control and signaling a credible threat.[6] An application of game theory with particular emphasis on reputation capital would be very useful in understanding why the use of torture is so persistent. The conflict literature might also provide some answers. For instance, Hirschleifer (1995) contends that anarchy is especially susceptible to conflict unless there are strong diminishing returns to fighting and incomes exceed the viability minimum. Fearon (1995) suggests that peaceful bargaining may not occur because of commitment problems due to incentives to renege on the bargain terms, issue indivisibilities (such as to legalize or not to legalize abortion), private information about relative military capabilities or resolve, and incentives to misrepresent such information. Furthermore, Garfinkel and Skaperdas (2000) demonstrate that conflict could be the rational equilibrium outcome if the long-run gains from defeating an opponent outweigh the short-run losses. Nafziger and Auvinen (2002), on the other hand, find that income inequality and pervasive rent-seeking by the ruling elites may lead to war and state violence. The logic for conflict provided by these studies can be extended to explain the persistence of torture.

7.6   THE DETERMINANTS OF TORTURE AND OTHER TYPES OF VIOLENCE

Whatever the true roots of violence and torture are, several studies show that geographical, institutional and economic factors affect conflict and might influence torture use as well. A growing list of studies finds that democracies may engage in different types of conflicts and utilize different military strategies compared to totalitarian states, which implies that democracies might differ from autocracies in torture practices as well. Filson and Werner (2004), Garfinkel (1994) and Mitchell, Gates and Hegre (1999) argue that democratic regimes tend to accept negotiated settlements over wars and choose to fight only low cost, short wars that they can win.

Persson (2002) and Mulligan, Giland Sala-i-Martin (2004) find that democracies differ significantly from autocracies when it comes to military spending, torture, execution, censorship and religious regulation. Mulligan and Tsui (2006) argue that democracies and non-democracies should have identical policies except for cases when these policies influence the threat of entry from political challengers. In support of Mulligan and Tsui's argument, Goldsmith (2003) and Yakovlev (2007) find that democracies spend proportionally less on national defense compared to dictatorships, holding everything else constant.

However, lower defense burdens as percentage of GDP do not turn democracies into weak military opponents. On the contrary, Biddle and Long (2004) argue that factors like superior human capital, harmonious civil–military relations, and Western cultural background are highly correlated with democracies and are largely responsible for democracy's apparent military effectiveness. Yakovlev (2008) finds that democratic and economic freedoms, volunteer armies, human capital and GDP per capita increase country's military capital intensity, which lowers conflict casualties. Horowitz, Simpson and Stam (2006) also find that democracies mitigate some of the conscription-induced casualties and are able to sustain high levels of casualties when targeted by authoritarian states. These findings suggest that torture and other forms of violence could have the same determinants.

A growing body of interdisciplinary research on the determinants of torture and other human rights abuses has been emerging in the last two decades. Factors such as democracy, economic development, population size, wars and acts of terrorism are typically found to have a significant effect on human rights violations (Poe and Tate 1994; Davenport 1995, 1996; Poe, Tate and Keith 1999; Richards, Gelleny and Sacko 2001; Bohara, Mitchell and Nepal 2006). Using district-level data on Maoist insurgency in Nepal, Bohara et al. (2006) find that an exchange of violence between government and opposition forces depends on the political and geographical factors. More specifically, their findings indicate that democracy and social capital have an inhibiting effect on the level of violence between government and opposition. In a cross-sectional time-series analysis of 137 countries from 1950 to 1982, Davenport (1999) finds that autocracies appear to escalate and democracies tend to pacify state repressions. Henderson (1991) finds that democracy, socioeconomic conditions, inequality, economic growth and economic development have a significant effect on the level of political repression. Democratic governments, as is commonly argued, tend to limit the use of violence against their own people (Henderson 1991, 1993; Poe and Tate 1994; Davenport 1995, 2004; Richards 1999; Zanger 2000; Davenport and Armstrong 2004). Supposedly, democracies prefer to resolve conflicts through compromise, dialogue, political participation, and decentralized decisions rather than violence (Gurr 1986; Poe 2004; Rummel 1997).

However, some studies find a non-linear relationship between government repression and political freedoms suggesting that most human rights violations occur in quasi-democratic countries (Fein 1995; Regan and Henderson 2002). Several studies indicate that even democratic countries can resort to repressions and torture when suffering from terrorist attacks, interstate conflicts and civil wars (Rasler 1986; Poe and Tate 1994; Krain 1997; Poe, Tate and Keith 1999; Zanger 2000; Sherborne 2003; Poe 2004). For instance, Dreher, Gassebner and Siemers (2007) discover that terrorist acts increase the probability of extrajudicial killings, political imprisonment and torture in countries where they are committed, but terror has no effect on political participation, freedom of religion, freedom of speech or freedom of movement. Hooks and Clayton (2005) argue that torture is not unique to autocracies as exemplified by systematical violence and prisoner abuse cases in supposedly democratic countries. According to Rejali (2007), most clean tortures (tortures that leave no permanent scars and therefore are hard to prove) were actually pioneered by imperial democracies such as Britain and France. Therefore, human rights groups may never be able to eradicate torture even in democratic societies because torturers resort to techniques that do not leave scars, like water boarding. Rejali (2007) concludes that most modern torture practices have strong historical path dependence and are passed on like a skill or craftsmanship.

Economic development is also found to have a strong connection to torture (Mitchell and McCormick 1988; Poe and Tate 1994; Davenport 1995; Poe et al. 1999; Carey 2004). According to Easterly, Gatti and Kurlat (2006), economic development leads to increased education, greater tolerance of other groups, higher productivity of labor and the value of human life. However, economic development could also make murderous political leaders more productive at killing since economic development brings with it advances in technology and social organization (Easterly et al. 2006). Abundance in natural resources may be less of a blessing and more of a curse when intense competition for resources in ethnically fragmented countries leads to ethnic cleansing, torture and other human rights abuses.

A pair-wise, cross-country correlation analysis in Table 7.1 reveals that the occurrence of torture decreases with increases in democracy, education, per capita income, military spending per soldier, and economic freedom index. On the other hand, torture appears to increase with an increase in energy consumption, total and urban population, government

Table 7.1   Selected pair-wise correlates for torture[1]

Democracy[2]	−0.3077*
Energy consumption per capita[3]	0.0539*
Total population[3]	0.1819*
Urban population[3]	0.1817*
Real GDP per capita[4]	−0.4871*
Government consumption, % of GDP[4]	0.1931*
Military spending per soldier[3]	−0.3563*
Economic freedom index[5]	−0.3908*
Average years of schooling[6]	−0.5415*
Elevation[7]	0.3583*
Percentage of population in tropical area[7]	0.2865*

Notes: * Statistically significant at the 5% level. The sample is an unbalanced panel of 200 countries from 1981 to 2006.

Sources: (1) Cingranelli and Richards, 2008; (2) Polity IV Project, 2000; (3) Singer, Bremer and Stuckey 1972; (4) Heston, Summers and Aten 2002; (5) Gwartney and Lawson, 2004; (6) Barro and Lee, 2000; (7) Gallup, Sachs and Melinger 1999.

size, geographic elevation and percentage of population living in the tropics. It could be argued that some of the above mentioned factors proxy for the level of economic development, resource scarcity, lack of government transparency and ethnic fractionalization that make violence, in general, and torture, in particular, more appealing.

The pair-wise correlations in Table 7.1 are consistent with the previous findings on the importance of terrain (Fearon and Laitin 2003), democracy and social capital (Putnam 1993; Weingast 1997; Russett and Oneal 2001) in affecting torture and violence.

7.7   ON THE ECONOMIC THEORY OF TORTURE (OR LACK THEREOF)

The literature on torture and conflict explored in the previous sections of this chapter raises a number of questions that warrant further empirical and theoretical research. For instance, why is torture so abundant despite its costliness and dubious effectiveness in gathering reliable information? Why does the treatment of POWs from different countries vary so much within one country (that is, the case of Nazi Germany)? How can one ensure that human rights treaties are binding? Attempts by economists to answer these questions would be very valuable.

The theoretical model developed by Wantchekon and Healy (1999) is a step in the right direction. They analyse the prevalence of torture in a dynamic game with incomplete information involving the state, the torturer and the victim. The results show that when the state endorses torture as a means of extracting information or intimidating political opposition, torture is carried out with positive probability and becomes more widespread and cruel. Wantchekon and Healy (1999) claim that the information-gathering use of torture can be reduced by an increase in an individual's ability to resist torture, perhaps, through a culture of solidarity and civil disobedience. When torture is used as a method of social control, only a revolt or international pressure can reduce torture.

Otherwise, very few economists have devoted sufficient efforts to this topic, especially when it comes to theorizing about torture in the context of rational and self-interested economic agents. In this section, I propose a simple model of torture and derive the optimal level of torture that will be chosen. I also suggest potential avenues for future theoretical research on torture.

Despite the overwhelming arguments made by economists in favor of free trade, anti-trade policies remain widespread and hard to eradicate. The conventional explanation for the persistence of anti-trade policies despite their negative welfare impacts is that the concentrated costs and widespread benefits of trade liberalization enable successful anti-trade lobbying. A similar argument can be made about torture. A soldier who tortures a prisoner of war for information gathering or other purposes opens the door to potential retaliation from the opposing side in the conflict (assuming perfect information). However, the same soldier is unlikely to be captured and administered the same punishment in retaliation to his decision to torture. Hence, the cost of potential retaliation from the enemy is spread across all soldiers who might be captured and tortured in return. The torturer captures full benefits from torturing a POW, but bears, at best, only a fraction of the costs from potential retaliation. If the person administering the torturous acts will never see a front line, then the retaliatory cost of torture for this individual is probably zero. The above argument is similar to the externality problem in economics where individual agents do not bear the full benefit or cost of their activity that generates that externality.

The following game theoretic exposition explores this tendency in more detail. Assume that the two opposing forces are made up of homogenous agents facing an identical level of torture or ability to torture t, weighted by an identical positive probability of being captured c. Now, imagine a hypothetical soldier trying to decide whether or not to torture a captured enemy soldier for the purpose of extracting valuable information

		Soldier 2	
		No torture	Torture
Soldier 1	No torture	q_1, q_2	$q_1 - ct, q_2 + t$
	Torture	$q_1 + t, q_2 - ct$	$q_1 + t(1 - c), q_2 + t(1 - c)$

Figure 7.1   Prisoner's dilemma applied to torture

that could save his life or the lives of his comrades. A soldier weighs the payoffs from torturing versus not torturing and chooses the highest payoff strategy. Suppose the payoff for not torturing is some positive value q when there is no retaliatory torture from the opposing side of the conflict either. If the opposing side in this conflict chooses to torture, the payoff for the torturer is $q + t$ and the payoff for the non-torturing enemy soldier is $q - ct$. If both sides of the conflict decide to torture, a soldier's payoff on either side becomes $q + t - ct$ or $q + t(1 - c)$. Figure 7.1 illustrates this payoff matrix for a soldier from side one and a soldier from side two of this hypothetical conflict. From these payoffs, which are reminiscent of the prisoner's dilemma game, it is obvious that the dominant strategy for both soldiers is to torture.

Moreover, for values of c and t such that $0 < c < 1$ and $0 < t < \infty$, the payoffs in Figure 7.1 indicate that the strategy to torture is not only dominant but also socially optimal.

This is where my analysis departs from the conventional prisoner's dilemma outcome. Recall that in the prisoner's dilemma game the socially optimal outcome is for both prisoners not to betray each other, but the individually optimal outcome is to betray each other, which is the correct solution. Both prisoners would be better off (that is, it would be socially optimal) if they could ensure that neither betrays the other, but because they cannot enforce this agreement, the outcome of the game is individually optimal but socially suboptimal. However, my model's solution differs from the prisoner's dilemma because the payoff to torturer and the cost of being tortured are equal, which eliminates the tradeoff between what is socially and individually optimal for the two soldiers involved. This leads to a rather dismal conclusion that the decision to torture is both individually and socially optimal and will be chosen with a positive probability. If torturer's payoff is lower than the cost to him of being tortured, the solution would be equivalent to the outcome in prisoner's dilemma game.

To describe the optimal level of torture to be chosen by each side of the conflict, let a soldier from side one (*Soldier 1*) maximize his utility by choosing the optimal level of torture that is constrained by the probability weighted retaliation from side two soldier (*Soldier 2*).[7] The objective function for *Soldier 1* can be stated as follows:

$$Max, \; U_1 = u_1(t_1) \text{ such that } c_1 t_2(t_1) \geq 0 \quad (7.1)$$

Let μ to be the Kuhn-Tucker multiplier on the constraint so that the Lagrangian takes the following form:

$$L = u_1(t_1) - \mu c_1 t_2(t_1). \quad (7.2)$$

The first order condition yields:

$$\frac{\partial u_1}{\partial t_1} = \mu c_1 \frac{\partial t_2}{\partial t_1}. \quad (7.3)$$

Soldier 2 solves a similar problem:

$$Max \; U_2 = u_2(t_2) \text{ such that } c_2 t_1(t_2) \geq 0. \quad (7.4)$$

Let μ to be the Kuhn-Tucker multiplier on the constraint. The second Lagrangian takes the following form:

$$L = u_2(t_2) - \mu c_2 t_1(t_2). \quad (7.5)$$

The first order condition for *Soldier 2* is:

$$\frac{\partial u_2}{\partial t_2} = \mu c_2 \frac{\partial t_1}{\partial t_2}. \quad (7.6)$$

When μ, c_1, c_2, t_1, $t_2 > 0$, the first order conditions suggest that the optimal level of torture will be reached when the marginal benefit of torture $\partial u_i / \partial t_i$ equals to the probability weighted, marginal torture retaliatory response $\mu c_i \partial t_j / \partial t_i$, where i = *Soldier 1* and j = *Soldier 2*. Now, one can evaluate how changes in probability c can affect the level of torture used. As shown in Figure 7.2, a lower probability of being captured alive such as $c^* < c^{**}$ would be associated with a higher level of torture such as $t^{**} > t^*$ because of the diminishing marginal utility of torture (concave utility function).

Figure 7.2 implies that a higher probability of being tortured by the opposing side reduces the level of desired torture. Alluding to the free trade analogy, a higher c_i would imply a more equal distribution of costs and benefits from trade openness. Similarly, an increase in the marginal retaliatory response $\partial t_j / \partial t_i$ by the opposing force j would also increase the

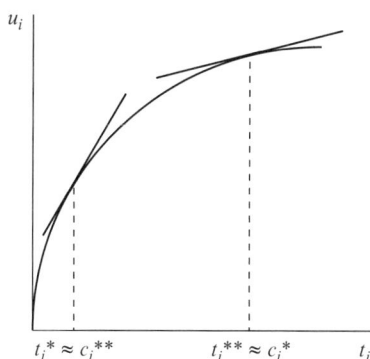

Figure 7.2   The optimal choice of torture under different probabilities

marginal utility of torture $\partial u_i/\partial t_i$ for side i, which means a lower level of torture due to diminishing marginal utility.

The above model can be made more intricate by incorporating asymmetric information about how, if at all, soldiers might be tortured and the importance of reputation capital in preventing the convergence of dominant strategy towards torture. This could be one of the avenues for future research. Since the role of government was omitted from this simple model, future studies could examine the effect of political regimes on the optimal level of torture. However, I suspect that the principal-agent problem would become a major obstacle in enforcing either domestic anti-torture policies or international treaties. Researchers may also want to examine how variations in the value of a statistical life across countries may affect their torture practices. For instance, if Soviet soldiers were relatively abundant compared to German soldiers in World War II, would that imply that they were proportionately less valuable than their German counterparts when it came to prisoner exchange and treatment of POWs? If so, this could explain the difference in treatment of the Soviet and American POWs in German prison camps.

7.8   CONCLUSION

This chapter presents an introduction to torture from the rational economic perspective. A multidisciplinary literature review reveals that torture continues to be a widely used method of information gathering, coercion and intimidation despite its questionable effectiveness and numerous treaties that prohibit it. Various economic, geographic, political and institutional factors are found to be significantly related to torture. However, some of these factors have rather intricate relationships with torture. Democracy, for instance, may have a non-linear effect on torture, which means that quasi-democratic countries may torture the most. Despite a wealth of empirical findings on torture, there is a lack of theoretical models of torture that rely on the rational agent framework. This chapter presents a simple model of torture between two warring countries based on the premise that torture costs are widespread and benefits are concentrated. The model's solution indicates that torture will be carried out with positive probability. The optimal level of torture depends on the probability weighted level of retaliation by the opposing side.

NOTES

1. The United Nations Convention Against Torture defines torture as any act by which severe pain or suffering, whether physical or mental, is intentionally inflicted on a person for such purposes as obtaining from him or a third person information or a confession, punishing him for an act he or a third person has committed or is suspected of having committed, or intimidating or coercing him or a third person, or for any reason based on discrimination of any kind, when such pain or suffering is inflicted by or at the instigation of or with the consent or acquiescence of a public official or other person acting in an official capacity.
2. Anti-torture treaties include but are not limited to Universal Declaration of Human Rights, UN Convention Against Torture, Third and Fourth Geneva Conventions.
3. For brevity, this chapter refers to the various articles and versions of the Hague and Geneva conventions simply as the Hague and Geneva conventions.
4. Alex Tabarrok argument can be found at http://www.marginalrevolution.com/marginal revolution/2005/11/torture_terrori.html.
5. James Miller's argument for torture can be found at http://www.overcomingbias. com/2007/08/bias-against-to.html.
6. Wantchekon and Healy (1999) claim that "Torture can be a rational choice for both the endorsing state and the individual torturer" (p. 596) without sufficiently explaining why.
7. Assume a utility function that is concave in torture and that $0 \le c \le 1$ and $0 \le t \le \infty$.

REFERENCES

Akerlof, G.A. (1970), "The market for 'lemons': quality uncertainty and the market mechanism", *Quarterly Journal of Economics*, **84** (3), 488–500.
Barro, R.J. and J-W. Lee (2000), "International data on educational attainment: updates and implications", CID Working Paper No. 42, available at http://www.cid.harvard.edu/cidwp/042.htm.
Beevor, A. (2001), *Stalingrad*. New York, NY: Penguin Press.
Biddle, S. and S. Long (2004), "Democracy and military effectiveness: a deeper look", *Journal of Conflict Resolution*, **48** (4), 525–46.
Bohara, A.K., N.J. Mitchell and M. Nepal (2006), "Opportunity, democracy, and the exchange of political violence: a subnational analysis of conflict in Nepal", *Journal of Conflict Resolution*, **50**, 108–28.

Carey, S.C. (2004), "Domestic threat and repression: an analysis of state responses to different forms of dissent", in S.C. Carey and S.C. Poe (eds), *Understanding Human Rights Violations*, Aldershot, UK: Ashgate, pp. 202–220.

Cingranelli, D.L. and D.L. Richards (2008), "The Cingranelli-Richards (CIRI) Human Rights Dataset", Version 2008.03.12, available at http://www.humanrightsdata.org.

Davenport, C. (1995), "Multidimensional threat perception and state repression: an inquiry into why states apply negative sanctions", *American Journal of Political Science*, **39** (3), 683–713.

Davenport, C. (1996), "The weight of the past: exploring the lagged determinants of political repression", *Political Research Quarterly*, **49** (2), 377–405.

Davenport, C. (1999), "Human rights and the democratic proposition", *Journal of Conflict Resolution*, **43**, 92–116.

Davenport, C. (2004), "Human rights and the promise of democratic pacification", International Studies Quarterly, **48** (3), 539–60.

Davenport, C. and D.A. Armstrong II (2004), "Democracy and the violation of human rights: A statistical analysis from 1976 to 1996", *American Journal of Political Science*, **48** (3), 538–54.

Dreher, A., M. Gassebner and L.R. Siemers (2007), "Does terror threaten human rights? Evidence from panel data", CESifo Working Paper Series No. 1935, available at http://ssrn.com/abstract=971454.

Easterly, W., R. Gatti and S. Kurlat (2006), "Development, democracy, and mass killings", Working Paper, Center for Global Development.

Evans, M.D. and R. Morgan (1998), *Preventing Torture: A study of the European Convention for the Prevention of Torture and Inhuman or Degrading Treatment or Punishment*, Oxford, UK: Clarendon Press, Oxford University Press.

Fearon, J.D. (1995), "Rationalist explanations for war", *International Organization*, **49**, 379–414.

Fearon, J.D. and D.D. Laitin (2003), "Ethnicity, insurgency and civil war", American Political Science Review, **97**, 75–90.

Fein, H. (1995), "More murder in the middle: life-integrity violations and democracy in the world, 1987", *Human Rights Quarterly*, **17** (1), 170–91.

Filson, D. and S. Werner (2004), "Bargaining and fighting: the impact of regime type on war onset, duration, and outcomes", *American Journal of Political Science*, **48**, 296–313.

Fujiwara, A. (1995), *Nitchû Sensô ni Okeru Horyo Gyakusatsu, Kikan Sensô Sekinin Kenkyû*, **9**, 22.

Gallup, J.L., J.D. Sachs and A. Mellinger (1999) "Geography and economic development", CID Working Paper No. 1, available at http://www2.cid.harvard.edu/ciddata/geography-data.htm.

Garfinkel, M.R. (1994), "Domestic politics and international conflict", *American Economic Review*, **84**, 1294–1309.

Garfinkel, M.R. and S. Skaperdas (2000), "Conflict without misperception or incomplete information: how the future matters", *Journal of Conflict Resolution*, **44**, 793–807.

Goldsmith, B.E. (2003), "Bearing the defense burden, 1886–1989: why spend more?" *Journal of Conflict Resolution*, **47**, 551–73.

Gourevitch, P. and E. Morris (2008), *Standard Operating Procedure*, 1st edition, New York, NY: Penguin Press HC.

Gurr, T.R. (1986), "The political origins of state violence and terror: a theoretical analysis", in M. Stohl and G.A. Lopez (eds), *Government Violence and Repression: An Agenda for Research*, Westport, CT: Greenwood, pp. 45–72.

Gwartney, J. and R. Lawson (2004), "Economic freedom of the world: 2004 annual report", Vancouver: The Fraser Institute, data retrieved from www.freetheworld.com.

Hafner-Burton, E.M. and K. Tsutsui (2007), "Justice lost! The failure of international human rights law to matter where needed most", *Journal of Peace Research*, **44** (4), 407–25.

Hathaway, O.A. (2002), "Do human rights treaties make a difference?", *The Yale Law Journal*, **111** (8), 1935–2042.

Hathaway, O.A. (2003), "The cost of commitment", *Stanford Law Review*, **55** (5), 1821–62.
Hathaway, O.A. (2007), "Why do countries commit to human rights treaties?" *Journal of Conflict Resolution*, **51**, 588–621.
Henderson, C.W. (1991), "Conditions affecting the use of political repression", *Journal of Conflict Resolution*, **35** (1), 120–42.
Henderson, C.W. (1993), "Population pressures and political repression", *Social Science Quarterly*, **74** (2), 322–33.
Heston, A., R. Summers and B. Aten (2002), *Penn World Table*, Version 6.1, Center for International Comparisons at the University of Pennsylvania (CICUP), available at http://pwt.econ.upenn.edu/.
Hirshleifer, J. (1995), "Theorizing about conflict", in K. Hartley and T. Sandler (eds), *Handbook of Defense Economics*, Vol.1, Amsterdam: North-Holland, pp. 165–92.
Hooks, G. and M. Clayton (2005), "Outrages against personal dignity: rationalizing abuse and torture in the war on terror", *Social Forces*, **83** (4), 1627–45.
Horowitz, M., E. Simpson and A. Stam (2006), "Domestic institutions and wartime casualties", Unpublished Draft Working Paper. Harvard University.
Koppl, R. (2005), "Epistemic systems", Game Theory and Information 0510001, EconWPA.
Krain, M. (1997), "State-sponsored mass murder: the onset and severity of genocides and politicides", *Journal of Conflict Resolution*, **41** (3), 331–60.
McCoy, K.E. (2005), "Trained to torture? The human rights effects of military training at the school of the Americas", *Latin American Perspectives*, **32** (6), 47–64.
Mitchell, N.J., and J.M. McCormick (1988), "Economic and political explanations of human rights violations", *World Politics*, **40** (4), 476–98.
Mitchell, S.M., S. Gates and H. Hegre (1999), "Evolution in democracy: war dynamics", *Journal of Conflict Resolution*, **43**, 771–92.
Mulligan, C.B., R. Gil and X. Sala-i-Martin (2004), "Do democracies have different public policies than nondemocracies?" *Journal of Economic Perspectives*, **18**, 51–74.
Mulligan, C.B. and K.K. Tsui (2006), "Political competitiveness", NBER Working Papers 12653, National Bureau of Economic Research, Inc.
Nafziger, E.W. and J. Auvinen (2002), "Economic development, inequality, war and state violence", European Union, Working Paper, *World Development*, **30**, pp. 153–163.
Neumayer, E. (2005), "Do international human rights treaties improve respect for human rights?" *Journal of Conflict Resolution*, **49**, 925–53.
North, J. (2006), Hitler's forgotten victims, *World War II Magazine*, January/February, 26–32, 80.
Persson, T. (2002), "Do political institutions shape economic policy?" *Econometrica*, **70**, 883–905.
Poe, S.C. and C.N. Tate (1994), "Repression of human rights to personal integrity in the 1980s: a global analysis", *American Political Science Review*, **88**, 853–900.
Poe, S.C., C.N. Tate and L.C. Keith (1999), "Repression of the human right to personal integrity revisited: a global cross-national study covering the years 1976–1993", *International Studies Quarterly*, **43** (2), 291–313.
Poe, S.C. (2004), "The decision to repress: An integrative theoretical approach to the research on human rights and repression", in S.C. Carey and S.C. Poe (eds), *Understanding Human Rights Violations*, Aldershot, UK: Ashgate, pp. 16–38.
Polity IV Project (2000), "Political regime characteristics and transition, 1800–2000", Electronic data (version p4v2000), College Park, MD: CIDCM, University of Maryland.
Putnam, R.D. (1993), *Making Democracy Work: Civic Traditions in Modern Italy*, Princeton, NJ: Princeton University Press.
Rasler, K. (1986), "War, accommodation, and violence in the United States, 1890–1970", *American Political Science Review*, **80** (3), 921–45.
Regan, P. and E. Henderson (2002), "Democracy, threats and political repression in developing countries: are democracies internally less violent?" *Third World Quarterly*, **23** (1), 119–36.
Reid, P. (1953), *The Colditz Story*, Oxford, UK: Greenwood Publishing Group.

Rejali, D. (2004), "Does Torture Work?" *Salon.com*, 21.

Rejali, D. (2007), *Torture and Democracy*, Princeton, NJ: Princeton University Press.

Richards, D.L. (1999), "Perilous proxy: human rights and the presence of national elections", *Social Science Quarterly*, **80** (4), 648–65.

Richards, D.L., R.D. Gelleny and D.H. Sacko (2001), "Money with a mean streak? Foreign economic penetration and government respect for human rights in developing countries", *International Studies Quarterly*, **45** (2), 219–39.

Rolf, D. (1998), *Prisoners of the Reich: Germany's Captives, 1939–1945*, Barnsley, UK: Pen and Sword Books.

Rummel, R. (1997), *Power Kills: Democracy as a Method of Nonviolence*, New Brunswick, NJ: Transaction Publishers.

Russett, B. and J.R. Oneal (2001), *Triangulating Peace: Democracy, Interdependence, and International Organizations*, New York, NY: W.W. Norton.

Schelling, T. (1960), *The Strategy of Conflict*, Cambridge, MA: Harvard University Press.

Sherborne, L. (2003), "An integrated model of political repression: theory and model development", Ph.D. dissertation, University of Houston, Houston.

Shue, H. (1978), "Torture", Philosophy and Public Affairs, **7** (2), 124–43.

Singer, J.D., S. Bremer and J. Stuckey (1972), "Capability distribution, uncertainty, and major power war, 1820–1965", in B. Russett (ed.) *Peace, War, and Numbers*, Beverly Hills, CA: Sage, pp. 19–48.

Vreeland, J.R. (2008), "Political institutions and human rights: why dictatorships enter into the United Nations Convention Against Torture", *International Organization*, **62**, 65–101.

Wantchekon, L. and A. Healy (1999), "The 'game' of torture", *The Journal of Conflict Resolution*, **43** (5), 596–609.

Weingast, B.R. (1997), "The political foundations of democracy and the rule of law", *American Political Science Review*, **91** (2), 245–63.

Yakovlev, P.A. (2007), "Arms trade, military spending, and economic growth", *Defense and Peace Economics*, **18** (4), 317–38.

Yakovlev, P.A. (2008), "Saving lives in armed conflicts: what factors matter?" *Economics of Peace and Security*, **3** (2), 68–73.

Zanger, S.C. (2000), "A global analysis of the effect of political regime changes on life integrity violations, 1977–1993", *Journal of Peace Research*, **37** (2), 213–33.

8   Terrorism in rational choice perspective
William F. Shughart II

8.1   INTRODUCTION

In the economist's model of rational human behavior, all individuals are assumed to be motivated by self-interest. They seek to maximize their senses of personal well-being, or utility, an objective that includes not only the satisfaction derived from consuming goods and services purchased on the market, but also the psychic pleasure associated with the attainment of any other desired end. What is of chief importance here is that self-interest is not to be understood narrowly as selfishness; the aim of economically rational economic man (or woman) is not solely to maximize private income or wealth. Other-regarding preferences indulged by actions such as providing aid and comfort to family and friends, bestowing charity on strangers or supporting a revolutionary cause fall within the ambit of the rational-choice model. So, too, does striving to gain entrée to a believed-in afterlife. Faced with a limited budget and unlimited wants, the problem confronting abstract economic man simply is to select the particular combination of market and non-market goods that, in the chooser's own judgment, yields the greatest possible level of satisfaction.

Terrorists are rational actors on that definition. Rationality in the spirit of *Homo oeconomicus* is not necessarily to be found in terrorists' stated intentions, though. Indeed, living in a "fantasy world" (Laqueur 1999, p. 28), the Red Army Faction (Baader-Meinhof Group), Italy's *Brigate Rosse*, France's *Action Directe* and other left-wing terror groups of the 1960s and 1970s generally had no well-articulated purposes beyond "destruction of the current Western system" of liberal democracy (Kellen 1990, p. 55) and no practical plans for replacing it, except perhaps, as in the pipedreams of their Russian nihilist forebears, with a "universally all-human social republic and harmony" (Dostoevsky [1872] 1994, p. 53).

But terrorists are rational in two important means-ends senses. First, while the globe is terrorist-target-rich, the resources commanded by individual terrorists and terrorist groups unavoidably are limited. Every terrorist faces a budget constraint and, whether acting alone or in concert with others, consequently must deploy money, munitions and manpower cost-effectively, allocating the available resources over time and space so as to maximize terrorism's net returns, in whatever form those returns are expected to materialize. Second, terrorists respond rationally to measures taken to counter them. When some targets are hardened, they shift attention to softer ones. If a country elevates its counterterrorist efforts, terrorists move their operations to less vigilant states. Terrorists, in short, behave as if they are guided by the same rational-choice calculus that animates human action in more ordinary settings. They evaluate the alternatives available to them and choose the option that promises the largest expected benefit relative to cost; they respond, moreover, "in a sensible and predictable fashion to changing risks" (Enders and Sandler 2006, p. 11) and, one might add, to changing rewards. Many of the causes and consequences of terrorism are, in short, amenable to explanation by the economist's model of demand and supply.

This chapter summarizes the theory and evidence that situates terrorism in a rational choice context.[1] Terrorism is first defined more precisely in Section 8.2. Attention then turns, in Section 8.3, to discussions of terrorists' rationality in selecting their targets and in responding to defensive countermeasures. Section 8.4 explores the logic of suicide terrorism. Section 8.5 concludes.

8.2   TERRORISM DEFINED

Irrational as it may seem at first blush, terrorist acts are goal-oriented. As defined by the US Department of State, terrorism is "premeditated, politically motivated violence perpetrated against noncombatant targets by subnational groups or clandestine agents, usually intended to influence an audience" (Office of the Coordinator of Counterterrorism 1997, p. vi)

While other definitions of terrorism certainly have been advanced and, as a matter of fact, it is at times difficult to distinguish its perpetrators from "revolutionaries,"[2] "insurgents," "freedom fighters," "martyrs" or ordinary criminals, modern scholarship attributes at least four distinctive characteristics to the terrorist program. First and foremost, terrorism is violence – or its threat – for political effect (Hoffman 1998, p. 15; Sandler 2005). (In light of the emergence of Islamist terrorism and of the bloodshed caused by the Unabomber, Timothy McVeigh, and the assassin of a guard at Washington DC's Holocaust Museum, one could well add religious and social goals to the list.) Second, terrorism is "a planned, calculated, and indeed systematic act" (Hoffman 1998, p. 15). Third, terrorists are not bound by established rules of warfare or codes of conduct (Ibid., p. 35)[3] and, fourth, terrorism is "designed to have far-reaching psychological repercussions beyond the immediate target or victim" (Ibid., p. 43).

"Terrorism is theater", as Brian Jenkins once said (Coll 2004, p. 139; also see Enders and Sandler 2006, p. 3).

8.2.1   The Psychology and Sociology of Terrorism

It once was thought that terrorism's origins could be located in personal character traits predisposing individuals to rebellious and violent behavior, in conditions of poverty and powerlessness leading to disaffection and disengagement from society at large, and in the social dynamics of terrorist groups themselves: subservience to a charismatic leader or the solidarity and brotherhood – the "primary group cohesion" (McPherson 1997, p. 85) – that in small-numbers settings often leads those in harm's way to place the welfare of their comrades above their own (for example, Reich 1990; Turk 2004).[4]

Scholarly work aimed at developing a composite personality profile of the archetypal terrorist has by and large been unsuccessful, however. Although "most terrorists have been young, some very young," and "the vast majority have been male" (Laqueur 1999, p. 80), no aspects of race, ethnicity, education, income, employment or social status conclusively can be said to distinguish terrorists from non-terrorists, either now or in the past. Nor, apparently, does terrorism have roots traceable to "genetic factors, psychological difficulties in early childhood, a disturbed family life, or identification with the underclass" (Ibid., p. 79). As a unique personality type, the representative terrorist does not exist: "there never was such a person" (Ibid.).

Even suicide attackers defy neat categorization: they "are not mainly poor, uneducated, immature religious zealots or social losers" (Pape 2005, p. 216). Indeed, if any conclusion can be drawn from the data on suicide terrorism since 1980, in which, except for attacks intended to advance the interests of Islamic extremists, women have played ever more prominent roles, it is that, "especially given their education, they resemble the kind of politically conscious individuals who might join a grassroots movement more than they do wayward adolescents or religious fanatics" (Ibid.).[5]

8.2.2   Economic Models of Terrorism

In contrast to psychological and sociological approaches to the problem, economists attempt to understand terrorism's origins (as well as its targets) by focusing on relevant incentives and constraints.[6] As it initially developed, the economics literature on terrorism divided along the lines of the subject's two main fields of study. One strand of the literature adopts a microeconomics perspective by assessing the costs and benefits of terrorist activity at the level of individual actors. The other strand examines the causes and effects of terrorism through the lens of macroeconomics by asking whether terrorism is more likely to emerge in conditions of high unemployment, slow or stagnant rates of economic growth and other indicators of poor national economic performance. An important related question is whether terrorism impairs a nation's economic performance; so, too, is the political economy question whether terrorism is driven by poor institutions of governance which, in addition to inhibiting economic development, block some individuals and groups from expressing their grievances at the polls, petitioning their political representatives or pursuing other, non-violent courses of remedial action.

Micro terrorism

Terrorism has swept the globe in three distinctive, albeit overlapping, waves since the end of World War II.[7] The first of these terrorist waves arguably began on VE Day (8 May 1945) in the small North African market town of Sétif, when Muslim demonstrators demanding Algerian independence spontaneously turned violent, triggering a nearly week-long cycle of bloodthirsty outrages against their *pied-noir* compatriots and indiscriminant reprisal by the French troops dispatched to restore order (Horne [1977] 2006, pp. 23–8; Shughart 2006, pp. 7–8). Aroused by the self-determination language of the Atlantic Charter and unleashed by the post-war shrinking of the British and French colonial empires, the events at Sétif helped launch a wave of terrorist violence motivated in large part by the goals of ethnic separatism and national liberation. That first wave, which saw terrorist tactics deployed decisively in expelling foreign rulers and creating the new states of Algeria, Cyprus, Ireland and Israel, among others (Rapoport 2004, p. 53), ended with the airlifting to safety of the last American diplomat from the rooftop of the US embassy in Saigon.[8]

The second post-war wave of terror was by then already well underway. It started on 22 July 1968, when Palestinian terrorists, acting to avenge Egypt's stunning defeat by Israel in the 1967 Six-Day War, hijacked an El Al passenger aircraft en route from Rome to Tel Aviv. Although it, too, was influenced to greater or lesser extent by ethno-nationalistic goals, the second wave precipitated by the hijacking elevated terrorism to the international stage as never before. The Popular Front for the Liberation of Palestine's (PFLP) publicity coup, which demonstrated the value of galvanizing public opinion, produced spillover effects by emboldening copycat terrorist groups in The Netherlands, Turkey and elsewhere. Left-wing movements in Europe and North America, frequently aided and abetted by the PFLP, the Palestine Liberation Organization (PLO) and other Palestinian terrorist groups, animated by opposition to the Vietnam

War and by anti-Americanism in general, and claiming solidarity with oppressed peoples of the Third World, embarked on self-styled revolutionary campaigns of political assassinations, bombings and hijackings (Kellen 1990). That wave of terror, also marked by hostage-taking extortion and garden-variety bank robbery, continued until the fall of the Berlin Wall in 1989, when the members of Italy's Red Brigade, West Germany's Red Army Faction,[9] and their sister organizations no longer could be assured of financial support from – or safe haven in – the East.

The third wave of terror was set in motion prior to the Soviet Union's collapse by the Iranian Revolution of 1979 (Enders and Sandler 2000). It is still ongoing, pushed forward in Central Asia by the withdrawal of Soviet troops bloodied in their decade-long war against the *mujahiddin*, in the Middle East by hostility to American support for Israel, and inspired everywhere – from Algeria to Chechnya, Kashmir, Indonesia, the Philippines and beyond – by pan-Islamic visions of a new world order in which the fundamentalist Muslim faithful, freed from Western cultural contamination, would be united under a resurrected Caliphate and strictly enforced *Shar'ia* law.[10]

Whether the objective is to wreck the "system," to liberate a repressed ethnic or religious minority by creating a new nation-state, or to redress real or imagined grievances against an established governmental regime or colonial power, an individual's decision to engage in terrorist activity, alone or in an organized group, requires a weighing of the probable benefits and costs to himself or herself personally. Consistent with the rational-choice model, the terrorist may gain psychic rewards from successful commission of a violent act. The expected payoff might also be in the form of bounties or similar financial rewards; elevated status within the terrorist organization; appointment to public office if the group seizes political power; access to education, job training or social services otherwise unavailable to themselves and their families (Zakaria 2003, p. 142); compensation to relatives in the event of disablement or death; and even the promise of a martyr's paradise.[11]

As a matter of fact, because the fruits of terrorism are something of a public good – the benefits of a successful terrorist act will be shared by all who support the terrorist's cause – such "selective incentives" often will be necessary to mitigate the free-rider problem that inevitably plagues collective action (Olson 1965; Rathbone and Rowley 2004). Russell Hardin (1995, p. 5) argues that "self-interest can often successfully be matched with group interest" when the members of one group become convinced that they are engaged in a zero-sum game, that is, that the expected gains from collective action depend on "the suppression of another group's interest." The salient selective incentives may include sticks as well as carrots: the now-vanquished Tamil Tigers, for instance, allegedly recruited suicide terrorists by threatening their loved ones and by exploiting other means of coercion (Berman and Laitin 2006, pp. 25–6).

To an economist, the costs of becoming a terrorist include, first and foremost, the income that could have been earned in legitimate lines of work.[12] It is for this reason that Frey and Luechinger (2003) propose that policies increasing the opportunity cost of terrorists are more effective in curbing terrorism than is increasing the material cost of terrorism through deterrence alone.[13] Faria and Arce (2005) elaborate on this theme by providing a theoretical model where both more effective deterrence and higher opportunity costs lessen the popular support that is essential for recruiting potential terrorists. Other explicit costs relevant to the terrorist's rational-choice calculus are exposure to the risks of arrest, imprisonment, torture, bodily injury and, ultimately, loss of life.

Engaging in terrorism is not simply an either–or decision, however. Individuals can remain on the sidelines of a terrorist campaign, supply clandestine support to a terrorist group or join the opposition to it. Avoiding active participation may be the optimal choice if terrorism ultimately is suppressed, but also raises one's chances of becoming a statistic in the collateral damage of a terrorist attack. Should a terrorist campaign succeed, on the other hand, bystanders and latecomers will be denied opportunities to share in the spoils distributed among those who zealously backed the cause from the beginning. The members of the opposition face a similar social dilemma: rewarded if terrorism is effectively countered and subject to reprisal if not (Tullock 1974).

To paraphrase Carl von Clausewitz ([1832] 1976, p. 87), terrorism merely is a continuation of policy by other means. Animated during much of recent history by the goals of redressing the grievances of oppressed ethnic minorities or of achieving independence from colonial rule, terror often is the best available course of action because the supporters of the status quo control the levers of established governing power and can mobilize police and military forces that are larger, better equipped and better trained than are the cadres seeking to effect change. Moreover, as we have seen, the tactical and strategic advantages of asymmetrical warfare, as opposed to regular warfare, have proven to be successful in the terror campaigns leading to the independence of, among others, Algeria, Israel and Cyprus. The British and Soviet experiences in Afghanistan likewise are apt (Shughart 2002, 2006).

Target selection is among the most important of terrorists' comparative advantages. Because nation-states seeking to protect their homelands cannot possibly safeguard people and property everywhere, terrorist groups can attack wherever countermeasures remain ineffectual.[14] Terrorists are well-positioned to exploit existing vulnerabilities because they typically are better informed about the strengths and weaknesses of a nation's defensive measures than the government is about the sizes, locations and resources available to terrorist cells. Terrorist groups also are organizationally less hierarchical, operationally more independent and, hence, more innovative and more nimble in acting than public law enforcement and counterterrorism agencies are in reacting to threats (Sandler 2005). Jack Hirshleifer (1991) calls this asymmetry the *paradox of power*: "They strike at the outskirts of the camp. Then when we sound the call to arms, they vanish. This is the most demoralizing kind of warfare" (Vidal [1964] 1986, p. 428).

Terrorists do not have to defeat the governing regime militarily; they only have to avoid losing (Hoffman 1998, p. 52).[15] In order to achieve their goals, however, they must marshal public opinion. Media attention is essential to the terrorist enterprise because terrorist groups do not in general aim to influence policy directly or necessarily even to elicit widespread sympathy for their cause. Terrorists instead choreograph their attacks mainly to intimidate, to produce "massive fear" (Cooper 2001, p. 883), thereby panicking an alarmed citizenry into demanding that national leaders stop the violence by somehow putting right the perceived wrongs that, at least in the minds of the perpetrators, justify their terror campaign. Creating a climate of fear requires fostering the belief that everyone is a potential target: "A man can face known danger. But the unknown frightens him" (Heinlein [1966] 1994, p. 75). Or, in terms more familiar to an economist, "there are few incentives more powerful than the fear of random violence – which, in essence, is why terrorism is so effective" (Levitt and Dubner 2005, p. 62).

It is for this reason that concentrating attacks on urban centers and targeting civilians are two of the prongs of a rational terrorist strategy. Incidents committed in metropolitan areas disrupt daily life there and command immediate media attention, both nationally and internationally. Publicity for "dramatic, well-orchestrated and appropriately timed acts of violence" (Rapoport 2004, pp. 57–8) both draws attention to the terrorist group's cause and raises popular estimates, perhaps overly so (Kahneman and Tversky 1979), of the risks to which ordinary people are exposed. Focusing on urban centers may also, as it did in Cyprus, hamstring official responses to terrorist threats by forcing troops to be dispersed citywide on static guard duty missions at scores of potential targets, none of which likely will be hit on any given day (Rapoport 2004, p. 58).

Target selection inevitably demands a weighing of expected costs and benefits because terrorist violence can, by producing indiscriminant death and destruction, turn public opinion against the responsible group (Crenshaw 1990, p. 17), compromising its ability to operate clandestinely, to raise needed funds and to recruit new members, all of which reduce its chances of success. Tradeoffs of similar kinds face those in charge of the counterterrorism effort. Governments, especially democratic governments, likewise are constrained by popular opinion. In addition to fostering a climate of fear, terrorist groups consequently can advance their interests by provoking officials into adopting repressive countermeasures that undermine civil liberties or simply inconvenience ordinary people enough that demands for protection from terrorism are transformed into opposition to the policies adopted to suppress it. Brutal reprisals and extensive security precautions may also serve a terrorist group's cause by contributing to public perceptions of its power (Ibid., p. 19), its "apparent ability to strike anywhere, anytime" (Rapoport 2004, p. 59), thereby making it easier to recruit new members.

There were 5431 transnational terrorist incidents during the 1980s, claiming in total 4684 lives (Pillar 2001, p. 42).[16] Terrorism's highwater mark during the post-World War II period was reached in 1987, which recorded nearly 700 attacks (Enders and Sandler 2006, p. 41). Transnational terrorism has declined fairly steadily since then – the last decade of the twentieth century witnessed 3824 incidents and 2468 terrorism-related fatalities (Pillar 2001, p. 42) – but terrorism has become more lethal. While 19 percent fewer terrorist events occurred in the second half of the 1990s than in the first half, the number of people killed by terrorists more than doubled (Ibid.; Enders and Sandler 2000).[17] Terrorism's rising butcher's bill coincides with growth in the incidence of suicide attacks, which kill, on the average, anywhere from four (Hoffman and McCormick 2004, p. 269) to thirteen people, compared with the one person who typically dies in a more ordinary event (Pape 2003). Suicide terrorism, which accounts for just three percent of the terrorist attacks of the past 25 years, is 12 times more deadly than other forms of terrorism if 9/11 is excluded (Pape 2005, p. 8).

Although the rational-choice model generates predictions about terrorist behavior not amenable to explanation by other social sciences, information on individual terrorists is hard to come by, Pape (2003, 2005) perhaps being the outstanding, but not entirely criticism-free exception. Economists and other scholars attempting to understand the historical patterns in the numbers and types of terrorist incidents therefore have devoted their attention to available aggregate datasets that track terrorism's countries of origin and targets over time. Such macroeconomic analyses have contributed important insights into terrorism's causes and consequences.

Macro terrorism

It is by now well-established that liberal states uniquely are vulnerable to terrorist attacks (Wilkinson 1986; Weinberg and Eubank 1987; Eubank and Weinberg 1994, 2001; Li 2005).[18] With their open borders, their respect for individual freedoms and the constitutional protections they offer for the rights of the accused, including those of non-citizens, democratic states supply favorable environments for terrorist groups, not only in which locate their operations but also in which to wage their violent campaigns (Enders and Sandler 2006, p. 24).[19] The institution of a free press maximizes the opportunities available to terrorists for publicizing their grievances and creating a climate of fear in which everyone, no matter how low the risk actually may be, sees himself or herself as a potential target; democracies are especially vulnerable to hostage-takers owing to popular concern for citizens' lives (Rapoport [1992] 2004, p. 1064).

It is important to emphasize in this regard that terrorists do not tend to select targets in liberal states because they want to unseat those nations' democratically elected governments, but rather because they want to induce policy changes compatible with their interests by influencing audiences there. That objective explains why the United States, France and Great Britain are the major net "importers" of terrorism (Blomberg and Hess 2008b, p. 128)[20] and why in the recent past Americans overwhelmingly have been the targets of terrorist attacks. More than half of the international terrorist incidents in 1982, for instance, were directed against US citizens or property on foreign soil. Those terrorist events "occurred in 78 different countries and 45 percent of them took place in Western Europe" (Wilkinson 1986, pp. 105–106).[21]

Terrorism also can be quite costly. It impairs private capital investment and, hence, economic growth. Indeed, one estimate suggests that world GDP would have been US$3.6 trillion greater in 2002 had there been no terrorist incidents that year. That sum equals about one-third of US GDP and exceeds the gross domestic products of Argentina, Italy and the United Kingdom combined. Put differently, reducing the number of terrorist attacks on the United States from three to two would have increased fixed capital investment there by US$5 billion and GDP by US$40 billion in 2002 (Crain and Crain 2006). The social costs of terrorism are considerably larger if one counts subjective losses in "life satisfaction" among survey respondents in terror-prone nations (Frey, Luechinger and Stutzer 2009).

Most of the existing scholarly literature finds the macroeconomic effects of terrorism generally to be quite modest and of limited duration, however. Despite the media attention paid to them, terrorist attacks are in fact quite rare and they have immediate impacts on people and property that, tragic as they may be, almost always are local in scope. The large and well-diversified economies of the developed world consequently are able to absorb the damage and recover from terrorist incidents fairly rapidly. The direct and indirect costs of 9/11, for example, estimated to have amounted to at most US$90 billion, represented a very small fraction of that year's US$10 trillion American economy (Sandler and Enders 2008, p. 17). Real US GDP growth dipped briefly in the third quarter of 2001, but then rebounded in short order (Ibid., pp. 26–8).

The evidence from studies tracking the experiences of large numbers of countries over long time horizons suggests that per capita income growth is lower in nations on the receiving end of terrorist attacks, but that terrorism's macroeconomic impact is small and its statistical significance is sensitive to the inclusion of other control variables (Blomberg, Hess and Orphanides 2004; Tavares 2004). More substantial effects are found when the focus is narrowed to smaller nations or to specific sectors of their economies. Abadie and Gardeazabal (2003), for example, find that GDP per capita in Spain's Basque region was 10 percent below predicted trend over 20 years of the terror campaign launched by ethnic separatists. Eckstein and Tsiddon (2004) report the same 10 percent reduction in per capita GDP for Israel during the period of the second Intifada, which began in the third quarter of 2000 and ended in the fourth quarter of 2003; in percentage terms, fixed capital investment and exports both fell by twice as much (for estimates of the economic and political costs of the Intifada of 1987, see Fielding 2003). The evidence from small countries also suggests that tourism (Enders and Sandler 1991; Enders, Sandler and Parise 1992; Fleischer and Buccola 2002; Drakos and Kutan 2003), the commercial airline industry (Drakos 2004; Ito and Lee 2004), foreign direct investment (Enders and Sandler 1996) and international trade (Nitsch and Schumacher 2004) are particularly vulnerable to terrorist activities.

The political economy of terrorism

Numerous studies find that healthier domestic economic performance – higher per capita incomes and faster rates of economic growth – lowers the risk of violence of various kinds, including hate crimes (Green, Glaser and Rich 1998); "conflict," broadly defined (Blomberg and Hess 2002; Blomberg, Hess and Thacker 2006); civil war (Collier and Hoeffler 2004) and terrorism (Krueger and Malecková 2003; Blomberg, Hess and Weerapana 2004a; Blomberg and Hess 2008a, 2008b).[22] But such evidence begs an important question: Nations that rank near the top on indicators of economic development tend to have "good" institutions (Easterly 2000). The richer countries of the world are characterized by governments that safeguard citizens' political and civil rights. Individuals are afforded opportunities freely to speak, peaceably to assemble, to vote in competitive elections and to petition the representatives they have chosen. Constitutional rules guarantee a free press, an independent judiciary and impose other constraints, including provisions for impeaching and removing public officials from their posts, which limit government's ability to override the popular will. Perhaps it is not economic development per se, but rather the institutions of liberal constitutional democracy that mitigate the chances that differences between individuals and groups will spill over into bloody conflict, civil war and terrorist violence?

Answers to that question become all the more important owing to evidence that greater fractionalization along ethnic, linguistic or religious lines raises the probability that a nation either will be plagued by civil war (Montalvo and Reynal-Querol 2005)[23] or become a terrorist target (Kurrild-Klitgaard, Justesen and Klemmensen 2006).[24] Indeed, Easterly (2000) has suggested that ethnic fractionalization is an important driver of recurrent bloodshed on the African continent.[25] The reason seems to be grounded in politics: as Horowitz ([1985] 2000, p. 39) puts it, "a profusion of dispersed groups usually creates such great ethnic heterogeneity at the center that when the center intervenes it may do so as a neutral arbiter." On the other hand, "in those states where a few groups are so large that their interactions are a constant theme of politics at the center[,] . . . the claims of one group tend to be made at the expense of another: mutually exclusive demands characterize political debate" (Ibid.). Indeed, Esteban and Ray (1994) conclude that ethnic polarization – and its propensity for triggering violence – is greatest when a society is divided into two groups of similar size.

Building on the work of Krueger and Malecková (2003), Krueger and Laitin (2008) report evidence that terrorism is more likely to originate in countries where civil liberties are denied than where the people are divided sharply along sectarian lines (measured in terms of national population percentages of Muslims, Buddhists, Hindus and "other" religious groups). Krueger and Laitin (2008, p. 150) conclude from their analysis that, for reasons given earlier, the citizens of "open" democratic societies are more likely to be terrorism's victims (Ibid., p. 167), but what is more important, that the origins of terrorism can be traced to "countries that suffer from political oppression" – those that deny "civil liberties" (Ibid., p 172). A key implication of Krueger and Laitin's empirical study is that the threat of both domestic and transnational terrorism can be lowered by policies that advance the political and civil liberties of the peoples now living under repressive regimes which quash political opposition, actively sponsor the activities of terrorist groups (Iran, Saudi Arabia and Hamas's "governors" of the Gaza Strip , for instance) or offer aid and comfort to terrorism's perpetrators (Lebanon, Libya, North Korea, Pakistan and Somalia, to name a few).

But there is another important set of institutions that distinguish nation-states from one another. It is true that "poor" democratic governments and non-democratic governments alike are characterized by public corruption, low bureaucratic quality, pervasive disrespect for the rule of law and studious inattention to broader measures of policy accountability, such as rates of secondary school enrollments (Keefer and Loayza 2008, p. 8). It is also true, however, that governments can promote development by protecting economic liberties, that is, by respecting the rights of private property, resisting the temptation to expropriate it and refraining from repudiating contracts entered voluntarily by competent individuals.

Exploiting a dataset comprising observations on 118 countries from 1982 through 1997, Basuchoudhary and Shughart (2010) report evidence consistent with the ideas that transnational terrorism is more likely to originate in ethnically tense states and that "good" institutions can help break that link. They also find, however, that property rights may be more important than civil rights in reducing the odds that terrorism will find fertile ground where ethnic tensions are high. Indeed, while liberal political institutions were associated with the launching of significantly fewer transnational terrorist acts in the period following the end of the Cold War, that result did not hold prior to 1990. Stronger protections for economic liberties, on the other hand, lowered the number of attacks originating in a country throughout the full sample. As a matter of fact, when the quality of a nation's economic institutions was controlled for, perceived ethnic tensions no longer explained transnational terrorism's countries of origin.

The obvious policy implication of these findings is that the reforming of political institutions in states that now deny citizens' civil liberties may be less effective in curbing transnational terrorism than the reforming of their economic institutions. It is well-known, after all, that, because of the advantages of incumbency, rational voter ignorance and the irrationality of voting in the first place (Downs 1957), elections alone do not tightly constrain governmental behavior, especially in a heterogeneous society where vote tallies often are nothing more than ethnic "head counts" – "the election is a census, and the census is an election" (Horowitz [1985] 2000, p.196). Offering stronger protections for private property rights, which provide incentives for starting businesses and interacting peacefully with others, may prevent ethnic differences from spilling over into ethnic violence and transnational terrorist activity. In any case, the definition of "good" institutions merits further scholarly study.

8.3   RATIONAL TERRORISTS

As mentioned at the outset, terrorists are rational in two important means-ends senses. Owing to the superior numbers, training and firepower that can be brought to bear by the regular army and police forces arrayed against them, terrorists must select their targets and time their attacks carefully, searching out the most vulnerable of them, or what, in the context of public goods provision, Jack Hirshleifer (1983) calls the "weakest link." Rationality in target selection also influences terrorists' modes of attack – although detonating explosive devices historically has been the most common method of sowing terror,[26] aircraft hijackings, assassinations, kidnappings and hostage-takings are among the other available options – as well as their responses to the security measures adopted to thwart them. Terrorists and their opponents thus are engaged in a repeated game, characterized by a sequence of moves in which a terrorist incident elicits a defensive response and the countermeasure, in turn, prompts the attackers to shift to "softer" targets, to change their method of attack, or both.[27] As we shall see, such "policy-induced substitution" (Enders and Sandler 2006, p. 112) not only impacts the effectiveness of any one nation's counterterrorism efforts, but also hinders international cooperation in the fight against terrorism. More to the point, scientific studies showing that terrorists actually do respond to counterterrorism polices in the predictable ways supply evidence that terrorists are in fact rational.

Analysing a dataset comprising all hijackings of US commercial aircraft between 1961 and 1976, William Landes (1978) found that countering that threat by installing metal detectors at domestic airports to screen boarding passengers early in 1973 resulted in between 41 and 50 fewer such incidents over the next four years. In showing that acting to make one method of spreading terror more personally costly – increasing the chances of being arrested and prosecuted for attempting to carry weapons on board – reduced the number of hijackings originating at domestic US airports significantly, Landes provided the first systematic test of the rational-choice model of terrorist behavior. The idea of policy-induced substitution predicts, however, that terrorists would have responded to the installation of metal detectors by reallocating their resources toward other targets.

Enders and Sandler (1993) estimate the interrelations among four types of terrorist incidents occurring over the period running from the first quarter of 1970 through the second quarter of 1988: skyjackings, kidnappings and hostage-takings, attacks against protected personnel (official representatives of heads of state, such as ambassadors and diplomats, along with their accompanying family members) and all other transnational terrorist attacks, including bombings, threats and hoaxes. They also estimate the effects of four US counterterrorism policy interventions introduced over the same period: the installation of metal detectors at domestic airports on 5 January 1973 – an innovation quickly emulated at commercial airfields worldwide – a doubling of spending, beginning in October 1976, to fortify US embassies around the globe, the appropriation in October 1985 of additional resources to secure US embassies and their personnel, and airstrikes against Libyan targets on 15 April 1986, in retaliation for that nation's involvement ten days earlier in the bombing of Berlin's La Belle discotheque, in which American military personnel accounted for many of the 230 people who were injured in the attack and two of the three who were killed.

Enders and Sandler's analysis confirms Landes's finding that the installation of metal detectors reduced the number of aircraft hijacking incidents significantly. Above and beyond that, other results of the study are consistent with the prediction of policy-induced substitution.[28] In particular, the advent of airport metal detectors led to significantly more terrorist hostage-taking and, perhaps because the same technology also was deployed at US embassies, military bases and various other government facilities both at home and abroad, to fewer attacks on protected American personnel. On the other hand, Enders and Sandler do not find that additional spending to fortify US embassies around the globe, either in 1976 or 1985, had statistically significant effects on any of the four types of terrorist incidents they examined. One possible explanation here is that in response to the hardening of those targets, terrorists shifted their attacks against embassy personnel to venues outside the walls of diplomatic compounds where countermeasures remained comparatively weak. They do report, though, that the Libyan airstrikes caused a large, but temporary spike in the number of transnational terrorist bombings, threats and hoaxes. Revenge, obviously, is a powerful motive for terrorists and counter-terrorists alike.

Enders and Sandler (2006, p. 133) conclude from this evidence that "piecemeal policies, designed to thwart only one attack mode, are shown to induce a substitution into other, similar modes, whose unintended consequences may be quite harmful."[29] Hence, "an effective counterterrorism policy is one that raises the costs of *all* attack modes or reduces the overall resource level of the terrorists (Ibid., pp. 122–124; emphasis in original).

The substitution possibilities open to terrorists also mean that if one nation enhances the effectiveness of its counterterrorism policies, terrorist groups rationally will shift their bases of operation or the locations of their primary targets to less cautious countries. Such strategic responsiveness undermines unilateral efforts to suppress terrorist activities and, at the same time, makes it more difficult to organize multilateral (that is, collective) action to counter them (Sandler 2005). If successful in diminishing or eliminating the threat posed by a particular terrorist group, the counterterrorism efforts of one nation confer an external benefit on all countries that otherwise would be vulnerable to its attacks. Because the gains from suppression are shared, but the costs are borne by the taxpayers of a single state, an incentive exists for other nations to free-ride by reducing their own investments in counterterrorism. But they increase their exposure to attack if they do so; alternatively, they can shift terrorists' attention elsewhere by strengthening their own homeland security measures. The interdependencies among national counterterrorist policies help explain why it is that, unless a country frequently is the target of transnational terrorist attacks, its own policies primarily will be defensive rather than proactive: the lion's share of the benefits of the former can be captured locally, whereas those of the latter must be shared more widely (Enders and Sandler 2006, p. 85).[30] Just as obviously, however, the defensive measures taken by one nation can impose negative externalities on others by making them more inviting targets.

Another strategy for responding to the threat of terrorism is what Lee (1988) calls the "paid-rider option." In exercising that option, a nation offers sanctuary to a foreign terrorist group in return for assurances that the group will refrain from striking targets in its safe haven. East Germany provided such refuge to the Red Army Faction (Baader-Meinhof Group) and to other perpetrators of left-wing terror during the 1960s and 1970s (Shughart 2006). Lee (1988, p. 24) cites France's harboring of both Arab and Basque terrorists as well as Cypriot and Italian accommodation of Palestinian terrorist groups as additional cases in point.[31] Failed states, such as Palestine itself, Lebanon, Afghanistan and Pakistan likewise have served as launching pads for transnational terror.

Given that the world's sovereign nations cannot even agree on the identities of terrorist groups – the members of the European Union did not consider Hamas to be a terrorist organization until very recently, for instance (Enders and Sandler 2006, p. 142) – it should not be surprising that the logic of collective action (Olson 1965) supplies terrorists with significant competitive advantages over the governments they threaten. The terrorist group typically has few members or, if not, is organized into compact, independently operating cells. Small numbers facilitate agreement on strategy and tactics and lower the costs of monitoring individual contributions to the collective effort and of controlling incentives to free-ride. Limiting group membership to people bound and, hence, easily identified by common ties of blood, ethnicity, faith or long-term friendship promotes solidarity and limits infiltration by outsiders who may be agents of the opposition or susceptible to becoming informants (Enders and

Sandler 2006, p. 88). Because they have interests that are more diffuse and less well-aligned, governments, in contrast, have fewer incentives to mount coordinated responses to terrorist threats.[32]

The asymmetric warfare characteristic of terrorist campaigns thus has two distinct aspects. One of these is found in the imbalance between the richness of the terrorist target environment and the inability of defenders to protect all potential victims of terror. The other asymmetry relates to organizing collective action: compared with the nation-states that are threatened by terrorist violence, terrorist groups enjoy a comparative advantage in capturing its benefits as well as in controlling its costs.

8.4   THE LOGIC OF SUICIDE TERRORISM

Rational individuals often place themselves in harm's way. They voluntarily choose to earn livings as firefighters or police officers; they willingly become soldiers or sailors; they endanger their own lives in order to rescue others, including strangers, from peril; and they join terrorist groups. Many of the activities engaged in by rational human beings involve trade-offs between risk and reward. A decision to drive rather than to fly to grandma's house for Thanksgiving, even though the chooser is much more likely to be injured or killed in an automobile accident than in an airplane crash, can, for example, be fully rational if the (normally) lower out-of-pocket costs of car travel more than offset the higher opportunity costs of the driver's time as well as his greater exposure to risk.

So, too, does a weighing of expected benefits and expected costs inform an individual's decision to participate – or not – in a terrorist campaign. But suicide terrorists seem to be wildly irrational – to place themselves beyond explanation by the economist's rational-choice model. It is, after all, one thing to risk capture, serious bodily harm or even death in a planned attack on a target selected by the terrorist group's leader; it is quite another purposely to die by detonating a bomb carried in one's vehicle or on one's person with the object of "influencing an audience" that, it is hoped, will then demand governmental action favorable to the group's cause. While it is true that for technical reasons the bomb may not explode, it is also true that that possibility is remote. The suicide terrorist is almost certain to die.

Suicide terrorism thus poses the gravest challenge to the rational-actor model. One explanation for it is that it works: suicide attacks have been successful in compelling "American and French forces to abandon Lebanon in 1983, Israeli forces to leave Lebanon in 1985, Israeli forces to quit the Gaza Strip and the West Bank in 1994 and 1995, [and] the Sri Lankan government to create an independent Tamil state from 1990 on"

(Pape 2005, p. 22). In recent memory, suicide terrorism in the late 1990s failed (so far) in convincing Turkey to grant autonomy to the Kurds (Ibid.). Neither has it caused Israel to accede to Palestinian territorial demands. But success or failure must have been cold comfort to the individual terrorists who died in these suicide campaigns.

As noted earlier, suicide terrorists do not fit any tidy demographic characterization: "they have been college educated and uneducated, married and single, men and women, isolated and socially integrated; they have ranged in age from fifteen to fifty-two" (Ibid., p. 17). Pape (Ibid., p. 23) concludes "that suicide terrorism is mainly a response to foreign occupation" and Wintrobe (2006) sees such behavior as being driven by a form of solidarity with an authoritarian leader so extreme that the leader's beliefs become the disciple's own and, hence, produce a willingness to die to advance the leader's goals. Solidarity, purchased in Wintrobe's model by trading individual beliefs for group beliefs, is fostered by repeated interaction between the leader and his followers, which helps explain why newcomers rarely are selected for suicide missions and also why the threat of punishment for failing to carry out an attack sometimes is necessary (Enders and Sandler 2006, p. 125).

But economic incentives offer a potentially more fruitful avenue for understanding the rationality of suicide terrorism. The available evidence suggests that terrorist groups offer tangible rewards to suicide attackers' kin. Under the regime of Saddam Hussein, for example, the family of a suicide bomber was paid US$25000, whereas the relatives of terror group members killed in more regular battleground encounters received US$10000 (Ibid., p. 126). Iannaccone and Berman (2006) argue, as does Zakaria (2003), that terrorist groups supply social welfare benefits to members and their families in return for compliance with the group's demands, including orders leading to certain death.

Such observations supply support for Azam's (2005) model of suicide terrorism as an intergenerational investment – an extreme form of saving. Suicide terrorists transfer wealth to their parents, their siblings and their children, if any. In addition to the private benefits accruing to family members, suicide attackers also may be motivated by the prospect of bequeathing a public good – increasing the likelihood of the withdrawal of foreign occupation or of the creation of an independent political state – to the next generation. Terrorists' regard for the welfare of their family members helps explain why it is Israel's policy to destroy the homes of suicide attackers.

A terrorist act carrying with it certain death may be rational in an evolutionary perspective. Genes can be thought of as self-interested actors that "want" to maximize their chances of survival (Dawkins [1976] 1989).[33] And in that context,

> the minimum requirement for a suicidal altruistic gene to be successful is that it should save more than two siblings (or children or parents), or more than four half-siblings (or uncles, aunts, nephews, nieces, grandparents grandchildren) or more than eight first cousins, etc. Such a gene, on average, tends to live on in the bodies of enough individuals saved by the altruist to compensate for the death of the altruist itself. (Ibid., p. 97)

Hence, under the right conditions,[34] the selfish gene can be an altruist.

Suicide terrorism is not yet well-understood by economists – or anyone else for that matter. It poses a serious challenge to their rational-choice model (Caplan 2006). But, rather than relying on religious zealotry, group cohesion or other psycho-social factors to explain its origins and growing importance as a terrorist strategy, it is worth keeping the following salient attributes of suicide attacks in mind. They are more lethal than other kinds of terrorist tactics and, because so, are more likely to achieve a terrorist group's goal of "influencing an audience." Suicide attacks often have succeeded in forcing concessions from targeted governments, Exhibit A being the withdrawal of a multinational peacekeeping force from Lebanon in early 1984, following Hezbollah's suicide bombing of the US Marine Corps' barracks in Beirut, which claimed 240 lives, combined with its abduction of western hostages, its murdering of American and French soldiers, and its attacks on the embassies of both nations (Laqueur 1999, p. 137; Pillar 2001, p. 20). In addition to the private benefits for family members, suicide attacks offer at least two more advantages to the terrorist groups that orchestrate them: they are more difficult to thwart than other terrorist methods and the attackers themselves are less likely to be apprehended, thereby lowering the risk that the identities of other group members or the group's planned operations will be exposed (Enders and Sandler 2006, p. 126). Dead men (and women) tell no tales.

8.5   CONCLUDING REMARKS

No matter how terrorism is defined, it is increasingly clear that many of its facets can be comprehended by modeling terrorists as rational actors, animated by the same kinds of incentives and constraints that influence the behavior of individuals in more ordinary pursuits. Terrorism, it is important to emphasize, does not arise in a vacuum. It emerges from inter-group conflict over things such as the distribution of land or other natural resources and the control of the levers of political power, including appointments to public office and access to the largesse of the welfare state: "Gain (or avoidance of loss) is the common reason for undertaking warfare" (Tullock 1974, p. 87). Terrorism differs from full-blown war in means and in scale, but not in ends.

Applying the rational-choice model to terrorism supplies insights into the emergence of terrorist groups, the targets they select and their modes of attack not amenable to explanation by other social-science methodologies. Its lessons, especially the model's prediction of policy-induced substitution, are of critical importance in formulating public policies intended to counter the terrorist threat. Actions undertaken to suppress one mode of attack may provoke terrorists to shift to other, perhaps more deadly tactics. Indeed, past efforts to clamp down on skyjackings and to protect embassies, other government installations and their personnel from kidnapping and assassination may well be responsible for the rise of suicide bombing, which is the most difficult mode of terrorist operations to defeat.

Most of the evidence adduced thus far in the rational-choice research program suggests that terrorism is more likely to arise in ethnically fragmented nation-states that lack "good institutions", implying that policies promoting transitions from authoritarianism to liberal constitutional democracy will, by providing non-violent options for expressing grievances against the incumbent regime, reduce terrorism's threat. But the holding of (superficially) competitive elections is only the window-dressing of the classical liberal state. Equally and perhaps more important, are the respect for private property rights, freedom of contract and the rule of law that allow ordinary citizens to improve their standards of living without fear of public confiscation of their private gains (Basuchoudhary and Shughart 2010). Moreover, most of the "countries" that have been the launching pads of terror are artificial constructs, whose boundaries were drawn by colonial powers in the sequels to the two world wars of the twentieth century (Shughart 2002, 2006; Ferguson 2006). Rather than trying to export democracy to the rest of the world, largely unsuccessfully (Coyne 2008), perhaps it is time to promote the economic liberties of the peoples of the globe's authoritarian or "failed" states by engaging in trade with them and encouraging the adoption of constitutional solutions to factional problems, confining central governments to issues of truly overarching national interest, endowing ethnic homelands with substantial regional autonomy, and in the event that differences cannot be reconciled, establishing a mechanism for orderly political secession.

ACKNOWLEDGEMENTS

I benefited considerably from the comments and suggestions of Daniel Arce, Michael Reksulak, Charles Rowley, Todd Sandler and Robert

Tollison. As is customary, however, I accept full responsibility for any remaining errors of omission or commission.

NOTES

1. A caveat: The literature surveyed herein focuses on nonstrategic approaches to terrorism, generally confining the reader's attention to the results of partial equilibrium models. To conserve space, studies of terrorism that adopt game-theoretic perspectives are for the most part ignored.
2. As Yassir Arafat once said, "the difference between the revolutionary and the terrorist lies in the reason for which each fights. For whoever stands by a just cause and fights for the freedom and liberation of his land from the invaders, the settlers and the colonialists, cannot possibly be called a terrorist" (quoted in Hoffman 1998, p. 26). Similarly, Conor Cruise O'Brien refuses to attach the terrorist label to anyone resisting an authoritarian regime (Crenshaw 1990, p. 13).
3. "*Collateral damage* is not in [terrorism's] lexicon" (National Commission on Terrorist Attacks upon the United States 2004, p. xvi; emphasis in original).
4. Gabel (1990) describes masterfully how such characteristics are fostered during the training exercises of elite military units. McPherson (1997, p. 170) nevertheless concludes that, along with the avoidance of personal dishonor, devotion to the same "holy cause" – an "ideological commitment to liberty, independence, and self-government" – animated the combatants on both sides of the War Between the States. Also see McPherson (1994). Some scholars of terrorism (for example, Hoffman and McCormick 2004; Gambetta 2005) have echoed this point of view in arguing that terrorists love their group or their cause – and hate their enemies – more than they love themselves.
5. Pape's (2003, 2005) widely cited work on suicide terrorism, about which more below, has provoked considerable controversy. See Ashworth et al. (2008), who contend that Pape's dataset, which includes every identifiable suicide terror attack between 1980 and 2001, "samples on the dependent variable" and, hence, suffers from sample-selection bias. Pape (2008) counters that criticism by arguing that he collected information on the universe of suicide terrorists over the period studied.
6. A pioneering contribution to the literature is Sandler, Tschirhart and Cauley (1983). Enders and Sandler (1995) summarize the rational choice approaches to terrorism, which nowadays has begun infiltrating the literature of political science (see Bueno de Mesquita 2005). Leeson's (2009) recent study of piracy during its "golden age," circa 1716–26, supplies an important and insightful application of the rational-choice model to another form of superficially aberrant human behavior.
7. An earlier anarchist wave of terror reached its highpoint in the 1890s, a period sometimes referred to as the "Golden Age of Assassination" (Rapoport [1992] 2004, p. 1053).
8. The Atlantic Charter gave new life to the "post-colonial" or "anti-colonial" terrorism that emerged in the 1920s out of decisions taken at the Paris Peace Conference leading to the Treaty of Versailles and the conclusion of World War I (Rapoport 2004, p. 52). Surveying the war's geopolitical wreckage, President Woodrow Wilson had proclaimed en route to Paris that "we now say that all these people have the right to live their own lives under governments which they themselves choose to set up" (quoted in Macmillan 2002, p. 11). In the event, unwilling to compromise and seriously weakened by illness, Wilson returned home to witness the US Senate's failure to ratify the Treaty and to see his dream of making the world safe for democracy crippled by fulfillment, under the auspices of the newly established League of Nations, of the terms of the secret Sykes-Picot Treaty of 1916, which assigned governing mandates to Britain and France in the non-European territories of the defeated Ottoman and Habsburg empires. Local resistance to the mandatory powers surfaced in short order as the subject peoples, resentful

of unbidden administration from London or Paris, began demanding the home rule Wilson had promised. Terror campaigns, including assassinations of British and French military and civilian personnel as well as attacks on their governmental installations, engulfed much of the Middle East and Central Asia in the Great War's aftermath. See Fromkin (1989).

9. Detailed portraits of these two exemplary left-wing terrorist groups can be found in Weinberg and Eubank (1987) and Aust ([1987] 2008).

10. See Rowley and Smith (2009) for an analysis of the contributions of fundamentalist Islamic beliefs to the terrorism of the late twentieth and early twenty-first centuries.

11. According to Al-Khatib Al-Tibrizi's *The Niches of Lamps*,
    The Messenger of God said: "A martyr has six privileges with God. He is forgiven his sins on the shedding of the first drop of his blood; he is shown his place in paradise; he is redeemed from the torments of the grave; he is made secure from the fear of hell and a crown of glory is placed on his head of which one ruby is worth more than the world and all that is in it; he will marry seventy-two of the huris with black eyes; and his intercession will be accepted for seventy of his kinsmen. (Quoted in Rapoport 1990, pp. 117–118)

12. Anecdotally, Collier and Hoeffler (2004) point out that, during the Russian civil war following the revolution orchestrated by V.I. Lenin, the desertion rates in the two contending armies (the Reds and the Whites) were about ten times higher during summertime than wintertime because the income foregone by the peasant rebels was much larger when fields needed to be plowed and harvests gathered.

13. Frey and Luechinger (2003, p. 247) offer "three specific [counterterrorism] strategies: visits to other countries, principal witness programmes, and formal contact, discussion processes and access to normal political participation." The underlying analysis is elaborated in Frey (2004). Anderton and Carter (2005) present a more rigorous analysis of the tradeoffs that emphasizes the importance of cross-price elasticities, expenditure shares and income elasticities in evaluating the effectiveness of "benevolence" versus deterrence as counterterrorism strategies.

14. Consistent with public choice reasoning, Coats, Karahan and Tollison (2006) report evidence suggesting that, in the wake of the shocking events of 9/11, grants to the US states by the newly created Department of Homeland Security were influenced to a greater extent by presidential electoral politics than by independent measures of states' vulnerability to terrorism.

15. Paraphrasing a letter published by the Irish Republican Army after learning that its bombing of Brighton's Grand Hotel had failed to kill Prime Minister Margaret Thatcher, Enders and Sandler (2006, p. 143) write that, "governments have to be fortunate on a daily basis, while terrorists only have to be lucky occasionally."

16. Transnational terrorism refers to incidents that originate in one country and target another; "its ramifications transcend national boundaries" (Mickolus, Sandler and Murdock 2003, p. 2). Attacks by Algerian terrorists on Metropolitan France supply one graphic example (Horne [1977] 2006). September 11, 2001, also exemplifies, as do the Madrid train bombings on 11 March 2004, and the July 2005 terrorist attack on London's Underground. The release of sarin nerve gas into a Tokyo subway by Aum Shinrikyo in March 2005, killing 12 and injuring thousands more, and Timothy McVeigh's bombing of the Alfred P. Murrah Federal Building in Oklahoma City on 13 April 1995, causing 168 fatalities, are examples of domestic terrorism, which, by definition, starts and ends in the same nation. In terms of raw numbers, domestic terrorism outpaces transnational terrorism worldwide by a factor of nine (Enders and Sandler 2006, p. 22).

17. During the 1990s, 70 percent of the terrorism-related injuries and 19 percent of the fatalities were caused by less than 0.01 percent of the terrorist attacks (Johnson 2001, p. 905).

18. Li (2005) also finds that, owing to the opportunities they afford for minority parties to secure seats in the national legislature, parliamentary (proportional representation)

systems of government experience significantly less terrorism than alternative, mainly presidential democracies. Regime stability likewise reduces a nation's vulnerability to terrorist attacks at home.

19. Wilkinson (1986, p. 39) argues that there is little moral justification for violence as a means of expressing political demands in a liberal democracy, where the civil rights of minorities are protected and the personal safety of members of minority groups is not in question. But based on evidence from Italy – hardly a stable democracy – Weinberg and Eubank (1987) report evidence suggesting that "rebel terror" occurs most frequently in democratic nation-states, independent of whether the state actually is democratic, is transitioning toward democracy, or has suddenly arrested a pro-democracy movement.

20. Israel, for somewhat different reasons, also belongs on the list. Notable net exporters of terrorism are Ireland, Iran and Cuba (Blomberg and Hess 2008b, p. 128).

21. According to Enders and Sandler, 40 percent of the transnational terrorist attacks between 1969 and 2005 targeted US interests.

22. Grossman (1991) supplies the underlying theoretical model. Also see Blomberg, Hess and Weerapanna (2004b). Llussá and Tavares (2008) provide a detailed review of the relevant empirical literature.

23. But see Sambanis (2008, p. 175), who contends that, "while civil wars can easily generate conditions that favor terrorism", the two are quite distinct and, hence, the conditions that produce the first will not necessarily foster the second.

24. "Fractionalization" typically is measured on the basis of a Herfindahl-Hirschman index, constructed as the sum of squares of the population percentages of a country's ethnic, linguistic or religious groups. A nation is more heterogeneous on such a calculation the larger is the number of different groups it contains and, hence, the less likely it is that any two people belong to the same group. The alternative concept of "ethnic polarization" stands on a theoretically stronger footing (Esteban and Ray 1994; Montalvo and Reynal-Querol 2005). An ethnic polarization index is constructed by summing the (absolute values) of the distances with respect to a set of distinguishing attributes between groups of relatively uniform size, internally homogeneous with respect to the attributes, but differing significantly on the same attributes from other groups. The index takes a maximum at 0.5. Ethnic polarization thus is greatest when a society is divided into two groups of equal size. So, too, is ethnic conflict (Esteban and Ray 1999), a result consistent with Horowitz's ([1985] 2000) claim that disputes are more likely when an ethnic majority faces a *large* ethnic minority. Thus one expects, and finds, that ethnic polarization is a much better predictor of conflict than ethnic fractionalization (Montalvo and Reynal-Querol 2005).

25. The growth-reducing impacts of ethnic fractionalization (Easterly and Levine 1997; Easterly 2000) and of ethnic polarization (Keefer and Knack 2002) are fairly well-established. Cashdan (2001) is an exception.

26. Bombings account "for about half of all terrorist incidents" (Sandler and Enders 2004) largely because they are cheap: the bomb exploded underneath the World Trade Center in 1993 "cost only US$400 but caused over US$500 million in damages" (Enders and Sandler 2006, p. 149).

27. The "game" may not have lasted very long during the 1960s and 1970s. Rapoport ([1992] 2004, p. 1064) reports that 90 percent of "Third Wave" (that is, "New Left") terrorist groups did not survive more than one year and that half of the surviving groups had been disbanded within a decade of their birth.

28. Enders, Sandler and Cauley (1990a) likewise report evidence that the introduction of metal detectors at airports prompted terrorists to engage in more kidnapping and barricade-and-hostage-taking missions. Also see Enders and Sandler (2004).

29. An additional "unintended" consequence of metal detectors is that the types of attack modes into which terrorists subsequently shifted were on the average more deadly than those employed beforehand (Enders and Sandler 2000), a tendency reinforced by the rise of Islamist terrorism (Enders and Sandler 2005).

30.   In contrast, nation-states pursue domestic terrorist groups aggressively when their attacks primarily target interests at home (Enders and Sandler 2006, p. 85).

31.   John le Carré (2008, pp. 56–57) supplies a fictional account of the paid-rider option circa 9/11:

> Okay, [Hamburg] harbored a few Islamist terrorists, and a trio of them had gone off and blown up the Twin Towers and the Pentagon. So what? It was what they'd come here to do, and they'd done it. Problem solved. They'd struck at the heart of the Great Satan, and they'd killed themselves in the process. We were their *launchpad* for Christ's sake, not their target! Why should *we* worry? So we lit candles for the poor Americans. And we *prayed* for the poor Americans. And we showed them a lot of *free solidarity*. . . And when the Iraq War came along, and we good Germans stayed aloof from it, that made us even *more* immune. Madrid happened. Okay. London happened. Okay. But no Berlin, no Munich, no Hamburg. We were too . . . immune for *any* of it. (emphasis in original)

The phrase "a few Islamist" was deleted from the first line of this passage in the audio-book version of *A Most Wanted Man*; one word has been omitted from the final sentence here in order to avoid offending sensitive readers.

32.   The divergent interests of individual governments explain why Enders, Sandler and Cauley (1990b) were unable to find any significant differences in transnational terrorist activity following the adoption of numerous regional and international agreements designed to counter various terrorist threats.

33.   But see Demsetz (2008), who attempts to restore individuals as the principal actors by allowing genes to appoint the person within whose body they reside as a central planner or agent, imperfect though the agent may be, for taking decisions on their behalf. However, Demsetz does not inquire into the mechanism (voting rule) by which genes collectively chose the actions they want their agent to take.

34.   The right conditions follow from "Hamilton's Rule . . ., [which] states that, other things equal, evolutionary selection will lead a Donor organism D to aid a recipient organism R if the *cost–benefit ratio* c_D/b_R is less than their *relatedness* r_{DR}", where "cost c_D and benefit b_R are measured in increments to the 'fitness' (i.e., reproductive survival) of Donor and Recipient, respectively" (Hirshleifer 2001, p. 21; emphasis in original). In the original version of this contribution to the literature (Hirshleifer 1998), the comma following "i.e." improperly is missing.

REFERENCES

Abadie, A. and J. Gardeazabal (2003), "The economic cost of conflict: a case study of the Basque country", *American Economic Review*, **93**, 113–32.

Anderton, C.H. and J.R. Carter (2005), "On rational choice theory and the study of terrorism", *Defence and Peace Economics,* **16** (4), 275–82.

Ashworth, S., J.D. Clinton, A. Meirowitz and K.W. Ramsay (2008), "Design, inference, and the strategic logic of suicide terrorism", *American Political Science Review*, **102** (2), 269–73.

Aust, S. ([1987] 2008), *Baader-Meinhof: The Inside Story of the R.A.F.*, A. Bell (trans.), Oxford, UK: Oxford University Press.

Azam, J.P. (2005), "Suicide bombing as intergenerational investment", *Public Choice*, **122**, 177–98.

Basuchoudhary, A. and W.F. Shughart II (2010), "On ethnic conflict and the origins of transnational terrorism", *Defence and Peace Economics*, **21**(1), 65–87.

Berman, E.B. and D. Laitin (2006), "Hard targets: Evidence on the tactical use of suicide attacks", available online http://dss.ucsd.edu/~elib/RatMartyrs.pdf; accessed 16 June 2009.

Blomberg, S.B.and G.D. Hess (2002), "The temporal links between conflict and economic activity", *Journal of Conflict Resolution*, **46** (1), 74–90.

Blomberg, S.B. and G.D. Hess (2008a), "From (no) butter to guns? Understanding the economic role in transnational terrorism", in P. Keefer and N. Loayza (eds), *Terrorism, Economic Development, and Political Openness*, Cambridge, UK: Cambridge University Press, pp. 83–115.

Blomberg, S.B. and G.D. Hess (2008b), "The Lexus and the olive branch: globalization, democratization, and terrorism", in P. Keefer and N. Loayza (eds), *Terrorism, Economic Development, and Political Openness*, Cambridge, UK: Cambridge University Press, pp. 116–47.

Blomberg, S.B., G.D. Hess and A. Orphanides (2004), "The macroeconomic consequences of terrorism", *Journal of Monetary Economics*, **51**, 1007–32.

Blomberg, S.B., G.D. Hess and S. Thacker (2006), "On the conflict-poverty nexus", *Economics and Politics*, **18** (3), 237–67.

Blomberg, S.B., G.D. Hess and A. Weerapana (2004a), "Economic conditions and terrorism", *European Journal of Political Economy*, **20**, 463–78.

Blomberg, S.B., G.D. Hess and A. Weerapana (2004b), "An economic model of terrorism", *Conflict Management and Peace Science*, **21**, 17–28.

Bueno de Mesquita, E. (2005), "Conciliation, commitment and counterterrorism: a formal model", *International Organization*, **59** (1), 145–76.

Caplan, B. (2006), "Terrorism: the relevance of the rational choice model", *Public Choice*, **128** (1–2), 91–107.

le Carré, J. (pseud.) (2008), *A Most Wanted Man*, New York, NY: Scribner.

Cashdan, E. (2001), "Ethnocentrism and xenophobia: a cross-cultural study", *Current Anthropology*, **42** (5), 760–66.

Clausewitz, C. von ([1832] 1976), *On War*, M. Howard and P. Paret (trans. and eds), Princeton, NJ: Princeton University Press.

Coats, R.M., G. Karahan and R.D. Tollison (2006), "Terrorism and pork-barrel spending", *Public Choice*, **128** (1–2), 275–87.

Coll, S. (2004), *Ghost Wars: The Secret History of the CIA, Afghanistan, and bin Laden, from the Soviet Invasion to September 11, 2001*, New York, NY: Penguin.

Collier, P. and A. Hoeffler (2004), "Greed and grievance in civil war", *Oxford Economic Papers*, **56**, 563–95.

Cooper, H.H.A. (2001), "Terrorism: the problem of definition revisited", *American Behavioral Scientist*, **44** (6), 881–93.

Coyne, C.J. (2008), *After War: The Political Economy of Exporting Democracy*, Stanford, CA: Stanford University Press.

Crain, N.V. and W.M. Crain (2006), "Terrorized economies", *Public Choice*, **128** (1–2), 317–49.

Crenshaw, M. (1990), "The logic of terrorism: terrorist behavior as a product of strategic choice", in W. Reich (ed.), *Origins of Terrorism: Psychologies, Ideologies, Theologies, States of Mind*, Washington DC: Woodrow Wilson Center and Baltimore and London: Johns Hopkins University Press, pp. 7–24.

Dawkins, R. ([1976] 1989), *The Selfish Gene*, Oxford and New York: Oxford University Press.

Demsetz, H. (2008), *From Economic Man to Economic System*, Cambridge and New York: Cambridge University Press.

Dostoevsky, F. ([1872] 1994), *Demons: A Novel in Three Parts*, R. Pevear and L. Volokhonsky (trans.), New York, NY: Knopf.

Downs, A. (1957), *An Economic Theory of Democracy*, New York, NY: Harper & Row.

Drakos, K. (2004), "Terrorism-induced structural shifts in financial risk: airline stocks in the aftermath of the September 11th terrorist attacks", *European Journal of Political Economy*, **20**, 435–46.

Drakos, K. and A.M. Kutan (2003), "Regional effects of terrorism on tourism in three Mediterranean countries", *Journal of Conflict Resolution*, **47**, 621–41.

Easterly, W. (2000), "Can institutions resolve conflict?", *Economic Development and Cultural Change*, **49** (4), 687–706.

Easterly, W. and R. Levine (1997), "Africa's growth tragedy: policies and ethnic divisions", *Quarterly Journal of Economics*, **112** (4), 1203–50.

Eckstein, Z. and D. Tsiddon (2004), "Macroeconomic consequences of terror: theory and the case of Israel", *Journal of Monetary Economics*, **51**, 971–1002.
Enders, W. and T. Sandler (1991), "Causality between transnational terrorism and tourism: the case of Spain", *Terrorism*, **14**, 49–58.
Enders, W. and T. Sandler (1993), "The effectiveness of antiterrorism policies: a vector-autoregression approach", *American Political Science Review*, **87** (4), 829–44.
Enders, W. and T. Sandler (1995), "Terrorism: theory and applications", in K. Hartley and T. Sandler (eds), *Handbook of Defence Economics*, Vol. I, Amsterdam: North-Holland, pp. 213–49.
Enders, W. and T. Sandler (1996), "Terrorism and foreign direct investment in Spain and Greece", *Kyklos*, **49**, 331–52.
Enders, W. and T. Sandler (2000), "Is transnational terrorism becoming more threatening? A time-series investigation", *Journal of Conflict Resolution*, **44** (3), 307–32.
Enders, W. and T. Sandler (2004), "What do we know about the substitution effect in transnational terrorism?", in A. Silke and G. Ilardi (eds), *Researching Terrorism: Trends, Achievements, Failures*, Ilford, UK: Frank Cass, pp. 119–37.
Enders, W. and T. Sandler (2005), "After 9/11: is it all different now?", *Journal of Conflict Resolution*, **49** (2), 259–77.
Enders, W. and T. Sandler (2006), *The Political Economy of Terrorism*, Cambridge, UK: Cambridge University Press.
Enders, W., T. Sandler and J. Cauley (1990a), "Assessing the impact of terrorist-thwarting policies: an intervention time series approach", *Defence Economics*, **2** (1), 1–8.
Enders, W., T. Sandler and J. Cauley (1990b), "UN conventions, technology, and retaliation in the fight against terrorism: an econometric evaluation", *Terrorism and Political Violence*, **2** (1), 83–105.
Enders, W., T. Sandler and G. F. Parise (1992), "An econometric analysis of the impact of terrorism on tourism", *Kyklos*, **45**, 531–54.
Esteban, J.-M. and D. Ray (1994), "On the measurement of polarization", *Econometrica*, **62**, 819–51.
Esteban, J.-M. and D. Ray (1999), "Conflict and distribution", *Journal of Economic Theory*, **87** (2), 379–415.
Eubank, W.L. and L.B. Weinberg (1994), "Does democracy encourage terrorism?", *Terrorism and Political Violence*, **6** (4), 417–35.
Eubank, W.L. and L.B. Weinberg (2001), "Terrorism and democracy: perpetrators and victims", *Terrorism and Political Violence*, **13** (1), 155–64.
Faria, J.R. and D.G. Arce M. (2005), "Terror support and recruitment", *Defence and Peace Economics*, **16** (4), 263–73.
Ferguson, N. (2006), *The War of the World: Twentieth-Century Conflict and the Descent of the West*, New York, NY: Penguin.
Fielding, D. (2003), "Counting the cost of the Intifada: consumption, saving and political instability in Israel", *Public Choice*, **116**, 297–312.
Fleischer, A. and S. Buccola (2002), "War, terror, and the tourism market in Israel", *Applied Economics*, **34**, 1335–43.
Frey, B. S. (2004), *Dealing with Terrorism: Stick or Carrot?* Cheltenham, UK and Northampton, MA: Edward Elgar.
Frey, B.S. and S. Luechinger (2003), "How to fight terrorism: alternatives to deterrence", *Defence and Peace Economics* , **14** (4), 237–49.
Frey, B.S., S. Luechinger and A. Stutzer (2009), "The life satisfaction approach to valuing public goods: the case of terrorism", *Public Choice*, **138**, 317–45.
Fromkin, D. (1989), *A Peace to End All Peace: The Fall of the Ottoman Empire and the Creation of the Modern Middle East*, New York, NY: Henry Holt.
Gabel, K. (1990), *The Making of a Paratrooper: Airborne Training and Combat in World War II*, ed. with and introduction and epilogue by W.C. Mitchell, Lawrence, KS: University Press of Kansas.

Gambetta, D. (ed.) (2005), *Making Sense of Suicide Missions*, Oxford and New York: Oxford University Press.

Green, D.P., J. Glaser and A. Rich (1998), "From lynching to gay bashing: the elusive connection between economic conditions and hate crimes", *Journal of Personality and Social Psychology*, **75** (1), 82–92.

Grossman, H.I. (1991), "A general equilibrium model of insurrection", *American Economic Review*, **81** (4), 912–21.

Hardin, R. (1995), *One for All: The Logic of Group Conflict*, Princeton, NJ: Princeton University Press.

Heinlein, R. A. ([1966] 1994), *The Moon is a Harsh Mistress*, New York, NY: Tom Doherty.

Hirshleifer, J. (1983), "From the weakest-link to best shot: the voluntary provision of public goods", *Public Choice*, **41** (3), 371–86.

Hirshleifer, J. (1991), "The paradox of power", *Economics and Politics*, **3** (3), 177–200.

Hirshleifer, J. (1998), "The bioeconomic causes of war", *Managerial and Decision Economics*, **19** (7–8), 457–66.

Hirshleifer, J. (2001), *The Dark Side of the Force: Economic Foundations of Conflict Theory*, Cambridge and New York, NY: Cambridge University Press.

Hoffman, B. (1998), *Inside Terrorism*, New York, NY: Columbia University Press.

Hoffman, B. and G. McCormick (2004), "Terrorism, signaling, and suicide attack", *Studies in Conflict and Terrorism*, **27**, 243–81.

Horne, A. ([1977] 2006), *A Savage War of Peace: Algeria, 1954–1962*, New York, NY: New York Review Books.

Horowitz, D.L. ([1985] 2000), *Ethnic Groups in Conflict*, Berkeley, CA: University of California Press.

Iannaccone, L.B. and E.B. Berman (2006), "Religious extremism: the good, the bad, and the deadly", *Public Choice*, **128** (1–2), 109–29.

Ito, H. and D. Lee (2004), "Assessing the impact of the September 11 terrorist attacks on US airline demand", *Journal of Economics and Business*, **57**, 75–95.

Johnson, L.C. (2001), "The future of terrorism", *American Behavioral Scientist*, **44** (6), 894–913.

Kahneman, D. and A. Tversky (1979), "Prospect theory: an analysis of decision under risk", *Econometrica*, **47**, 263–91.

Keefer, P. and S. Knack (2002), "Polarization, politics and property rights: links between inequality and growth", *Public Choice*, **111**, 127–54.

Keefer, P. and N. Loayza (eds) (2008), *Terrorism, Economic Development, and Political Openness*, Cambridge, UK: Cambridge University Press.

Kellen, K. (1990), "Ideology and rebellion: terrorism in West Germany", in W. Reich (ed.), *Origins of Terrorism: Psychologies, Ideologies, Theologies, States of Mind*, Washington DC: Woodrow Wilson Center and Baltimore and London: Johns Hopkins University Press, pp. 43–58.

Krueger, A.B. and D.D. Laitin (2008), "*Kto kogo*? A cross-country study of the origins and targets of terrorism", in P. Keefer and N. Loayza (eds), *Terrorism, Economic Development, and Political Openness*, Cambridge, UK: Cambridge University Press, pp. 148–73.

Krueger, A.B. and J. Malecková (2003), "Education, poverty and terrorism: is there a causal connection?", *Journal of Economic Perspectives*, **17** (4), 119–44.

Kurrild-Klitgaard, P., M.K. Justesen and R. Klemmensen (2006), "The political economy of freedom, democracy and terrorism", *Public Choice*, **128** (1–2), 289–315.

Landes, W.M. (1978), "An economic study of US aircraft hijackings, 1961–1976", *Journal of Law and Economics*, **21** (1), 1–31.

Laqueur, W. (1999), *The New Terrorism: Fanaticism and the Arms of Mass Destruction*, Oxford and New York: Oxford University Press.

Lee, D.R. (1988), "Free riding and paid riding in the fight against terrorism", *American Economic Review Papers and Proceedings*, **78** (2), 22–6.

Leeson, P.T. (2009), *The Invisible Hook: The Hidden Economics of Pirates*, Princeton and Oxford: Princeton University Press.

Levitt, S.D. and S.J. Dubner (2005), *Freakonomics: A Rogue Economist Explores the Hidden Side of Everything*, New York, NY: William Morris/HarperCollins.

Li, Q. (2005), "Does democracy promote transnational terrorist incidents?", *Journal of Conflict Resolution*, **49**, 278–97.

Llussá, F. and J. Tavares (2008), "Economics and terrorism: what we know, what we should know, and the data we need", in P. Keefer and N. Loayza (eds), *Terrorism, Economic Development, and Political Openness*, Cambridge, UK: Cambridge University Press, pp. 253–96.

Macmillan, M. (2002), *Paris 1919: Six Months that Changed the World*. New York, NY: Da Capo Press.

McPherson, J.M. (1994), *What They Fought For, 1861–1865*. New York, NY: Anchor Books.

McPherson, J.M. (1997), *For Cause and Comrades: Why Men Fought in the Civil War*, New York and Oxford: Oxford University Press.

Mickolus, E.F., T. Sandler and J.M. Murdock (2003), *International Terrorism: Attributes of Terrorist Events, 1968–2003*, Dunn Loring, VA: Vinyard Software.

Montalvo, J.G. and M. Reynal-Querol (2005), "Ethnic polarization, potential conflict, and civil wars", *American Economic Review*, **95** (3), 796–816.

National Commission on Terrorist Attacks upon the United States (2004), *The 9/11 Commission Report: Final Report of the National Commission on Terrorist Attacks upon the United States*, New York and London: W.W. Norton.

Nitsch, V. and D. Schumacher (2004), "Terrorism and international trade: an empirical investigation", *European Journal of Political Economy*, **20**, 423–33.

Office of the Coordinator of Counterterrorism (1997), *Patterns of Global Terrorism, 1986*, US Department of State Publication 10433, Washington, DC: US Department of State.

Olson, M. (1965), *The Logic of Collective Action: Public Goods and the Theory of Groups*, Cambridge, MA: Harvard University Press.

Pape, R.A. (2003), "The strategic logic of suicide terrorism", *American Political Science Review*, **97**, 343–61.

Pape, R.A. (2005), *Dying to Win: The Strategic Logic of Suicide Terrorism*, New York, NY: Random House.

Pape, R.A. (2008), "Methods and findings in the study of suicide terrorism", *American Political Science Review*, **102** (2), 275–77.

Pillar, P.R. (2001), *Terrorism and US Foreign Policy*, Washington DC: Brookings Institution.

Rapoport, D.C. (1990), "Sacred terror: a contemporary example from Islam", in W. Reich (ed.), *Origins of Terrorism: Psychologies, Ideologies, Theologies, States of Mind*, Washington DC: Woodrow Wilson Center and Baltimore and London: Johns Hopkins University Press, pp. 103–30.

Rapoport, D.C. ([1992] 2004), "Terrorism", in M. Hawkesworth and M. Kogan (eds), *Encyclopedia of Government and Politics*, Vol. 2, 2nd edn, London and New York: Routledge, pp. 1049–77.

Rapoport, D.C. (2004), "The four waves of modern terrorism", in A.K. Cronin and J.M. Ludes (eds), *Attacking Terrorism: Elements of a Grand Strategy*, Washington DC: Georgetown University Press, pp. 46–83.

Rathbone, A. and C.K. Rowley (2004), "Terrorism", in C.K. Rowley and F. Schneider (eds), *The Encyclopedia of Public Choice*, Vol. II, Dordrecht, Boston and London: Kluwer Academic Publishers, pp. 558–63.

Reich, W. (ed.) (1990), *Origins of Terrorism: Psychologies, Ideologies, Theologies, States of Mind*, Washington DC: Woodrow Wilson Center and Baltimore and London: Johns Hopkins University Press.

Rowley, C.K. and N. Smith (2009), "Islam's democracy paradox: Muslims claim to like democracy, so why do they have so little?", *Public Choice*, **139** (3–4), 273–99.

Sambanis, H. (2008), "Terrorism and civil war", in P. Keefer and N. Loayza (eds), *Terrorism, Economic Development, and Political Openness*, Cambridge, UK: Cambridge University Press, pp. 174–206.

Sandler, T. (2005), "Collective versus unilateral responses to terrorism", *Public Choice*, **124** (1–2), 75–93.

Sandler, T. and W. Enders (2004), "An economic perspective on transnational terrorism", *European Journal of Political Economy*, **20** (2), 301–16.

Sandler, T. and W. Enders (2008), "Economic consequences of terrorism in developed and developing countries", in P. Keefer and N. Loayza (eds), *Terrorism, Economic Development, and Political Openness*, Cambridge, UK: Cambridge University Press, pp. 17–47.

Sandler, T., J.T. Tschirhart and J. Cauley (1983), "A theoretical analysis of transnational terrorism", *American Political Science Review*, **77** (1), 37–54.

Shughart, W.F. II (2002), "September 11, 2001", *Public Choice*, **111** (1–2), 1–8.

Shughart, W.F. II (2006), "An analytical history of terrorism, 1945–2000", *Public Choice*, **128** (1–2), 7–39.

Tavares, J. (2004), "The open society assesses its enemies: shocks, disasters and terrorist attacks", *Journal of Monetary Economics*, **51**, 1039–70.

Tullock, G. (1974), *The Social Dilemma: The Economics of War and Revolution*, Blacksburg, VA: University Publications.

Turk, A.T. (2004), "Sociology of terrorism", *Annual Review of Sociology*, **30**, 271–86.

Vidal, G. ([1964] 1986), *Julian*, New York, NY: Ballentine Books.

Weinberg, L.B. and W. Eubank (1987), *The Rise and Fall of Italian Terrorism*, Boulder, CO: Westview Press.

Wilkinson, P. (1986), *Terrorism and the Liberal State*, 2nd edn, New York, NY: New York University Press.

Wintrobe, R. (2006), "Extremism, suicide terror, and authoritarianism", *Public Choice*, **128** (1–2), 169–95.

Zakaria, F. (2003), *The Future of Freedom: Illiberal Democracies at Home and Abroad*, New York and London: W.W. Norton.

9 The political economy of conscription
Panu Poutvaara and Andreas Wagener

9.1 INTRODUCTION

Forced labor is no longer exacted by today's non-totalitarian states –
except in the forms of compulsory military service and its unarmed cor-
ollaries such as civil, alternative or social service. Conscription (military
draft) is the legal obligation for persons from a certain demographic
subgroup to perform military service; in practice this obligation is usually
imposed on young men.[1] Non-compliance with the draft is typically considered a felony, punishable by imprisonment or, in case of war, even
death. After their active duty, conscripts often remain in military reserve
for some additional period.

Historically, conscription is quite novel (see Keegan 1993, for a thorough account). While rulers at all times pressed their subjects into military service whenever they wished so,[2] such draft schemes (*militias*) were
occasional, selective and non-systematic. In fourteenth-century Italy,
hired professionals started to replace citizen militias; mercenaries and
commercialized warfare dominated the European battlefields until the late
eighteenth century. The birth of general military conscription is usually
dated back to 1793 when the French National Convention called a *levée en
masse*. However, in 1800 the generality of the French conscription scheme
was abandoned when citizens were allowed to buy themselves out of
military service. Basically, it was Prussia under its king Friedrich Wilhelm
III that in 1814 first installed a universal scheme of conscription without
exceptions (apart for those found unable to deliver military service). The
military successes of the Prussian and Napoleonic conscripted armies
inspired many countries to adopt universal conscription, and the industrialized, high-intensity mass wars of the late nineteenth and twentieth
centuries were only feasible because compulsory military service made
available millions of young men as soldiers. During and after World War
II, military conscription was the dominant recruitment method for armies
around the world, in democratic as well as in authoritarian regimes. With
the end of the Cold War, draft systems are in retreat in democratic countries (Haltiner 2003). Several countries abolished the military draft in
favor of a professional army while others are debating such a step. Six out
of the 28 NATO members[3] still run their armies with conscripts, and the

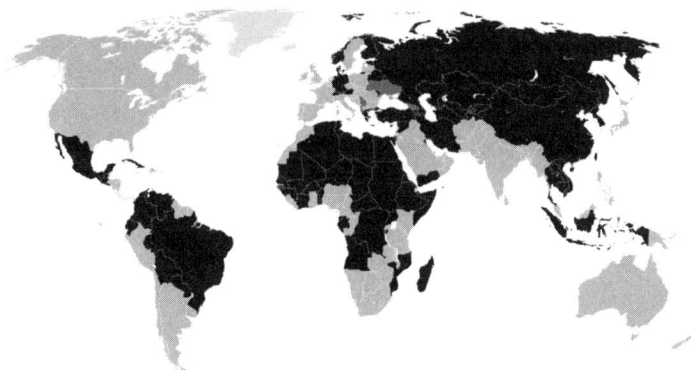

Notes:
Light: No conscription
Dark: Conscription
Medium: Plan to abolish conscription within 3 years
Exceptions: Costa Rica, Greenland, Haiti, Iceland, Panama (no own armed forces), Iraq,
             Western Sahara (no official information)

Source: Wikipedia (2010)

Figure 9.1   Conscription throughout the world, 2010

draft heavily intrudes into the lives of young men in many Asian countries (including China), in most successor states of the Soviet Union, as well as throughout Latin America, Africa and the Middle East (see Figure 9.1).

While the duration of military service is currently one year or less in most European countries, it is typically between 18 and 24 months elsewhere; some countries have even longer periods of service.[4]

Historically, the rise of military conscription coincided with the emergence of the nation state and the idea of citizen rights. Military service was considered as one of the duties by which citizens paid for their increased rights of political participation (Levi 1998). Likewise, the emergence of professional soldiers and the commercialization of warfare in Renaissance Italy were associated with the expansion of the economic powers of merchants and bankers; by hiring foreign mercenaries locals bought themselves out of direct involvement in warfare and could fully specialize in trade and banking (McNeill 1982). These observations indicate a strong linkage between various military recruitment formats and the political economy, which we survey in this chapter. Our main goal is to shed light on the question of why countries continue to embrace military conscription.

Our analysis proceeds as follows. We argue that the military draft is a tax. While appearing inefficient relative to an all-volunteer army, which also requires the government's power to tax, the draft comes with a specific incidence within and across age cohorts: it primarily burdens young males (Section 9.2). From the perspective of political economy (in its version of public choice), this implies that the introduction and the maintenance of military draft would always find support by a majority of the population, at least in the absence of sufficiently strong intergenerational altruism (Section 9.3.1). However, the empirical evidence for this conclusion appears to be mixed (Section 9.3.2). While parts of the decline of conscription may be attributed to a change in military threats, it also seems that political preferences against conscription involve concerns about its unfairness and questionable record on social accounts (Section 9.4). Still, societal groups (for example, trade unions, the military, bureaucracy or the welfare industry) that benefit from military conscription may form special interest groups that actively lobby against its abolition (Section 9.5). Sections 9.6 and 9.7 discuss the military record of conscription and the political economy of mercenaries. Section 9.8 concludes.

It should be noted that most democratic countries with conscription grant the right to conscientious objectors against military service to comply with their duty to serve in the form of an alternative service, sometimes called civil or social service. If available, unarmed alternative service is typically longer than military service. All economic arguments against, and most aspects of political economy associated with military conscription apply, *mutatis mutandis*, also to alternative service.

9.2   THE DRAFT AS A TAX: EFFICIENCY AND INCIDENCE

Currently, the most common alternative to military conscription for recruiting personnel into armies (as well as into reserves) are volunteers, hired for a certain period on the labor market and financed out of general tax revenues.[5] Pure conscript armies do not exist; some career officers are always needed to train conscripts and to command the troops. Yet we speak of a conscript army when at least part of the army and reserves consist of citizens who are ordered to serve. Moreover, we use the terms "volunteer force" and "professional army" interchangeably and apply them both to standing armies and to reserves. Figure 9.2 visualizes various military recruitment formats.

The relative merits of military draft and professional armies have been debated for centuries by military strategists, historians, political scientists and economists (for recent surveys see Sandler and Hartley

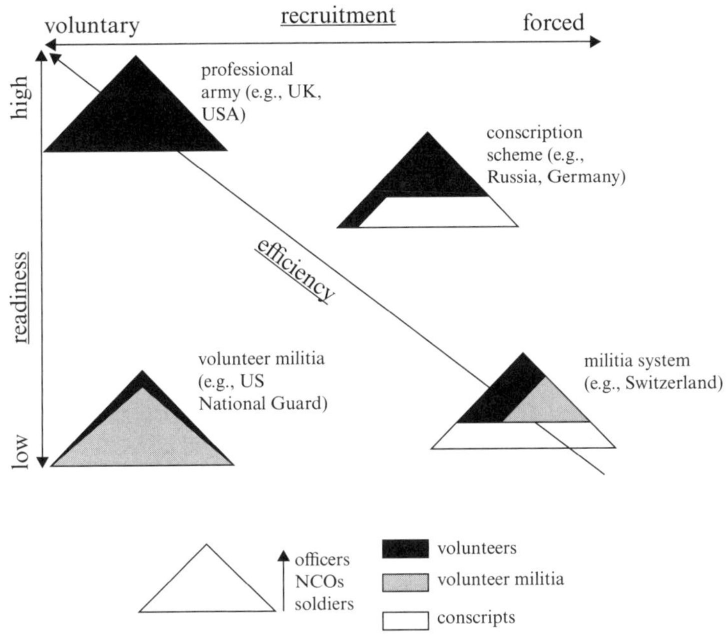
voluntary
recruitment
forced
high
readiness
low
professional army (e.g., UK, USA)
conscription scheme (e.g., Russia, Germany)
efficiency
volunteer militia (e.g., US National Guard)
militia system (e.g., Switzerland)
officers
NCOs
soldiers
volunteers
volunteer militia
conscripts

Source: Adapted from Haltiner (1998).

Figure 9.2 Military recruitment formats

1995, Chapter 6; Warner and Asch 2001; or Poutvaara and Wagener 2007a). Economically, a military draft is a tax in the form of coerced and typically underpaid labor services. Its alternative, the professional army, compensates soldiers with the revenues from fiscal (that is, money) taxes. Conscript forces and professional armies, thus, represent two different tax modes to "finance" military personnel: in-kind or fiscal.

9.2.1 Specialization and Production Efficiency

Economists generally hold that a military draft is the inferior way to raise an army. Adam Smith made a clear case against conscription and found an "irresistible superiority which a well-regulated standing [that is, all-volunteer] army has over a militia [that is, temporary conscription]" (Smith [1776] 1976, p. 701). Smith's arguments focus on comparative advantage and the benefits from specialization.

The principle of comparative advantage demands that jobs be assigned to individuals who are relatively more productive than others in doing them. By forcing everybody into a military occupation, irrespective of their relative productivities, military conscription violates that principle and involves an inefficient match between people and jobs. Benefits from specialization arise when individuals, after being employed for a single set of tasks over a longer period, become more productive than those with less experience. Effective warfare or defense operations require a considerable degree of training and mastery in handling complex weapon systems. By lack of specialization, drafted short-term soldiers are inferior to long(er)-term professionals. Societies that rely on military conscription thus forego productivity gains. In total, armies tend to be economically more efficient the more they are based on volunteerism and the more permanent they are. In Figure 9.2, this is indicated by the diagonal arrow.

9.2.2 Opportunity Costs and Excess Burden

In terms of the government budget, operating a draft system is generally cheaper than a professional army: conscripts are only paid some pocket money rather than the market value of their labor service, and fringe benefits such as health plans, family support, old-age provisions and so forth are granted to draftees on a much smaller scale than for professional soldiers (if at all).[6] However, accounting costs do not reflect the real opportunity costs of a conscript army; the use of compulsion in itself suggests that real costs are higher. The social cost of drafting someone to be a soldier is not what the government chooses to pay him but the minimum amount for which he would be willing to join the army voluntarily. The discrepancy between budgetary and opportunity costs is substantial. For example, Kerstens and Meyermans (1993) estimate that the social cost of the (now abolished) Belgian draft system amounted to twice its budgetary cost.

A military draft shares with all other taxes the feature that it is not neutral but rather induces substantial avoidance activities and, thus, causes economic distortions and deadweight losses. For example, conscription goes along with various ways of "dodging," inefficient employment, preemptive emigration, pretend schooling, hasty marriages and other reactions. Young Russians avoid their country's statutory one-year draft in large numbers, using means such as fake medical certificates, university studies, bribery or simply not showing up at drafting stations (Lokshin and Yemtsov 2008). Maurin and Xenogiani (2007) find that higher education enrollment of males in France has decreased since conscription was (de facto) abolished in 1997 for men born in 1979 or later. The study points to the fact that some men may have attended higher education to postpone their military duties, possibly hoping to completely circumvent service at a later date. A similar effect is shown by Card and

Lemieux (2001) for males who were at risk of being drafted into the US Army during the Vietnam War.

An all-volunteer force also inflicts distortionary effects on the economy through the taxes needed to finance the system. From an economic perspective the question of "military draft versus professional army" is a problem of optimal taxation: select that type of taxation that minimizes distortions. In general, conscription appears to be inferior and, thus, should be avoided. However, Lee and McKenzie (1992), Warner and Asch (1995) and Gordon, Bai and Li (1999) argue that a military draft could, under certain circumstances and beyond some recruitment level, be the less costly tax instrument – for example, if the level of fiscal taxation (to finance non-military expenditure) is already very high. Warner and Negrusa (2005) suggest that differences in deadweight losses (for example, through evasion) for fiscal taxes could rationalize why some countries rely on conscripts and others do not.

Clearly, the amount of resources that have to be provided for the military may affect the optimal tax mix (Friedman 1967). Also countries without conscription during peacetime retain the option to re-introduce conscription in case of war – when it might be infeasible to mobilize the necessary resources through fiscal taxes alone. Similar arguments may explain the use of conscription in countries such as Israel, where the military doctrine relies on the ability to mobilize most citizens to military service in case of a large-scale conflict. Mjoset and van Holde (2002) recount plenty of historical anecdotes that suggest a positive correlation between the military threat perceived by countries and their use of conscription. The recent abolishment of military draft in several European countries can then be explained – from an optimal tax perspective – by (the perception of) decreasing threats to national security in the wake of the collapse of the communist block.

9.2.3   Dynamic Effects

In wartime, conscripts are forced to risk life and limb, and being drafted in peacetime at least means losing discretion over one's use of time. The specific timing of military service at an early age of economic adulthood entails dynamic extra costs which have to be added to the static opportunity costs. Draftees, when forced to work in the army at a young age, have to postpone or interrupt college or university education, fall behind in experiences on their normal jobs, or see parts of the human capital they accumulated before the draft depreciating during military service.

On the individual level, a draft system results in a substantially lower lifetime wage profile (with income losses of between 5 and 15 percent), an effect which is also documented empirically (Angrist 1990; Imbens and van der Klaauw 1995; Buonanno 2006).[7] These effects are not confined to males, but seem to matter society-wide. For example, in the case of a local and temporary abolition of military conscription in Italy, Cipollone and Rosolia (2007) show it increased educational attainment of both males and females. They explain this contagion by peer-group effects and social interaction: when teenage boys stayed longer at high school, girls also increased their participation.

On the macroeconomic level, the disruption of human capital investments by military conscription translates into lower stocks of human capital, reduced labor productivity and substantial losses in GDP (Lau, Poutvaara and Wagener 2004). From 1960 to 2000, GDP growth rates in OECD countries with conscription were lower by around a quarter percent than in OECD countries with professional armies (Keller, Poutvaara and Wagener 2009), which is remarkably large given that military expenditure or the size of the military labor force *per se* do not seem to exert any systematic effect on GDP and its growth (Dunne, Smith and Willenbockel 2005).

9.2.4   Intergenerational Issues

Economically, but also from a political perspective, a military draft shares many features of government debt or of pay-as-you-go pension schemes. In both cases its introduction is a (temporary) way around higher fiscal taxes, the static inefficiencies will remain largely unnoticed, and its dynamic costs will only start to become visible after a time lag that by far exceeds the usual presidential or parliamentary terms. The draft involves intergenerational redistribution to the extent that it one-sidedly levies parts of the costs for the provision of government services on young cohorts. Like an unfunded pension scheme, starting a draft scheme amounts to giving a "present" (in the form of a reduced fiscal tax burden) to the cohorts that are beyond draft age at that moment. Such a gift may be handed over from cohort to cohort, but it can never be accomplished such as to make everybody in the future equally well off as without the gift (Poutvaara and Wagener 2007b).

9.3   THE PUBLIC CHOICE PERSPECTIVE ON MILITARY CONSCRIPTION

9.3.1   Theory

The military draft is a highly discriminatory tax with respect to age, gender and social status.[8] From the perspective of political economy, the specific (statutory or economic) incidence is precisely what might make military conscription politically attractive.

The public choice approach to political economy posits that, regardless of the (likely) inefficiency or injustice of the military draft, democratic regimes will choose to establish or maintain conscription if the majority of voters find it less costly or more socially beneficial than a professional army. As argued before, those directly burdened by the draft (namely, males at and below draft age) are largely outnumbered by those who are not directly affected by the draft (that is, all males above draft age and all females). By contrast, the fiscal bill for the higher tax burden involved with a professional army would visibly hit everybody. In a simple majority vote among selfish taxpayers, a military draft is a winning alternative over a professional army (see Oi 1967; Tollison 1970).[9] This holds even when taxpayers anticipate that the budgetary cheapness of military conscription is a fiscal illusion (Posner 2003, pp. 490f.). For reasons of minimizing political resistance non-democratic regimes may also find military conscription attractive (apart from allowing for political indoctrination or the build-up of numerically large armies) as only a small fraction of the population with political relevance is at or below the draft age. Such a tendency could be mitigated by intergenerational altruism if parents dislike the idea of forcing their children or grandchildren to perform military service.

The similarity of military conscription with a pay-as-you-go pension scheme and its intergenerational incidence also helps to explain why draft systems continue to be maintained though they impose a higher future burden on the economy than an all-volunteer force. Given its dynamic inefficiency, a draft system, once introduced, could be replaced by an all-volunteer force in a Pareto-improving manner (that is, with unanimous political support) – but only if age-specific fiscal taxes are available.[10] Given that such taxes are infeasible and given that age cohorts beyond the draft age largely outnumber younger cohorts at or below the draft age, both the continuation and the introduction of the military draft garner widespread political support in democratic as well as in non-democratic regimes. The casual observation that the staunchest advocates of conscription usually come from an age group well above draft age supports this view.

The draft's specific incidence makes it especially appealing in ageing societies where older cohorts gain in political weight. Ironically, however, it is ageing societies for which military draft is a particularly bad idea (in spite of its potential to deliver a large number of conscientious objectors who are cheaply employable in old-age homes, care units and similar welfare institutions). Not only are the distortions in the allocation of human and physical capital more damaging when young people become relatively scarcer; in ageing societies that already load the lion's share of the burden of demographic transitions on younger generations via pay-as-you-go financing of pensions and health care, draft systems unduly acerbate intergenerational imbalances.

9.3.2   Empirical Evidence

There are only a limited number of studies on public support for the military draft. Attitudes appear to differ widely across countries and over time. Surveying polls among young citizens from EU countries in the late 1990s (especially from a Eurobarometer study in 1997), Manigart (2003) finds that support for a re-introduction of military conscription in countries that had recently abolished it was very low. For countries that were (then) running a draft scheme, approval rates varied considerably, ranging from 79 percent in Greece to 13 percent in Spain. Cronberg (2006) reports conscription in Finland enjoys the full support of 79 percent of the Finnish population, while the number for Sweden was 36 percent. Subsequently, Sweden decided to abolish conscription during peacetime, while Finland maintains it. For Russia, opinion polls in 2002 and 2003 found that 60 percent of the population would have supported transition to a professional army (Gerber and Mendelsohn 2003); still the country is running a draft scheme (supported by 30 percent). In Germany the picture is less clear-cut, with changing majorities for and against military conscription every now and then.[11] Flynn (1998, 2001) documents that military conscription in France (1996), Britain (1960) and the United States (1973) was abolished although the draft had public support from a majority of voters in principle; what made the draft so highly unpopular in the US was its biased selectiveness in the Vietnam War.[12]

Based on expert questionnaires in 22 European countries from 2001 and 2005, Haltiner and Szvircsev Tresch (2008) find that the incidence of the draft tax and the implied inequality in burden-sharing (a constantly diminishing number of young men are drafted) are a major cause for the waning support for military conscription in Europe.[13] The other causes are a lack of military threat after the end of the Cold War and the increased frequency of overseas operations. Taken together, these findings suggest only a limited support for the hypothesis that the military draft is supported as a way for taxing a minority. It appears that those European countries in which the draft receives the widest popular support, like Finland, Greece and Switzerland, are all relatively small and adhere to a military doctrine that requires being able to defend against a large-scale invasion by land. By contrast, popular support for conscription in larger countries with a military draft (say, Russia or Germany) seems to be lower. From the political economy perspective of taxing a minority this is puzzling, since the size of the country should not matter for that argument.

Age-related issues of military conscription may matter for political economy. Flynn (2001, p. 226) reports for France in the 1990s that two-thirds of all Frenchmen who had already delivered military service were in favor of conscription, but only 40 percent of those who had not yet done so had a favorable view. This age pattern is in line with the predictions from public choice theory.

9.4 SOCIAL AND POLITICAL RECORD OF MILITARY CONSCRIPTION

The public choice perspective presented above implicitly assumed that political agents are self-concerned and care for their own welfare only ("pocketbook voting"). Yet there is ample evidence of other-concerning preferences which then might give rise to unselfish (sociotropic) political attitudes, thereby voters care about society at large, rather than their narrow self-interest. The military draft, in particular, is often debated in non-individualistic terms. Social, moral, political and military aspects may add to (or subtract from) the political allure of the military draft and, thus, contribute to an explanation as to why countries opt for that recruitment scheme. In this section, we ask whether equity considerations, social cohesion and national identity, or democratic control of the army, could explain the use of military conscription.

9.4.1 Equity Issues

Advocates of the military draft argue that a conscript military is more "representative" of society than a professional army that (allegedly) preys disproportionately on the poorly educated, the lower classes, ethnic minorities or otherwise marginal(ized) strata of society. Conscription appears more egalitarian since all are included in universal service. It is seen to instill a sense of the moral duties of citizenship from which nobody is exempted (see Sandel 1998; or Galston 2004).

In fact, there is hardly any reason to believe that conscription makes the military (more) representative.[14] First, to have a genuine cross-section of the population in the army was never the aim in conscription countries: Even at its peak, conscription covered substantially less than 50 percent of the population; it excluded women, migrants, and often certain religious groups, fathers, or gays (Leander 2004). Second, even within its target group (young males), the military draft is biased. For the US, today blamed for staffing their professional army mainly with underprivileged minorities and lower-class whites, analysis of Vietnam era veterans indicates that individuals of high socioeconomic status were widely underrepresented among draftees (Angrist 1990). In Germany, males with higher educational status are *more* likely to be called to service than their peers with lower status (Schneider 2003). In the Philippines, military training is compulsory for male college and university students while conscription for other groups in the population does not exist (WRI 2009). By contrast, 24 out of the 95 countries with a military draft covered in Mulligan and Shleifer (2005) have shorter terms for college students, 11 of them with complete exemption. Legal and illegal buyout options favor wealthy, urban and well-educated citizens.

9.4.2   Social Cohesion and National Identity

Conscription is sometimes viewed as a "melting pot" for diverse ethnic or social groups that would otherwise have little mutual contact, thereby forging national identity, loyalty to the nation or social respect.[15] Military service is often hailed as the "school for the nation", and civic, political and historical education often is a formal requirement for conscripts.

Empirical evidence for the military's power as a socializing agent is, at best, mixed (for an extensive survey see Krebs 2004). Moreover, it may be questioned whether forced labor in a military environment is an appropriate means to promote social cohesion, even when combined with deliberate civic instruction. Primary and secondary schooling, integration of minorities, policies targeted at underprivileged groups in society and so forth appear to be far more promising, in particular as they approach the root of the problem.

9.4.3   Armed Forces and Democracy

Military conscription is often attributed with a greater affinity with democracy than an all-volunteer force. Army structures, which operate on the basis of order and command rather than on voting, are inherently non-democratic. Still conscripts may act as mediators between a society and its army, while a professional military tends to alienate from society and form a "state within a state."

However, the "isolation" of the military from the rest of society may be indicative of an increased division of labor. In a certain sense, employees in bakeries, courts of justice and universities are also alienated in their work from the rest of society, but calls for compulsory internships of all members of society in such sectors have so far been unheard of. Even if one views the alienation of the military from the rest of society as particularly undesirable, conscription does not offer a solution. Praetorian tendencies are most likely to emerge from the officers' corps (the "warrior caste") which in any case consists of professional soldiers. Moreover, the democratic controls arising from a draft are open to debate. Not only were conscript forces used by totalitarian regimes (Nazi-Germany, the Soviet Union or Fascist Italy) without noticeable resistance from within the army, but also democratic countries like Argentina (in 1976), Brazil (in 1963), Chile (in 1973), Greece (in 1967) and Turkey (in 1980) used conscription at the time of their military coups. Combined with the fact that many democracies have adopted the all-volunteer system without ever facing the risk of military coups, these observations as well as the econometric evidence established by Mulligan and Shleifer (2005) indicate that no causality in whatever direction exists between the form of government and the structure of armed forces in a country.

9.5   CONSCRIPTION AND SPECIAL INTERESTS

The military draft does not burden all segments of society or sectors of the economy equally. Such differential incidence gives rise to special interests – which might shape the political process.

For Anglo-Saxon countries, Levi (1996) finds that decisions in favor or against military conscription are not so much driven by strategic, military or fiscal factors but rather by the ability of the opponents of conscription to transform their views into political clout. The cleavages against the draft fell into three main categories: ideological groups (left-wing political parties, anarchists and pacifists); economic groups (some labor unions and farmers' lobbies) that feared to be the primary losers from universal conscription; and religious, ethnic, and other cultural groups (the Irish in Britain or the Francophones in Canada) that had lost confidence in government promises.

Anderson, Halcoussis and Tollison (1996) suggest that members of labor unions will favor conscription as it keeps potential competitors off the private labor market, thus allowing for a higher wage for unionized workers. In fact, empirical evidence in Anderson et al. (1996) reveals a positive correlation between the percentage of the workforce in labor unions and the use of conscription.

When available, the option to do alternative rather than military service is exercised by a considerable share of draftees. For their employers, conscientious objectors to military service – who mainly deliver their duties in the social sector – are quite attractive staff as they are cheap, have to work on order and their employment is not subject to the restrictions imposed by labor laws. This adds issues of rent-seeking to the debate on military conscription. The disappearance of alternative service (which, by legal design, is only a corollary to compulsory military service), is used as an argument against the abolition of military conscription. Afraid of losing economic rents, the welfare industry actively lobbies for conscription (or even for a universal national service to be delivered by youths of both genders), arguing that many nursing and care services could not be upheld in their present form without conscription, with the cost falling mainly on the most needy and disadvantaged people in society. Interestingly, such argumentation suggests that it is easier to finance the care for the elderly by imposing the costs disproportionately on the young, rather than sharing the fiscal burden over the whole population.

The military itself might also have vested interests in the conscription debate. Because conscription affects quite a large stratum in society, it gives the military a high visibility. The military might view conscription as a means to convey the importance of national defense and security to the minds of young draftees or to use its greater visibility to lobby for more resources. Conscription might also be used as an advertising mechanism for would-be professional soldiers. However, in certain circumstances the military might also be against conscription. The high administrative burden, permanent low-level training of conscripts, and the dubious military value of draftees may be seen as a distraction from the military's proper tasks. Further, the equipment of the army including weapons, materials and personnel suitable for draftees may come at the expense of more prestigious or sophisticated items. Frequently publicized reports by draftees about the tedium of their service (not to speak of abuses of draftees by officers) may also backfire on the perceived attractiveness of the army as a potential employer. Unfortunately, a systematic account or comparative study of the attitude towards conscription in the military itself does not currently exist.

From an organizational perspective, professional armies differ from conscript forces in that the latter need a larger administrative apparatus to operate (for example, to register the population, enforce the draft and so forth). Hence, bureaucracies may play a role. Mulligan and Shleifer (2005) argue that countries with a lot of other government regulation are also more likely to use draft. They trace this correspondence back to the legal system under which a country is operating – either common law systems (originating from England) or civil law systems (originating mainly from Napoleonic France). Common law countries rely to a greater extent on contracts and decentralized conflict resolution, while civil law countries rely on regulation, state involvement, and public administration. Given this logic, when choosing between military conscription and professional armies, countries with larger public administrations (that is, the civil law countries) find it more attractive to set up a conscription scheme as compared to common law countries which prefer a professional army.

9.6   THE MILITARY RECORD OF THE DRAFT

In the early nineteenth century, military conscription gained popularity among political leaders because of the military successes of Prussia's and France's conscript armies. However, this initial battlefield dominance later came at the huge cost of millions of deaths which at least partly can be attributed to the "cheap-labor fallacy" with conscription. Observing the carnage of Napoleon's poorly prepared winter campaigns in Russia, nineteenth-century German economist J.H. von Thuenen argued that this negative outcome could only happen after soldiers became easily available through the system of conscription. Von Thuenen (1875, pp. 154f) reasoned that the scandalous misperception in military recruitment of those times was to view human life as a commodity and not as a capital good (see also Kiker 1969; Spencer and Woroniak 1969; Knapp 1973).

Compulsory service and the perception of draftees as cheap labor are likely to lead to an inefficient organization within the military. In peacetime, this excessive labor-to-capital ratio manifests itself in an often-lamented tedium of service, the over-manning of army units, and the excessive maintenance devoted to weapons and materials (Straubhaar 1996). In wartime, the use of less advanced military technology, lack of experience and training, poor equipment and the easy availability of apparently expendable soldiers leads to a larger number of casualties and "cannon-fodder"-type battlefield tactics (for example, trench wars, human-wave attacks etc.).

Despite the use of conscription in most wars in the nineteenth and twentieth centuries, advocates of conscription sometimes contend that using a military draft breaks militaristic ideologies of societies and limits the inducement for aggressive foreign interventions. By imposing casualties on all groups of society, military adventurism is politically less sustainable and faces greater public resistance with a draft system. Hence, a peace-loving population would opt for military conscription rather than for professional soldiers. Empirically, this "peacemaker" argumentation is questionable. As argued by many opponents of conscription, the draft may actually contribute to a militarization of society. By teaching all (male) citizens how to use weapons and kill, and instilling in them the view that killing for the home country is a patriotic duty, draft fosters processes by which civil societies organize themselves for the production of violence, and thereby increases the likelihood and severity of armed conflicts.[16] Between 1800 and 1945, basically all wars in Europe were fought with conscript armies, and democratic countries like the US and France later used conscript military in their colonial wars in Vietnam and Algeria. Analysing militarized interstate disputes from 1886 to 1992 systematically, Choi and James (2003) find that a military manpower system based on conscripted soldiers is associated with more military disputes than professional or voluntary armies. Based on cross-sectional data from 1980, Anderson et al. (1996) also conclude that "warlike" states are more likely to rely on conscription.

Interacting conscription with democracy seems to change the picture somewhat. Vasquez (2005) demonstrates that, in the second half of the twentieth century, the recruitment of military draftees, as compared with volunteer soldiers, tended to have a mediating effect on the number of casualties that democratic countries were likely to suffer in military disputes. He argues that democracies with conscription pursue casualty-averse policies out of concern for political backlash that could come from the most powerful segments of society that contribute troops to the force.

Another consideration is that compulsory military service provides manpower reserves to augment the army in the case of military emergency. This might provide a precautionary motive for using the draft. The validity of this argument depends on whether reservists are indeed suitably trained for their assignments in the case of mobilization, which may be doubtful, given the concerns about the inadequacy of conscripts' training for the requirements in modern armies even during peacetime. Moreover, establishing an all-volunteer army in no way implies giving up reserves, provided that reservists are paid sufficient compensation for their participation in regular exercises. Contracted (as contrasted to conscripted) reservists would render the full opportunity costs of alternative military strategies visible and help to allocate resources more efficiently between personnel and material.

9.7   MERCENARIES

Historically, military conscription emerged from an era of commercialized warfare that heavily relied on mercenaries. Given the questionable record of forced labor in the military on several accounts, "market solutions" appear more attractive. This is not only evidenced by the recent shifts in many countries from the military draft to professional armies, but is also reflected in the fact that private military companies, which operate on a

world-wide scale, have recently been booming (Singer 2004).[17] This trend
has raised serious concerns among many observers, but the question of
what precisely makes mercenaries morally or politically questionable is
complicated (Sandel 1998; Percy 2007).

From the viewpoint of political economy, hiring (foreign) mercenaries
in armed conflicts might reduce the political costs of casualties and also of
committing atrocities; after all, it is only a contracted hireling who loses his
health or life or who "misbehaved." Reluctance to employ mercenaries on
a large scale may stem from severe principal-agent problems. Machiavelli
(1532, Ch. 12) favored conscription as the way to raise an army, arguing
that, by virtue of their citizenship, even comparatively untrained militia
conscripts were better defenders than professional hirelings from abroad.
While defection of mercenaries merely amounts to non-compliance with
the terms of a labor contract, desertion of citizens from their country's
army is typically heavily penalized, stigmatized and often goes along with
abandoning one's home country. The higher exit costs and, arguably,
the higher idealistic motivation provide two arguments for why national
soldiers are a better option than mercenaries.[18]

Armies staffed by non-citizens are not doomed to be unreliable. While
an Italian state in Machiavelli's time would typically contract an entre-
preneurial commander with a mercenary army of unspecified origins,
the French government directly hires individual soldiers into its Légion
étrangère. Admission to the legion is (nowadays) severely restricted and
recruits, who come from diverse backgrounds and nationalities, undergo
a unifying training to generate a strong *esprit de corps*. The legion's composition and structure follow that of a regular army, and commanding
positions are trusted only to long-serving soldiers with a reliable record,
mainly to French citizens. After three years of service (or after being
injured in a battle for France), foreign legionnaires can apply for French
citizenship. These structures and incentives help to avoid that mercenaries
would organize themselves against the state that hired them.

9.8   CONCLUSION

We have documented that the normative case for conscription is weak,
both from efficiency and from non-economic perspectives. The inefficiency
of conscription results to a great extent from ignoring comparative advantage and specialization, thereby resulting in higher social costs than a voluntary army. At the same time, there is no empirical support for the claim
that the use of conscription would help to protect democracy, promote
social cohesion or tame belligerence. Political economy explanations for

the use of conscription in democratic regimes have a somewhat mixed record. While some evidence suggests that conscription is welcomed as a way to shift a tax burden to a minority, the changes in public opinion suggest that this is only part of voter considerations. Conscription tends to be more popular the more universal it is among young men. Fairness concerns requiring equal treatment of youngsters seem to stop at the gender line as voters by and large seem to accept conscription affecting only men. In democratic systems, the military draft continues to be maintained not least due to some inertia in the political process. The draft cannot be abolished in an intergenerationally Pareto-improving manner and special interest groups voice their "concerns" against its abolition loudly which contributes to the maintenance of the status quo.

In non-democratic regimes – which are currently the dominant users of conscription – popular support for conscription is less politically relevant. In these cases, aspects of indoctrination (or even intimidation), as well as the desire to maintain numerically large armies, seem to be important factors for relying on the draft. For developing countries, with their inability to raise enough fiscal revenues to finance an all-volunteer force and with their generally lower opportunity costs of labor, the military draft could even be economically attractive.

In democratic countries with developed economies, military conscription has run its course. Historically, it might have been a useful and even popular military recruitment device when these countries were involved in mass warfare or nation building or only had limited capacities to raise fiscal taxes. With the possible exception of states that view themselves under permanent military threat that requires all citizens to be militarily trained, the present-day political, economic and military conditions are unfavorable for the survival of the draft.

ACKNOWLEDGEMENTS

We are grateful for helpful comments by Chris Coyne, Jan Fidrmuc, William A. Fischel, Katarina Keller, and Vasily Zatsepin. Panu Poutvaara gratefully acknowledges financial support from the Yrjö Jahnsson Foundation.

NOTES

1. Unlike the rest of the world, Eritrea, Israel, Libya, Malaysia, North Korea, Taiwan and Tunisia currently also draw women into compulsory military service or its equivalents.

Formally, compulsory military service for women also exists in China (but has never been enforced).

2. Examples include feudal levies, military slaves, serfs with lifetime conscription, allotment systems or armed peasants.

3. These are Denmark, Estonia, Germany, Greece, Norway and Turkey.

4. Most notably: North Korea (3 to 10 years of compulsory military service), South Korea (24–28 months), or Syria (30 months). See https://www.cia.gov/library/publications/the-world-factbook/fields/2024.html.

5. In a volunteer system, reservists also receive compensation for being available in case of an armed conflict. Perhaps the best-known example is the system of National Guards in the United States that, in addition to serving as military reserves, help to respond to domestic disasters.

6. According to Oneal (1992), budgetary savings from conscription in NATO states reduced from an average of 9.2 percent of national military expenditures in 1974 to only 5.7 percent in 1987. Warner and Asch (2001) report that the budgetary costs of moving to a volunteer force in the USA in 1973 came at 10 to 15 percent of the 1965 military budget (which was chosen as a reference point to exclude the effect of the Vietnam War).

7. With generally low educational attainment of the young male workforce, spending some time in the military may increase the quality of human capital by providing training opportunities for self-discipline, communicative skills or problem-solving techniques. This seems to be empirically relevant for African and Latin American countries (Stroup and Heckelman 2001).

8. Also see Section 9.4.1. In addition, the draft tax generally involves an unequal treatment even within its original target group. As cohort sizes outnumber requirements for military personnel, typically only a fraction of those who are legally subject to the draft are indeed called to service.

9. As voting age was 21 at that time, most US draftees in the Vietnam War era were not yet allowed vote. Fischel (1996) notes that it might not have been coincidental that the lowering of voting age to 18 and the end of military conscription in the US came at the same time.

10. See Poutvaara and Wagener (2007b). Tax exemptions for cohorts beyond draft age are needed to avoid a double burden on those who have already delivered their military service and who would, upon abolition of draft, suffer from the higher fiscal taxes that go to finance the all-volunteer force.

11. According to Infratest (2003), 54 percent of the Germans supported abolition of conscription in December 2003; a month later (and without apparent reason) that rate dropped to 41 percent. In 2010, 43 percent of Germans supported the abolition of conscription, while 51 percent preferred to maintain it (Focus 2010).

12. The US draft during the Vietnam War had escape clauses that favored young men from the upper and middle classes and from wealthy backgrounds. In particular, deferments were available to all full-time college and graduate students (but not for part-time students). For college graduates, further deferments were available if one worked in a defense-related industry, or in exempted professions, like teaching.

13. The violation of fairness perceptions has already been identified as an extra social cost of selective conscription schemes by Fischel (1996). By "demoralization costs" he denotes the disutility, experienced by draftees, of having "to shoulder an obligation that most other members of the community do not have to bear and in fact apparently gain by your having borne it" (p. 43). Referring to examples of expropriation in contexts not related to military conscription, Fischel (1996) argues that the demoralization costs could be substantial.

14. This point was forcefully made by the Gates Commission, whose report led to the abolition of the draft in the US in 1970 (Gates et al. 1970, pp. 63f). But even if military conscription were egalitarian, that would not be a convincing argument in its favor. The existence of a civic duty (for example, to defend one's country) does not imply that

the burden from that duty be shared equally. Arguably, contributing to the financing of government is also a civic duty – but the idea that everybody pays the same amount of taxes is neither a logical nor probably a socially desirable implication of that duty.
15.   See Peled (1998). The "melting pot" argument is part of the official doctrine of military conscription in Malaysia, Singapore, South Africa and Israel.
16.   This point is most voicefully made in the famous Anti-Conscription Manifesto (see http://www.themanifesto.info/manifesto.htm). For a thorough historical account for Germany, see Frevert (2004).
17.   As Saudi Arabia evidences, even standing armies can be staffed with hired foreigners. Also, the Vatican City's picturesque Swiss Guard is a professional army exclusively hired from abroad.
18.   For a government, hiring mercenaries means outsourcing parts of its monopoly over (armed) violence. In low-intensity conflicts and temporarily, this might be hardly noticeable. Van Creveld (1991) argues, however, that over time selling away the monopoly of power inevitably threatens sovereignty and the existence of the state as such.

REFERENCES

Anderson, G.M., D. Halcoussis and R.D. Tollison (1996), "Drafting the competition. labor unions and military conscription", *Defence and Peace Economics*, **7**, 189–202.
Angrist, J.D. (1990), "Lifetime earnings and the Vietnam era draft lottery: evidence from social security administration records", *American Economic Review*, **80**, 313–35.
Buonanno, P. (2006), "Costs of conscription: lessons from the UK", University of Bergamo, Department of Economics Working Paper No. 04/2006.
Card, D. and Th. Lemieux (2001), "Going to college to avoid the draft: the unintended legacy of the Vietnam War", *American Economic Review*, **91**, 97-102.
Choi, S.-W. and P. James (2003), "No professional soldiers, no militarized interstate disputes? A new question for neo-Kantianism", *Journal of Conflict Resolution* **47**, 796–816.
Cipollone, P. and A. Rosolia (2007), "Social interactions in high school: lessons from an earthquake", *American Economic Review*, **97**, 948–65.
Cronberg, T (2006), "The will to defend: a nordic divide over security and defence policy", in A.J.K. Bailes et al. (eds), *The Nordic Countries and the European Security and Defence Policy*, Oxford, UK: Oxford University Press, pp. 315–22.
Dunne, J.P., R.P. Smith and D. Willenbockel (2005), "Models of military expenditure and growth: a critical review", *Defence and Peace Economics*, **16**, 449–61.
Galston, W.A. (2004), "Thinking about the draft", *Public Interest*, **154** (Winter 2004), 61–73.
Fischel, W.A. (1996), "The political economy of just compensation: lessons from the military draft for the takings issue", *Harvard Journal of Law and Public Policy*, **20**, 23–63.
Flynn, G.Q. (1998), "Conscription and equity in Western democracies, 1940–75", *Journal of Contemporary History*, **33**, 5–20.
Flynn, G.Q. (2001), *Conscription and Democracy: The Draft in France, Great Britain, and the United States*, Westport, CN: Greenwood Press.
Focus (2010), "Streit um Wehrpflicht spaltet Deustschland", *Focus*, **31**, 47.
Frevert, U. (2004), *A Nation in Barracks: Modern Germany, Military Conscription and Civil Society*, Oxford, UK: Berg.
Friedman, M. (1967), "Why not a volunteer army?", *New Individualist Review*, Spring 1967, 3–9.
Gates, T. et al. (1970), *The President's Commission on an All-Volunteer Armed Force*. Washington DC: US Government.
Gerber, Th.P. and S.E. Mendelson (2003), "Strong public support for military reform in Russia", PONARS Policy Memo 288, Centre for Strategic and International Studies, Washington DC.
Gordon, R.H., C.-E. Bai and D.D. Li (1999), "Efficiency losses from tax distortions versus government control", *European Economic Review*, **43**, 1095–113.

Haltiner, K.W. (1998), "The definite end of the mass army in Western Europe?", *Armed Forces & Society*, **25**, 7–36.

Haltiner, K.W. (2003), "The decline of the European mass armies", in G. Caforio (ed.), *Handbook of the Sociology of the Military*, New York, NY: Kluwer/Plenum Publishers, pp. 361–84.

Haltiner, K.W. and T. Szvircsev Tresch (2008), "European civil–military relations in transition: the decline of conscription", in G. Caforio et al. (eds), *Armed Forces and Conflict Resolution: Sociological Perspectives*, Bingley, UK: Emerald Publishing Group, pp. 165–182.

Imbens, G. and W. van der Klaauw (1995), "Evaluating the cost of conscription in the Netherlands", *Journal of Business and Economic Statistics*, **13**, 207–15.

Infratest (2003), "Deutschland TREND' (Dezember 2003)", available at http://www.infratest-dimap.de/uploads/media/dt0312.pdf, accessed 20 August 2009.

Keegan, J. (1993), *A History of Warfare*, New York, NY: Alfred Knopf.

Keller, K., Poutvaara, P. and A. Wagener (2009), "Military draft and economic growth in OECD countries", *Defence and Peace Economics*, **20**, 373–93.

Kerstens, K. and E. Meyermans (1993), "The draft versus an all-volunteer force: issues of efficiency and equity in the Belgian draft", *Defence Economics*, **4**, 271–84.

Kiker, B.F. (1969), "Von Thünen on human capital", *Oxford Economic Papers*, **21**, 339-43.

Knapp, C.B. (1973), "A human capital approach to the burden of the military draft", *Journal of Human Resources*, **8**, 485–96.

Krebs, R. (2004), "A school for the nation? How military service does not build nations, and how it might", *International Security*, **28**, 85–124.

Lau, M.I., P. Poutvaara and A. Wagener (2004), "Dynamic costs of the draft", *German Economic Review*, **5**, 381–406.

Leander, A. (2004), "Drafting community: understanding the fate of conscription", *Armed Forces & Society*, **30**, 571–99

Lee, D.R. and R.B. McKenzie (1992), "Reexamination of the relative efficiency of the draft and the all-volunteer army", *Southern Economic Journal*, **59**, 646–54.

Levi, M. (1996), "The institution of conscription", *Social Science History*, **20**, 133–67.

Levi, M. (1998), "Conscription: the price of citizenship", in R.H. Bates et al. (eds), *Analytic Narratives*, Princeton, NJ: Princeton University Press, pp. 109–48.

Lokshin, M. and R. Yemtsov (2008), "Who bears the costs of Russia's military draft?", *Economics of Transition*, **16**, 359–87.

McNeill, W.H. (1982), *The Pursuit of Power: Technology, Armed Force, and Society Since A.D. 1000*, Chicago, IL: The University of Chicago Press.

Machiavelli, N. ([1532, written in 1515] 2001), *Il Principe*, in George Bull (trans. and ed.) (2001), *The Prince*, Harmondsworth, UK: Penguin.

Manigart, P. (2003), "Public opinion on defence policy in the countries of European Union", in M. Vlachová (ed.), *The Public Image of Defence and the Military in Central and Eastern Europe*, DCAF and Centre for Civil-Military Relations: Geneva/Belgrade, pp. 27–46.

Maurin, E. and Th. Xenogiani (2007), "Demand for education and labor market outcomes: lessons from the abolition of compulsory conscription in France", *Journal of Human Resources*, **42**, 795–819.

Mjoset, L. and S. van Holde (2002), "Killing for the state, dying for the nation: an introductory essay on the life cycle of conscription into Europe's armed forces", in L. Mjoset and S. van Holde (eds), *The Comparative Study of Conscription in the Armed Forces*, Amsterdam: JAI Press, pp. 4–98.

Mulligan, C. and A. Shleifer (2005), "Conscription as regulation", *American Law and Economics Review*, 85–111.

Oi, W.Y. (1967), "The economic cost of the draft", *American Economic Review*, **57**, 39–62.

Oneal, J.R. (1992), "Budgetary savings from conscription and burden sharing in NATO", *Defense and Peace Economics*, **3**, 113–25.

Peled, A. (1998), *A Question of Loyalty: Military Manpower Policy in Multiethnic States*, Ithaca, NY: Cornell University Press.

Percy, S. (2007), *Mercenaries. The History of a Norm in International Relations*, Oxford/New York: Oxford University Press.

Posner, R.A. (2003), *Economic Analysis of Law*, 6th edition, New York, NY: Aspen Publishers.

Poutvaara, P. and A. Wagener (2007a), "Conscription: economic costs and political allure", *Economics of Peace and Security Journal*, **2**, 5–15.

Poutvaara, P. and A. Wagener (2007b), "To draft or not to draft: inefficiency, intergenerational incidence, and political economy of military conscription", *European Journal of Political Economy*, **23**, 975–87.

Sandel, M.J. (1998), "What money can't buy: the moral limits of markets", Tanner Lectures on Human Values, University of Utah, available at www.tannerlectures.utah.edu/lectures/documents/sandel00.pdf, accessed 20 August 2009.

Sandler, T. and K. Hartley (1995), *The Economics of Defense*, Cambridge, UK: Cambridge University Press.

Schneider, T., (2003), "Wehr- und Zivildienst in Deutschland: Wer dient, wer nicht? [Military and alternative service in Germany: Who serves and who doesn't?]", *Jahrbücher für Nationalökonomie und Statistik*, **223**, 603–22.

Singer, P.W. (2004), *Corporate Warriors: The Rise of the Privatized Military Industry*, Ithaca, NY: Cornell University Press.

Smith, A. ([1776] 1976), *An Inquiry into the Nature and Causes of the Wealth of Nations*, reprinted in W.B. Todd (ed.), *Glasgow Edition of the Works and Correspondence of Adam Smith*, Vol. I, Oxford, UK: Oxford University Press.

Spencer, D.L. and A. Woroniak (1969), "Valuing transfer of military-acquired skills to civilian employment", *Kyklos*, **22**, 467–92.

Straubhaar, T. (1996), "Einsparpotenziale bei den Verteidigungsausgaben: Die allgemeine Wehrpflicht" [Potential economies in defense expenditures: military conscription], in D. Fritz-Assmus and T. Straubhaar (eds), *Sicherheit in einem neuen Europa*, Berne, Germany: Haupt, pp. 267–99.

Stroup, M.D. and J.C. Heckelman (2001), "Size of the military sector and economic growth: a panel data analysis of Africa and Latin America", *Journal of Applied Economics*, **4**, 329–60.

Thuenen, J.H. von (1875), *Der isolierte Staat in Beziehung auf Landwirtschaft und Nationalökonomie* (3rd edition), Berlin: Wiegardt, Hempel & Parey. (English edition: *Isolated State* (1966), Pergamon Press: Oxford/New York).

Tollison, R.D. (1970), "Political economy of the military draft", *Public Choice* **9**, 67–78.

Van Creveld, M. (1991), *The Transformation of War*, New York, NY: The Free Press.

Vasquez, J.P. (2005), "Shouldering the soldiering: democracy, conscription, and military casualties", *Journal of Conflict Resolution*, **49**, 849–73.

Warner, J.T. and B.J. Asch (1995), "The economics of military manpower", in K. Hartley and T. Sandler (eds), *Handbook of Defense Economics*, Vol. 1, Amsterdam: Elsevier, pp. 347–98.

Warner, J.T. and B.J. Asch (2001), "The record and prospects of the all-volunteer military in the United States", *Journal of Economic Perspectives*, **15**, 169–92.

Warner, J. and Negrusa, S. (2005), "Evasion costs and the theory of conscription", *Defense and Peace Economics*, **16**, 83–100.

Wikipedia (2010), Keyword "Conscription", http://en.wikipedia.org/wiki/Conscription, accessed 2 August 2010.

WRI (2009), *World Survey of Conscription and Conscientious Objection to Military Service*, War Resister's International: London, available at http://www.wri-irg.org/co/rtba/index.html, accessed on 20 August 2009.

PART III

CIVIL WAR AND REVOLUTION

10 Economic perspectives on civil wars
Nathan Fiala and Stergios Skaperdas

10.1 INTRODUCTION

Since the end of World War II, civil wars have taken place in over 70 countries, resulting in millions of human deaths and high economic costs.[1] In the Democratic Republic of the Congo (formerly Zaire) alone, more than four million human beings have perished and many others have been displaced or completely impoverished since 1998 (Prunier 2009).[2] The countries that have experienced civil wars are poor and there is a high correlation between per capita income and the incidence of civil war (see, for example, Collier et. al. 2003, p. 55). Even though traditional growth theory and development economics do not take into account the economic effects of civil wars, it would be hard to argue that countries involved in civil wars are not harmed economically. Moreover, low levels of per-capita income and economic shocks can feed back into inducing civil wars (see Miguel, Satyanath and Sergenti 2004). Thus, civil wars have high costs that cannot but impair economic performance whereas bad economic performance and lower levels of income increase the risk of civil war.

We review some of the costs of civil wars, following Skaperdas (2009), in Section 10.1 of this chapter. Direct costs include destroyed public infrastructure, factories, machinery, housing and other physical property; deaths, physical and mental injuries and the future costs of caring from those who become disabled; and the extra costs of arming and lost equipment. Indirect or induced costs of civil wars include population displacement; reduced production and trade due to violence or its threat; lower current and future physical investment; reduction in educational opportunities and brain drain; and other macroeconomic effects including reduced economic growth. Even by conservative measures these costs are much higher than other measured deadweight costs in economics and are therefore economically very significant. Trying then to understand why wars occur in the first place is important for economic reasons as well.

Wars violate a central simplifying assumption of neoclassical economic theory, that property rights on all endowments are perfectly and costlessly enforced. Studying and modeling civil wars from an economic perspective requires relaxing that assumption, something that has been attempted by an increasing number of scholars over the past two decades.[3] A critical ingredient in relaxing the assumption is that individuals and groups cannot just produce and trade in order to make a living but also by taking or *appropriating* the production of others. The inputs to appropriation are costly as they involve labor, arming and other activities that divert resources from direct production. The capability of appropriation, however, is not sufficient by itself to induce arming and war. Since arming and war are costly activities, all potential adversaries could in principle write a contract that would prevent such losses. The impossibility of finding and writing such contracts, often attributed to the catch-all term of "transaction costs," has spawned a considerable literature on incomplete contracting in economics, mostly associated with the theory of the firm (for example, Hart 1995). Consequently, the second ingredient of the approach adopted here is *incomplete contracting*; that is, long-term contracting on arming and war is difficult or impossible. Implicit in the idea of incomplete contracting is that individuals are not all-knowing, so that they cannot anticipate every possible contingency and write it down in a contract.

The idea of incomplete contracting has essentially its synonym in the political science literature in the problem of *commitment* (for example, Fearon 1995), the inability of adversaries to commit to an agreement about arming and peace without having the incentive to renege on it once the time to implement it comes.

Following the review of the costs of civil wars in Section 10.1, in Section 10.2 we show how adversaries might to choose to go to war, instead of negotiating and settling, despite the extra costs that war might induce. In addition to incomplete contracting, we discuss asymmetric information, which is the reason for war that has been most emphasized in the economics literature. In Section 10.3, we discuss more concretely some sources of incomplete contracting that increase the chance of civil war, including ethnic and religious differences, geography, economic and social change and the role of foreign actors.[4]

Before proceeding we should refer to at least one definition of civil war: "[C]ivil war occurs when an identifiable rebel organization challenges the government militarily and the resulting violence results in more than 1000 combat deaths, with at least 5 percent on each side" (Collier et al. 2003, p. 11). Whereas the threshold is in terms of combat deaths or even the degree to which the government is involved does not directly concern us here, as the analysis in this chapter can well apply to a wider set of internal conflicts.

10.2 ON THE COST OF CIVIL WARS

The cost of a public building that has been destroyed during war and the loss of the benefit of its services can be calculated relatively easily. The cost of lost trade in a volatile region or the psychological costs of the brutality of warfare on a country's residents are more difficult to estimate and depend in part on the method of measurement and empirical model employed by the researcher. The range of probable values of such costs can then vary widely. In this way, a continuum of possibilities exists in estimating the costs of violence, from considering only the most direct costs that are easy to calculate to estimating different indirect costs that depend on the channels of causality, scenarios and counterfactuals that are assumed or which models are estimated.

Collier et al. (2003) provide a comprehensive discussion of the different types of costs associated with civil wars and offer an overview of different quantitative estimates. The two edited volumes by Stewart and Fitzgerald (2001) also contain a number of country studies and overall evaluation of the effects of war on economic development. Two recent overviews are Blattman and Miguel (2009), a survey of the theory, causes and consequences of civil wars, and Collier, Chauvert and Hegre (2008), a policy-oriented piece that includes estimates of the costs of civil wars.

Before accounting for the destruction and other costs, the extra *budgetary cost* due to increased military and other security expenditures is the first cost to consider. Collier et al. (2003) estimate that the average extra cost of military expenditures due to civil wars was 2.2 percent of GDP for a country with a GDP per capita of US$3000 in 1995. Additionally, other government revenues and expenditures – and, therefore, the public goods they supply – tend to decrease with the length of the war. Then, reductions in the fiscal capacity of states to provide for public goods such as basic health care and other social services induces various indirect effects on the population to withstand disease, injury, malnutrition and poverty.

Infrastructure – roads, bridges, railroads, public buildings, hospitals – are often battlegrounds in the fighting between rebels and governments. *Private capital*, such as factories, housing and cattle are also often subject to significant destruction. Surprisingly, to our knowledge, there are no studies that systematically quantify these costs and compare them across countries, but in nations that have experienced long wars, these costs are high. In Nicaragua, for instance, Fitzgerald and Grigsby (2001) have estimated that, over the years of most intense conflict (1987–89), the cumulative total economic damages were equal to about one year's GDP. Collier et al. (2003) also reports estimates of *capital flight* for countries in civil war. In these, the share of private wealth held abroad goes from

9 percent before the war to 20 percent by its end. Moreover, as far as capital is concerned, war according to Collier et al. has lasting effects – by the end of first decade of postconflict peace, capital flight rises to 26.1 percent. However, Blomberg, Hess and Weerapana (2004) find neither a statistically nor economically significant effect of internal conflict on investment.

We expect that long-lasting wars would induce *lower levels economic of growth*. Stewart, Huang and Wang (2001) calculate the difference in growth rates for 14 countries at war and compare them with those of comparable countries. They found them lagging on average about 3.4 percentage points in GDP. Cerra and Saxena (2008) estimate the effect of civil wars on economic growth using the beginning of civil war as a shock in a VAR model. Using impulse response functions, the immediate effect of a civil war is estimated to induce a reduction of 6 percentage points in GDP, although almost half of that loss is recovered after about six years, and the long-run estimates are imprecise. In the event of a long civil war, these negative effects on growth can be expected to compound over time and it is not clear to what extent output can be expected to partially recover in the long run. Country experiences in terms of growth of course can vary widely. Miguel and Roland (2006) exploit the regional variation of the air bombing campaign of the US in Vietnam in order to estimate long-run effects of conflict. They find that areas that suffered heavy bombing did not suffer a long-run negative impact on poverty rates, consumption levels, infrastructure or literacy. It could be that this finding is due to the absence of long-run effects from bombing. Nevertheless, it is also likely that the Vietnamese government directed more resources towards the areas that were heavily bombed – they may have built more modern infrastructure that enhanced the growth potential of these areas over those that were not as heavily bombed, and thus retained their older infrastructure. In addition, Vietnam has been a rather poor country in terms of absolute levels of income since the war ended, and the war likely had an effect on its growth rate. The possible diversion of resources to the more heavily bombed areas likely reduced the country's overall growth rate.

Civil wars of course cause *death, injuries* and other long-term deteriorations in *health*. A conservative estimate of the deaths directly attributable to civil war between 1945 and 1999 is 16.2 million (Fearon and Laitin 2003), whereas we mentioned earlier (Footnote 2) that the International Rescue Committee estimates that 5.4 million people have died from war-related causes in the Democratic Republic of the Congo since 1998 alone. For public policy purposes, the cost of death in rich countries is usually monetized using estimates of the value of life. For instance, to estimate the cost of US soldiers' deaths, Bilmes and Stiglitz (2008) use US$7.2 million as the Value of Statistical Life (VSL), which is consistent with recent usage.

Clearly it would be inappropriate to value the life of a US citizen more than those of citizens of other countries, but given that economic opportunities are much lower in some countries we could at least try to provide a sense of comparison of the human cost by trying different numbers. Even if we were to value the life of a citizen of the Democratic Republic of Congo at 1/72 of that of an American citizen (that is, US$100 000), the total cost would be US$540 billion over the past ten years (for comparison, the CIA World Factbook estimated the GDP of the country in 2007 to be a little over US$19 billion at purchasing power parity). Even if the value of life in the Democratic Republic of the Congo were considered at 1/720 of an American life (US$10 000), still the cost would be US$54 billion. What such numbers indicate is that no matter how one views the loss of life in civil wars, these losses pose an immense cost to both the deceased's loved ones and their country.

In addition to death and injury, civilian populations plagued by war suffer disproportionately from *disease* as a result of worse nutrition, living conditions in camps or deteriorating health care. Malaria, diarrhea, respiratory infections, AIDS, even measles and meningitis occur more frequently during wartime and result in higher death rates than in times of peace (Collier et al. 2003). Measures exist for aggregating the impact of different diseases, such as disability-adjusted life years (DALYs). For 1999 alone, 8.44 million DALYs were directly attributed to wars (Ghobarah, Huth and Russett 2003). Moreover, during the same year an additional 8 million DALYs were lost as a result of wars that ended in the years 1991–97. In principle, one could use such estimates, along with their value in terms of prevailing wages and estimates for pain and suffering, to arrive at dollar estimates of the cost of disease.

Another effect of civil war is *population displacement*. The number of refugees around the world has barely fallen below 10 million for over two decades (United Nations High Commission for Refugees [UNHCR] 2007). By the end of 2006, the number of UNHCR "persons of concern" (which includes refugees, and Internally Displaced Persons [IDPs], and others) reached 32.9 million, whereas it hovered around 20 million for the preceding decade. The number of IDPs rose the most in 2006. Displaced persons and refugees are often unable to find work, and also need to be fed and housed. Thus, an accounting of the costs of population displacement should include both the cost of their care and at least a partial measure of the opportunity cost of the population.

Other costs and negative economic effects of civil war include: emigration of the educated and skilled members of the work force; mental illness and destruction of community life and social capital (see Collier et al. 2003, p. 21); the lingering effects of landmines (for example, Merrouche

2008); and chronic poverty (Justino 2006). It is difficult to estimate, monetize, compare and add many of the costs of civil wars. Blomberg and Hess (2006) employ an indirect method to measure the welfare costs of conflict (that include not just civil wars, although they represent the biggest source of conflict in their data set).[5] According to Blomberg and Hess's estimates, someone living in a country that experienced some conflict would permanently give up at least 8 percent of current consumption to live in a peaceful world; this figure is calculated as a lower bound of the true welfare cost of conflict. The variation across countries is very wide, with no high-income country having a high cost, whereas countries like Angola having costs of over 40 percent of annual consumption. The lower bound of the total world cost of conflict in 1985 dollars is estimated by Blomberg and Hess to be close to US$400 billion to be paid every year, with that payment growing at the rate of population growth.

Such numbers can be roughly compared to Collier et al.'s (2008) overall conservative estimate of the yearly costs of civil wars, which at over US$120 billion is about the same order of magnitude as the total annual development aid. Collier et al.'s (2008) average estimate is actually close to US$500 billion. Therefore, regardless of how one measures the costs of civil wars, at a minimum they exceed total development aid and they are likely much higher than that, especially if one were to attempt to include effects that are difficult to measure and monetize.

10.3   WAR VERSUS ARMED PEACE

Given that wars are so costly why do they occur in the first place? Is it irrationality or other non-economic factors that can only explain that? Even when long-term contracts on arming and peace are considered impossible, a series of short-term truces by adversaries who are armed could well be feasible and mutually desirable, yielding an outcome that Jack Hirshleifer has described (orally) as *Armed Peace*. The Cold War between the United States and the Soviet Union is an example of such an outcome. Warfare involves destruction, reduction of trade and other direct costs beyond those of arming, and its outcome is uncertain. Why not then agree on a settlement so that all sides avoid the direct costs and risks of war? Rationally, then, the case for compromise can be overwhelming.

In practice, when arms are taken up, avoiding civil war or ending it soon after often becomes difficult. To see why war occurs and continues despite its large direct costs, then, without invoking irrationality, hate, revenge or other preferential externalities, we briefly discuss two sets of explanations that have been explored in the economics and rational-choice literatures.[6]

10.3.1   Absence of Common Knowledge and Incomplete Information

To make detailed analysis possible in basic economic models of conflict, the adversaries are typically supposed to know the exact size of the contested surplus or the level of production, if there is one; the number of their adversaries and their preferences; the exact nature of the conflict that determines the disposition of the surplus; and in the case of negotiation and settlement they are supposed to share a norm about how to divide up the surplus. That is, they face what economists and game theorists refer to as complete information about all aspects of the game. Moreover, all this information is common knowledge, in the sense that everybody knows that everyone knows, that everyone knows and so on.

In reality, adversaries face incomplete information in, at least, one of the above dimensions. In addition, the requirement of common knowledge is rather stringent. They might have only a general estimate of the size of the surplus, the strengths and preferences of their adversaries, the nature of the contest, and they might have no shared norms, or at least they are not sure about them, in the event of negotiations. If the beliefs of the adversaries about any of these dimensions deviate significantly from one another, then it would be perfectly possible to have equilibria (in appropriately defined games) in which overt conflict is the outcome despite the presence of incentives to compromise. Bester and Warneryd (2006), for example, examine environments where there is war because at least one side rationally underestimates the strength of the other, and there is much other research that shows how suboptimal outcomes occur under incomplete information in many different contexts.

Many wars can at least partly be attributed to the presence of incomplete information. World War I, for instance, has been described to have occurred after a series of misunderstandings, miscalculations and even inattention to details by some leaders at a time that trade and other interdependencies among the future combatants made war unthinkable in the minds of opinion-makers on all sides (see Joll, 1992, pp. 10–41). If war could occur, then, between the great powers of Europe that had established channels of communication, regular diplomatic exchanges and norms of conduct that had been evolving for centuries, it would be far easier to take place between loosely organized groups that face a far less predictable environment, possibly without regular channels of communication and without established norms of conduct to guide many of their critical moves. Furthermore, as Chwe (2000) has argued attaining common knowledge itself is non-trivial, and again the anarchic environments in which civil wars emerge are not as conducive to the attainment of that condition.

10.3.2   Incomplete Contracting and Commitment Problems

We have already mentioned in the introduction how incomplete contracting on arming and peace is a succinct way of expressing (in economists' language) the similar idea of the difficulties entailed in making commitments without facing the temptation of reneging on them in the future. However, even if there are difficulties in making long-term commitments, it might well be possible to have a series of short-term series of truces under the threat of going to war. The adversaries would still arm, in order to maintain the credibility of the threat of fighting that also provides one with a stronger negotiating position in any short-term bargaining that might take place.

Under such conditions, on the one hand adversaries face a series of short-term truces ("armed peace") with the cost of arming in each period in order to maintain their bargaining position. On the other hand, they face the possibility of going to war, with certain chances of winning and losing; in the event of winning they enjoy the immediate benefits of victory minus the costs of destruction but they will also be in better strategic position in the future, having a greater resource and arming capability against their opponent. That is, by pursuing war now, one side could weaken its adversaries permanently or even possibly eliminate them and take control well into the future. Therefore, a party that values the future highly could indeed take the chance of war instead of pursuing negotiation and compromise, despite the short-term benefits of compromise, because the expected long-run profits could be higher if the opponents become permanently weakened or eliminated as they reduce or eliminate the future arming costs that are needed to maintain the credibility of armed peace. In environments in which those who win gain an advantage well into the future, both the intensity of conflict, as measured by the amount of resources devoted to it, increases (Powell 1993; Skaperdas and Syropoulos 1996) and the choice of overt conflict over negotiation becomes more common (Garfinkel and Skaperdas 2000; Powell 2006; McBride and Skaperdas 2007) as the future becomes more important.

For concreteness, consider the following simple example. Suppose there are two adversaries and they care about what happens today and about what happens in the future; that is, for simplicity, we can think of the game as having two periods. In each period there is an economic surplus of 100 units. Because of incomplete contracting on arming, each side has to devote 20 units of resources to guns in each period. Given the guns they have there are two options, war and compromise. If they were to compromise and have an armed peace, each side would receive half of the surplus for a net payoff of 30 units ($(1/2)100 - 20$). If they were to engage in war, each adversary would have half a chance of winning and half a chance of losing the entire surplus, which would however be reduced by 20 units as a result of the destruction that war would bring. The expected payoff of each side under war in a particular period would then be $(1/2)(100 - 20 - 20) + (1/2)(0 - 20) = 20$. Therefore, because war is destructive both sides would have the short-term incentive to compromise. War, however, has long-term effects on the relative power of the adversaries. For simplicity and starkness, suppose that if there were war today, the loser would be eliminated and the winner could enjoy whole the surplus by itself in the future and do that without having to incur the cost of arming in the future. The expected payoff from compromise under armed peace as of today – which would also imply compromise in the future – would be $30 + 30 = 60$. The expected payoff from war, again as of today, would be $20 + ((1/2)100 + (1/2)0) = 20 + 50 = 70$ Thus, war would be preferable to compromise by both adversaries since $70 > 60$.

This simple example assumes that arming under armed peace is the same as under war. It is possible, though, that the adversaries could make "partial" commitments using third parties, social and political institutions that are part of the country's history and traditions, or elements of the state that might have the independence and strength to partially guarantee peace agreements. Then, the adversaries would need less arming to sustain armed peace and as a result armed peace would become less costly and more likely to be chosen. We next discuss in more detail the factors that do influence the likelihood of peace and war, largely through this degree of commitment or incomplete contracting that the adversaries face.

10.4 COMMITMENT PROBLEMS AND SOURCES OF CIVIL WARS

Given that the interaction among sovereign states is characterized as "anarchic" and the contractual possibilities between states can be considered to be fewer than those within states, international wars could be expected to emerge more frequently than civil wars. That was true, however, before World War II, but has not been the case afterwards. A thicket of transnational institutions, from the UN to the World Trade Organization (WTO), the World Bank and the International Monetary Fund (IMF) and norms of "collective security" have channeled differences among states in the diplomatic and legal arena and less in the battlefield. The civil wars themselves have taken place within countries without what we call "modern states," by which we mean the richer states that typically have in place functioning institutions of conflict management and enforcement like constitutions, legislative processes, bureaucratic procedures, laws and courts. Such institutions tend to channel contests for power through politics and legal competition instead of through the barrel of a gun. Then, a combination of insufficient institutional development and changing circumstances and opportunities that create demands that cannot be accommodated peacefully create the mix that leads to warfare. But the first step towards civil war is the creation of a power vacuum, of anarchy, whereby for a combination of reasons the state effectively cedes control, and physical and contractual insecurity become rampant. Some of the factors that can contribute to increased contractual incompleteness and to civil wars can be correlated or act synergistically with one another and typically more than one of them is to be found in circumstances where war has broken out.

10.4.1   Ethnic and Religious Contention

Ethnic or religious differences, either real or imagined, can be used as a focal point for rallying support for one's cause and inciting violence against others. Ethnicity, even if we were to consider it a constructed attribute, can be used more easily than class (Esteban and Ray 2008) to rally support and create oppositional organizations. Through a threshold or "tipping" process described by Granovetter (1978), Kuran (1989) and others, small initial events can quickly lead to segregation and hostility between groups that were formerly living peacefully with one another. Precipitating events can include a small piece of legislation that can be seen as targeting an ethnic group or a particularly virulent speech by a politician who is in power. Although such small events could be thought of as epiphenomena of essentially doomed relationships, the separation of ethnicities in different states and even the delineation of ethnic identities in the first place are not cast in stone. Much historical contingency, it can be argued, plays a role on which ethnicities manage to get their own ethnic state, which ones peacefully become absorbed and integrated into another state or which ones receive formal status within a multi-ethnic or explicitly non-ethnic state.

Ethnic groups for which absorption within the dominant culture or integration within the state has been minimal often face distrust of state institutions by its members, thus marking the beginnings of a process that can easily lead to armed resistance. The distrust of the police implies that physical security depends on the social cohesion of the group and possibly, in urban settings, on more organized protection groups that could easily turn into mafias and later transform themselves into guerrilla groups. When members of the ethnic group might also stop using the courts, contractual insecurity becomes an additional problem which, in cases where the state was previously functioning reasonably well, can reduce economic activity and lead to the emergence of parallel, more informal, less predictable and less efficient institutions.

In terms of econometric evidence, a well-known exploration of the effect of ethnicity on *economic growth* is Easterly and Levine (1997), who constructed a dataset of ethnic fractionalization based on the likelihood that two people drawn at random in a country are of the same ethnicity for countries around the world. They found that "ethnic diversity is closely associated with low schooling, underdeveloped financial systems, distorted foreign exchange markets, and insufficient infrastructure" (1997, p. 1241). They do not discuss the effect of ethnic distance on conflict in much detail, though they do note that there is a strong correlation with the incidence of genocide. Easterly (2000) discussed the impact on war deaths and finds that "ethnic fractionalization increases the likelihood of war casualties. However . . . good institutions are effective in mitigating this threat" (2000, p. 699).

10.4.2   Geography

Geographic distance, jungle for cover and mountainous terrain can all make conflict easier for certain groups to become organized and seek shelter. This has become a very popular variable in most regressions on conflict and, as far as we know, was first discussed in that type of literature by Fearon and Laitin (1999).

States, contrary to the common Weberian definition, can never literally have the absolute monopoly in the use of force within their territories. A power vacuum often exists in distant areas that become the breeding ground initially for brigandage and later for rebellions and independence movements. The Congolese jungle in which large movements of troops and material can effectively go only slowly up the Congo river is one recent example of geographic distance contributing to political fragmentation and civil war. On the other extreme is Rwanda, which has also experienced a civil war of the most violent type – a genocide – but that was rather brief and it also happens to have probably the strongest state in sub-Saharan Africa.[7] The Amazon jungle as well has been a vast area over which the governments of Brazil, Colombia, Equador and Peru have had tenuous control over their respective areas. The vacuum is often filled by guerrillas and the private armies of landlords and drug traffickers who fight amongst themselves and against the police and the militaries of their governments. When the fighting takes a more overt political character, as it did at the time of the Shining Path's insurrection in Peru, and a greater number of military forces are involved, as it has been the case intermittently in Colombia, the conflict can be characterized as a civil war. But the difference from the less organized, more atomized, anarchy that exists otherwise in such areas is often not large.

Mountainous terrain also contributes to distance from state control. The Caucasus is a well-known example. The Russian czars were finally able to control Chechnya in the nineteenth century only after many decades of attempts and only after they systematically cut down the dense beech forest in which the Chechen guerrillas were able to hide (Lieven 1999, p. 310). And, of course, more than a century afterwards and still without the forest, the current Russian government does not have complete control over Chechnya. Similarly, the mountains both gave refuge to the resistance movements and facilitated the beginnings of civil wars in Greece and Yugoslavia during World War II.

10.4.3   Economic Shocks and Social Change

For the first half of the nineteenth century, slavery and other contentious issues between the North and the South in the United States were kept in the background through the agreement that no free state would be admitted to the union without a slave state also being admitted. The arrangement gave veto power to Southern States in the Senate and ensured that no legislation that was vital to the South's interests would pass (see Weingast 1998). The North in the meantime had much faster population growth and an industrializing economy, whereas the expansion of slavery to the West was economically unprofitable. These were changes that made the political agreement between the South and the North nonviable, leading not to a revised agreement but to Civil War.

Economic change brings social change, and the changing economy and society precipitate demands for political change as well. New markets need new institutions to govern them and perhaps more importantly a changing social landscape often involves new groups and social classes demanding representation and political accommodation. As has been argued by Acemoglu and Robinson (2000), the extension of the democratic franchise in Britain and other Western European countries can be considered to be a response to the potential for social conflict, which in turn was a result of the rapidly changing economic and social landscape brought about by the second, capital-goods based, phase of the industrial revolution.

Outside Britain this process, however, was not achieved easily at all. In addition to the two world wars of the twentieth century, there was much internal turmoil in all of Europe. Russia, of course, experienced revolution and civil war. And, during the interwar years in all of continental Europe democratic institutions were under siege (see the graphic account of the time in Mazower 1998, Chapter 2). In Spain, which along with Russia had more ossified state institutions than Northwest Europe, no compromise was found and civil war ensued after its brief experiment with democracy (for a comparison of civil wars in Southern Europe, see Minehan 2006). In others, rapidly changing governments, parliamentary fights, street protests and economic depression led to dictatorial governance in most countries on the eve of World War II.

There have been some recent econometric studies providing evidence of how changes in market conditions, economic shocks and replacement of institutions can lead to conflict. This idea has been explored by Djankov and Reynal-Querol (2007), who use the colonial origins dataset of Acemoglu, Johnson and Robinson (2001) to argue that poor institutions lead to civil conflict. Besley and Persson (2008) have also explored the likelihood of conflict arising due to price shocks from other countries and find that an increase in the international price of commodities can lead to increased incidence of conflict. Likewise, Dube and Vargas (2008) examined the effect of shocks to prices in Colombia and find that a decrease in coffee prices and an increase in oil price increased the incidence of conflict. Economic shocks could induce conflict by changing the relative costs between conflict and peaceful production. Perhaps the leading paper methodologically is from Miguel et al. (2004), who use rainfall as an instrumental variable for shocks to the economy. This is possibly the best causal understanding of the causes of civil wars, though it comes with its own problems.

10.4.4 The Role of Outsiders: Geopolitics, Natural Resources, and Other Rents

During the Cold War, the United States and the Soviet Union were seeking to expand their respective spheres of influence around the world by propping up friendly governments and undermining unfriendly ones. From Nicaragua and El Salvador to Angola, Mozambique or Vietnam, the two great powers were at least indirectly involved in civil wars. Sometimes, as in the cases of Vietnam and Afghanistan, the internal conflicts expanded to become international wars, even though the two great powers never directly faced one another in these wars.

The Cold War was not a historically unique period for the effect it had in the rest of the world. Before World War I, competition among the great powers of the time was associated with large areas of unstable governance. For example, at the turn of the nineteenth century, the area from today's Pakistan, to Afghanistan, Iran, the Ottoman Empire all the way to the border of Austria–Hungary was the buffer zone between the British and Russian Empires and subject to numerous interventions from both of these Empires in what came to be called as the "Great Game." Regardless of the problems that governments in these areas might have had without any outside influence, great power rivalry could hardly have made their condition better. Official pronouncements, of course, were phrased as if the actions of the great powers were in the interests of the locals, but it would be hard to imagine that such actions could be induced by anything other than the perceived interest of these powers.

The effect of great power competition can be thought to come from a mixture of long-term strategic state interests ("geopolitics") and of more direct material interests, possibly involving natural resources, lucrative contracts and other rents. Similar motives can exist for intervention in other countries not just on the part of great global powers but also by regional powers or even by any neighbor with the capacity of intervene. The ongoing civil war in the Democratic Republic of the Congo, a country with the aforementioned problem of geography, has involved the direct military intervention of countries like Rwanda, Uganda and Angola and the indirect interventions of others from Libya in the north all the way to South Africa. The same mixture of perceived long-term strategic interests and the opportunity to exploit Congo's mineral wealth have been factors in the intervention of different countries in varying degrees (Prunier 2009).

In more recent years non-state foreign actors have started to become more important in influencing civil wars: non-governmental organizations (NGOs) with varied agendas, multinational corporations, private security firms (Singer 2003), international organizations and even the international press as it affects through TV images and other ways how the amorphous "international community" perceives developments in far-off places. While some of the interests and objectives of such actors are shaped by the interaction of states, or can even be proxies of states, they still exert some independent influence, sometimes in unpredictable ways. For example (see Prunier 2009), after the genocide in Rwanda the former government (that perpetrated the genocide) essentially compelled more than two million Rwandan Hutus to join them in refugee camps in the Eastern Congo. The TV images of suffering refugees, who were confounded with the victims of genocide by the international public, filled the coffers of many NGOs to the brim with donations. The NGOs spent large amounts on the refugee camps while allowing the perpetrators of genocide, who were controlling the camps, to skim off a considerable percentage of the expenditures. At the same time, foreign aid to the victims of genocide inside Rwanda was minimal, though urgent. Thus, many of the NGOs with ostensibly human-itarian objectives were in effect supporting the regrouping of the perpetra-tors of genocide in the Congo.[8] In turn, that presence induced the new government of Rwanda to support the overthrow of Mobutu Sese Seko, precipitating the war that has been continual since then in the Congo.

On the positive side, outsiders can be a source of good as well, and that is what tends to be the dominant media view of international intervention. Rich countries and international organizations provide financial, technical and administrative assistance that in many instances could reduce the chance of civil war. In the end, it would be very difficult, if not impossible, to empirically assess whether the presence of the outside world has made civil war more or less likely in specific countries. After all, today's world cannot be globalized just economically. The greater flow of goods, services and credit across countries implies the need for governing those transactions, of having "property rights" defined at the transnational level. Inevitably then, politics has to become more globalized and the effect of the rest of the world on individual countries – especially the smaller, poorer, and less institutionally developed ones – has to be large with an accompanying risk of civil war.

10.5 CONCLUDING REMARKS

There are very high costs associated with civil wars and therefore these wars are of high significance to the economy. While traditional economics has ignored the study of wars, we can understand why wars occur by simply invoking the "dark side" of self-interest, as human beings can make a living not by producing and trading but by appropriating the production of others. We have demonstrated why wars can occur in such settings and what the risk factors are that may lead to war.

Civil wars have not been common just during the modern era. History is full of examples of time periods during which civil wars have been endemic, from the warring states in Ancient China to the internal conflicts of late-medieval Italian city states, the English civil wars during the seventeenth century and the Spanish civil war and other internal conflicts in much of Europe during the interwar period. Civil wars and other violent internal conflicts can go on intermittently for decades – essentially between political entities that have state-like properties – or be resolved through a centralization of power by the state until the next crisis, perhaps after centuries of relative stability, until a new cycle of violence may appear. Given their high economic significance and the fact that they can be analysed used basic tools of economics, it is surprising that so little research had been conducted on the topic up to relatively recently. There is still much to be done, especially about the mechanisms through which wars affect the economy and the feedbacks from the economy to the likelihood of peace and war.

We have discussed a number of the reasons for this conflict arising and have presented both the theoretical and empirical evidence behind these causes. Empirical work on this question is though plagued by a number of statistical problems, most importantly being able to identify the *causes* of conflict rather than simply correlations. Overcoming this identification problem will likely remain an area of fruitful research for the foreseeable future.

NOTES

1. For overviews of the empirical evidence on civil wars, see Collier et. al. (2003) Fearon and Laitin (2003) and Blattman and Miguel (2009). This last reference is the most comprehensive and up-to-date overview of civil wars and the interested reader would profit from reading it as a complement to this chapter which is more focused on problems of commitment as a cause of civil wars and on the industrial organization of civil war combatants. For an overview of the literature that estimates the economic costs of civil wars as well as other forms of organized violence, see Skaperdas (2009).
2. The International Rescue Committee estimates the considerably higher number of 5.4 million people having died from war-related causes in the Democratic Republic of the Congo. (See http://www.theirc.org/special-report/congo-forgotten-crisis.html)
3. The earlier literature includes Hirshleifer (1988, 1995), Garfinkel (1990), Grossman (1992), Skaperdas (1992) and Neary (1997). For an overview of the theoretical literature, see Garfinkel and Skaperdas (2007).
4. Sections 10.2 and 10.3 partly draw on Skaperdas (2008).
5. Blomberg and Hess adapt a model of Lucas (1987) that was meant to measure the costs of business cycles and use it to estimate the impact of conflict, regarded as a "shock," to consumption and welfare. They then compare the expected welfare of each country's actual path of consumption – that may include conflict – to another counterfactual path of consumption where there is no state of war.
6. We do not dispute that psychological factors like hate, revenge or irrationality might not play a role in instigating and propagating war, but we do not discuss them here both because these effects have not been studied much by economists with respect to war and because some of the resulting effects appear to be qualitatively similar to those of incomplete information and lack of common knowledge.
7. The connection between Rwanda's geography and its strong state has been discussed by Prunier (1997, 2009) and others.
8. Some of the NGOs, like "Doctors without Borders," that saw the effect of this policy decided to leave the refugee camps in the Eastern Congo.

REFERENCES

Acemoglu, D., S. Johnson, J. Robinson (2001), "The colonial origins of comparative development: an empirical investigation", *American Economic Review*, **91** (5), 1369–401.
Acemoglu, D. and J. Robinson (2000), "Why did the West extend the franchise? Democracy, inequality and growth in historical perspective", *Quarterly Journal of Economics*, **115**, 1167–99.
Bester, H. and K. Warneryd (2006), "Conflict and the social contract", *Scandinavian Journal of Economics*, **108** (2), 231–49.

Besley, T. and T. Persson (2008), "The incidence of civil war: theory and evidence", NBER Working Papers 14585, National Bureau of Economic Research, Inc.

Bilmes, L. and J. Stiglitz (2008), *The Three Trillion Dollar War: The True Cost of the Iraq Conflict*. New York, NY: W.W. Norton.

Blattman, C. and E. Miguel (2009), "Civil war", NBER Working Paper No. w14801.

Blomberg, S.B. and G.D Hess (2006), "How much does violence tax trade?", *The Review of Economics and Statistics*, **88** (4), 599–612.

Blomberg, S.B., G. Hess and A. Weerapana (2004), "An economic model of terrorism", *Conflict Management and Peace Science*, **21** (1), 17–28.

Cerra, V. and S.C. Saxena (2008), "The monetary model strikes back: evidence from the world", IMF Working Papers 08/73, International Monetary Fund.

Chwe, M. (2000), "Communication and coordination in social networks", *Review of Economic Studies*, **67**, 1–16.

Collier, P., V.L. Elliott, H. Hegre, A. Hoeffler, M. Reynal-Querol and N. Sambanis (2003), "Breaking the conflict trap; civil war and development policy", World Bank Policy Report, Washington DC: World Bank and Oxford University Press.

Collier, P., L. Chauvet and H. Hegre (2008), "The security challenge in conflict-prone countries", Prepared for Copenhagen Consensus 2008 Challenge Conference, April 2008.

Djankov, S. and M. Reynal-Querol (2007), "The colonial origins of civil war", Working Paper, available at: http://ssrn.com/abstract=1003337.

Dube, O. and J.F. Vargas (2006), "Resource curse in reverse: the coffee crisis and armed conflict in Colombia", Royal Holloway, University of London: Discussion Papers in Economics 06/05, Department of Economics, Royal Holloway University of London, revised Dec 2006.

Easterly, W. (2000), "Can institutions resolve ethnic conflict?", *Economic Development and Cultural Change*, **49** (4), 687–706.

Easterly, W. and R. Levine (1997), "Africa's growth tragedy: policies and ethnic Divisions", *Quarterly Journal of Economics*, **CXII** (4), 1203–50.

Esteban, J.M. and D. Ray (2008), "On the salience of ethnic conflict", *American Economic Review*, **98** (5), 2185–202.

Fearon, J.D. (1995), "Rationalist explanations for war", *International Organization*, **49** (3), 379–414.

Fearon, J. and D. Laitin (1999), "Weak states, rough terrain, and large-scale ethnic violence since 1945", Annual Meeting of the American Political Science Association, 2–5 September 1999.

Fearon, J.D. and D.D. Laitin (2003), "Ethnicity, insurgency, and civil war", *American Political Science Review*, **97** (1), 75–90.

Fitzgerald, V. and A. Grigsby (2001), "Nicaragua: the political economy of social reform and armed conflict", in Frances Stewart and Valpy Fitzgerald (eds), *War and Underdevelopment, Volume 2: Country Experiences*, New York, NY: Oxford University Press, pp. 119–54.

Garfinkel, M.R. (1990), "Arming as a strategic investment in a cooperative equilibrium", *American Economic Review*, **80** (1), 50–68.

Garfinkel, M.R. and S. Skaperdas (2000), "Conflict without misperceptions or incomplete information: how the future matters", *Journal of Conflict Resolution*, **44** (6), 792–806.

Garfinkel, M.R. and S. Skaperdas (2007), "Economics of conflict: an overview", in T. Sandler and K. Hartley (eds), *Handbook of Defence Economics*, Vol. II, New York, NY: Elsevier, pp. 649–709.

Ghobarah, H., P. Huth and B. Russett (2003), "Civil wars kill and maim people – long after the shooting stops", *American Political Science Review*, **97**, 189–202.

Granovetter, M. (1978), "Threshold models of collective behavior", *American Journal of Sociology*, **83** (6), 1420–43.

Grossman, H.I. (1992), "A general equilibrium model of insurrections", *American Economic Review*, **81**, 912–21.

Hart, O. (1995), *Firms, Contracts, and Financial Structure*, New York, NY: Oxford University Press.

Hirshleifer, J. (1988), "The analytics of continuing conflict", *Synthese*, **76**, 201–33.
Hirshleifer, J. (1995), "Anarchy and its breakdown", *Journal of Political Economy*, **103**, 26–52.
Joll, James (1992), *The Origins of the First World War*, 2nd edn, New York, NY: Longman.
Justino, P. (2006), "On the links between violent conflict and chronic poverty: how much do we really know?", HiCN Working Papers 18, Households in Conflict Network.
Kuran, T. (1989), "Sparks and prairie fires: a theory of unanticipated political revolution", *Public Choice*, **61**, 41–74.
Lieven, A. (1999), *Chechnya: The Tombstone of Russian Power*. New Haven and London: Yale University Press.
Mazower, M. (1998), *Dark Continent: Europe's Twentieth Century*, New York, NY: Vintage Books.
McBride, M. and Skaperdas, S. (2007), "Explaining conflict in low-income countries: incomplete contracting in the shadow of the future", in M. Gradstein and K.A. Konrad (eds), *Institutions and Norms in Economic Development*, Cambridge, MA: MIT Press, pp. 141–61.
Merrouche, O. (2008), "Landmines and poverty IV: evidence from Mozambique", *Peace Economics, Peace Science and Public Policy*, **14** (1), Article 2.
Miguel, E., S. Satyanath and E. Sergenti (2004), "Economic shocks and civil conflict: an instrumental variables approach", *Journal of Political Economy*, **112** (4), 725–53.
Miguel, E. and G. Roland (2006), "The long run impact of bombing Vietnam", NBER Working Papers 11954, National Bureau of Economic Research, Inc.
Minehan, P.B. (2006), *Civil War and World War in Europe: Spain, Yugoslavia, and Greece, 1936–1949*. New York, NY: Palgrave Macmillan.
Neary, H. (1997), "Equilibrium structure in an economic model of conflict", *Economic Inquiry*, **35**, 480–94.
Powell, R. (1993), "Guns, butter, and anarchy", *The American Political Science Review*, **87** (1), 115–32.
Powell, R. (2006), "War as a commitment problem", *International Organization*, **60**, 169–203.
Prunier, G. (2009), *Africa's World War: Congo, the Rwandan Genocide, and the Making of a Continental Catastrophe*. New York, NY: Oxford University Press.
Singer, P.W. (2003), *Corporate Warriors: The Rise of the Privatized Military Industry*. London: Cornell University Press.
Skaperdas, S. (1992), "Cooperation, conflict, and power in the absence of property rights", *American Economic Review*, **82**, 720–39.
Skaperdas, S. (2008), "An economic approach to analysing civil wars", *Economics of Governance*, **9** (1), 25–44.
Skaperdas, S. (2009), "The costs of organized violence: a review of the evidence", Working Papers 080924, University of California-Irvine, Department of Economics.
Skaperdas, S. and C. Syropoulos (1996), "Can the shadow of the future harm cooperation?", *Journal of Economic Behavior and Organization*, **29**, 355–72.
Stewart, F. and V. Fitzgerald (2001), *War and Underdevelopment*, New York, NY: Oxford University Press.
Stewart, F., C. Huang and M. Wang (2001), "Internal wars in developing countries: an empirical overview of economic and social consequences", in. F. Stewart and V. Fitzgerald (eds), *War and Underdevelopment, Volume 2: Country Experiences*, New York, NY: Oxford University Press, pp. 67–103.
United Nations High Commission for Refugees (UNHCR) (2007), "2006 Global trends: refugees, asylum seekers, returnees, internally displaced persons, and stateless persons", Geneva: United Nations High Commission for Refugees, available at http://www.unhcr.org/statistics/STATISTICS/4676a71d4.pdf.
Weingast, B. (1998), "Political stability and civil war: institutions, commitment, and American Democracy", in R. Bates, A. Greif, M. Levi, J.-L. Resenthal, and B.R. Weingast (eds), *Analytic Narratives*. Princeton, NJ: Princeton University Press, pp. 148–93.

11 Political economy of Third World revolutions
Misagh Parsa

11.1 INTRODUCTION

Social theorists define revolutions in two alternative ways. Some analysts provide a political definition of revolution characterized by the forcible transfer of state power. Charles Tilly (2006, p. 159) defines revolution as forcible transfer of power in the course of a struggle involving at least two distinct blocs of contenders that make incompatible claims to control the state with some significant segments of the population supporting the claims of the rival contenders. Other theorists define revolutions in terms of broader economic and political outcomes. Theda Skocpol (Skocpol 1979, p. 4) is interested in social revolutions, that is, alterations in both the political and economic structures of society. Skocpol's definition requires a rapid, basic transformation of state and class structures that are carried out in part through class-based revolts from below. Jeffery Paige even went further and defined revolution as "a rapid and fundamental transformation in the categories of social life and consciousness, the metaphysical assumptions on which these categories are based, and the power relations in which they are expressed as a result of widespread popular acceptance of a utopian alternative to the current social order" (Paige 2003, p. 24). Though rare phenomena, social revolutions have produced the most fundamental changes in the modern world and social life.

Although several generations of social scientists have attempted to explain the causes, processes and outcomes of revolutions (Goldstone 1980), no general theoretical consensus has emerged. In a recent work, Charles Tilly argued that it was not possible to specify the necessary and sufficient conditions for revolutions. He noted, "regimes vary and change historically. As a result, so do the conditions for violent seizure of state power. No natural history of all revolutions, specifying necessary or sufficient conditions that are not true by definition, is possible" (Tilly 2006, p. 159). Tilly's pessimism has not prevented scholars of revolution to continue studying the causes, processes, and outcomes of revolutions. Fortunately, structural models of revolution have greatly advanced our understanding of revolutions in developing countries. Several influential works, focusing on variables such as the nature of the state, economy, classes and international conditions, have gone a long way toward explaining social revolutions (Moore 1966; Paige 1975; Skocpol 1979; Goldstone 1991). Analyses of state vulnerabilities, internally and externally within the world system, their internal structures and relations to economy and society have proved very fruitful in studying large-scale social conflicts and revolutions. Yet, despite great advances, structural models by themselves cannot explain the complexity of social revolutions in developing countries. Although structural conditions set the stage for conflicts, they do not determine the revolutionary process or outcome. Thus, if a structural analysis of revolutionary conflicts and their outcome is to be comprehensive, it must rely on additional variables.

Karl Marx has greatly influenced theories of revolutions and understanding of social revolutions. Marx's focus on social classes certainly deepened scientific analysis of revolutionary conflicts, processes, and outcomes. But, Marx's central claim on the role of class conflict is insufficient to account for social revolutions. Marx's theory of revolution focused primarily on social classes and assumed that class conflict in the economic sphere would inevitably find expression in the political sphere. The central argument of Marx's analysis was that class exploitation in the context of economic crisis would result in rebellion and revolution (Boswell and Dixon 1990). Although some degree of class antagonism characterizes most revolutions, class conflict by itself does not produce social revolution in contemporary developing countries. In fact, intense class conflict may actually reduce the likelihood of revolutions because in the absence of state breakdowns class coalitions have been crucial for the overthrow of the state. The present work will demonstrate that, contrary to Marx's theory, a high level of working class militancy and an ideological shift against the capitalist class and system may actually impede the formation of broad coalitions, which are necessary for revolutions. Because revolutions in the twentieth century have occurred only where major social classes succeeded in consolidating and forming broad coalitions, any theory of revolution must also focus on the state, its nature and its vulnerability to revolutionary conflicts (Goldfrank 1979, p. 141; Skocpol 1979; Goldstone 1980, 1986; Rueschmeyer and Evans 1985; Parsa 1985, 1989).

Skocpol's influential work (1979) makes an important contribution and shifts the focus of analysis back to the state and allows for its potential autonomy. She maintains that social-revolutionary conflicts involve a struggle over the forms of state structures (Skocpol 1979, p. 29). According to Skocpol, military pressures and defeat in wars may undermine the state's coercive apparatus and lead to revolution. In agrarian bureaucracies, external pressures combined with state efforts to promote industrial development may generate schisms between the state and the dominant class, with each sector competing to extract greater resources from the peasantry. In such conflicting situations, dominant classes may be able to block state policies and frustrate government attempts at economic transformation. Such conflicts between the state and the dominant class may result in state breakdown paving the way for revolutionary upheavals. Peasants may be able to revolt and bring about a revolution if they have communal solidarity and strength.

But Skocpol's formulation is somewhat problematic because it relies heavily on the relationship between the dominant class and the state. It locates the center of the conflicts around the dominant class and the state. It is true that, as the present work will show, the capitalist class often joins the insurgency primarily to change the power structure. But, as Skocpol has argued, revolutionary struggles always involve multiple conflicts and multiple actors with diverse interests and cannot be reduced to merely one set of conflicts. Furthermore, many states in developing countries do not rule in alliance with the upper classes. Thus, the simple withdrawal of support by the capitalist class from the state may increase state vulnerability but may not result in revolutions. In addition, despite autonomy, many governments in developing countries in the latter part of the twentieth century pursued economic strategies that served the economic interests of large capital and landlords. Although serving the interests of at least segments of large capital, state policies could not prevent revolutions in many developing countries.

Skocpol's analysis also suffers from the fact that her formulation does not sufficiently analyse the role of other classes and actors. Working class insurgency may threaten the capitalist class and prevent the capitalists from opposing the state even in the face of rising conflicts between the dominant class and power-holders. Thus, capitalists' defection from the state and their mobilization against the government may be affected by the intensity of class conflict and threats posed by other classes. Labor radicalism, particularly in the presence of powerful, revolutionary challengers, may prevent capitalists or dominant classes from attacking the state and generating a revolutionary outcome. In the Philippines, labor militancy and ideological shift to the left along with rising class conflict threatened the capitalists and landlords and prevented class coalition against Marcos after the assassination of Benigno Aquino (Parsa 2000, p. 232).

Finally, Skocpol's structural model suffered from a lack of an analysis on the role of ideology in revolutions. Skocpol's original formulation claimed that revolutionary movements rarely begin with revolutionary intentions. Surprised by the outcome of the Iranian revolution, Skocpol revised her model and presented an analysis of the role ideas play in revolutions. In a new formulation, she argued that ideas played an important role. In fact, she assigned sweeping powers to ideology. She asserted that Shi'a Islam justified resistance against unjust authority and legitimized religious leaders as competitors to the state. Specifically, Husayn's myth of martyrdom inspired devout Iranians to oppose the Shah in the face of repression and death (Skocpol 1982, p. 275). Skocpol claimed that the Iranian willingness to face the army repeatedly eventually resulted in disobedience among the military rank and file that hesitated shooting into the crowds.

Skocpol's ideological explanation ignores the complexity of the revolutionary processes. Like many other ideologically driven explanations, Skocpol's reasoning has a tautological character. She begins with the outcome of the revolution, victory of a segment of the Shi'a clergy and their fundamentalist ideology, and uses it as part of the explanation of the revolution. Skocpol uses a number of religious principles to explain the revolution. But, the myth of Hussayn's martyrdom and the significance of the clergy represent constant features of Shi'a Iran. As such, they should have produced a revolution in 1963 when Ayatollah Khomeini opposed the Shah's reforms and, in fact, called for his removal, particularly at a time when Iranians were more religious and traditional. Furthermore, if the number of deaths determine the likelihood of revolution, Iran should have had another revolution after 1981, when Ayatollah Khomeini's regime killed at least 15000 people, considerably more than the Shah's 3000 (it is noteworthy that in 1979 Somoza's National Guard killed about 50000 people in Nicaragua, a country that constituted 10 percent of Iran's population). It is also important to note that Skocpol's emphasis on the Shi'ite culture of martyrdom is vastly exaggerated. During the revolutionary struggles, the clergy and Iranian people consistently condemned the killings of the civilians; they did not call for martyrdom. Finally, Skocpol's ideologically driven analysis cannot explain the complexities of the revolutionary struggles, as various collectivities entered the revolutionary struggles at different times and presented diverse claims and demands. The majority of those involved in the Iranian struggles did not volunteer to give their lives, but expected to improve their lives. Their deaths were the result of political repression not desire for martyrdom. In fact, they mobilized through the mosque because of the relative safety and security it provided for mobilization.

More recently, John Foran (2005) developed another theory of social revolution in Third World countries. His model focused on the role of a large number of variables including dependent capitalist development, exclusionary states, culture of opposition, economic downturn and world systemic opening in producing revolutionary outbreaks. He maintained that dependent development generated social and economic grievances, such as high inflation and growing inequality, among diverse sectors of the population. Where dependent development was combined with exclusionary and personalist political systems, it provided the necessary conditions for revolutions (Foran 2005, pp. 18–20). For revolutions to take place, however, Foran argued such structural conditions had to be accompanied with an active human agency. To overcome the weaknesses of some structural models, Foran incorporated an analysis of political cultures of opposition and resistance into his model of social revolution. He asserted that the notion of "political cultures of opposition and resistance" was responsible for converting the grievances generated by structures into a revolution. Significantly, Foran insisted on the irreducible role of human agency and meaning in the making or not making revolutions (Foran 2005, p. 22). Combined with a domestic economic downturn and a world systemic opening, these variables produced revolutionary outbreaks.

Foran's model of social revolution raises interesting questions that need to be addressed. He is right in pointing out that rising inequalities and recurrent economic downturns and exclusionary political systems are important aspects of development in many Third World countries. These conditions certainly generate a great deal of conflicts. The causal arrows in his model (2005, p. 18) seem to suggest that dependent capitalist development and exclusionary states lead to the formation of political cultures of opposition. Yet, he also insists on the irreducible role of human agency and culture (2005, p. 22). To prove his case, Foran should provide evidence and cases in which dependent capitalism and exclusionary states did not produce conflict and political opposition, and thus did not experience "revolutionary outbreak." On the other hand, Foran's concept of the "culture of opposition and resistance" seems to have a tautological tone. He seems to claim that if aggrieved populations in a country have a culture of opposition and resistance, then, they may succeed in launching resistance and revolution. In this formulation, Foran appears to claim that the presence of a culture of opposition and resistance predicts its recurrence. This appears to be circular reasoning: what else one should expect from a culture of opposition and resistance. And, by definition, revolutions would have to be carried through popular mobilization, collective action and resistance. Furthermore, it is not clear why Foran places greater significance on the pre-existing cultures, underestimating the capacity of the current contenders in producing their own culture of opposition and repertoire of resistance. This is particularly interesting given the rapid rise and spread of modern social movement due to the availability of communication networks and international support for social justice and democracy.

Finally, it is not clear in Foran's model why the mere presence of cultures of opposition and resistance, combined with an economic downturn and world systemic opening should lead to a revolution. By itself, the concept of cultures of political opposition does not imply revolutionary ideology. Generally speaking, conflicts that result in revolutionary outcomes do not begin with revolutionary intentions. An analysis of revolutions in various countries reveals that ordinary people do not join protests with the goal of overthrowing a government. With the exception of students and intellectuals, most protestors mobilize and engage in collective action to condemn violations of established rights and interests, and demand redress of grievances. Foran's model does not explain the mechanism by which protestors shift their claims from concrete demands within the existing system to supporting alternative political systems or social revolutions.

I do not mean to discount the role of ideas and ideologies in revolutions. Clearly, theories of revolutions should take into account the role of ideology. In fact, in developing countries in the twentieth century, ideologically driven intellectuals and students stood at the forefront of revolutionary struggles. Thus, it is important to analyse the role of the ideologically driven revolutionaries in large-scale social conflicts and understand the conditions where they manage to seize power and transform the social structure. But, an appropriate analysis of the role of ideology has to place the emphasis elsewhere.

11.2   AN ALTERNATIVE THEORETICAL MODEL FOR REVOLUTIONARY SITUATIONS

Although Charles Tilly warned against developing general theories of revolutions, I will attempt to specify some of the conditions that produce revolutionary situations in developing countries. Following Tilly, I define a revolutionary situation in terms of the appearance of revolutionary challengers who claim exclusive state power and receive backing by a sizeable portion of the population that render the existing regime unwilling or incapable to repress them. In the following, I will present an alternative model for explaining the rise of revolutionary situations in developing countries. The model focuses on the nature of the state and its relationship to the economy, and the rise of broad coalitions that can disrupt the social structure, heightening the likelihood of the overthrow of the state. Finally, I will examine the role of ideology and ideologically driven challengers in social revolutions.

11.3 STATE INTERVENTION AND TARGET OF SOCIAL CONFLICTS

The relationship between the state and economy has crucial consequences for social conflicts. Although virtually ignored by structural theorists of revolution, state intervention in capital allocation and accumulation has profound consequences for social conflicts. Basically, state intervention in capital accumulation converts the government into a major economic actor and thus affects the nature of social conflicts by providing a visible, concrete target for challenge and attack. State intervention has an impact on social and political conflicts by affecting the interests of various social classes and collectivities, and thus setting the stage for conflicts. Furthermore, the level of state intervention affects the nature and likelihood of class conflict. These variables in turn affect the outcome of social conflicts.

The degree of state intervention in the economy can be analysed by means of a simple typology categorizing the level of government involvement in the process of capital accumulation. Based on such criteria, three types of states can be distinguished: regulative states, administrative states and hyperactive states.[1] Regulative states intervene minimally in the economy, limiting their activities to enforcing rules and assuring "efficient" operation of the market, often through fiscal and monetary policies. Administrative states intervene moderately in economic matters. In addition to regulative activities, they initiate planning, pursue corporatist policies, and may provide economic incentives to certain sectors. Hyperactive states intervene extensively in capital allocation and accumulation, thus limiting the scope of the market's operation. In addition to extensive regulating and planning, hyperactive states often own and control vast economic resources and, consequently, become major economic actors.

In general, social conflicts may lead to revolution only when contending collectivities and classes view the state as responsible for the conflicts and target the state to effect change. Although many factors contribute to struggle over state power, certain state structures seem to be more vulnerable to social conflicts than others. The level of state intervention affects the nature and outcome of social conflicts. In general, a low level of state intervention in capital accumulation, as exists in regulative states, reduces the probability that the state will become the direct target of collective action and thus, in turn, diminishes the likelihood of revolutionary conflicts. In this case, capital allocation and accumulation are determined by an abstract, decentralized, depoliticized and "self-regulating" market system, which tends to defuse and privatize conflicts, confining them to the civil society. Because it is abstract, decentralized and depoliticized, the market cannot be attacked or overthrown. As a result, the regulative state is unlikely to attract direct attacks or challenges because class conflict remains confined within the economic sphere and the civil society. Should such conflicts escalate, aggrieved groups may clamor for the state to intervene on their behalf against their adversaries. Because aggrieved groups solicit help from the state, rather than attacking it, they are far more likely to be reformist than revolutionary. Furthermore, when state intervention is low, the regulative state tends to be perceived as an autonomous entity that serves general, societal interests. In such cases, the state may become an integrative, rather than a divisive force. Finally, a low level of state intervention in capital accumulation may increase the likelihood and intensity of class conflict. Intensification of class conflict, in turn, removes the state from being the principal target of attack and thus reduces the likelihood of revolution.

In contrast, states that intervene to a great extent in the economy render themselves more vulnerable to challenge and attack. Hyperactive states tend to become major economic actors, control a great deal of economic resources and intervene extensively in capital allocation and accumulation. As loci of accumulation, hyperactive states may become direct producers and financiers. In extreme cases, a hyperactive state may even become the single largest entrepreneur, industrialist, banker and landowner in its domain. These states also tend to institute regulative mechanisms, which intervene extensively in multitudinous aspects of the economy in order to promote economic development.

High levels of intervention entail significant political consequences for interventionist states. High state intervention replaces the abstract, decentralized and depoliticized market mechanism with a visible, concrete, social entity, which can be targeted for attack during conflict or crisis (Parsa 1985, 1989; Rueschemeyer and Evans 1985, p. 69). High state intervention expands the extent of political conflicts because of the convergence of economic and political conflicts in the political arena. In addition to ordinary political conflicts, states also become the center for economic conflicts. Thus, at times of economic crisis, the state, rather than market forces will be held accountable for failure and mismanagement, once again making the government vulnerable to challenge and attack. Furthermore, hyperactive states in developing countries often pursue development strategies that serve narrow and particular, rather than general societal, interests. Such strategies are often accompanied by rapid accumulation of resources in some sectors in contrast to others, thus widening social, economic and regional inequalities. State power in such conditions becomes visibly and directly linked to privilege and disprivilege and inevitably politicizes the development process. If inequalities and disadvantages were generated by the market mechanism, adversely affected groups would not blame the state; rather, aggrieved segments of the population would demand state intervention to redress their grievances. But when rising inequality is directly and visibly linked to state policies, politicization may be inevitable and the hyperactive state cannot escape liability.

Finally, a high level of state intervention affects the nature of economic and political conflict. Hyperactive states that employ sizable segments of the workforce inevitably tend to become the target of workers' economic conflicts. Workers' attacks against the state may reduce the intensity of class conflict. Reduction in the intensity of class conflict, in turn, increases the likelihood of coalition formation and revolutions.

States in developing countries became heavily involved in the economy in the twentieth century. To promote economic development, governments in developing countries after World War II expanded intervention in the economy and restricted the market mechanism. Whether in the form of import-substitution industrialization or expansion of state enterprises, states became major actors in the economy of developing countries until at least the early 1990s. Many governments in developing countries also became direct producers and owned the largest industrial enterprises in their countries. During this period, governments in the developing countries received a great deal of foreign aid and development assistance, which transformed them into major financial players.

In general, high state intervention increases the likelihood that social conflicts will become politicized and, given the appropriate conditions, target the state. High levels of state intervention in capital accumulation in developing countries often have negative consequences for many social groups and classes, thereby weakening political support for the regime across the board and setting the stage for social conflict. State accumulation policies often serve narrow interests and thus heighten inequalities in the distribution of income and wealth. Furthermore, state intervention may increase inequalities among different sectors.

For example, state intervention during the 1960s and 1970s adversely affected the agricultural sector in many developing countries that pursued import-substitution industrialization. These governments either ignored the agrarian sector or failed to carry out substantial reforms to improve conditions of the peasantry. In fact, in most cases, government intervention served the interests of large producers at the expense of smaller ones. State intervention in the industrial sector may also adversely affect working class interests when hyperactive states promote capital accumulation by banning strikes, keeping wages down and restricting or prohibiting working class organizations. Although ordinarily workers may accept these policies, in times of crises, these policies constitute grounds for working class mobilization. The likelihood of workers' politicization increases particularly in conditions where state intervention is high and the government is the principal employer. In such cases, the state will become the direct target of workers' attacks.

High levels of state intervention may also negatively affect the capitalist class. State policies may split the interests of this class. While state intervention may protect and promote nascent industries, some capitalists may oppose regulative activities, for example, limited licensing and high protective tariffs, which may reduce potential entry into such sectors. While these policies may prove highly lucrative for a small segment of capitalists who are protected from competition and the vagaries of the market, the vast majority of small- and medium-sized capital may oppose such privileges because they may be compelled to operate without protection and advantages. Capitalists may likewise oppose state intervention in capital allocation, which often politicizes the financial process, because segments of the capitalist class are likely to be excluded from government resources. Although large, favored enterprises may be granted access to state resources, small- and medium-sized businesses may be excluded, placed in precarious circumstances and may turn to bribery to gain advantage. These capitalists often condemn corruption because it imposes an additional cost on their businesses. Exclusion of these smaller entrepreneurs from the most favorable loans and subsidies may reduce the hyperactive state's base of social support, making it vulnerable in times of conflict.

Finally, the hyperactive state may also become a target of attack if it pursues inappropriate economic and financial policies that increase the country's economic vulnerability in the world market.[2] States that heavily rely on external sources of capital and technology may become vulnerable during unfavorable economic conditions and experience a debt crisis (Walton 1989, p. 299; Foran 1993, 1997). Of course, government mismanagement of resources often intensifies the debt crisis. The vulnerability is especially acute for developing countries that rely heavily on exports of a few raw materials and primary commodities. An economic downturn may produce falling prices for these goods and a decline in demand on the world market. Mono-crop economies can be devastated by such world market fluctuations, and even oil-rich countries are susceptible. A decline in the world market can negatively affect those segments of the population that produce a single export and may even threaten broad segments of the population. In the context of declining resources, a highly indebted country may experience a balance of payments crisis and may be required to initiate "structural adjustment" and currency devaluation, often with adverse effects on the country's entire economic structure.

11.4   EXCLUSIVE STATES, CENTRALIZATION OF POWER, AND VULNERABILITY

States that are characterized by exclusive rule tend to become vulnerable to challenge and attack in times of crisis. Such states contract the scope of the polity and block access to the state and the centers of political power. They often tend to eliminate or render irrelevant formal democratic institutions. In extreme cases, highly exclusive states may develop an exceedingly personalistic rule, which virtually excludes most of the population, even the economic elite, from decision-making processes (Goodwin 2001, pp. 210–13). "Sultanic" regimes (Linz 1975, pp. 259–63) and "autonomous personalist" regimes (Roberts and Midlarsky 1986, pp. 24–7) are extreme examples of exclusive rule. Under such regimes, rule is based on personal characteristics (Chehabi and Linz 1998, p. 7). Such regimes also tend to minimize or eliminate accountability to the public and rule independently of the underlying population (McDaniel 1991, p. 6). Centralized, dynastic regimes are especially vulnerable because they restrict elite access to the polity and remain exclusive for prolonged periods without providing any option or outlet for change (Goodwin 1994, p. 758; Foran 1997, p. 229; Snyder 1998, p. 56).

The emergence of exclusive rule and centralization of power in the context of large-scale social conflicts often have several crucial consequences. First, in such conditions, states may have to continually resort to violence and repression to demobilize or eliminate their opponents or insurgents. The continuous use of repression may reduce social support for the regime and force it to become dependent on both the military and external support to maintain power. State reliance on military coercion may enable governments to hold on to power in the short run, but such reliance may prove to be inadequate in the long term. When challenged by broad coalitions that disrupt the social order, governments may not enjoy the loyalty of the armed forces particularly if rulers do not completely control the armed forces or if the armed forces lack cohesion. In times of crises, preexisting divisions may render the military vulnerable to schisms and defection. For example, armies that are based on conscripts are often vulnerable to schisms and defection especially because they may retain regular contact with the civilian population. Second, government repression may weaken or eliminate elite or moderate challengers and consequently polarize the opposition in favor of the hegemony of radical or revolutionary challengers.

Exclusive states may also attempt to rely on external support to maintain power (Snyder 1998, p. 58). External dependence may render exclusive states vulnerable, as such reliance can be a double-edged sword. Although such relations may protect dependent states in the international state system, shifts in international alignments may expose them to unfavorable political decisions made beyond their borders. Support may be eroded during times when major powers are preoccupied with war or urgent internal conflicts. Additionally, dependent states may be at an obvious disadvantage when they receive less external support than do the armed rebel groups within their borders seeking to overthrow them (Goldfrank 1979, p. 149). External support may even be withdrawn in the face of a forceful internal opposition, especially when continued support for the existing regime could potentially spawn a more radical alternative that may pose a greater threat to the old regime's external allies. Thus, a high level of dependence on external sources may prove distinctly detrimental in times of conflicts and crisis.

But structural vulnerabilities by themselves do not inevitably produce social conflict, let alone revolution. The history of the world is replete with examples of states that were highly centralized and interventionist and also excluded and adversely affected large segments of the population. Many of these states had only limited social support, yet only a few actually experienced social revolution. In short, structural theories by themselves are inadequate to explain the eruption, nature, timing and outcome of social conflicts (Walton 1984; Aya 1990; Kim 1991, p. 10). Although structural factors set the stage for conflict and restrict certain options by affecting the interests and capacities of different collectivities for mobilization and action, they cannot determine the complex revolutionary processes and actual outcomes. There is always more than one potential outcome present in any conflictual situation (Kimmel 1990, pp. 185–86). Similar structural conditions may give rise to different outcomes (Selbin 1993, p. 29). Thus, any analysis of revolution must also take into account the revolutionary process and the role of revolutionary challengers in order to explain revolutionary outcomes.

11.5   CONSOLIDATION AND COALITION FORMATION

Revolutions erupt when challengers and collective actors can consolidate and form broad coalitions, and disrupt the social structure. The formation of broad coalitions are essential where highly repressive regimes, with monolithic elite and loyal armed forces and paramilitary entities erect enormous obstacles to democratization. Consolidation of opposition and formation of broad coalitions tend to reduce or eliminate the social base of support for the regime leaving it isolated and vulnerable. Broad-based coalitions and movements have a high likelihood of success because they can potentially disrupt the normal functioning of the social structure through large-scale collective action including general strikes and popular uprisings. Disruption of the social structure and likely attacks against economic targets may broaden the scope of the conflicts and result in the defection of some members of the polity leading to political instability. More importantly, formation of broad coalitions may signal instability and cause defections in the armed forces rendering the state incapacitated.

Consolidation of opposition and formation of broad coalitions is often rare because of the diversity of interests and capacity for mobilization and collective action among various social classes and collectivities in the social structure. Intensification of class or ethnic conflicts often impedes the formation of broad coalition and consolidation of opposition. Class and ethnic conflicts often fail to target the state and thus do not result in democratization. Intensification of class conflict may also prevent democratization by forcing the capitalist class to rely on the state for protection and thus impede the formation of a broad democratic coalition (Parsa 2000). On the other hand, broad coalitions tend to emerge during periods of national economic and political crises that threaten or adversely affect the interests of broad segments of the population. National economic crises tend to reduce state resources and may disrupt the pact between the authoritarian regime and their backers in the private sector. Thus, economic decline may result in a loss of confidence in the private sector and capitalist refusal to invest, leading to further instability (Haggard and Kaufman 1995, pp. 7–8, 29–30), increasing the likelihood of consolidation and coalition formation. During economic downturns, an authoritarian government may pursue policies that adversely affect the established interests of powerful social entity in order to solve the problem. Violation of the established interests of powerful collectivities may in turn instigate challenges drawing other classes with preexisting grievances against the state to join in a coalition. More importantly, national economic crises tend to stimulate the formation of broad coalitions because they adversely affect the interests of broad segments of population, and particularly impose heavy costs on disadvantaged collectivities. Finally, economic downturns and crises exacerbate disparities in the distribution of income and wealth, leading the adversely affected populations to join in a broad coalition to demand egalitarian distribution of resources.

National political crises also affect the interests, opportunities and capacities of major social groups, encouraging them to mobilize and engage in collective action. Political divisions and schisms among the ruling elite over alternative policies may encourage popular mobilization and formation of coalitions. In particular, the rise of a reformist faction and reduction of repression certainly provide favorable opportunities for political mobilization and opposition. Political crises may also stimulate the rise of radical political challengers demanding fundamental political changes. The rise of radical challengers may in turn contribute to the mobilization of excluded collectivities that are incapable of independent action. Finally, intensification of repression against members of powerful or resourceful collectivities may be construed as violation of established rights and instigate collective action, providing a favorable opportunity for popular collective action, given preexisting conflicts. Consolidation of these forces and formation of a broad coalition may have great potential in fundamentally transforming the political system.

In the absence of a political compromise, coalition allies may have to escalate the conflicts and disrupt the social structure to overthrow the regime. Disruptive collective action can make the state extremely vulnerable (Schwartz 1988; Piven and Cloward 1977; McAdam 1982; Jenkins 1985). Prolonged structural disruptions may have a serious impact especially on societies that are characterized by an urban economy. When production, distribution and services are interrupted, the social structure may be destabilized to the point of economic crisis, which may deprive the state of revenues and resources necessary for its continued operation. A state's inability to prevent sustained, large-scale disruptions may itself signal political instability, which may, in turn, intensify the crisis and precipitate mobilization by groups that have not yet engaged in collective action.

State impotence in the face of growing conflict may lead dissatisfied members of the polity to defect. Such defections reduce support for the state at the same time that they augment the opposition's resources. The most dangerous defections at this stage are those from the armed forces, paralyzing the coercive apparatus. With intensification of conflicts, preexisting divisions within the armed forces may widen and result in state breakdown. The probability of defection increases if relatively close links exist between members of the armed forces and the civilian population. Armies largely staffed by conscripts are especially vulnerable to defection because the recruits maintain contact with the rest of population. As defections increase, the armed forces may become paralyzed, declare neutrality or even join insurgents to expedite a transfer of power. Defections may not increase in armies that are staffed by professional soldiers. In the absence of defection, insurgents may have to initiate armed struggle and attack the armed forces in the context of large-scale disruptive actions. A combination of armed struggle combined with popular uprising may defeat or neutralize the military. Increased external support and resources for insurgents combined with a decline of support for the state increases the likelihood that a transfer of power will occur.

11.6 IDEOLOGY AND SOCIAL REVOLUTION

Ideologically driven explanations of revolutions tend to claim that spread and adoption of revolutionary ideologies often precede social revolutions. Some analysts seem to claim that adoption of these ideas or ideals should be considered as a cause of the revolution. My own analysis of the collective actions of major classes and collectivities in revolutions in Iran, Nicaragua and the Philippines does not support the exaggerated ideological explanations of revolutions. While it is true that revolutionary challengers often emerge and attempt to overthrow the state long before revolutions, in prerevolutionary situations only a minority of the population subscribes to revolutionary ideologies. The seizure of state power by radical revolutionary challengers does not always imply popular conversion to the ideology of the new power holders. In fact, often a revolutionary coalition emerges and enables radical challengers to seize state power. Thus, it is important to distinguish between situations where an ideological conversion is involved and where a coalition is formed.

Major social classes and collectivities have different interests and propensities in supporting radical or revolutionary ideologies because of their varying position in the social structure. During the twentieth century, students and intellectuals in developing countries were generally open to adopt radical political ideologies. They often led the ideological struggles and adopted radical perspectives to transform the social structure. Students and intellectuals also took a leading role in mobilizing and initiating collective action against the existing regimes in favor of ideologically driven, radical challengers. But, the collective actions of other major collectivities and their support for ideologically driven, radical challengers were more complex. Specifically, industrial workers and capitalists in developing countries mobilized and engaged in collective action in response to violations of their established rights and interests rather than ideological causes. Although working classes had greater propensity in supporting radical movements, their shift often depended on the solidarity structures and strength of their preexisting organizations. Furthermore, the timing of the collective actions of these actors coincided with the reduction of repression, and increased state vulnerability due to internal and external pressures and developments. When the three conditions met, they produced intense mobilization, collective action and conflicts. These major classes and collectivities demonstrated interest in supporting radical political organizations when authorities or governments failed to respond to their demands. The timing of the shift to supporting revolutionary challengers often depended on the availability of options, the extent of organization of the collectivity and the degree of state vulnerability.

Finally, whether large-scale social conflicts will result in only political change or eventually transform the entire social structure depends, at a minimum, upon the ideology of the challengers that ultimately seizes power. If the new leaders are moderate with ties to the dominant class, the revolution will result only in changes in the political system, possibly accompanied by some social reforms. If, on the other hand, the new leaders are radical revolutionaries, the outcome may be a social revolution, large-scale transformation of the state and class structure. Thus, the ascendancy of ideologically driven challengers, that is, revolutionaries, is critical in determining whether the conflicts will culminate in social revolution.

In theory, challengers that possess crucial resources, those that are well organized and unconstrained by repression are in a better position to lead the insurgency and seize power. Thus, moderate challengers have a greater potential than do revolutionaries to gain power. They have greater economic resources, which can be used offensively in times of conflicts. They are often mobilized because they are permitted to form occupational or economic organizations to defend their interests, which also serve to enhance their capacity for collective action. They may be less restricted by repression because they do not advocate fundamental change in the social structure. At best, they favor political rather than social revolutions. Finally, elite challengers may have allies within the government with whom they can form coalitions to advance their cause. But it is important to note that such challengers, by definition, do not mobilize to bring about social revolutions. At best, they may advocate the expansion of the polity and democratization.

In contrast, radical challengers that advocate social revolutions often lack adequate resources and are forced to operate underground to escape repression. Furthermore, ideologically driven challengers generally do not have allies within the government to advance their interests. Thus, most revolutionary challengers in the developing countries in the twentieth century failed to seize power and were repressed. Only a few revolutionary organizations were successful in seizing power in developing countries.

It is noteworthy that during the twentieth century revolutionary organizations and challengers initiated political activities long before popular struggles erupted. These challengers were interested in mobilizing the people to seize state power. These challengers were often ideologically driven intellectuals and students inspired in part by the success of revolutionaries elsewhere and antagonized by domestic economic structures, rising income inequalities, political repression and the closing of the political system. Most of the revolutionary organizations were repressed or failed to mobilize the people. The revolutionary challengers that survived were successful in gaining the support of dissident intellectuals and students or some segments of the population who contributed resources and new recruits. Revolutionary challengers became serious contenders for power where they acquired adherents among major classes or collectivities such as workers, peasants or segments of the middle class. Radical challengers particularly succeeded in seizing power where elite opposition broke away from the existing regime but failed to remove the power-holders. The chances of revolutionaries improved in seizing power where they could forge a coalition with moderate or elite challengers or obtain their implicit support. To form such coalitions, revolutionary challengers had to tone down their radical ideologies and compromise, or totally conceal, their ideology from the public.

Future studies of revolutions should pay close attention to the role of revolutionary ideology and mobilization options in the final stages of revolutionary struggles. The immediate political outcome of revolutions is not easily predictable at the outset of revolutionary struggles. While it is true that revolutionary ideologies have always played a role in mobilizing certain segments of the population and in complex ways affected outcomes of revolutions, mobilization options in the last phase of revolutions have also contributed to the outcome of revolutions. But, political ideology and the organizational strength of challengers do not always affect the outcome of revolutions. The available mobilization options in the final phase of revolutions may be central in determining which challengers will be victorious. Where government intransigence refuses to compromise with moderate opposition and uses indiscriminate violence and repression against the people, armed struggle may be the only option for revolution. In Nicaragua, Somoza's refusal to hold elections and permit the moderate opposition to contest his rule provided an opportunity for the Sandinistas to use armed struggle and seize power. In Iran, the Shah's policies weakened the moderate opposition, but left the mosques open for political mobilization, thus providing an opportunity for a segment of the clergy to seize power. In the Philippines, the powerful leftist-nationalist coalition failed to seize power because Marcos agreed to hold an election that enabled the moderate opposition to win, eliminating the chance of the radicals to bring about a social revolution. Future scholarship on revolutions should distinguish between the impact of ideology and mobilization options in order to understand the impact of each on the outcome of revolutions.

NOTES

1. I have borrowed the first two terms from the work of Zysman (1983), although he may not agree with my definitions.

2. Dependence may generate economic difficulties and render Third World countries to political conflicts; see Eckstein (1989), Foran (1993, 1997), Wolf (1969), Paige (1975), Walton (1989) and Boswell and Dixon (1990).

REFERENCES

Aya, R. (1990), *Rethinking Revolutions and Collective Violence: Studies on Concept, Theory, and Method*, Amsterdam: Het Spinhuis.

Boswell, T., and W.J. Dixon (1990), "Dependency and rebellion: a cross-national analysis", *American Sociological Review*, **55**, 540–59.

Chehabi, H. and J. Linz (1998), *Sultanic Regimes*, Baltimore, MD: The Johns Hopkins University Press.

Eckstein, S. (1989), "Power and protest in Latin America", in S. Eckstein (ed.), *Power and Popular Protest: Latin American Social Movements*, Berkeley, CA: University of California Press.

Foran, J. (1993), *Fragile Resistance: Social Transformation in Iran from 1500 to the Revolution*, Boulder, CO: Westview Press.

Foran, J. (1997), "The comparative-historical sociology of Third World revolutions: why a few succeed, why most fail", in J. Foran (ed.) *Theorizing Revolutions*, New York, NY: Routledge, pp. 227–67.

Foran, J. (2005), *Taking Power: On the Origins of Third World Revolutions*, Cambridge, UK: Cambridge University Press.

Goldfrank, W. (1979), "Theories of revolution and revolution without theory: the case of Mexico", *Theory and Society*, **7**, 135–65.

Goldstone, J. (1980), "Theories of revolution: the third generation", *World Politics*, **32**, 425–53.

Goldstone, J. (1986), "The Comparative and Historical Study of Revolutions", in J. Goldstone (ed.), *Revolutions: Theoretical, Comparative, and Historical Studies*, San Diego, CA: Harcourt Brace Jovanovich.

Goldstone, J. (1991), "Ideology, cultural frameworks, and the process of revolution", *Theory and Society*, **20**, 405–55.

Goodwin, J. (1994), "Toward a new sociology of revolutions", *Theory and Society* **23**, 731–66.

Goodwin, J. (1997), "State-centered approaches to social revolutions: strenghts and limitations of a theoretical tradition", in J. Foran (ed.), *Theorizing Revolutions*, New York, NY: Routledge, pp. 11–37.

Goodwin, J. (2001), *No Other Way Out: States and Revolutionary Movements, 1945–1991*, Cambridge, UK: Cambridge University Press.

Haggard, S. and R. Kaufman (1995), *The Political Economy of Democratic Transitions*, Princeton, NJ: Princeton University Press.

Jenkins, J.C. (1985), *The Politics of Insurgency: The Farm Worker Movement in the 1960s*, New York, NY: Columbia University Press.

Kim, Q.-Y. (1991), "Paradigms and revolution: the societal and statist approaches reconsidered", in Q-Y Kim (ed.), *Revolutions in the Third World*, Netherlands: E.J. Brill, pp. XXX

Kimmel, M. (1990), *Revolution: A Sociological Interpretation*, Philadelphia, PA: Temple University Press.

Linz, J. (1975), "Totalitarian and authoritarian regimes", in F. Greenstein and N. Polsby (eds), *Macropolitical Theory*, Reading, MA: Addison-Wesley, 175–412.

McAdam, D. (1982), *Political Process and the Development of Black Insurgency, 1930–1970*, Chicago, IL: University of Chicago Press.

McDaniel, T. (1991), *Autocracy, Modernization, And Revolution In Russia And Iran*, Princeton, NJ: Princeton University Press.

Midlarsky, M. and K. Roberts (1986), "Inequality, the state, and revolution in Central America", in M. Midlarsky (ed.), *Inequality and Contemporary Revolutions*, Denver, CO: University of Colorado Press, pp. 11–33.

Moore, Jr., B. (1966), *Social Origins of Dictatorship and Democracy: Lord and Peasant in the Making of the Modern World*, Boston, MA: Beacon.

Paige, J. (1975), *Agrarian Revolution: Social Movements and Export Agriculture in the Underdeveloped World*, New York, NY: The Free Press.

Paige, J. (2003), "Finding the revolutionary in the revolution: social science concepts and the future of revolution", in J. Foran (ed.), *The Future of Revolutions*, London: Zed Press.

Parsa, M. (1985), "Economic development and political transformation: a comparative analysis of the United States, Russia, Nicaragua, and Iran", *Theory and Society* **14**, 623–75.

Parsa, M. (1989), *Social Origins of the Iranian Revolution*, New Brunswick, NJ: Rutgers University Press.

Parsa, M. (2000), *States, Ideologies and Social Revolution: A Comparative Analysis of Iran, Nicaragua, and the Philippines*, Cambridge, UK: Cambridge University Press.

Piven, F.F. and R.A. Cloward (1979), *Poor Peoples' Movements: Why They Succeed, How They Fail*, New York, NY: Vintage Books.

Rueschemeyer, D. and P. Evans (1985), "The state and economic transformation: toward an analysis of the conditions underlying effective intervention", In P. Evans, D. Rueschemeyer, and T. Skocpol (eds), *Bringing the State Back*, Cambridge, UK: Cambridge University Press, pp. 44–77.

Schwartz, M. (1988), *Radical Protest and Social Structure: The Southern Farmers' Alliance and Cotton Tenancy, 1880–1890*, Chicago: The University of Chicago Press.

Selbin, E. (1993), *Modern Latin American Revolutions*, Boulder, CO: Westview Press.

Selbin, E. (1997), "Revolution in the real world: bringing agency back", in J. Foran (ed.), *Theorizing Revolutions*, New York, NY: Routledge, pp. 123–36.

Skocpol, T. (1979), *States and Social Revolutions: A Comparative Analysis of France, Russia, and China*, Cambridge: Cambridge University Press.

Skocpol, T. (1982), "Rentier State and Shi'a Islam in the Iranian Revolution", *Theory and Society*, **11**, 265–83.

Snyder, R. (1998), "Paths out of sultanic regimes: combining structural and voluntarist perspectives", in H. Chehabi and J. Linz (eds), *Sultanic Regimes*, Baltimore, MD: The Johns Hopkins Press, pp. 49–81.

Tilly, C. (2006), *Regimes and Repertoires*, Chicago, IL: The University of Chicago Press.

Walton, J. (1984), *Reluctant Rebels: Comparative Studies of Revolution and Underdevelopment*, New York, NY: Columbia University Press.

Walton, J. (1989), "Debt, protest, and the state in Latin America", in S. Eckstein (ed.), *Power and Popular Protest: Latin American Social Movements*, Berkeley, CA: University of California Press, pp. 299–328.

Wolf, E. (1969), *Peasant Wars of the Twentieth Century*, New York, NY: Harper Torchbooks.

Zysman, J. (1983), *Governments, Markets, and Growth: Financial Systems and the Politics of Industrial Change*, Ithaca, NY: Cornell University Press.

PART IV

THE ARMS TRADE

12 The arms trade
David Kinsella

12.1 INTRODUCTION

The Book-of-the-Month Club's April selection in 1934 was *Merchants of Death*. In that best-selling volume, H.C. Engelbrecht and F.C. Hanighen argued that the activities of arms merchants undermine the policies of national governments to whom they owe allegiance. Part of their message was, in essence, that American neutrality was compromised during World War I by weapons manufacturers whose strict adherence to commercial principles in peddling their wares left them little incentive to ponder the political or moral implications of their profession. The arms business is exactly that – a business – and business is good when nations are at war, or when they fear it.

Merchants of Death figured prominently among the polemics that fueled the flames of American isolationism, culminating in the Neutrality Acts of 1935–39. Prior to the passage of the Neutrality Acts and the formation of the Munitions Control Board, the export of weaponry by American merchants was essentially unregulated. By the outbreak of a second World War in Europe, the US Government had established controls over private arms sales, and thus what was for the arms merchants a means of profit became for the government an instrument of foreign policy. This new role for arms transfers was inaugurated with the signing of the Lend-Lease Act of 1941, in the hopes that direct American involvement in the European war could be avoided, and that the country would remain merely the great *arsenal* of democracy. With the passing of international arms marketing from the private to the public sphere, so withered public vigilance.

George Bernard Shaw appears to have foreseen this transition in the final act of *Major Barbara*, which opened in London in 1906. It includes this exchange between Andrew Undershaft, the arms manufacturer, and Adolphus Cusins, a professor of Greek and Undershaft's prospective son-in-law and inheritor:

CUSINS: What on earth is the true faith of the Armorer?
UNDERSHAFT: To give arms to all men who offer an honest price for them, without respect of persons or principles: to aristocrat and republican, to Nihilist and Tsar, to Capitalist and Socialist, to Protestant and Catholic, to

> burglar and policeman, to black man, to white man and yellow man, to all sorts
> and conditions, all nationalities, all faiths, all follies, all causes and all crimes. . .
> CUSINS: [A]s to your Armorer's faith, if I take my neck out of the noose of
> my own morality I am not going to put it into the noose of yours. I shall sell
> cannons to whom I please and refuse them to whom I please. So there!

During the cold war that followed World War II, the major powers, and
especially the superpowers, provided and refused weapons to whom they
pleased, and often with little regard for whether clients could offer an
honest price for them. The arms business ceased to be solely a business; it
also became an instrument of foreign policy and geopolitical competition.

The social scientific literature on the arms trade began to take shape
during the height of the cold war and is now quite extensive. The purpose
of this chapter is to survey some of the main themes in this literature and
to suggest at least a couple directions for future social scientific research.
Scholars, policymakers and activists who examine the arms trade do so
for any number of reasons: to identify important actors in the arms trade,
whether states or nonstate actors; to illuminate the decision-making processes driving arms imports and exports; to examine political–military
relationships between suppliers and recipients; to identify global and
regional trends in arms flows and the diffusion of arms export capacity;
to ascertain the impact of arms transfers on interstate conflict, civil war or
government repression; to evaluate the prospects for arms control and disarmament in both pre- and post-conflict environments. Thus, the aims of
those contributing to the arms trade literature are descriptive, explanatory
and normative. Of course, I cannot in this brief survey hope to do justice
to the scope and nuance of such a vast body of research and writing, one
spanning multiple social scientific disciplines as well as the policy, activist
and legal fields. But I will identify several of the most important topics
tackled by arms trade researchers and try to give some sense of what we
know (and don't know) about the issues that have animated this active
research community.

The next three sections will address descriptive, explanatory and
normative questions, respectively. Generally speaking, the descriptive
literature endeavors to identify the main players in the arms trade, their
arms-transfer policies and relationships, and patterns or trends in global
and regional arms flows. The explanatory literature consists of research
designed to uncover the causes and consequences of the arms trade, especially the relationships between arms transfers and violence between or
within states. The normative literature not only aims to expose the economic, political, and humanitarian ills associated with arms transfers, but
also the prospects for developing international rules and institutions for
the purpose of curbing the arms trade and thereby mitigating these ills.

Before turning to the question of arms control, this last section will focus specifically on the illicit arms trade and what might be learned from the application of social network analysis.

12.2 ACTORS, FLOWS AND STRUCTURES

We might start by distinguishing the trade in finished weapons systems and ammunition from the trade in components and spare parts, the provision of military training and other services, and the general diffusion of military and dual-use technology (nuclear and non-nuclear). It is probably fair to say that most arms trade research, including major data collection efforts, focus on finished conventional weapons systems, although both theoretical treatments and empirical analyses often address these other dimensions of proliferation secondarily or by implication. In any event, I limit my attention in this literature survey to the trade in finished systems.

A second useful distinction is that between major conventional weapons and small arms and light weapons (SALW). According to a UN panel of experts, "small arms are those weapons designed for personal use, and light weapons are those designed for use by several persons serving as a crew." Small arms include pistols, rifles, carbines and light machine guns; light weapons include heavy machine guns, grenade launchers, portable anti-aircraft and anti-tank systems, and mortars of less than 100 mm caliber. This category of weaponry also includes ammunition and explosives: cartridges, shells and missiles, anti-personnel and anti-tank grenades, landmines and other explosives (UN 1997, pp. 11–12). Most SALW research adopts this or a very similar working definition. Of course, everything else short of nuclear, chemical and biological weapons would count as major conventional weapons systems.

Until the end of the cold war, the social science literature (which dates back to the late 1960s) was concerned mainly with the trade in major weapons systems, for several reasons. First, the volume of that trade had been rising substantially since the end of World War II, peaking in the early 1980s at 60 to 70 billion dollars per year (at today's price levels), and thus represented what many considered to be an alarming trend in the proliferation of destructive military capability. Second, the major weapons trade was dominated by the two superpowers and their closest allies and was thus a central manifestation of cold war dynamics for both academic researchers and policy analysts.[1] Third, for many the supply of major conventional weaponry seemed to feed interstate rivalry in the developing word and arguably contributed to the outbreak of wars in the Middle East, South Asia, the Horn of Africa and elsewhere. Fourth, as a practical matter, those collecting hard data on the arms trade could (and still can) be much more confident of the accuracy of information pertaining to major weapons transfers than to the SALW trade, which is diffuse, less closely monitored by governments and easier to conceal by those not wanting the attention and scrutiny. Researchers who made use of arms trade data for either descriptive or explanatory purposes had to adjust the scope of their inquiries accordingly.

The end of the cold war ushered in a new focus on the SALW trade. The US–Soviet competition was no longer the core organizing force behind global security relations and, whether there was a causal connection or not, violent interstate conflict was becoming increasingly rare. Instead, internal war was accounting for a far larger proportion of armed violence and it was SALW, not major conventional weapons, that were doing most of the killing. Humanitarian crises precipitated by the most relentless of these internal conflicts gave added urgency to this reorientation of arms trade research. Thus, since the early 1990s, the literature on the SALW trade has burgeoned and is now quite substantial. This has been accompanied by new and continuing data collection efforts, which will help to place SALW research on an increasingly firm social scientific footing.

12.2.1 Hierarchies in Arms Supply

The state of social science theory pertaining to the arms trade is relatively underdeveloped compared to some other areas of inquiry within the disciplines of political science, economics and sociology. Nevertheless, the literature has seen the development of some noteworthy conceptual frameworks that might be best described as "pre-theoretical." In a path-breaking study of the arms trade, researchers at the Stockholm International Peace Research Institute (SIPRI) identified three patterns of arms supply. The *hegemonic* pattern, which they said was epitomized by the United States and Soviet Union during the cold war, involves the use of arms transfers "to support a particular group in power, or to prevent the emergence of an alternative group which might be willing to accept the dominance of another country" (SIPRI 1971, p. 17). This is not the case for *industrial* patterns of supply, where exporting states are concerned primarily with maintaining the economic viability of their own defense industries, or for *restrictive* patterns of supply, where producing states seek to minimize their involvement in local conflicts by refusing to equip actual or potential belligerents. The three patterns are, to be sure, ideal types: political, economic and even humanitarian considerations factor into any given supplier's decision to arm any given client at any given time.

Other studies offer fairly comprehensive historical–structural frameworks situating the arms trade within world politics and the evolution of the international system over time. In a comparative analysis of the inter-war and post-World War II arms trade, Harkavy (1975) examined supplier and recipient market structures and showed how they corresponded to the shifting distribution of power during these two periods. During the inter-war years, supplier markets were only moderately oligopolistic, a larger proportion of importing states maintained multiple-supplier relationships, and arms acquisitions that cut across alliances were frequent. These patterns reflected not only a more diffused distribution of capabilities among the major suppliers, but also a lesser degree of state involvement in the market as compared to subsequent years. After World War II, the supplier market became more tightly oligopolistic and increasingly dominated by the United States and Soviet Union. Cross-bloc arms transfers were virtually nil, and even importing states in the periphery generally did not mix acquisitions from the opposing cold war alliances – unless a change in government leadership brought about a major ideological reorientation. As Harkavy (1975, p. 11) remarked, the cold war arms trade was reflective of a "concatenation of factors involving bipolarity, stable hegemonic alliances under the leadership of the two major powers, an ideological locus of conflict, and a zeitgeist of total war."[2]

A more sweeping historical–structural framework was provided by Krause (1992), who sketches three waves in global arms transfer and production system. The first wave began with the so-called Military Revolution of the fifteenth century and lasted until the seventeenth century. This was followed by a two-century long period of relative stasis in military-technological development. Arms were indeed produced and traded, but the pace of technological change was slow in comparison to the preceding period, and especially subsequent periods. The second wave began in the middle of the nineteenth century and was associated with the rapid advance of the Industrial Revolution. There was no period of technological stasis between the second wave and the current third wave; rather, the end of one and the beginning of the next were condensed by the transformative event of World War II.

Within each of these three historical waves, Krause identifies a similar evolutionary dynamic consisting of five phases. In phase one, significant military-technological innovation is realized by a select group of states that then become the leading centers of global arms production. In phase two, rising demand for advanced weaponry produced by this first tier drives a rapid expansion of the arms trade and, in phase three, rising demand for arms production technology accompanies the demand for finished systems. This gives rise to a second tier of arms producing states able to manufacture a wide range of military equipment, including the most advanced systems, but generally limited in their capacity to innovate at the military-technological frontier. Next, in the fourth phase, the international arms market becomes characterized by fiercer competition among a larger number of suppliers. The transfer of arms accelerates, as does the diffusion of arms production capacity, and there now emerges a third tier of weapons manufacturing states. Capacity varies in the third tier, but a common characteristic is the need to import designs, machinery, and often the key components necessary for domestic production of the most technologically advanced systems, if such systems can be produced at all. In the fifth and final phase, military-technological diffusion slows and the three-tier arms-production hierarchy solidifies (Krause 1992, pp. 26–32).

This evolving three-tier structure among arms producers is complemented by a lower echelon of states with no significant arms-manufacturing capacity. If these states elect to maintain any military capability at all, they must import it. All states that achieved independence as a result of decolonization after World War II were in this position, as were many other states, like those in Latin America, that received independence earlier. Indeed, most developing states are still in this position; a rather limited number even now have the military-industrial capacity associated with third-tier arms production. Although this evolutionary pattern, as described by Krause (1992), has been repeated in three waves during the history of the contemporary state system, it is also the case that the second iteration was more compressed than the first, and the third – which some would argue is now yielding to a fourth – has been shorter still. Analysts debate the nature, timing and implications of military-technological innovations for the global arms trade (for example, Carus 1994; Buzan and Herring 1998; Zarzecki 2002), but Krause's general depiction of the *longue durée* is enlightening and has not been the subject of sustained criticism.

A more recent study by Bourne (2007) examines the structural features of the SALW trade and is thus indicative of the shifting focus of arms trade researchers. Bourne confronts what he calls the "amorphous image" of SALW diffusion in which virtually no structural constraints impede the global flow of SALW, especially to regions of conflict. This image was embraced by the academic and policy communities because SALW diffusion did not seem to conform to the patterns observed for the conventional arms trade generally or for the more closely scrutinized trade in nuclear, biological and chemical (NBC) weapons.[3] If these structures did not apply to the SALW trade, then was it not reasonable to conclude that there was no discernible structure at all? Although the amorphous image – in which SALW spread in accordance with market forces of supply and demand, unconstrained by the normative or policy concerns of states and intergovernmental organizations – is consistent with many of the arguments found in the literature on globalization, Bourne's examination suggests that it is exaggerated. There is no denying that constraints on SALW proliferation are fragmented and porous and do allow for a wide range of state and nonstate participants in the legal and illicit SALW trade. But structures do exist, at both the global and regional levels.

Bourne's (2007) complex and nuanced analysis defies easy summary, but some specific elements of it are worth noting here. First, compared the arms trade in general, the global SALW trade is not dominated by the major supplier countries to nearly the same extent. This is not surprising given the less demanding military-technological capabilities required to produce SALW, and has been observed in earlier periods by Harkavy (1975), Krause (1992) and others who have described the tiered structure of arms production and supply in the international system (for example, Anthony 1993). Second, in contrast to the amorphous image of the SALW trade, Bourne argues that the illicit market is not globalized, but is primarily a regional phenomenon (the infamy of such globe-trotting arms brokers as Victor Bout and Monzer al-Kassar notwithstanding). Third, although the amorphous image seems to imply a rather homogenized process whereby SALW flow into ongoing conflict areas, Bourne suggests that the character of proliferation very much depends on specific factors like the type of states, insurgencies and war economies that compose the conflict complex.

12.2.2 Data Collections

These and the relatively few other broad conceptual frameworks found in the arms trade literature tend to be inductive, relying on historical and contemporary data to help identify major and minor actors in the arms trade, patterns of arms flows and discernible global and regional structures. This section briefly introduces the most important sources of contemporary arms trade data, both qualitative and quantitative.

There are three main sources of quantitative information on conventional arms transfers. The US Department of State's Bureau of Verification, Compliance, and Implementation publishes *World Military Expenditures and Arms Transfers* (*WMEAT*). Previously compiled by the Arms Control and Disarmament Agency, an independent agency within the US Government until it was subsumed within the State Department in 1999, *WMEAT* was released annually and reported arms imports and exports for all states in dollar-valued aggregates as well as counts of weapons transfers by category (aircraft, tanks, submarines and so forth). In recent years, however, *WMEAT* releases have been sporadic and less comprehensive in their coverage and consequently this data source is less often used in academic research than it once was.[4] The Congressional Research Service (CRS), a research arms of the US Congress, also publishes arms trade data in its annual report, *Conventional Arms Transfers to Developing Nations* (for example, Grimmett 2009). These data are limited to transfers by major suppliers to developing countries only, but are noteworthy for distinguishing between arms agreements and arms deliveries.

The most authoritative source of both quantitative and qualitative information on the arms trade is the yearbook published by SIPRI, *Armaments, Disarmament and International Security*.[5] SIPRI relies exclusively on open sources for its data and focuses its attention on the kind of information consistently available to the public, namely major weapons systems. These include aircraft, armor and artillery, guidance and radar systems, missiles and ships. In addition to those items physically transferred to recipients, SIPRI includes weaponry manufactured by the recipient under license. The data come in two forms: "trade registers" of transferred military hardware broken down by model (F-16 aircraft, M-60 tanks, Patriot surface-to-air missile systems and so forth), and dollar-valued aggregates. The latter are what SIPRI calls its "trend indicator values" (TIVs). These figures do not represent what the recipient paid for arms, as this sort of information is exceedingly difficult to gather on a consistent basis, or even an assessment of the market value of the weapons. Rather, SIPRI applies a pricing procedure intended to index the military resource value of transferred weaponry based on a set of core weapons about which price and performance information is fairly reliable. Thus, TIVs are suitable for the analysis of trends, but not for establishing the financial value of arms transfers or their value in relation to other types of expenditure. They are, however, well-suited to various forms of econometric analysis and continue to be used extensively in a academic research.

As the attention of the academic and policy communities has turned increasingly to SALW, there has been a great deal of interest in the collection and distribution of systematic information (qualitative and quantitative) on this aspect of the arms trade. Because the SALW trade is much less regulated by state authorities than the major weapons trade, and because the weapons themselves are smaller and harder to observe by journalists and others who might want to document their movement, reliable information is very difficult to gather on a consistent basis. But researchers are now beginning to accumulate and release pertinent data.[6] Several significant data collection efforts could be mentioned, covering various dimensions of the SALW trade and its potential consequences, but two stand out as sustained and fairly comprehensive. The Small Arms Survey, located at the Graduate Institute of International Studies in Geneva, is a clearing house for public information on SALW production and transfers. The Survey's staff conduct in-depth country studies and other analyses focusing on various dimensions of the legal and illicit SALW, many of which are reported in its annual review along with limited amounts of quantitative data (for example, Small Arms Survey 2009). The Norwegian Initiative on Small Arms Transfers (NISAT), located at the International Peace Research Institute in Oslo, also issues reports on a variety of SALW issues. In addition to its document library, NISAT maintains an online database of SALW transfers, with some records dating back to 1962. These data are likely to feature in future academic and policy research.[7]

12.3   CAUSES AND CONSEQUENCES

The broad conceptual frameworks discussed in the previous section are among the very few that have appeared in the arms trade literature. A far larger share of the work produced by scholars, policy analysts and activists consists of investigations into the arms export or import policies of particular states, historical and contemporary studies of the flow of weapons to regions plagued by violent conflict, primers on the workings of the arms trade and its role in international politics, and exposés of arms manufacturers or traders engaged in questionable dealings. This literature is voluminous and is not reviewed here.[8] Rather, I limit the survey in this section mainly (but not exclusively) to work that attempts to model, formally or statistically, factors driving the arms trade and especially the impact of arms transfers on violent conflict.

12.3.1   Strategic Interaction in the Arms Market

Compared to some other subject areas related to the political economy of war – conflict processes and arms racing, for example – formal modeling has not been used extensively in the arms trade literature. The primary exception is the work by Levine and collaborators, which models the decisions of arms producers, exporters and importers as games of strategic interaction with consequences for the security and welfare of participating states (for example, Levine, Sen and Smith 1994; Levine and Smith 1997; García-Alonso and Levine 2002, 2007). Early models tended to treat suppliers and recipients as unitary actors pursuing both economic and security objectives, but current models include additional layers of strategic interaction: between exporting states, between exporter governments and their domestic arms manufacturers, between the arms manufacturers themselves, and between importing states and their adversaries.

These models of strategic interaction have also evolved to include a range of competing incentives on the part of suppliers and recipients. For example, suppliers have incentives to subsidize their own arms manufacturers in order to increase international market share, yet arms exports generate negative externalities for suppliers and other countries (although exports to allies can offset these for suppliers). Negative externalities provide incentives for coordinated restraint among suppliers, but collective action is difficult in this realm for the same reasons that it is hard to achieve when confronting international terrorism, environmental degradation or other global problems (Sandler 2000). Recipients, of course, want to import weapons for reasons of national security, but they also have incentives to build their own arms production capacity, especially if suppliers have imposed export controls (Brauer 2000; Levine and Smith 2000; Mouzakis 2002). Formal models show how regional arms races and other unintended consequences may follow. In addition to export controls, this literature has also sought to model the impact of changing security perceptions, military-industrial policies, market concentration and other variables.

At this time, these models are mainly the purview of those working within the discipline of economics. It remains to be seen whether their methods and insights gain traction among scholars in other social science disciplines who share a substantive interest in the arms trade and its impact on the security and well-being of governments and their populations, but who are less likely to command the skills required for formal modeling.

12.3.2   The Arms Trade and Interstate Conflict

When considering the arms trade, it is no surprise that scholars writing about security in the developing world tend to highlight its harmful consequences. Ross (1990, p. 22), for instance, states that "while arms, whether domestically produced or imported, do not inevitably lead to military conflict, they exacerbate existing tensions and contribute to the perceptions and misperceptions that lead to war." Ayoob (1995, p. 102) has put it similarly: "whereas weapons transfers even on such a large scale should not be seen as substituting for the root causes on conflict inherent in Third World historical situations, the relatively easy availability of sophisticated weaponry certainly contributed to regional arms races and to the escalation and prolongation of conflicts in the Third World." Thus, despite the presupposed harmful effects of arms transfers, there is a recognition that factors driving state leaders to resort to military conflict as a means of redressing grievances – or factors prompting them to stumble into military conflict unintentionally – are complex and multifaceted. Any monocausal argument, whether it highlights arms supplies or some other contributor, is likely to prove incomplete at the very best. Add to this questions regarding the role of arms transfers on the course of military hostilities once begun, as well as the bargaining process leading to a settlement, and the issues confronting the empirical analysis of even a single historical case become that much more numerous and complex.

Some of the most careful empirical work on the subject has been conducted by Pearson and associates. In focused chronologies of six interstate conflicts in Africa, Pearson, Baumann and Bardos (1989) compared the timing of arms transfers with changing levels of fighting and progress during settlement talks. They did not find that arms transfers closely preceded crisis escalation or intensified fighting, but rather that arms flows increased only after conflicts were well underway. Nor were peace negotiations significantly affected by the arrival of weapons shipments. However, they did find an association between weapons agreements (often in the context of friendship treaties) and increased risk taking by the recipient, suggesting that the security commitments implied by arms deals may have more of an impact on the onset of conflict than actual arms deliveries. But in an expanded study covering multiple regions, Brzoska and Pearson (1994, pp. 214, 215) concluded that "arms deliveries clearly were a factor in decisions to go to war, because of considerations about military superiority, perceptions of changes in the balance of power, and interest in establishing links with supporting states" and that "arms deliveries during wars generally prolonged and intensified the fighting" (see also Pearson, Brzoska and Crantz 1992).

The commonly held view that arms transfers are partly to blame for the frequency, duration and severity of armed conflict in the developing world does withstand close empirical scrutiny in many cases. This finding has motivated a number of other researchers to explore the robustness and generalizability of the association between arms transfers and conflict using statistical techniques, given that quantitative data on both are available for most countries. Although statistical studies of war and lesser forms of international conflict often span two or more centuries, inquiries into the role of arms transfers tend to concentrate on the post-World War II period. As with the case-study literature, the results of these studies are not always unambiguous, and our cumulative understanding is probably well short of satisfactory, but the empirical results reported in the quantitative literature have been compelling enough to sustain continued interest in this analytical approach to the problem.[9]

Craft (1999) examines the relationship between arms transfers and military conflict at the global level of analysis. Based on data covering the 1950–92 period, Craft reports positive correlations between the total value of arms transferred between all states in the international system and the number of wars erupting in subsequent years, as well as the number of states involved in war. Although the implications of these finding seem to be, at first glance, rather obvious, when Craft takes a closer look at the behavior of arms recipients – as opposed to the incidence of war in the international system – his findings temper those initial conclusions. There is only a very weak association between arms imports and recipients' involvement in warfare, even among importers with higher-than-average propensities to be engaged in military conflict due to unresolved grievances with neighboring states. Furthermore, Craft found no relationship at all between weapons transfers and the duration of the wars that recipients became involved in, or the number of casualties produced by those wars. In view of these findings, Craft (1999, p. 75) acknowledges the element of truth in the common rejoinder to arms controllers that "weapons don't make wars, men do."

The quantitative results reported by Durch (2000) exhibit similar patterns and lead to similar conclusions. He reports a strong positive correlation between the total dollar value of arms transfers to the developing world and the number of states involved in external conflict, but then shows that this relationship weakens or disappears when the focus shifts from the developing world as an aggregate to the behavior of arms recipients. In delving further, Durch analyses the number of systems delivered in various heavy-weapon categories (instead of dollar values) and introduces controls for past conflict and regional locale. His conclusion: "conflict per se is not an adequate explanation for the arms trade, nor is the arms trade an adequate explanation for conflict within and among developing states" (Durch 2000, p. 104).

Other researchers have approached the question of arms transfers and instability by examining the political and military relations between particular pairs of states over time. Even if more aggregated analyses of the type conducted by Craft (1999) and Durch (2000) reveal at best weak associations between arms transfers and military conflict, the connection may still be strong in certain instances and we would like to know at what point the generalizability of such findings breaks down. Sanjian (1999), for instance, has constructed formal models of cold war arms transfers to rival states (using fuzzy sets) that correspond rather well to the historical data. He evaluates two competing models. His "instability model" treats conflictual political relations between two rivals as an increasing function of their arms-supply relationships with the superpowers (as well as third parties), and cooperative political relations between them as a decreasing function of arms supplies. The "stability model" does the reverse. Sanjian is interested in the impact of transfers on the entire range of interstate behavior, diplomatic as well as military, and his empirical results for three different interstate rivalries – India–Pakistan, Iran–Iraq, and Ethiopia–Somalia – consistently support the instability rather than the stability model (see also Sanjian 1998).

The quantitative literature covering the cold war period generally has not distinguished the impact of US arms transfers from Soviet transfers. Sanjian (1999) reports some distinctive results for third party transfers, but his models treat the outcomes of arms supply relationships with the two superpowers as symmetrical. Some of my own research, however, suggests that the superpowers' arms-supply relationships affected regional security in distinct ways. For example, in relations between the Arab states and Israel or between Iraq and Iran, Soviet arms transfers were associated with subsequent increases in hostility levels between rival states. Sometimes hostility was initiated by the recipient of Soviet weaponry, and sometimes by its opponent. That is, although opponents were themselves the recipients of US arms, my time-series analyses suggest that their conflict initiation tended to be a preemptive response to Soviet transfers to the other side, not a response to their own arms acquisitions (Kinsella 1994, 1995; Kinsella and Tillema 1995).

12.3.3 Arms Transfers, Internal Conflict and Repression

Compared to the literature examining the relationship between arms transfers and interstate conflict, there is considerably less research that attempts to model the linkages between the arms trade and internal conflict. Practical matters explain this in large part. Formal and statistical approaches to the study of internal war are themselves of fairly recent vintage, certainly relative to the study of interstate war. Also, as discussed above, there are as yet few sources of SALW data that are sufficiently developed to be useful for systematic spatial or longitudinal analysis, and this is the type of weaponry that seems most important to consider in the context of internal conflict and rebellion.[10] There are some studies worth mentioning here, however, and there is reason to expect that more will be forthcoming as SALW data are further developed and distributed to the research community.

Sislin and Pearson (2001) consider several hypotheses on the impact of arms transfers on the onset of ethnic uprisings; the intensity, duration and escalation of ethnopolitical violence; and the involvement of third parties in the resolution of internal wars. In addition to examining a number of cases of internal conflict in some detail, they also test some of their propositions by constructing various categorical measures of ethnopolitical violence and arms acquisition and cross-tabulating them. They show that higher levels of weapons accumulation by ethnic groups in conflict zones are a good predictor of subsequent ethnopolitical violence. Although Sislin and Pearson do not differentiate between internal and external arms supply in their analysis of conflict onset, they do consider the source of both rebels' and governments' weaponry when they turn to the question of conflict duration and intensity. Arms importation by ethnic groups is not correlated with conflict duration; importation by governments, on the other hand, is associated with longer internal wars. Causation could run in both directions, as the authors point out, but it is probable that arms transfers to governments facing rebellions prolongs these violent internal struggles. The intensity of violence, measured in terms of casualties, correlates with arms importation as well, but here it is the rebels' imports (not the government's) that seem to make a difference. Finally, Sislin and Pearson find that arms imports by rebel groups are associated with costly but indecisive internal conflicts commonly called "hurting stalemates" in the conflict resolution literature (for example, Zartman 2000).

The linkage between arms transfers and state repression, accompanied or not by rebellion and warfare, has also been the subject of social scientific investigation. In an analysis of developing countries over the 1982–92 period, Blanton (1999) finds that increased arms imports correlate with a higher incidence of human rights violations, even after controlling for governmental involvement in internal and external conflict. In other studies, Blanton (2000, 2005) flips the causal arrow and asks whether US arms supplies have been responsive to the human rights records of importing states, as well as their degree of democratic governance. Her argument, supported by the evidence, is that US arms transfers during the cold war were driven more by realpolitik considerations than by humanitarian or governance concerns. However, since the end of the cold war, both the level of democracy and the protection of human rights have become significant considerations in US arms export policy. Where these considerations come into play is at the gatekeeping ("selection") stage – who qualifies to be admitted to the club of arms recipients – not in determining how much a recipient gets. Interestingly, at this second ("amount") stage, Blanton shows that realpolitik considerations still dominate.

A survey of social scientific research into some of the most important causes and consequences of the arms trade suggests that despite an awareness of the potentially harmful repercussions of arms transfers, and the corresponding temptation of supplier states to exercise some restraint, weaponry has flowed rather freely to even the most volatile regions of the world. The results – not always and everywhere, but often and in very many places – have been predictable: an increase in repression, violence and warfare. The empirical evidence is not unambiguous, nor does theory or research imply that the arms trade provides any more than a partial explanation for these societal ills. Furthermore, systematic research examining the link between SALW and internal conflict is underdeveloped, not least due to data limitations. But the arms trade has been the preoccupation of many social science researchers and activists, perhaps because it is the product of policy choices that might be subject to influence.

12.4   SOME FUTURE DIRECTION FOR ARMS TRADE RESEARCH

This last section considers two areas that are likely to see a fair amount of continued research, especially given the emphasis that the SALW trade has received since the end of the cold war. One, the illicit arms trade, which (for obvious reasons) is not amenable to systematic observation and measurement, requires sustained descriptive research in the years ahead. The other, international norms limiting the SALW trade, engages the aspirations of a substantial subset the research and activist communities. Future work in this area will help to develop both the explanatory literature, to the extent that it can account for success and failure in norm-building processes, and the normative literature, to the extent that theory and research are deployed to advance the small-arms control agenda.

12.4.1   Illicit Arms Transfers and Social Network Analysis

The value of the SALW trade amounts to roughly US$4 billion per year, and probably 10 to 20 percent of this occurs in the black and gray markets. Generally speaking, legal arms transfers are sanctioned by states and are often (but not always) elements in an ongoing military relationship between governments. Illicit transfers, on the other hand, may be state-sanctioned, but usually they are not.[11] Although the illicit arms trade is driven on the supply side mainly by the profit motive, it nevertheless requires a degree of shared commitment (possibly even trust) on the part of buyers, sellers, brokers and other intermediaries to an underground system of economic exchange. I have argued that this feature of black and gray arms markets lends them to conceptualization as social networks, and to empirical examination using the tools of social network analysis (Kinsella 2006).

Curwen's (2007) examination of illicit arms transfers to Liberia provides a good illustration of the application of social network analysis (SNA) in an effort to identify key actors and their placement in these underground networks. Based on UN reports documenting arms embargo violations,

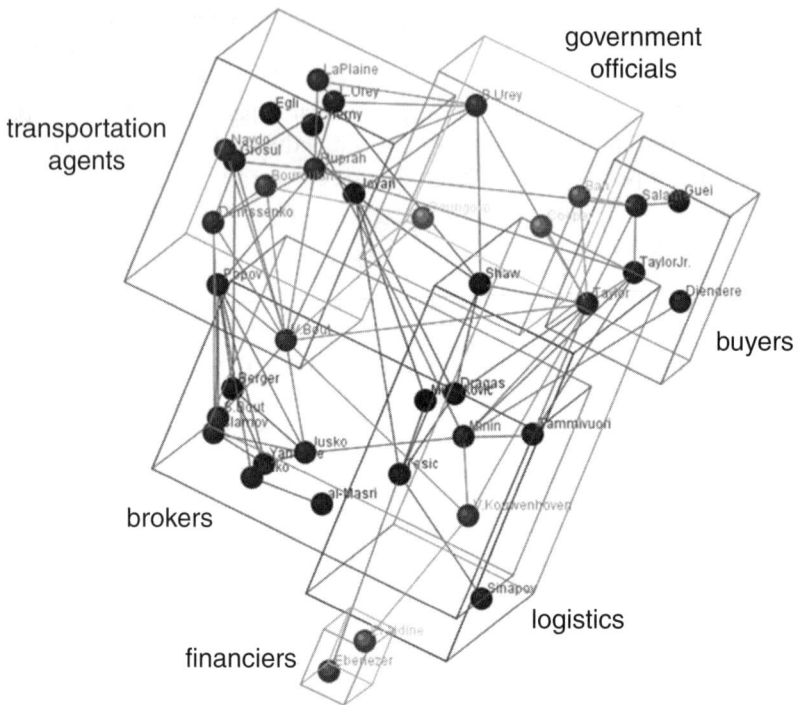

Source: Based on data in Curwen (2007)

Figure 12.1   Actors in illicit arms transfers to Liberia

Curwen identifies the individuals and transactions involved in four arms-transfer events occurring between 1999 and 2002. All together, 38 individuals comprise the nodes of this network – brokers, transportation agents, buyers (including Liberian President Charles Taylor himself and his son, Chuckie) and so on. The 78 ties between the nodes are operationalized as the presence of contractual, business, or employer–employee relationships between individuals. This illicit arms transfer network is depicted in Figure 12.1.[12] From the mapping of actors (clustered according to role) and ties – called a "sociogram" or "network graph" – we get a good sense of network structure and the most connected individuals.

Social network data are arranged as a square "sociomatrix" in which there is both a row and a column for each node in the network. A cell in the matrix contains a 1 if the actor represented by row i, designated n_i, had a relationship with the actor represented by column j, designated n_j, in which case $x_{ij} = 1$; otherwise $x_{ij} = 0$. Curwen's (2007) data are nondirectional in that a tie between two nodes represents a relationship rather than a sent or received communication or other exchange; thus, $x_{ij} = x_{ji}$. But in other SNA applications to the study of illicit arms transfers, it may be useful to consider directional ties. In this case, an actor's *outdegree*, $d(n_i)$, is the number of other actors to whom that actor has directed some form of communication or exchange (for example, delivered weapons); *indegree*, $d(n_j)$, is the number of actors from whom a communication or exchange has been received. That is,

$$d(n_i) = \sum_{\forall i \neq j} x_{ij} \text{ and } d(n_j) = \sum_{\forall j \neq i} x_{ji}, \qquad (12.1)$$

which are, respectively, the row i and column j totals of the sociomatrix. If there are s actors in the network, the maximum number of directed ties between them is $s(s-1)$.

In most social networks, certain actors are more prominent than others and the evidence of their prominence is often the number and type of social ties they maintain with other actors. The *centrality* of a network actor is sometimes indexed as its outdegree or indegree (or both), but since these measures are greatly affected by the number of actors in a network, it is useful to normalize the index. Thus, the normalized outdegree and indegree centrality indexes can be computed as

$$C'_{D}(n_i) = \frac{\sum_{\forall j \neq i} x_{ij}}{s-1} \text{ and } C'_{D}(n_j) = \frac{\sum_{\forall i \neq j} x_{ji}}{s-1}. \qquad (12.2)$$

Again, because Curwen's (2007) data are nondirectional – the sociomatrix is symmetric – the formulas in (12.2) give the same result. Figure 12.2 arranges the nodes so that the actors with the highest centrality measures are positioned nearer the center of five concentric rings, while those with lower scores are positioned nearer the periphery. Not surprisingly, the most central actors in the network examined by Curwen are Charles Taylor (a buyer) and Victor Bout (a broker).

Another SNA concept useful for the study of illicit arms trade networks is "brokerage." Brokers are actors positioned between nonadjacent actors and through which a directional interaction takes place. Social network analysts have gone on to specify particular brokerage roles based on the actors' membership in groups or other attribute categories. For instance, a node occupies a "coordinator" role when it is interposed between nodes within its same group or organization; when the three nodes are members of different groups, the broker acts as a "liaison." Other brokerage roles are defined when the broker and one actor are members of one group

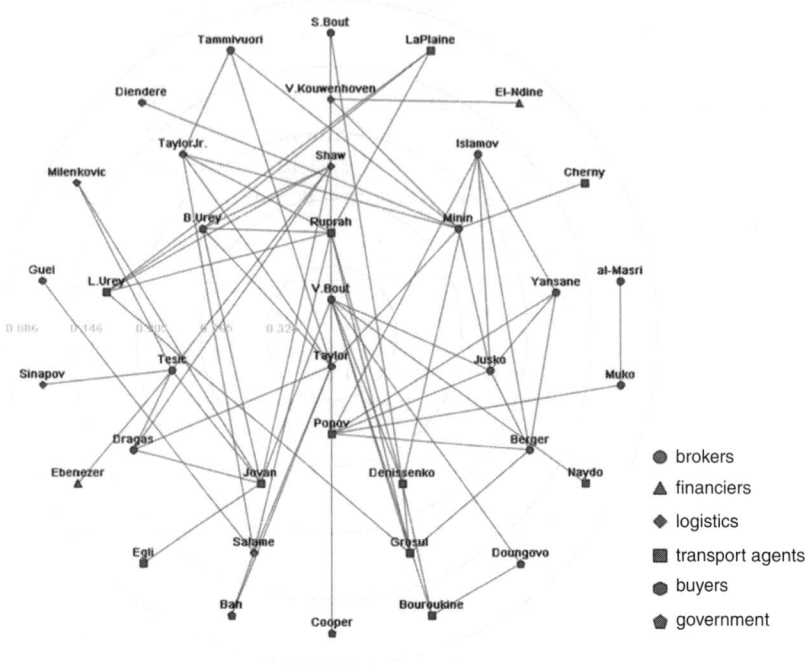

Source: Based on data in Curwen (2007)

Figure 12.2   Actor centrality in Liberia's illicit arms trade

and the other actor is a member of a second group: brokers that mediate inflows into their group are "gatekeepers"; those that mediate outflows from their own group are "representatives." Identifying important brokers in a social network involves counting the number of triads in which that node is positioned as an intermediary. I do not pursue brokerage concepts any further here, except to suggest their face validity when Curwen's (2007) data are analysed. Of the ten actors with the highest brokerage scores, all but two are coded (a priori) by Curwen as either arms brokers or transportation agents.[13] These are precisely the sort of intermediaries we want the analysis to identify.

SNA need not be limited to networks composed of individuals. Curwen (2007) also analyses ties between individual and organizations (a two-mode network) and international relations researchers have applied SNA methods to relations between states (for example, Hoff and Ward 2004; Maoz et al. 2006; Hafner-Burton, Kahler and Montgomery 2009). Some of my own research on the illicit arms trade, while built upon a dataset

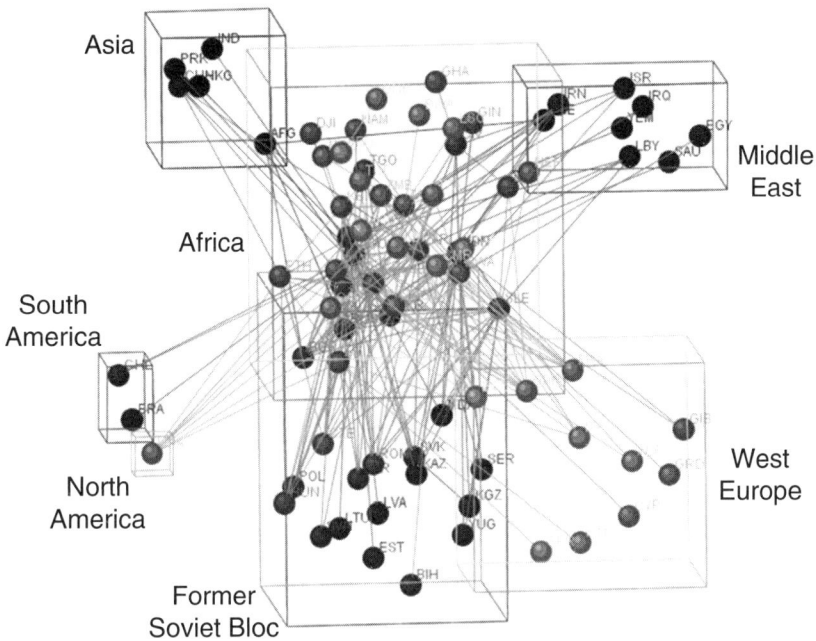

Source: Based on data in the Illicit Arms Transfers Dataset (Kinsella 2008)

Figure 12.3   State locales in the illicit arms trade with Africa

that includes information (where available) on individuals and organizations, has operationalized network nodes as the state locales where arms transfers originate, transit and arrive.[14] For example, Figure 12.3 maps state locales (grouped by geographic region) involved in illicit arms transfers ultimately arriving in Africa from the late 1990s through 2005. This network consists of 80 nodes (labeled with three-letter country codes) and 270 links. States appear as nodes in the network if they were involved in at least one illegal arms transfer during the period and if there is sufficient information to identify the locale at both ends of the transfer.

As with the network of individuals involved in illicit arms transfers to Liberia, the most prominent state locales in Africa's illicit arms trade can be identified by examining centrality scores. Figure 12.4, like Figure 12.2 above, places the most connected nodes at the center, but in this case the data are directional and the positioning is based on outdegree centrality scores. Thus, the figure identifies the most prominent exporter locales.[15] It is noteworthy that several former Soviet bloc countries appear rather central in Africa's illicit arms trade: Russia (RUS), Ukraine (UKR),

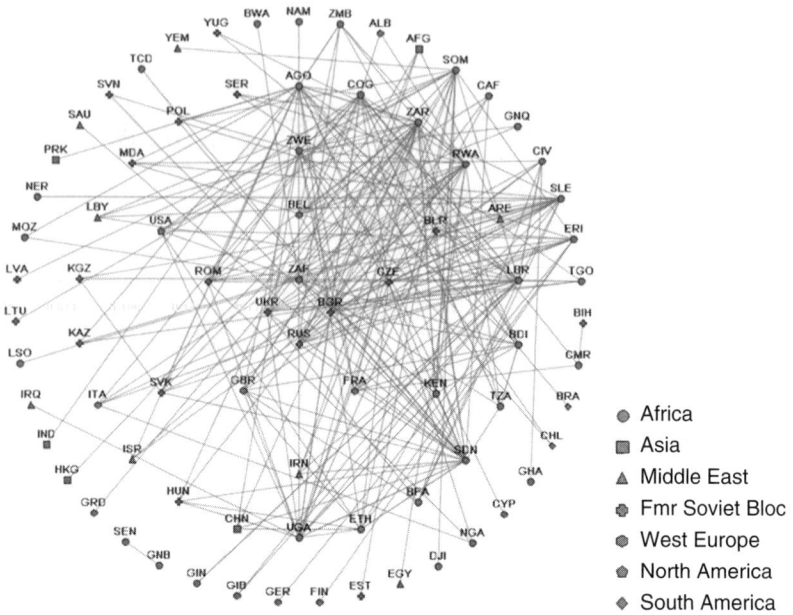

Source: Based on data in the Illicit Arms Transfers Dataset (Kinsella 2008)

Figure 12.4   Exporter centrality in Africa's illicit arms trade

Bulgaria (BGR) and, to a somewhat lesser extent, Romania (ROM) and Belarus (BLR). One explanation for their centrality may be the availability of cold war surplus and a black market infrastructure nurtured originally by their communist economic systems. This, at least, is a reasonable working hypothesis for subsequent empirical research. South Africa (ZAF) is also central in the illicit arms trade to other African countries, and West European countries – Belgium (BEL), Britain (GBR) and France (FRA) – are important locales as well.

The utility of SNA methods for illuminating the illicit arms trade obviously hinges on the quality of data that can be collected. Mapping the structure of the black market is hampered by the secrecy with which deals are concluded and the duplicity of the actors involved. What we do know about it is due mainly to the perseverance of enterprising activists and investigative reporters and, as with any data source, this information is subject to measurement error and selection bias. More sophisticated SNA methods will become useful as our data collections improve. Rather than simply identifying individuals and locales in the illicit arms trade, it will become possible to model the linkages among them as a function of factors on both the supply and demand side. The role of ongoing conflict, social and economic deprivation, weapons surpluses, criminal networks and other conditions conducive to proliferation have been highlighted by small arms researchers and activists. The cause of arms control will be advanced to the extent that we can identify the most important forces driving proliferation, especially those that are most subject to policy intervention and manipulation, and the individuals and locales that figure prominently as hubs in the arms supply network.

12.4.2   International Norms and Arms Control

This chapter has not surveyed the arms control literature as it pertains to the weapons trade, but I do want to conclude with some observations on future social science research in this area. It is safe to say that a substantial majority of those in the academic community who conduct research on the SALW trade share a normative commitment – among themselves and with those in the activist community and many others in policymaking circles – that SALW proliferation needs to be curbed and that some sort of international action is necessary. That does not mean that international action is likely. Researchers have begun to examine the hurdles along the path to successful arms control, especially in the light of an evolving body of theory from international sociology and political science.

Grillot, Stapley and Hanna (2006) compare the small arms movement with the International Campaign to Ban Landmines (ICBL), which now serves as a benchmark for measuring the success of transnational advo-cacy networks. Drawing on work of Keck and Sikkink (1998) and other contributors to the literature on global civil society, Grillot at al. (2006, pp. 68–72) argue that despite certain similarities, there are key differences in the arms control issues and the movements themselves that account for the achievements of the ICBL in comparison (thus far) to those of small arms movement. For example, although small arms, like landmines, are linked to the death and maiming of innocents, there is no "short and clear causal chain" given that "gun violence may be the result of a multitude of factors, such as instability, corruption, and poverty, as well as gun avail-ability and build-up." As a transnational network, the ICBL is also less diverse more centralized than the small arms movement, which is com-posed of many more groups and organization and lacks a core leadership – notwithstanding direction provided by the International Action Network on Small Arms (IANSA).

Further research on the small arms movement and the prospects for the controlling the SALW trade will continue to engage constructivist approaches to the study of world politics, which focus on the domestic, international and transnational processes by which states' interests are defined and evolve (for example, Finnemore and Sikkink 1998; Adler 2002). The failure of multilateral arms control negotiations to yield an international treaty limiting the SALW trade would seem to provide confirmation for a rationalist argument that such an outcome is to be expected given the distribution of interests and influence among states engaged in the negotiations. But as Krause (2002) points out, understanding the norm-building process on this issue requires that we consider more than these multilateral interactions. We must also examine the domestic and transnational political processes that have prompted many states to formulate positions and policies on SALW proliferation and have encouraged them to undertake various initiatives, including at the regional level (see also Garcia 2006, 2009).

Progress in our understanding of norm-building and the role of transnational advocacy networks will advance the theoretical development of the arms trade literature. It will also provide new and interesting questions for empirical research – and, we can hope, opportunities for social science to help advance the cause of arms control and conflict resolution.

NOTES

1. This connection between the superpower rivalry and the global arms trade is implicit, if not explicit, in much of the research covering all or part of the cold war period. Studies that investigate this connection explicitly include Neuman (1986), Mintz (1986), Sanjian (1988, 1998), Kinsella (1994, 1995, 2002).
2. Harkavy (1994) applied his basic comparative framework to the immediate post-cold war period, concluding that there were certain resemblances to the interwar arms trade, especially to the extent that contemporary arms transfers are less politicized than before. Transfers in the post-cold war years lost much of the geopolitical and ideological content they had acquired during the long US–Soviet rivalry.
3. Bourne also refers to the amorphous image of SALW spread as the "diffusion image" – in contrast to the "proliferation image" that applies to the more restrictive, state-centric spread of NBC weapons and ballistic missiles, or the "trade image" that applies to the similarly state-centric, if somewhat less restrictive, spread of major conventional weapons (see Bourne 2007, Chapter 2).
4. The 2005 edition is the most recent, the first since 2000, but as of this writing its phased online release does not yet include any arms transfer data. See US Department of State (2009).
5. Originally called *World Armaments and Disarmament*, the SIPRI Yearbook has been published since 1969. Data on arms transfers to the developing world during the cold war have been collected in two separate volumes (see SIPRI 1975; Brzoska and Ohlson 1987). These and other data can also be retrieved from the "SIPRI Arms Transfers Database" online at www.sipri.org/databases/armstransfers.
6. States are invited to provide information on their conventional arms transfers for the

UN Register of Conventional Arms, and although the UN register originally recorded only major weapon transfers, nearly 60 states have now provide information on their SALW transfers as well. This reporting is completely voluntary, however, and it is clear from the database that only a fraction of SALW exports and imports have been recorded. See Holtom (2009), UN Department of Disarmament Affairs (2002).

7. Much of the data compiled and distributed by both the Small Arms Survey and NISAT are drawn from customs information in the UN's Commodity Trade Statistics Database (Comtrade). The NISAT "Small Arms Trade Database" can be accessed at www.prio.no/NISAT/Small-Arms-Trade-Database/.

8. The best of this work is often to be found in the annual reviews published by SIPRI and the Small Arms Survey.

9. The first wave of interest in using quantitative analysis to assess the impact of arms transfers on interstate conflict occurred in the late 1970s and early 1980s, motivated at least in part by the rethinking of arms transfers as a tool of American foreign policy that grew out of the Carter administration's emphasis on human rights. That literature is reviewed in Gerner (1983) and is well represented in the special issue of *International Interactions* in which Gerner's review appears (e.g., Baugh and Squires 1983; Schrodt 1983; Sherwin 1983).

10. As Krause (2002, p. 251) observes, "small arms and light weapons are implicated in complex causal pathways with these various problems, although little work has yet been done to trace systematically these pathways to assess the relative weight of small arms (compared to other factors) or to evaluate the effectiveness of particular policy measures."

11. An arms transfer may be authorized by the government, but still violate the state's laws or international arms embargoes. Although illegal, some researchers regard these as covert transfers rather than illicit transfers. Illicit transfers would be those undertaken by private actors without legal authorization, even though the transactions may involve the participation of corrupt government officials. The term "gray market" is often used to refer to arms transfers that are not clearly illegal (that is, when pertinent laws are ambiguous) or wholly illegal (that is, when authorized transfers are later diverted in unauthorized directions). There is no absolute consensus in the arms trade literature on these use of these terms (see, for example, Bourne 2007, pp. 39–42; Naylor 2004, pp. 88–132; Marsh 2002).

12. I have generated Figures 12.1 and 12.2 from the raw data contained in Curwen (2007, Appendix B). Clearly, there were more than 38 individuals involved in these four events, so the network that Curwen reconstructs is represents only the most visible (to UN experts) of the real-world network. The study of illicit networks must therefore contend with questions of sampling (for example, Rothenberg 1995; Frank 2005).

13. These results are available upon request.

14. The *Illicit Arms Transfers Database* (IATD) is an evolving dataset consisting of information gleaned from news and other reports of illegal arms shipments crossing interstate borders. At this stage of development, the IATD project has relied primarily on NISAT's "Black Market File Archive," a collection of news stories and investigative reports on the illicit arms trade. The unit of observation in IATD is an illicit arms transfer "event," defined as coterminous with a particular arms shipment's journey from source to recipient, possibly intercepted along the way. Each record in the dataset consists of data describing that event, including the actors and locations involved in the shipment's journey from originator to recipient (or interceptor). Most variables are event descriptors and can be grouped as they pertain to (1) the *source* of the arms shipment, (2) those involved in the arms *deal*, (3) the *characteristics* of the arms shipped, (4) the *journey* that the shipment took after leaving the source, and (5) the shipment's *destination*. See Kinsella (2008) for a complete description.

15. Here, "exporter" means the state locale serving as the starting point for a shipment of illicit weaponry arriving in an African country, not necessarily the country that manufactured the weaponry. Also, I am using the terms "prominent" and "central" to

describe state locales that served as starting points for shipments of arms to the largest
number of the other countries, not necessarily starting points for the largest volume of
transferred weaponry. However, I suspect that there is a correlation.

REFERENCES

Adler, E. (2002), "Constructivism and international relations", in W. Carlsnaes, T. Risse and
B. Simmons (eds), *Handbook of International Relations*, London: Sage, pp. 95–118.
Anthony, I. (1993), "The 'third tier' countries: production of major weapons", in H. Wulf
(ed.), *Arms Industry Limited*, Oxford, UK: Oxford University Press, pp. 362–83.
Ayoob, M. (1995), *The Third World Security Predicament: State Making, Regional Conflict,
and the International System*, Boulder, CO: Lynne Rienner.
Baugh, W.H. and M.J. Squires (1983), "Arms transfers and the onset of war. Part II: wars in
third world states, 1950–1965", *International Interactions*, **10** (1), 129–41.
Blanton, S.L. (1999), "Instruments of security or tools of repression? Arms imports and
human rights conditions in developing countries", *Journal of Peace Research*, **36** (2),
233–44.
Blanton, S.L. (2000), "Promoting human rights and democracy in the developing world: US
rhetoric versus US arms exports", *American Journal of Political Science*, **44** (1), 123–31.
Blanton, S.L. (2005), "Foreign policy in transition? Human rights, democracy, and US arms
exports", *International Studies Quarterly*, **49** (4), 647–67.
Bourne, M. (2007), *Arming Conflict: The Proliferation of Small Arms*, New York, NY:
Palgrave Macmillan.
Brauer, J. (2000), "Potential and actual arms production: implications for the arms trade
debate", *Defence and Peace Economics*, **11** (5), 461–80.
Brzoska, M. and T. Ohlson (1987), *Arms Transfers to the Third World 1971–85*, Oxford, UK:
Oxford University Press.
Brzoska, M. and F. S. Pearson (1994), *Arms and Warfare: Escalation, De-escalation, and
Negotiation*, Columbia, SC: University of South Carolina Press.
Buzan, B., and E. Herring (1998), *The Arms Dynamic in World Politics*, Boulder, CO: Lynne
Rienner.
Carus, W.S. (1994), "Military technology and the arms trade: changes and their impact",
Annals of the American Academy of Political and Social Science, **535**, 163–74.
Craft, C. (1999), *Weapons for Peace, Weapons for War: The Effects of Arms Transfers on War
Outbreak, Involvement, and Outcomes*, New York, NY: Routledge.
Curwen, P.A. (2007), "The social networks of small arms proliferation: mapping an aviation
enabled supply chain", Master's thesis, Naval Postgraduate School.
Durch, W.J. (2000), *Constructing Regional Security: The Role of Arms Transfers, Arms
Control, and Reassurance*, New York, NY: Palgrave.
Engelbrecht, H.C. and F.C. Hanighen (1934), *Merchants of Death: A Study of the
International Armament Industry*, New York, NY: Dodd, Mead and Company.
Finnemore, M. and K. Sikkink (1998), "International norm dynamics and political change",
International Organization, **52** (4), 887–917.
Frank, O. (2005), "Network sampling and model fitting", in P. J. Carrington, J. Scott and
S. Wasserman (eds), *Models and Methods in Social Network Analysis*, Cambridge, UK:
Cambridge University Press, pp. 31–56.
Garcia, D. (2006), *Small Arms and Security: New Emerging International Norms*, New York,
NY: Routledge.
Garcia, D. (2009), "Arms transfers beyond the state-to-state realm", *International Studies
Perspectives*, **10** (2), 151–68.
García-Alonso, M.D.C. and P. Levine (2002), "Domestic procurement, subsidies, and the
arms trade", in J. Brauer and J.P. Dunne (eds), *Arming the South: The Economics of*

Military Expenditure, Arms Production and Arms Trade in Developing Countries, New York, NY: Palgrave, pp. 161–91.

García-Alonso, M.D.C. and P. Levine (2007), "Arms trade and arms races: a strategic analysis", in T. Sandler and K. Hartley (eds), *Handbook of Defense Economics, Volume 2: Defense in a Globalized World*, Amsterdam: Elsevier, pp. 941–71.

Gerner, D.J. (1983), "Arms transfers to the third world: research on patterns, causes and effects", *International Interactions*, **10** (1), 5–37.

Grillot, S.R., C.S. Stapley and M.E. Hanna (2006), "Assessing the small arms movement: the trials and tribulations of a transnational network", *Contemporary Security Policy*, **27** (1), 60–84.

Grimmett, R.F. (2009), "Conventional arms transfers to developing nations, 2001–2008", CRS Report R40796. Washington DC: Congressional Research Service.

Hafner-Burton, E.M., M. Kahler, and A.H. Montgomery (2009), "Network analysis for international relations", *International Organization*, **63** (3), 555–92.

Harkavy, R.E. (1975), *The Arms Trade and International Systems*, Cambridge, MA: Ballinger.

Harkavy, R.E. (1994), "The changing international system and the arms trade", *Annals of the American Academy of Political and Social Science*, **535**, 11–28.

Hoff, P.D. and M.D. Ward (2004), "Modeling dependencies in international relations networks", *Political Analysis*, **12** (2), 160–75.

Holtom, P. (2009), "Reporting transfers of small arms and light weapons to the United Nations Register of Conventional Arms, 2007", SIPRI Background Paper, February 2009.

Keck, M. and K. Sikkink (1998), *Activists Beyond Borders: Advocacy Networks in International Politics*, Ithaca, NY: Cornell University Press.

Kinsella, D. (1994), "Conflict in context: arms transfers and third world rivalry during the cold war", *American Journal of Political Science*, **38** (3), 557–81.

Kinsella, D. (1995), "Nested rivalries: superpower competition, arms transfers, and regional conflict, 1950–1990", *International Interactions*, **21** (2), 109–25.

Kinsella, D. (2002), "Rivalry, reaction, and weapons proliferation: a time-series analysis of global arms transfers", *International Studies Quarterly*, **46** (2), 209–30.

Kinsella, D. (2006), "The black market in small arms: examining a social network", *Contemporary Security Policy*, **27** (1), 100–117.

Kinsella, D. (2008), "Illicit arms transfers dataset: coding manual", available at web.pdx.edu/~kinsella/iatcode.pdf.

Kinsella, D. and H.K. Tillema (1995), "Arms and aggression in the Middle East: overt military interventions, 1948–1989", *Journal of Conflict Resolution*, **39** (2), 306–29.

Krause, K. (1992), *Arms and the State: Patterns of Military Production and Trade*, Cambridge, UK: Cambridge University Press.

Krause, K. (2002), "Multilateral diplomacy, norm building, and UN conferences: the case of small arms and light weapons", *Global Governance*, **8** (2), 247–63.

Levine, P., S. Sen and R. Smith (1994), "A model of the international arms market", *Defence and Peace Economics*, 5 (1), 1–18.

Levine, P. and R. Smith (1997), "The arms trade", *Economic Policy*, **25**, 337–70.

Levine, P. and R. Smith (2000), "Arms export controls and proliferation", *Journal of Conflict Resolution*, **44** (6), 885–95.

Maoz, Z., L.G. Terris, R.D. Kuperman and I. Talmud (2006), "Structural equivalence and international conflict, 1816–2001: a network analysis of affinities and conflict", *Journal of Conflict Resolution*, **50** (5), 664–89.

Marsh, N. (2002), "Two sides of the same coin? The legal and illegal trade in small arms", *Brown Journal of World Affairs*, **9** (2), 217–28.

Mintz, A. (1986), "Arms exports as an action–reaction process", *Jerusalem Journal of International Relations*, **8**, 102–113.

Mouzakis, F. (2002), "Domestic production as an alternative to importing arms", in J. Brauer and J.P. Dunne (eds), *Arming the South: The Economics of Military Expenditure,*

Arms Production and Arms Trade in Developing Countries, New York, NY: Palgrave, pp. 129–159.

Naylor, R.T. (2004), *Wages of Crime: Black Markets, Illegal Finance, and the Underworld Economy*, Ithaca, NY: Cornell University Press.

Neuman, S.G. (1986), *Military Assistance in Recent Wars: The Dominance of the Superpowers*, New York, NY: Praeger.

Pearson, F.S., R.A. Baumann and G.N. Bardos (1989), "Arms transfers: effects on African interstate wars and interventions", *Conflict Quarterly*, **9** (4), 36–62.

Pearson, F.S., M. Brzoska and C. Crantz (1992), "The effects of arms transfers on wars and peace negotiations", in *SIPRI Yearbook 1992: World Armaments and Disarmament*, Oxford, UK: Oxford University Press.

Ross, A.L. (1990), "Do-it-yourself weaponry", *Bulletin of the Atomic Scientists*, **46** (4), 20–2.

Rothenberg, R.B. (1995), "Commentary: sampling in social networks", *Connections*, **18** (1), 104–110.

Sandler, T. (2000), "Arms trade, arms control, and security: collective actions issues", *Defence and Peace Economics* **11** (5), 533–48.

Sanjian, G.S. (1988), *Arms Transfers to the Third World: Probability Models of Superpower Decisionmaking*, Boulder, CO: Lynne Rienner.

Sanjian, G.S. (1998), "Cold war imperatives and quarrelsome clients: modeling US and USSR arms transfers to India and Pakistan", *Journal of Conflict Resolution*, **42** (1), 97–127.

Sanjian, G.S. (1999), "Promoting stability or instability? Arms transfers and regional rivalries, 1950–1991", *International Studies Quarterly*, **43** (4), 641–70.

Schrodt, P.A. (1983), "Arms transfers and international behavior in the Arabian Sea area", *International Interactions*, **10** (1), 101–27.

Sherwin, R. (1983), "Controlling instability and conflict through arms transfers: testing a policy assumption", *International Interactions*, **10** (1), 65–99.

Sislin, J. and F.S. Pearson (2001), *Arms and Ethnic Conflict*, Lanham, MD: Rowman and Littlefield.

Small Arms Survey (2009), *Small Arms Survey 2009: Shadows of War*, Oxford, UK: Oxford University Press.

Stockholm International Peace Research Institute (1971), *Arms Trade Registers: The Arms Trade with the Third World*, Stockholm: Almqvist and Wiksell.

Stockholm International Peace Research Institute (2009), *SIPRI Yearbook 2009: Armaments, Disarmament and International Security*, Oxford, UK: Oxford University Press.

United Nations (1997), "Report of the Panel of Governmental Experts on small arms", Report A/52/298, 27 August 1997.

United Nations Department of Disarmament Affairs (2002), "Transparency in armaments: United Nations Register of Conventional Arms", available at disarmament.un.org/cab/register.html, accessed 1 September 2009.

United States Department of State (2009), "World military expenditures and arms transfers", available at www.state.gov/t/vci/rls/rpt/wmeat/, accessed 31 August 2009.

Zartman, I.W. (2000), "Ripeness: the hurting stalemate and beyond", in P.C. Stern and D. Druckman (eds), *International Conflict Resolution after the Cold War*, Washington, DC: National Academy Press, pp. 225–50.

Zarzecki, T.W. (2002), *Arms Diffusion: The Spread of Military Innovations in the International System*, New York, NY: Routledge.

13 Arms trade offsets: what do we know?
Jurgen Brauer and John Paul Dunne

13.1 INTRODUCTION

In September 2002, an international conference on arms trade offsets and economic development was held in Cape Town, South Africa, and subsequently an edited collection was produced, drawn from selected conference contributions as well as other solicited papers (Brauer and Dunne 2004). All contributions represented original work and were peer-reviewed and thoroughly edited before inclusion in the volume. The authors include a sweep of top-notch experts in the field. Their institutional affiliation ranges from university professors to think-tank fellows, consultants in private practice and personnel at defense institutes and defense academies. The geographic origin or current location of the authors spans all continents. Likewise, the case studies include countries from across the globe. In alphabetical order they are: Argentina, Australia, Belgium, Brazil, Denmark, Finland, Germany, India, Indonesia, Japan, the Netherlands, New Zealand, Norway, Poland, Singapore, South Africa, South Korea, Sweden, Taiwan, the United Kingdom and the United States. The volume was published by Routledge in 2004. This chapter is our summary of the state-of-the-art as reflected in the book's chapters, supplemented by an updated literature search and review (through to July 2009) and by a discussion of emerging issues and policy recommendations.

Although both topics are treated in the book, we do not review here the *theory* of offsets nor the theory of the economic *consequences* of offsets. The literature search for 2004–2009 did not yield new *empirical* papers on arms trade offsets. We are aware of some work being conducted in East and Central Europe and of isolated interest in the topic in India and elsewhere but to our knowledge there has been no readily accessible, peer-reviewed literature in English since the chapters we commissioned for our 2004 book were published. This book still appears to be the latest word on the subject matter. In terms of *policy*, however, both the United States and the European Union now officially declare offset deals to be undesirable; this is explained and explored in the main text of this chapter. The next section considers the nature of offsets, followed by a section discussing the mechanics of offset deals and then one reviewing the evidence of their impact on both sellers and procurers, before concluding with a discussion of the issues involved and lessons to be learned. Where we make use of references to our book, we cite them as (author, page), for example, (Markusen, p. 81), so that readers can to look up specific details in the book.

13.2 WHAT ARE OFFSETS?

13.2.1 Definition

The very definition of what offsets are is disputed. Nonetheless, the main idea is this: ordinarily, a country that wishes to spend, say, $100 million to import arms from another country transfers $100 million worth of funds to the arms seller, the only value gained in return being the putative national security-value of the imported arms.[1] To increase the exchange value, the importing country may stipulate that the arms exporting country or firm must take some portion of its $100 million revenue to set up arms co-production facilities in the arms importing country, or else to commit itself to any of a variety of other possible activities that would secure a flow-back of some or all of the $100 million to the arms purchasing country. If this flow-back is made part of the arms trade contract, we call this an offset. The advertised benefit is that the importing country obtains not only the arms but that some of the public funds expended on the arms purchase "remain" in the country and are thus expected to stimulate domestic economic development, just as if they had been spent domestically in the first place.

13.2.2 Motivation

To be able to double-dip – to get the arms and yet to keep the money at home – is seductive for politicians, especially in democracies, who must justify expenditure of public funds, usually in the face of crying social need. The logic sounds so convincing: sign a contract that requires the arms selling party to use some or all of the expended funds to set up arms production facilities in the purchasing country or to make nonmilitary purchases in or from the arms acquiring country that otherwise would not have been made. In the post-Cold War buyers' market, buyers have the upper hand and can extract substantial rents and benefits. Offset demands have therefore become universal.

13.2.3 Magnitude

The use of offsets is by no means restricted to the field of arms trade. Offsets, and related forms of countertrade, constitute a vast, pervasive business practice involving tens of thousands of people around the globe, reaching far beyond the market for military-related items. The size of the trade is variously estimated at ranging between 5 and 30 percent of world trade. However, governments and international organizations do not track the value of offset trade separately. All estimates offered in the literature and press are guesses and it is by no means clear how they are arrived at.

With regard to the arms trade, some countries do undertake efforts to track the value of offsets, especially the United States where legislation mandates offsets tracking and an annual report to Congress.[2] The implementing agency is the Bureau of Industry and Security (BIS) within the Department of Commerce. The thirteenth annual report was issued in December 2008 and covers the 15-year span from 1993 to 2007.[3] For example, for 2007 alone, total US defense-related merchandise exports were $16.7 billion of which contracts to the value of $6.7 billion came with an offset obligation agreement (ca. 40 percent). The value of the agreements amounted to $5.4 billion (ca. 80 percent). Thus, for 2007 the value of agreements over total exports was $5.4/$16.7 billion, or 32.3 percent.

For this entire 1993–2007 time period, BIS reports 9249 arms trade offset transactions (rather than agreements, promises which may or may not be fulfilled in future), affecting 53 companies and 48 countries for an actual transactions value of $45.73 billion and an offsets value of $53.61 billion. The offsets value is higher than the actual value because of the use of multipliers whereby an actual value is multiplied to count toward offset obligation (usually if it is in a preferred industry/product group, as explained below). In this case, the ratio of 53.61/45.73 implies an average multiplier of 1.17. Actual transaction values have been on the order of about $2 billion a year with a marked rise toward $4–5 billion in the 2000s (see Figure 13.1). On average, across all the years covered, US defense exports with an offset obligation make up about 40 percent of all defense export sales and of those, offsets values are the order of 70 percent of the arms contract value.

If one makes the assumption that the United States accounts for one-third of the world arms trade (Brauer 2007, p. 979 based on a 55-year record of SIPRI arms transfer values data) and that importing countries' average offset demands are reflected in what they demand from the United States then an initial guess at the dollar value of worldwide offset *transactions* values would run to about $135 billion (3 × $45 billion) over this 15-year period, or about $9 billion per year.

However, the sum of offsets *agreements* (transactions to be fulfilled in future) was about $65 billion for the United States (BIS 2008, p. 4, Table 3.1); thrice that would be $195 billion worldwide, or about $13 billion per

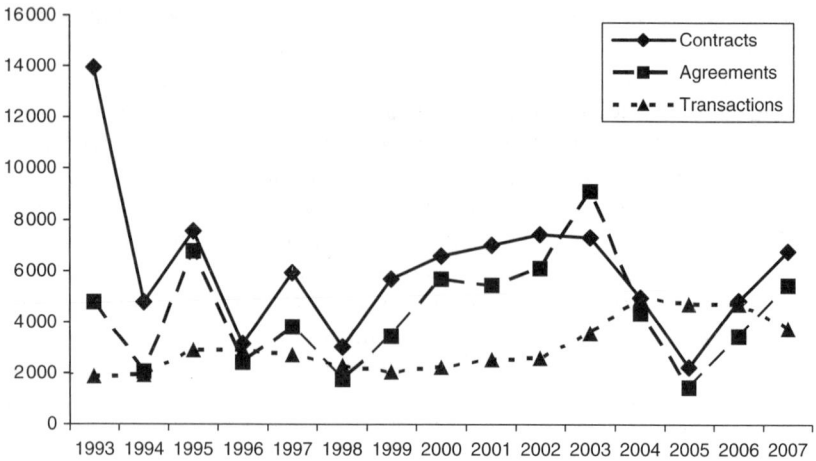

Source: BIS (2008)

Figure 13.1   US offset contracts, agreements, transactions, 1993–2007 in US$ million

year, a not insubstantial sum.[4] Because agreements include an offsets multiplier, the $13 billion needs to be "discounted" accordingly. If one uses the 1993–2007 average of 1.17 for the United States, one arrives at about $11 billion of worldwide annual offset agreements resulting in *future actual offset transaction values*, still an appreciable sum.

13.2.4   Countries' Objectives and Strategies

Arms importing countries' offset objectives do, of course, evolve over time and their strategies change as their objectives evolve. Some states target certain arms niches that they wish to learn to master for themselves and they structure arms import acquisition and offset demands toward the fulfillment of this goal (for example, Singapore, Taiwan). Other countries have well-developed specialized arms production niches and use arms trade offsets to assist them to maintain international competitiveness in that niche. Their objective has evolved from vaguely promoting general economic development to the development and maintenance of specific arms-production competences (for example, Sweden, the Netherlands). Still other countries (for example, Brazil, India, Indonesia) appear driven by regional power ambitions that would dictate the development of an indigenous ability to produce a sweeping plate of weapon systems in-country, and they therefore pursued or pursue an arms sourcing and offset strategy with broad technology transfer requirements. Yet other states (for example, South Korea) seek an ability to produce a wide spectrum of systems not because of regional power ambitions but because of a general desire and increasing ability to broadly participate in all industrial markets. Still other states appear to view arms offsets as an opportunity to revive a collapsed or failed indigenous arms industry (for example, Poland). Other states (for example, the United Kingdom) view offsets as a tool toward reaching an ever more advanced state of a globally integrated arms manufacturing system in which producers residing in various states produce components for sometimes this and sometimes that lead-manufacturer. The primary objective is joint production parceled out to competitive, cost-minimizing producers across the globe (Mawdsley and Brzoska, p. 106), and offsets can help states to position themselves at the top of the arms supply chain. And still other countries appear to more naively view arms offsets as a way to simply get the arms and keep the money at home as well (as, for example, South Africa did).[5]

13.2.5   Offset Characteristics

While countries' offset objectives are codified in arms offset policies that naturally vary among states and vary within states over time, a set of universal characteristics that define countries' offset arrangements in practice can be discerned. These characteristics include: (1) that importing countries generally mandate offset requirements by law, often to 100 percent of the arms contract value; (2) that offset requirements start at some minimum contract value, often as low as $5 million; (3) that multipliers are frequently attached to offset deals, meaning that a specific transaction value (say, $10 million) can be multiplied to count toward a higher value (say, $15 million) in fulfillment of the offset obligation; (4) that virtually all arms trade contracts now contain clauses that subject arms exporters to a variety of penalties for nonfulfillment of offset obligations (for example, exclusion from consideration for future contracts). In addition, there are expectations (5) that offsets will reduce arms acquisition costs; (6) that job creation and generalized economic development will result in the arms acquiring country; (7) that the offset will result in new and sustainable work (that is, that the offset not merely replace work that would have been sourced in-country anyway and that it not be one-off but continuous work); and (8) that the offsets result in general and specific technology transfers since technology is seen as a key component of future economic prosperity.

Elements crucially missing in these offset characteristics are offset contract monitoring, auditing and feedback to the importing country's defense contract-issuing organization and a plain economic valuation of whether or not the stated military and economic objectives associated with offsets have been met. Tellingly, very few countries have ever carried out even a single formal and independent offset-contract audit to determine to what degree, if any, the hopes with which offset contracts are invested come to fruition.

13.3   THE MECHANICS

13.3.1   Offset Mandates

As a rule, importing countries mandate offsets formally or informally, frequently to 100 percent of the arms contract value. For example, the United Kingdom typically asks for 100 percent (Mawdsley and Brzoska, p. 107). Likewise, Germany typically asks for 100 percent offset both during its rearmament period as well as today (p. 110). The Nordic countries (Denmark, Finland, Norway, Sweden) all have minimum contract values at which 100 percent offsets are demanded (Hagelin, p. 138).

Some countries ask and receive (promises) for more than 100 percent offsets. For example, when Poland signed an aircraft deal with an American company valued at $3.5 billion offsets were to amount to a value of $5.5 billion (Markowski and Hall, pp. 172, 181; the US values these offsets even higher). In one spectacular deal, South Africa is supposed to receive offsets valued at several times the value of the underlying arms import contract. Under a new EU offsets code of conduct, effective 1 July 2009, participating states agree to place a cap of 100 percent on offsets (more on the EU code later on in the chapter). But other countries ask for less than 100 percent offsets. Ordinarily, this happens in small economies whose industrial structure may have difficulty absorbing huge offset deals. For example, for contracts beyond about $13 million, Denmark's offset demands drop to 30 percent on the recognition that Denmark cannot absorb large offset programs (Hagelin, p. 139). In fact, offset demands can drop to zero, as in the case of Finland and Norway (Hagelin, p. 143). In Taiwan, in contracts above $50 million, "the government seeks between 30 to 60 percent in offsets" (Chinworth, p. 245). For a time, Australia asked for only 30 percent offsets on contracts valued at AU$2.5 million or above (Markowski and Hall, p. 272). Similarly, New Zealand generally asks for around 30 percent (Markowski and Hall, p. 275).

Most countries have formal offset laws, policies or regulations. There are exceptions, however. These include, for example, Germany (Mawdsley and Brzoska, p. 108), India (Baskaran, p. 217) and Japan (Chinworth, p. 237). In these cases, there nonetheless exist well-understood informal offset policies. Germany, for instance, effectively runs a procurement cartel to which foreign suppliers gain access only by joining a German-led consortium such that foreign-sourced items are channeled via German (co)production. Singapore, likewise, has no formal offsets policy but channels most contracts through a special corporation set up to deal with arms production issues (Bitzinger, p. 262).

During the 1990s, a number of countries shifted emphasis from a lofty general economic development goal to more narrowly conceived objectives, seeking special technology transfer assistance via offsets for their own military equipment production. These countries include, for example, all of the Nordic countries (Hagelin, p. 143; Sköns, p. 152). Poland's recent aircraft and armored vehicle deals are specifically tied to a hoped-for reinvigoration of its moribund post-Communist arms production industry (Markowski and Hall, Chapter 12).

If not specifically tied to military industry, many countries focus their offset efforts on technology transfers tied to local industry (military or otherwise). This would include for instance Taiwan, Australia and New Zealand. Only a few countries now, such as South Africa, still seem to believe that offsets can result in across-the-board generalized economic development and job creation.

13.3.2 Minimum Offset-contract Values

Countries recognize that offset administration involves fixed and marginal costs. They therefore stipulate minimum arms contract values at which offset requirements kick in. For example, in Denmark foreign-sourced military contracts up to about $3 million are offset free; beyond that offset requirements are applied (Hagelin, p. 139). In the United Kingdom, the minimum value is set at £10 million (£50 million for France and Germany under a reciprocal waiver agreement) although Britain automatically asks for offsets on any deal, regardless of the amount, involving the United States (Mawdsley and Brzoska, p. 106). For Poland, the minimum at which 100 percent offsets are demanded is set at contracts valued above $5 million of which at least half must benefit the defense industry (Markowski and Hall, p. 179). In Brazil, offsets are asked for contracts over $1 million, and 100 percent offsets for contracts over $5 million (Perlo-Freeman, p. 192). South Korea, "applies offset requirements for any defense transaction in excess of $10 million. The minimum required offset is 30 percent, "but has been raised to 70 percent for some recent, high-profile programs" (Chinworth, p. 241). Taiwan "seeks between 30 to 60 percent in offsets in arms sales above $50 million" (Chinworth, p. 243). And in South Africa, contracts above US$50 million are "subject to a fifty percent offset or industrial participation policy" (Haines, p. 302).[6]

13.3.3 Multipliers

Many countries apply multipliers to offset fulfillment. This means that if an arms exporter invests say $50 million in an activity that is particularly desired by the importing country (often some form of technology transfer), the $50 million may be counted at some multiple toward offset fulfillment. This multiple can range from some very small number such as 0.1 (that is, an extra 10 percent) to numbers as large as 5, 6 or even higher. In the Nordic countries, the size of multipliers is falling: in Finland from 20+ to now as low as 0.5; in Denmark no multipliers are offered at all except for high tech cases; Sweden's maximum multiplier is 3 but is restricted to limited cases; Norway's maximum is 5 and goes as low as 0.1 (Hagelin, p. 140). Poland uses multipliers of 0.5 to 2 and exceptionally of up to 5 (Markowski and Hall, p. 179). New Zealand uses multipliers between 1 and 3 (Markowski and Hall, p. 275). Like Denmark, the United Kingdom offers no multipliers at all. Moreover, offsets are credited to the arms seller only when transferred technology is actually used by a UK firm (Mawdsley and Brzoska, p. 107).

All-in-all, we gain the impression that the size of multipliers has been falling over the decades. For the United States for 1993–2007 offset multipliers applied to only 12.4 percent of arms offset contracts (1145/9249 contracts). In the other 87.6 percent, US arms exporters had to deliver the full offset value. For the same time period, in value terms – that is, offset credit value over transaction value – the average multiplier amounts to about 17 percent. As smaller contract and value numbers imply that more actual offset value must be delivered, this means that buying states play a relatively strong hand against US arms exporters.[7]

13.3.4 Penalties

Arms offset contracts routinely contain clauses that subject arms exporters to a variety of penalties for nonfulfillment of offset obligations such as exclusion from consideration for future contracts in the country or cash penalties (enforcement, of course, is an entirely different matter). Norway for instance imposes a penalty of not less than 10 percent of the contract value[8] and Denmark simply blacklists or bans the supplier (Hagelin, p. 141), as does South Korea (Chinworth, p. 241). In Poland, the offset provider may be held liable for "liquidated damages equivalent to 100 percent of the outstanding offsets obligation" (Markowski and Hall, p. 179). But in practice, Markowski and Hall write (p. 182), "liquidated damages are set initially at 4 percent for four years – not 100 percent as required under the Act – and subsequently at 3 percent." Likewise, Australia and New Zealand use liquidated damages as their penalty option (Markowski and Hall, pp. 272, 275).

13.4 THE EVIDENCE

13.4.1 Cost Reduction?

In the political and news media arenas, the expectation is that offsets will reduce arms procurement costs to the importing country; and certainly that there be no cost premium as compared to off-the-shelf arms purchases. Australia for instance has an explicit "no cost premium" expectation (Markowski and Hall p. 272). But this is illusionary. The administrative cost of offsets alone is believed to cost arms sellers anywhere from 7 to 10 percent of contract value (Markusen, p. 71), and this cost must be recovered in some form.

In practice, many countries recognize and pay for the additional cost. For example, Germany asked for 100 percent offsets during its rearmament period and additional costs were accepted if this led to technology transfers, that is, long-term gains (Mawdsley and Brzoska p. 110). When several European nations bought F-16 aircraft from General Dynamics in 1975 they paid an extra 34 percent, an estimate that does "not include the costs of the extra time and delays involved in the F-16 coproduction program compared with a direct buy from the USA (for example, the costs of running-on old equipment)" (Hartley, p. 130). Even worse, in the context of intra-European collaborative projects, Hartley reports cost premium estimates ranging from 33 to 100 percent for certain collaborative arms acquisition projects (for example, the Merlin helicopter, the Eurofighter Typhoon) as compared to projections for go-it-alone acquisition (Hartley, p. 119). OCCAR, a four-nation procurement agency (France, Germany, Italy, UK), is an attempt to base procurement awards on competition rather than *juste retour* but its success is to be awaited (Hartley, p. 120), as is that of a yet to be established pan-European Arms Procurement Agency.

Even the UK's participation in the US-dominated Joint Strike Fighter (JSF) program is estimated to be 4 percent more expensive than outright purchase. The extra 4 percent will buy access to participation and technology, and a go-it-alone program would cost Britain 60 to 105 percent more

(Hartley, p. 123). One risk is that already announced reductions in the number of units to be acquired by the United States will raise unit costs for the United Kingdom and other JSF partner nations (Hartley, p. 126) so that the ultimate cost may be much higher than anticipated.

For the Nordic countries, Hagelin reports that Denmark now acknowledges that offsets result in added costs and Finland estimates 10 to 15 percent added cost per offset contract (Hagelin, p. 143). For Finland and Sweden, Sköns reports that for both mandatory and voluntary offsets costs are higher as compared to off-the-shelf purchases (p. 150). The Finnish F/A-18 Hornet deal added between $100 and $200 million in contract administration cost alone that the Finnish government agreed to bear. This amounted to 3 to 6 percent of the contract value (Sköns, p. 154). In both Finland and Sweden, part of the motivation to switch from vaguely defined general economic development offsets to purely defense-oriented offsets was not only the difficulty to properly target general offsets but also their associated cost (Sköns, p. 160).

For Belgium, Struys reports offset-related "overcosts" estimated at 20 to 30 percent of imported items (Struys, pp. 166–167). Poland's public procurement law of 1994 aimed at competitive tendering and transparency contains certain crucial exemptions with regard to defense acquisitions so that cost savings are unlikely to be achieved; they cannot, at any rate, be monitored because transparency rules have been undermined for defense acquisitions (Markowski and Hall, pp. 178, 182).

In Brazil, Perlo-Freeman reports that "the sheer size and complexity of major warship projects has given rise to serious cost inflation and delays, unmitigated by export orders" (p. 197) and across all arms acquisition categories he notes "the added cost of such deals compared with off-the-shelf procurement" and that "this was accepted by the government as a necessary price for obtaining technology" (p. 197). This assessment also reflects India's experience where licensed technology programs in tanks, aircraft and naval vessels "faced delays and cost overruns, and resulted in spectacular failures" (Baskaran, p. 218). In its dealings with Western suppliers, such as Britain, France and Sweden, India tended to make use of credit arrangements "to cover the foreign exchange burden. However, evidence suggests that such arrangements resulted in increased selling prices" (Baskaran, p. 221). Likewise, India's arms relation with Russia and eastern Europe "appears to have resulted in a significant burden on the Indian economy" (pp. 223–4).

Regarding South Korea, Chinworth writes that it "would be premature to label the country's policies and experiences as a collective failure, but it also would be generous to characterize them as a success" (p. 243). For Indonesia's civilian aircraft program, based on offset deals, Bitzinger reports that its "apparent success was illusory . . . In reality, [it] was a bloated, state-owned white elephant, employing many more workers than it needed and was awash in excess production capacity" (p. 264). For instance, the government poured about $1 billion into a particular civilian airliner that eventually failed to receive FAA certification and thereby made it impossible to bring the aircraft to market anywhere.

For Australia as well, a form of offsets called Strategic Industry Development Activities (SIDAs) are thought to contain a cost premium (Markowski and Hall, pp. 273–274), although mostly of unspecified and uncertain size. In one case, the Australian Department of Defense "itself calculated that the cost premium paid for local industry participation in assembly of F/A-18 aircraft in the late 1980s amounted to 29 percent of the value of the additional work required to be done in Australia (Markowski and Hall, p. 280). The authors note that "industry outcomes associated with offsets have failed to live up to their promise" and they make the important point that mere "compliance with offset requirements should not be interpreted to benefit the defense department and/or the economy at large" (p. 280).

Finally, a South African arms procurement deal with certain European nations was trumpeted to generate some 65000 new jobs but Dunne and Lamb point out that while "this sounds impressive [it] amounts to a cost of R1.6 million per job and is extremely high, nearly 20 times the average cost per job in South Africa's defense industry" (p. 288). As in the case for other countries, the authors argue that "the arms deal has had a positive effect on South Africa's economy, particularly in defense-related industry – after all, the billions must buy something – but there is little evidence that the predicted level of benefits have been or will be reached" (p. 289). In 2000, personnel at the South African ministries of finance and of trade and industry estimated the overall return on the arms deal "to be on the order of 94.5 percent . . . [and] that during the duration of the deal, anticipated exports would be in the region of 280 percent of the original purchase price" (Haines, p. 303). But in his case study, Haines finds "substantial hidden costs associated with offsets" (p. 312). For example, substantial state investment in regional infrastructure and other resources would be needed for offsets to work as planned but were not forthcoming for the cases and regions he examined. "Yet this kind of cost is not factored into official assessments of the Strategic Defense Program and the associated offset work" (p. 312).

Suppose country A procures $1 billion worth of arms from country B with a 100 percent offset requirement to be fulfilled in the form of arms co-production in country A. Also suppose that there is a 30 percent cost premium. One way to view the cost aspect of offsets then is to say that since country B returns funds to country A, the net external cost to A is if not zero than certainly smaller as compared to a pure off-the-shelf purchase.[9] There is thus no question that offsets work in the sense that funds are returned to the importing country,[10] although it has never yet been shown – and often been questioned (for example, Brauer, 2002) – just what this foreign-exchange saving would amount to. But another view is to observe that country A spent a fiscal total of $1.3 billion ultimately to be raised from its taxpayers. The scant evidence we have suggests that the extra $300 million – the offset "overcost" – does not buy general economic development, does not buy new and sustainable work and, except for limited, specific cases does not result in appreciable technology transfer. This is explored in the next subsections.

13.4.2   Generalized Economic Development?

Even if offsets result in higher total contract cost this could be justified if general economic development is stimulated, as politicians claim and as the news media repeat. The evidence is mixed, however, with the balance of evidence pointing to adverse experiences. In the United Kingdom, for instance, offsets are generally directed at small- and medium-sized enterprises (SMEs) and as a consequence of involvement in the American C-130J Hercules transport aircraft "some UK SMEs are now embedded in the supply chain" (Mawdsley and Brzoska, p. 107). But the objective here centered on getting UK companies embedded in supply chains whether or not offsets were offered (in fact, in this particular case direct offsets were very small).

Emphasis on SMEs was also important to Denmark and Finland (Hagelin, p. 139) but with little evidence that this strategy worked. To the contrary, a 1999 Finnish offset audit acknowledged that except for some degree of technology transfer, other anticipated offset gains were not realized (Hagelin, p. 143). This is echoed by Sköns, whose review of offset audits in Finland and Sweden finds mostly negative experiences that led both countries to shift offset objectives from vague, general economic development objectives toward narrowly defined military-industry related offsets (p. 160).

Germany appears to have taken a more practical approach from the start of its rearmament program by locating and tightly integrating military technology and defense production in civilian firms, often in peripheral areas to assist regional economic development.[11] A similarly focused approach, in this case targeted on certain key industries, has been taken by Taiwan. This differs from Japan and South Korea, both of which have aimed – without success – at self-sufficient production in all defense systems (Chinworth, p. 245). Not unlike Denmark, Belgium and New Zealand today, Taiwan realized early on that certain "practical obstacles exist that limit the economic impact of offset agreements with Taiwan. Analysts have noted that few companies or research organizations within Taiwan have sufficient capability to manage large military programs" (Chinworth, p. 245). But limiting work directed toward its civilian sector to 15 percent of all offset work "minimizes the multiplier effects of offsets" (Chinworth, pp. 245–6). In Poland, offsets are seen as a way to rebuild its ailing defense industry (Markowski and Hall, p. 172) but whether this succeeds and how many sustainable jobs are to be created remains to be seen. The Poles at least appeared to have learned from other countries' experiences that promises of general economic development will likely go unfulfilled.

Whatever the official rhetoric for public consumption, a number of countries have been clear that their primary purpose with arms trade offset work regards not general economic development but development of the indigenous arms industry, for example, Japan, South Korea, Taiwan and Poland. This is also true of Brazil where "offset policy and practice . . . involving licensed production, coproduction, and technology transfer has been pursued not so much for direct economic benefit but to develop Brazil's arms industry to fulfill a certain view of its place in the world" (Perlo-Freeman, p. 199).

As mentioned, countries that did harbor and pursue general economic development appear to have given up on this objective (for example, the Nordic countries). Nonetheless, some countries still pursue this dream. These include Indonesia and South Africa. The case of Indonesia also illustrates a particular vulnerability. Bitzinger writes: "The 1997–98 Asian financial crisis was the defining event that forced Jakarta to reexamine and ultimately dramatically scale back its ambitious plans for its aerospace industry and instead to greatly downsize its arms industry" (p. 264). South Africa also has yet to learn from the prevailing experience. Its officials sought to link offset projects "with other national economic and industrial policy initiatives, such as . . . Spatial Development Initiatives and Industrial Development Zones," even though analysts suggested that many of the promised investments were dubious and now seem to have been correct (Dunne and Lamb, p. 288). In his study on regional economic development in South Africa, Haines, for instance, finds few, if any, positive effects. To the contrary, "the recent arms deal will probably reinforce the current economic situation and existing [regional and other] inequalities in South Africa" (Haines, p. 303). The lesson is that virtually no evidence exists that general economic development goals are ever achieved via offsets. Germany may be the exception, back in the 1950s.

13.4.3 New and Sustainable Work?

Another criterion often expressed by officials is that offsets not merely replace work that would have been sourced in-country anyway and that it not be one-off but continuous work. Mawdsley and Broska for instance write that the United Kingdom requires new work for its defense-related industry, moreover new work that is of equivalent technical quality than would otherwise be bought off-the-shelf. This is to avoid offset in-sourcing of inappropriately low-tech work (p. 106). This resulted from the UK's disagreeable experience with its Boeing AWACS purchase in the 1980s. In that case, the UK agreed to 130 percent offset work but little genuinely new work resulted. For instance, Rolls-Royce aircraft engines that Boeing bought for its commercial airlines were counted as offset work – accounting in fact for half of the entire offset obligation – even though these civilian airliner engines would have been bought anyway (Hartley, pp. 120–21). For examples like these, it is estimated that offset work in developed countries brings in perhaps only 25 to 50 percent genuinely new but not necessarily sustained or sustainable work (Hartley, p. 121).

Mawdsley and Brzoska write that in spite of decades of arms licensing and co-operation with Germany, Argentina received virtually no long-term benefit (p. 114). This underscores Brauer's argument and evidence that a minimum condition for successful indigenous arms production efforts is that existing civilian industry must already exist from which a state may branch out into military-related work (Brauer 1991, 2000). Sköns cites "extremely limited" job and export creation for SMEs on account of Finland's Hornet F/A-18 deal (p. 153). Struys emphasizes that Belgium practices an explicit regional political sharing of offsets among its Flemish, Walloon and Brussels regions. This contributes to offset-related overcosts since work allocation decisions are made on the basis of a political rather than economic calculus (p. 167). Perlo-Freeman reports that Brazil's anticipated Mirage fighter replacement (on the order of $700 million) is not thought likely to result in sustainable work unless unexpected export orders were to come in (p. 195). Indeed, of all of Brazil's extensive indigenous arms production ventures started since the 1930s with various forms of offsets only a single one – Helibras – might be deemed commercially viable (p. 196).

Indonesia's attempt to create an indigenous military and civilian air-craft industry collapsed in the wake of the 1997 financial crisis in East Asia. The main aircraft corporation, IPTN, was forced to restructure and, by 2000, accumulated a debt of $570 million. It also had to lay off "around one-third of its workforce, or 5000 employees" and anticipates cutting an additional 3500 jobs in the near future (Bitzinger, p. 264). The most egregious recent job generation claim is that of South Africa. It claimed that its arms offset deal will result in 65000 new jobs over seven years. As quoted before, to Dunne and Lamb, "this sounds impressive but amounts to a cost of R1.6 million per job and is extremely high, nearly 20 times the average cost per job in South Africa's defense industry" (p. 288) and it is "not clear that the companies will be internationally competitive to allow follow-on industrial development to be sustainable" (p. 290).[12]

Once more, the main lesson is that there is virtually no positive and certainly no compelling evidence that offsets create new, let alone sustainable jobs. The mere, but very common, assertion of states and their offsets agencies claiming "success" is not evidence. For example, the United Arab Emirates' (UEA) Offset Program Bureau (OPB) reports in its issue 3, April 2008, newsletter on Nextcare Administrative Services (NAS), a healthcare claims administrator. This is "incorporated in Abu Dhabi as a joint venture between the Alfia Investment Company LLC, a company under the UAE Offset Program umbrella, and the National Investor, a leading UAE investment firm."[13] It is utterly unclear why, in the absence of offsets, a healthcare claims processor could not have been established anyway. Likewise, OPB proudly reports the creation of a new holding company – Tawazun Holding – in October 2007 that promptly bought "Caracal International, the first national arms manufacturer in the United Arab Emirates." Jobs and assets already existed, and the newsletter reader must remain mystified as to the exact nature of the "success" of the offsets program.

13.4.4 Technology Transfer

With regard to general and specific technology transfer directed either toward military or civilian industry the record is also mixed. Military-offsets are considered highly desirable, for instance, to help maintain the UK defense industrial base (Mawdsley and Brzoska, p. 106) but the quality of that transfer must frequently be doubted. With regard to the aforementioned Boeing AWACS deal, Hartley writes that UK work on aircraft galleys and on-board toilets was counted as "high technology" (p. 121). During the competition to supply replacement fighter aircraft for the Royal Air Force in the UK, Lockheed Martin made certain claims in favor of its advanced F-16 aircraft. But Hartley writes that "these claimed benefits are rarely supported with empirical evidence . . . for example, reference to the technology benefits of offsets rely on *ad hoc* examples, such as the transfer of US production and management technology to European co-producers. Rarely is consideration given to assessing the market value of such technology and who pays for these benefits (governments or firms)" (p. 130).

The experience with civilian-oriented technology transfers appears to be worse than the examples with military-offset technology transfers already suggest. This is the reason why all Nordic countries, but especially Sweden, are now primarily interested in technology transfers that support indigenous military industry (Hagelin, p. 139). Sköns adds that while technology transfer and export promotion are "complicated to evaluate" (p. 156) Sweden's experience with civilian offset attempts have been most negative (p. 159).

In contrast, a number of authors report that military-directed technology transfers originating with offset deals are considered successful in some country's own terms, at least in certain cases, for example, in the case of Brazil, which as a result of technology transfer strategy ended up with a world leader in the regional Embraer. This was, however, achieved through massive government investment and subsidy and Brazil is still nowhere near having fully autonomous arms production in any sector.

Likewise for India. Baskaran's assessment is that while there is no question that certain technologies were successfully transferred, "the industry failed to acquire capabilities sufficient to close the technology gap with developed countries and keep pace with technological change in weapon systems" (p. 219, also p. 224). A particular problem seemed to be that "technology transfers at the level of whole systems worked less efficiently than at component level as sellers tended to withhold core technologies" (Baskaran, p. 220). This hints at what Chinworth found for the case of Taiwan. He writes that its "efforts to develop indigenous systems in the 1990s resulted in items that remained heavily dependent on imported technology; not all domestic development programs were successful" (p. 246).[14] A response to or proper anticipation of such experiences explains the relatively more successful cases of Singapore and Germany. With regard to the former, Bitzinger's view is that "Singapore's defense industry appears to be thriving, largely because of its core competencies/niche production business strategy" (p. 264). The available offset work is limited in scope but sustainable, even spilling into the nondefense sector. Tellingly, the requirement rather than consequence of this strategy is its "significant impact on further diminishing the nation's already low attachment to offsets as an industrial policy," and in the case of its participation in the US JSF project the country explicitly rejected the idea of offsets (pp. 265–6). Germany was "unusually successful" with its objective of integrating offsets resulting from post-World War II rearmament but almost certainly not only because of its own careful planning but because of NATO's interest in successfully binding Germany into the alliance (Mawdsley and

Brzoska, pp. 108–10). Even so, reflecting its civilian-industrial strengths Germany's defense work today is niche production in the automotive and marine industries (tanks, ships) rather than in aircraft and electronics.

Finally, with regard to South Africa, it must be acknowledged that the country has some indigenous industrial capacity that could be exploited if South African firms were to be integrated into an emerging European or global arms production supply chain (Dunne and Lamb, p. 288). But potential need not and may not translate into actual experience. As regards the non-defense industry, the authors question the offset deal. For instance, they write that "it is not clear whether South Africa is getting state-of-the-art technology in areas of growth, or old technology in areas of overcapacity (for example, stainless steel)" (Dunne and Lamb, p. 290). In fact, the BIS reports that "anecdotal information obtained from industry suggests that 'cutting edge' or nascent technologies under development in the United States are less likely to be transferred to foreign companies in fulfillment of offset obligations than 'older' technologies" (BIS 2008, p. 19).

13.5 LESSONS AND ISSUES

Although for many countries this may reasonably be disputed (Dumas, Chapter 1), assume that arms imports are in fact needed for legitimate defense purposes. There is nonetheless a crying need for countries to obtain a much better idea of what works under what circumstances, and what does not work (Taylor, Chapter 2, and Markowski and Hall, Chapter 3, offer some guidelines). To date, the evidence does not suggest that offsets advance countries' long-term goals. To summarize this evidence, it is now quite clear that offsets do not result in arms acquisition cost reductions, that offsets do not stimulate broad-based civilian economic development, that neither substantial nor sustained job creation occurs, not even within the military sector, that almost no successful technology transfer into the civilian sector is observed, and that only limited technology transfer into the military sector occurs, often over decades and at high cost. Moreover, whatever technology is transferred is quickly outpaced by continuous technology advances in the main developed countries, especially the United States.

These lessons can be drawn in spite of severe data problems (for example, Baskaran, p. 217, on India; Dunne and Lamb, p. 289, on South Africa; Hagelin, p. 143, on Norway; and Hartley, p. 118, generally). But from what data points are available, the general picture can be pieced together. The onus to prove otherwise lies with those who would champion the case of offsets. Regrettably, their case relies on pre-offset assertions, rather than post-offset evidence. As Hartley points out, the incentive is to exaggerate benefits and understate or ignore the costs (p. 121).

The case studies raise several additional issues:

1. *Data, access and audits*: As mentioned, the data situation is poor. So is countries' willingness to allow researchers access to offset-related data, even in democracies. This is difficult to justify. Any country ought to be interested whether or not policies work and what their costs are. Where public funds are expended, public accounting is needed. There is no reason to treat the military any different. The press widely reports on offset deals so that there can be no fear about military secrets being revealed. Even for their own internal use, governments ought to want to know what offsets cost their countries. This would improve decision-making. From the country case studies it appears that only Australia, Finland and Sweden have ever carried out official audits of specific arms trade offset contracts (in Finland 1 out of 20 offset deals since 1977; in Australia and Sweden 3 out of 15 since 1983).

   Audits need to be done on economic principles, counting *all* economic costs (Brauer, Chapter 4). This would include for instance environmental costs associated with weapon production, the cost of manpower training, special infrastructure construction and other resource uses to support offset work, as well as the opportunity cost of directing resources to offset rather than other work. All this requires a sophisticated set of monitoring tools and abilities by the relevant state agencies which, especially in developing countries, may not be readily available. Still, expert consultants could be hired to take at least a partial look at things. Offsets should not be excluded from the planning, execution and feedback loop.

2. *Vulnerabilities*: Data apart, the case studies lead to a striking observation: Brazil's arms industry collapsed post-1988 with the end of the Iran–Iraq war; Argentina's vanished, Poland's folded, Western Europe's bent, post-1991, following the dissolution of the Soviet bloc, and South Africa's industry faltered post-1994 with the end of apartheid. Unsurprisingly for an industry that thrives on latent and actual conflict, less or less intense conflict lowers demand for its products. It seems absurd then that some countries still intend to build the industry and that offsets are thought (and sought) to promote this. In a declining market, exit not entry has to occur. Thus it is virtually certain that even as developing countries are trying to build arms industries, the industry will decline and some producers be withdrawn

from the market, as Argentina and Belgium already all but completely have (for evidence of exit, see Brauer 2007). Tellingly, where tensions remain – the Indian subcontinent, the Korean peninsula, Taiwan – costly arms industry efforts continue.

Vulnerability stems not only from lack of demand but also from other market forces such as the collapse of Indonesia's arms industry post-1997 in the wake of the East Asian financial crisis illustrates. A third vulnerability comes from the growing technology gap between developed and developing countries. Even if some militarily-relevant technology is transferred, it is illogical to believe that leading countries will voluntarily surrender their technology lead. (Indeed, any truly remarkable advances appear to have come from illegally transferred technologies or from exceedingly costly ones unrelated to any officially sanctioned offsets, for example, rockets, missiles, nuclear technology.)

3. *Military Malthusianism*: A further vulnerability is compellingly illustrated by Scheetz's case study of Argentina (Chapter 14). "Military Malthusianism" arises from a single inescapable fact, namely that the unit-cost of major weapon systems rises faster than government budget revenues (geometric against arithmetic series). When even well-developed, industrialized countries such as those of Western Europe cannot cope anymore with spiraling unit-costs, it is fantastic to believe that developing states will be able to do so. Even the United States cannot entirely cope with the extraordinary cost in all weapons classes, hence its invitation to select countries from across the globe to join it in the development of its Joint Strike Fighter program.

As a consequence of this military Malthusianism, states are left with four options (Hartley, p. 118): (1) the "equal misery" option in which a state's defense programs are cut across the board; (2) the "defense review" option that would reduce states' defense commitments; (3) the "increased defense budget" option which would come at the expense of non-defense programs or a higher tax-take; and (4) the "increased efficiency" option to obtain economies by globalizing arms production and arms acquisition. Options 1 to 3 have variously been tried or are not feasible. Option 4 would make countries' arms industries mutually dependent, and although that is the current trend, the long-run consequence would be that countries cannot fight when important arms component production sites are located in each others' territories. Military Malthusianism thus raises the tantalizing hope that as unit-costs of weapon systems become unaffordable we might be spending ourselves to peace.

But this will not happen for there is a fifth option, not noted by

Hartley. That is that states or other actors will offend, deter and defend differently. They will, in a word, find substitutes. In fact, this has been going on for some time as the examples of state-sponsored or state-supported terrorism, guerrilla warfare, low-intensity warfare, low-tech warfare, proxy wars and the use of private military companies illustrate. Military Malthusianism implies that we will see more non-conventional conflict.

4. *The strong and the weak*: To be sure, there is concern that offsets help create international competitors in the short term. But offsets combined with the vulnerabilities listed in points 2 and 3 create not merely an increasing number of arms producers but an enfeebled number of state-based arms industries, kept alive by an infusion of costly state aid as in Brazil, India, Indonesia, South Africa, South Korea and other countries. It is not surprising then that a number of arms producing countries turn out to be too weak to survive in the arms market (Brauer 2007). They become infant industries that never grow up and drain the economies of the mother state. Some of these infants have died (for example, Argentina); others survive by becoming "orphans," adopted by strong industrial powerhouses that integrate the weak into a global supply-chain (for example, Singapore, an increasing number of Western European countries and, to a lesser extent, Taiwan and South Korea).[15]

5. *Arms globalization*: The most likely of Hartley's four options to be adopted in the short-run – at least in the European context – is increased arms internationalization. Gradually, EU members will drift toward a European Arms Procurement Agency with competitively let contracts.[16] Certain developing countries or countries in the Far East will seek to become part of the supply-chain either with US or EU firms, or both, much as is the case now with the commercial aircraft of Boeing and Airbus. In this case, offsets for major weapon systems would largely disappear, and the defense industry would become just another industry, much like globalized automobile or consumer electronics design, manufacturing and distribution.

This is not to say that we will see a two-bloc system, the United States against the European Union. The Joint Strike Fighter model, although led by the US already involves several European and non-European partners, and it is not inconceivable that in future the EU will take the lead in other projects, such as armored vehicles. Joining an arms supply chain may, at any rate, be the only remaining realistic option for several small, industrialized European and non-European countries (for example, Australia, Denmark, Finland, Norway, New Zealand, South Korea, Taiwan). As Chinworth writes

(p. 247), "typically, offsets have been post-production agreements but increased globalization results in more pre-production agreements that determine work share and technology transfers," most likely based on market competition.

6. *Offsets will not disappear but may be in retreat*: The United States' government officially regards offsets to be "economically inefficient and trade distorting" (BIS 2008, p. i). More pointedly, it is concerned about the viability of its defense industrial base when bits of the defense supply chain may be undermined by shipping defense-export work abroad. For example, for 2004–2007, the estimated dollar value of domestic work accruing to defense-export sales in the US aerospace sector was $18.4 billion, half of which was lost (transferred abroad) due to offset contracts (BIS 2008, p. 17, Table 5.4). Put differently, defense exports do result in a net economic gain to the economy of the United States but only by half as much as would have been the case in the absence of offset agreements. A US government "interagency team was able to conclude that the United States is not alone in its concerns about the use of offsets in defense procurement. Other industrialized nations, which also are major providers of offsets, expressed concerns about the adverse effects of offsets on their sales of defense weapons systems. These provider nations expressed interest in a multinational dialogue to address their concerns. From both providers and demanders of offsets, most nations agree with the United States' view that there is a real cost associated with offsets."[17]

Correspondingly, 26 states have subscribed to the European Defense Agency's "Code of Conduct on Offsets," which took effect on 1 July 2009. The Code (1) provides for a bit of transparency (collecting states' basic offset information on a common web site), (2) strives to avoid undue competition by collecting defense work across the member states without distorting offsets, that is, to promote the development of a European Defense Technological and Industrial Base (EDTIB), (3) limits offsets to a cap of 100 percent of contract value, and (4) puts a reporting and monitoring system in place. In an interview the director of EDA's Defence Industry and Market Directorate, Arturo Alfonso-Meirino, acknowledged however, that the Code applies only to its subscribing states and the non-members, that is, major arms buyers such as India, China and Middle Eastern states still will demand offsets.[18] Arms trade offsets thus will not just disappear. Nonetheless, that both the United States and the European Union (through EDA) at the highest government levels steer against the use of arms trade offsets suggests that economic arguments would appear to have carried the day.

ACKNOWLEDGEMENTS

This chapter is based on a paper first delivered at the 8th Annual Defence Economics and Security Conference, University of the West of England, Bristol, June 2004.

NOTES

1. Unless otherwise noted, all dollar-values in this chapter refer to US dollars.
2. Section 309 of the Defense Production Act of 1950, as amended.
3. See   http://www.bis.doc.gov/defenseindustrialbaseprograms/osies/offsets/default.htm, accessed 13 July 2009.
4. When the nominal dollar figures are deflated using 2000 as the base-year, the totals are nearly identical to those reported in the text, probably because the year 2000 lies about half-way between 1993 and 2007.
5. On the arms exporting side of the ledger, arms exporters (for example, in the US, UK, Sweden, and others) almost always see offset requirements as a costly distraction and nuisance (for example, Mawdsley and Brzoska, p. 106), something that has to be done to win contracts but that they would prefer to be able to avoid.
6. For certain EU states, updated information may be obtained from http://www.eda. europa.eu/offsets/, the European Defense Agency's web page on offsets, accessed 16 July 2009. The EDA was established on 12 July 2004.
7. Information extracted from BIS (2008).
8. See EDA (2009), then click on "Norway."
9. In practice net external, that is, foreign exchange, costs are never zero since domestic co-production invariably requires at least some imports of weapon system components.
10. In 1996–97 in Australia, for example, as a consequence of offset regulations, "87 percent of expenditure on defense logistics was spent in-country, 55 percent of capital equipment was sourced locally, and 99 percent of expenditure on capital facilities was spent in-country" (Markowski and Hall, p. 273).
11. Germany does not have pure defense firms; instead defense work is carried out in firms that are primarily civilian (Mawdsley and Brzoska, pp. 108–109).
12. An earlier case study on defense offsets in Saudi Arabia "reveals that instead of a projected 75 000 local jobs, the various programs generated employment in the region of 2000" (Matthews 2002).
13. Available via www.offset.ae, accessed 16 July 2009.
14. The Indigenous Fighter Aircraft, for example, ran into cost and quality control problems limiting its production run.
15. "The number of competitors in the world arms market has imploded even though each has somewhat greater access to each others' domestic markets. The competition remains oligopolistic but is more international in scope" (Markusen, p. 81).
16. Whether beyond that there will perhaps lie a genuine EU-wide defense and foreign policy with defense functions turned over to the EU as well is beyond the scope of chapter to discuss.
17. BIS (2008, Appendix F, p. 3).
18. EPICOS newsletter, 4 March 2009, p. 4; available on www.epicos.com, accessed 16 July 2009.

REFERENCES

Brauer, J. (1991), "Arms production in developing nations: the relation to industrial structure, industrial diversification, and human capital formation", *Defence Economics*, **2** (2), 165–75.

Brauer, J. (2000), "Potential and actual arms production: implications for the arms trade debate", *Defence and Peace Economics*, **11** (5), 461–80.

Brauer, J. (2002), "The arms industry in developing nations: history and post-Cold War assessment", in J. Brauer and J.P. Dunne (eds), *The Economics of Military Expenditure and Arms Production and Trade in Developing Countries*, London: Palgrave, pp. 101–127.

Brauer, J. (2007), "Arms industries, arms trade, and developing countries", in T. Sandler and K. Hartley (eds), *Handbook of Defense Economics*, Vol. 2, Amsterdam: Elsevier, pp. 973–1015.

Brauer, J. and J.P. Dunne (eds) (2004), *Arms Trade and Economic Development: Theory, Policy, and Cases in Arms Trade Offsets*, London: Routledge.

Bureau of Industry and Security [BIS] (2008), "Offsets in defense trade. Thirteenth study," Washington DC: Bureau of Industry and Security, US Department of Commerce, available at http://www.bis.doc.gov/defenseindustrialbaseprograms/osies/offsets/default.htm, accessed 13 July 2009.

EDA. (2009), "Code of Conduct on Offsets" Brussels: European Defense Agency, available at http://www.eda.europa.eu/offsets/, accessed 16 July 2009.

Matthews, R. (2002), "Saudi Arabia: defense offsets and development", in J. Brauer and J.P. Dunne (eds), *The Arms Industry in Developing Nations: History and Post-Cold War Assessment*, London: Palgrave, pp. 195–219.

PART V

POLITICAL AND ECONOMIC SYSTEMS

14 The capitalist peace
Erich Weede

14.1 THE CONCEPT AND THE CONTEXT

The capitalist peace is a comprehensive idea. It is not limited to assertions that economic freedom or capitalism,[1] trade, foreign investment, financial openness or the avoidance of state property ownership promotes peace, but it also includes the democratic peace. If democracy itself is a descendant of economic freedom or a "contract-intensive economy" (Mousseau 2009) and the prosperity generated by it, then the democratic peace becomes a mere component of the capitalist peace. Then capitalism and economic interdependence promote peace by two or even three routes, directly and indirectly, via democracy and, possibly, by common memberships in intergovernmental organizations, too. Admittedly, this argument relies on compiling lots of diverse evidence some of which is still debated in the scientific community (Weede 2005). Not all of it is quantitative, some of it is historical and qualitative. It derives from different disciplines: in particular, economics, sociology and political science. It supports the idea that capitalism is more important than democracy for two reasons. First, without capitalism and the prosperity it promotes, democracy is unlikely to exist. Second, democratic peace theory invites the misconception that one might promote democracy by war. After all, the pacific benefits of democracy did not convince the Taliban or Saddam Hussein that they should retire. By contrast, capitalism expands by the power of successful examples. The Chinese and Vietnamese *communist parties* accepted it because they were no longer satisfied by equality in poverty. The best thing about economic freedom or capitalism is that it does not only benefit those who enjoy it, but even those where the government still obstructs it (Hayek 1960). Ultimately, even the most robust determinant of economic growth, the level of economic development which provides potential advantages of backwardness, may be understood as an external benefit of economic freedom (Weede 2006). Whichever economic miracle in Asia might be one's favorite, it could not have happened without economic freedom in the West. Although a full appreciation of the capitalist peace rests on combining the study of economic growth and prosperity with the study of war, here the focus is *primarily* on the *direct* determinants of war and peace rather than on their more distant background conditions.

14.2   A REVIEW OF ECONOMETRIC STUDIES

Political scientists have investigated the issue of whether democracy or capitalism promote peace or the avoidance of war. As suggested above, peace is most effectively promoted by the establishment and expansion of a capitalist economic order. Whether democracy or some other characteristics of a capitalist order, like a contract-intensive economy or free trade, private property in the means of production, foreign direct investment or financial openness promote peace has been investigated by quantitative or econometric methods. The most frequently used approach is the dyadic design. The dyad is a pair of nations, say Georgia and Russia. Other dyads are, for example, Germany and France, or the United States and China. If there are hundred states at some point of time, then there are 4950 dyads, or 100 times 99 divided by two. If one considers the question whether a military conflict begins in a specific year, if one investigates a data set of 100 years, then one may ask the question, in which year a military conflict begins in which dyad. Such a data set can be huge and contain about half a million dyad-years which are the units of observation. The research task is to decompose the huge data set into component data sets where some contain most of the dyads and almost all of them are peaceful, and where other sets contain most of the military conflicts. Since war itself is a rare event, most empirical work replaces war with less disastrous events, such as militarized interstate conflict. Conceivable criteria for partitioning the entire set of dyad-years include democracy and free trade.[2]

The most frequently investigated hypothesis has been that democracy promotes peace. More exactly, military conflict becomes extremely unlikely if both countries in a dyad are democracies (Russett 1993; Ray 1995; Lipson 2003). Another hypothesis is that war becomes less likely, if two states trade a lot with each other, if their economies depend on this trade (Russett and Oneal 2001). It is not enough, however, to investigate only pacifying conditions, like free trade or democracy. We need to know which dyads are at risk, that is, which ones are likely to be involved in war (Bremer 1992). Take the dyad of Finland and Portugal where military conflict is unlikely. Is it because of the fact of both being democracies? Or, is it because of their trade within the European Community framework? A more obvious explanation of peace between Finland and Portugal than both of the explanations referred to above is the lack of opportunity for fighting. Similarly, one may confidently predict everlasting peace between South Korea and India irrespective of the regimes or the amount of trade between these two countries. Thus, if one wants to study the impact of conceivable pacifying conditions on the risk of military conflict, one also has to control for those background conditions which make conflict possible and likely: contiguity or distance, enforced transfers of territory in the past (because of resentment and the desire to recover the lost territories), one member of the dyad being a major power (because major powers have always been great fighters), or the balance of power within the dyad (because a preponderance of one nation over the other reduces the risk of war).

Concerning the pacifying conditions of democracy or capitalism, this type of research has led to the following conclusions: The risk of war between two democracies is extremely small, much smaller than between two autocracies (Russett 1993; Ray 1995; Russett and Oneal 2001; Lipson 2003). A major objection against this finding arises from the fact that most of the supporting evidence comes from the period after World War II (Gowa 1999). Since there have been few stable and contiguous democracies before 1945, this criticism is not very damaging to the democratic peace proposition. Some arguments do not deny the democratic peace, but instead qualify it and restrict its applicability. Mansfield and Snyder (2005) accept the argument for mature democracies, but reject it for recently established, unstable and immature regimes. Although the suspicion that young and imperfect democracies are more likely than others to become involved in war is not replicable (Narang and Nelson 2009), the democratic peace is less effective where the democracies are less stable and less perfect. Based on qualitative evidence, Mandelbaum (2007, p. 176) contends that liberty (or limited government) rather than popular government promotes peace. Since the establishment of the rule of law and limited government might need much more time than merely electing a government the arrival of full and mature democracies might need a generation or so. Then, democratization is no quick fix for the problems of world politics.[3]

Another qualification of the democratic peace (Mousseau, Hegre and Oneal 2003; Mousseau 2005) argues that it seems to apply more strongly among developed or rich countries than among the poorest ones where the pacification effects might vanish. In recent work, the democratic peace seems to become ever more conditional. It seems to be most effective and beyond dispute only in rich and mature democracies. A more devastating objection (Gibler 2007; Mousseau 2009) argues that the democratic peace, even at the dyadic level where its support is strongest, might be *spurious*. According to Gibler (2007), secure and stable borders which do not divide nations might promote democratic performance and the avoidance of war at the same time. According to Mousseau (2009), the contract-intensity of economies[4] determines whether or not a nation is a democracy as well as its avoidance of fatal conflicts and wars. Mousseau (2009, p. 5) claims, "From 1961 to 2001, democratic nations engaged in numerous fatal conflicts with each other, including at least one war, yet not a single fatal militarized incident occurred between nations with contract-intensive economies – where most people have the opportunity to participate in the market."[5] On the one hand, these are very serious objections, on the other hand, one still hesitates to give up one of the most robust findings in quantitative work on the causes of war on the basis of a few empirical studies.[6]

Some authors (Rummel 1995; Benoit 1996; Souva and Prins 2006; Boehmer 2008) have asserted that the pacification effect of democracy is *not* restricted to relations between democracies. Democracies as such might be less warlike than autocracies. Although there is some evidence in favor of this view, it is much less solid and robust than the evidence in favor of the dyadic democratic peace is. McDonald (2009) even argues that democracies actually were more war-prone during the nineteenth century than other states, and that pacifying effects of democracy depend on the *avoidance* of much state ownership in the economy.

There is little agreement on whether the risk of war between democracies and autocracies is higher than between two autocracies or lower.[7] My personal reading of the evidence favors the first and more pessimistic point of view. If the risk of war between democracies and autocracies is higher than between two democracies, then inserting a democracy into a solidly autocratic region does *not* improve, but reduces the prospects of peace. So, there is another reason to be skeptical about the benefits of democratization under all circumstances. Worse still, the frequency of war between strong democracies (like the US) and much weaker autocracies (like Afghanistan or Iraq) permits a very unfavorable interpretation (Waltz 2003–2004, p. 181): "The weaker can hardly threaten the stronger, yet democratic countries go to war against them. If this is true, it tells us something frightening about the behavior of democratic countries; namely, that they excel at fighting and winning unnecessary wars."[8]

Another finding of quantitative research is that military conflict becomes less likely, if the constituent nations of a dyad trade a lot with each other (Oneal and Russett 1997, 2003a, 2003b; Russett and Oneal 2001; Gartzke and Li 2003; Oneal 2003; Oneal, Russett and Berbaum 2004; Dorussen 2006; Xiang, Xu and Keteku 2007). One may label this effect "peace by free trade."[9] Studies which call the peace by trade proposition into question (most famous: Barbieri 2002) are likely to suffer from at least one of the following defects. Either they do not adequately control for conditions which raise the risk of war in a dyad, such as contiguity, distance, power balance or one of them being a big power. It simply does not make sense to study the effect of pacifying conditions, if one implicitly starts from the assumption that war is as likely between Switzerland and Sweden as it is between Armenia and Azerbaijan.[10] Or, some studies do not distinguish carefully between those military conflicts which remain at the level of exchanging threats and those which lead to fatalities. There is another design characteristic which affects results. Where dyadic trade is standardized by GDP (instead of foreign trade), there the peace by trade proposition is supported. If design defects are avoided, then almost all studies support the proposition 'peace by free trade'.[11]

Quantitative research has demonstrated that the risk of war between nations is reduced, if they trade a lot with each other. There is something like a commercial peace or peace by trade. Foreign investment has some beneficial impact, too (Souva and Prins 2006). Moreover, economic freedom reduces involvement in military conflict, and financial market openness reduces the risk of war (Gartzke 2005, 2007, 2009).

Until about three or four years ago, it looked as if the democratic peace were solid and robust, whereas the commercial peace between free traders was less so. Now, however, the democratic peace looks ever more conditional: it is not only restricted to relations between democracies, but also most effective with developed or market democracies or contract-intensive economies, or with mature rather than new democracies. By contrast, peace by free trade or economic freedom looks ever more robust.[12] It is supported by dyadic and monadic research designs, i.e., pacifying effects are not restricted to relationships between free traders on both sides of a dispute.[13] Moreover, trade to GDP ratios are no longer the only or even the best ways to document the pacifying effects of economic freedom or the invisible hand. By applying innovative measures of free markets, such as avoidance of public property ownership and protectionism, McDonald (2009) argues convincingly in favor of much more robustly pacifying effects of economic freedom than of political freedom. His argument relies on quantitative analyses as well as on a couple of qualitative or historical case studies.

The idea of a capitalist peace is related to, but different from the ideas of a Kantian or liberal peace advocated by Russett and Oneal (2001, 2006). The Kantian peace refers to three pacifying condition: (dyadic) democracy, trade or economic interdependence, and common memberships in intergovernmental organizations (IGOs). This package of propositions says nothing about the roots of democracy. In capitalist peace theory, as advocated here, it is argued that democracy is promoted by capitalism or economic freedom or contract-intensive societies, by trade and prosperity. Thus, capitalism, trade, the avoidance of state ownership and financial openness reduce the risk of war by two routes: directly as well as indirectly via democracy. Until recently, I hesitated to include IGOs in capitalist peace theory because I distrusted treating all IGOs as equally relevant, as has been implicitly done in much earlier research. Some of the most recent research disaggregates IGOs by issue area and level of institutionalization. Thereafter, Boehmer and Nordstrom (2008, p. 282) arrive at the following conclusion: "Trade ties, however, are the most important determinant of joint memberships between states in the most institutionalized IGOs." Tentatively, capitalist peace theory may be expanded by asserting that there are three routes from capitalism or free trade to the avoidance of conflict, directly as well as indirectly, where the indirect effects run through democracy as well as common IGO memberships.[14]

14.3   HISTORICAL ARGUMENTS

The occurrence of World War I is the standard argument against peace by trade or the capitalist peace because economic interdependence between the Western powers and the Central European powers before it was quite substantial. Certainly, World War I serves as a useful reminder that, at best, the capitalist peace works like an inoculation: useful, but not failsafe. Moreover, World War I is not as unexplainable even by the short version of capitalist peace theory provided above. After all, there was no democratic contribution to pacification because the Central European powers were, at best, imperfect democracies. By contemporary standards, even the democratic character of the United Kingdom was not beyond suspicion because of franchise limitations. As far as trade linkages were concerned (Russett and Oneal 2001), it is noteworthy that Germany traded much more with its Austrian-Hungarian ally in the war to come than with its French opponent in the war to come, that France traded much more with its British ally in the war to come than with its German opponent in the war to come. So, the strongest shots of the capitalist peace inoculation have not been delivered where needed most.

As Lindsey (2002, Chapter 4) and McDonald (2009) point out, sceptics rightly observe that increasing trade to GDP ratios did not prevent World War I, but they overlook that trade volumes increased because of falling transportation costs, but *in spite of* protectionist policies. Finally, capitalist peace theory is an admittedly incomplete theory. It says only how risks of war may be reduced but it says nothing about what generates them in the first place. But capitalist peace theory is easily compatible with World War II which was even bloodier than the previous war. There was little trade between the Western powers and the Axis powers (Germany, Italy and Japan). Since the Axis powers were no democracies, the democratic peace could also not apply between the Axis and the West.

The different long-term effects of the settlements of both world wars may be explained by differences in the application of the capitalist peace strategy toward the losers of the wars. After World War I France influenced the settlement more than anyone else. The French intended to weaken Germany in order to be prepared for the next war. France did not even think of a capitalist peace strategy. Misery and desperation within Germany contributed to Hitler's empowerment and indirectly to World War II in which France had to be saved by its Anglo-American allies. After World War II, the United States, however, pursued a capitalist peace strategy toward the vanquished. It promoted global free trade and subsidized even the recovery of the losers of the war. Germany and Japan became prosperous and allies of the United States.

14.4   CONCLUSION

The most important contemporary application of peace by trade may be the Sino-American relationship. Economic cooperation pacifies the relationship between rising China and the West. Already now, trade between the United States and China as well as American investment in China and profits made by American enterprises in China may pacify an otherwise competitive relationship. Moreover, economic interdependence between China and Taiwan might be the most important pacifying influence in an otherwise truly dangerous relationship (McDonald 2009). If the Chinese economy prospers, if China outgrows poverty, then Mainland China may begin a process of democratization, say, in about two decades.

There are two reasons why one should refer to a capitalist peace rather than a democratic peace. First, the balance of the evidence has been shifting from supporting pacifying effects of democracy towards supporting pacifying effects of capitalism. Whereas research until recently investigated only pacifying effects of trade, more recent work also looks at contract-intensity, capital market integration, protectionism, state ownership or economic freedom. It is too early to say which specific feature of capitalism is most effective in underwriting peace. But one may dare to say that capitalism promotes peace. Second, the democratic peace – where it works most effectively, that is, among mature and prosperous market-oriented democracies themselves – is an effect of capitalism. Without capitalism and free trade, there is little economic development and prosperity. Without economic development and prosperity, democracy is unlikely to be established and to survive. It has even been suggested (Mandelbaum 2007, p. 92): "The school for democracy was the free-market economy." In this perspective, the democratic peace is little more than a component of the capitalist peace.

The promotion of peace by peaceful means is obviously preferable to the promotion of peace by war.[15] The export of democracy is unlikely to appeal to autocrats in power. That is why a policy of democratization easily degenerates into a crusade, or another war to end wars. The US waged such wars from World War I to the most recent Iraq War. By contrast, capitalism is exportable because it provides a model for emulation. China's turn to creeping capitalism since the late 1970s, capitalist reforms in many former Warsaw Pact member states and in India in the early 1990s – however imperfectly implemented in some countries – document the appeal of capitalism. The shining example of capitalist prosperity in the West, together with the demonstration by East Asian economies that a hegemonic West permits poor countries to catch up, sufficed to elicit home-grown reforms which improved the material conditions of life of hundreds of millions of people.

There is one major difference between the promotion of peace by capitalism and its promotion by democratization. If one wants to enforce democratization by military means, then one may run into severe problems of implementation, as the United States is finding out in Afghanistan and Iraq (Weede 2007; Moon 2009). But politicians in democratic countries seem to be in control. They can pick the targets of their efforts. If capitalism spreads by the sheer power of example, then the locals and their frequently autocratic leaders decide the pace of events alone. The democratic peace proposition too easily gets married with a crusading spirit. By contrast, the capitalist peace requires nothing more than the virtue of patience. It relies on limited government, whereas war easily expands the scope of government.

On the one hand, globalization promises to enlarge the market and therefore to increase the division of labor and to speed productivity gains and economic growth. On the other hand, it remains under attack from special-interest groups and misguided political activists. Critics of globalization not only forget both the benefits of free trade and globalization for developing countries and for their poor and underemployed workers and the benefits of free trade to consumers everywhere (Weede 2008), but they know almost nothing about the international security benefits of free trade. The least enlightened opponents of globalization still think in Leninist terms about capitalism, imperialism and war. Historical evidence properly analysed, however, suggests the opposite: by promoting capitalism, economic freedom, trade and prosperity, we simultaneously promote peace.

Conceivable instruments to promote capitalism, freedom and prosperity include advice about the legal foundations of capitalism and economic policies. Open markets in rich countries for exports from poor countries generate credibility for free market institutions and policies. They complement export-oriented growth strategies in poor countries. Foreign direct investment by private enterprises and donations from private Western sources to poor countries are more likely to have a positive effect on the growth path of poor countries than will official aid, which tends to strengthen the state at the expense of free markets. The more capitalist the rich countries become, the more they provide a model for emulation by poor countries as well as a market for their products and a source of technology and investment for them. By resistance to protectionism Western nations may simultaneously strengthen their own economies, improve the lot of the poor in the developing world, and contribute to the avoidance of conflict and war. In a period of financial distress or during a global economic crisis, resistance to protectionism and other attempts to roll back capitalism are the most important tasks for those who prefer prosperity and peace over poverty and war.

NOTES

1. In my view, capitalism and economic freedom refer to the same thing. Economic freedom scales have been produced by establishments, such as the Fraser Institute and its collaborators worldwide, or the Heritage Foundation in collaboration with the *Wall Street Journal*. None of them may be accused of enmity towards capitalism.
2. Although it is much easier to verbally describe the outlines of the research design, *as if* all variables were dichotomies, this is not true for most independent variables in most studies. Nevertheless the description might be useful to those not familiar with the underlying research designs without irritating the cognoscenti too much.
3. For a policy relevant elaboration of the time needed for full democratization in long-lasting and extreme autocracies (whether Afghanistan, Iraq or Saudi Arabia), see Moon (2009).
4. This variable is operationalized by life insurance contracts.
5. "At least one war" refers to the Kargil War between India and Pakistan. In my view, it is questionable whether Pakistan should be coded as a democracy. Mousseau (2009, p. 69, note 54) also discusses the Turkish invasion of Cyprus where he expresses doubts whether Cyprus was a democracy when the war broke out. I might add my own doubts about Turkey's regime. Although Mousseau might defend himself by pointing to the need to stick to coding rules, such rules might nevertheless be questionable. Investigations of the robustness of findings across coding rules might be as important in studies of rare events (like wars) as the more popular analyses of robustness across specifications.
6. Gartzke's (2007, 2009) work also reinforces doubts about the democratic peace, even at the dyadic level. It is discussed below.
7. Although Russett and Oneal (2001, p. 116) did not accept the view that autocratic–democratic dyads suffer from a higher risk of war than purely autocratic dyads, some of their earlier *and later* work supports this view (Oneal and Russett 1997; Oneal and Russett 2005; Russett and Oneal, 2006; Russett 2009, p. 13).
8. Levy (2008) points out that democracy is compatible even with waging preventive wars. Reiter and Stam (2002) argue that democracies tend to pick vulnerable and weak opponents and therefore win most of their wars. Downes (2009), however, could not confirm this conclusion.

9. As suggested by Dorussen (2006), the kind of trade might matter, too.
10. Similarly, you do not study the impact of vaccinations without considering the infection risk within a population.
11. Admittedly, this conclusion relies on empirical studies which build on a questionable data base. For a discussion of the shortcomings of our trade data, see Barbieri, Keshk and Pollins (2009). If one assumes that trade to GDP data are more reliable than dyadic trade data, as I do, then a monadic finding is very important: trading states tend to be less frequently involved in military disputes or war than more autarkic states.
12. This conclusion rests on my rejection of research designs which use directed dyads where dispute initiation instead of involvement becomes the dependent variable. Gelpi and Grieco (2008) apply such a design and find much stronger and more general effects of democracy than of trade on less dispute initiation. First, I doubt whether codings of "initiation" can be as objective as those of involvement. Second, "initiation" elicits connotations of "guilt" or "responsibility." In my view, these concepts rarely justify a zero or hundred percent attribution to one party while absolving the other one.
13. This contrast has been admitted by Russett (2009, p. 19) who resists the subordination of the democratic peace to the capitalist peace advocated here.
14. Although one should not exaggerate the consensus among researchers, there is a need to summarize mainstream findings. Gartzke (2007, 2009), for example, finds that controlling for financial market openness (which he sometimes labels "production") makes the direct effects of democracy insignificant. If these findings become replicated again and again, then "the democratic peace" would have to be discarded whereas the package of propositions constituting "the capitalist peace" would need only some modification.
15. Gleditsch (2008) acknowledges that "the capitalist peace" is a theoretical rival to the liberal or Kantian peace. Strangely, he does not analyse the divergent policy implications of the two conceptions. The capitalist peace is less prone to encourage adventurous security policies than the democratic peace which may nourish a crusading spirit.

REFERENCES

Barbieri, K. (2002), *The Liberal Illusion. Does Trade Promote Peace?* Ann Arbor, MI: The University of Michigan Press.

Barbieri, K., O.M.G. Keshk and B.M. Pollins (2009), "Trading data: evaluating our assumptions and coding rules", *Conflict Management and Peace Science,* **26** (5), 471–91.

Benoit, K. (1996), "Democracies really are more pacific (in General)", *Journal of Conflict Resolution,* **40** (4), 636–57.

Boehmer, C.R. (2008), "A reassessment of democratic pacifism at the monadic level of analysis", *Conflict Management and Peace Science,* **25** (1), 81–94.

Boehmer, C. and T. Nordstrom (2008), "Intergovernmental organization memberships. Examining political community and the attributes of political organizations", *International Interactions,* **34** (3), 282–309.

Bremer, S.A. (1992), "Dangerous dyads: interstate war, 1816–1965", *Journal of Conflict Resolution,* **36** (2), 309–341.

Dorussen, H. (2006), "Heterogeneous trade interests and conflict", *Journal of Conflict Resolution,* **50** (1), 87–107.

Downes, A.B. (2009), "How smart and tough are democracies? Reassessing theories of democratic victory in war", *International Security,* **33** (4), 9–51.

Gartzke, E. (2005), "Freedom and peace", in J.D. Gwartney and R.A. Lawson (eds), *Economic Freedom in the World,* Vancouver, BC: Fraser Institute and Potsdam: Liberales Institut der Friedrich-Naumann-Stiftung, pp. 29–44.

Gartzke, E. (2007), "The capitalist peace", *American Journal of Political Science,* **51** (1), 166–91.

Gartzke, E. (2009), "Production, prosperity, preferences, and peace", in P. Graeff and

G. Mehlkop (eds), *Capitalism, Democracy and the Prevention of War and Poverty*, Abingdon, UK: Routledge, pp. 31–60.

Gartzke, E. and Q. Li (2003), "Measure for measure: concept operationalization and the trade interdependence: conflict debate", *Journal of Peace Research*, **40** (3), 553–71.

Gelpi, C.F. and J.M. Grieco (2008), "Democracy, interdependence and the sources of the liberal peace", *Journal of Peace Research*, **45** (1), 17–36.

Gibler, D.M. (2007), "Bordering on peace: democracy, territorial issues, and conflict", *International Studies Quarterly*, **51** (3), 509–532.

Gleditsch, N.P. (2008), "The liberal moment fifteen years on", *International Studies Quarterly*, **52** (4), 691–712.

Gowa, J. (1999), *Ballots and Bullets. The Elusive Democratic Peace*, Princeton, NJ: Princeton University Press.

Hayek, F.A. von (1960), *The Constitution of Liberty*, Chicago, IL: The University of Chicago Press.

Levy, J.S. (2008), "Preventive war and democratic politics", *International Studies Quarterly*, **52** (1), 1–24.

Lindsey, B. (2002), *Against the Dead Hand. The Uncertain Struggle for Global Capitalism*, New York, NY: Wiley.

Lipson, C. (2003), *Reliable Partners. How Democracies Have Made a Separate Peace*, Princeton, NJ: Princeton University Press.

McDonald, P. (2009), The Invisible Hand of Peace, Cambridge, UK: Cambridge University Press.

Mandelbaum, M. (2007), *Democracy's Good Name. The Rise and Risks of the Worlds Most Popular Form of Government*, New York, NY: Public Affairs Press.

Mansfield, E.D. and J. Snyder (2005), *Electing to Fight. Why Emerging Democracies Go to War*, Cambridge, MA: MIT Press.

Moon, B.E. (2009), "Long time coming: prospects for democracy in Iraq", *International Security*, **33** (4), 115–48.

Mousseau, M. (2005), "Comparing new theory with prior beliefs. Market civilization and the liberal peace", *Conflict Management and Peace Science*, **22** (1), 63–77.

Mousseau, M. (2009), "The social market roots of the democratic peace", *International Security*, **33** (4), 5 and 52–86.

Mousseau, M., H. Hegre, and J.R. Oneal (2003), "How the wealth of nations conditions the liberal peace", *European Journal of International Relations*, **9** (2), 277–314.

Narang, V. and R. Nelson (2009), "Who are these belligerent democratizers? Reassessing the impact of democratization on war", *International Organization*, **63** (2), 357–79.

Oneal, J.R. (2003), "Measuring interdependence and its pacific benefits", *Journal of Peace Research*, **40** (4), 721–5.

Oneal, J.R. and B.M. Russett (1997), "The classical liberals were right", *International Studies Quarterly*, **40** (2), 267–94.

Oneal, J.R. and B.M. Russett (2003a), "Assessing the liberal peace with alternative specifica-tions", in G. Schneider, K. Barbieri and N.P. Gleditsch (eds), *Globalization and Armed Conflict*, Lanham, MD: Rowman and Littlefield, pp. 143–63.

Oneal, J.R. and B.M. Russett (2003b), "Modelling conflict while studying dynamics", in G. Schneider, K. Barbieri and N.P. Gleditsch (eds), *Globalization and Armed Conflict*, Lanham, MD: Rowman and Littlefield, pp. 179–88.

Oneal, J.R. and B. Russett (2005), "Rule of three, let it be. When more really is better", *Conflict Management and Peace Science*, **22** (4), 293–310.

Oneal, J.R., B. Russett, and M.L. Berbaum (2004), "Causes of peace: democracy, interde-pendence, and international organizations, 1885–1992", *International Studies Quarterly*, **47** (3), 371–93.

Ray, J.L. (1995), *Democracy and International Conflict*, Columbia, SC: University of South Carolina Press.

Reiter, D. and A.C. Stam (2002), *Democracies at War*, Princeton, NJ: Princeton University Press.

Rummel, R.J. (1995), "Democracies ARE less warlike than other regimes", *European Journal of International Relations*, **1** (4), 457–79.

Russett, B.M. (1993), *Grasping the Democratic Peace.* Princeton, NJ: Princeton University Press.

Russett, B.M. (2009), "Democracy, war and expansion through historical lenses", *European Journal of International Relations*, **15** (1), 9–36.

Russett, B.M. and J.R. Oneal (2001), *Triangulating Peace: Democracy, Interdependence and International Organizations*, New York, NY: Norton.

Russett, B.M. and J.R. Oneal (2006), "Seeking peace in a post-Cold War world of hegemony and terrorism", in B.M. Russett (ed.), *Policy and Purpose in the Global Community,* New York, NY: Palgrave Macmillan, pp. 231–52.

Souva, M. and B. Prins (2006), "The liberal peace revisited: the role of democracy, dependence, and development in militarized interstate dispute initiation, 1950–1999", *International Interactions*, **32** (2), 183–200.

Waltz, K.N. (2003–2004), "Fair fights or pointless wars", *International Security*, **28** (3), 181.

Weede, E. (2005), *Balance of Power, Globalization and the Capitalist Peace.* Berlin: Liberal Verlag (for the Friedrich Naumann Foundation).

Weede, E. (2006), "Economic freedom and development", *CATO Journal*, **26** (3), 511–24.

Weede, E. (2007), "Capitalism, democracy and the war in Iraq", *Global Society*, **21** (2), 219–27.

Weede, E. (2008), "Globalization and inequality", *Comparative Sociology*, **7** (4), 415–33.

Xiang, J., X. Xu and G. Keteku (2007), "Power: the missing link in the trade conflict relationship", *Journal of Conflict Resolution*, **51** (4), 646–63.

15 On the democratic peace

Sebastian Rosato

15.1 INTRODUCTION

Democratic peace theory – the claim that democracies rarely fight one another because they share common norms of live-and-let-live and domestic institutions that constrain the recourse to war – is the most powerful liberal contribution to the debate on the causes of war and peace.[1]

Its impact on American foreign policy is manifest. President George H.W. Bush was clearly convinced of the link between democracy and peace. "A democratic Russia," he announced soon after the end of the Cold War, "is the best guarantee against a renewed danger of competition and the threat of nuclear rivalry." Secretary of State James Baker concurred: "shared democratic values can ensure an enduring and stable peace in a way the balance of terror never could." Underlying his statement was the belief that "real democracies do not go to war with each other" (quoted in Russett 1993, p. 129). This was also the view of the Clinton administration whose campaign of "democratic enlargement" was premised on the belief that democracies are "far less likely to wage war on one another." Enlarging the community of democracies, noted National Security Adviser Anthony Lake, "protects our interests and security" (quoted in Henderson 2002, pp. 19–20). As Deputy Assistant Secretary of Defense Joseph Kruzel put it, "the notion that democracies do not go to war with each other. . .has had a substantial impact on policy" (quoted in Ray 2000, p. 299). The belief that spreading democracy would perform the dual task of enhancing American national security and promoting world peace arguably peaked during the George W. Bush presidency. The president himself was convinced that, "The best hope for peace in our world is the expansion of freedom in all the world" (quoted in Weeks 2008, pp. 60–61). This was not "some moralistic flight of fancy," asserted Secretary of State Condoleezza Rice (2005, p. B7) in the *Washington Post*. The democratic transformation of the Middle East was the "only realistic path to security." In short, it is hard to argue with a recent review of the field when it concludes that democratic peace theory provides the "clearest recent example of basic political science research that has influenced US foreign policy" (Bennett and Ikenberry 2006, p. 655).

For all its policy import, democratic peace theory is even more influential within the academy. According to Jack Levy (1994, p. 352), "the idea that democracies almost never go to war with each other is now commonplace. The skeptics are in retreat and the proposition has acquired a nearly law-like status." Similarly, Bruce Russett (1990, p. 123) describes the democratic peace finding as "one of the strongest nontrivial and nontautological generalizations that can be made about international relations." More recently, Charles Lipson (2003, p. 1) has concluded that the "democratic peace is now one of the best established regularities in international politics, perhaps the best established." The theory's prominence derives at least in part from the fact that it poses a direct challenge to realism, long considered the dominant approach for understanding international politics. To be sure, not all realists disagree with the theory's emphasis on regime type as a key driver of state behavior.[2] However, it directly contradicts structural realists such as Kenneth Waltz and John Mearsheimer, who argue that the prevailing balance of power is more important than variation in domestic political institutions and norms in explaining state behavior (Waltz 1979; Mearsheimer 2001). If it is true that democracies have forged a durable peace based on common institutions and norms, then this undermines both the realist claim that states are condemned to exist in a constant state of security competition and its assertion that the distribution of power, rather than state type, should be central to our understanding of state behavior. As Russett and James Lee Ray (1995, p. 323) note, if democratic peace theory is correct, "the theoretical edifice of various varieties. . .of realism is fundamentally in doubt."

In this chapter, I offer a description and evaluation of democratic peace theory. I focus on the theory's core empirical claim – democracies rarely fight one another – and on the causal mechanisms that have been adduced to explain it.[3] As regards the empirical finding, I find scant support for the two claims that typically fall under this rubric, namely that democracies have rarely if ever gone to war with one another, and that democracies are significantly less likely to engage one another in militarized disputes short of war than other pairs of states. Nor are the causal mechanisms underlying these claims convincing. The mechanisms, which focus on the foreign policy effects of democratic norms and institutions, do not operate as stipulated by their proponents, and cannot therefore explain why democracies remain at peace with one another. In short, there are good reasons to doubt the democratic peace.

The remainder of this chapter proceeds in five sections. First, I unpack the claim that democracies rarely fight each other. Second, I evaluate the claim and conclude that it is unconvincing. Third, I lay out the causal mechanisms that have been provided to explain why democracies do not fight one another. Fourth, I demonstrate that these mechanisms do not provide a compelling explanation for inter-democratic peace because they do not operate as their proponents claim they do. In the final section, I speculate as to why democratic peace theory continues to dominate policy and scholarly debates despite the lack of evidence for its core claim and for the mechanisms underpinning it.

15.2   THE CLAIM

At the core of democratic peace theory lies a simple claim: democracies rarely fight one another. This is not to say that they do not fight at all, but they do not fight their own kind. Strictly speaking, the claim is comprised of two elements: democracies have rarely if ever gone to war with one another; and pairs of democracies are significantly less likely than other pairs of states to engage one another in militarized disputes short of war.

15.2.1   War

Democratic peace proponents assert that democracies rarely if ever go to war with one another, where a war is usually defined as an interstate conflict resulting in more than 1000 battle fatalities. According to Michael Doyle (1983a, p. 213), "constitutionally secure liberal states have yet to engage in war with one another."[4] Although he focuses on democracies rather than liberal states, Russett (1993, p. 11) concurs: "there are no clearcut cases of sovereign stable democracies waging war with each other in the modern international system." His analysis of politically relevant dyads – pairs of states that are contiguous or contain a major power and therefore for whom war is a real possibility – yields no wars between democracies during the Cold War. Nils Petter Gleditsch (1995, pp. 315–16) makes the more modest claim that democratic states "very rarely" go to war against each other, but points out that the cases he codes as democratic wars can easily be explained away. Charles Gochman (1996/97, p. 179) offers a neat summary of the common view: "wars between democracies have been extremely rare (and, perhaps, non-existent)."

   Democratic peace theorists assert that these findings are statistically significant, which is to say that it is unlikely that they are due to random chance. Zeev Maoz and Nasrin Abdolali compare the actual number of democratic dyads at war between 1816 and 1976 with the expected number if wars were distributed simply according to the proportion of democratic dyads in the entire population, and conclude that the difference is significant (Maoz and Abdolali 1989, pp. 24–5). Although he claims that democracies "very rarely" go to war with one another, Stuart Bremer (1992, pp.

325–30) also asserts that democracies were significantly less likely to wage war against one another than other pairs of states between 1816 and 1965. Maoz and Russett (1992, pp. 253–4) argue that this was also the case for politically relevant dyads during the Cold War.

The findings also appear to be robust. For one thing, the relationship between joint democracy and peace cannot be attributed to some third variable. As Gleditsch notes, the absence of war between democracies cannot be attributed to the fact that they have tended to be far apart. Democracies have not been further apart than the average interstate dyad since the Congress of Vienna. Thus the suggestion that democracies have remained at peace because they are far apart can "be rejected out of hand" (Gleditsch 1995, pp. 316–17). The finding also appears to hold regardless of research design or methodological approach. Russett, for example, retests the claim using "regime-dyads" rather than the more conventional "dyad-years" as his unit of analysis and reconfirms his original finding. Democracies have never gone to war with one another and this is highly significant (Russett 1995, pp. 173–4). Although Arvid Raknerud and Havard Hegre (1997, pp. 394–5) identify a series of methodological problems inherent in most analyses of the democratic peace and develop an alternative model to deal with them, they still find that democratic dyads are half as likely to go to war with one another as other pairs of states. The finding is significant and cannot be attributed to the fact that democracies are far apart or that they tend to have "histories" of peaceful interaction.

Democratic peace theorists have supplemented these findings with case studies in which they examine the handful of conflicts that, at least on the surface, appear to be wars between democracies. Russett (1993, pp. 11–20) identifies 12 such "candidate" wars and concludes that none violate the core claim. By his criteria, it is "impossible to identify unambiguously *any* wars between democratic states in the period since 1815" (Russett 1993, p. 16, emphasis in original). Similarly, Ray (1993, p. 269) lists 20 potential cases and concludes that "none of [them]. . . should be categorized as international wars between democratic states." The conflicts can be dismissed because they were not sufficiently violent, were civil conflicts or involved at least one state that was not truly democratic. Finally, although Spencer Weart (1998, p. 13) identifies three-dozen borderline cases by setting the war threshold at 200 battle deaths, he too finds that "well-established democracies have never made war on one another."

In sum, there appears to be abundant evidence that democracies have rarely if ever gone to war with one another. The finding is unlikely to have been generated by chance, cannot be attributed to some other factor and does not depend on the research design or method employed.

15.2.2 Militarized Disputes

Democratic peace theorists assert that the pacifying effect of joint democracy is not restricted to large scale war: pairs of democracies are significantly less likely to engage one another in conflicts short of war than other pairs of states. Maoz and Russett, for example, conclude that "democracy. . . has a consistent and robust negative effect on the likelihood of conflict." Their analysis of politically relevant dyads between 1946 and 1986 confirms that "the more democratic are both members of a pair of states, the less likely it is that militarized disputes break out between them" (Maoz and Russett 1993, pp. 624, 627). Moreover, the association between democracy and the absence of conflict remains even after accounting for the influence of other variables commonly thought to contribute to peace, including wealth, economic growth, alliances, contiguity and power asymmetries.

This basic claim has received repeated confirmation. In a seminal analysis, Russett and John Oneal use an "improved" measure of joint democracy, extensively revised data on political regimes and militarized disputes, the same controls as previous analyses and a new control for economic interdependence, and find powerful support for the democratic peace. Between 1950 and 1985, "increasing the constraint on the use of force, by augmenting . . . democratic institutions in the state that is freer to resort to violence, reduces the likelihood of dyadic conflict." Arguing that they have found "strong support for the democratic peace," they conclude that "in all our analyses, the probability of a dispute is strongly associated with the continuous measure of the political character of the less democratic state" (Oneal and Russett 1997, pp. 273, 279, 288).[5] Their subsequent work suggests that the finding holds regardless of time period, research design or statistical estimator (Oneal and Russett 1999a, 1999b).

Others have provided abundant evidence to support these claims. Although he uses different control variables, a different statistical estimator and a different research design, Michael Mousseau "reconfirms the democratic peace." Even adding a control for economic development does not fundamentally alter the basic finding: "we can safely conclude that democracy appears to have a significant pacifying effect among all democracies, rich and poor" (Mousseau 2000, pp. 490, 492). This is also the conclusion of David Rousseau and his colleagues even though their analysis differs substantially from most studies of the democratic peace. Rousseau et al. use the nation state rather than the dyad as their unit of analysis, focus on who initiated violence rather than simply when violence broke out, control for what they believe is an important confounding variable – satisfaction with the status quo – and use the International Crisis Behavior

(ICB) dataset rather than the more traditional Militarized Interstate Dispute (MID) dataset to identify violent conflicts. Nevertheless, their findings offer strong support for the democratic peace: "democratic states are clearly less likely to initiate force against other democracies" (Rousseau et al. 1996, p. 521). Vesna Danilovic and Joe Clare (2007) evaluate the behavior of liberal as well as democratic states using a similar approach and come to much the same conclusion: liberal states and democracies are significantly less likely to initiate conflict against their own kind than they are against other kinds of states.

Again, the finding appears to be robust. Nathaniel Beck and his colleagues note that most scholars treat their observations as if they are independent of one another when, in fact, they are not. However, when they reanalyse the data using what they claim is a more appropriate statistical test they still find evidence for a democratic peace. Oneal and Russett's "findings about the [democratic] peace . . . are upheld" (Beck et al. 1998, p. 1278). Similarly, Scott Bennett and Allan Stam point out that researchers can adopt several different research designs and statistical estimators and that these choices can substantially affect their results, but find "little change in our estimates of how democracy affects conflict across either research design or estimator choices." The "findings on democracy are the most statistically robust and among the most substantively powerful relationship of any in our analysis" (Bennett and Stam 2000, p. 676).

In sum, the claim that democratic pairs are less conflict prone than other kinds of dyads has received what one observer has described as "painstaking confirmation" (Henderson 2002, p. 24). The finding has been repeatedly confirmed, is highly significant, cannot be attributed to other factors and holds regardless of definitions, datasets, research designs or statistical models.

15.3   EVALUATING THE CLAIM

In this section, I evaluate the empirical claims at the core of democratic peace theory. I find scant support for both of them. Democracies do go to war with one another and attempts to prove that they do not have the unintended consequence of making the no war claim uninteresting. Moreover, there is little evidence that democracies are less likely to engage each other in militarized disputes than other pairs of states because of their shared regime type. The finding is either statistically insignificant or explained by factors other than democracy.

15.3.1 War

The claim that democracies rarely if ever go to war with one another is either incorrect or unsurprising. A careful review of the evidence suggests that contrary to the assertions of democratic peace proponents, there have been a handful of wars between democracies and these can only be excluded by imposing a highly restrictive definition of democracy. This would not pose a problem were it not for the fact that by raising the requirements for a state to be judged democratic, the theory's defenders reduce the number of democracies in the analysis to such an extent that the finding of no war between them is wholly to be expected.

Democratic wars
There is considerable evidence that the absence of war claim is incorrect. As Christopher Layne (2001, p. 801) notes, "The most damning indictment of democratic peace theory, is that it happens not to be true: democratic states have gone to war with one another." For example, categorizing a state as democratic if it achieves a democracy score of six or more in the Polity dataset on regime type – as several analysts do – yields three inter-democratic wars: the American Civil War, the Spanish–American War and the Boer War.[6] This is something defenders of the theory readily admit – adopting relatively inclusive definitions of democracy, they themselves generate anywhere between a dozen and three dozen cases of inter-democratic war.

In order to exclude these anomalies and thereby preserve the absence of war claim, the theory's defenders restrict their definitions of democracy. In the most compelling analysis to date, Ray (1993, pp. 256–9, 269) argues that no two democracies have gone to war with one another as long as a democracy is defined as follows: the members of the executive and legislative branches are determined in fair and competitive elections, which is to say that at least two independent parties contest the election, half of the adult population is eligible to vote and the possibility that the governing party can lose has been established by historical precedent. Similarly, Doyle (1983a, pp. 216–17) rescues the claim by arguing that states' domestic and foreign policies must both be subject to the control of the citizenry if they are to be considered liberal. Russett, meanwhile, argues that his no war claim rests on defining democracy as a state with a voting franchise for a substantial fraction of the population, a government brought to power in elections involving two or more legally recognized parties, a popularly elected executive or one responsible to an elected legislature, requirements for civil liberties including free speech and demonstrated longevity of at least three years (Russett 1993, pp. 14–16).

Despite imposing these definitional restrictions, proponents of the democratic peace cannot exclude up to five major wars, a figure which, if confirmed, would invalidate the democratic peace by their own admission (Ray 1995, p. 27). The first is the War of 1812 between Britain and the United States. Ray argues that it does not contradict the claim because Britain does not meet his suffrage requirement. Yet this does not make Britain any less democratic than the United States at the time where less than half the adult population was eligible to vote. In fact, as Layne (2001, p. 801) notes, "the United States was not appreciably more democratic than unreformed Britain." This poses a problem for the democratic peace: if the United States was a democracy, and Ray believes it was, then Britain was also a democracy and the War of 1812 was an inter-democratic war. The second case is the American Civil War. Democratic peace theorists believe the United States was a democracy in 1861, but exclude the case on the grounds that it was a civil rather than interstate war (Russett 1993, pp. 16–17). However, a plausible argument can be made that the United States was not a state but a union of states, and that this was therefore a war between states rather than within one. Note, for example, that the term "United States" was plural rather than singular at the time and the conflict was known as the "War Between the States."[7] This being the case, the Civil War also contradicts the claim.[8]

The Spanish–American and Boer wars constitute two further exceptions to the rule. Ray excludes the former because half of the members of Spain's upper house held their positions through hereditary succession or royal appointment. Yet this made Spain little different to Britain, which he classifies as a democracy at the time, thereby leading to the conclusion that the Spanish–American War was a war between democracies. Similarly, it is hard to accept his claim that the Orange Free State was not a democracy during the Boer War because black Africans were not allowed to vote when he is content to classify the United States as a democracy in the second half of the nineteenth century (Ray 1993, pp. 265, 267; Layne 2001, p. 802). In short, defenders of the democratic peace can only rescue their core claim through the selective application of highly restrictive criteria.

Perhaps the most important exception is World War I, which, by virtue of the fact that Germany fought against Britain, France, Italy, Belgium and the United States, would count as five instances of war between liberal states in most analyses of the democratic peace.[9] As Ido Oren (1995, pp. 178–9) has shown, Germany was widely considered to be a liberal state prior to World War I: "Germany was a member of a select group of the most politically advanced countries, far more advanced than some of the nations that are currently coded as having been 'liberal' during that period." In fact, Germany was consistently placed toward the top of that group, "either as second only to the United States . . . or as positioned below England and above France." Moreover, Doyle's assertion that the case ought to be excluded because Germany was liberal domestically, but not in foreign affairs, does not stand up to scrutiny. As Layne (1994, p. 42) points out, foreign policy was "insulated from parliamentary control" in both France and Britain, two purportedly liberal states (see also Mearsheimer 1990, p. 51, fn. 77; Layne 2001, pp. 803–807). Thus it is difficult to classify Germany as non-liberal and World War I constitutes an important exception to the finding.

Small numbers
Even if restrictive definitions of democracy enable democratic peace theorists to uphold their claim, they render it unsurprising by reducing the number of democracies in any analysis. As several scholars have noted, there were only a dozen or so democracies in the world prior to World War I, and even fewer in a position to fight one another. Therefore, since war is a rare event for any pair of states, the fact that democracies did not fight one another should occasion little surprise (Mearsheimer 1990, p. 50; Cohen 1994, pp. 214, 216; Layne 1994, p. 39; Henderson 1999, p. 212).[10] It should be a source of even less surprise as the number of democracies and the potential for conflict among them falls, something that is bound to happen as the democratic bar rises. Ray's suffrage criterion, for example, eliminates two great powers – Britain and the United States – from the democratic ranks before World War I, thereby making the absence of war between democracies eminently predictable.[11]

A simple numerical example should serve to illustrate the point. Using a Polity score of six or more to designate a state as a democracy yields 716 purely democratic dyads out of a total 23240 politically relevant dyads between 1816 and 1913. Assuming that wars are distributed according to the proportion of democratic dyads in the population and knowing that there were 86 dyads at war during this period, we should expect to observe three democratic–democratic wars between the Congress of Vienna and World War I.[12] If we actually observed no wars between democracies, the democratic peace phenomenon might be worth investigating further even though the difference between three and zero wars is barely statistically significant.[13] Increasing the score required for a state to be coded as a democracy to eight – a score that would make Britain democratic from 1901 onwards only and eliminate states like Spain and the Orange Free State from the ranks of the democracies – makes a dramatic difference. The number of democratic dyads falls to 171, and the expected number of wars is now between zero and one. Now the absence of war finding is to be expected. In short, by adopting restrictive definitions of democracy, proponents of the democratic peace render their central claim wholly unexceptional.

In sum, proponents of the democratic peace have unsuccessfully attempted to tread a fine line in order to substantiate their claim that democracies have rarely if ever waged war against one another. On the one hand, they admit that inter-democratic war is not an unusual phenomenon if they adopt relatively inclusive definitions of democracy. On the other hand, in their attempts to restrict the definition of democracy and thereby save the finding they inadvertently make the absence of war between democracies trivial.

15.3.2   Militarized Disputes

There are at least two reasons to doubt the claim that pairs of democracies are less prone to conflict than other pairs of states. First, despite their assertions, it is not clear that democratic peace theorists have established the existence of a powerful association between joint democracy and peace. Second, there is good evidence that factors other than democracy – many of them consistent with realist expectations – account for the peace among democratic states.[14]

Significance
Democratic peace theorists have yet to provide clearcut evidence that there is a significant relationship between their independent and dependent variables, joint democracy and peace. It is now clear, for example, that Maoz and Russett's analysis of the Cold War period, which claims to establish the existence of a joint, separate peace, does not in fact do so. In a reassessment of that analysis, which follows the original as closely as possible save for the addition of a control for economic interdependence, Oneal et al. (1996) find that a continuous measure of democracy is not significantly correlated with peace. Moreover, a supplementary analysis of contiguous dyads – those that experience most of the conflicts – also finds no significant relationship between a continuous measure of joint democracy and peace whether a control for economic interdependence is included or not. This finding is particularly damaging because democratic peace theorists argue that "most theoretical explanations of the separate peace imply a continuous effect: the more democratic a pair of states, the less likely they are to become involved in conflict" (Oneal and Ray 1997, p. 752).

Oneal and Ray (1997, pp. 756–7) conclude that the original Maoz and Russett finding does not survive reanalysis because it is based on a joint democracy variable that, although widely used, is poorly calculated and constructed, and they therefore propose a new democracy measure that they claim does achieve statistical significance. Their new measure of joint democracy uses the democracy score of the less democratic state in a dyad on the assumption that conflict is a function of the regime type of the less constrained of two interacting states. This "weak link" specification appears to provide powerful support for the democratic peace finding: "As the less democratic state becomes more democratic, the likelihood of conflict declines. This is clear evidence of the pacific benefits of democracy." The new variable provides "corroboration of the democratic peace" (Oneal and Ray 1997, pp. 764–5). Oneal and Russett concur with this conclusion in a separate analysis that also uses the weak link assumption. An increase in democracy in the state that is "freer to resort to violence, reduces the likelihood of dyadic conflict" (Oneal and Russett 1997, p. 279).

Although the weak link measure is widely accepted as the gold standard in studies of the relationship between democracy and a variety of international outcomes, it does not provide evidence that joint democracy is significantly related to peace. Even as they developed it, Oneal and Ray admitted that the weak link was not a pure measure of joint democracy. What it really revealed was that the probability of conflict was "a function of the average level of democracy in a dyad . . . [and] *also the political distance separating the states along the democracy–autocracy continuum*" (1997, p. 768, emphasis added). The problem, of course, is that the logics advanced to explain the democratic peace refer to the effects of democracy on state behavior; none refer to the effects of political similarity. Thus findings generated using the weak link specification – which is to say all the major assessments of the democratic peace – may not actually support the central democratic peace claim that it is something about the norms and institutions of democracies that enables them to remain at peace.

This is precisely the conclusion that Errol Henderson reaches in his compelling assessment of Oneal and Russett's work. His analysis replicates theirs precisely with two minor modifications: he includes only the first year of any dispute because democratic peace theory is about the incidence of disputes, not their duration, and he introduces a political similarity variable in order to disentangle the effects of joint democracy and political distance on conflict. His central result is striking: democracy "is not significantly associated with the probability of dispute onset." "What is apparent from the results," he concludes, "is that in the light of quite reasonable, modest, and straightforward modifications of Oneal and Russett's . . . research design, there is no statistically significant relationship between joint democracy and a decreased likelihood of militarized interstate conflict" (Henderson 2002, pp. 37–9). Mark Souva (2004) reaches essentially the same conclusion in an analysis of the relationship between domestic institutions and interstate conflict using the weak link specification. In a model that includes variables for political and economic institutional similarity, both of which are significantly associated with peace, there is no significant relationship between joint democracy and the absence of conflict.

Other factors

There is considerable evidence that factors other than democracy account for the peace among democratic states. As a prelude to elaborating on this point, a few words are in order about the temporal scope of the finding. It is generally agreed that there is scant evidence of mutual democratic pacifism prior to 1945. Henry Farber and Joanne Gowa (1995, p. 143) adopt the most extreme position, claiming that democratic dyads were significantly *more* likely to fight between 1816 and 1913 than other pairs.[15] However, even proponents of the theory admit that there is no clearcut evidence for a democratic peace before the Cold War. Thus Oneal and Russett (1999b, pp. 226–7) find that if they exclude all but the first year of the wars in their sample – a move that is wholly appropriate given that the theory refers only to the incidence of conflict – there is scant support for the democratic peace between 1870 and 1945. Elsewhere, they are more bullish about the democratic peace, arguing that double democratic "dyads . . . were the most peaceful after about 1900," though it is worth noting that this period constitutes a small fraction of the entire multipolar era for which data are available (1816–1945) (Oneal and Russett 1999a, p. 28). This is not surprising. As Russett (1993, p. 20) observes, the nineteenth century was a period of "very imperfect democracy," therefore we should expect to find a number of inter-democratic rivalries, violent conflicts and, as some have suggested, even wars. When coupled with the fact that there were few democracies in the world at the time, this observation suggests that we are unlikely to find a democratic peace before 1945.

There is widespread agreement that, in contrast to the pre-World War II period, there is good evidence of a democratic peace during the Cold War. Henderson (2002, p. 15), for example, describes the postwar period as "the period within which the democratic peace is most evident." Indeed, even Farber and Gowa (1995, p. 145) admit that "after World War II, there was a marked and statistically significant lower probability of disputes short of war between democracies." Proponents of the theory attribute this to two changes at mid-century: the number of democratic states increased markedly, and democratic norms and institutions became stronger and more entrenched, thereby exerting a greater restraining effect on conflict (Maoz and Russett 1993, p. 627; Oneal and Russett 1997, p. 273).

The problem for democratic peace theory is that there are several factors other than democracy that plausibly account for the peace among democratic states after World War II. Farber and Gowa (1995), for example, attribute the democratic peace not to joint democracy, but to alliance ties brought on by the Cold War conflict. Proponents of the democratic peace respond by claiming that in their analyses joint democracy is still related to peace even when controlling for alliance ties. But Henderson (2002, p. 134) refutes this claim, noting that in his replication of Oneal and Russett, "alliance membership, more than joint democracy, contributed to peace in the postwar era." Crucially, Farber and Gowa and Henderson demonstrate that it is not shared democracy that causes democracies to ally with one another in the first place – thus democracy does not have even an indirect effect on peace.

Another research tradition argues that the inter-democratic peace can be attributed to economic factors, specifically economic interdependence and development. Solomon Polachek, for example, finds that "introducing trade explains away democracy's impact" on conflict in his analysis of interstate disputes between 1958 and 1967. "Democracy *per se* does *not* reduce conflict. Instead a more fundamental factor than being a democracy in causing bilateral cooperation is trade" (1997, p. 306, emphasis in original). Similarly, Erik Gartzke (2007) finds that adding variables for financial and monetary integration and economic development to the standard Oneal and Russett model renders the effect of joint democracy insignificant. Thus he concludes that "capitalism, and not democracy, leads to peace" (2007, p. 180). Mousseau (2009) makes a similar argument, claiming that it is advanced capitalist states – he refers to them as contract intensive economies – rather than democracies that do not fight one another. His analysis suggests that the democratic peace is spurious – contract intensive economies caused democracy and peace between 1961 and 2001 (2009, pp. 53–4).

Scholars have come up with several other purported causes of the democratic peace that do not fit neatly into the security or economic categories. For Gartzke (2000), the finding can be attributed to the fact that democracies tend to have similar preferences. Adding a control for "preference affinity" makes the relationship between democracy and peace insignificant. Importantly, there is only a modest correlation between preference affinity and democracy. Thus he concludes that, contrary to the views of his critics, the effect of preferences on conflict is not largely a by-product of regime type. His results "challenge the notion that the democratic peace is due largely, or even substantially, to democracy" (2000, p. 209).[16] Douglas Gibler (2007, p. 529), meanwhile, concludes that the democratic peace is "in fact a stable border peace." After adding a control for stable borders on the assumption that the removal of territorial issues has a pacifying effect on interstate relations, Gibler finds that democracy has little or no effect on conflict.

Most of these findings – and therefore the postwar peace among democracies – can plausibly be explained by realism. The argument goes as follows. Beginning in 1945, the United States found itself in a life and death struggle with the Soviet Union. In order to compete and ultimately prevail in that contest, Washington implemented a two-pronged strategy. First, it established a far-reaching network of military alliances to resist Soviet aggression wherever it might occur. Second, it created an open economic order designed to generate enough wealth to fund the military effort and to combat communist subversion. In other words, it was the exigencies of the Cold War that generated the alliances, economic integration, advanced economies, and perhaps even the preference affinity that scholars have found to be powerfully associated with the peace among democracies since 1945.[17]

In sum, there are good reasons to doubt the claim that democracies are less likely to engage each other in violent disputes short of war than other pairs of states. The evidence that there is a significant relationship between joint democracy and peace is not strong. Moreover, scholars have uncovered several other factors that plausibly account for the peace among democracies, many of which can be explained by realism.

15.4   THE CAUSAL MECHANISMS

Proponents of the theory have developed two sets of causal mechanisms to explain the democratic peace. The first focuses on the effect of democratic norms on foreign policy behavior. The second attributes the separate peace to the effect of democratic institutions.

15.4.1   Norms

The normative argument begins with the premise that democratic leaders are socialized to act on the basis of democratic norms whenever possible. These norms stress the importance of nonviolent conflict resolution and negotiation in a spirit of live-and-let-live. Because they have been socialized to adhere to these norms, democratic elites try to adopt them in the international arena if they can. Consequently, democracies trust and respect one another when a conflict of interest arises. They respect one another because they believe that the other is committed to the same norms of behavior and is therefore worthy of accommodation. And they trust one another because they believe that the other respects them and is normatively proscribed from using violence. Together these *norm exter-nalization* and *trust and respect* mechanisms make up the normative logic (Russett 1993, pp. 31–5; Dixon 1994, pp. 16–18; Weart 1998, pp. 77–8, 87–93).

The normative logic also explains why democracies are not especially peaceful toward nondemocracies. Antagonists that are not democratic are not trusted because they are presumed not to respect democracies and because their leaders are not inclined toward peaceful conflict resolution. And they are not respected because their domestic systems are unjust. Thus democracies will act violently toward nondemocracies in order to defend themselves from attack, to preempt aggressive action, or in order to introduce human rights and representative government (Doyle 1983b, pp. 323–37; Russett 1993, pp. 32–5).

15.4.2 Institutions

Although there are several variants of the institutional argument, all of them begin with the premise that democratic leaders are accountable to a wide variety of social groups that may, under various conditions, oppose the use of force. Their *accountability* derives from their desire to remain in office, from the fact that there are opposition parties ready to capital-ize on unpopular policies, and from the fact that democratic publics can periodically remove leaders who are judged not to have acted in their best interests. In addition, the freedom of speech and open political processes that are characteristic of democracy make it possible for the public to rate the government's performance. In short, democratic institutions make it possible for publics to monitor and sanction their leaders (Lake 1982, pp. 25–6; Russett 1993, pp. 38–40; Owen 1997, pp. 41–3).

Conscious of their accountability, democratic elites will only use force abroad if there is widespread support for doing so. This support is vital if they are not to be removed from office for waging an unpopular war or to encounter opposition from various social groups for committing the state to a costly violent conflict. Democratic peace theorists focus on four spe-cific groups that must be mobilized to support a war: the general public, constituencies that benefit from an open international economic order, opposition parties and liberal opinion leaders. These groups are likely to oppose war because it is costly in terms of blood, treasure, or expected profits, because they can gain electorally from doing so, or because they deem it morally unacceptable (Doyle 1983a, pp. 229, 231–2; Russett 1993, pp. 38–9; Owen 1997, pp. 19, 37–9, 45–7; Schultz 1998, pp. 831–2).

Six causal mechanisms flow from the elite accountability claim, each of which traces a different path to peace between democracies. The first two suggest that democracies are constrained from using force in the international arena. According to the *public constraint* mechanism, democratic elites shy away from the use of force in response to the public's aversion to war, which is itself driven by a reluctance to incur the costs associated with large scale interstate violence. The *group constraint* mechanism is similar: democratic leaders carry out the wishes of various antiwar groups. Thus in a standoff involving two democracies both sides are constrained, believe the other also to be constrained and seek an agreement short of war (Bueno de Mesquita and Lalman 1992, pp. 155–8; Russett 1993, pp. 38–40).

Two further mechanisms focus on the claim that accountability makes democratic leaders slow to resort to force. According to the *slow mobilization* mechanism, persuading the public and potential antiwar groups to support the use of force is a long, complex process and therefore democracies cannot mobilize quickly. This is also the core of the *surprise attack* mechanism, which also notes that the mobilization process takes place in the open, thereby precluding the possibility that a democracy can launch a surprise attack. In a crisis involving two democracies, then, the antagonists have the time to come to a mutually acceptable agreement and can negotiate without fearing attack (Russett 1993, pp. 38–40; Bueno de Mesquita, Koch and Siverson 2004, pp. 256–7).

The fifth mechanism zeroes in on the advantages that democracies have in revealing *information* about their resolve in a crisis. Because they are accountable to their citizens and can expect opposition parties to oppose unpopular policies, democratic leaders are cautious about escalating a crisis or launching a war. In fact, they will only fight if the stakes in a conflict are important to them. This provides valuable information to an opponent: if a democracy refuses to back down or escalates a crisis, then it is resolved. In purely democratic crises, then, both states will have good information about the other's resolve, are unlikely to misrepresent their own resolve and can reach a settlement without risking war (Schultz 1998, pp. 840–1; Bueno de Mesquita et al. 1999, pp. 802–803).

The final mechanism focuses on democratic expectations of *victory*. Because they are accountable to their citizens and various domestic groups, democratic leaders will only choose to fight when they believe that their chances of victory in the ensuing war are high. It follows that when two democracies face off against one another, the odds that both believe they have a good chance of prevailing in battle are exceedingly low. Therefore pairs of democracies in a crisis will negotiate rather than fight (Bueno de Mesquita et al. 1999, p. 799; Bueno de Mesquita 2006, p. 640).

These mechanisms also explain why democracies fight nondemocracies. Leaders of nondemocratic states are not as accountable as their democratic counterparts and are therefore less constrained, quicker to act, unable to signal their resolve and prepared to fight even when their chances of victory are modest. This being the case, democracies are likely to use force against nondemocracies for three reasons: they may have to fight in self-defense; they may conclude that they have to preempt aggressive action by striking first; or because they misread their opponents' resolve, they may mistakenly believe that peaceful bargains are not available (Lake 1982, pp. 26–30; Bueno de Mesquita and Lalman 1992, pp. 158–60; Russett 1993, pp. 38–40; Bueno de Mesquita 2006, p. 640).

15.5   EVALUATING THE CAUSAL MECHANISMS

15.5.1   Norms

The causal mechanisms that comprise the normative logic do not appear to operate as stipulated. The available evidence suggests that democracies do not reliably externalize their domestic norms of conflict resolution, nor do they tend to treat each other with trust and respect when their interests clash.

Externalization

Democracies have often failed to externalize their domestic norms of conflict resolution. These norms justify the use of force under only two conditions: self-defense, and intervention to prevent gross human rights violations or impose democracy. However, there is good evidence that democracies have frequently waged war for reasons other than these.[18]

Between 1815 and 1975, Europe's most liberal states fought 33 "imperial" wars against previously independent polities, and 33 "colonial" wars against their own possessions. None of the imperial wars can be justified in terms of self-defense. Several, such as the First Opium War (1839) and Dutch–Achinese War (1873), were driven by the desire for profit or in order to extend a sphere of influence. Another set of cases that includes the British–Afghan War (1838) and the Franco–Tunisian War (1881) was driven by imperial competition: a liberal great power conquered an independent people in order to prevent it falling into the hands of another state. Some commentators justify these as defensive wars, arguing that the democracy in question was attempting to protect its empire. However, most were preventive rather than defensive: there was no imminent threat to either Afghanistan or Tunisia, for example. Moreover, in launching these wars Britain and France eschewed an obvious liberal alternative to conquest such as offering the non-European entity a defensive alliance.

A final set of cases, including the British–Zulu War (1838) and Franco-Tonkin War (1873), involves wars fought against independent peoples bordering democratic empires. Several of these have also been erroneously categorized as defensive. In most cases, the democratic imperial power acted preventively or deliberately provoked the non-European polity into attacking as a prelude to conquering it. And in the few cases where the non-European power initiated the war it, and not the democracy, was acting in self-defense. Nor were any of the wars, colonial or imperial, fought in order to prevent human rights violations or inculcate liberal values. All of the colonial wars were waged expressly to perpetuate autocratic rule. The imperial wars, meanwhile, simply had the effect of replacing indigenous illiberal governments with European authoritarian rule. Where this rule was not direct, the Europeans supported local autocratic elites, thereby effectively underwriting autocratic rule.

In short, there is good evidence that the norm externalization mechanism does not operate as advertised. Britain and France, generally viewed as classic examples of liberal states, have frequently violated liberal norms in their foreign affairs, thereby casting doubt on the claim that democracies externalize their internal norms of conflict resolution. As Dan Reiter and Allan Stam (2002, p. 151) note, "The essential parts of the norms explanation argue that democracies engage in wars out of fear of exploitation by nondemocratic states. However, the initiation of wars of empire against weaker states to expand democracy's interests and influence at the expense of weaker societies is inexplicable from the liberal norms perspective."

Trust and respect
Democracies do not have a powerful inclination to treat each other with trust and respect when their interests clash. Good evidence for this claim comes from a review of American interventions to destabilize fellow democracies during the Cold War. Three features of these cases warrant attention. First, all of the regimes that the United States sought to undermine – Iran (1953), Guatemala (1954), Indonesia (1957), British Guyana (1961–64), Brazil (1961, 1964), Chile (1973) and Nicaragua (1984–90) – were established or fledgling democracies and all were replaced by authoritarian regimes. Second, although the interventions were often justified as attempts to combat communism, none of the targets were communist, intended to impose a communist model, or were actively courting the Soviet Union. In other words, the United States did not trust and respect other democracies even when the issues at stake were relatively minor. Third, in the cases of Iran, Guatemala, Brazil and Chile support for democracy appears to have been subordinated to naked economic interests.

Democratic peace theorists deny that these examples damage the theory. First, they argue that the target governments were not sufficiently democratic. Second, they argue that the United States government acted covertly precisely because of democratic norms: the public would have viewed overt action as illegitimate. Thus the cases do not contradict the theory. Neither argument stands up to scrutiny. In some instances, the targets may not have been fully democratic, but they were more democratic than the regimes that preceded or succeeded them. As for the claim that the covert nature of these operations actually supports democratic peace theory, it is worth noting that the theory explicitly asserts that it is the leaders of democracies who are most likely to be socialized to and abide by liberal norms. That they did not do so *and* misled a liberal public is a powerful indictment of the theory. But this is of little consequence: whether or not normative considerations affected the *type* of violence employed, the fact is that the United States, perhaps the most liberal state in the system, did not trust or respect these states, even though they were democratic, and used military force in order to destabilize them.

Further evidence against the trust and respect claim comes from several analyses of diplomatic crises involving Britain, France, Germany and the United States. Layne looks at four crises where democratic states almost went to war with each other and concludes that they offer scant support for the mechanism: "In each of these crises, at least one of the democratic states involved was prepared to go to war. . . In each of the four crises war was avoided not because of the 'live and let live' spirit of peaceful dispute resolution at democratic peace theory's core, but because of realist factors" (Layne 1994, p. 38).[19] Similarly, Stephen Rock (1997) finds little evidence that shared liberal norms helped to resolve any of the nineteenth century crises between Britain and the United States. In later cases, where they do appear to have contributed to resolving divisive conflicts, "liberal values and democratic institutions were not the only factors inclining Britain and the United States toward peace, and perhaps not even the dominant ones" (Rock 1997, p. 146). In short, the trust and respect mechanism does not appear to work as specified.

Faced with these anomalies, democratic peace theorists argue that democracies will only trust and respect one another if they *perceive* each other to be democratic. This is only a convincing amendment, however, if democracies tend to form coherent, accurate, and stable opinions of the regime types of other states. They do not. Even John Owen (1997), in his sympathetic analysis of the democratic peace, is forced to admit that, more often than not, liberal elites fail to form coherent or accurate assessments of the regime type of their adversaries. Meanwhile, Oren (1995) has shown that these assessments are far from stable: democracies frequently redefine who is or is not democratic and they do so based on strategic considerations rather than on the democratic attributes of those states. Thus the introduction of perceptions has done little to strengthen the democratic peace case.

15.5.2   Institutions

The available evidence suggests that the institutional argument does not work as specified. For one thing, democratic leaders are no more accountable than their autocratic counterparts. Nor does the evidence support the institutional mechanisms that purportedly flow from democratic accountability. Pacific publics and antiwar groups rarely constrain decisions for war, democracies are not slow to mobilize or incapable of surprise attack, democratic states are not especially good at revealing their resolve in a crisis, and they are not especially likely to win their wars.

Accountability
It is generally accepted that democracies do not fight each other, but autocracies do. Therefore, if accountability is a key mechanism in explaining the separate peace between democracies, democratic leaders must be more accountable than autocratic leaders. If they are not, then accountability – the key to all the institutional arguments – cannot be a prime cause of the democratic peace.

In assessing whether leaders are accountable, proponents of the democratic peace focus exclusively on their chances of losing office as a result of waging a losing or costly war (Bueno de Mesquita et al. 1999, p. 794). Logically, however, accountability depends on a leader's likelihood of removal *and* the costs that he or she will incur when removed. It is not clear, for example, that leaders who are likely to be voted out of office for prosecuting a losing or costly war, but are unlikely to be exiled, imprisoned or killed in the process will feel more accountable than leaders who are unlikely to lose office, but can expect severe punishment in the unlikely event that they are in fact removed. Put somewhat differently, it is not clear that their expected costs, which are a function of the likelihood that they will be removed and the costs they will incur if they are removed, are substantially different.[20]

If we focus on expected costs, democrats do not appear to be more accountable than autocrats. An analysis of the fate of all leaders in all the wars in the Correlates of War (COW) dataset, reveals that democratic leaders who lose a war or embroil their state in a costly war are marginally more likely to be removed from office than their autocratic counterparts (37 percent to 35 percent), but considerably less likely to be exiled, imprisoned, or killed (5 percent to 28 percent).[21] Thus there is little evidence that democratic leaders face greater expected costs for waging losing or costly wars and are therefore more accountable than their autocratic counterparts. Giacomo Chiozza and Hein Goemans reach a similar conclusion in their examination of how defeat in war affects the tenure of democratic and nondemocratic leaders between 1919 and 1999. Defeat in war does not significantly affect the tenure of democrats, but does significantly reduce the tenure of autocrats (Chiozza and Goemans 2004, p. 613). Similarly, in her analysis of domestic audience costs, Jessica Weeks (2008, p. 59) finds that leaders in most nondemocracies are just as accountable as their democratic counterparts.

Faced with this argument, democratic peace theorists provide alternative evidence that democratic leaders are more accountable than their autocratic counterparts. Noting that democracies rarely lose their wars, proponents of the democratic peace assert that this must be because they are more accountable than autocrats and therefore tend to choose winnable wars. (Slantchev, Alexandrova and Gartzke 2005, p. 461). There are several problems with this new body of evidence. First, it does not contradict the finding about the fate of leaders described above. That body of evidence, which provides a more direct test of the accountability claim, suggests that there is little difference between democrats and autocrats in terms of accountability. Second, as I argue below, there is little evidence that democracies are more likely to win their wars than autocracies, and scant support for the claim that democrats carefully select wars that they can win because they are aware of their accountability. As Michael Desch (2003, p. 188) points out, democratic peace theorists are content to "infer" careful selection "rather than directly testing these propositions."

Public constraint

The claim that public opinion can be expected to restrain leaders considering war suffers from several weaknesses. First, only a tiny fraction of the public is likely to experience the costs of war directly and therefore have a reason to oppose a conflict. Excluding the World Wars, democratic fatalities in war have tended to be quite low. In 60 percent of cases, losses amounted to less than 0.01 percent of the population, or 1 in 10 000 people. Indeed, the casualty rate only exceeded 0.1 percent, or 1 in 1000 people, in 6 percent of cases. As for militarized disputes, Britain and the United States have suffered less than one hundred total battle fatalities in 97 percent of them. Thus the vast majority of citizens do not experience the costs of war. Moreover, those who are directly affected – the families and friends of military personnel – are the least likely to oppose a war. Because most democracies have professional standing armies and members of the military sign up voluntarily, they and those close to them tend to be imbued with a powerful spirit of patriotism and self-sacrifice, and they are therefore unlikely to speak out against a government that chooses to go to war.

Second, cost aversion is often trumped by nationalism. The growth of nationalism is one of the most striking features of the modern period. Its effect is so powerful, in fact, that ordinary citizens have repeatedly demonstrated a willingness to fight and die in order to defend their state and co-nationals. This being the case, it is likely that if they believe the national interest is at stake, as it is in most interstate conflicts, the citizens of democracies will ignore the costs associated with a decision for war. Third, democratic leaders can often lead the public rather than follow it. Their reputation as foreign policy experts and their privileged access to relevant information give them ample opportunity to stoke nationalistic fervor, shape public opinion and suppress dissent despite the obligation to allow free and open discussion.[22]

There is good evidence that cost considerations are often trumped by nationalism or elite entrepreneurship. Between 1815 and 1991, the world's five most militarily active democracies – the United States, Britain, France, India and Israel – went to war 30 times. In half of those cases, they were the victims of aggression and therefore we should not be surprised that their publics reacted in a nationalistic fashion or were persuaded to support decisions for war. In the other fifteen cases, however, there was no obvious threat to the homeland or vital national interests. Nevertheless, on 12 of these occasions (80 percent) the outbreak of war was greeted by a spontaneous and powerful nationalistic response, or in the absence of such a response, leaders persuaded the public to support the use of force. This kind of reaction has been common even in clashes between democracies. The available evidence reveals that public opinion was highly bellicose and nationalistic on at least a dozen occasions where democracies came to the brink of war with one another.

Group constraint

For the group constraint mechanism to be a plausible explanation of the democratic peace, there must be good evidence that antiwar groups will, more often than not, dominate the policy process. There are theoretical and empirical reasons to doubt this claim. As far as theory goes, it is generally agreed that groups that are better organized and have more at stake in a given situation are more likely to influence policy. This being the case, there is no reason to believe that pacific groups will generally prevail over bellicose ones. When it comes to issues of war and peace, international traders and the military industrial complex will both have a great deal at stake and are likely to be equally well organized.

The historical record also suggests that prowar groups often win out in the foreign policy process. Owen (1997) identifies four nineteenth century examples in which the American political elite was deeply divided about going to war and finds that in each case the prowar group won out over the antiwar group. Similarly, Jack Snyder (1991) provides abundant evidence of bellicose groups capturing the foreign policy making process in Britain and the United States over the last 200 years. Imperialist groups managed to dominate British policymaking in the middle of the nineteenth century due to "their apparent monopoly on expertise and effective organization." The US case is even more damaging to the group constraint claim. Despite a consensus *against* involvement in "high cost, low benefit endeavors" the United States became embroiled in Korea and Vietnam as a result of coalitional logrolling among prowar groups (Snyder 1991, pp. 206, 209). In short, it is not clear that pacific interest groups tend to dominate the democratic policy process even in the most mature and stable democracies.

There is also little evidence for the other implication of the group constraint claim, namely that group constraints must be weaker in autocracies than in democracies. If the mechanism is to explain why democracies remain at peace but autocracies do not, then there must be good evidence that democratic leaders face greater group constraints. The evidence suggests, however, that autocratic leaders often respond to groups – themselves or their supporters – that have powerful incentives to avoid war.

One reason for autocrats to shy away from conflict is that wars are expensive and the best way to pay for them is to move to a system of consensual taxation, which in turn requires the expansion of the franchise. In other words, autocratic leaders have a powerful incentive to avoid wars lest they trigger political changes that may destroy their hold on power. Another reason to avoid war is that it allows civilian autocrats to maintain weak military establishments, thereby reducing the chances that they will be overthrown. Different considerations inhibit the war proneness of military dictators. First, because they must often devote considerable effort to domestic repression, they have fewer resources available for prosecuting foreign wars. Second, because they are used for repression their militaries often have little societal support, which makes them ill equipped to fight external wars. Third, military dictators are closely identified with the military and will therefore be cautious about waging war for fear that they will be blamed for any subsequent defeat. Finally, time spent fighting abroad is time away from other tasks on which a dictator's domestic tenure also depends. Thus there may be fewer groups with access to the foreign policy process in autocracies – in extreme cases only the autocrat himself has a say – but these often have a vested interest in avoiding war. This being the case, it is not clear that group constraints are weaker in autocracies than they are in democracies.

Slow mobilization

There is scant support for the claim that democracies are slow to use force because of the complexity of mobilizing multiple domestic groups behind the war effort. American presidents, for example, have routinely circumvented or ignored the checks and balances that are supposed to restrain their decisions to use force. For proof we need look no further than the following fact: most of the 200 American uses of force in the last two centuries were authorized unilaterally by the president and only five of them were wars declared by Congress. Presidents have circumvented the democratic process in several ways: by asserting that national security is more important than observing the constitution; by redefining the action in question as anything but a war, thereby obviating the need for consultation; by putting troops in harm's way in order to spark a wider conflict; and, at times, by simply ignoring Congress. Even the passage of the War Powers Resolution (1972), which was designed to make war decisions subject to open debate, has had little effect. When presidents have determined that national security depends on swift and decisive action they have been willing to bypass the democratic imperatives of open debate and consensus decision making. That this kind of behavior is routine in perhaps the most democratic state of the last two centuries suggests that slow mobilization is not a feature of democracies as a whole.

Surprise attack

There is also scant support for the claim that democracies are less able to launch surprise attacks. There have been ten surprise attacks since 1939, two of which have been launched by democracies – the British–French–Israeli attack on Egypt in 1956 and the Israeli initiation of the Six Day War (1967). Because there are so few cases, it is impossible to determine whether this finding is significant, but it is worth noting that democracies have made up approximately one-third of the state years since 1939, which suggests that they are as likely to launch surprise attacks as nondemocracies. Moreover, there does not appear to be a great deal of evidence for the claim at the core of the surprise attack mechanism, namely that democracies cannot keep their war deliberations secret. The United States kept its decision for war from the British before the War of 1812, Lord Grey did not publicize his agreement to defend French Channel ports before World War I and Roosevelt did not reveal his agreements with Churchill prior to World War II. In short, democratic leaders will eschew open debate and maintain secrecy whenever they believe that doing so will improve their chances of military success.

Information

Democracies do not appear to be especially good at revealing their level of resolve in a crisis. The first reason is that although their open political systems can provide a great deal of information, this is not the same as providing good information. In a standoff against a democracy, the other state will receive signals from numerous sources, including the government, the opposition, interest groups, public opinion and the media. Discerning which signal is representative of the democracy's true position is likely to be a difficult task. There is good evidence for this claim. In their analysis of seven interstate crises between 1812 and 1969, for example, Bernard Finel and Kristin Lord (1999) find that democracies do indeed provide a great deal of information, but also that its sheer volume has either confused observers or served to reinforce prior misconceptions.

Democratic peace theorists have responded that opponents are not confused by the multitude of signals that they receive from democracies. If the opposition party supports the government then the democracy is committed, otherwise it is not. It is not clear, however, that the opposition's stance in a crisis reveals a great deal about a democracy's resolve. For one thing, the opposition almost invariably supports the government either as a result of the familiar "rally round the flag" effect or because the administration persuades it to do so. In fact, as Kenneth Schultz (2001, p. 167) has shown, opposition parties support their governments' deterrent threats 84 percent of the time. What this means is that democracies are rarely able to signal their level of resolve – since the opposition almost always supports the government, opponents glean little information when they see an opposition party doing exactly that. Nor do they gain valuable information when the opposition party opposes the government. On the few occasions that opposition parties have opposed military action, thereby presumably signaling that the democracy is not resolved, the government has instead gone ahead and initiated hostilities. Presidents Madison, Truman, and George H.W. Bush and Prime Minister Anthony Eden, to name a few, all went to war despite resistance from their respective opposition parties. In short, there does not appear to be a strong correlation between declarations by opposition parties and decisions for war.

Victory

For the victory mechanism to explain the democratic peace there must be good evidence that democracies win most of their wars and that their victory propensity can be attributed to the fact that they carefully select wars they can win.[23]

All else equal, democracies are not more likely to win their wars than autocracies. As Alexander Downes (2009) has shown, the evidence that democracies are more likely to win their wars is critically affected by two debatable choices: the decision to code all states that did not initiate a war as targets and the exclusion of all wars that ended in draws. When he divides states into initiators, targets and joiners, and adds draws to the dataset, he finds that democracies are not significantly more likely to win their wars. Thus the finding does not appear to be robust. Desch (2002) reaches a similar conclusion using a different approach. Focusing only on cases that provide fair tests of the war-winning proposition, he concludes that the "historical data do not strongly support the triumphalists' claim that democracies are more likely to win wars than nondemocracies" (Desch 2002, p. 20).

Nor is there strong support for the claim that democratic leaders carefully select wars that they can win because they are aware of their domestic accountability. In his statistical analysis of war decisions, Desch (2003, pp. 187–92) finds that democracy has one of the smallest effects of any variable on whether a state wins a war that it initiates. His case studies of democratic war initiations buttress this finding: in half of the cases, democratic leaders' decisions for war were not affected by calculations of accountability or the operation of a robust marketplace of ideas. Meanwhile, Downes (2009) finds little evidence for the corollary of the careful selection argument, namely that democracies will shy away from wars that they are not confident of winning. Finally, democracies appear to engage in as many costly wars as autocracies, thereby suggesting that they are not especially selective about the wars that they fight.

In conclusion, the causal mechanisms that purport to explain the democratic peace do not appear to operate as stipulated by the theory's proponents. Democracies do not reliably externalize their domestic norms of conflict resolution and do not trust and respect one another when they have a conflict of interest. Moreover, democratic leaders are not more accountable than their autocratic counterparts, democratic publics are not reliably peaceful, pacific groups do not have privileged access to decision-making and democracies are not especially slow to mobilize, incapable of surprise attack, adept at revealing their resolve, or good at fighting wars.

15.6 THE DURABILITY OF THE DEMOCRATIC PEACE

There are good reasons to doubt that joint democracy causes peace. Although the empirical claim that democracies rarely fight one another is generally considered to be the most compelling element of democratic peace theory, it does not survive close examination. The finding that democracies rarely if ever go to war with one another is either incorrect or unexceptional. Meanwhile, the claim that they are less likely to engage each other in militarized disputes than other pairs of states turns out to be statistically insignificant or attributable to something other than their democratic nature. Nor does there appear to be a causal relationship between joint democracy and peace. Contrary to the assertions of democratic peace theorists, shared norms and institutions do not seem to work to inhibit violence among democracies. In short, the data do not support the claim that democracies rarely fight and even if they did there is no compelling explanation for why this should be the case.

Given that there is good evidence contradicting democratic peace theory, how can we explain its prominence and durability in policymaking circles and within the academy? The first reason is that it is a liberal theory of war and peace and, at least in America, liberalism is the dominant framework of political discourse. Indeed, Louis Hartz (1991, pp. 3, 57) goes so far as to argue that liberalism is the only political tradition of any importance in the United States.[24] This dominance derives from its fundamentally optimistic view of the world, a view that fits neatly with the optimism that pervades American society. As Mearsheimer (2001, p. 24) notes, "Americans are basically optimists. They regard progress in politics, whether at the national or international level, as both desirable and possible." This view dovetails neatly with liberal political thought, which Keith Shimko (1992, p. 283) describes as "ultimately dependent upon an optimistic assessment of man and his potential." It is this connection that gives democratic peace theory its staying power. After all, Shimko (1992, p. 285) notes, "Theoretical perspectives, particularly in the social sciences, thrive not merely because of their scientific superiority, but also because they are consonant with a society's prevailing values and beliefs."

The second reason that the democratic peace continues to thrive is that the research program is considered to be an exemplar of "good" scientific inquiry. There is a growing consensus among students of international politics that, in order to be compelling, theories must meet two and only two criteria: their independent and dependent variables must be significantly correlated and their explanations must be logically consistent (Slantchev et al. 2005, p. 462). Democratic peace theory appears to meet these criteria. For one thing, there seems to be abundant evidence of a powerful association between joint democracy and peace. Moreover, there is nothing illogical, for example, about the claim that states that trust and respect one another will remain at peace or the claim that states with leaders accountable to pacific publics will remain at peace.

Because they are wedded to this conception of scientific inquiry, proponents of the democratic peace dismiss most critiques of the theory as illegitimate. Critics tend to focus on establishing whether the theory's causal mechanisms actually function as advertised. In my critique of the theory, I sought to determine whether the "causal mechanisms operate as stipulated" (Rosato 2003, p. 586). Similarly, Desch (2003, p. 187) was concerned with establishing whether the "causal mechanisms really explain why these democracies won their wars." However, because these analyses do not fit with the "instrumentalist-empiricism" approach that dominates the field, they are rejected out of hand. Thus Branislav Slantchev (2005, p. 462) and his colleagues accuse me of "legitimizing a fundamentally incorrect method of evaluating social science theory." Similarly, David Lake (2003, p. 155) dismisses Desch's critique as "ill-conceived." But there is a flaw in these defenses: contrary to the assertions of democratic peace theorists, their approach is not axiomatically superior to others. Critics of the democratic peace who evaluate theories based on the operation of their causal mechanisms are working within a powerful and established tradition in the philosophy of science, that of "scientific-realism." Democratic peace theorists cannot claim that this approach is inferior to their own preferred way of doing business. As Paul MacDonald (2003, p. 563) points out, "there is no objective" way to "adjudicate between competing epistemologies." Scholarly communities settle on the "proper" way to conduct scientific inquiry for various reasons none of which rest on a "foundational notion of an absolute *a priori* standard."

In sum, democratic peace theory continues to prosper because it is consonant with Americans' views about themselves and the wider world, and because it is based on a particular interpretation of science. Indeed, democratic peace theorists accuse critics of having "a normative aversion to the democratic peace or the scientific method" (Slantchev et al. 1995, p. 462). While this kind of argument may satisfy the theory's proponents, others would do well to doubt a theory that derives its strength from inherent normative appeal and a narrow conception of science.

ACKNOWLEDGEMENTS

I thank Paul Avey, Michael Bocchino, Michael Desch and John Schuessler for their comments and suggestions.

NOTES

1. For a similar formulation, see Russett (1993, p. 4).
2. Regime type is, for example, central to Snyder (1991) and Schweller (1992).

3. This emphasis means that I ignore several related literatures. I do not, for example, evaluate the "monadic" peace claim that democracies are more peaceful than other kinds of states in general and not just in their relations with one another. For this claim, see Oneal and Ray (1997, p. 765) and Oneal and Russett (1999a, p. 27). Nor do I enter the debate about the war proneness of democratizing states. For a summary of the debate, see Mansfield and Snyder (2005). Finally, because I take democratic peace theory to be fundamentally about domestic regime type and its impact on foreign policy, I touch only tangentially on the "liberal" argument that democracy and interdependence combine to produce peace. On the liberal peace, see Oneal and Russett (1997).

4. Although democracy and liberalism are not equivalent, democratic peace proponents tend to equate the two. I therefore use the terms interchangeably throughout.

5. For statements about the centrality of Russett and his colleagues' work to the democratic peace research program, see Henderson (2002, p. 16) and Beck, Katz and Tucker (1998, p. 1274).

6. The US scored an 8 in 1860, Spain scored a 6 and the US scored a 10 in 1898, and Britain and the Orange Free State both scored a 7 in 1899. For my defense of the Civil War as an example of an interstate war, see below.

7. Ray (1993, p. 262) agrees that excluding the Civil War on the grounds that it was not an interstate war properly defined would constitute a "rather technical victory."

8. Defenders of the democratic peace may counter that I have violated the accepted definition of independent states used by the Correlates of War (COW) project, but this is no different to their practice of altering the equally accepted Polity definition of democracy in order to buttress their own claims.

9. I focus on *liberal* states in this paragraph because Doyle mentions World War I as a possible exception to his liberal peace claim – proponents of the *democratic* peace do not view it as a marginal case.

10. I do not deny that the no war finding is significant after World War II (see also Farber and Gowa 1995, pp. 141–2). For my analysis of this period, see below.

11. Oneal and Russett (1999a, p. 12) note that 40 percent of British males (and all females) were disenfranchised in Britain before 1918. Meanwhile, blacks were denied the vote in most southern states of the United States.

12. A politically relevant dyad (PRD) is a pair of states that is contiguous by land or less than 400 miles of water or that contains a major power. I generated the PRD total using EUGene and the democratic PRD total using the Polity IV and COW System Membership, Direct Contiguity and Major Power datasets. EUGene undercounts the number of PRDs by 1390, however the results reported here hold whether or not these dyads are included. The number of wars is from the COW Interstate War dataset. In cases where a war involved more than two combatants, I paired all states on one side with all states on the other side in order to generate the number of dyads at war. I deleted two wars because they involved dyads that were not politically relevant. An analysis of all mathematically possible dyads yielded identical results. The data are from www.correlatesofwar.org, www.systemicpeace.org/polity/polity4.htm, and www. eugenesoftware.org.

13. A finding of zero wars would be significant only at the 10 percent level. In fact, there *was* one war between states scoring six or more on the Polity scale – the Spanish–American War. For different analyses that also conclude that a finding of zero wars between democracies before 1913 is insignificant, see Farber and Gowa (1995, pp. 141–2; 1997a, pp. 405–406) and Spiro (1994, pp. 66–8). For a critique of these findings, see Maoz (1997, pp. 164–73). For the claim that democracies were not significantly less warlike than other pairs between 1870 and 1946, see Barbieri (1996, pp. 42–3).

14. For methodologically driven critiques of the democratic peace finding, see James, Solberg and Wolfson (1999); Green, Kim and Yoon (2001); Ray (2003, 2005); Ward, Siverson and Cao (2007). For rejoinders to all but the last of these, see Oneal and Russett (2000, 2001, 2005).

15. This is the conclusion Farber and Gowa derive from their bivariate analysis. In their

multivariate analysis, democratic dyads are also significantly more conflict prone, but only at the 10 percent level (Farber and Gowa 1995, pp. 144–5). William Thompson and Richard Tucker (1997) argue that democratic dyads do not appear more conflict prone when other types of dyads are disaggregated into their various sub-types (for example, autocratic–autocratic, autocratic–democratic and so forth) or when a control variable is introduced for interstate rivalries. As Farber and Gowa (1997b) point out, neither critique is either theoretically or methodologically sound.

16. For the original finding, see Gartzke (1998) and for a critique, see Oneal and Russett (1999b).

17. For a similar claim, see Rosato (2003, pp. 599–600). See also Henderson (1999, 2002, pp. 125–43). The Cold War argument may also explain another finding in the literature, namely that peace is a condition for democracy. In an effort to prosecute the Cold War as effectively as possible, the United States imposed stability within its bloc and this stability was in turn the key precondition for the emergence of democracy. For the claim that peace is a condition for democracy, see Thompson (1996), James et al. (1999, p. 30) and Reuveny and Li (2003, p. 343).

18. For the argument, examples and analysis in this section, see Rosato (2003, 2005). Here and elsewhere, I test democratic peace theory's causal logics as if they are monadic. Some proponents of the democratic peace contend that this is inappropriate because the logics are in fact dyadic. This is a mistaken interpretation of the logics underpinning the democratic peace: the finding is dyadic, but the logics are not. See Rosato (2005, pp. 467–8). For further support of my claim that the logics are monadic in nature, see Muller and Wolff (2006). Critics also contend that my analysis of the causal mechanisms treats them as if they are deterministic when they are in fact probabilistic. Again, the criticism is unwarranted. I agree that theories are probabilistic and go to great lengths to challenge democratic peace theory on those grounds. Thus I cite large numbers of anomalies rather than selected historical cases in order to demonstrate that the mechanisms *rarely* operate as stipulated. Moreover, I focus my attention on sets of cases that are most likely to support democratic peace theory, reasoning that if there is little evidence that the mechanisms work in these easy cases then this casts serious doubt on the theory. Finally, in several cases (the accountability, surprise attack and information mechanisms) my claims are based on an analysis of the entire universe of cases as recommended by my critics. See Rosato (2005, pp. 468–9).

19. Layne (1997) comes to the same conclusion after analysing three further Franco-British crises in the 1830s and 1840s. In a similar vein, Macmillan (1996, pp. 282–3) argues that democratic Italy seriously considered going to war with democratic France in 1914–15, but decided against it because the Italian government did not believe that it could win.

20. This approach draws on Goemans (2000).

21. For evidence that war substantially increases the chances of domestically instigated violent regime change and that most violent regime changes occur in nondemocracies, see Bueno de Mesquita, Siverson and Woller (1992).

22. For an analysis of how democratic leaders shape public opinion, see Kaufmann (2004).

23. For evidence in support of the victory mechanism, see Lake (1982) and Reiter and Stam (2002).

24. For the claim that the United States' international behavior has been shaped by liberalism, see Kennan (1951, p. 46).

REFERENCES

Barbieri, K. (1996), "Economic interdependence: a path to peace or source of interstate conflict?", *Journal of Peace Research*, **33** (1), 29–49.

Beck, N., J.N. Katz and R. Tucker (1998), "Taking time seriously", *American Journal of Political Science*, **42** (4), 1260–88.

Bennett, A. and G.J. Ikenberry (2006), "The *Review's* evolving relevance for US foreign policy 1906–2006", *American Political Science Review*, **100** (4), 651–8.

Bennett, D.S. and A.C. Stam (2000), "Research design and estimator choices in the analysis of interstate dyads: when decisions matter", *The Journal of Conflict Resolution*, **44** (5), 653–85.

Bremer, S.A. (1992), "Dangerous dyads: conditions affecting the likelihood of interstate war 1816–1965", *Journal of Conflict Resolution*, **36** (2), 309–41.

Bueno de Mesquita, B. (2006), "Game theory, political economy, and the evolving study of war and peace", *American Political Science Review*, **100** (4), 637–42.

Bueno de Mesquita, B., M.T. Koch and R.M. Siverson (2004), "Testing competing institutional explanations of the democratic peace: the case of dispute duration", *Conflict Management and Peace Science*, **21** (4), 255–67.

Bueno de Mesquita, B. and D. Lalman (1992), *War and Reason: Domestic and International Imperatives*, New Haven, CT: Yale University Press.

Bueno de Mesquita, B., J.D. Morrow, R.M. Siverson and A. Smith (1999), "An institutional explanation of the democratic peace", *American Political Science Review*, **93** (4), 791–807.

Bueno de Mesquita, B., R.M. Siverson, and G. Woller (1992), "War and the fate of regimes: a comparative analysis", *American Political Science Review*, **86** (3), 638–46.

Chiozza, G. and H.E. Goemans (2004), "International conflict and the tenure of leaders: is war still *ex post* inefficient?", *American Journal of Political Science*, **48** (3), 604–19.

Cohen, R. (1994), "Pacific unions: a reappraisal of the theory that democracies do not go to war with each other", *Review of International Studies*, **20** (3), 207–23.

Danilovic, V. and J. Clare (2007), "The Kantian liberal peace", *American Journal of Political Science*, **51** (2), 397–414.

Desch, M.C. (2002), "Democracy and victory: why regime type hardly matters", *International Security*, **27** (2), 5–47.

Desch, M.C. (2003), "Democracy and victory: fair fights or food fights?", *International Security*, **28** (1), 180–94.

Dixon, W.J. (1994), "Democracy and the peaceful settlement of international conflict", *American Political Science Review*, **88** (1), 14–32.

Downes, A.B. (2009), "How smart and tough are democracies? reassessing theories of democratic victory in war", *International Security*, **33** (4), 9–51.

Doyle, M.W. (1983a), "Kant, liberal legacies, and foreign affairs, Part 1", *Philosophy and Public Affairs*, **12** (3), 205–35.

Doyle, M.W. (1983b), "Kant, liberal legacies, and foreign affairs, Part 2", *Philosophy and Public Affairs* **12** (4), 323–53.

Farber, H.S. and J. Gowa (1995), "Polities and peace", *International Security*, **20** (2), 123–46.

Farber, H.S. and J. Gowa (1997a), "Common interests or common polities? Reinterpreting the democratic peace", *Journal of Politics*, **59** (2), 393–417.

Farber, H.S. and J. Gowa (1997b), "Building bridges abroad", *Journal of Conflict Resolution*, **41** (3), 455–6.

Finel, B.I. and K.M. Lord (1999), "The surprising logic of transparency", *International Studies Quarterly*, **43** (2), 315–39.

Gartzke, E. (1998), "Kant we just all get along? Opportunity, willingness, and the origins of the democratic peace", *American Journal of Political Science*, **42** (1), 1–27.

Gartzke, E. (2000), "Preferences and the democratic peace", *International Studies Quarterly*, **44** (2), 191–212.

Gartzke, E. (2007), "The capitalist peace", *American Journal of Political Science*, **51** (1), 161–91.

Gibler, D.M. (2007), "Bordering on peace: democracy, territorial issues, and conflict", *International Studies Quarterly*, **51** (3), 509–32.

Gleditsch, N.P. (1995), "Geography, democracy, and peace", *International Interactions*, **20** (4), 297–323.

Gochman, C.S. (1996/97), "Democracy and peace", *International Security*, **21** (3), 177–87.

Goemans, H.E. (2000), *War and Punishment: The Causes of War Termination and the First World War*, Princeton, NJ: Princeton University Press.

312   *The handbook on the political economy of war*

Green, D.P., S.Y. Kim and D.H. Yoon (2001), "Dirty pool", *International Organization*, **55** (2), 441–68.
Hartz, L. (1991), *The Liberal Tradition in America: An Interpretation of American Political Thought Since the Revolution*, San Diego, CA: Harcourt Brace Jovanovich.
Henderson, E.A. (1999), "Neoidealism and the democratic peace", *Journal of Peace Research*, **36** (2), 203–31
Henderson, E.A. (2002), *Democracy and War: The End of an Illusion?* Boulder, CO: Lynn Rienner.
James, P., E. Solberg and M. Wolfson (1999), "An identified systemic model of the democracy-peace nexus", *Defence and Peace Economics*, **10** (1), 1–37.
Kaufmann, C. (2004), "Threat inflation and the failure of the marketplace of ideas: the selling of the Iraq War", *International Security*, **29** (1), 5–48.
Kennan, G. (1951), *American Diplomacy, 1900–1950*, Chicago, IL: University of Chicago Press.
Lake, D.A. (1982), "Powerful pacifists: democratic states and war", *American Political Science Review*, **86** (1), 24–37.
Lake, D.A. (2003), "Fair fights? Evaluating theories of democracy and victory", *International Security*, **28** (1), 154–67.
Layne, C. (1994), "Kant or cant: the myth of the democratic peace", *International Security*, **19** (2), 5–49.
Layne, C. (1997), "Lord Palmerston and the triumph of realism: Anglo-French relations, 1830–48", in M.F. Elman (ed.), *Paths to Peace: Is Democracy the Answer?* Cambridge, MA: MIT Press, pp. 61–100.
Layne, C. (2001), "Shell games, shallow gains, and the democratic peace", *International History Review*, **23** (4), 799–813.
Levy, J.S. (1994), "The democratic peace hypothesis: from description to explanation", *Mershon International Studies Review*, **38** (2), 352–4.
Lipson, C. (2003), *Reliable Partners: How Democracies Have Made a Separate Peace*, Princeton, NJ: Princeton University Press.
MacDonald, P.K. (2003), "Useful fiction or miracle maker: the competing epistemological foundations of rational choice theory", *American Political Science Review*, **97** (4), 551–65.
Macmillan, J. (1996), "Democracies don't fight: a case of the wrong research agenda?" *Review of International Studies*, **22** (3), 275–99.
Mansfield, E.D. and J. Snyder (2005), *Electing to Fight: Why Emerging Democracies Go to War*, Cambridge, MA: MIT Press.
Maoz, Z. (1997), "The controversy over the democratic peace: rearguard action or cracks in the wall?", *International Security*, **22** (1), 162–98.
Maoz, Z. and N. Abdolali (1989), "Regime types and international conflict, 1816–1976", *Journal of Conflict Resolution*, **33** (1), 3–35.
Maoz, Z. and B. Russett (1992), "Alliance, contiguity, wealth, and political stability: is the lack of conflict among democracies a statistical artifact?", *International Interactions*, **17** (3), 245–67.
Maoz, Z. and B. Russett (1993), "Normative and structural causes of democratic peace, 1946–1986", *American Political Science Review*, **87** (3), 624–38.
Mearsheimer, J.J. (1990), "Back to the future: instability in Europe after the Cold War", *International Security*, **15** (1), 5–56.
Mearsheimer, J.J. (2001), *The Tragedy of Great Power Politics*, New York, NY: W.W. Norton.
Mousseau, M. (2000), "Market prosperity, democratic consolidation, and democratic peace", *Journal of Conflict Resolution*, **44** (4), 472–507.
Mousseau, M. (2009), "The social market roots of democratic peace", *International Security*, **33** (4), 52–86.
Muller, H. and J. Wolff (2006), "Democratic peace: many data, little explanation?", in A. Geis, L. Brock and H. Muller (eds), *Democratic Wars: Looking at the Dark Side of Democratic Peace*, New York, NY: Palgrave Macmillan, pp. 41–73.

Oneal, J.R. and J.L. Ray (1997), "New tests of the democratic peace: controlling for economic interdependence, 1950–85", *Political Research Quarterly*, **50** (4), 751–75.

Oneal, J.R. and B. Russett (1997), "The classical liberals were right: democracy, interdependence, and conflict, 1950–1985", *International Studies Quarterly*, **41** (2), 267–93.

Oneal, J.R. and B. Russett (1999a), "The Kantian peace: the pacific benefits of democracy, interdependence, and international organizations, 1885–1992", *World Politics*, **52** (1), 1–37.

Oneal, J.R. and B. Russett (1999b), "Is the liberal peace an artifact of Cold War interests? Assessing recent critiques", *International Interactions*, **25** (3), 213–41.

Oneal, J.R. and B. Russett (2000), "Comment: why an identified systemic model of the democracy-peace nexus does not persuade", *Defence and Peace Economics*, **11** (1), 197–214.

Oneal, J.R. and B. Russett (2001), "Clear and clean: the fixed effects of the liberal peace", *International Organization*, **55** (2), 469–85.

Oneal, J.R. and B. Russett (2005), "Rule of three, let it be? When more really is better", *Conflict Management and Peace Science*, **22** (4), 293–310.

Oneal, J.R., F.H. Oneal, Z. Maoz and B. Russett (1996), "The liberal peace: interdependence, democracy, and international conflict, 1950–85", *Journal of Peace Research*, **33** (1), 11–28.

Oren, I. (1995), "The subjectivity of the 'democratic' peace: changing US perceptions of Imperial Germany", *International Security*, **20** (2), 147–84.

Owen, J.M. (1997), *Liberal Peace, Liberal War: American Politics and International* Security, Ithaca, NY: Cornell University Press.

Polachek, S.W. (1997), "Why democracies cooperate more and fight less: the relationship between international trade and cooperation", *Review of International Economics*, **5** (3), 295–309.

Raknerud, A. and H. Hegre (1997), "The hazard of war: reassessing the evidence for the democratic peace", *Journal of Peace Research*, **34** (4), 385–404.

Ray, J.L. (1993), "Wars between democracies: rare, or nonexistent?", *International Interactions*, **18** (3), 251–76.

Ray, J.L. (1995), *Democracy and International Conflict: An Evaluation of the Democratic Peace Proposition*, Columbia, SC: University of South Carolina Press.

Ray, J.L. (2000), "Democracy: on the level(s), does democracy correlate with peace?" in J.A. Vasquez (ed.), *What Do We Know about War?* New York, NY: Rowman and Littlefield, pp. 299–316.

Ray, J.L. (2003), "Explaining interstate conflict and war: what should be controlled for?", *Conflict Management and Peace Science*, **20** (2), 1–32.

Ray, J.L. (2005), "Constructing multivariate analyses (of dangerous dyads)", *Conflict Management and Peace Science*, **22** (4), 277–92.

Reiter, D. and A.C. Stam (2002), *Democracies at War*, Princeton, NJ: Princeton University Press.

Reuveny, R. and Li, Q. (2003), "Joint democratic-dyadic conflict nexus: a simultaneous equations model", *International Studies Quarterly*, **47** (3), 325–46.

Rice, C. (2005), "The promise of democratic peace", *Washington Post*, December 11, B7.

Rock, S.R. (1997), "Anglo-US relations 1845–1930: did shared liberal values and democratic institutions keep the peace?", in M.F. Elman (ed.), *Paths to Peace: Is Democracy the Answer?*, Cambridge, MA: MIT Press, pp. 101–50.

Rosato, S. (2003), "The flawed logic of democratic peace theory", *American Political Science Review*, **97** (4), 585–602.

Rosato, S. (2005), "Explaining the democratic peace", *American Political Science Review*, **99** (3), 467–72.

Rousseau, D.L., C. Gelpi, D. Reiter and P.K. Huth (1996), "Assessing the dyadic nature of the democratic peace, 1918–88", *American Political Science Review*, **90** (3), 512–33.

Russett, B. (1990), *Controlling the Sword: The Democratic Governance of National Security*, Cambridge, MA: Harvard University Press.

Russett, B. (1993), *Grasping the Democratic Peace: Principles for a Post-Cold War World*, Princeton, NJ: Princeton University Press.

Russett, B. (1995), "And yet it moves", *International Security*, **19** (4), 164–77.

Russett, B. and J.L. Ray (1995), "Raymond Cohen on pacific unions: a response and a reply", *Review of International Studies*, **21** (3), 319–25.

Schultz, K.A. (1998), "Domestic opposition and signaling in international crises", *American Political Science Review*, **92** (4), 829–44.

Schultz, K.A. (2001), *Democracy and Coercive Diplomacy,* Cambridge, UK: Cambridge University Press.

Schweller, R.L. (1992), "Domestic structure and preventive war: are democracies more pacific?" *World Politics*, **44** (2), 235–69.

Shimko, K.L. (1992), "Realism, neorealism, and American liberalism", *Review of Politics*, **54** (2), 281–301.

Slantchev, B.L., A. Alexandrova and E. Gartzke (2005), "Probabilistic causality, selection bias, and the logic of the democratic peace", *American Political Science Review*, **99** (3), 459–62.

Snyder, J. (1991), *Myths of Empire: Domestic Politics and International Ambition,* Ithaca, NY: Cornell University Press.

Souva, M. (2004), "Institutional similarity and interstate conflict", *International Interactions*, **30** (3), 263–80.

Spiro, D.E. (1994), "The insignificance of the liberal peace", *International Security*, **19** (2), 50–86.

Thompson, W.R. (1996), "Democracy and peace: putting the cart before the horse?", *International Organization*, **50** (1), 141–74.

Thompson, W.R. and R. Tucker (1997), "A tale of two democratic peace critiques", *Journal of Conflict Resolution*, **41** (3), 428–54.

Waltz, K.N. (1979), *Theory of International Politics,* New York, NY: McGraw-Hill.

Ward, M.D., R.M. Siverson and X. Cao (2007), "Disputes, democracies, and dependencies: a reexamination of the Kantian peace", *American Journal of Political Science*, **51** (3), 583–601.

Weart, S.R. (1998), *Never at War: Why Democracies Will Not Fight One Another*, New Haven, CT: Yale University Press.

Weeks, J.L. (2008), "Autocratic audience costs: regime type and signaling resolve", *International Organization*, **62** (1), 35–64.

16 International conflict and leadership tenure
Randall J. Blimes

16.1 INTRODUCTION

For the last several decades, neorealist approaches to explaining international relations have been at the forefront of academic research. These approaches make the assumption that domestic politics is irrelevant to explaining foreign policy patterns because the anarchic nature of the international system constrains all states to act alike, regardless of variation in domestic-level factors. More recently, this approach has come under intense scrutiny and more and more scholars, notably those writing in the liberal tradition, have begun to argue that variation in domestic institutions plays a large role in explaining variation in foreign policy. Research areas such as the dyadic democratic peace and the diversionary theory of war, for example, have suggested that leaders take domestic preferences and opinions into account in forming foreign policy. However, while research along these lines has been both productive and plentiful, there is still a great deal of theoretic and empirical disagreement about exactly how and why domestic politics matters.

This chapter focuses on exploring the relationship between international conflict and leadership tenure. Broadly defined, this subject encompasses some of the most fruitful and important literatures within international relations study. I divide the research done on conflict and leadership tenure into two categories. The first category is what I refer to as "indirect" analysis. This body of research views leadership tenure as a cause of international conflict. It asks such questions as: do leaders use war as an instrument to increase domestic support and make their tenure more secure? Or, on the other hand, does fear from being removed from office restrain leaders from engaging in conflict they otherwise would? Do leaders' concerns about remaining in office explain the timing of wars? Are these issues solely the concern of democratic leaders?

I refer to this line of study as indirect because much of this literature relies on assumptions about how international conflict affects leadership tenure. The research within this category suggests, for example, that a defeat in a war should decrease an incumbent leader's likelihood of being retained, and then asks what implications this has for how leaders act. Therefore, the empirical tests are one step removed from the theoretical underpinnings. The empirical tests of the arguments within this literature are thus indirect tests of the effect of international conflict on leadership tenure. For example, if democracies tend to have fewer casualties in wars than autocracies, this may be taken as indirect evidence that democratic leaders fear being removed from office after a costly war. Certainly this seems a plausible argument to make; nevertheless, it does not provide direct evidence.

The category of the international conflict and leadership tenure literature is by far the bigger category. In fact, with such literatures as democratic peace and diversionary war, it could be argued that this body of literature is one of the most important in the discipline. In this chapter, I will cover four basic bodies of literature that fall within the indirect analysis approach: public constraints (which includes institutional explanations for the democratic peace), audience costs, diversionary war and electoral cycles.

The second category of the international conflict and leadership tenure literature I will cover is what I refer to as "direct" analysis. This body of literature views leadership tenure as an effect or consequence of international conflict. It asks such questions as: does international conflict affect leadership tenure? If so, how and when? Is the effect mitigated by domestic institutions?

I refer to this line of study as direct because it seeks to directly test the assumptions about how international conflict affects leadership tenure. Empirical tests used in this category tend to rely on survival analysis, a statistical technique designed to directly test how a set of factors affects the duration of some phenomenon.

The direct analysis literature is far smaller than that of the indirect analysis, but in recent years it has asserted its importance. Significantly, the empirical results within the direct analysis literature have been highly contradictory. This suggests that the assumptions made by the indirect analysis literature are, at the very least, not as straightforward as have been argued. A deeper understanding of exactly how international conflict affects leadership tenure will bring significant insights into all areas of indirect analysis.

I proceed by exploring each of the categories of literature. I begin with the indirect analysis, covering public opinion constraints, audience costs, diversionary war and electoral cycles. I then cover the direct analysis and offer ideas for advancement of this body of research.

16.2 PUBLIC OPINION CONSTRAINTS

The first body of literature within the indirect analysis category focuses on public opinion constraints. This body of literature proposes that (1) decision-makers take domestic politics into account rather than using a cost–benefit analysis based strictly on a national interest and (2) that different types of domestic institutions result in different foreign policy outcomes.

The public opinion constraints models rest on the assumption that leaders in power wish to remain in power. Especially in democratic states, retention of power is contingent upon maintaining some minimum level of domestic support. Therefore, leaders are constrained in their actions by the fear that the public will retrospectively punish a leader for engaging in an unpopular foreign policy. Because populations bear the costs of war, democratic leaders should therefore only engage in wars where these costs can be minimized, thus making it more likely that the public will view the benefits as greater than the costs. Gartner and Segura (1998) found that the popularity of wars within democracies declines as casualties mount. Therefore, democratic countries should tend to fight shorter wars (Bennett and Stam 1996; Slantchev 2004); they also should fight wars with fewer casualties[1] (Siverson 1995; Goemans 2000); and they should be more likely to compromise to end a long war (Bennett and Stam 1998).

Similarly, because continuation in office relies on avoiding negative foreign policy outcomes for democratic leaders, they will be more cautious about the types of conflicts they get involved with than their autocratic counterparts. In other words, while autocratic leaders may engage in highly risky foreign policy adventures, democratic leaders may select themselves only into conflicts with a very high likelihood of victory to avoid negative feedback from the voting public. This suggests that democratic countries would be more likely to win the conflicts they do get involved in (Rioux 1998; Gelpi and Griesdorf 2001; Reiter and Stam 2002), while autocratic leaders will be more likely to lose conflicts (even those conflicts which they choose to initiate) (Reed and Clark 2000; Clark and Reed 2003; Reiter and Stam 2003).

But scholars disagree on whether domestic constraints on leaders always produce more peaceful foreign policy. While some have argued that domestic constraints may make democratic leaders less likely to initiate conflicts (Schultz 2001a; Huth and Allee 2002), others have argued that nationalism within democracies may be more likely to lead to conflict (Braumoeller 1997) or that democracies will be more aggressive toward non-democracies (Werner 2000; Reiter and Stam 2003; Bennett and Stam 2004).

One of the most important and productive bodies of literature within the public opinion constraints model is that of the dyadic democratic peace (the proposition that democratic states do not fight other democratic states).[2] Explanations for the democratic peace are generally categorized as either normative or institutional. Institutional explanations rely heavily on the assumption that democratic populations hold leaders accountable for foreign policy decisions and may remove the leaders from office for unpopular actions or outcomes. Thus concerns about continued leadership tenure play the driving theoretical force in much of the democratic peace literature.

The empirical finding that democracies do not fight other democracies is quite strong. The question, however, is why. The constraints that democratic institutions place on incumbent leaders outlined above have two very important effects which may account for the democratic peace. First, fears that an international conflict could end in defeat and therefore bring removal from office decreases the expected utility of leaders making the decision to go to war. Autocratic leaders are believed to be largely insulated from these fears due to the absence of voter feedback. Therefore, democratic leaders are more cautious than autocratic leaders, and it is unlikely that two highly cautious states will go to war.

Second, because failed policy is likely to result in removal from office in democratic states, democratic institutions create a need for success as defined by voters. Therefore, democratic leaders are unwilling to fight each other because each knows the other's future in office depends on a successful outcome. This would likely lead to a costly war for both sides. Democratic leaders may fear removal from office even after a victory if the war is long or costly. This is consistent with Bennett and Stam's (1998) finding that democratic states prefer short conflicts and become anxious to end wars that drag on. Again, autocratic leaders should be insulated from these concerns.

Nor will two democratic populations likely have the high degree of support necessary for a democratic leader to carry out a war when fighting another country believed to also be democratic. Combining a normative argument, which suggests that democratic populations will tend to view war as an illegitimate policy tool, with a public constraints argument, Owen (1997) suggests that liberal populations will oppose any use of violence against another population considered to also be liberal (which explains why democratic states are still willing to fight autocratic states).

While there has been a great deal of empirical investigation into the democratic peace (and the public opinion constraints models in general), two fundamental assumptions remain largely unsupported.[3] The first assumption is that democratic leaders are electorally punished as a result of international conflict, and that leaders are aware of this possibility and act accordingly. Chan and Safran (2006) find that many democratic leaders choose to go to war despite significant public opposition and that certain types of democratic institutions insulate leaders from electoral consequences. Further, the empirical results directly testing whether leaders are more likely to be removed after an unsuccessful international conflict have produced mixed results (Bueno de Mesquita et al. 2003; Chiozza and Goemans 2004; Colaresi 2004a).

The second assumption that the dyadic democratic peace rests on is that autocratic leaders are not likely to be removed from office as a result of international conflict. However, some empirical studies have found that autocratic leaders are not less likely to be held accountable for international conflicts (Rosato 2003; Chiozza and Goemans 2004; Colaresi 2004a), or that while autocratic leaders are less likely to face punishment after an unsuccessful international conflict, the consequences when they do can be extreme (Goemans 2000).

While the democratic peace has become one of the most influential and certainly most written about theories of international relations, there is still a great deal of disagreement about exactly *why* democracies do not tend to fight other democracies. To truly understand the causal mechanism behind the strong empirical regularity which the democratic peace rests on, more attention must be paid to the direct relationship between international conflict and leadership tenure, especially focusing on the differences between democratic and autocratic institutions.

16.3   AUDIENCE COSTS

The second body of literature within the indirect analysis is that of audience costs. This literature argues that war is an inefficient means by which two countries may resolve differences, but suggests that some bargain that is preferable (for all parties) to war always exists (Fearon 1994a; Fearon 1994b; Fearon 1995). In effect, war is a "mistake" that occurs because one or more parties are unable to credibly signal intentions. According to this reasoning, if states were better able to signal their true intentions (despite incentives to misrepresent these intentions) war would occur less frequently.

Audience costs are the costs that a leader incurs if she publicly makes a statement and then fails to follow through.[4] The leader's audience[5] may decide that a leader who does not follow through on public statements should be removed from power. Because incumbent leaders wish to remain in power, they therefore avoid making threats and then backing down. Thus democratic leaders, who are assumed by most scholars to be most sensitive to audience costs, are deterred from bluffing. Democratic leaders should therefore have an advantage when it comes to issuing credible commitments.

For the logic of audience costs to produce the expected results, domestic audiences must (1) decide that backing down is an undesirable trait that should be punished and (2) have the ability to remove the incumbent leader from office.

Addressing the first issue, Smith (1998) asks why individuals in a state would punish an incumbent leader for backing down from a threat and thereby avoiding a costly conflict. After all, audiences should prefer to avoid conflict whenever possible and may realize the benefits of bluffing from time to time. However, Smith argues that there is an incentive for individuals to punish a leader who backs down because only the least competent type of leader makes false promises. Because audiences prefer to remove incompetent leaders, there is an incentive to give an ex post punishment to leaders who bluff.

Tomz (2007) provides direct evidence for audience costs using embedded experiments in public opinion data. He finds that individuals were likely to punish leaders who backed down from threats or promises because individuals care about the reputation of their country and their leaders.

Empirical tests have also provided a certain degree of evidence suggesting that democratic leaders act in a manner consistent with the audience costs logic (Eyerman and Hart 1996; Partell and Palmer 1999; Gelpi and Griesdorf 2001; Prins 2003). In addition, Schultz (1999) finds that disputes initiated by democratic states are less likely to be reciprocated by non-democratic states and takes this as evidence that democratic states are better able to communicate resolve to potential opponents.

However, Slantchev (2006) argues that democratic leaders are not necessarily vulnerable to audience costs. Rather, Slantcher argues that democratic leaders are only able to generate audience costs in the presence of a free media.

Weeks (2008) also provides a critique by pointing out that the audience costs literature overestimates the extent to which autocratic leaders are immune to audience costs. She argues that when elites are able to solve their coordination dilemmas, autocratic leaders are just as vulnerable to audience costs as democratic leaders.

While a logical direction to take the audience costs literature would be to directly test whether (1) democratic leaders are less likely to make hollow threats than autocratic leaders and (2) whether leaders who back down from public statements are more likely to lose office, these direct tests are very difficult due to selection problems (Schultz 2001b). Audience costs can only be observed when they occur, but leaders will likely avoid audience costs in all situations in which they believe those audience costs will be significant. In other words, the likelihood of a leader incurring audience costs is a function of the severity of those audience costs. Therefore, the observed cases of incurred audience costs are a strategically selected set of cases, and analysis based on these cases will provide biased results.

Solutions for this problem are difficult. One answer is in increasingly sophisticated statistical estimators to account for selection problems. In addition, Schultz (2001b) offers three suggestions. First, decrease noise in empirical estimates by improving the specification of models of political survival. Second, use historical case studies to supplement and compliment large-N statistical analysis. Third, continue to employ indirect tests of the implications of audience costs.

16.4   DIVERSIONARY WAR

The third category of indirect analysis is diversionary war theory. While the previously discussed literature on international conflict and leadership tenure focuses on leaders making conflict decisions in order to avoid electoral punishments, the diversionary war literature focuses on the use of conflict to provide electoral rewards.

A large body of international relations scholarship has grown up around the idea that (democratic) leaders may use foreign policy to distract public attention away from domestic troubles.[6] Several scholars have noted the "rally-round-the-flag" effect, in which public support for leaders increases during times of international crisis. Leaders should be able to anticipate the rally effect and use foreign policy actions to boost popularity at home during times of, for example, economic troubles.

Empirical evidence for the diversionary theory is quite mixed. While there is a large number of studies which offer support for the theory (Ward and Widmaier 1982; Stoll 1984; Ostrom and Job 1986; Russett 1990; James and Oneal 1991; Morgan and Bickers 1992; DeRouen 1995; Hess and Orphanides 1995; Miller 1995; Enterline and Gleditsch 1996; Gelpi 1997; Fordham 1998; Dassel and Reinhardt 1999; Miller 1999; Fordham 2002), there is also a good deal of evidence refuting the theory (Meernik 1994; Meernik and Waterman 1996; Leeds and Davis 1997; Gowa 1998; Meernik 2000; Mitchell and Moore 2002; Chiozza and Goemans 2003). These contradictory results suggest that the use or effectiveness of diversionary war may be conditioned upon a further set of variables.

For example, one approach scholars have taken to explain the diversionary war hypothesis suggests that the quality of the opponent is critical to the effectiveness of diversionary war. This line of reasoning relies on principal–agent models. These models assume that populations prefer to retain competent leaders and remove incompetent ones. However, because competence is not directly observable, populations have to look for clues which may provide information about how competent a leader is. Leaders may therefore choose to engage in interstate conflict to demonstrate competence to a population, especially if other signals, such as a poor economy, signal incompetence.

Two articles in this tradition, one by Richards et al. (1993) and the other by Tarar (2006), make an important contribution to the diversionary literature by noting that the quality of the opponent is an important, and generally overlooked, aspect of the diversionary war theory. A leader who defeats a weak target state does not demonstrate competence in the same way that a leader who defeats a strong target does. This important point is absent from most of the theoretic diversionary literature and all of the empirical studies. However, given the diversity of empirical findings in many of the literatures examining the relationship between international conflict and leadership tenure, it seems more appropriate to begin to ask questions such as "under what circumstances can wars be diversionary," rather than "are wars diversionary."

16.5   ELECTION CYCLES

The fourth category of indirect analysis is that of election cycles. In states with exogenously determined electoral timing, the election cycles may be a significant factor affecting international conflict decision-making. Even in states with endogenously determined electoral timing, there is often a significant period of time before the actual election in which anticipation of the election may affect decision-making.

Gaubatz (1999) finds that international conflict is less likely to occur in the period leading up to an election. Smith (1996) also suggests that the election cycle may affect foreign policy behavior, but provides a specific condition when this is most likely to occur. Smith argues that when there is a high degree of certainty in the outcome of an election, the electoral cycle should be unrelated to conflict decisions. However, when neither victory nor defeat in an election are certain, and therefore foreign policy might play a crucial role in determining the outcome of an election, the incumbent leader will be biased toward aggressive, bellicose behavior leading up to the election.

Other scholars have taken a strategic approach to explaining how elections affect foreign policy. Gelpi and Greico (2001) suggest that relatively inexperienced leaders may make highly attractive targets to other states. Because new leaders fear their inexperience may lead to poor conflict outcomes, they may feel it would be cheaper to offer concessions to the aggressor state. This suggests that a state should attract more challenges shortly after an election which results in a new leader.

Wolford (2007) also suggests that outside states have incentives to test the resolve of new leaders. However, Wolford also points out that these new leaders have an incentive to meet all challenges aggressively to ward off future challenges. This provides a "turnover trap" resulting in conflict after changes in leadership.

In contrast to these studies, Gowa (1998) finds no evidence of a relationship between electoral cycles (or government partisan make-up) for the United States. Gowa suggests that attempts to manipulate the public and gain goodwill through the use of violence abroad are bound to fail. Rather, she finds power politics the best explanation for US foreign policy.

16.6   THE DIRECT EFFECT OF INTERNATIONAL CONFLICT ON LEADERSHIP TENURE

I now turn to the relatively new and growing body of literature which directly tests the effect of international conflict on leadership tenure.

Most, if not all, of the literature linking domestic politics to international relations rests on the assumption that leaders prefer to remain in power and act accordingly. This argument is the driving theoretical explanation for each of the bodies of literature outlined above. Institutional explanations for the democratic peace suggest that the threat of being voted out of office causes democratic leaders to avoid specific types of conflicts. The audience costs literature argues that democratic leaders are able to make credible commitments because of a fear of losing office. Diversionary war theory also explicitly links leaders' foreign policy actions with the desire to remain in office. And the electoral cycles literature suggests the timing of war is explained by leaders considerations for doing well in the next election.

One potential criticism of most of the indirect analysis literature is that although the theoretical unit of analysis is the leader, the empirical unit of analysis has most often been the country (Chiozza and Goemans 2004). The research outlined below represents what I call the direct approach to studying the link between international conflict and leadership. This literature uses the same theoretical and empirical unit of analysis, namely the leader or leader-year, and seeks to *directly* address the question of whether or how international conflict affects leaders' likelihoods of remaining in office. Given the vast amount of research that relies on assumptions or indirect tests of how conflict affects leadership tenure, it is surprising that relatively little direct research has been conducted. However, this body of literature is growing, and it has the potential to greatly affect how the discipline views many of its most important theories.

Early investigations into political survival were often focused on explaining the shape of the hazard rate (the probability distribution for removal from office) of both individual leaders and cabinets, but did not offer much in the way of the determinants of political survival (Browne, Frendreis and Gleiber 1986; Bienen and Van deWalle 1992; Warwick 1995; Diermeier and Stevenson 1999; Grofman and Van Roozendaal 1999). More recently scholars have begun to explicitly examine the relationship between foreign policy and leadership tenure. For example, Marinov (2005) finds that economic sanctions destabilize target regimes. Horowitz, McDermott and Stam (2005) find a link between the age of a leader and the likelihood of that leader initiating and escalating interstate conflict. Boehmer (2007) finds that both high rates of economic growth and interstate conflict reduce the likelihood of a leader losing power.

In the mid 1990s, a series of articles was published that directly examined the effect of international conflict on leadership tenure that culminated in Bueno de Mesquita et al.'s book, *The Logic of Political Survival*. Bueno de Mesquita et al. ask why some leaders are able to engage in costly or unsuccessful foreign policy adventures and are able to retain power, while other leaders experienced more success and are removed. They find that variation in domestic political institutions accounts for these confusing cases. They argue that the key is the size of a country's selectorate (the portion of the population that has some part in choosing the leader) and the winning coalition (the subset of the selectorate whose support is necessary for a leader to maintain power). Democratic states have large selectorates (all eligible voters) and large winning coalitions (the portion of the population whose vote is necessary to win the election), while autocratic countries tend to have small selectorates and winning coalitions.

Bueno de Mesquita et al. argue that leaders with small winning coalitions maintain the necessary support by providing private benefits to the relatively small number of individuals in their winning coalition. Leaders with very large winning coalitions, on the other hand, are unable to provide enough private benefits to win the necessary support, and therefore these leaders are forced to focus on providing public benefits. In this argument, foreign policy is considered a public good, and therefore leaders with large selectorates and winning coalitions are (1) cautious in their foreign policy decision and (2) make a very high effort to succeed when they do get involved in an international conflict. When these leaders produce failed foreign policy, the likelihood of removal from office is high, while leaders with small selectorates and winning coalitions are able to insulate themselves from these consequences by providing private goods to their winning coalition members. This line of argument became known as the selectorate theory and has gained a great deal of attention.

The selectorate theory is not without criticism however. Clarke and Stone (2008) point out that Bueno de Mesquita et al. may have inflated the importance of their key independent variables by using a process called residualization. In their empirical work, Bueno de Mesquita et al. regress a measure of democracy on measures of a state's selectorate and winning coalition size, and use the residuals as control variables in their analyses (rather than controlling for democracy directly). Clarke and Stone argue that this induces significant omitted variable bias into their results. When they re-ran Bueno de Mesquita et al.'s models controlling for democracy, the important results disappeared. However, Bueno de Mesquita et al. responded to Clarke and Stone by running additional tests using different measures of democracy as a control and found their results highly robust to the changes (Morrow et al. 2008).

Perhaps a more surprising critique of both Bueno de Mesquita et al.'s work, and much of the literature connecting domestic politics and international conflict, came from other empirical studies. Chiozza and Goemans (2004), using an improved dataset[7] and sophisticated empirical analysis, test the effects of both international crises and wars on leadership tenure. Surprisingly, they find that democratic leaders are less likely to be affected by the outcome of interstate conflicts than autocratic leaders. In fact, in most cases democratic leaders are not any more or less likely to retain office regardless of whether an international conflict is a win, a loss or a draw. These findings call into doubt some of the most basic assumptions that much of the literature linking domestic politics and international relations rests on.

Chiozza and Goemans also reject the notion that a selection process was responsible for their results. If, as is often argued, democratic leaders are careful about selecting themselves into conflicts which have a low likelihood of resulting in loss of office, then the empirical results should have shown that incumbent leaders are rewarded for a victory, but are not punished for a loss. The lack of any significant results for democratic leaders, therefore, is taken as evidence against a selection effect.

Colaresi (2004a) also finds empirical evidence suggesting there is no difference between how international conflict affects democratic and autocratic leaders. Colaresi tests the likelihood of an incumbent being removed from office after a war, and found no significant interaction between war outcome and regime type, suggesting that a military defeat has the same impact on leadership tenure for both autocrats and democrats.

With such strong, contradictory findings, how are researchers to progress in the study of international conflict and leadership tenure? One potential answer is that there are different methods of removal for leaders which are conceptually distinct. Goemans (2008) distinguishes regular removal (removal mandated by election, and so forth) of leaders from irregular removal (coups, and so forth). He then argues that international conflict outcomes affect the likelihood of irregular removal (which also entails serious risks of significant punishment for the removed leader), but not regular removal.

Another strategy taken to begin to reconcile the contradictory empirical results is to look at outside environmental factors. Most of the international conflict and leadership tenure literature has assumed that a victory should be associated with a lower likelihood of being removed from office, while a defeat should be associated with a higher risk. However, Colaresi (2004b) found that incumbent leaders who lose a war to a rival state are significantly less likely to be removed from office than those who lose a war to a non-rival. This suggests that domestic audiences may prefer to fight and lose to a rival than to not fight. Therefore the standard to judge whether a given conflict is a success or failure is more complex than a simple "win, lose or draw" measurement.

Johnson and Tierney (2006) have also noted this subjective aspect of judging success or failure. They argue that, because individuals see gains or losses in relation to some reference point (Levy 2000), judgments of whether an interstate war is a success or a failure can be different in different situations. In fact, Johnson and Tierny go so far as to call the mental process by which individuals determine what constitutes a success "match fixing," denoting the process as highly biased by a variety of factors.

Johnson and Tierney offer a wealth of inspiration for researchers wishing to add to the growing body of literature empirically testing the effect of international conflict on leadership tenure using large-N statistical techniques. While the precise arguments made in their book, *Failing to Win*, may be too complex to effectively opperationalize and measure for quantitative study, perhaps the biggest contribution of the book to the direct analysis literature is to remind us that judgments of success and failure are relative. Individuals do not make such judgments in a vacuum. There must be some standard, for which outcomes that exceed the standard are considered successes and outcomes that fall below are considered failures. The question then is what sets the standard?

I suggest that one likely answer is a simple ex-ante expectation that can be compared to the actual outcome of the conflict. Before any conflict begins, an individual voter could make a guess about how the conflict would most likely end. This individual will fall somewhere on a continuum from optimistic to pessimistic in his expectations. This expectation provides the standard for judging success or failure. Individuals may form expectations based on a number of factors, but two simple and measurable factors include the balance of military power between the conflicting states and the past history of the dyad.

Taking this approach can help clear up many confusing cases in which the simple model (victory = reward / defeat = punishment) cannot explain. For example, suppose two states, A and B, are involved in a crisis that escalates to war. If State A is significantly more powerful than State B, and State A wins the conflict, would the population of State A determine that the victory over State B demonstrated competent leadership and therefore reward Incumbent A with more time in office? In fact, it is more likely that the victory was simply a result of the superior military power of State A, and the population is not given any additional information about the competency of Incumbent A.

Likewise, would the population of State B determine that the defeat was due to Incumbent B's lack of competency? Again, the outcome is most likely attributable to military power and therefore the population of State B gains no new information about incumbent B.[8] In fact, if State B loses, but puts up a better fight than expected, the outcome may be considered a success from State B's point of view.

In each of these cases, the outcome of the conflict would seem confusing to a model that simply expected a victory to be associated with a reward and a defeat to be associated with a loss. Leader A would likely not be affected at all despite her victory, while Leader B might be rewarded despite his defeat.

Similarly, a past history should also have a strong effect on the formation of expectations. If a state has achieved a great deal of success in international conflict in the past, the standard of success will be higher than a state that has suffered more defeats. For example, the Yom Kippur War was viewed as a victory by Egypt and a disastrous loss by Israel. This is surprising given the military situation at the end of the war. After initial losses, the Israeli army regrouped and forced the Egyptians to retreat back across the Suez, cut off a sizable portion of the Egyptian army and threatened Cairo. From a pure military standpoint, the Yom Kippur War was a success for the Israelis. However, it was Golda Meir, the Israeli Prime Minister, who was strongly criticized and eventually resigned in the wake of the conflict.

The impact of the Yom Kippur War was to shatter the impression of an invincible Israel, a reputation that had been established in the decades leading up to 1973. Because Israel had a history of quick, decisive victories, that is what was expected and anything less was considered a defeat. Without taking ex-ante expectations into account as the standard against which success and failure are measured, the Yom Kippur War is a confusing example for scholars of international conflict and leadership tenure.

Another yet underexplored avenue of research is an increase in the scope of independent variables used to explain leadership turnover. While scholars have suggested that, for example, democratic countries need to fight short wars lest the leader be punished (Bennett and Stam 1996; Slantchev 2004), scholars directly studying leadership tenure have focused on "win, lose or draw" measurements. Likewise, while scholars have noted that mounting casualties may affect public opinion (Gartner and Segura 1998), it is not clear whether this dip in public opinion actually translates to a higher likelihood of leadership turnover.

It seems likely that an incumbent leader may win a war, but if she wins at great cost, her population may take that as a sign of incompetence and remove her from office anyway; however, this line of argument has not been included in the direct analyses of leadership tenure. Like war outcomes, war costs should also be measured on a sliding scale, with different standards of success in different situations. Once again, populations will have some expectation about what constitutes an appropriate cost. Populations may be willing to bear increased costs in conflicts they deem more important, or in conflict they believe will eventually be successful (Feaver and Gelpi 2004). And again, military power and history should both provide a base for individuals to form some expectation about what seems likely.

This suggests that leaders who wish to hedge their bets should encourage populations to have relatively low expectations at the start of a conflict, thereby lowering the standard for success. Notwithstanding the pervasive argument that leaders tend to be overconfident about international conflict,[9] leaders have, indeed, shown themselves supremely "underconfident" when it serves their purposes. For example, in the late stages of World War II, German radio broadcasted highly inflated casualty reports after allied air raids. Several days after these initial reports were made new reports gave estimates closer to the actual number of fatalities suffered. The purpose of these inflated reports was to make actual losses seem less by comparison. A thousand deaths does not seem as great a loss if you initially thought the losses were ten times that great.

Another example of this type of manipulation of expectations may be seen in the greatly overestimated losses the US made public before the 1991 Gulf War. Published estimates of the probable number of US fatalities ranged from 1000 to 10 000, while the actual number of fatalities suffered by US troops was 146 (Achenbach 1991; Royko 1991;Weisberg 1991). On the other hand, Mearsheimer (1991) predicted fewer than 500 US fatalities. Did Mearsheimer know something that those making the official estimates were ignorant of, or did political motivations give incentives for the official estimates to be vastly overinflated?

Compare public reaction to the 146 deaths in the 1991 Gulf War to the deaths of 18 US soldiers in Somalia in 1993. While the American public took the Gulf War deaths in their stride, the far smaller number of casualties in Somalia generated a public outcry. One possible explanation for this difference is that the American public expected, and therefore was willing to tolerate, more deaths in the Gulf War than in the Somali peacekeeping operation. The publication of the grossly over-inflated casualties estimates in the case of the Gulf War indicates that leaders are aware that expectations are important in how individuals judge the success or failure of outcomes and that leaders are able to appear underconfident if it suits their purpose.

16.7   CONCLUSION

If the analysis of the relationship between international conflict and leadership tenure is to move forward, scholars need to continue to focus more on asking "under what conditions" rather than "if" war affects leadership tenure. Under what conditions might a leader successfully use war to divert attention away from domestic trouble? Under what conditions do democratic institutions prevent two democracies from going to war? Under what conditions does the outcome of a war affect a leader's likelihood of retaining office? Simply asking "if" has led to a host of contradictory findings which have not moved the discipline forward. The most interesting and important works have asked "under what conditions?"

Within the indirect study, a great deal of research has made interesting and important contributions by asking under what conditions leaders' concerns for retaining office will lead to certain types of foreign policy.

To this point, the most striking weakness in the direct analysis literature is the general lack of research. While there has been some effort to explore whether and under what conditions war affects leadership tenure directly, it is surprising there has not been a greater effort given the importance of the issue and the weight of the literature which rest upon arguments concerning how leaders attempt to retain office. While this review of the literature is not a call for less work to be done within the indirect analysis framework, it does represent a call for the direct analysis literature to catch up. The emergence of new and increasingly accurate datasets and the application of increasingly sophisticated statistical techniques allow scholars to better address the significant problems associated with the direct study of conflict and leadership tenure (including selection problems, endogeneity and measurement issues).

Thus far, scholars working within the direct analysis framework asking "under what conditions" have focused mainly on regime type. This has proved unsatisfactory however, as empirical results have been contradictory. It seems that the answer to the question "under what conditions does war affect leadership tenure?" needs a more complex answer than simply "democracy." Therefore, until we are able to better answer this question, we must hold some of our most fruitful and influential theoretical developments, or rather the assumptions upon which many of our theories rest, suspect.

NOTES

1. However, Feaver and Gelpi (2005) found that populations may be tolerant of casualties so long as victory seems likely.
2. This short section will barely scratch the surface of the vast body of literature on the democratic peace. For a more thorough review, see Chan (1997).
3. There are, of course, some significant exceptions. See the direct analysis section below.
4. In addition to Fearon 1995, see Martin 1993; Leeds 1999; McGillivray and Smith 2000; Martin 2000; Dorussen and Mo 2001; Schultz 2001a; Jensen 2003; Lipson 2003; and Leventoglu and Tarar 2005.
5. While most of the audience costs literature focuses on the mass public as the important audience, some work focuses on different audiences. For example, Martin (2000) examines the role of the legislature in generating credible commitments.
6. See Levy (1989) for a review of this literature.
7. See Goemans, Gleditsch and Chiozza (2009).
8. Incumbent B might, however, be punished for getting involved in a conflict with a stronger state. However, especially if State A was the aggressor, the population of State B may prefer to fight and lose than to not fight and suffer reputational consequences.
9. Van Evera, for example, states that "At least some false optimism about relative power preceded every major war since 1740" (1999, p. 16).

REFERENCES

Achenbach, J. (1991), "The experts, in retreat: after-the-fact explanations for the gloomy predictions", *Washington Post*, February 28, p D1.
Bennett, D.S. and A.C. Stam (1996), "The duration of interstate wars, 1816–1985", *American Political Science Review*, **90** (2), 239–57.
Bennett, D.S. and A.C. Stam (1998) "The declining advantages of democracy: a combined model of war outcomes and duration", *Journal of Conflict Resolution*, **42** (3), 344–66.
Bennett, D.S and A.C. Stam (2004), *The Behavioral Origins of War*, Ann Arbor, MI: The University of Michigan Press.
Bienen, H. and N. Van de Walle (1992), "A proportional hazard model of leadership duration", *The Journal of Politics*, **54** (3), 685–717.

Boehmer, C. (2007), "The effects of economic crisis, domestic discord, and state efficacy on the decision to initiate interstate conflict", *Politics and Policy*, **35** (4), 774–809.

Braumoeller, B.F. (1997), "Deadly doves: liberal nationalism and the democratic peace in the soviet successor states", *International Studies Quarterly*, **43** (3), 375–402.

Browne, E.C, J.P. Frendreis and D.W. Gleiber (1986), "The process of cabinet dissolution: an exponential model of duration and stability in Western democracies", *American Journal of Political Science*, **30** (3), 628–50.

Bueno de Mesquita, B.A. Smith, R.M. Siverson and J.D. Morrow (2003), *The Logic of Political Survival*, Cambridge, UK: Cambridge University Press.

Chan, S. (1997), "In search of democratic peace: problems and promise", *Mershon International Studies Review*, **41** (1), 59–91.

Chan, S. and W. Safran (2006), "Public opinion as a constraint against war: democracies' response to Operation Iraqi Freedom", *Foreign Policy Analysis*, **2** (2), 137–56.

Chiozza, G. and H.E. Goemans (2003), "Peace through insecurity: tenure and international conflict", *Journal of Conflict Resolution*, **47** (4), 443–67.

Chiozza, G. and H.E. Goemans (2004), "International conflict and the tenure of leaders: is war still ex post inefficient?", *American Journal of Political Science*, **48** (3), 604–619.

Clark, D.H. and W. Reed (2003), "A unified model of war onset and outcome", *The Journal of Politics*, **65** (1), 69–91.

Clarke, K.A. and R. Stone (2008), "Democracy and the logic of political survival", *American Political Science Review*, **102** (3), 387–92.

Colaresi M. (2004), "Aftershocks: postwar leadership survival, rivalry, and regime dynamics", *International Studies Quarterly*, **48** (4), 713–28,

Colaresi, M. (2004b), "When Doves Cry: International Rivalry, Unreciprocated Cooperation, and Leadership Turnover", *American Political Science Review*, **48** (3), 555–570.

Dassel, K. and E. Reinhardt (1999), "Domestic strife and the initiation of violence at home and abroad", *American Journal of Political Science*, **43** (1), 56–85.

DeRouen, K.R. (1995), "The indirect link: politics, the economy, and the use of force", *The Journal of Conflict Resolution*, **39** (4), 671–95.

Diermeier, D. and R.T. Stevenson (1999), "Cabinet survival and competing risks", *American Journal of Political Science*, **43** (4), 1051–68.

Dorussen, H., and J. Mo (2001), "Ending economic sanctions: audience costs and rent-seeking as commitment strategies", *Journal of Conflict Resolution*, **45** (4), 395–426.

Enterline, A. and K.S. Gleditsch (1996), "Threats, opportunity, and force: repression and diversion of domestic pressure, 1948–1982", *International Interactions*, **26** (1), 21–53.

Eyerman, J. and R.A. Hart, Jr. (1996), "An empirical test of the audience cost proposition: democracy speaks louder than words", *Journal of Conflict Resolution*, **40** (4), 597–616.

Fearon, J.D. (1994a), "Domestic political audiences and the escalation of international disputes", *The American Political Science Review*, **88** (3), 577–92.

Fearon, J.D. (1994b), "Signaling versus the balance of power and interests: an empirical test of a crisis bargaining model", *The Journal of Conflict Resolution*, **38** (2), 236–69.

Fearon, J.D. (1995), "Rationalist explanations for war", *International Organization*, **49** (3), 379–414.

Feaver, P.D. and C. Gelpi (2005), *Choosing Your Battles: American Civil-Military Relations and the Use of Force*, Princeton, NJ: Princeton University Press.

Fordham, B. (1998), "The politics of threat perception and the use of force: a political economy model of US uses of force", *International Studies Quarterly*, **42** (3), 567–90.

Fordham, B.O. (2002), "Another look at 'parties, voters, and the use of force abroad'", *Journal of Conflict Resolution*, **46** (4), 572–96.

Gartner, S.S. and G.M. Segura, (1998), "War, casualties, and public opinion", *The Journal of Conflict Resolution*, **42** (3), 278–300.

Gaubatz, K. (1999), *Elections and War: The Electoral Incentive in the Democratic Politics of War and Peace*, Stanford, CA: Stanford University Press.

Gelpi, C. (1997), "Democratic diversions: government structure and the externalization of domestic conflict", *Journal of Conflict Resolution*, **41** (2), 255–82.

Gelpi, C. and J. Greico (2001), "Attracting trouble: democracy, leadership tenure, and the targeting of militarized challenges, 1918–1992", *Journal of Conflict Resolution*, **45** (6), 794–817.

Gelpi, C.F. and M. Griesdorf (2001), "Winners or losers? Democracies in international crisis, 1918–1994", *The American Political Science Review*, **95** (3), 633–47.

Goemans, H.E. (2000), *War and Punishment: The Causes of War Termination*. Princeton, NJ: Princeton University Press.

Goemans, H.E. (2008), "Which way out?", *Journal of Conflict Resolution*, **52** (6), 771–94.

Goemans, H.E., K.S. Gleditsch and G. Chiozza (2009), "Introducing Archigos: a data set of political leaders", *Journal of Peace Research*, **46** (2), 269–83.

Gowa, J. (1998), "Politics at the water's edge: parties, voters, and the use of force abroad", *International Organization*, **52** (2), 307–24.

Grofman, B. and P. Van Roozendaal (1999), "Toward a theoretical explanation of premature cabinet termination", *European Journal of Political Research*, **26** (2), 155–70.

Hess, G.D. and A. Orphanides (1995), "War politics: an economic, rational-voter framework", *American Economic Review*, **85** (4), 828–46.

Horowitz, M., R. McDermott and A.C. Stam (2005), "Leader age, regime type, and violent international relations", *Journal of Conflict Resolution*, **49** (5), 661–85.

Huth, P.K. and T.L. Allee (2002), *The Democratic Peace and Territorial Conflict in the Twentieth Century*. Cambridge, UK: Cambridge University Press.

James, P. and J.R. Oneal (1991), "The influence of domestic and international politics on the President's use of force", *Journal of Conflict Resolution*, **35** (2), 307–32.

Jensen, N.M. (2003), "Democratic governance and multinational corporations: political regimes and inflows of foreign direct investment", *International Organization*, **57** (3), 587–616.

Johnson, D.P. and D. Tierney (2006), *Failing to Win: Perceptions of Victory and Defeat in International Politics*, Cambridge, MA: Harvard University Press.

Leeds, B.A. (1999), "Domestic political institutions, credible commitments, and international cooperation", *American Journal of Political Science*, **43** (4), 979–1002.

Leeds, B.A. and D.R. Davis (1997), "Domestic political vulnerability and international disputes", *Journal of Conflict Resolution*, **41** (6), 814–32.

Levenotoglu, B. and A. Tarar (2005), "Prenegotiation public commitment in domestic and international bargaining", *American Political Science Review*, **99** (3), 419–33.

Levy, J.S. (1989), "The diversionary war theory: a critique", in M.I. Midlarski (ed.), *The Handbook of War Studies*, London: Unwin-Hyman.

Levy, J.S. (2000), "Loss aversion, framing effects, and international conflict", in M.I. Midlarski (ed.), *The Handbook of War Studies 2*, Ann Arbor, MI: University of Michigan Press.

Lipson, C. (2003), *Reliable Partners: How Democracies Have Made a Separate Peace*, Princeton, NJ: Princeton University Press.

McGillivray, F. and A. Smith (2000), "Trust and cooperation through agent-specific punishments", *International Organization*, **54** (4), 809–24.

Marinov, N. (2005), "Do economic sanctions destabilize country leaders?", *American Journal of Political Science*, **49** (3), 564–76.

Martin, L. (1993), "Credibility, costs, and institutions: cooperation on economic sanctions", *World Politics*, **45** (3), 406–32.

Martin, Lisa (2000), *Democratic Commitments*, Princeton, NJ: Princeton University Press.

Mearsheimer, J.J. (1991), "A war we can win–decisively", *Chicago Tribune*, January 15.

Meernik, J. (1994), "Presidential decision making and the political use of military force", *International Studies Quarterly*, **38** (1), 121–38.

Meernik, J. (2000), "Modeling international crises and the political use of military force by the USA," *Journal of Peace Research*, **37** (5), 547–62.

Meernik, J. and P. Waterman (1996), "The myth of the diversionary use of force by American presidents", *Political Research Quarterly*, **49** (3), 573–90.

Miller, R. (1995), "Domestic structures and the diversionary use of force", *American Journal of Political Science*, **39** (3), 760–85.

Miller, R.A. (1999), "Regime type, strategic interaction, and the diversionary use of force", *Journal of Conflict Resolution*, **43** (3), 388–402.

Mitchell, S.M. and W.H. Moore (2002), "Presidential uses of force during the Cold War: aggregation, truncation, and temporal dynamics", *American Journal of Political Science*, **46** (2), 438–52.

Morgan, T.C. and K.N. Bickers (1992), "Domestic discontent and the external use of force", *Journal of Conflict Resolution*, **36** (1), 25–52.

Morrow, J.D., B. Bueno de Mesquita, R.A. Siverson and A. Smith (2008), "Retesting selectorate theory: separating the effects of W from other elements of democracy", *American Political Science Review*, **102** (3), 393–400.

Ostrom, C.W., Jr. and B.L. Job (1986), "The president and the political use of force", *American Political Science Review*, **80** (2), 541–66.

Owen, J.M. (1997) *Liberal Peace, Liberal War: American Politics and International Security*. Ithaca, NY: Cornell University Press.

Partell, P.J. and G. Palmer (1999), "Audience costs and interstate crises: an empirical assessment of Fearon's model of dispute outcomes", *International Studies Quarterly*, **43** (2), 389–405.

Prins, B.C. (2003), "Institutional instability and the credibility of audience costs: political participation and interstate crisis bargaining, 1816–1992", *Journal of Peace Research*, **40** (1), 67–84.

Reed, W. and D.H. Clark (2000), "War initiators and war winners", *Journal of Conflict Resolution*, **44** (3), 378–95.

Reiter, D. and A.C. Stam (2002), *Democracies at War*, Princeton, NJ: Princeton University Press.

Reiter, D. and A.C. Stam (2003), "Identifying the culprit: democracy, dictatorship, and dispute initiation", *American Political Science Review*, **97** (2), 333–6.

Richards, D., T.C. Morgan, R.K. Wilson, V.L. Schwebach and G.D. Young (1993), "Good times, bad times, and the diversionary use of force: a tale of some not-so-free agents", *Journal of Conflict Resolution*, **37** (3), 504–35.

Rioux, J. (1998), "A crisis-based evaluation of the democratic peace proposition", *Canadian Journal of Political Science*, **31** (2), 263–83.

Royko, M. (1991), "Most experts really blew it this time", *Chicago Tribune*, February 28.

Rosato, S. (2003), "The flawed logic of democratic peace theory", *American Political Science Review*, **97** (4), 585–602.

Russett, B. (1990), *Controlling the Sword: The Democratic Governance of National Security*, Cambridge, MA: Harvard University Press.

Schultz, K.A. (1999), "Do democratic institutions constrain or inform? Contrasting two institutional perspectives on democracy and war", *International Organization*, *53* (2), 233–66.

Schultz, K.A. (2001a), *Democracy and Coercive Diplomacy*, Cambridge, MA: Cambridge University Press.

Schultz, K.A. (2001b), "Looking for audience costs", *Journal of Conflict Resolution*, **45** (1), 32–60.

Siverson, R.M. (1995), "Democracies and war participation: in defense of the institutional constraints argument", *European Journal of International Relations*, **1** (4), 481–9.

Slantchev, B.L. (2004), "How initiators end their wars: the duration of warfare and the terms of peace", *American Journal of Political Science*, **48** (4), 813–29.

Slantchev, B.L. (2006), "Politicians, the media and domestic audience costs", *International Studies Quarterly*, **50** (2), 445–77.

Smith, A. (1996), "Diversionary foreign policy in democratic systems", *International Organizations*, **40** (1), 133–53.

Smith, A. (1998), "International crises and domestic politics", *American Political Science Review*, **92** (3), 623–38.

Stoll, R.J. (1984), "The guns of November: presidential reelections and the use of force", *Journal of Conflict Resolution*, **28** (2), 231–46.

Tarar, A. (2006), "Diversionary incentives and the bargaining approach to war", *International Studies Quarterly*, **50** (1), 169–88.

Tomz, M. (2007), "Domestic audience costs in international relations: an experimental approach", *International Organization*, **61** (4), 821–40.

Van Evera, S. (1999), *Causes of War: Power and the Roots of Conflict*. Ithaca, NY: Cornell University Press.

Ward, M.D. and U. Widmaier (1982), "The domestic–international conflict nexus: new evidence and old hypotheses", *International Interactions*, **9** (1), 75–101.

Warwick, P.V. (1995), *Government Survival in Parliamentary Democracies*, Cambridge, MA: Cambridge University Press.

Weeks, J.L. (2008), "Autocratic audience costs: regime type and signaling resolve", *International Organization*, **62** (1), 65–101.

Weisberg, J. (1991), "Gulfballs: how the experts blew it–big time", *New Republic*, March 25.

Werner, S. (2000), "The effects of political similarity on the onset of militarized disputes, 1816–1985", *Political Research Quarterly*, **53** (2), 343–74.

Wolford, S. (2007), "The turnover trap: new leaders, reputation, and international conflict", *American Journal of Political Science*, **51** (4), 772–88.

17 A public choice perspective on defense and alliance policy
Bernhard Klingen

17.1 INTRODUCTION

Public choice analyses of defense and alliance policy are fairly scant. More than 20 years ago Hartley (1987, p. 399) "recognised that the analytical and empirical work is still in its infancy." This has not changed significantly since that time. However the neglect stands in sharp contrast to the share a public choice approach could have in explaining defense and alliance policy.

Defense as well as alliance policy have some distinct specifics. Informational asymmetries are exceptionally strong, ties between government, bureaucracy, industry and the military are tight, and the production of defense goods is hardly market-based. Moreover there are complex inter-state dynamics, and international organizations play an important role. In this environment the political actors' scope for diverting the political outcome from public interest is extremely large.

This is where the public choice approach comes in. Therefore this chapter will review the political economy literature on defense and alliance policies as well as theories which could usefully be applied to them. Furthermore the specific features of these policy fields will be elaborated, and suggestions for future research will be proposed.

17.2 THE ACTORS

Public choice theory focuses explicitly on the political actors. Most important are the voter, the politician,[1] the public servant[2] and the lobbyist. Just like for any other policy field the relevant actors are assumed to maximize their utility from defense and alliance policy by trying to affect the political process.

17.2.1 The (Median) Voter

The (median) voter has a vital interest in a high degree of external security to assure his properties and physical integrity.[3] Given the "price" in terms of taxes and the perceived external threats he chooses the optimal level of security.

However the median voter is in an unfavorable position to pursue his interests. Since the issue space is multidimensional, the preferences regarding defense and security cannot accurately be expressed with a single vote (Hartley 1998, p. 133). Especially in peacetime, defense issues play a minor role in election campaigns and thus they are unlikely to dominate voting decisions. In addition, the ex ante probability to be pivotal is infinitesimal so that the potential median voter has no incentives to collect the information necessary to effectively control the government (for example, Downs 1957; Riker and Ordeshook 1968). Information on defense is much more scant than in other policy fields. Owing to an often multi-partisan consensus on questions of "raison d'Etat" and strategic nondisclosure, debates on defense policy issues are infrequent and information on the process of security production is hardly available. In effect, the only indicator easily accessible to the voting public is the defense budget.

This low level of information on defense issues increases the role of ideology. Since "hard facts" are unavailable, party affiliation, patriotism, pacifism and the like are important for the voter's position on defense policy. The lack of information may also be the reason for the fact that voters tend to gather behind their political leaders when external security is assumed to be at stake (see Mueller 1970).

17.2.2   The Politician

The politician plays an ambiguous role. Besides personal goals he has to be concerned about his reelection and thus has to consider the position of the other actors in defense policy. He needs the approval of the voters as well as the support of the bureaucracy and campaign contributions from industry. Therefore he has to find the compromise which maximizes his probability to stay in office.

The politician can expand his room for manoeuvre by disseminating selective information. Since the voting public is poorly informed, government information can strongly affect its threat perception and increase its willingness to pay for the defense budget. Moreover a feigned external crisis may help to shift the voter's attention away from bad government performance in other policy fields and may even increase the general readiness to support the political leadership.

Apart from the reelection concern the politician pursues personal goals: maximizing power and prestige as well as protecting the tax base.[4] Defense policy may be an instrument to increase power, especially in international relations. Being commander-in-chief of strong military forces confers prestige on a politician.[5] Moreover Holcombe (2008) suggests that the main incentive to provide national security is to protect the tax base against foreign aggressors.

17.2.3 The Public Servant

The public servant primarily pursues the goals of maximizing budget, personnel, and "organizational slack" of his agency since he tends to have little control of his income[6] (Downs 1967; Niskanen 1971; Migué and Bélanger 1974). A large budget increases the bureaucrat's power, a large staff enhances social prestige. By gaining organizational slack the public servant reduces his work load and limits his risks.

In the context of defense policy the room for such discretionary behavior is especially large since the bureaucracy's final output "security" is neither clearly defined nor measurable (Hartley 1987, p. 405). To maximize budget and personnel the public servant has an incentive to deliberately overestimate both the external threats and the need for armament and man power.

17.2.4 The Defense Lobbyist

The defense lobbyist represents the interests of a highly regulated industry.[7] The armament market is characterized by little domestic competition, large public R&D funding, low transparency in contracting and a high degree of protectionism. Against this background the defense industry has an incentive to put strong emphasis on lobbying to maximize its profit. Since the defense lobby is a small and homogenous group, such activities are likely to be successful (Olson 1982, pp. 29–34).

The defense lobbyist will primarily try to influence the government with campaign contributions. Besides, he aims to ease the politician's reelection constraint by funding studies which call for a stronger defense policy and thereby may increase the willingness to pay.

17.3 CONFLICTS IN NATIONAL DEFENSE POLICY

The different political actors' interests in national defense policy tend to clash. The deepest rift is probably between the median voter and the other actors. Thereby the most important issues at stake are: How much should be spend on security? How should the expenditures be allocated to different purposes? From whom should defense goods be purchased? And finally, when should military means be used?

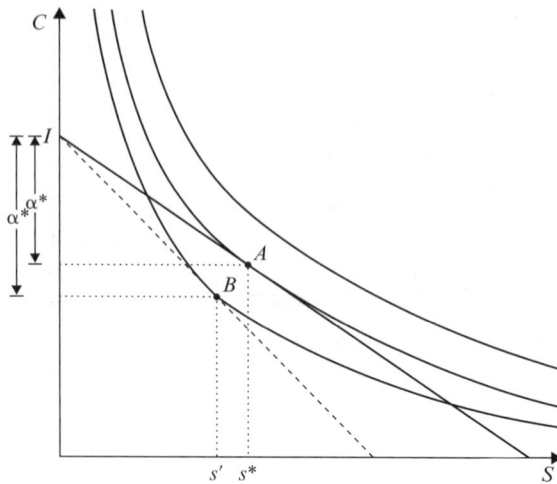

Figure 17.1   The defense budget and the voter's demand for security

17.3.1   Guns or Butter?

The search for a balance between national security and civilian needs is often referred to as the choice between "guns and butter." Although national defense is a textbook example of a public good,[8] the "publicness" of defense is of minor importance for a positive analysis from a public choice perspective (Holcombe 2008, pp. 12–13). What has to be revealed instead is the political process that leads to the bundle of "guns" and "butter" we actually observe.

The voter's optimization calculus

The voter's optimization calculus is to find the bundle of security S and consumption C which maximizes his utility. As shown in Figure 17.1 he chooses point A, the point of tangency of his highest indifference curve with the solid budget line, the corresponding amount of security is s^*. The median voter allocates the share α^* of his income I to defense and the share $(1-\alpha^*)$ to civilian consumption.

The solid budget line assumes a perfect political process in which a benevolent dictator guarantees an efficient use of the budget to maximize external security. However since the voter cannot control the process of security production, special interests of the industry, public administrations and the government will lower efficiency. In Figure 17.1 the budget line shifts to the steeper dashed line. A rational voter will anticipate this increase of the de facto price of security and reduce his demand to s'. Although he gets a smaller amount of security than in the benevolent dictator case, this does not necessarily mean a cut of the defense budget. If the price elasticity of the voter's demand for security is low, he will respond to the efficiency loss by demanding higher defense spending. Figure 17.1 shows this scenario: the effciency loss leads to a higher defense budget α'.

Hence the price elasticity of demand for security has a strong impact on the distribution of power in the struggle for the defense budget. In the case of an inelastic demand the divergence from the initial mandate is "rewarded" by higher spending. Thus the defense industry can push through its interests quite successfully and in some cases may even choose the level of compliance quasi monopolistically. The existing literature on the demand for military expenditures (for example, Dudley and Montmarquette 1981; Murdoch and Sandler 1984b; Gonzalez and Mehay 1990) does barely account for this effect.

The voter's preference for security and his threat perception

The voter's preference for security and his threat perception influence the shape of his indifference curve. Both factors lead to a higher expected defense budget α. Hence the other actors have an incentive to expand their room of manoeuvre by influencing the preferences and the threat perception of the voters.[9]

The voter's preference for security depends on his safety needs as well as his potential pacifism and patriotism. A patriotic or even nationalist voter has an additional benefit from "guns" since they increase his own country's influence and prestige on the international stage. Therefore the politician, the public servant and the lobbyist have an interest in strengthening such attitudes[10] to implement a high defense budget. Using panel data future research might be able to test whether there is a relationship between defense spending and patriotic feelings.

The voting public's threat perception may be influenced even more easily. The more the voter feels threatened, the more "guns" he will demand. Thus the lobbyist and the public servant[11] have an incentive to exaggerate potential threats and to bias information.[12] During the Cold War, for example, the public administrations and the industry of Western countries used the numerical superiority of the Warsaw Pact forces as an argument to increase or maintain the level of defense spending while ignoring their lower effectiveness. Since the end of the Cold War many lobbyists and administrators claim that the world has become "more dangerous" (Sandler and Hartley 1999, p. 127).

Moreover, not only the perceived threat but the threat itself might be influenced by the political actors to increase the demand for defense spending. Future research could elaborate on this by applying public choice theory to arms race analysis.[13]

17.3.2   Soldiers or Missiles?

After a decision on the defense budget has been reached, the resources have to be allocated to the various purposes. Needless to say the voter asks for the allocation that maximizes security. As mentioned above, however, the public can hardly control the process of security production. Therefore the other political actors may behave in a discretionary way.

A basic decision has to be taken about the capital–labor mix. In other words, it has to be decided how much to spend on military personnel and how much on sophisticated weapons. This choice may be a cause of conflict between the military[14] and the industry. The controversies about the appropriate strategy for the Iraq War between the US Secretary of Defense Donald Rumsfeld and the generals may exemplify this conflict. Having close links to the arms industry the Department of Defense favored a small-scale invasion relying on high-precision air strikes and intercontinental missiles, whereas the army called for a more conservative strategy with more troops.

Moreover a choice has to be made which armament goods should be procured. That may cause conflicts between the military services. However Hartley (1987, p. 412) suggests that army, navy and air force tend to collude calling jointly for more and better equipment since he finds remarkably stable budget shares of the military services in the UK. As a matter of course the defense industry pushes for the allocation of resources to new armaments. Thus it may support frequent changes in strategies and doctrines since such changes require the procurement of new equipment. For example, the recent vogue of military crisis management and peacekeeping demands increased air- and sealift capabilities (Sandler and Hartley 1999, p. 127).

An additional bias in defense procurement may occur due to the widespread usage of cost plus contracts (Sandler and Hartley 1995, pp. 137–40). For the defense industry, this contract type provides an incentive to obtain orders by underestimating project costs. After signing the contract any cost escalations[15] have to be borne by the government. A bias toward too high quality,[16] however, may even occur when the political actors have no private consumption value of sophisticated weapons (Rogerson 1990).

17.3.3   Import or Domestic Production?

Leaving aside complete autarky, a further decision has to be taken: which defense goods should be imported and which are to be produced domestically?[17]

The government generally prefers to buy armament goods from its domestic defense industry since it aims to maintain a defense industrial base and cater for special interests. Taxpayer resistance, however, limits the price which can be paid. In the following the largest politically feasible difference between the world price and the price paid to the national defense industry will be called "domestic premium." The size of this "premium" depends on the political influence of the defense lobby and the supposed importance of a national defense industrial base as well as the basic trade paradigm. Lobbying activities of the defense industry will aim to increase the "domestic premium." At the same time the defense industry has a strong interest in exporting its products. Below, this will be regarded in more detail.

17.3.4   War or Peace?

Answering exhaustively why states go to war is certainly beyond the scope of this chapter. Nonetheless there are a few insights from public choice theory which shall be presented, in particular electoral cycles as well as the analyses of peace keeping and reconstruction.

Electoral cycles
Electoral cycles are an extensively investigated field of economic research.[18] This research concentrates on discretion in economic policy. Nonetheless discretionary powers in foreign and security policy may also be used to secure reelection.

Missions abroad possibly follow electoral cycles since the government hopes to avail itself of the so-called "rally 'round the flag" effect. Mueller (1970) indicates that international crises boost the president's popularity in the short run. This effect is supposed to be due to voter irrationality or asymmetric information about threats.[19] Hess and Orphanides (1995), however, show that electoral cycles may even occur when neither is present. An incumbent who has performed poorly in economic policy may have an incentive to go to war to improve his reelection prospects by revealing competency in security issues. In the empirical testing of this model, Hess and Orphanides (1995, p. 836) use different proxies for economic activity given in the first column of Table 17.1: NBER is a dummy for economic troughs as determined by the NBER chronology, RGNP

Table 17.1   Probability of US presidents going to war (1953–88)

Variable for RECESSION	$\hat{\alpha} + \hat{\beta}$	$\hat{\alpha}$	*p* value
NBER	1.000	0.364	0.064
RGNP (mean)	0.700	0.307	0.039
RGNP (MA-8)	0.667	0.333	0.087
IP (mean)	0625	0.357	0.171
IP (MA-8)	0667	0.333	0.039
–UN (mean)	0.667	0.333	0.087
–UN (MA-8)	0.700	0.307	0.039
APPROVAL (mean)	0.500	0.393	0.441
APPROVAL (MA-8)	0.583	0.333	0.141

Source: Hess and Orphanides (1995, Table 2)

is a below average real growth rate, IP a below average index of industrial production, –UN an above average increase of unemployment and
APPROVAL a below average approval rating from Gallup Poll Survey
data; Mean and MA-8 indicate the comparison with the sample mean and
an eight year moving average, respectively. As can be seen, the conditional
frequency of starting or significantly escalating a war is approximately
twice as large when a president seeks reelection and the economy is weak
in a year $(\hat{\alpha} + \hat{\beta})$ to when these conditions do not coincide $(\hat{\alpha})$. The difference is significant and fairly robust across the different measures of
economic activity (Hess and Orphanides 1995, p. 837).[20]

Further research should try to check this result with an international
panel including more recent data. Moreover, the increase in peacekeeping
missions raises the question of whether these missions also follow electoral
cycles.

Peacekeeping
Peacekeeping missions and reconstruction efforts recently moved into
the focus of political economy research. This new emphasis reflects the
growing importance of such missions since the fall of the iron curtain (for
example, Solomon 2007, pp. 748–51).

Peacekeeping missions are characterized by a high degree of publicness. Both non-excludability and non-rivalry are assumed to be strong.
Therefore the analysis of these missions is of special interest under a collective good perspective. In line with the *Economics of Alliances* literature,
which will be discussed in greater detail in the following section, Khanna
and Sandler (1997) analyse NATO burden sharing. While showing that
there is no general asymmetry in defense spending, they find evidence for

free riding with regard to peacekeeping. Moreover, Hartley and Sandler (1999, p. 674) note that NATO's *strategic crisis management* doctrine may provide a free ride to the UN.

Similar to the increase in peacekeeping activities there is a growing number of peace building or regime change missions followed by reconstruction efforts, for example, in Somalia, Haiti, Afghanistan and Iraq. This increase is mainly due to the fact that, especially since the 9/11 attacks, many scholars identify failed and failing states as the biggest threat to the West. In the light of Tullock's (1965) *Politics of Bureaucracy* Coyne (2008), however, shows that these missions are likely to fail since the occupational forces and bureaucracy have neither the information nor the incentives[21] necessary to successfully establish liberal democratic institutions. Accordingly the role of the winning forces' administrations was relatively limited in Germany and Japan, the two outstanding historical examples of successful reconstruction, compared to recent missions (Coyne 2008, pp. 19–20).

17.4   THE ALLIANCE DIMENSION

Defense policy is seldom a purely national task. Alliances are formed to counter common threats and to gain international influence. The comprehensive literature on the *Economics of Alliances* has contributed to the understanding of alliance policy focussing on burden sharing while the public choice analysis of federalism and international organizations has concentrated on the political actors' incentives in an international environment. Regarding defense policy, a few recent studies offer some specific insights.

17.4.1   The Economics of Alliances

The seminal paper by Olson and Zeckhauser (1966) analyses alliance defense as a collective good. Since defense is public among allies, small and poor countries have an incentive to free ride on the financial contributions[22] of the large and rich. This leads to "exploitation" (Olson 1965, p. 29) by the small allies and underprovision of defense.

Olson and Zeckhauser's (1966) results[23] have been criticized by follow-up studies. Sandler (1977), for example, argues that defense efforts also render benefits which are private among allies. He models alliance defense as a "joint product" finding that the asymmetry in the burden share is less severe than assumed by the Olson-Zeckhauser paper (Sandler 1977, p. 456).[24] Many studies find empirical evidence for Sandler's model (for example, Gonzalez and Mehay 1990; Sandler and Murdoch 1990).

The "publicness" of defense has been extensively questioned along the non-rivalry dimension while the non-excludability dimension, by contrast, has been largely ignored. In a recent paper, Klingen (2008), however, argues that exclusion is at least partly possible since treaties may very well be terminated and guarantees to assist may be withdrawn. In a simple model it can be shown that this opportunity has potentially strong implications for the outcome of the burden sharing conflict within military alliances.[25]

17.4.2   Share of Spending and Share of Costs

The *Economics of Alliances* provides valuable insights into the burden sharing process but it does not explain very well why military alliances exist. Why should states be member of an alliance when they are "exploited"? The public choice answer is: because they want to.

Jones (2007, p. 320) notices that a large and rich member state's defense industry does not object to a disproportionate burden share because this raises the demand for its products. The industry obtains an internal transfer of rents from taxpayers. Therefore, a large member state's share of the alliance's defense spending is larger than its share of the costs (Jones 2007, p. 330). Moreover asymmetries in spending may be outweighed by asymmetries in trade. Since large and rich member states typically dominate the intra-alliance arms trade, they earn high export profits (Jones 2007, p. 328). Therefore their armament lobbies tend to support alliance enlargements to further increase exports (Hartley 1998, p. 132). The US defense industry, for example, lobbied strongly for the entry of the small and potentially free-riding Eastern European candidate countries into NATO (Jones 2007, p. 320).

17.4.3   The Demand for Security

Another explanation of defense cooperation is provided by Riker's (1964) work on federalism. Riker identifies the quest for security as the most important motive for the formation of federations and alliances. The theory implies that alliances are in the interest of the citizens who demand security.

Analysing survey results for the EU-25 member states Klingen (2009), however, shows that popular support for military alliances can not only, not even primarily, be explained by the respondents' security interest. Instead, it is significantly affected by ideology. As can be seen from the mixed effects logistic regression results in Table 17.2 there is little evidence that the support for (1) the European Security and Defence Policy (ESDP), (2) NATO and (3) for ESDP and/or NATO in 2005 is driven by

Table 17.2   Explaining support for ESDP and NATO (2005)

	Support for ESDP	Support for NATO	Support for ESDP or NATO
Fixed Part			
Constant	−0.875**	−0.795*	0.222
	(−2.98)	(−2.36)	(0.75)
Population	−0.001	−0.005	−0.006
	(−0.29)	(−0.94)	(−1.35)
GDP p.c.	−0.002	0.011	0.008
	(−0.23)	(1.29)	(1.09)
Distance to Moscow	−0.139	−0.371*	−0.373**
	(−1.08)	(−2.39)	(−2.94)
Europhilia	0.647***	0.031	0.731***
	(12.53)	(0.34)	(18.98)
Anti-Americanism	0.253***	−0.182**	0.179**
	(4.53)	(−3.09)	(2.72)
Neutrality	−0.006	−1.571***	−0.777**
	(−0.02)	(−5.07)	(−3.11)
Age	−0.003***	−0.004*	−0.005***
	(−2.90)	(−2.13)	(−3.57)
Gender (male=1)	0.211***	0.222***	0.373***
	(5.74)	(5.08)	(11.63)
Education	0.038***	−0.002	0.046***
	(7.29)	(−0.32)	(7.50)
Random Part			
Θ	0.377	0.436	0.332
μ[Europhilia]	0.211	0.286	0.117
μ[Anti-Americanism]	0.259	0.207	0.289
μ[Age]	0.004	0.007	0.005
μ[Gender]	0.117	0.103	0.062
μ[Education]	0.019	0.012	0.022
Log likelihood	−15,665.997	−10,023.403	−14,419.274

Notes:
*   Significance at 5% level
**   Significance at 1% level
***   Significance at 0.1% level
z-values in brackets

Source: Klingen (2009)

security relevant variables. Only proximity to non-allied Russia seems to play a role.[26] At least for ESDP security issues appear to be completely irrelevant. In contrast, the respondent's identification with Europe, his anti-American feelings as well as his country's neutrality status influence his opinion on these alliances significantly.

Thus these results do not support the view that Western defense cooperation is mainly due to the voter's quest for security. Other interests in establishing and maintaining international ties seem to be crucial.

17.4.4   The Centralization of Decision-making

To form a military alliance is to found an international organization with its own administration and and to shift decision-making competencies to the international level. Therefore public choice theories of international organizations and federalism apply.

For the politician centralization may be a means to ease the reelection constraint. Voter control through the ballot box diminishes and so does his incentive to become informed. Moreover his cost of information raises because international decision-making reduces the scope for comparison and yardstick competition.[27] In this respect, international organizations may be interpreted as cartels of national governments (Vaubel 1986, pp. 44–7). They reduce the domestic pressure to choose the level and allocation of defense spending efficiently. In addition, an international organization may be used as a scapegoat for unpopular policies (Vaubel 1986, pp. 45–6). Probably many European ministers of defense welcome pressures for higher defense spending from NATO, for example, because this enhances their potential for dealings with interest groups.

Evading public control[28] also appeals to the bureaucrat.[29] Vaubel, Dreher and Soylu (2007) show empirically that staff size in international organizations is significantly affected by the member states' incentives to monitor. Enlargement, for example of NATO, plays an important role in this context.[30] The alliance officials have an incentive to underestimate the costs of enlargement and overestimate the benefits (Hartley and Sandler 1999, p. 670).[31]

A strong defense bureaucracy is also in the interest of the defense industry. An empirical analysis by Crain and McCormick (1984, pp. 298–301) reveals that appointed officials are more open to lobbying than elected politicians. However the implications of potential market integration on its competition position is surely of much greater importance to the armament industry.

17.4.5   The Armament Cartel Hypothesis

If the allies integrate their markets for defense goods, the "domestic premium" loses relevance for exports to other member states. Therefore exporters from allied states obtain a competitive advantage vis-à-vis suppliers from non-allied countries who still have to pay the "premium." Even though market integration raises competition within the alliance the defense industries of the member states may thus support the integration of its national armament markets to reduce imports from third countries.[32]

Figure 17.2 shows the two country case. The demand for the armament good x is D^i in country i and D^j in country j. Before a common market is established, i's defense industry can sell good x on the domestic market if it chooses the price $P^i \leq \min(P^{int} + d, MC^i + d)$ whereas P^{int} is the world market price, MC^j the marginal costs of j's defense industry and d the "domestic premium." Otherwise i's government prefers to buy on the world market or to import from j respectively. Accordingly, the defense industry of country i can export to j at any price $P^j \leq \min(P^{int}, MC^j - d)$. In the given example country i's defense industry can satisfy the national demand due to the "domestic premium." As shown by Figure 17.2a it chooses the output quasi monopolistically identifying marginal revenue[33] MR^i and marginal costs MC^i. Hence it realizes the profit Π_1^i given as the hatched area in Figure 17.2a. In contrast j's defense industry is too inefficient to compete for its domestic market as can be seen in Figure 17.2b. Since $MC^i > P^{int}$, country j chooses to buy x_1^j on the world market.

After integrating the armament markets domestic supply and exports from allied states are treated equally. Therefore the defense industry from country i can export to j at any price $P^j \leq \min(P^{int} + d, MC^j)$ and vice versa. Figure 17.2c shows that this change has no effect on i's armament market. However due to the distortion of competition with regard to third country suppliers the defense industry of country i can capture j's market. As can be seen in Figure 17.2d country i sells x_2^j to country j and realizes the export profit[34] $\tilde{\Pi}_2^i$.

Given the above scenario with $P^{int} < MC^i < P^{int} + d < MC^j$ the effect of market integration on the total profit of the alliance's defense industries is positive.[35] Additional profits may be distributed among the member states' industries since the relative efficiency varies between different defense goods.[36] If, for example, the European Union furthers the integration of its national armament markets, Germany has a competitive advantage vis-à-vis the United States selling tanks to France, whereas the French defense industry has better prospects to sell aircrafts in the German armament market.

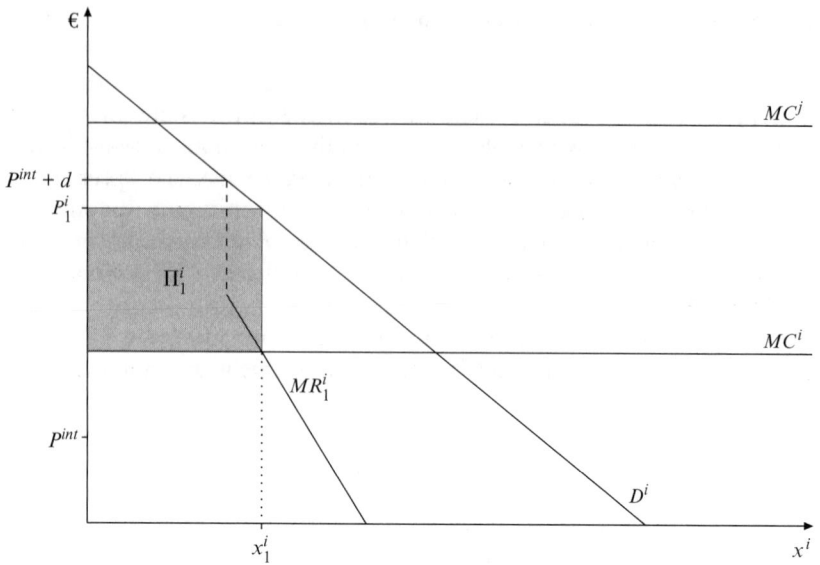

(a) Country i without common defense market

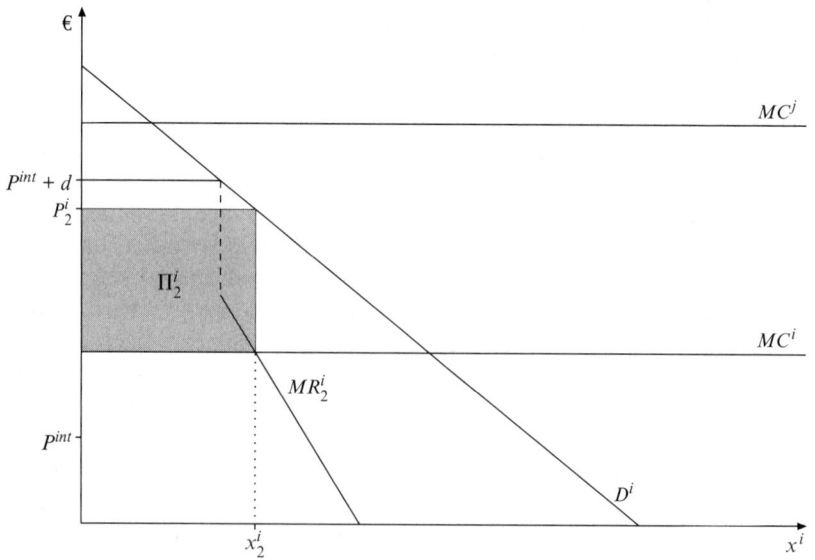

(c) Country i with common defense market

Figure 17.2   Rents of the arms industry with and without a common defense market

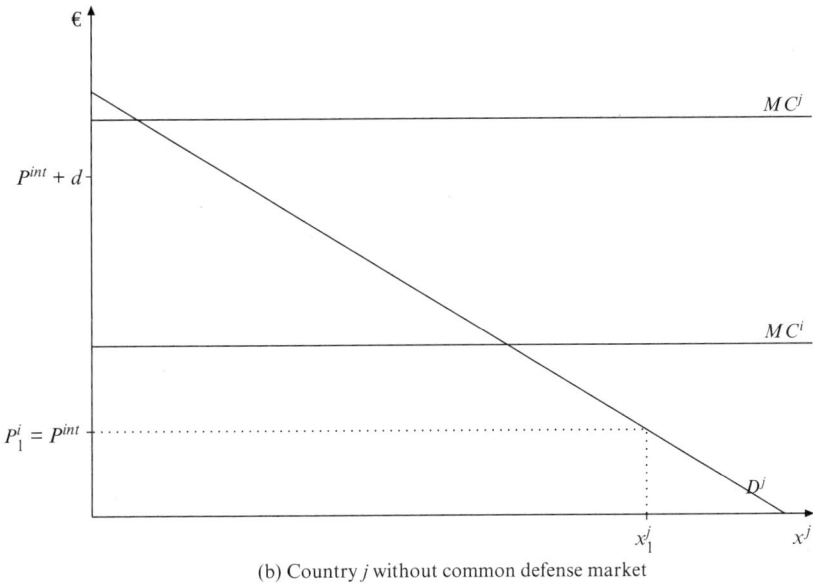

(b) Country *j* without common defense market

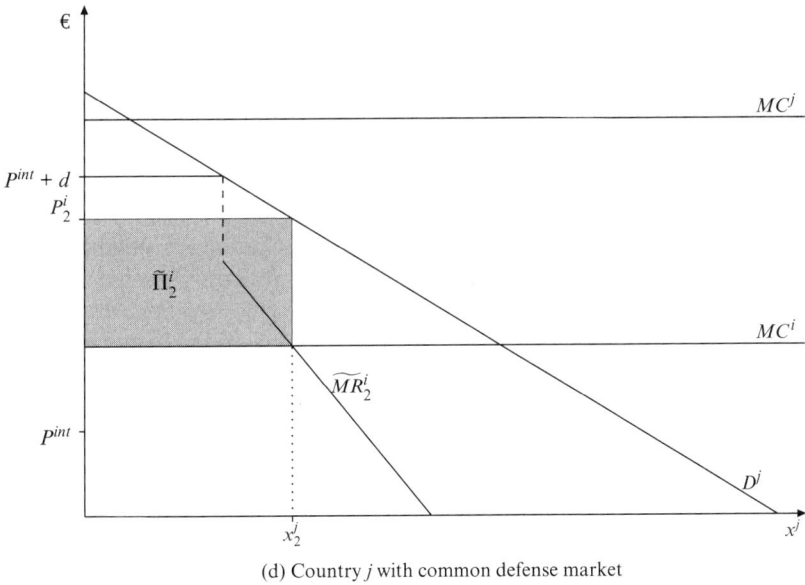

(d) Country *j* with common defense market

Figure 17.2   (continued)

Further research might elaborate a general model dropping the assumptions about MC^i, MC^j, P^{int} and d.[37] In such a general model two opposing effects of market integration are observable: constrained competition on the market of the ally by crowding out third country imports[38] on the one hand and intensified competition on the domestic market by opening it to imports from allied countries[39] on the other hand. Building on such a generalized model the two opposing effects have to be analysed empirically. Such an analysis would clarify whether the arms industry may also support alliance formation if it is connected with the integration of defense markets.

17.5 CONCLUSION

This chapter has reviewed and developed public choice approaches to defense and alliance policy. It has drawn on relevant case studies, discussed electoral cycles in mission orders and analysed peacekeeping and reconstruction. With regard to military alliances, the *Economic Theory of Alliances* has been criticized from a public choice perspective and the public choice approach to federalism and international organizations has been applied.

Thereby, some distinct specifics of defense and alliance policy are revealed. Hardly knowing anything else than a digit for defense spending, the median voter faces extraordinary information problems which give the other actors much room for discretion. Nondisclosure may also fuel collusion between the politician, the public servant and the lobbyist. Furthermore protectionism and state direction are probably stronger than in any other part of the economy.

The public choice approach to defense and alliances is still incomplete. The most important gaps concern the voter's influence on defense spending, the effect of informational asymmetries and electoral cycles, as well as discussing the "armament cartel hypothesis." A very important task will be to test the hypotheses empirically. However, this task may also be the most ambitious one. The lack of data is probably the main reason why the economic analysis of alliance and defense policy is often regarded as a sour grape. Yet the subject is of considerable relevance and further research is definitely worthwhile.

NOTES

1. It is a strong simplifcation to regard "the politician" as a unitary actor. However, conflicts between government and legislature, regarding parliamentary scrutiny, for

example, as well as conflicts between different ministries are beyond the scope of this chapter.

2. With regard to his interests in defense and alliance policy "the public servant" is a fairly heterogenous actor. Interests will especially differ between bureaucrats and the military as well as between the separate services. However, at least army, navy, and air force can collude at moderate cost (Hartley 1997, p. 24).

3. Security may not be the only goal the voter pursues. For example, pacifists are supposed to prefer a reluctant defense policy, whereas patriotic voters possibly tend to favor a strong and prestigious role of their home country on the global stage. Moreover, in some cases the income motive may also play a role: one can think of scenarios in which a country has the possibility to increase its wealth by military means.

4. Since the politician acts in a non-market environment, income maximization is subordinate. However a goal which may also play an important role in the politician's calculations is the expected utility at the end of his mandate. This utility can be increased by securing lucrative job offers from the industry or public administrations.

5. However the prestige from being commander-in-chief may be of decreasing importance, at least in the Western hemisphere. Nowadays annual military parades, the most evident demonstration of this form of prestige, take place only in Ankara, London, Madrid, Paris and Vienna.

6. An important exception may be business appointments. Hartley (1987, p. 417) notices that contact and expertise of senior staff is very valuable to the defense lobby.

7. The arms industry is not the only interest group trying to influence defense policy. For example Hartley (1987, p. 405) regards supporters of disarmament as a lobby group trying to influence policy outcomes with demonstrations and civil disobedience. The following analysis, however, will concentrate on lobbying by the defense industry.

8. In contrast most defense economists do not regard defense as a "pure" public good (for example, Sandler 1977, pp. 444–8). Nevertheless its "publicness" is commonly ranked higher than that of many other goods supplied by the public sector (see Brown and Jackson 1992, p. 42). In a public choice framework, however, underprovision may be offset by the rent-seeking activities of producers. Jones (1999) argues that producers' pressure for the provision of public goods is higher than that for the provision of private goods since, due to non-rivalness in consumption, higher prices per unit are more readily accepted by the public.

9. An empirical analysis by Hartley and Russett (1992) shows that defense spending in fact reflects public opinion.

10. A very subtle channel which can be used to rouse patriotism is revealed by Regan (1994). For the US he finds that the popularity of war toys and movies as well as a pro-military bias in the mass media are correlated with the degree of militarization and public opinion towards defense spending.

11. Apart from the defense lobby and the bureaucracy, the politicians in government may also have an incentive to emphasize potential threats. At the same time, they want to create the impression of competency in security matters. This can be illustrated by a statement by the former national security advisor Condoleezza Rice during the election campaign 2004: "This country is safer than we were on 9/11 but we're not yet safe" (quoted from Fox News, "The O'Reilly Factor," 2 August 2004, http://www.foxnews.com/story/0,2933,127847,00.html).

12. The information policy of the industry and public administrations does not concentrate solely on external threats. Hartley (1987, p. 412) points out that potential effects on employment and high technology development are used as arguments for higher defense spending too.

13. The arms race literature going back to Richardson (1960) analyses the interaction between states building up arms. However, the bulk of this literature has so far not accounted for the role of special interests.

14. The position of the military, however, is ambiguous. It has an interest in high quality equipment as well as large troops. The desired mix may differ between the services,

especially between the capital intensive air force and the labor intensive army (Hartley 1987, p. 412).

15. Due to the special interests of involved scientists, managers and workers, projects are difficult to stop once started (Sandler and Hartley 1999, p. 125). Therefore the government can hardly apply any pressure to avoid so-called "gold plating."

16. As an example for too high quality Tobias, Goudinoff and Leader (1982, pp. 211–7) point to a series of mock air battles organized by the US air force in 1978. These showed that one fighting jet of the F14 or F15 type, the premiere fighters at that time with unit costs of US$30 million and US$47 million respectively, were inferior to two much cheaper jets of the export type F5E costing only US$5 million each. Currently the wisdom of purchasing the costly F22 jets is discussed in the United States.

17. Certainly these two possibilities are not mutually exclusive. If a defense lobby cannot avert the import of a certain defense good, it will push for work-sharing (Hartley 1987, p. 417).

18. At first Nordhaus (1975) identified business cycles resulting from the manipulation of fiscal and monetary policy. Before the election the government tries to stimulate the economy to improve its reelection prospects while cutting spending and fighting inflation afterwards. Such political business cycles may also occur in defense spending. Possibly more weapons are contracted prior to elections. Moreover the contracts are likely to be allocated to firms in areas of high unemployment and in swing constituencies (Hartley 1987, p. 407).

19. The "patriotism" explanation states that in times of international crisis people support the government rather instinctively to demonstrate unity. Alternatively, the "opinion leadership" explanation assumes asymmetric information. According to this latter approach people do not react to the international crisis in itself but to information from the government, the opposition and the media. Baker and Oneal (2001) show that this "opinion leadership" explanation outperforms the "patriotism" hypothesis empirically.

20. Hess and Orphanides (1995) use a Fisher's exact right-tailed test for $\hat{\beta} = 0$. The results are even stronger than those reported in Table 17.1 when, in line with the political business cycles literature, only election and preelection years are included (Hess and Orphanides 1995, Table 4).

21. For example the lobbying of the occupant's domestic industry for lucrative orders in the reconstruction process (Coyne 2007, p. 98) may harmfully bias the bureaucracy's incentives.

22. Goff and Tollison's (1987) analysis of casualties in the Vietnam War reveals that burden sharing conflicts may not only be about financial contributions. An ally may also try to minimize the risks to its military personnel in joint actions of the alliance.

23. The results of Olson and Zeckhauser (1966) strongly depend on the historical context of the *mutual assured destruction* doctrine NATO ascribed to from 1957–67. This doctrine was based on nuclear deterrence which is fairly non-rival among allies (Sandler and Hartley 1999, pp. 37–40).

24. Murdoch and Sandler (1984a, pp. 89–90) show that the disproportionality can even be completely offset when the public and the private good output of defense spending are complements.

25. For example a large and rich member state located in the hinterland may free ride on an allied front-line state's contributions even if this ally is relatively small and poor (Klingen 2008, pp. 9–11).

26. When the variable "Distance to Moscow" is replaced by a dummy for former Warsaw Pact member states, this dummy does not appear to be significant (Klingen 2009).

27. Besley and Case (1995), for example, show empirically that reelection prospects are influenced by the policies of neighboring constituencies.

28. The growth of an international organization weakens the voters' and the national politicians' incentive to control it (Frey 1984, pp. 220–1).

29. Sandler and Hartley (1999, p. 127) point out that not only the civil servant but also

    military personnel may benefit from alliance formation, for example, by increasing travel opportunities associated with overseas postings.

30. Vaubel et al. (2007, pp. 283–4) find that the elasticity of an international organization's personnel to its membership is much larger than unity. This finding is consistent with the assumed decrease of control over the organization's administration. NATO, however, is not included in the sample since annual staff growth in the Secretariat of the North Atlantic Treaty Organization has been negative after 1985 (Vaubel et al. 2007, pp. 279–80). More recent data are needed to check if this tendency has been reversed by NATO's Eastern enlargement in the 2000s.

31. Hartley and Sandler (1999, p. 670) note that the offcial NATO forecast of enlargement costs is the lower bound of different estimates ranging from US$1.5 billion to US$125 billion.

32. The basic idea of the "armament cartel hypothesis" goes back to Viner (1950). He argues that the creation of customs unions may also have a negative welfare effect due to a demand shift to less efficient suppliers: the so-called "trade diversion" effect.

33. MR^i has an unusual shape due to the upward price limit. In the example given in Figure 17.2a, however, this restriction is not binding.

34. The defense industry of country i chooses the profit maximizing amount x_2^i by identifying MC^i with its marginal export revenue $\overline{MR}_2^i$.

35. While the defense industry maximizes its rent, the tax payer of country j loses. The consumer surplus in country j decreases by $\int_{x_2^j}^{x_1^j} D^j + P_2^j x_2^j - P^{int} x_1^j$.

36. However it may be suffcient that one strong national defense lobby is interested in a free trade zone for defense goods. As long as the costs are spread widely among tax payers, this national defense lobby has a good chance to lobby for market integration successfully.

37. A general model should even account for different "domestic premia" d^i and d^j since the relative influence of the defense industry and the taxpayer may vary among countries.

38. Market integration leads to additional export profits for country i as shown in Figure 17.2 if the reduction of competitive pressure on j's market is relevant. This condition is fulfilled if $MC^i < \min(P^{int} + d, MC^j)$ and $P_2^j > P^{int}$.

39. The profit of i's defense industry on the domestic market decreases if the additional competitive pressure is relevant. This is the case if $MC^i < \min(P^{int} + d, MC^j + d)$ and $P_1^i > MC^i$.

REFERENCES

Baker, W.D. and J.R. Oneal (2001), "Patriotism or opinion leadership? The nature and origin of the 'rally 'round the flag' effect", *Journal of Conflict Resolution*, **45** (5), 661–87.

Besley, T. and A. Case (1995), "Incumbent behavior: vote-seeking, tax setting, and yardstick competition", *American Economic Review*, **85** (1), 25–45.

Brown, C.V. and P.M. Jackson (1992), *Public Sector Economics*, Oxford, UK: Basil Blackwell.

Coyne, C.J. (2007), "Deconstructing reconstruction: the overlooked challenges of military occupation", *Economics of Peace and Security Journal*, **2** (2), 94–100.

Coyne, C.J. (2008), "The politics of bureaucracy and the failure of post-war reconstruction", *Public Choice*, **135** (1–2), 11–22.

Crain, W.M. and R.E. McCormick (1984), "Regulators as an interest group", in J.M. Buchanan and R.D. Tollison (eds), *The Theory of Public Choice II*, Ann Arbor, MI: University of Michigan Press, pp. 287–304.

Downs, A. (1957), *An Economic Theory of Democracy*, New York, NY: Harper & Row.

Downs, A. (1967), *Inside Bureaucracy*, Boston, MA: Little, Brown.

Dudley, L. and C. Montmarquette (1981), "The demand for military expenditures: an international comparison", *Public Choice*, **37** (1), 5–31.

Frey, B.S. (1984), "The public choice view of international political economy", *International Organization*, **38** (1), 199–223.

Goff, B.L. and R.D. Tollison (1987), "The allocation of death in the Vietnam War: a public choice perspective", *Southern Economic Journal*, **54** (4), 316–21.

Gonzalez, R.A. and S.L. Mehay (1990), "Burden sharing in the NATO alliance: an empirical test of alternative views", *Public Choice*, **68** (1–3), 107–16.

Hartley, K. (1987), "Reducing defense expenditure: a public choice analysis and a case study of the UK", in C. Schmidt and F. Blackaby (eds), *Peace, Defense and Economic Analysis*, New York, NY: St. Martin's Press, pp. 399–423.

Hartley, K. (1997), "Defence market", *Economic Affairs*, **17** (4), 22–7.

Hartley, K. (1998), "State budget in a changing economic and security environment", in 1998 NATO Economics Colloqium. Economic Developments and Reforms in Cooperation Partner Countries: The Role of the State with particular Focus on Security and Defence Issues, NATO Economics Directorate and NATO Offce of Information and Press, pp. 127–43.

Hartley, K. and T. Sandler (1999), "NATO burden sharing: past and future", *Journal of Peace Research*, **36** (6), 665–80.

Hartley, T. and B. Russett (1992), "Public opinion and the common defense: Who governs military spending in the United States?", *American Political Science Review*, **86** (4), 905–15.

Hess, G.D. and A. Orphanides (1995), "War politics: an economic, rational-voter framework", *American Economic Review*, **85** (4), 828–46.

Holcombe, R.G. (2008), "Why does government produce national defense?", *Public Choice*, **137** (1–2), 11–9.

Jones, P.R. (1999), "Rent seeking and defence expenditure", *Defence and Peace Economics*, **10** (2), 171–90.

Jones, P.R. (2007), "Colluding victims: A public choice analysis of international alliances", *Public Choice*, **132** (3–4), 305–18.

Khanna, J. and T. Sandler (1997), "Conscription, peace-keeping, and foreign assistance: NATO burden sharing in the post-Cold War era", *Defence and Peace Economics*, **8** (1), 101–21.

Klingen, B. (2008), "Disproportionality and exclusion: reconsidering the theory of alliances", 17th Workshop on Political Economy, Silvaplana, 25 July 2008, available at SSRN: http://ssrn.com/abstract=1448042.

Klingen, B. (2009), "Is Riker right? Explaining preferences for common defence", Working Paper, 12 August 2009, available at SSRN: http://ssrn.com/abstract=1448030.

Migué, J-L. and G. Bélanger (1974), "Toward a general theory of managerial discretion", *Public Choice*, **17** (1), 27–43.

Mueller, J.E. (1970), "Presidential popularity from Truman to Johnson", *American Political Science Review*, **64** (1), 18–33.

Murdoch, J.C. and T. Sandler (1984a), "Complementarity, free riding, and the military expenditures of NATO allies", *Journal of Public Economics*, **25** (1–2), 83–101.

Murdoch, J.C. and T. Sandler (1984b), "A theoretical and empirical analysis of NATO", *Journal of Conflict Resolution*, **26** (2), 237–63.

Niskanen, W.A. (1971), *Bureaucracy and Representative Government*, Chicago, IL: Aldine Atherton.

Nordhaus, W.D. (1975), "The political business cycle", *Review of Economic Studies*, **42** (2), 169–90.

Olson, M. (1965), *The Logic of Collective Action*, Cambridge, MA: Harvard University Press.

Olson, M. (1982), *The Rise and Decline of Nations: Economic Growth, Stagflation, and Social Rigidities*, New Haven, CT: Yale University Press.

Olson, M. and R. Zeckhauser (1966), "An economic theory of alliances", *The Review of Economics and Statistics*, **48** (3), 266–79.

Regan, P.M. (1994), "War toys, war movies, and the militarization of the United States, 1900–85", *Journal of Peace Research*, **31** (1), 45–58.

Richardson, L.F. (1960), *Arms and Insecurity: A Mathematical Study of the Causes and Origins of War*, Pittsburgh, PA: Homewood.

Riker, W.H. (1964), *Federalism: Origin, Operation, Significance*, Boston, MA: Little, Brown and Company.

Riker, W.H. and P.C. Ordeshook (1968), "A theory of the calculus of voting", *American Political Science Review*, **62** (1), 25–42.

Rogerson, W.P. (1990), "Quality vs. quantity in military procurement", *American Economic Review*, **80** (1), 83–92.

Sandler, T. (1977), "Impurity of defense: an application to the economics of alliances", Kyklos, **30** (3), 433–60.

Sandler, T. and K. Hartley (1995), *The Economics of Defense*, Cambridge, UK: Cambridge University Press.

Sandler, T. and K. Hartley (1999), *The Political Economy of NATO: Past, Present, and into the 21st Century*, Cambridge, UK: Cambridge University Press.

Sandler, T. and J.C. Murdoch (1990), "Nash-Cournot or Lindahl behavior? An empirical test for the NATO allies", *The Quarterly Journal of Economics*, **105** (4), 875–94.

Solomon, B. (2007), "Political economy of peacekeeping", in K. Hartley and T. Sandler (eds), *Handbook of Defense Economics, Vol. 2 Defense in a Globalized World*, Amsterdam: Elsevier, pp. 741–74.

Tobias, S., P. Goudinoff and S. Leader (1982), *The People's Guide to National Defense: What Kinds of Guns Are They Buying for Your Butter?* New York, NY: Quill.

Tullock, G. (1965), The Politics of Bureaucracy, Washington DC: Public Affairs Press.

Vaubel, R. (1986), "A public choice approach to international organization", *Public Choice*, **51** (1), 39–58.

Vaubel, R., A. Dreher, and U. Soylu (2007), "Staff growth in international organizations: a principal-agent problem? An empirical analysis", *Public Choice*, **133** (3–4), 275–95.

Viner, J. (1950), *The Customs Union Issue*, New York, NY: Carnegie Endowment for International Peace.

18 International regimes and war
James Ashley Morrison and Avery F. White

18.1 INTRODUCTION

This chapter analyses the relationship between international regimes and war. Following a new branch of scholarship that questions the traditional distinction between domestic and international order, we compare several of the most prominent theories of international regimes to the political theories of Thomas Hobbes, John Locke and Max Weber. We find that each of these theories of domestic political order provides new insight into the role international regimes can play in generating order – and minimizing war – in the international system. Based on this, we suggest that the sharpest division may not be between theories of domestic and international politics, as has been traditionally assumed. Instead theories of order may be better organized according to the assumptions they make about material circumstances – specifically the distribution of power – and the relative importance of actors' understandings of those circumstances. This insight recasts the debate about the design and operation of international regimes. Scholars and policymakers must now grapple with the amount of hierarchy they would like to order the international system.

The chapter proceeds as follows. We begin by defining our variables and presenting our argument. We go on to consider the parallels between the theories of John Locke and those of the neoliberal institutionalists. Next we highlight the similarities between the theories of Thomas Hobbes and those following in the tradition of hegemonic stability theory. Then we consider the similarities between the theories of Max Weber and those of the constructivists. Lastly we consider the implications of the finding that the difference between international and domestic order is one of type rather than degree.

18.2 OUR ARGUMENT

We have elected to use broad renderings of both our independent and dependent variables. Our independent variable is the robustness of *international regimes*. Following the convention in the study of international politics, we treat international regimes as "sets of implicit or explicit principles, norms, rules and decision-making procedures around which actors' expectations converge in a given area of international relations" (Krasner 1983, p. 2). Our *dependent variable* is war. By "war" we mean something akin to "a state of war", which includes not just open combat but also, as Thomas Hobbes put it, "the known disposition thereto" (Hobbes [1651] 1996, p. 88).

We argue that international regimes influence the likelihood of nations entering into states of war via two pathways. First, international regimes affect the material realities that influence the likelihood of war. A long, distinguished line of thought contends that the distribution of power among states is the most influential variable in international politics. While debate continues to rage over which distributions tend to generate peace and which tend to generate war, few deny the importance of the distribution of power in shaping international relations.[1] We argue that international regimes can serve to enhance the benefits – and minimize the failings – of both multipolar and unipolar distributions of power. In the case of the former, regimes can provide the assurances that facilitate dealings among equals. In the case of the later, regimes can curb the potential excesses of hegemony while still providing the hegemon with incentives to provide order.

In addition to altering the material circumstances of states, international regimes can also affect their interpretation of these circumstances. Constructivists have long argued the perception of force is that which is most important in creating international order rather than raw power itself. In the famous words of Alexander Wendt (1992), "anarchy is what states make of it." International regimes play a role in how states interpret their surroundings by providing new frameworks of legitimacy, law and authority (Barnett and Finnemore 2004). These norms serve to change how states perceive other actors and therefore determine how states construct international order, placing international regimes at the forefront of both regulating and constructing international politics.

Recognizing these parallels between theories of domestic and international politics leads us to draw several conclusions. First, there are potentially considerable returns to synthesizing these theories, which were conceived in distinct intellectual traditions. Hobbes, Locke and Weber may have as much to tell us about international politics as they do about domestic. Second, the traditional distinction between theories of domestic and international politics is less significant than are the distinctions between all such theories' assumptions about material conditions like the distribution of power and actors' understandings of those circumstances. Finally, the designers of our international regimes must also recognize that the distinction between domestic and international order is one of degree rather than type. This forces us to evaluate the amount of hierarchy we hope to establish in the international system.

18.3   THEORIES OF DOMESTIC AND INTERNATIONAL ORDER

Traditionally anarchy has been the defining feature of the international system. By definition, domestic politics is the realm of peace and order while the international system is host to war and disorder. The increasing "institutionalization" of the international system, however, has called this distinction into question. A growing number of scholars have suggested that the differences between domestic and international politics may be ones of degree rather than type. The stakes in this debate are considerable. First, it has implications for how we understand international order. Do we need a separate theory of international politics or can we leverage the insights from domestic politics to understand the international system? Additionally, the nature of international order determines how we pursue order. If the distinction between international and domestic politics is continuous, then it is not inevitable that the international system should remain fully "anarchic." By invigorating international regimes, we may reduce the amount of anarchy in the international system and, with it, the amount of war. This section considers this debate.

For centuries virtually every theory of international politics has begun with the assumption that there is a difference of type between the order generated in domestic politics and the order generated in international politics. In this formulation, the international society is an "anarchical society," meaning that it is characterized by "the absence of government or rule" (Bull [1977] 2002, p. 44). Or as Kenneth Waltz succinctly put it, "The difference between national and international politics lies not in the use of force but in the different modes of organization for doing something about it" (1979, p. 103). The result is that "[n]ational politics is the realm of authority, of administration, and of law. International politics is the realm of power, of struggle, and of accommodation" (1979, p. 113).

This "classical" perspective is organized around the concept of sovereignty. Among its earliest apostles, Jean Bodin defined "sovereignty" in 1576 as "the absolute and perpetual power of a commonwealth" ([1576] 2004, p. 345). Simply put states were sovereign and sovereigns were states.[2] This meant both that states enjoyed "absolute" authority over matters within their borders and that there could be no higher power to constrain states.[3] Kenneth Waltz argued that this axiom necessarily implied that the anarchic international system was a "self-help" system, a system in which each actor must "spend a portion of [its] efforts . . . in providing the means of protecting itself" (1979, p. 105). After all, sovereign states cannot rely on protection via supranational regimes since the very concept of sovereignty denies the possibility of a higher authority. Sovereignty also ensured that states were legally equal to another.[4] If a state were sovereign, it could not, by definition, be subject to hierarchy, to impositions by others. This traditional perspective then concluded that domestic order was the product of sovereignty; and international order – insofar as there is international order – must be the product of something else.

Waltz inferred that this essential difference necessitated distinct theories for each realm of politics. Arguably, his whole purpose in drafting the *Theory of International Politics* was to develop a theory of distinctly *international* politics. Too many of the "reductionist" theories, Waltz claimed, had attempted to import into international politics assumptions that only held in domestic politics. He suggested that his theory – the balance of power theory – might be the first truly "systemic theory," the first theory to "conceive of causes operating at the international level" (1979, p. 2–4).

Recently, however, several prominent scholars have challenged the axiom that the international system is thoroughly "anarchic." These attacks grew out of challenges to the classical understanding of sovereignty as monolithic and indivisible. In several studies on the changing "geography of money," Benjamin J. Cohen (1998, 2004) argued that states' "monetary sovereignty" must be considered separately from national political sovereignty. Following Cohen, Stephen Krasner (1999) grouped different types of autonomy into four broad forms of sovereignty. Perhaps the most interesting implication of this perspective is that states are recognized as often choosing to surrender one form of sovereignty in order to increase their autonomy in other areas. States, for instance, frequently choose to exercise their international legal sovereignty "to create international institutions, some of which have compromised their Westphalian sovereignty by establishing external authority structures" (Krasner 1999, p. 13–14). The famed "Westphalian system" of nation-states enjoying "exclusive control over a given territory" was a myth. "[P]olitical entities with exclusive control over a well-defined territory existed well before the Peace [of Westphalia of 1648]," Krasner explained, "and feudal and universal institutions . . . continued well after it" (Krasner 1993, p. 235).

David Lake has argued that there continues to be hierarchy in the international system today. "International hierarchies," he insisted, "are pervasive. Both in the past and present, states subordinate themselves in whole or part to the authority of other, dominant states" (Lake 2009, p. 2). Rather than seeing international and domestic politics as two distinct realms, each with their own logic, Lake suggested that all political orders exist on a continuum between hierarchy and anarchy. In both domestic and international politics at various times and places, one can find every-thing from anarchic alliance structures to hierarchical empires (Lake 2003, p. 312). As John Ikenberry observed, "In some countries, politics can be extremely ruthless and coercive, whereas some areas of international poli-tics are remarkably consensual and institutionalized" (Lake 2001, p. 21). In the end, the differences between some domestic and some international relations may even be less than the differences in the political systems across different states.

Recognizing that the differences between international and domes-tic politics are differences of degree rather than type affects the way we approach the international system. Lake and Ikenberry do not deny that states are more likely to enter "states of war" in international politics than are individuals or factions in domestic politics. However, they do insist that we do not require a separate theory of "international politics" divorced from theories of "domestic politics" to understand international relations. Many of the insights we have developed into domestic politics could prove vital in understanding and shaping the international system.

While scholars of international politics have not hesitated to invoke seminal theorists of domestic politics, most of these references have been explicitly used "merely as metaphors or stylized representations" claiming "no close adherence to [the theorists'] views" (Wendt 1999, p. 247).[5] In the several sections that follow, we attempt to systematically investigate the parallels between three of the most influential theories of domestic order – those of Thomas Hobbes, John Locke and Max Weber – and the most prominent "schools" of international relations.

18.4   ORDER VIA EQUALITY

The first distribution of power we consider is that of equality, meaning that a number of actors enjoy roughly equal capacities. In domestic poli-tics, this corresponds to the "equality" of individuals' capacities to defend themselves and attack others, which has often been hypothesized to exist in the state of nature. In international politics, this corresponds to the "equality" of states' military capabilities that is endemic to multipolar distributions of power.

John Locke maintained that the inherent equality of individuals in the state of nature formed a basis for their peaceful coexistence (Locke [1690] 1967, p. §6).In Locke's original state of nature – prior to the invention of money – there was little need for rivalry. He denied that an individual's "appropriation of any parcel of Land, by improving it, [was] any prejudice to any other Man, since there was still enough, and as good left; and more than the yet unprovided could use . . . For he that leaves as much as another can make use of, does as good as take nothing at all" (Locke [1690] 1967, p. §33). Later Locke went even further, suggesting "that he who appropriates land to himself by his labour, does not lessen but increase the common stock of mankind. For the provisions serving to the support of humane life, produced by one acre of inclosed and cultivated land, are . . . ten times more, than those, which are yielded by an acre of Land, of an equal richnesse, lyeing wast in common" (Locke [1690] 1967, p. §37).

Locke held that individuals should and do care more about their *absolute* gain than their *relative* gain. This is apparent in the many contrasts Locke drew between the experience of the Native Americans and that of "the Civiliz'd part of mankind" (Locke [1690] 1967, p. §30). Locke stressed that "a King of a large and fruitful Territory [in America] feeds, lodges, and is clad worse than a day Labourer in England" (Locke [1690] 1967, p. §41). Despite the Native American king's superior status relative to his compatriots, Locke suggested that this king would actually prefer the greater absolute gain enjoyed by the lowest ranks of English society.

Locke admitted that there might be some conflict in the state of nature. But he insisted that the relative equality of individuals and their focus on absolute rather than relative gains combined with the plenty available to ensure that whatever disputes did arise could be resolved without recourse to third parties. Locke's state of nature was rarely a "state of war" (Locke [1690] 1967, Chapter 3).

Several of the most prominent theories of international politics turn on some of the same assumptions as those employed by Locke. Proponents of "balance of power theory" hold that maintaining a relatively equal distribution of power among states is the best way to secure peace. George Kennan went so far as to argue that the *Pax Britannica* of the nineteenth century actually depended on the careful balancing of power among the major European states (Kennan 1984, p. 69–70; see also Jervis 1985). He proposed "containing" Soviet expansion in part to ensure that a balance of power was maintained between East and West (Kennan 1984, Part II). Kenneth Waltz similarly celebrated the balance of power: "If there is any distinctively political theory of international politics, balance-of-power theory is it" (Waltz 1979, p. 117). States, according to Waltz, seek to maintain balance within the international system rather than "bandwagon" onto coalitions of the strong because "[t]he first concern of states is not to maximize power but to maintain their positions in the system." "States can seldom afford to make maximizing power their goal," Waltz added. "International politics is too serious a business for that" (Waltz 1979,

p. 127).Thus states' preeminent goal is the maintenance of their relative "equality" as this is assumed to generate peace.

Equality however does not always lead to peace. As Locke recognized, equality fosters peace only when individuals' pursuits are *non-rivalrous*, meaning only when the satisfaction of one's pursuits does not come at the expense of others' pursuits. For Locke, this condition held true prior to the invention of money. Money, however, gave individuals both the incentive and the means to "enlarge their possessions" to the point of creating scarcity (Locke [1690] 1967, p. §48). Once land and other goods became "scarce," their consumption became rivalrous; and, under those conditions, even those individuals focused on absolute gains find they cannot gain but at another's expense.

International security is almost certainly a rival good. Because increasing security usually means increasing one's arms, states frequently face a "security dilemma" whereby "many of the means by which a state tries to increase its security decrease the security of others" (Jervis 1978, p. 169).Robert Jervis has suggested that key variables – such as the relative potency of offensive and defensive weapons – may exacerbate or mitigate this dilemma (Jervis 1978, p. 186–210). But few weapons are purely defensive; and, frequently, offensive weapons are required to achieve defensive political objectives.[6] This ambiguity combines with the high stakes of international security to ensure that a "balanced" distribution of power must always be a precarious one.

There is no way to make the rival good of security non-rivalrous. The increase of security by one state must always come at the expense of the security of other states. But there is a certain class of challenges to order created as a result of rivalry that *can* be remedied. In many situations in both international political economy and security, actors face a "prisoner's dilemma" in which they enjoy a long-term interest in cooperating but find they have short-term incentives to "defect," or cheat. Perhaps as important as any actor's own incentives to defect, every actor knows that every other actor possesses these strong incentives to cheat as well. Thus, even "honest" actors focused exclusively on absolute gains find that rivalry decreases the likelihood that cooperative outcomes will be achieved.

Regimes can help to ensure cooperation given such conditions. In terms of domestic politics, John Locke saw the "great and chief end . . . of Mens uniting into Commonwealths" as "the Preservation of their Property. To which in the state of Nature there are many things wanting." First, there is no "common measure to decide all Controversies between [men]." Second, there is no third party to settle disputes. Finally, there is no power to execute judgments (Locke [1690] 1967, pp. §§124–26). Interestingly these failings prevented cooperation among not just "degenerate Men" but also among honest individuals who could not be relied upon to serve as impartial judges in their own cases.[7] Here Locke may have been thinking of the difficulties of resolving disputes about contracts. Such intertemporal agreements, which are more likely after the introduction of money (the concomitant of political society), are particularly subject to disagreement and outright reneging (North 1990, p. 50–1). In such cases individuals enjoyed a long-term incentive to cooperate but wanted clear standards of behavior and the sticks and carrots requisite to aligning short-term and long-term interests. Locke saw political society as the means to remedy those failings.

Just as domestic regimes can help to ensure cooperation among equal individuals focused on absolute gain, so too can international regimes. In *After Hegemony*, Robert Keohane elucidated a number of mechanisms by which relatively equal states can achieve cooperation in anarchy.[8] International regimes – one type of those mechanisms – perform some of the same functions for Keohane as political society did for Locke. Regimes establish "legal liability," or, in other words, define "property rights." They also provide both "guidelines for actors' behavior" and some measure of adjudication and enforcement.[9] All told, "international regimes can facilitate cooperation by reducing uncertainty" – uncertainty about the standards of behavior and uncertainty about the consequences of defection (Keohane 1984, p. 97). The principal difference between Keohane's international regimes and Locke's political society might simply be that international regimes "cannot establish patterns of legal liability that are as solid as those developed within well-ordered societies" – a difference in the *degree* to which international regimes work (as compared to domestic regimes) rather than a difference in the *way* they work (Keohane 1984, p. 88).[10]

So-called "realists" have been quick to point out the limited usefulness of international regimes as conceptualized by Keohane and the other "liberal institutionalists." These critics suggest that the insights derived from considering international political economy do not translate well to the realm of security affairs where the stakes are altogether different. After all, falling victim to defection in a trade agreement might cost a state a few percentage points of GDP. Being the "sucker" in a security agreement, on the other hand, could "result in a devastating military defeat" and perhaps even ensure a state's ultimate "destruction" (Mearsheimer 1994, p. 19). These high stakes follow directly from the want of hierarchy in the international system, one of the primary functions of which is to limit the stakes of interactions by limiting the returns on power.[11]

Realist scholars have also questioned institutionalists' assumption that states prioritize absolute over relative gains. Joseph Grieco contends that there may be good reasons in both security and economic affairs for states to care more about their relative status than their absolute gain or loss (Grieco 1988). And given the spillovers between the economic and security realms, states facing a security dilemma may be forced to pursue relative economic gains even where they might otherwise prefer to focus on absolute gains (Mearsheimer 1994, p. 20).

The institutionalist surrejoinder to these criticisms has generally focused on elucidating the material conditions in which regimes still prove useful. Robert Powell suggested that states' concern with relative versus absolute gains ultimately depends on "the cost of fighting." This largely turns on "the underlying technology of war" – which might be another way of saying the offense–defense balance (Powell 1991, p. 1311–12; see also Mearsheimer 1994, p. 22). Duncan Snidal argued that relative gains matter little in what were essentially the conditions of Locke's state of nature: a multipolar system where a large number of actors enjoy roughly equal power. He reasoned that "more actors enhance the possibilities of protecting oneself through forming coalitions; and, generally, the less well united one's potential enemies, the safer one is" (Snidal 1991, p. 716). In so far as the "relative-gains problem" in the "liberal institutionalist" literature has been resolved, it has been so on the basis of realist premises about the importance of structural conditions (Grieco, Powell and Snidal 1993).

18.5   ORDER VIA INEQUALITY

Perhaps the structural conditions in which regimes prove the most beneficial are those of inequality rather than equality. This section examines the role of regimes in such distributions in both domestic and international politics.

Thomas Hobbes had a rather different view of the implications of the equal distribution of power among individuals than did Locke. For Hobbes, equality was the principle problem with the state of nature. "From this equality of ability," Hobbes argued, "ariseth equality of hope in the attaining of our Ends. And therefore if any two men desire the same thing, which neverthelesse they cannot both enjoy, they become enemies; and in the way to their End . . . endeavour to destroy, or subdue one an other" (Hobbes [1651] 1996, p. 87). Unlike Locke, Hobbes assumed that rivalry was endemic to the state of nature. Hobbes concluded that as soon as individuals recognized this danger, they would collectively "conferre all their power and strength upon one Man, or upon one Assembly of men, that may reduce all their Wills, by plurality of voices, unto one Will." The "leviathan" would then enjoy "the use of so much Power and Strength conferred on him, that by terror thereof, [it] is inabled to conforme the wills of them all, to Peace at home, and mutuall ayd against their enemies abroad" (Hobbes [1651] 1996, p. 120–1). In other words, Hobbes reasoned that the solution to the problem of constant warfare among relative equals was the generation of radical inequality.

Similar logic has been applied to the international system by the hegemonic stability theorists. While there are important differences between these theorists, they all agree on the core assumption that hegemonic powers – states which enjoy a disproportionate share of global power – possess both the incentives and the capacity to foster a state of peace across the international system. In Charles Kindleberger's formulation, the hegemon is responsible for providing the leadership that undergirds a stable global financial system (Kindleberger 1973, p. 14). For Stephen Krasner, the hegemon used sticks and carrots to open foreign markets, which fostered global economic integration (Krasner 1976, p. 321–3). Robert Gilpin extended this theory from the realm of economic relations to include security affairs. Gilpin argued that hegemons not only provide international political stability but may also coerce subordinate states into helping underwrite the cost of providing that stability (Gilpin 1983, p. 1; see also Snidal 1985, p. 587). In all of these theories, the hegemon acts as a "quasi-government," as Duncan Snidal put it, that provides stability in a more or less centralized manner using some mixture of benevolence and coercion. (Snidal 1985, p. 587–90).

There are, however, several pitfalls in relying on hegemony to generate peace. First, hegemonic stability depends to some extent on the cooperation of subordinate states. Even where stability is generated solely through the beneficence of the hegemon – without any coercion of the subordinate states – the system functions better when the small states participate willingly. But these subordinate states understandably fear subsequent domination by the hegemon.[12] As a result, they may choose to participate in the hegemon's order the minimum amount necessary. Thus the asymmetry of power that inspires the hegemon to promote stability also encourages the subordinate states to resist that order.

Second, hegemony simply is not durable.[13] While there may indeed be a tendency for scholars to find hegemonic decline everywhere they look for it, no one disputes that every previous hegemon has eventually fallen from its perch (Strange 1987). Yet if peace, stability and order depend on hegemony, how are states to preserve these benefits after the hegemon declines?

International regimes have the potential to resolve both of these problems. By locking states into clear agreements, international regimes can be used to create a more mutually beneficial and durable international order. John Ikenberry has argued that the postwar settlements after major wars provide a unique opportunity to form international regimes. After victory, he suggests, wise states will agree to form a "mutually acceptable postwar order" which will "establish a set of rules and arrangements that are durable and legitimate" that bind both winners and losers into a cooperative order (Ikenberry 2001, p. 50). This "constitutional" order forces the victor to sacrifice some of its current power in order to "lock in" a favorable order. At the same time the lesser powers have their subordination ameliorated by the victor's self-imposed limitations (Ikenberry 2001, p. 56–7). In such orders, international regimes limit the ability of the hegemon to dominate subordinate states without limiting the hegemon's capacity or incentive to foster peaceful relations. In doing so they create incentives for smaller states to invest in the order. This combines with the "stickiness" of institutions to ensure that the order created during the hegemon's reign continues after the hegemon's decline.

International regimes play a decisive role in these constitutional arrangements, enabling cooperation much as they do in Keohane's formulation. Regimes for Ikenberry, however, are far more robust than they are in Keohane's rendering. Rather than merely coordinating states, Ikenberry holds that regimes have "an independent ordering impact on states." They impinge on state sovereignty by limiting the stakes of winning and losing in both security and economic affairs, just as domestic constitutional orders limit the losses incurred by political parties in an election (Ikenberry 2001, p. 41–2).[14]

These claims appear to have been confirmed empirically. Ikenberry found that the orders created after the previous two centuries' major wars were increasingly "constitutionalized," Elsewhere Goldstein and Gowa (2002) similarly showed that the postwar United States chose to use international regimes to engage in "strategic restraint" for the reasons Ikenberry suggested. In his study comparing the periods of British and American hegemony David Lake found that "the greater reliance of American hegemony on international regimes can be expected to preserve the liberal international economic order for some unspecifiable period . . . America's hegemonic afterglow may well be longer than Britain's" (Lake 1991, p. 115).[15]

18.6   ORDER VIA NORMS

It is clear at this point that the domestic theories of order propounded by Locke and Hobbes have strong parallels to structuralist theories of international regimes. The same sorts of parallels can also be found in a comparison between domestic and international theories which focus not on the distribution of capabilities but on norms of behavior. Indeed, the similarities between the theories of sociologists like Max Weber and international constructivist theorists are so great as to make any distinction negligible, adding further credence to the "revisionist" approach.

Max Weber is credited with what may be the most well known definition in political science: "a state is a human community that (successfully) claims the *monopoly of the legitimate use of physical force* within a given territory." While Weber's state might appear at first blush to be merely an updated version of Hobbes's Leviathan, the inclusion of the concept of "legitimacy" is notable. Hobbes's state maintains order via power. Weber's does so via the *right* to use force. In a modern state, "the right to use physical force is ascribed to other institutions or to individuals only to the extent to which the state permits it. The state is considered the sole source of the 'right' to use violence." While Weber's state is still based on "men dominating men," this relationship is "supported by means of legitimate (i.e. considered to be legitimate) violence." (Weber [1919] 1991, p. 78)

The significance of this concern with legitimacy is that Weber sees the *idea* of a state's right to power as its defining characteristic, rather than the state's power itself. Order in Weber's state rests not just on power itself but also on that power being perceived as "legitimate." Such legitimacy stems from three sorts of authority: "traditional," "charismatic," and "legal" – all of which are based not in power but on socially constructed norms of behavior. Traditional authority is based in "the unimaginably ancient recognition and habitual orientation to conform," charismatic authority in "absolute personal devotion and personal confidence in revelation, heroism, or other qualities of individual leadership" and legal authority in "the validity of legal stature and functional 'competence' based on rationally created rules." What is notable about these foundations of authority is firstly that they describe an order based on the perception of force rather than force itself and secondly that there are multiple, and presumably malleable, normative frameworks for the creation of order via the perception of force. (Weber [1919] 1991, pp. 78–9)

Weber's idea that political order rests on norms of authority rather than raw power bears remarkable similarities to the constructivist approach to international relations. The first principle of the constructivist approach is that states' behavior is a product not of the structure of the international system but of the socially learned behavior produced by interactions between both individuals and groups within a state and between states. Alexander Wendt suggested that "if we want to say a small number of big and important things about world politics we would do better to focus first on states' ideas and the interests they constitute, and only then worry about who has how many guns" (Wendt 1999, p. 256). Peter Katzenstein observed that "[t]he international and domestic societies in which states are embedded shape their identities in powerful ways. The state is a social actor." (Katzenstein 1996, p. 23) Anarchy is not directly responsible for the behavior of states. It "plays only a permissive role" according to Wendt (Wendt 1992, p. 403). As John Ruggie argued, "Power may predict the *form* of the international order, but not its *content*" (Ruggie 1982, p. 382). Power is merely a means to socially determined ends.

In constructivism, just as in Weber, it is the perception of force which matters more than force itself. Wendt suggests that different "cultures" of international politics determine different logics of order and perceptions of force, just as with Weber's various conceptions of authority. In Wendt, we find cultures described as "Hobbesian," "Lockean," and "Kantean" "Each." according to Wendt, "involves a distinct posture or orientation of the Self towards the Other with respect to the use of violence." Hobbesian "enemies" are "threatening adversaries who observe no limits in their violence towards one another." Lockean "rivals" are "competitors who will use violence to advance their interests but refrain from killing each other." Kantian "friends" are "allies who do not use violence to settle their disputes and work as a team against security threats." All of these perceptions of "other" are possible in anarchy, according to Wendt, but they clearly provide radically different possibilities for order. (Wendt 1992, p. 256–7) This idea of various possible orders clearly mirrors Weber's various forms of authority, in which the possibilities for institutions and politics vary from authority to authority. The modern state, for example, is dependent on legal authority, as it allows for "organized domination" via "continuous administration" (Weber [1919] 1991, p. 80). These parallels are acknowledged obliquely by Wendt, who points out that "the proposition that structures can be analysed in terms of roles is hardly radical. Sociologists routinely think this way about structure," with Weber of course being one of the foremost sociologists (Wendt 1999, p. 258). Similarly Michael Barnett and Martha Finnemore use Weber's work on bureaucracy as a framework for their own constructivist analysis of international organizations (Barnett and Finnemore 2004, p. 3).

International regimes can thus be understood as products of a socially constructed system of norms and rules, much as Weber's bureaucratic institutions are products of a legal system of authority. Bureaucracy, Weber argues, is the product of the need to administer a "body of law" which "consists essentially in a consistent system of abstract rules" (Weber [1922b] 1978, p. 217). This requirement means that "the typical person in authority occupies an 'office'. . . subject to an impersonal order to which his actions are oriented" (Weber [1922b] 1978, p. 330). In other words, authority is vested with bureaucrats holding offices rather than "warlords" leading based on charisma or chiefs leading based on tradition (Weber [1922b] 1978, p. 1154). Thus, bureaucracies are born out of the normative need for the objective, impersonal application of rules. They are an institutionalization of legal authority.

In a similar fashion Martha Finnemore explains international regimes governing humanitarian interventions as a product of changing norms of "identification or *empathy*" with others. The effect of "decolonization and the expansion of human rights" in the twentieth century was to expand this identification to groups which were previously considered to be "barely human" by white Europeans. These "individual level affect and cognitive changes" were then turned into "larger social structures" by international regimes. Examples include the United Nations and "the elaborate web of human rights treaties" now in existence (Finnemore 2003, pp. 144–5). Just as Weber's bureaucracy was the institutionalization of the norms of legal authority, so too are Finnemore's international regimes institutionalizations of new norms of identity.

But both international regimes and Weber's bureaucracy are more than the products of constructed normative systems. Weber believed that bureaucracy, while a necessary component of legal authority and the most rational possible administrative system, was also capable of affecting social norms itself. Bureaucracy was therefore not merely an institutional reaction to norms of legal authority, but also a source of new norms and ideas. One example among many is the tendency of bureaucracies towards "keeping their knowledge and intentions secret" in order to "increase the superiority of the professionally informed," Since bureaucracies will be the dominant form of public administration in the modern state, the bureaucratic desire for secrecy will change the very nature of public discourse. "Prussian church authorities," for example, "threaten to use disciplinary measures against pastors who make reprimands or other admonitory measures in any way accessible to third parties." Similar actions will be taken in "the management of diplomacy" and by "the military administration" and "political parties." In this manner bureaucracy tends to impose the norm of secrecy on an entire society (Weber [1922a] 1991, p. 233).

Finnemore and Barnett come to similar conclusions in their study of international regimes, an unsurprising result given that they characterize international organizations themselves as "bureaucracies" (Barnett and Finnemore 2004, p. 3). International organizations are capable of both "regulative" and "constitutive" effect. Regulative effect refers to "the ability of an actor to manipulate incentives to shape the behavior of another actor." Regulative effect would influence both the material realities discussed by structural theories of international regimes and the processes of "normative institutionalization" described by constructivists. Constitutive effect refers to "the ability to create, define, and map social reality." Essentially, international organizations, just like domestic bureaucracies, are capable of using "their authority, knowledge and rules to regulate and constitute the world that subsequently requires regulation" (Barnett and Finnemore 2004, pp. 30–31). This ability to not only regulate but actually reconstitute international norms is not limited to bureaucratic international organizations. The regimes which govern humanitarian intervention, which consist of not only international organizations but also international legal and moral norms, have "reconstituted legitimate intervention practice" by changing the norms of authority and legitimacy governing humanitarian intervention, and have thus enabled the increasing number of such interventions seen today (Finnemore 2003, pp. 144–5). Thus, just as Weber's domestic bureaucracy both regulates and reconstitutes, so too do international regimes.

Weber's theories of domestic sociology and constructivist theories of international politics are nearly identical. Indeed, the similarities are so great that the constructivist approach anticipates much of what a "revisionist" approach could offer. Many constructivists have already made their debt to Weber clear. The real import of Weber's theory may lie in his idea that bureaucracies and other agents of social reconstruction "have a mind of their own," a point echoed by Finnemore and Barnnet, but which has important consequences for all attempts to chart the future of international regimes.

18.7   INTERNATIONAL REGIMES: BETWEEN ANARCHY AND HIERARCHY

The three previous sections have shown that international regimes can be used to generate the same kind of order generated by domestic political regimes. Regimes can work both by affecting material circumstances and by affecting actors' interpretations of and reactions to those circumstances. Confronted with this reality, the natural tendency may be to assume that it would be desirable to change both material circumstances and the interpretation of those circumstances to increase the amount of hierarchy in the international system. There is some sense to that conclusion. After all anarchy does invite – if not necessitate – violent dispute resolution. Given the current potential for conflict to spiral into nuclear warfare, why would we not invigorate our international regimes toward the end of making them as robust as our domestic regimes – as Woodrow Wilson and the 'neo-Wilsonians' have long advocated (Wilson 1918; Holmes 1993)?

There are several reasons to think twice before we embark on a crusade of international regime-building. First, there may be practical limits to the amount of hierarchy we can generate in the international system. For one thing it is not clear that we could all agree on the content of any such global governing regime. How could a world government be established when many "failed" states remain bitterly divided? Any idealist attempts to impose order via force must be considered carefully. As Waltz reminds us, such "projected crusades . . . may lead to perpetual war for perpetual peace" (Waltz 1959, p. 113). Alexander Wendt similarly argues that even just attempting to reconstruct identities toward solidarity and cooperation may prove counterproductive. Instead, he sees the invigoration of sovereign identities as the "social basis for the individuality and security of states" (Wendt 1992, p. 412). It has been when that norm is weak "that only power matters, not the world of today" (Wendt 1992, p. 415).

Additionally some of the most important conditions fostering governmental formation may be found wanting in the international system. Thomas Hobbes particularly emphasized the existence of foreign threats as one of the major motivations in the creation of political society (Hobbes [1651] 1996, pp. 118–20). But, as Hedley Bull put it, "It is . . . one of the classic obstacles to the political unity of mankind as a whole that no external enemy exists against which a common defense is needed" (Bull [1977] 2002, p. 726). According to this logic, establishing complete hierarchy in international politics will remain unlikely until Mars attacks.

It is also not clear that establishing a single "world government" would be desirable even if it were possible. For one thing, the bulk of our current international regimes are "unabashedly undemocratic" (Barnett and Finnemore 2004, p. 172). The United Nations is largely governed by the five permanent members of the Security Council. The International Monetary Fund relies on weighted voting. And the World Trade Organization, while nominally governed by consensus decision-making, is in fact dominated by those members with the largest economies (Barton et al. 2006, p. 64).Thus, while these regimes work to spread the liberal values of "human rights" and "growth through markets," they are all marred by what Barnett and Finnemore call "undemocratic liberalism" (Barnett and Finnemore 2004, p. 172).

Finally, there may be advantages to preserving some measure of states' sovereignty. Federalism, as Justice Louis D. Brandeis famously observed in 1932, allows states to experiment and develop: "It is one of the happy incidents of the federal system that a single courageous state may . . . serve as a laboratory; and try novel social and economic experiments without risk to the rest of the country" (*New State Ice Co. v. Liebmann* 1932).

Similarly, sovereignty could allow states to "specialize," carving out distinct niches that appeal to the different orientations of individuals across the world. Lastly, federalism might also encourage states to "compete" as firms compete in the marketplace. Such healthy competition could increase the "efficiency" with which states perform their functions (Schultz and Weingast 2003).

18.8   CONCLUSION

At this point it should be clear that there is real utility in applying domestic theories of order to the international sphere. There are indeed clear parallels between the theories of domestic order propounded by Locke, Hobbes and Weber and mainstream theories of international order, suggesting that hierarchy is not so foreign to international politics as classical scholars like Kenneth Waltz suggested. Regardless of one's approach to international order – whether it be based on material circumstances or the interpretation of those circumstances – theories of domestic order seem to offer applicable frameworks which expand the depth of our understanding of international order.

This conclusion, that hierarchy is a present and future possibility in international politics, cannot help but have consequences for international regimes in our attempts to create a cooperative international order. Some general discussion of these effects has been presented here. Once the choice between anarchy and hierarchy is made apparent, we are presented with a normative question which has enjoyed little prominence in international politics up to this point. We must now consider how much hierarchy we desire in the international system and what paths we will take to establish that level of hierarchy. Developing a more integrated theory of "order" in general – rather than distinct theories of "domestic" and "international" order – would surely advance both of those ends.

NOTES

1. See, for instance, Waltz (1979) and Mearsheimer (2001). Even Alexander Wendt accepts the role played by material factors (Wendt 1999, p. 256).
2. As Louis XIV later put it, "L'état, c'est moi."
3. In fact, Bodin did not go as far as is typically thought. Bodin specified that "every earthly prince is subject to the laws of God and of nature and to various human laws that are common to all peoples" ([1576] 2004, p. 357). He provided little detail, however, on the content of these laws.
4. The doctrine of sovereign equality was enshrined two centuries after Bodin by Emmerich de Vattel (1758, Bk. II, Chapter 3).

5. Our use of Hobbes and Locke is rather different from the rendering given by Wendt. See further discussion below.
6. Jervis himself acknowledged that weapons may be difficult to class and may be used toward varied strategic ends. Scott Sagan framed the US commitment to protect NATO allies as a case in which "it will be necessary to have offensive military capabilities even if NATO has defensive political objectives" (Sagan 1986, p. 175).
7. In §128, Locke suggests that "were it not for the corruption, and vitiousness of degenerate Men, there would be . . . no necessity that Men should separate from this great and natural Community, and . . . combine into smaller and divided [political] associations," This seems to stand in contrast, however, to his previous discussion, where he suggests that men (in general) are "biased by their Interest" and "partial to themselves." These failings prevent cooperation even among "the Industrious and the Rational" (Locke [1690] 1967, p. §34; §§124–5).
8. Despite Keohane's empirical suggestion that regimes are frequently created by hegemons, his theoretical model is based on the prisoner's dilemma (Keohane 1984, p. 100). That model assumes that actors are relatively equal. Here we treat that model.
9. "Regimes facilitate agreements," Keohane explained, "by raising the anticipated costs of violating others' property rights, by altering transaction costs through the clustering of issues, and by providing reliable information to members" (Keohane 1984, p. 84, 88–89, 97).
10. At one point, Keohane explicitly stated that these "international regimes should not be interpreted as elements of a new international order 'beyond the nation-state,'" which would seem to place him among systemic theorists like Kenneth Waltz (Keohane 1984, p. 63). There is nothing essential in Keohane's framework, however, that leads invariably to the conclusion that domestic order is different in type from international order. Indeed, as we have seen, many of the same mechanisms are used to generate both types of order.
11. This finding is compatible with our contention that the order of the international system, like the order of domestic political systems, exists on a continuum between hierarchy and anarchy. Further discussion below details the role of regimes in limiting the stakes of politics.
12. Both the proponents and critics of hegemonic stability theory have acknowledged this fear (Krasner 1976, p. 319–321; Ikenberry 2001; Goldstein and Gowa 2002, p. 154–157). Further discussion follows below.
13. As Rousseau put it, "The strongest is never strong enough to be always the master, unless he transforms strength into right, and obedience into duty." (Rousseau [1762] 1997, Bk. I, Chapter 3)
14. Ikenberry relied in particular on Adam Przeworski's suggestion that constitutions limit the implications of winning (Przeworski 1993, p. 36; Ikenberry 2001, p. 23–4).
15. Robert Keohane made similar arguments (Keohane 1984, p. 101).

REFERENCES

Barnett, M. and M. Finnemore (2004), *Rules for the World: International Organizations in Global Politics*, Ithaca, NY: Cornell University Press.
Barton, J.H. et al. (2006), *The Evolution of the Trade Regime: Politics, Law, and Economics of the GATT and the WTO*, Princeton, NJ: Princeton University Press.
Bodin, J. ([1576] 2004), *On sovereignty: four chapters from the six books of the commonwealth*, J.H. Franklin (ed.), New York, NY: Cambridge University Press.
Bull, H. ([1977] 2002), *The Anarchical Society: A Study of Order in World Politics*, A. Hurrell and S. Hoffmann (eds), New York, NY: Columbia University Press.
Cohen, B.J. (1998), *The Geography of Money*, Ithaca: Cornell University Press.
Cohen, B.J. (2004), *The Future of Money*, Princeton, NJ: Princeton University Press.

Finnemore, M. (2003), *The Purpose of Intervention: Changing Beliefs About the Use of Force*, Ithaca, NY: Cornell University Press.

Gilpin, R. (1983), *War and Change in World Politics*, New York, NY: Cambridge University Press.

Goldstein, J. and J. Gowa (2002), "US national power and the post-war trading regime", *World Trade Review*, **1** (2), 153–70.

Grieco, J., R. Powell and D. Snidal (1993), "The relative-gains problem for international cooperation", *The American Political Science Review*, **87** (3), 727–43.

Grieco, J.M. (1988), "Anarchy and the limits of cooperation: a realist critique of the newest liberal institutionalism", *International Organization*, **42** (3), 485–507.

Hobbes, Thomas ([1651] 1996), (1996), *Leviathan*, R. Tuck (ed.), New York, NY: Cambridge University Press.

Holmes, S.A. (1993), "Choice for national security adviser has a long-awaited chance to lead", *New York Times*, 3 January 1993.

Ikenberry, G.J. (2001), *After Victory: Institutions, Strategic Restraint, and the Rebuilding of Order after Major Wars*, Princeton, NJ: Princeton University Press.

Jervis, R. (1978), "Cooperation under the security dilemma", *World Politics* **30** (2), 167–214.

Jervis, R. (1985), "From balance to concert: a study of international security cooperation", *World Politics* **38** (1), 58–79.

Katzenstein, P.J. (1996), "Introduction: alternative perspectives on national security", in *The Culture of National Security: Norms and Identity in World Politics*, New York, NY: Columbia University Press, p. 1–32.

Kennan, G.F. (1984), *American Diplomacy*, Chicago, IL: University of Chicago Press.

Keohane, R.O. (1984), *After Hegemony: Cooperation and Discord in the World Political Economy*, Princeton, NJ: Princeton University Press.

Kindleberger, C.P. (1973), *The World in Depression, 1929–1939*, Berkeley, CA: University of California Press.

Krasner, S. (ed.) (1983), *International Regimes*, Ithaca, NY: Cornell University Press.

Krasner, S.D. (1976), "State power and the structure of international trade", *World Politics*, **28** (3), 317–47.

Krasner, S.D. (1993), "Westphalia and all that", in J. Goldstein and R.O. Keohane (eds) *Ideas and Foreign Policy: Beliefs, Institutions, and Political Change*, Ithaca, NY: Cornell University Press, p. 235–64.

Krasner, S.D. (1999), *Sovereignty: Organized Hypocrisy*, Princeton, NJ: Princeton University Press.

Lake, D.A. (1991), "British and American hegemony compared: lessons for the current era of decline", in M.G. Fry (ed) *History, the White House, and the Kremlin: Statesmen as Historians*, New York, NY: Pinter Publishers, p. 106–22.

Lake, D.A. (2003), "The new sovereignty in international relations", *International Studies Review*, **5** (3), 303–23.

Lake, D.A. (2009), *Hierarchy in International Relations*, Ithaca, NY: Cornell University Press.

Locke, J. ([1690] 1967), *Second Treatise*. In *Two Treatises of Government*, P. Laslett (ed.), London: Cambridge University Press.

Mearsheimer, J.J. (1994), "The false promise of international institutions", *International Security*, **19** (3), 5–49.

Mearsheimer, J.J. (2001), *The Tragedy of Great Power Politics*, New York, NY: W.W. Norton and Company.

(1932), *New State Ice Co. v. Liebmann*, 285 US 262.

North, D.C. (1990), *Institutions, Institutional Change and Economic Performance*, Cambridge, UK: Cambridge University Press.

Powell, R. (1991), "Absolute and relative gains in international relations theory", *The American Political Science Review*, **85** (4), 1303–20.

Przeworski, A. (1993), *Democracy and the Market*, New York, NY: Cambridge University Press.

Rousseau, J-J. ([1762] 1997), *Of the Social Contract*, in V. Gourevitch (ed.), *The Social Contract and Other Later Political Writings*, New York, NY: Cambridge University Press.

Ruggie, J.G. (1982), "International regimes, transactions, and change: embedded liberalism in the postwar economic order", *International Organization*, **36** (2), 379–415.

Sagan, S.D. (1986), "1914 revisited: allies, offense, and instability", *International Security*, **11** (2), 151–75.

Schultz, K.A., and B.R. Weingast, (2003), "The democratic advantage: institutional foundations of financial power in international competition", *International Organization*, **57** (1), 3–42.

Snidal, D. (1985), "The limits of hegemonic stability theory", *International Organization*, **39** (4), 579–614.

Snidal, D. (1991), "Relative gains and the pattern of international cooperation", *The American Political Science Review*, **85** (3), 701–26.

Strange, S. (1987), "The persistent myth of lost hegemony", *International Organization*, **41** (4), 551–74.

de Vattel, E. (1758), *The Law of Nations: Or, Principles of the Law of Nature, Applied to the Conduct and Affairs of Nations and Sovereigns*.

Waltz, K.N. (1959), *Man, the State, and War: A Theoretical Analysis*, New York, NY: Columbia University Press.

Waltz, K.N. (1979), *Theory of International Politics*, Reading, UK: Addison-Wesley Publishing Co.

Weber, M. ([1919] 1991), "Politics as a vocation", in H. H. Gerth and C. Wright Mills (eds), *From Max Weber: Essays in Sociology*, New York, NY: Routledge, p. 77–128.

Weber, M. ([1922a] 1991), "Bureaucracy", in H.H. Gerth and C. Wright Mills (eds) *From Max Weber: Essays in Sociology*, New York, NY: Routledge, p. 196–244.

Weber, M. ([1922b] 1978), *Economy and Society: An Outline of Interpretive Sociology*, G. Roth and Claus Wittich (eds), Berkeley, CA: University of California Press.

Wendt, A. (1992), "Anarchy is what states make of it: the social construction of power politics", *International Organization*, **46** (2), 391–425.

Wendt, A. (1999), *Social Theory of International Politics*, New York, NY: Cambridge University Press.

Wilson, W. (1918), "The Fourteen Points", in E.D. Cronon (ed.) (1965), *The Political Thought of Woodrow Wilson*, Indianapolis, IN: Bobbs-Merrill, p. 438–45.

PART VI

POST-CONFLICT RECONSTRUCTION AND NATION BUILDING

19 Fixing failed states: a dissenting view
Justin Logan and Christopher Preble

19.1 INTRODUCTION: THE PRETENSE OF KNOWLEDGE[1]

Few foreign-policy arguments are more widely accepted than the related claims that "failed states" present a global security threat and that, accordingly, powerful countries should "fix" the failed states (Helman and Ratner 1992–93; Rotberg 2003; Fukuyama 2004a; Fearon and Laitin 2004; Krasner and Pascual 2005; Scowcroft and Berger 2005; Ghani and Lockhart 2008). Despite their widespread currency, these ideas are based on a sea of confusion, poor reasoning and category errors. In an earlier work, we criticized the idea that state failure poses a threat on two main grounds. First, we examined existing lists of failed states and scrutinized the common claims about the relationship between "failedness" and threat. A cursory look at the Failed States Index or any other list of failed states makes eminently clear that failedness is not so much as correlated with, let alone the cause of, threats to faraway countries. (Logan and Preble 2006; *Economist* 2009) States that regularly rank highly on failedness indicators included Côte d'Ivoire, the Democratic Republic of the Congo and Haiti, which belonged clearly in the "non-threat" category. (Patrick 2007)

Second, we argued that even in the anecdotal case where a failed state did pose an important threat, Afghanistan, the failure itself did not produce the threat and moreover, attempting to repair the state would not have eliminated the threat. Indeed, Afghanistan was both less failed and more threatening once the Taliban took power. As we wrote at the time, attacking a threat rarely involves paving roads or establishing new judicial standards (Logan and Preble 2006).

Scholarship on state failure had begun before September 11, but the terrorist attacks that day provided a huge boost to the topic. Analysts concluded *en masse* that since Afghanistan was both a failed state and a threat, failed states were threatening. Moreover, after the United States toppled the rickety structure of the Iraqi state, it became clear that attempting to administer a failed state was difficult. The role these political events played in boosting interest in the topic of failed states is hard to overstate. Accordingly, it is difficult, and we do not attempt, to separate the discussion of state failure from recent US efforts to form viable states in Iraq and Afghanistan. Similarly, we treat counterinsurgency and stabilization and reconstruction operations as close neighbors on an operational continuum rather than as separate categories.

Analysts have drawn one major lesson from the 9/11 terrorist attacks and the subsequent difficulties with the American response to them: if the United States could prevent state failure or repair failed states, it would reap gains not just in terms of international development but also in national security. Below we attempt to clarify both the concept of failed states and the likely implications of attempting to fix them.

This chapter proceeds in three sections. First, we outline the methodological and empirical problems with the scholarship on state failure and argue that, contrary to the conventional wisdom, state failure in itself poses no security concerns to foreign countries. Second, we show that attempts to fix failed states have a poor track record, and argue that reorienting national security bureaucracies toward a focus on state building is both unlikely and unwise. We conclude with a policy recommendation: given the minimal threat posed by state failure itself, and the difficulty in attempting to create viable states, foreign countries would be wise to avoid attempting to repair failed states.

19.1.1 What is a Failed State and Why Should Anyone Care?

Several elementary problems have hindered the study of state failure. The most significant is the fact that there is no agreed upon definition of the term "failed state." Analysts have created a number of listings of failed states, which have, in fairness, overlapped considerably: all are populated by poor countries, many of which have been wracked by interstate or civil violence. (SFTFR 2000; DFID 2005; FSI 2009) However, instead of adhering to basic social-scientific standards of inquiry in which questions or puzzles are observed, and then theories are described and tested using clearly defined independent and dependent variables, analysts began by fabricating a category – failed state – and then attempted to create data sets from which theoretical inferences could be induced.

To take one prominent case, the authors of the "State Failure Task Force Report" contracted by the Central Intelligence Agency's Directorate of Intelligence dramatically expanded their definition of "failed state" after their initial criteria did not produce an adequate data set for the quantitative tests the researchers wanted to perform. Working with the greatly expanded definition, the task force produced almost six times more countries that could be coded "failed" as compared with their original criteria, and then proceeded with their statistical analysis. They justified this highly questionable decision on the judgment that "events that fall beneath [the] total-collapse threshold often pose challenges to US foreign policy as well." (SFTFR 2000) Subsequently, the task force changed its name to the "Political Instability Task Force," and appeared to back away from the term "failed state" (Call 2006). Still, one of the principal authors of the index persists in using the term, still without a clear, bounded working definition (Goldstone 2008).

Beyond methodological shortcomings, the lists of failed states reveal only that there are many countries plagued by severe problems. The top ten states in the 2009 Failed States Index include two countries the United States occupies (Iraq and Afghanistan), one country without any central government to speak of (Somalia), four poor African states (Zimbabwe, Chad, the Democratic Republic of the Congo and the Central African Republic), two resource-rich but unstable African countries (Sudan and Guinea) and a nuclear-armed Muslim country, population 176 million (Pakistan). The sheer diversity of the countries on the lists makes clear that few policy conclusions could be drawn from a country's designation as a failed state.

Repeatedly, though, US government agencies and officials have endorsed the notion that state failure is threatening. For example, the George W. Bush administration's 2002 *National Security Strategy* was based on the argument that "America is now threatened less by conquering states than we are by failing ones" (Bush 2002, p. 1). Senator Richard Lugar, in support of the creation of the State Department's nation-building office, claimed that "international crises are inevitable, and in most cases, US security interests will be threatened by sustained instability" (NPR 2004). The 2005 *National Intelligence Strategy* claimed that "the lack of freedom in one state endangers the peace and freedom of others, and . . . failed states are a refuge and breeding ground of terrorism" (ODNI 2005). Barack Obama argued in 2007 that "since extremely poor societies and weak states provide optimal breeding grounds for disease, terrorism, and conflict," the United States must "invest in building capable, democratic states that can establish healthy and educated communities, develop markets, and generate wealth" (Obama 2007). The 2009 "whole-of-government" counterinsurgency manual claims that "in today's world, state failure can quickly become not merely a misfortune for local communities, but a threat to global security" (USICI 2009).

Prominent foreign-policy scholars agree. *Eminences grises* such as Samuel "Sandy" Berger and Brent Scowcroft reached across the political aisle to intone in unison that "[a]ction to stabilize and rebuild states marked by conflict is not 'foreign policy as social work,' a favorite quip of the 1990s. It is equally a humanitarian concern and a national security priority."

(CFR 2005, p. 6) In 2005, Stephen Krasner and Carlos Pascual claimed that "weak and failed states pose an acute risk to US and global security" (Krasner and Pascual 2005, p. 153). According to Francis Fukuyama, "it should be abundantly clear that state weakness and failure is [sic] the single most critical threat to US national security" (Fukuyama 2004c). Similarly, Pauline Baker of the Fund for Peace references the Afghanistan example, arguing that if a threat could arise from "that war-torn, shattered country, it can happen in virtually any decayed state" (Baker 2005).

In particular, the concept of the "war on terror" has become, in the minds of many experts, a war to fix failed states (Jones 2008). David Kilcullen, a former adviser to former Secretary of State Condoleezza Rice and CENTCOM commander General David Petraeus, has described the fight against terrorism as a "global counterinsurgency," and argues that it is "corruption, bad policies, poor governance, and lack of development that generate the threat in the first place" (Kilcullen 2009, p. 289). Counterinsurgency, in Kilcullen's telling, constitutes "armed social work; an attempt to redress basic social and political problems while being shot at" (Kilcullen 2006, p. 8). As another scholar of counterinsurgency stated the case:

> Victory in the Long War requires the strengthening of literally dozens of governments afflicted by insurgents who are radicalised by hatred and inspired by fear. The soldiers who will win these wars require an ability not just to dominate land operations, but to change whole societies. (Nagl 2008, p. 83)

Many of the arguments about the alleged relationship between state failure and international security threats are framed in peculiarly ordinal terms. For instance, the Bush administration's argument that "America is now threatened less by conquering states than we are by failing ones" cannot tell us much about the absolute value of the danger posed by failing states – or the resulting costs policymakers should be prepared to incur to attempt to protect against it. America faces an extraordinarily low threat of being overcome by a conquering state. Accordingly, identifying failed states as posing a more significant problem than the trivial danger posed by conquering states tells us little about how threatening they are, let alone what sorts of opportunity costs would be worth paying to counter the threat.

Similarly, the whole-of-government COIN guide's claim that "in today's world, state failure can quickly become . . . a threat to global security" is logically valid but practically worthless (USICI 2009). Any number of problems *could* evolve into threats, but this is only the beginning of analysis. The job of the intelligence analyst, foreign-policy scholar, or policymaker is to attempt to determine the likelihood of such a scenario coming to pass. Unfortunately, however, these claims rooted only in relative threat and logical possibility have been taken to inform policy without engaging contrary theories or empirical realities – or engaging seriously with the likely costs of attempting to fix failed states.

A recent study by James A. Piazza offers a quantitative analysis of the relationship between state failure and terrorism. The study represents a real methodological leap forward, clearly defining independent and dependent variables and performing regression analysis to attempt to link incidence of terrorism with ranking on the Failed States Index. Piazza concludes that state failure is a powerful predictor of the incidence of terrorism and offers a policy argument that "addressing the problem of failed and failing states should be the key strategy in the war on terror, rather than a mere acknowledgement found in anti-terrorism strategy documents" (Piazza 2008, p. 483).

Piazza's work adds considerably more social-scientific rigor to the study of failed states, but the article itself suffers from important flaws. First, for its dependent variable, the study uses a database containing recorded terrorist plots against all countries, of wildly varying degrees of lethality. However, the "war on terror" is concerned primarily with attacks targeted at the United States and its allies rather than terrorism in the abstract. Similarly, countries generally place higher priority on countering more lethal attacks. By counting all incidents of terrorism equally as US or global concerns, Piazza draws inappropriate inferences from his data.

Second, the study produced noteworthy results from its control variables, many of which wound up as significant predictors of whether a particular country would produce transnational terrorists. Based on Piazza's research, if policymakers had concerns about preventing terrorism, they should consider, in addition to state failure, the following factors: countries in which the executive branch has few constraints produce fewer terrorists (FSI 2008, p. 69);[2] countries with newer regimes produce fewer terrorists; countries with smaller populations produce fewer terrorists; countries with greater land area produce fewer terrorists; and countries that are less developed produce fewer terrorists (Piazza 2008, p. 482–3). While one could argue that some of these attributes are beyond outside control and others are outweighed by other considerations, one could level the same protests at Piazza's policy argument that fixing failed states should be at the center of US counterterrorism strategy.

As this discussion makes clear, research on failed states constitutes "an eminently political discourse, counseling intervention, trusteeship, and the abandonment of the state form for wide swaths of the globe" (Gourevitch 2005). The category "failed state" is itself a construction that opens the door for such norms to be imported and provides justification to a variety of Western interventions. The lack of conceptual and theoretical clarity defies even correlation between the supposed independent (failedness) and dependent (threat) variables, reducing the concept itself to something more like "countries with important problems."

The obvious conclusion that should be drawn from the efforts to generate lists and rankings of failed states is that the category itself is not particularly useful and hopelessly broad. Interestingly, the proponents of the "failed state" construction acknowledge that there is extraordinary variance among failed states and little that ties them together.

For instance, the 2007 update of the *Fund for Peace/Foreign Policy* magazine "Failed States Index" promises on the magazine's cover to explain "why the world's weakest countries pose the greatest danger." The opening lines of the article declare that failed states "aren't just a danger to themselves. They can threaten the progress and stability of countries half a world away." Strikingly, then, the article does little to back up or even argue these claims. It instead concedes that "failing states are a diverse lot" and that "there are few easy answers to their troubles" (FSI 2007, pp. 54, 56) By 2009, the Index was conceding that "greater risk of failure is not always synonymous with greater consequences of failure," and that the state failure-terrorism link "is less clear than many have come to assume" (FSI 2009, p.82).

Given these concessions undermining the validity of the category "failed state," one wonders why scholars continue to study failed states at all. The purpose, one would think, of creating a new category of states would be to unify countries that share attributes that can inform either how we think about these states (for academic purposes) or how we craft policies toward these states (for policy purposes). By the standards that have characterized the scholarship on state failure, Washington think tanks and academics could begin drawing up lists of "Countries that Begin with the Letter I," or "Countries between the 35th and 70th Meridians," and simply begin drawing up policy proposals for dealing with the states in question, while conceding the extreme variance inherent in their categories. But the category "failed state" has produced an assumption in Western policy circles that state failure represents a particular sort of problem that diplomats, military officials, and scholars must attempt to solve. Despite repeated assertions and insinuations to the contrary, learning that a task force has deemed a particular state "failed" is not useful for threat assessment.

19.2   THE ILLUSION OF CONTROL[3]

Rooted in the flawed theorizing on failed states, foreign-policy experts have proposed a variety of strategies for targeting and repairing them. In general, however, analysts who grasp the scale of the challenge of assembling viable states have converged on policy proposals that bear a startling resemblance to colonialism.

Some scholars have proposed a policy of simply seizing political control of failed states for some period of time – or indefinitely. To take one prominent example, political scientists James Fearon and David Laitin propose a policy of "neotrusteeship, or more provocatively, postmodern imperialism" as the solution to weak states. For Fearon and Laitin, after foreign powers have seized political control of a country, "the search for an exit strategy is delusional, if this means a plan under which full control of domestic security is to be handed back to local authorities by a certain date in the near future." Rather, the endgame is "to make the national level of government irrelevant for people in comparison to the local and supranational levels" (Fearon and Laitin 2004).

Policy practitioners have endorsed a similar view. Stephen Krasner, a scholar who would later become the director of policy planning in the Bush administration's State Department, wrote that foreign countries should seek to "eliminate the international legal sovereignty of the entity or control treaty-making powers in whole or in part (for example, in specific areas such as security or trade). There would be no assumption of a withdrawal in the short or medium term." Krasner also offered advice on how to avoid charges of colonialism:

> For policy purposes, it would be best to refer to shared sovereignty as "partnerships." This would more easily let policymakers engage in organized hypocrisy, that is, saying one thing and doing another . . . Shared sovereignty or partnerships would make no claim to being an explicit alternative to conventional sovereignty. It would allow actors to obfuscate the fact that their behavior would be inconsistent with their principles. (Krasner 2004)

Development experts with interest in state failure agree. Paul Collier, for example, writes that outside powers should take on the responsibility of providing public goods in failed states, including security guarantees to indigenous governments that pass Western democracy tests, and the removal of guarantees coupled with the encouragement of coups against governments that fail such tests (Collier 2009).

In part, these sweeping admonitions to simply seize politico-military control of the countries in question result from the failure to determine which, if any, of the "failedness" indicators should be addressed first, or whether there is any order at all. While some studies have proposed hierarchies of objectives, starting with security and ending with development (Dobbins et al. 2007, p. 14–15), it is clear that for many analysts, the causal arrows zigzag across the diagram. Each metric is tangled up with others, forcing those arguing for intervention to advocate simultaneous execution of a number of extraordinarily ambitious tasks. David Kilcullen lists "cueing and synchronization of development, governance, and security efforts, building them in a simultaneous, coordinated way that supports the political strategy" as only one of eight "best practices" for counterinsurgents (Kilcullen 2009, p. 265).

Discussing this dilemma of these interlocking objectives in the context of Afghanistan, Rory Stewart remarks that:

> Policymakers perceive Afghanistan through the categories of counter-terrorism, counter-insurgency, state-building and economic development. These categories are so closely linked that you can put them in almost any sequence or combination. You need to defeat the Taliban in order to build a state and you need to build a state in order to defeat the Taliban. There cannot be security without development, or development without security. If you have the Taliban you have terrorists, if you don't have development you have terrorists, and as Obama informed the *New Yorker*, "If you have ungoverned spaces, they become havens for terrorists." (Stewart 2009)

Not only do all bad things go together in these analyses, but it becomes difficult if not impossible to discern which objective should be the primary focus of state-building efforts. Similarly, on the issue of state building and democracy, Francis Fukuyama informs readers that "before you can have a democracy, you must have a state, but to have a legitimate and therefore durable state you must have democracy." Those who dizzily fall off this logical merry-go-round are then helped up and reassured with the admonition that "the two are intertwined, but the precise sequencing of how and when to build the distinct but interlocking institutions needs very careful thought" (Fukuyama 2005, p. 88). Such advice should be cold comfort to policymakers who are being urged forward by the same experts to perform these ambitious tasks.

Fixing failed states promises to be an extraordinarily complex, difficult and potentially violent enterprise. Existing national-security institutions are ill-suited for success in this task. The most powerful (and most active) Western militaries were designed to pursue the object of killing enemy forces and destroying material assets. Similarly, the diplomatic corps of Western countries were designed for relating to foreign countries rather than governing them. Accordingly, a number of policy reports have called for radical reforms of the national security establishment, particularly in the United States, so that it can be better tailored to repair failed states (Fukuyama 2005, p. 88).

The history of state formation has been violent and protracted, however, and there are few examples of foreign powers successfully fashioning and implanting a functioning, self-sustaining state. Two large problems inhibit successful state building. First is the inexistence in many countries of a nation, as discrete from the institutions of statehood. Second, and equally important, is the high cost of pressing together the disparate tribes and factions that populate many failed states. The formation of European states is a highly imperfect but helpful tool of comparison.[4]

Historically, few states emerged with citizens shuffling out of the previous order of indirect rule and fragmented sovereignty to sign on the dotted line of a national social contract. To the contrary, most modern states – and certainly most nations, in Western Europe – emerged from the exigencies of preparations for war against outside powers. Writing of the emergence of national states in Europe, Charles Tilly observes that "war wove the European network of national states, and preparation for war created the internal structures of the states within it" (Tilly 1990, p. 76). Very little of the literature urging a strategy of state building across poorly governed nations grapples with the fact that effective institutions of domestic governance emerged in Europe *alongside* military institutions. Tilly suggests that in the developing world, the disproportionate power and influence of military institutions as compared with civilian ones can help explain much of the problem of poor governance (Tilly 1985, p. 186).

Tilly referred to two crucial tactics employed by European state makers: homogenization and bargaining. Homogenization describes leaders' efforts to create "a linguistically, religiously, and ideologically homogenous population" (Tilly 1990, p. 186). In other words, a nation. Bargaining constituted buying off capital-holders by agreeing to provide a number of public goods in cities, including "pensions, payments to the poor, public education, city planning, and much more" (Tilly 1990, p. 186). This bargaining created an interface between citizens and the central state. The bureaucracies and agencies that administered these programs were tied, ultimately, to a central, national body that gave states a new immediacy in the lives of their citizens.

In most failed states, neither homogenization nor bargaining has happened in a meaningful way. Accordingly, Francis Fukuyama explicitly rejects the term "nation building": "nation building in the sense of the creation of a community bound together by shared history and culture is well beyond the ability of any outside power to achieve . . . only states can be deliberately constructed. If a nation arises from this, it is more a matter of luck than design" (Fukuyama 2004a, p. 99).

Fukuyama's call for state building begs two questions, then: first, can a cohesive state be built where there is no nation? Second, can outside powers implant the institutions of statehood and form a country without the homogenization and bargaining processes having first taken place?

Iraq is a disheartening indication that state building is both more difficult and of limited utility without the preexistence or building of a nation. As President Bush remarked on al Arabiya in 2005, "the future of Iraq depends on Iraqi nationalism and the Iraq character – the character of Iraq and Iraqi people emerging" (Bush 2005).

In addition to the nation/state dilemma there is the problem of costs. Assuming the reader is unconvinced by our arguments that the "failed state" category is a meaningless construct and that failed states are not inherently threatening, he or she may be inclined to press for state building. It is then important to examine the historical record and attempt to determine what the costs of such a policy would be.

It is of course impossible to determine the cost of any mission beforehand. Historically, however, such operations have been extremely costly and difficult. Fukuyama writes that state building "has been most successful . . . where US forces have remained for generations. We should not get involved to begin with if we are not willing to pay those high costs" (Fukuyama 2004b, p. 162). In a study for the RAND Corporation, James Dobbins and his coauthors attempt to draft a rule of thumb measure for the costs of nation building in a hypothetical scenario involving a country of 5 million people and $500 per capita GDP (Dobbins et al. 2007, pp. 255–9). For less ambitious missions they calculate the need for 1.6 foreign troops and 0.2 foreign police per 1000 population, and $1.5 billion per year. In the more ambitious scenarios, they figure 13 foreign troops and 1.6 foreign police per 1000 population, and $15.6 billion per year (Dobbins 2007, pp. 256–7). Curiously, though, Dobbins et al. simply compose average figures from eight historical nation building missions, six of which they code as producing at best mixed results (Dobbins et al. 2003, p. xix). It is unclear why future missions should be based on historical experience when three-quarters of the missions have failed at least partly to reach their objectives.

Moreover, as David Kilcullen observes in the context of counterinsurgency, a corps of state builders should be available to stay in the country indefinitely. Kilcullen proposes that "key personnel (commanders, ambassadors, political staffs, aid mission chiefs, key advisers and intelligence officers) in a counterinsurgency campaign should be there 'for the duration'" (Kilcullen 2009, p. 266). But it is unlikely that Western governments possess large pools of workers willing and well-equipped to deploy to Bangladesh, the Democratic Republic of the Congo or Haiti "for the duration." Because of American nationalism and the central role of the military in the Iraq example, the command in that country has managed to hold together. But Western civil services – and even most, if not all, Western militaries – are not comprised of a separate class of citizens who live their lives in far-flung locales, away from family and country, indefinitely. As will be seen below, the actual changes in the US national security bureaucracy have been wholly inadequate to performing these tasks well.

19.2.1   Counterinsurgency and State Building: the US Military's Response to the Failed State Consensus

Despite the flaws in the theory and empirics underlying research on failed states, the US military has made significant changes to its doctrine in order to protect the United States from the threat posed by the alleged state failure/terrorism nexus. In particular, two new field manuals are rooted in the idea that in order to protect the country against terrorism, Washington will have to create effective governments in other countries.

The release in late 2006 of Field Manual 3-24, the US Army and Marine Corps' manual for waging counterinsurgency, was greeted with a fanfare typically reserved for Harry Potter novels. After being downloaded 1.5 million times within the first month from the Fort Leavenworth and Marine Corps websites, the manual was published by the University of Chicago Press, and reviewed by *The Chicago Tribune, The Los Angeles Times* and *The New York Times* where it was given an editors' choice award.

The interest is understandable. As field manuals go it is a page-turner. The writing team went out of its way to transcend the typically bland prose, and also reached out to civilian experts on matters of substance. Georgetown University professor Colin Kahl called the new field manual "the single best distillation of current knowledge about irregular warfare" (Kahl 2007, p. 171). Yale University's Stathis Kalyvas described the sweep and breadth of the document, noting that the manual was rooted in "a strategy of competitive state building combining targeted, selective violence and population control, on the one hand, with the dissemination of a credible mass ideology, the creation of modern state structures, the imposition of the rule of law, and the spurring of economic development, on the other" (Kalyvas 2008, p. 351).

The Army released FM 3-07, "Stability Operations," two years later. Lt. Gen. William B. Caldwell, IV, the commander of the US Army's Combined Arms Center, called the new manual "a roadmap from conflict to peace, a practical guidebook" that "institutionalizes the hard-won lessons of the past while charting a path for tomorrow." Perhaps anticipating public skepticism toward a repeat of recent wars, Gen. Caldwell predicted:

America's future abroad is unlikely to resemble Afghanistan or Iraq, where we grapple with the burden of nation-building under fire. Instead, we will work through and with the community of nations to defeat insurgency, assist fragile states, and provide vital humanitarian aid to the suffering. (Caldwell 2008)

The assumptions underlying these doctrinal developments are consonant with the emerging nation-building consensus in Washington. The Stability Operations field manual asserts, for example, that "the greatest threat to our national security comes not in the form of terrorism or ambitious powers, but from fragile states either unable or unwilling to provide for the most basic needs of their people" (US Army, p. vi). Senior military officers have taken their cues from civilian opinion leaders who contend that the US Government must improve its capacity for nation building.

As the lead authors of the COIN manual noted in *Military Review* "America's extraordinary conventional military power makes it likely that many of our future opponents will choose irregular means, including terrorism and insurgency, to achieve their political objectives and prevent us from achieving ours" (Cohen et al. 2006, p. 53). Accordingly, it is not surprising that military leaders are taking steps to prepare for waging counterinsurgency and post-conflict stabilization missions. Department of Defense Directive 3000.05 declares that "stability operations are a core US military mission" for the Department of Defense that "shall be given priority comparable to combat operations" (USDOD 2005). The 2010 Quadrennial Defense Review adopted similar assumptions.

19.2.2   Other US Government Agencies' Responses

In July 2004, with American policy elites reeling from the chaos in Iraq, the US State Department established a dedicated state-building office, the Office of the Coordinator for Reconstruction and Stabilization (S/CRS). As the Congressional Research Service noted at the time,

> For many analysts and policymakers, the ongoing Iraq operation illustrates a US government need for new planning and coordination arrangements that would provide a leadership role for civilians in post-conflict phases of military operations and new civilian capabilities to augment and relieve the military as soon as possible (Serafino and Weiss 2005).

Over time, however, it became clear that the fledgling office had neither the capacity nor the desire to take ownership of the Iraq project. Carlos Pascual, the first director of S/CRS, made clear that the office would have been "overwhelmed" by the demands of Iraq or Afghanistan, and they sought instead simply to "learn from those missions" (Chandrasekaran 2007). Subsequently, the office began forming contingency plans for

Sudan, Liberia, Haiti and other unrelated countries (Logan and Preble 2006, p. 22).

Over time, however, the office began to receive greater funding. The Obama administration's FY 2010 budget request included $323.3 million for the Civilian Stabilization Initiative (CSI), a nearly nine-fold increase over the Bush administration's budget for FY 2009. Obama's request included more than $200 million to expand the Civilian Response Corps (CRC), and nearly $25 million to add new positions and staff in Washington for CSI and S/CRS (Serafino 2009, pp. 16–17). Congress appears eager to support the Obama administration's request.

The administration envisions a 4250 member corps, including 250 active members, plus another 2000 standby component members and 2000 in a reserve status. CRC cuts across at least eight federal government agencies, including State, Justice, Treasury, Commerce, Agriculture, Homeland Security, Heath and Human Services and USAID (S/CRS 2009).

As the above numbers indicate, the US Government's state-building activities are still decidedly limited. As with the Bush administration, S/CRS is playing only a very minor role in Iraq and Afghanistan. An S/CRS team deployed to coordinate the US Government support for the Afghan presidential elections in August 2009, and has provided modest support for similar activities in Iraq. Excepting these missions, the office's activities have been limited to planning exercises and coordinating financial support in places such as Haiti, Congo and Bangladesh.

Similar gaps bedevil the US efforts to deploy so-called Provincial Reconstruction Teams (PRTs) in Iraq and Afghanistan. Despite forceful national-security appeals for Americans to join PRTs in those countries (Obama 2009), the results have been unimpressive. As of 2008, in the 12 US-led PRTs in Afghanistan, 34 of the 1055 personnel came from civilian agencies. In Iraq in 2008 the situation was somewhat better: roughly 450 Americans were serving in the 28 US-led PRTs, 360 of whom were from civilian agencies (US GAO 2008). Still, this result came only after top State Department officials toyed with the ideas of forcing Foreign Service personnel to deploy to Iraq and adopting military rather than diplomatic security standards governing their deployments (Kessler 2007a, 2007b). These proposals encountered significant resistance within the State Department, indicating an apparent institutional rigidity likely to hinder any effort to develop a workable and sizeable corps of nation-builders. While it is true that "by the turn of the twenty-first century the United States military had already appropriated the entire earth, and was ready to flood the most obscure areas of it with troops at a moment's notice," (Kaplan 2005, p. 3) the same cannot be said of the civil service.

19.3   RESISTING THE SIREN CALL OF IMPROVEMENT

Too frequently, Western analysts jump to conclusions about the security implications of this or that phenomenon. State failure is a hopelessly broad analytical concept and much of the theorizing on failed states and their supposed relevance to national security cannot withstand empirical scrutiny. By representing failed states as threats that we are ill-equipped to protect against, we convince ourselves of a false vulnerability. Put differently, "to say that militarily strong states are feeble because they cannot easily bring order to minor states is like saying that a pneumatic hammer is weak because it is not suitable for drilling decayed teeth" (Waltz 1979, p. 189).

The failed state debate is only one example of this phenomenon. Part of the reason that everything tends to become a security concern in Western capitals – particularly in Washington – is because publics tend, reasonably, to care most about foreign policy issues that have the potential to affect their lives in some way. Accordingly, for those tasks in which policymakers are interested but publics are not, framing the proposed problem as a threat becomes useful. But acknowledging that state failure poses no serious threat does not in itself preclude attempting to provide assistance to various governments or peoples in trouble.

Simple honesty would require just calling such policies what they are: philanthropy. And, as Barry Posen has observed, the injection of the military element complicates the philanthropic urge:

> When the United States is about to engage in armed philanthropy, it should not disguise the effort as the pursuit of a security interest. If the latter is required to sell the policy, then the policy is already in trouble. Once characterized as a security interest, the US Congress and the public expect that the United States will lead the fight; that decisive military means will be employed; and that victory will be achieved – all of which raises US military and political costs (Posen 2007).

As Stewart Patrick notes, "clear-headed analysis" could "help restrain the worst impulses of Northern governments" (Patrick 2007, p. 659). But there has been too little clear-headed analysis, and little restraint.

The reader may note a severe disconnect between the analytical judgments of scholars and policymakers regarding state failure and the resources that have been allocated to addressing the matter. Given the extraordinary expense and difficulty involved in building functional states, how do the resources dedicated to the task hold any promise of fulfilling the mandate of state building? Put differently, if state failure is such an important threat – Barack Obama tells us that "the safety of people around the world is at stake" (Obama 2009) – then why has there been so little willingness to devote adequate resources to the problem?

We do not have a satisfactory answer to this question, other than to suggest that state failure is obviously not the problem it is made out to be. Still, this leaves another question: why are the claims about state failure repeated with such frequency and vigor? We offer this chapter as a challenge for the proponents of fixing failed states to clarify their logic and to answer to empirics.

What would be more appropriate – and far less costly – than the dramatic changes that would be necessary to form a serious strategy of fixing failed states would be a fundamental rethinking of the role of nation building and the relevance of state failure to national security planning. Thrust forward by the claims of threat, but unequipped with the expensive tools necessary for the task, policymakers look likely to persist in the failed approach to the subject that they have followed in recent years.

NOTES

1. This phrase was the title of Friedrich Hayek's Nobel Prize Lecture, 11 December 1974.
2. Interestingly, the 2008 Failed States Index produces a significant finding that strong executive constraints make state failure less likely (FSI 2008, p. 69).
3. This heading title refers to the psychological tendency among humans to believe that events beyond their control are, in fact, within it. (Langer 1982)
4. It is important to note that the United States is essentially *sui generis* in terms of state formation. The foundation of the American Republic was at once an ideological crusade and the building of a state and a nation. Some scholars have suggested that the history of the United States has induced American foreign policymakers to believe that the American experience is easily replicable and that this explains the decades-long American infatuation with state or nation building. (Allouche 2008). For an opposing view of nation building in America, see Smith (1999).

REFERENCES

Allouche, J. (2008), "State-building and US foreign policy", MIT Center for International Studies, Audit of Conventional Wisdom series, November 2008.

Baker, P.H. (2005), "Threat convergence and failing states: a new agenda for analysts", paper presented to The Cornwallis Group X: Analysis for New and Emerging Societal Conflicts, The Canadian Royal Military College, Kingston, Ontario, Canada, March 21–24, 2005, available at http://www.thecornwallisgroup.org/pdf/CX_2005_08-Baker-CX-July22.pdf.

Bush, G.W. (2002), *The National Security Strategy of the United States of America*, Washington: The White House.

Bush, G.W. (2005), "Interview of the President by Al Arabiya Television", January 26, 2005, transcript available at http://georgewbush-whitehouse.archives.gov/news/releases/2005/01/print/20050126-7.html.

Caldwell, Lt. Gen. W.B., IV (2008), "Foreword", in *Stability Operations Field Manual* (FM 3-07), Washington DC: Headquarters Department of the Army.

Call, C. (2006), "The fallacy of the 'failed state'", paper presented at the annual meeting of the International Studies Association, San Diego, California, March 22, 2006.

Chandrasekaran, R. (2007), "Iraq rebuilding short on qualified civilians", *Washington Post*, 24 February 2007, p. 1.

Cohen, E., C. Crane, J. Horvath and J. Nagl (2006), "Principles, imperatives, and paradoxes of counterinsurgency", *Military Review* March/April, 49–53.

Collier P. (2009), "Development in dangerous places", *Boston Review*, July/August.

Council on Foreign Relations Task Force (CFR) (2005), *In the Wake of War: Improving US Post-Conflict Capabilities*, July 2005.

Department for International Development (DFID) (2005), "Why we need to work more effectively in fragile states", January 2005, available at http://www.dfid.gov.uk/Documents/publications/fragilestates-paper.pdf.

Dobbins, J., S.G. Jones, K. Crane and B.C. DeGrasse (2007), *The Beginners Guide to Nation Building*, Santa Monica, CA: RAND Corporation.

Dobbins, J., J.G. McGinn, K. Crane, S.G. Jones, R. Lal, A. Rathmell, R.M. Swanger A.R. Timilsina (2003), *America's Role in Nation-Building: From Germany to Iraq*, Santa Monica, CA: RAND Corporation.

Economist (2009), "Fixing a broken world", *Economist*, 31 January 2009, 65–7.

Fearon J.D. and D.D. Laitin (2004), "Neotrusteeship and the problem of weak states", *International Security* **28** (4) 5–43.

FSI (2007), "The Failed States Index", *Foreign Policy*, **161**, July/August, 54–63.

FSI (2008), "The Failed States Index", *Foreign Policy*, **167**, July/August, 64–73.

FSI (2009), "The Failed States Index", *Foreign Policy*, **173**, July/August, 80–93.

Fukuyama, F. (2004a), *State-Building: Governance and World Order in the 21st Century*, Ithaca, NY: Cornell University Press.

Fukuyama, F. (2004b), "Nation Building 101", *Atlantic Monthly* January–February, 159–62.

Fukuyama, F. (2004c), "Comment on Center for Global Development Task Force Report", *On the Brink: Weak States and US National Security*, available at http://www.cgdev.org/section/initiatives/_archive/weakstates.

Fukuyama, F. (2005), "'Stateness' first", *Journal of Democracy*, **16** (1) 84–8.

Ghani, A. and C. Lockhart (2008), *Fixing Failed States: A Framework for Rebuilding a Fractured World*, Oxford, UK: Oxford University Press.

Goldstone, J.A. (2008), "Pathways to state failure", *Conflict Management and Peace Science*, **25** (4) 285–96.

Gourevitch, A. (2005), "The myth of the failed state", paper presented at the Annual Meeting International Studies Association, March 3, 2005.

Helman, G.B. and S.R. Ratner (1992–93), "Saving failed states", *Foreign Policy*, **89** (Winter, 1992–1993), 3–20.

Jones, S.G. (2008), "The rise of Afghanistan's insurgency: state failure and jihad", *International Security*, **32** (4) 7–40.

Kahl, C.H. (2007), "COIN of the realm: is there a future for counterinsurgency?", *Foreign Affairs*, **86** (6), 169–76.

Kalyvas, S.N. (2008), "The new US Army/Marine Corps Counterinsurgency Field Manual as political science and political praxis", *Perspectives on Politics*, **6** (2) 351–3.

Kaplan, R.D. (2005), *Imperial Grunts*, New York, NY: Random House.

Kessler, G. (2007a), "Embassy staff in Baghdad inadequate, Rice is told", *Washington Post*, 19 June 2007, A01.

Kessler, G. (2007b), "Rice orders that diplomatic jobs in Iraq be filled first", *Washington Post*, 21 June 2007, A11.

Kilcullen, D. (2006), "Twenty-eight articles of company-level counterinsurgency", available at http://smallwarsjournal.com/documents/28articles.pdf.

Kilcullen, D. (2009), *The Accidental Guerilla: Fighting Small Wars in the Midst of a Big One*, Oxford, UK: Oxford University Press.

Krasner S.D. (2004), "Sharing sovereignty: new institutions for collapsed and failing states", *International Security*, **29** (2), 85–120.

Krasner S.D. and C. Pascual (2005), "Addressing state failure", *Foreign Affairs*, **84** (4), 153–63.

Langer, E. (1982), "The illusion of control", in D. Kahneman, P. Slovic and A Tversky, (eds), *Judgment under Uncertainty: Heuristics and Biases*, Cambridge, UK: Cambridge University Press, pp. 231–38.

Logan, J. and C. Preble (2006), "Failed states and flawed logic: the case against a standing nation-building office", *Cato Policy Analysis*, 560.

Nagl, J. (2008), "Review of *The Echo of Battle: The Army's Way of War*", *RUSI Journal*, **153** (2), 82–3.

National Public Radio (NPR) (2004), *Weekend All Things Considered*, 21 March 2004.

Obama, B. (2007), "Renewing American leadership", *Foreign Affairs*, **86** (4), 2–16.

Obama, B. (2009), "Remarks by the President on a new strategy for Afghanistan and Pakistan," 27 March 2009, available at http://www.whitehouse.gov/the_press_office/Remarks-by-the-President-on-a-New-Strategy-for-Afghanistan-and-Pakistan/.

Office of the Director of National Intelligence (ODNI) (2005), *The National Intelligence Strategy of the United States of America*, October 2005, available at http://www.dni.gov/NISOctober2005.pdf.

Patrick, S. (2007), "Failed states and global security: empirical questions and policy dilemmas", *International Studies Review*, **9** (4), 644–62.

Piazza, J.A. (2008), "Incubators of terror: do failed and failing states promote transnational terrorism?", *International Studies Quarterly*, **52** (3), 469–88.

Posen, B.R. (2007), "The case for restraint", *The American Interest*, November/December, 7–17.

Rotberg, R.I. (ed.), (2003), *State Failure and State Weakness in a Time of Terror*, Cambridge, MA: World Peace Foundation.

Scowcroft, B. and S.R. Berger (2005), "In the wake of war: getting serious about nation-building", *National Interest*, Fall, 49–53.

Serafino, N.M. (2009), "Peacekeeping/ stabilization and conflict transitions: background and congressional Action on Civilian Response Corps and other civilian stabilization and reconstruction capabilities", *CRS Report for Congress, Order Code RL32862*, 16 June 2009.

Serafino N.M. and M.A. Weiss (2005), "Peacekeeping and conflict transitions: background and congressional action on civilian capabilities", *CRS report for Congress Order Code RL32862*, 13 April 2005.

Smith, R. (1999), *Civic Ideals: Conflicting Visions of Citizenship in US History*, New Haven, CT: Yale University Press.

State Failure Task Force Report: Phase III Findings (SFTFR) (2000), 30 September 2000, available at http://globalpolicy.gmu.edu/pitf/SFTF%20Phase%20III%20Report%20Final.pdf

Stewart, R. (2009), "The irresistible illusion", *London Review of Books*, **31** (13), available at http://www.lrb.co.uk/v31/n13/stew01_.html.

Tilly, C. (1985), "War making and state making as organized crime", in P.B. Evans, D. Rueschemeyer and T. Skocpol (eds), *Bringing the State Back In*, Cambridge, UK: Cambridge University Press.

Tilly, C. (1990), *Coercion, Capital, and European States*, Cambridge, MA: Blackwell.

US Army (2008), *Stability Operations Field Manual (FM 3-07)*, Washington DC: Headquarters, Department of the Army.

US Army and Marine Corps (2006), *Counterinsurgency Field Manual (FM 3-24)*, Washington DC: Headquarters, Departments of the Army and Navy.

US Department of Defense (USDOD) (2005), "Directive 3000.05," November 28, http://www.dtic.mil/whs/directives/corres/pdf/300005p.pdf.

US Department of State, Office of the Coordinator for Reconstruction and Stabilization (S/CRS) (2009), "President's FY 2010 Budget Request for the Civilian Stabilization

Initiative", available at http://www.crs.state.gov/index.cfm?fuseaction=public.display& shortcut=4QJW.

US Government Accountability Office (USGAO) (2008), "Provincial reconstruction teams in Afghanistan and Iraq," GAO-09-86R, 1 October 2008, available at http://www.gao.gov/ new.items/d0986r.pdf.

US Interagency Counterinsurgency Initiative (USICI) (2009), *US Government Counterinsurgency Guide*, January 2009, available at http://www.state.gov/documents/ organization/119629.pdf.

Waltz, K.N. (1979), *Theory of International Politics* Reading, MA: Addison-Wesley.

20 Choice and consequence in strategies of transitional justice
Geoff Dancy

20.1 INTRODUCTION

More and more, today's hopes of erasing violent conflict and vitalizing democratic institutions are being pinned on transitional justice.[1] "Just as wounds fester when they are not exposed to the open air," one scholar writes, "so unacknowledged injustice can poison societies and produce cycles of distrust, hatred, and violence" (Kiss 2000, p. 72). However, this viewpoint and the practices to which it alludes are relatively new. Before 1990, only ten countries in the world had prosecuted human rights violators, and only five had formed truth commissions to systematically investigate their pasts. By 2007, these figures had spiked: trials had been initiated for 59 state jurisdictions, and at least one official truth-seeking body had been established in 33 states.[2] With these advancements, transitional justice shifted from a narrow area of advocacy to the strategic forefront of transnational democratic state-building, rule of law promotion and postconflict peacebuilding. First used in 1991,[3] the term "transitional justice" surfaced at the intersection of two emergent global phenomena: a strengthening human rights regime and the fourth wave of democratization (Aranhövel 2008; Arthur 2009). By the 1980s, moral indignation to repressive tactics like torture, disappearances and political imprisonment reached a fevered pitch, and the international community began to mobilize in response. Democratization, sweeping the world, was a multi-staged process – involving destabilization, a transitional sequence and consolidation – shepherded through by decision-making elites (O'Donnell, Schmitter and Whitehead 1986; Karl 2005). Transitional justice designated elites' efforts to settle accounts for the worst of past human depredations during the middle stage of this process.

The need to deal with human rights violations in the fragile and troubling temporal-political domain of transition was variously referred to as the "torturer problem" or the "transitional dilemma" on account of its precarious nature (Huntington 1991; Teitel 2000). In practice, a number of policy tactics were used: (1) amnesty laws that encouraged forgetting and reintegration of former torturers; (2) international and domestic trials which proceeded despite legal obstacles; (3) investigatory 'truth commissions' that aimed to lift the shroud of state secrecy; (4) lustration and vetting, which prevent former officials from serving in public posts; and (5) reparations to those vanquished by violence and repression.[4] (For the remainder of the chapter, I refer to options 2–5 as "accountability mechanisms.") Because each of these in isolation was deemed incapable of meting out full retribution while remaining politically salutary, justice in transition was imbued with limitations, paradoxes and imperfections. For example, not only might transitional justice sap resources in already beleaguered governing institutions – the state capacity paradox (Putnam 2002) – but it might also violate impunity laws on the books that legally protect perpetrators from criminal or civil prosecution – the rule of law paradox (McAdams 1997; Teitel 2000).

The 1990s, the "decade of international law," however, would witness the maturation of transitional justice despite these drawbacks. The watershed proceedings of the South African Truth and Reconciliation Commission, in tandem with widespread domestic trials in Latin America, and the ad-hoc international tribunals for Rwanda (ICTR) and the former Yugoslavia (ICTY), spurred a "cascade" of accountability mechanisms (Lutz and Sikkink 2001; Daly 2008). Transitional justice became normalized into a contemporary orthodoxy, even as its application in practice was still fraught with difficulty (Teitel 2003). Accompanying normalization are three additional developments. First, connotatively speaking, the term has broadened to mean something like *those strategies for reckoning with the wrongs of the past in times of political change.* Second, strategies of transitional justice have expanded to include what is now an impressive range of tactics across jurisdictions, including indictment and prosecution by the decade-old International Criminal Court (Schiff 2008); security sector reforms (Loden 2007); disarmament, demobilization and reintegration of armed groups (Theidon 2007); public memorialization projects (Jelin 2007); and history education reforms (Cole 2007). Third, and perhaps most significantly, transitional justice strategies have been decoupled from an exclusive relationship with democratization. Juan Mendez, President of the International Center for Transitional Justice, argued as early as 1997 that transitional justice should not be confined to the domain of democratization. De facto, it has not been. Practice has extended beyond paradigmatic transitory democracies; accountability mechanisms have been pursued in post-atrocity societies (Rwanda), new states (Timor L'este), "conflicted democracies" (Northern Ireland), occupied states (Iraq and Afghanistan) and even "pre-post-conflict" countries (Uganda).[5]

Popularity has brought with it introspection, along with calls for further scrutiny, which have coalesced into an academic field of transitional justice.

Within this field, the ability of accountability mechanisms to achieve macro-level social goals has been the subject of growing inquiry. To what end do leaders decide to institute such measures? At what price? Is transitional justice *effective*? Skeptics aver that these questions have been given insufficient attention, and as a result, transitional justice practices chug along without solid foundation. Furthermore, they argue that the costs of pursuing accountability could outweigh the benefits, and even worse, that strategies of transitional justice might be counter-productive to peace.

In this chapter, I argue that the field of transitional justice, and thus the answer to these questions, is lacking in two respects. First, the scholarly community has not converged on a consistent theoretical framework for understanding decisions made regarding transitional justice. It misinterprets the choice to pursue accountability in the wake of regime transition to be either a product of domestic political constraints or of diffusing behavioral norms, rather than one that is nested in larger processes of interaction between these two determinants. Second, empirical research lacks consistent metrics for sustaining large-scale comparisons and evaluations (that is, what is the universe of transition cases, and when do we know transitional justice has failed?). These issues have stacked the deck against positive evaluation.

I proceed in five sections. Section 20.2 will provide a heuristic for organizing the interdisciplinary "field" that has emerged around, and mirrored, transitional justice practices. Sections 20.3 and 20.4 will discuss two key elements of causal theories of transitional justice – choice and consequence – with an eye toward theoretical integration. Section 20.5 will present a brief re-assessment of the consequences of transitional justice strategies. Finally, Section 20.6 will conclude with suggestions for future research.

20.2   THE 'FIELD' OF TRANSITIONAL JUSTICE

A voluminous literature exists under the heading of transitional justice, one that extends beyond 2300 citations.[6] Interest in the topic has been responsible for numerous conferences, and has recently given birth to a specialist's journal, the *International Journal of Transitional Justice*. One could conclude on this basis that transitional justice has undergone a "dramatically compressed trajectory of fieldhood" (Bell 2008, p. 7). This field has two essential characteristics: interdisciplinarity and proximity to practice. Burgeoning research has relied on a blend of legal, comparative and philosophical approaches all centered on analysing course of action in transitional periods. Virtually impossible is maintaining a participant–observer distinction within this field. "Discourse about settling the past is," as one writer notes, "both political and academic, and mixes the roles of practitioners and theoreticians" (Forsberg 2003, p. 59). Because the full spectrum of this normative-intellectual literature is so wide, and because it resists domination by one discipline, arranging it in one singular framework presents great difficulties. An oversimplified but useful method for doing so is to classify research projects by what kinds of questions they ask, and how these questions correspond to ideal type academic approaches. Such a classification recognizes and accepts that theoretical inquiry (intentionally or not) mirrors closely on-the-ground developments in the use of accountability mechanisms. Table 20.1 represents a heuristic for organizing the field of transitional justice by four strands of inquiry which are discussed in more detail below.

20.2.1   Mechanism and Function

Strand I is where the lion's share of scholarship resides. The transitional justice literature conveys a kind of functionalist bias in that it reflects upon the use of certain mechanisms by asking, "what are they good for?", "what are they meant to do?" and "how do they do it?"[7] Research into these questions has performed two roles. First, it has exhaustively documented the legal and administrative procedure of different tools available to transitioning regimes. One foundational example is Priscilla Hayner's (2001) seminal treatment of truth commissions in *Unspeakable Truths.* Hayner traces the history of truth commissions across 21 cases, documenting their operational shortcomings and gesturing toward theory about the way that they affect victims and society.

The second contribution of "functionalist" studies is that they have produced a dense matrix of claims concerning the merits of certain tools in isolation. Amnesties, for example, are seen by some to be an effective method for getting junta regimes to exit (David and Holliday 2006), a way of facilitating demobilization of rebel groups (Mallinder 2008), and consequently, as midwives of peace and order that lay the groundwork for future democracy (Teitel 1995; Snyder and Vinjamuri 2003/4). Criminal trials have been promoted as a tool for producing a record of truth within due process (Scharf and Rodley 2002); as rituals of collective memory (Osiel 1997); as a deterrent of future abuse (see Mennecke 2007); or as a way of fostering democratic rule of law after impunity (McAdams 1997; Neier 1999). Truth commissions, the most celebrated innovation of the transitional justice movement, have been championed as a third way between pardoning criminals and punishing them through trials (van Zyl 1999; Boraine 2000b). These bureaucratic tools are said to support personal healing and victim recognition (Minow 2000; Hayner 2001); produce a true record of historical

Table 20.1 Framework for organizing research questions by approach

	Functionalism (I)	Normative Theory (II)	Historical/ Structuralism (III)	Causal Theory (IV)	
				Choice	Consequences
Questions	(1) How do different TJ mechanisms like trials and truth commissions operate? (2) What are they meant for? (3) Do they function to meet certain needs?	(1) Does "justice" belong to the individual, to the community, or to the state? (2) What is the nature of political "truth"? (3) How do former enemies reconcile? (4) What is an appropriate normative framework for TJ?	(1) What are the historical antecedents to TJ? (2) How does TJ fit into the current historical moment? (3) What is the menu of justice options available to leaders in given periods?	(1) Why do leaders choose to institute certain mechanisms instead of others?	(1) How do mechanisms meet certain goals? (2) What positive or negative ramifications do these TJ measures have?

Notes: TJ, transnational justice

401

events after a period of state secrecy (Zalaquett 1995); achieve a level of retribution by naming names of torturers (Popkin and Roht-Ariazza 1995); potentially instill democratic goods like a "moral economy of disagreement" (Gutman and Thompson 2000); or, more commonly, promote reconciliation, forgiveness, and civility in formerly fractured societies (Asmal, Asmal and Robert. 1996; Scharf 1996; Bhargava 2000; Amstutz 2005).[8]

Functionalist treatments have created a melting pot from which theorists of transitional justice can draw inferences. However, this frame of inquiry has a few shortfalls. First, because it has placed emphasis on the role of specific mechanisms in isolation, functionalist research is responsible for balkanizing the study of transitional justice. The search was originally for one type of mechanism that can be pre-configured and transplanted in a variety of social contexts. Recently, though, practitioners have discarded this "one-size-fits-all" approach in favor of a holistic or relational understanding of transitional justice mechanisms (Boraine 2006; de Greiff 2006; de Greiff and Duthie 2009). While also recognizing that there are valuable lessons to be learned from the use of formally similar tools across cases, policymakers are realizing that benefits that accrue to transitional justice practices are tied to the degree to which they are designed to reinforce one another in given contexts.

Second, for every claim about the proper function or promise of one mechanism, there is an equal and opposite counter-claim about its limitations. For example, where Payam Akhavan (2001, p. 8) writes that trials' effectiveness can be determined by whether they have "contributed to post-conflict peace-building and reconciliation," others write that "[r]econciliation is not the goal of criminal trials except in the most abstract sense" (Minow 1998, p. 26). Vectors of disagreement such as these have created inconsistent and untested expectations about the possible repercussions of transitional justice practices. Bronwyn Leebaw (2008, p. 97) argues on this basis that the continued promotion of accountability mechanisms is puzzling since "scholars have always had somewhat mixed views on the political and social role of these institutions." Contrariety, in this instance, does not reflect the frictions of scientific falsificationism. Few of these theories have been subject to rigorous testing, and by dint of their functionalism, they are causally ambiguous (Mendeloff 2004). Instead, differences over purpose reflect the legal, moral, philosophical – and ultimately conceptual – predispositions of those making claims.

20.2.2   Justice, Truth and Reconciliation

Many characterizations of the social utility and potency of transitional justice mechanisms are undergirded by legal and moral reasoning. Strand

II of inquiry centers on these normative concerns. Transitional justice practices have always been accompanied by a supportive legalism, which has served both as a source of demands for how leaders *should* make decisions, and as a language for post-hoc justification of practices already underway. Legalists like Diane Orentlicher (1991) proclaimed that the duty of the state is to roundly reject amnesties and pursue punishment for massive violations of human rights irrespective of the political situation it faces.[9] After their popularity rose, this rationale was also employed to justify the use of truth-seeking measures. For example, Argentine jurist Juan Mendez (1997, p. 261) made the case that there is an international "right to know truth," that has achieved the level of customary law, thereby it is the duty of a state to reveal the nature of its conduct toward its citizens. Scholars have also traced the hardening of this right through the rulings of international bodies and legal decisions made by regional high courts (see Wiebelhaus-Braum 2010). For legalists, developments in customary law and new interpretations of long-standing hard law ought to serve as a compass for future action by clarifying obligatory rules for behavior.

Legalist claims, though couched in positivist terms, typically correspond to normative conceptualizations of justice. In Strand II literature, justice has been separated into retributive, restorative, procedural and distributive types (Gibson and Gouws 1999), and attempts have been made to integrate these types into larger "rectificatory" (Mani 2002) or "transformational" frameworks (Lambourne 2009). Assimilating the full array of justice frameworks, which are ample, would be a paralyzing enterprise, so outlining the dimensions of the two most prominent will have to suffice. In the mid-1990s, retributive and restorative models monopolized thinking about the purpose of transitional justice. Retributivists, who have alternately been referred to as maximalists or purists, conceive of trial punishment both as an ideal way of serving up just desserts, and as a method for deterring future abuses (Malamud-Goti 1995). The restorative model, on the other hand, emerged in discussions of transitional justice as an alternative to retributive justice, which to some is more accurately framed as the expropriation of personal vengeance to the apparatus of the state (Minow 1998). Proponents of this model assert that "communities are the key stakeholders in justice" (Zehr and Mika 2003, p. 41). It follows that rituals of truth assertion and conflict mediation better serve justice if reconceived as community healing, societal restoration or reconstruction (du Toit 2000). This justice-as-social-restoration model is the foundation of the pedigreed socio-psychological truth and reconciliation framework that has come to dominate the field.[10]

Strand II also incorporates critical reflections on these normative constructions, specifically the deployment of certain discourses that justify transitional justice practices and support claims that are made about their social functions. Reconciliation has become, for better or worse, the single defining feature of the end state to which transitional societies should progress.[11] However, critical theorists have argued that the term itself remains elusive, resisting consensus and generating "varieties of reconciliation" (Meierhenrich 2008). One author points out that reconciliation, rather than being conceived as a discrete goal, would be more properly understood as an "epiphenomenal" condition which "supervenes" on life once other social pre-requisites are met (de Greiff 2008).[12] In this sense, reconciliation might be characterized as an empty signifier, in so far as its meaning defies fixity because its content is always subject to political contestation and mediation (see Zerilli 1998).[13] More pessimistic criticisms have derided the fascination with reconciliation in the practice of transitional justice as a "deeply illiberal," idealist obsession with unreachable harmony and erasure of the political (Ash 1997; Forsberg 2003). Reconciliation has also been treated cynically as a way to paper over the role impunity plays in *realpolitik* political negotiations (Dwyer 1999; Wilson 2001), or as a "dirty word" that masks state's desires to suppress difference and reform identity in the name of order in multi-national and multi-ethnic societies like that of Northern Ireland (McEvoy, McEvay and McConnachie 2006).

20.2.3   History

A criticism of both Strand I and Strand II scholarship is that it is decidedly presentist, looking to evaluate the contemporary uses of accountability mechanisms without an adequate grounding in the historical and structural contingencies that have contributed to their rise. In a corrective, some more recent studies have aimed to place the practice of transitional justice, writ large, in "historical perspective" (Strand III). Jon Elster (2004) finds precedent for the political balancing act between amnesty and punishment in Athens after the fall of the Thirty Tyrants and in England after the Restoration of Charles II. He concludes that these dilemmas have been present throughout the centuries. Other historical works have a more international structural bent. Catherine Turner (2008) situates transitional justice and international law within the current moment of liberal imperial order, arguing that accountability and human rights compliance is now linked to the "recognitional" legitimacy of states (Cf. Tully 2005).[14] In a related work, Christine Bell (2008) argues that transitional justice was born at a node in the evolution of peace agreements. As the demand rose for intrastate peace agreements, so too did the need to graft emergent human rights and constitutional legalism onto those agreements. The result, she argues, is a new international *lex pacificatoria*, or law of peace, of which transitional justice is a vital part.

Historical research of this sort forms a binary with functionalist and legalist inquiry. International structural accounts highlight the newfangled nature of transitional justice in the contemporary era, treating it as an aggregated body of globalized practices that is bound to a moment in the arc of history. Functionalist and legalist research, however, comes dangerously close to decontextualization, assuming away the political roots of transitional justice strategies; in a way, they treat these tools as items on a menu that may be chosen by fiat, however problematically, whenever they are deemed appropriate. Strands I–III, then, are less applicable when it comes to discerning the variation in decisions to use transitional justice mechanisms, or their effects, across countries. Speaking in reference to the South African TRC, Aletta Norval (1999, p. 505) writes that a focus on "ethical and historical functions" risks "losing sight of the manner in which political decisions have shaped the transition process." The remainder of this chapter will focus on Strand IV of the literature – empirical research that has examined questions of causality vis-à-vis the two elements of transitional justice process: choice and consequence.

20.3   CAUSAL THEORIES OF TRANSITIONAL JUSTICE

By virtue of its intellectual origins, the study of transitional justice is wedded to the study of regime change. The literature on regime change features a vacillation between structural and voluntarist accounts (Mahoney and Snyder 1999). Traditionally, Marxists favored structural accounts, visualizing change as the long-term unfolding of class conflicts and other slow-changing domestic economic forces (Moore 1966; Reuschmeyer, Stephens and Stephens 1992). But since the 1970s, with the work of Juan Linz (1978), focus has shifted toward the voluntarist perspective, from the "causes to the causers" within transition processes – individuals and institutions (Huntington 1991). From this perspective regime changes are seen as foundational moments where degenerative patterns of living are being discarded for new contracts of governance, and institutions are being intentionally re-molded from those that came before (Zalaquett 1998; Roeder 2001). "What matters most in such times of 'abnormal politics,'" writes Terry Karl (2005, p. 9), "are not the structural conditions that may subsequently shape a polity but rather the short-term strategic calculations of actors." Within these moments, transitional justice may be framed as an end in itself (Addison 2009), but it is more often seen as a means for reaching other ends. What role do accountability mechanisms play in transitional processes, and what factors determine actors' calculations?

20.3.1   Choice

At its crux, empirical research is preoccupied with assessing what sociologist Luc Huyse (1995, p. 51) succinctly described as the "choice successor elites make in dealing with the past." In the literature, two oppositional outlooks have formed around the nature of decision-making in transitional circumstances. Realists magnify the importance of the power constraints, whereas constructivists accentuate the role that behavioral norms have played in creating innovations in, and contributing to, the pervasiveness of accountability mechanisms.[15] These two schools, which share an interest in modeling the process of decision-making surrounding transitional justice, picked up cues from a debate that raged among practitioners and policymakers at the genesis of the field over how leaders *should* make decisions. Realists like Jose Zalaquett (1991) and Carlos Nino (1996), who had participated in decisions made within transitioning regimes in Latin America, countered "irrational" legalist demands for punishment by defending an "ethic of responsibility." For these intellectual practitioners, who passed along their knowledge to those in South Africa (Boraine 2000a), leaders should not involve themselves in the politics of *ressentiment* if it poses insurmountable risks to the short-term survival of the newly instituted regime (Linz 1978, p. 42).

Political scientists took the lessons of practicality from Latin America and generalized them. Not only *should* leaders pay heed to the circumstances of transition, the argument goes, but history will prove that their decisions *are* determined by domestic alignments of power. Based on the theoretical supposition that regimes are interested primarily in their own survival, political scientists generated a number of hypotheses. First, the kind of response to the past will be causally predicted by the character of the transition a country undergoes. Specifically, "justice [is] a function of political power" between the new regime and its predecessor (Huntington 1991, p. 228). Those transitions that make a clean rupture with the *ancien regime* will result in more punitive justice; those that follow pacted, or negotiated, transitions will be hamstrung into seeking amnesties and more diluted forms of justice like those served by truth commissions (Huntington 1991; Sutil 1997; Sieff and Wright 1999).[16] Modeled as such, choice was framed as static and dichotomous: leaders would either pursue trials or truth commissions, but not both. This notion gave rise to the truth versus justice binary that still lingers in discussions of transitional justice.[17] A second hypothesis that came from realist analysis is that if retributive trial justice is going to be sought in the aftermath of transition, it must happen quickly (within a few years) because the demand for prosecutions will abate as time drags on. A third and final hypothesis was one that dealt more with economic constraints. As the financial cost of accountability increases, so too will the unwillingness on the part of decision-makers to bank-roll expensive measures (Elster 2004).[18]

Unraveling the relationship between political economic constraints and transitional justice choices is, as Jon Elster writes, "a *positive* or explanatory task" (2004, p. 79), one that calls out for hard evidence. A scan of the empirical record[19], in combination with more recent quantitative research, yields a fairly consistent conclusion that challenges realist theoretical propositions: the character of power-political and economic constraints in the transition does create obstacles, but they are far less than determinative. First, in conflict with the binary thinking of early scholarship, truth procedures and punitive justice do not, and need not, trade off. Upward of 14 regimes have made use of both retributive and restorative forms, though many have done so in a staggered fashion.[20] Nor has a precise or statistically significant correlation been shown between types of regime change and types of transitional justice pursued, though this remains an area for more comprehensive future research. These simple observations have prompted some to push the bounds of the field beyond balance of power and truth versus justice thinking (for example, Roht-Arriaza and Mariezcurrena 2006).

Confounding the other two expectations of realists, the use of certain mechanisms continue to accelerate despite the number of years from transition or the financial costs. Sikkink and Walling (2007) propose that time does not quash the demand to seek accountability – a proposition that seems to be supported by the empirical record. Domestic trials, on average, take place 4.8 years after a regime transition (with a maximum of 18), and truth commissions are instituted an average of 4.7 years after transition (with a maximum of 15).[21] Additionally, in the current literature, economic factors maintain a yet indefinite relationship to transitional justice practices. Transitional justice measures no doubt require a good deal of public financing, and one group of scholars focused specifically on the economic determinants of transitional justice efforts found an empirical relationship between state-level economic wealth and the decision to institute transitional justice mechanisms (Olsen, Payne and Reiter 2007).[22] However, this relationship is not overwhelming or ineluctable. Though relevant as a "constraint on the pursuit of justice," writes Roger Duthie (2009, p. 21), a "country's level of development does not predict or determine the extent to which it will pursue transitional justice."

As research progresses, constraint-fixated realist propositions appear less valid. One reason is that their authors zoomed in too far on specific national events, leaving international aspects of transitional justice out of the picture. Mark Arenhövel (2008, p. 577) states the problem concisely: "In the vast majority of cases, transitional justice . . . has been seen as an exclusively domestic affair." Even more powerful than domestic material structures in transition, it seems, is the role of internationally derived behavioral norms in decision-making processes. One study shows that though the presence of a conflict stalemate is a statistically significant predictor of truth commission initiation, a much larger causal effect is exerted by the "normative international environment" in which the decision takes place (Dancy and Poe 2006).[23] In a mixed-method dissertation, Hunjoon Kim (2009) demonstrates quantitatively that the overwhelming predictor of truth or trial efforts is the number of state neighbors that have instituted similar policies, along with the presence of in-country activist groups pushing for government action.[24] By the end of the century, both trials and truth commissions, in so far as both strove toward answerability and responsiveness of the state to individuals, were viewed by transnational activists as complementary for achieving accountability, and the idea that they were mutually exclusive options began to fade. What this suggests, in support of social constructivist explanations, is that behaviorally prescriptive ideas of what transitional regimes should do have become self-perpetuating. According to Rama Mani (2002, p. 89) "The immense popularity of both mechanisms – trials and truth commissions – and the strong support they receive from the international, human rights, and donor communities have created an implicit obligation for countries newly emergent from conflict to adopt one or both."

At first blush, these contributions might seem academic. However, what is at stake is our outlook toward decision-making, which does not seem to be confined to power-laden interactions between new elites and old in financially prohibitive situations. These findings have produced a pushback from realist thinkers: if allowed to outpace reason and reflection, transitional justice decisions made under the influence of normative pressure could be construed as negligent or "seriously flawed" (Call 2004, p. 102). The following passage illustrates this fear:

> '. . .policymakers. . .have a vague sense that dealing with the past is appropriate but a government's decision to pursue a particular mechanism often depends less on well-grounded and proven policy considerations than on whether the junior staff member. . . has some experience with the South African TRC or another transitional justice process' (Kritz, 2009, p. 14)[25]

If this account is accurate, and these crucial decisions are made slapdash, then they are subject to the criticisms lodged by realist skeptics – that they do not follow a reasoned logic. They might be the product of blind emulation, misapplied emotion, or worse, top-down social experimentation at the behest of the international community (see Snyder 2000; Elster 2004; Vinjamuri and Snyder 2004; Chesterman 2007). Belief that decisions are not sufficiently forward-thinking, and that they are the product of "templatized" rule-following, has led some to caution practitioners against proceeding to urge justice without careful reflection (for example, Thoms, Ron and Paris 2008), or to read the spread of transitional justice as an instance of legalist norms run amok.

20.3.2 Transitional Justice as Nested

One sad truth of transitional justice efforts is that, to observers, they always are seen to fall short of the "ideal." Legalists and idealists typically chide leaders for shirking their duties, while realists find the pursuit of justice to be irrational (Linz 1978) or economically inefficient (for example, Boettke and Coyne 2007). Rather than advance the notion that power will be (or should be) the prime mover of decision-making, or proclaiming that the pursuit of accountability should follow a course dominated by norms, it is more fruitful to consider how these two interact. A good deal of scholarship over the years has made the case that both transnational political activism and domestic political structures combine to produce certain justice policies (Pion-Berlin 1994; Barahona de Brita 2003; Lutz and Sikkink 2001). However, they have not given equal treatment to how these conditions combine to produce decisions.[26] More integration of these two perspectives is needed.

It might be fruitful, for example, to think of the interplay between behavioral norms and domestic constraints as involving nested games in moments of institutional change (Tsebelis 1991). Nested games figure prominently in times when actors face uncertainty both over unsettled institutional rules of the game, and their strategic interaction within those contested rules (see Schedler 2002 for elections as nested games). In political transitions, policymakers may be straddling multiple-level interactions with international organizations, oppositional parties, the military, rebels groups, and mass actors, all at once. They know that the ability of their regime to sustain itself will be based on the way that it facilitates negotiations – which are increasingly featured in transitions – and the way that it adapts to a multitude of heavy demands. As norms reach a tipping point (Finnemore and Sikkink 1998), they generate a growing demand for accountability, which then feeds back into expectations that insert themselves into bargaining processes (for example, Cortell and Davis 2000). Global norms often travel through civil society and mass actors, who have become more active participants in democratic transitions (Diamond 2008; Simmons 2009) and post-conflict negotiations (Roht-Arriaza 2002; Bell 2008).[27] One blind spot for realist analyses of transitional justice is that, in its focus on the power between regime and opposition, they have not given equal treatment to the way that elites must also strategically interact with mass actors. When they do, realists tend to treat civil society as an instrument of elite manipulation (Snyder 2000) or as a polarizing spoiler in the process of change (Huntington 1968; cf. Bermeo 2003). A more acquiescent view is that mass actors are an independent source of democratic interests, and that they sit in judgment of regime legitimacy.

Transitional justice strategies are adopted as solutions to nested games between regime and opposition, and between regime and mass actors. These occur within meta-games like sustaining the peace, operating new liberal democracy and achieving economic development. Within the larger spectrum of sustaining peace, it has been shown that accountability measures are increasingly brought to the table in settlement processes involving third-party mediators, rebel groups and state forces (Williams 2002; Vinjamuri and Boesenecker 2007; Bell 2008; Mallinder 2008). Long and Brecke (2003) argue, based on 11 postconflict cases, that "reconciliation events" like those produced by truth-seeking bodies help facilitate the sending of costly signals between rivals as these situations unfold over time. Transitional justice measures could also be used instrumentally, and perhaps unflatteringly, by regimes to win in games with mass actors. Operational accountability mechanisms may provide for joint ownership of state bodies, or create the appearance thereof, between postconflict regime and interest groups. The mandate of the 2005 Liberian TRC, for example, clearly states that civil society and political parties will comprise a portion of the government selection panel for state commissioners.[28] By giving mass actors stakes in the performance of new state mechanisms, tactics of inclusion might help delegitimize competitive claims to rule or destabilize a situation of "dual sovereignty" (see Quinn, Mason and Gurses 2007).

Second, laws establishing transitional justice measures are often among the first acts of public policy that are trying to legitimately establish new democracy as the only game in town. Institutionalizing accountability through transitional justice mechanisms might serve as a method for signaling credible commitments to an expectant electorate, much as creating constitutions locks in regimes' recognition of individual rights (North and Weingast 1989; Moravscik 1997). This explains why some see the promise of transitional justice in its ability to generate stirrings of trust in nascent democratic institutions (de Greiff 2008; de Greiff 2009). Simultaneously, though, leaders must bargain with oppositions over the shape and reach of accountability efforts: Who will institute them? Which of the country's elites will be their subjects? What rules will they follow? Interacting across these two levels involves maximizing accountability while minimizing the chance that political extremists will defect. Third, transitional justice efforts normally take place in economically disadvantaged countries with high levels of inequality. For these countries, moving toward development involves interaction between foreign investors, weak public financing institutions, potentially corrupt leaders and weak private capital. Transitional justice measures cut across these interactions. They can, for example, be a tactic for shoring up outside foreign aid (Duthie 2008), which has been shown retrogressively to insulate African regimes from private capital (Widner 1994). Or alternatively, they can be seen as possibly issuing commitments to counteract rent-seeking and corruption, as discussions over transitional justice in contemporary Kenya reveal.[29] Moreover, reparations can also serve as a method of leveling the playing field for the economically disadvantaged (Duthie 2008).[30]

It is far beyond the scope of this chapter to provide a sufficiently rigorous game-theoretic analysis,[31] but simply modeling choices as a result of nested games is instructive in three ways. First, it helps conceptually arrange facts that we already know about transitional justice. To begin, transitional justice choices do not necessarily trade off between retribution and truth seeking (Sikkink and Walling 2007). Of the 59 regimes that have instituted some form of accountability mechanism, 14 have had both retributive and truth-seeking types. In Chile, for example, the transitional regime in 1990 established a truth and reconciliation commission, which was followed by the beginning of long-term domestic trials in 1991, along with various reparations policies passed in law starting in 1992. All this was followed by yet another truth commission on torture in 2004. Individual tools are thus sequenced into complex equilibrium strategies during uncertain initial stages of transition, and they constitute larger policies of accountability that can grow to be more institutionalized afterward.[32] Second, the embeddedness of individual transitional justice "tools" within larger strategies and institutional changes means that effects on the polity are the subject of endogeneity, that is their effects may be attributable to other changes concurrently taking place (Brahm 2007; cf. Call 2007). It might be difficult, for example, to disentangle the contributions of transitional justice mechanisms from those made by constitutional changes, institutional reforms and legalistic peace settlements.

Third and finally, assessments of usefulness of transitional justice decisions, *sui generis*, cannot be made in comparison to what seems most appropriate to activists or what seems most expedient to realists. To quote George Tsebelis (1991, p. 7) "if, with adequate information, an actor's choices appear to be suboptimal, it is because the observer's perspective is incomplete. The observer focuses attention on only one game, but the actors are involved in a whole network of games." Transitional justice policies are the result of decisions that incorporate a rational calculation of political-economic payoffs in a variety of arenas. Policymakers must weigh risks to institutional capacity and resumption of violence against the benefits of legitimacy and development that come from meeting swelling domestic demands for accountability. As such, their strategies are not necessarily stuck somewhere between principle and pragmatism, as some have suggested (Vinjamuri and Snyder 2004); they are themselves the essence of pragmatic action because they are made in the balance between multiple competing demands. Like all pragmatic strategies, they must be evaluated on the basis of their consequences.

20.3.3   Consequence

We saw that functionalist research has generated a number of hopeful claims about the overall social desirability of accountability mechanisms, while critics presume that they are only a global fad with unproven or inimical results. On the other hand, recognizing transitional justice as nested suggests that the appropriateness or the rationality of policies should not be judged outright, but rather on the basis of their strategic consequences over time. In the words of Cherif Bassiouni (2002, p. 40), we must look at each mechanism "as an instrument of social policy designed to achieve a particular set of outcomes which are not exclusively justice-based." Consequences, or more positively impact, may be assessed with individual, social structural or state level components (cf. van der Merwe, Baxter and Chapman 2009). At the individual level, a growing number of studies have looked directly at the effect of transitional justice policies on victim's attitudes and public opinion. James Gibson, for one, has built a productive survey research program in South Africa around the notion that successful reconciliation means that individuals in the aggregate positively value the work of the TRC and understand it to have served justice aims (Gibson 2002, 2004; cf. Pham and Vinck 2007). Harvey Weinstein, through extensive interview evidence, has argued that a hard test for effectiveness in reconstruction is whether individuals can learn to live aside one another in the aftermath of atrocity (Fletcher and Weinstein 2002; Halpern and Weinstein 2004).

Social structural approaches have looked more at the effect of transitional justice on the constitution of and relationship between groups. With mixed results, some have observed how trials and truth commissions stir up or marginalize nationalist and ethnic group politics (Weinstein and

Stover 2004; Stromseth, Wippman and Brooks 2006); whether official transitional justice policies can be localized or can reach group inequalities in rural areas (Shaw 2007; Arriaza and Roht-Arriaza 2008); or if gender relations are at all affected by accountability mechanisms (Askin 2003; Bell and O'Rourke 2007; Campbell 2007; Hamber 2007). Deep research into attitudes and group behavior is invaluable, but it is wont to produce larger, generalized conclusions about the strategic ramifications of accountability within transitional processes. If there is any conclusion that may be drawn from these studies, it is that individuals and groups experience conflict and its resolution in disparate, highly contingent ways.

Individual and group behavior collects to form state-level characteristics. If people do not operate within the rules outlined by institutions, this will lead to institutional deformity, dysfunction or collapse. If people re-arm, organize and fight, the expression of this will be macro-social instances of violence. Arguably, then, priority should be given to systematic research that can evaluate the macro-level costs or benefits that accrue to those transitional regimes which pursue strategies of accountability. The new vanguard of cross-national comparative research is performing this task, weighing out the independent and interactive effects of transitional justice measures on aggregated state features like democratic institutionalization, human rights compliance and absence of violent conflict. Some have generated positive assessments. In a scientifically rigorous study of 93 democratizing countries, Kim and Sikkink (2010) find that trials drive down repression levels, even controlling for the presence of violent conflict. Theoretically, the authors further argue that the threat of future trials serves to deter leaders from considering repressive policies.[33] In a World Bank working paper that modeled the presence of multiple accountability mechanisms, Lie et al. (2007) discovered a relationship between use of truth commissions and the duration of peace following conflict termination. The authors also show that amnesties exhibit a peace-shortening effect.

On the other side are those that issue a negative assessment based on the unnecessary risks accountability poses to peace. Most notably, Snyder and Vinjamuri (2003/4) issue an incisive statement against trials, claiming that they impose avoidable risks during peace processes by antagonizing potential spoilers. In their analysis of 32 post-conflict cases, they also write that whatever successes have been assigned to truth commissions are more likely attributable to amnesties, which facilitated bargaining between fighting groups.[34] Other large-N analyses have shown little to no effect for transitional justice of any kind on democracy or repression (Brahm 2006). Finally, though hypotheses concerning economic repercussions have been expounded, few studies have managed to demonstrate any clear linkage between the use of accountability mechanisms and the invigoration of hindrance of economic development.

Despite the promise of these studies, which tackle complexities of sequencing and interaction, there are three concerns with research performed thus far. First, just about every comparative assessment of transitional justice effects examines a different universe of cases. Where some look specifically at countries transiting to democracy (Kritz 1995), others analyse solely post-conflict or post-atrocity states (Bassiouni 2002). Ambiguities over what "a state is supposed to be transitioning *to*" have been built into the field since its emergence (Leebaw 2008, p. 101). One could fault the historical inaccuracies of the "transitions paradigm" itself because it tautologically assumes that regimes have a future evolutionary direction toward democratic consolidation, when in fact regime changes are resulting in institutionalized "gray zones" (Carothers 2002). Or, one could simply blame lack of clear classification of cases on the part of scholars examining these issues (Roht-Arriaza and Mariezcurrena 2006). Regardless, the expansive range of contexts in which transitional justice might apply has created inconsistency among empirical studies. In the words of one scholar, confusion exists over the questions of "when to compare" and "how to compare," which bear directly on the results of policy evaluation (Backer 2009).

Second, scholars diverge in their very definitions of successes and failures. For example, Snyder and Vinjamuri (2003/4, p.26) deem the Argentine case to be a failure because trials "risked provoking disturbances or even a coup by unreconciled elements of the officers corps." Sikkink and Walling (2007, pp. 439–41) disagree on this score. They view Argentina to be a success because no actual interruption of democracy ever occurred, repression scores indicate that abuses of rights are lower in the aftermath of trials, and trials allowed citizens to "discover rule of law."[35] That the same case is read in two different ways is a grave concern, one worth addressing in future treatments. An explanation for this divergence is that empirical researchers are observing different dependent variables. Some are focused on the sustainability of peace, while others are focused on the maintenance of institutional democracy and the protection of rights. This creates a moving target in terms of what transitional justice is supposed to accomplish.

Third and finally, newer empirical assessments face a negativity bias. Positive assessments are saddled with the burden of proving a progressive impact of embedded mechanisms, rather than simply proving the negative – that they do no unique harm amidst larger processes (that is, they must show that *increases* in transitional justice causally generate *increases* in democratic institutionalization, peace and so forth). Because it is difficult to hold all other sources of variation constant, especially in transitional scenarios when institutions and strategies are under simultaneous alteration, large scale empirical research has struggled to produce substantively significant findings, leading some to highlight their inconclusiveness (Thoms et al. 2008). However, few to no studies have shown, using statistical controls or counterfactuals, that accountability mechanisms actually create substantively *negative* effects on the polity. Instead, those studies that issue negative assessments simply elaborate the difficulties of pursuing accountability or the uncertainty of positive findings to illustrate their rationale.

20.4   REASSESSING TRANSITIONAL JUSTICE

Looking at these three issues with systematic research into consequences, and keeping in mind the embedded nature of transitional justice strategies, I make three suggestions for a comparative re-assessment of consequences. First, the cases in which "transitional justice" might apply should be better classified on the basis of type and timing of the political transition. Second, because the central axis of contention within studies of macro-social impact is over whether accountability mechanisms grease or derail larger democratic and peace-building processes of transition, one should retrospectively judge success and failure on the basis of whether accountability policies were part of a conglomerate strategy which has ultimately managed to sustain moves toward institutional liberal democracy and peace in the wake of transition. Furthermore, addressing the negativity bias means giving specific focus to failure, and the avoidance thereof. Rather than attempting to locate end points of unmitigated success like consolidation or stability, one should think of both democracy and peace as ongoing processes that are operational when they are not being disrupted.

20.4.1   Classifying Type of Transition

Influential transitional justice expert Neil Kritz (2009) writes that a main avenue for the future contribution of empirical scholarship on transitional justice practice will be the classification of types of transition.[36] This is important for two reasons, one methodological and one theoretical: first, defining a general set of cases is necessary for cross-national comparison that avoids selection on the dependent variable (Geddes 1990); second, an adequately detailed typology of transitions can create placeholder categories that correspond to constraining domestic structural configurations.

More research in the future should be devoted to this second issue, but I focus mainly on the first: how to construct a pool of comparable cases. The most exhaustive effort to generate a universe of potential transitional justice cases is provided by David Backer (2009, p. 27), who lists 114 transition cases based on their shared "experience of initiating a transition that could in principle permit or induce increased scrutiny of past injustices." Vague in this account, however, is what satisfies the "transition" or "in principle" clauses. I reproduce a list of cases, with regime as the unit, using more explicit inclusion criteria. Ni Aolain and Campbell (2005, p. 183) argue for "the need to conceive of transitional situations not as involving one single transition, but in terms of at least two primary sets: a movement towards democracy . . . and that towards peace" (cf. Karl 2005). Figure 20.1 presents a universe of transitional regimes that is organized along these two dimensions: whether they exhibited a 3-point move toward institutional democracy on the often-used Polity IV scale[37]; and whether they followed the sustained termination of a period of major, violent, intrastate conflict.[38]

Regimes that experience both types of transition within two years of one another are included in the middle of the Venn diagram.[39] Those that lie outside the diagram represent cases which have been treated as "transitional" cases by Backer, but did not experience a move toward minimal democracy or the termination of violent conflict. (In this sense, these may be seen as pre-transition cases.)

20.4.2   A Glance at Success and Failure

Within the entire universe of cases from 1970 to 2007, 64 of 151 total transitional regimes have made use of at least one measure to achieve human rights accountability.[40] Within the regimes that have experienced either of the two forms of transition, that number is 56. I use a hard test for success in reference to the 96 democratic transitions. If they either reverted to non-democratic forms of governance, or if they saw the continuation or resumption of violent conflict, I list them as failures.[41] For the 46 cases of conflict termination, I list them as failures simply if they later resume violent patterns of conflict. Finally, for the pre-transitional cases that match neither of the criteria, a general failure rate is not possible to determine because there had been no transition. However, it can be argued that those which instituted transitional justice and did not see a future democratic transition or end to violent conflict were failures.

Table 20.2 presents summary numbers on regimes which have experienced failure so defined. There are four tentative conclusions one can draw from these basic statistics. First, for each type of transition, the baseline failure percentage is lower for those regimes that have instituted some

Other

Afghanistan (2002)
Algeria (1999)
Angola (1994)
Burundi (1993)
Cambodia (1979)
Cameroon (1990)
Chad (1990)
Croatia (1991)
Ecuador (1996)
Gambia (1996)
Georgia (2003)
Gabon (1990)
India (1977)
N = 27

Iraq (2003)
Kazakhstan (1993)
Kenya (1992)
Kyrgyzstan (2005)
Madagascar (2002)
Mauritania (1992)
Morocco (1999)
Peru (1990)
Sri Lanka (1994)
Tanzania (1992)
Tunisia (1987)
Turkmenistan (1992)
Uganda (1985–1986)
Uzbekistan (1991)

Democratic Transitions

Albania (1990–1992)
Algeria (2004)
Argentina (1983)
Armenia (1991–1994)
Armenia (1998)
Azerbaijan (1992)
Belarus (1991)
Benin (1990–1992)
Bolivia (1982)
Brazil (1985)
Bulgaria (1990)
Burkina Faso (1978)
Burundi (2000)
Cambodia (1991)
CAR (1991)
Chile (1989)
Comoros (1990)
Comoros (2002)
Republic of Congo (1992)
Cote de Ivoire (2000)
Czech Republic (1993)
Dominican Republic (1978)
Djibouti (1999)
Ecuador (1979)
El Salvador (1980)

N = 98

Estonia (1991)
Fiji (1990)
Germany (1990)
Ghana (1992)
Greece (1974)
Guyana (1992)
Guinea-Bissau (1994)
Guinea-Bissau (2005)
Haiti (1991)
Haiti (1993–1994)
Haiti (2004)
Honduras (1980–1982)
Hungary (1989)
Indonesia (1999)
Kenya (2002)
Kyrgyzstan (2005)
Latvia (1991–1993)
Lebanon (2005)
Lesotho (1998–1999)
Lithuania (1992)
Macedonia (1991)
Madagascar (1991–1992)
Malawi (1994)
Mali (1990–1992)
Mauritania (2007)
Mexico (1994–1996)
Moldova (1992–1994)
Mongolia (1990)
Montenegro (2006)
Namibia (1990)
Nepal (1990)
Niger (1991–1992)
Nigeria (1979)
Nigeria (1998–1999)
Pakistan (1988)
Panama (1989–1991)
Philippines (1986)
Poland (1989)

Portugal (1974)
Romania (1989–1990)
Russia (1992)
Senegal (2000)
Sierra Leone (1996)
Slovakia (1993)
Solomon Islands (2004)
South Korea (1987)
Spain (1975)
Sudan (1986)
Taiwan (1992)
Thailand (1992)
Turkey (1983)
Ukraine (1991)
Uruguay (1985)
Zambia (1991)

Bangladesh (1992)
Cambodia (1999)
Croatia (1999)
DRC (2001–2004)
Ethiopia (1991–1994)
Georgia (1991–1993)
Guatemala (1994–1996)

Guinea-Buissau (1999)
Liberia (2003)
Mozambique (1992–1994)
Nepal (2006)
Nicaragua (1988–1990)
Niger (1996–1999)
Paraguay (1989–1992)
Peru (1999–2000)
Sierra Leone (2001)
South Africa (1991–1994)
Timor-Leste (1999)

Major Violent Conflict Termination

Argentina (1978)
Azerbaijan (1996)
Bosnia (1995)
Cameroon (1985)
DRC (1979)
El Salvador (1992)
India (1972)
Iraq (1998)
Serbia/ former Yugo (1991)
Laos (1974)
Laos (1991)
Lebanon (1989)
Liberia (1996)
Morocco (199)
Northern Ireland (1992)
Northern Ireland(1998)
Pakistan (1979)
Papua New Guinea (1996)
Republic of Congo (2003)

Rwanda (1994)
Rwanda (2003)
Sri Lanka (1972)
Tajikistan (1997)
Thailand (1983)
Yemen (1995)
Zimbabwe (1979)

N = 46

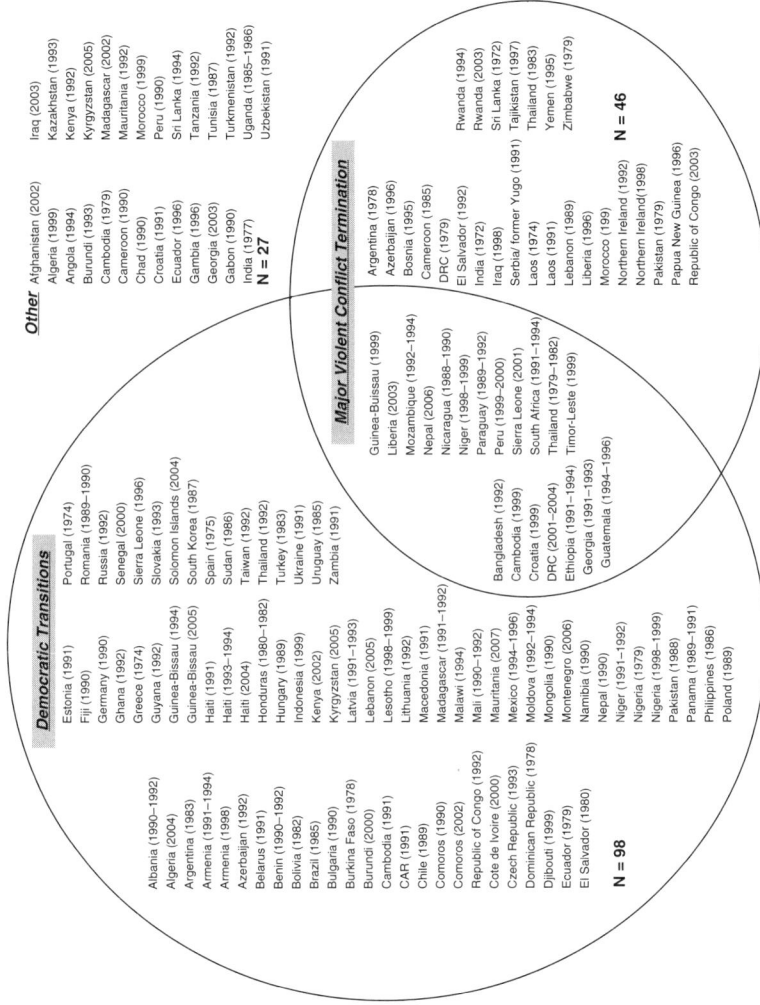

Figure 20.1   Universe of transition regimes, 1970–2007

Table 20.2.   Successes and failures of transitional regimes[42]

	(I) Total	(II) Failures	(III) % Total	(IV) TJ Regime	(V) TJ Failures	(VI) % TJ Failure
Democratization	98	36	36.7%	48	16	33.3%
Major termination	46	15	32.6%	20	4	20.0%
Double transitions	20	7	35.0%	12	2	16.7%
Total transitions	**124**	**47**	**37.9%**	**55**	**18**	**32.7%**
Pre-transitions	27	–	–	8	6	75.0%

form of transitional justice. For democratizations, it is only slightly lower (by 3.4 percent). But for those regimes emerging from major conflicts or experiencing double transitions, those that use transitional justice mechanisms have much lower failure percentage (12.6 percent and 18.3 percent lower, respectively). That it is possible to reach different conclusions about failure – and thus the capacities of accountability efforts – depending on what sample of regimes are analysed shows the importance of being careful and lucid when selecting which types of cases to compare. Also, from these findings one could argue that transitional justice is not necessarily as ill-equipped for addressing post-conflict situations as some have expected. In fact, in those cases where countries are simultaneously undergoing the termination of violent conflict and democratization, transitional justice strategies have a positive, fairly consistent track record.

Second, when totaled, the failure rate for all transitional justice regimes is still less by 5.2 percent, though some variation across transition types is lost. The reason the overall effect seems less is that that when failure rates are separated by type, double-transition regimes that resumed violent conflict or regressed into non-democracy are counted twice. Not so in the total figure, which shows that any transitional strategies that including accountability mechanisms are generally effective around 67 percent of the time. Third, 18 total transitional cases, and six pre-transitional cases, may be considered justice failures, yielding a definitive list of 24.[43] Fourth, pre-transitional regimes that pursued some form of accountability were much more likely to fail, indicating that at its best, accountability works in the context of already-existing transitions, rather than prior to their existence. Not shown in the table are similar figures on amnesty processes. Fifty-five transitional regimes used amnesties, and of these, 25 were failures (45.5 percent). However, it should be noted that of the 36 cases coded as successful transitional justice regimes, a clear majority of 21 also used amnesty somewhere along the process (58.3 percent).

I make no pretense that these statistics are overwhelmingly robust, nor are they intended to be. At best, they are suggestive. For one, they do not control statistically for the effects of other variables. Additionally, they cannot account for time, causality, the sequence of events or variation in accountability measures themselves. However, as described earlier, among different regimes, the use of various tactics follows highly dynamic variation. The contribution of this brief exposition is to show, first, how one might go about defining regime successes and failures in a systematic and exhaustive fashion. Second, it makes the case that accountability mechanisms, embedded within larger strategic efforts, do not seem to present uniquely insuperable costs to peace or democracy – or at least costs that go beyond those transitional regimes already face.

20.5   CONCLUDING REMARKS

Transitional justice practices are ensconced within multiple overlapping efforts to produce peace and good governance in the contemporary world. More civil wars are ending with negotiated settlements, more constitutions are being written, more elections are being held and more postconflict development programs are afoot. Amidst these trends, measures are being taken to ensure that people are held accountable for their derogations from international law. The question of primary focus has become, are accountability mechanisms effective? Do they quell conflict? Do they generate democratic values? Answers to these questions are mixed, partially because it is hard to isolate these mechanisms from their transitional surroundings, to place in stylized relief the impact of single policies. Though empirical research has presented only tenuous evidence of positive, progressive effects thus far, it should be stated that no systematic negative evidence regarding consequences has been produced. One cannot claim that transitional justice has led to the resumption of violent conflict, nor can one say that it has prevented the advance of liberal democracy or economic development. On this basis, what I argue is that efforts to achieve accountability do not necessarily present unique disruptions to the processes in which they are embedded. "The assumption should be," as former chief prosecutor of the ICTR Louise Arbour (2008) states, "that judicial and political processes can be allowed to advance simultaneously" At the same time, contending that transitional justice is a panacea, or a universal good, would be rash. This chapter is not meant to be a rearguard defense of all transitional justice practices. The argument that I present cannot address the economic efficiency or the quality of governance within post-transitional regimes. Nor does it speak to qualitative variations in accountability processes themselves. Sometimes transitional justice is "hijacked" by self-interested leaders in an effort to manipulate the public (Subotic 2009; also see Bell 2008, p. 256), and other times it is stillborn into underfunded and poorly sequenced mechanisms (Quinn 2004).

This review and brief assessment has a number of suggestive implications for future research. First, modelers of decision-making might delve deeper into the processes that bridge international norms and domestic transitional justice actions. Though some have done theory-building case study research in this regard (for example, Subotic 2005; Kim 2009), fewer efforts have been made to produce deductive logics that capture the interplay between levels of normative structure and intentional action. Second, the field ought to pay keener attention to developments in the literature on the political economy of regime change, which is moving back toward new and innovative ways that reintroduce structural factors in dynamic models (for example, Acemoglu and Robinson 2006). If economic structures are truly at root of regime change and institutional success, then it will become more important to draw theoretical "connections" between transitional justice, inequality and development (see de Greiff and Duthie 2009). Third, observers should study "failure" cases, those transitional regimes that were not able to sustain their moves toward democracy and cessation of violent conflict, and using counterfactual reasoning attempt to determine whether accountability played a role in their failures. Otherwise, claims about the inescapable dangers of pursuing justice amidst transition cannot be convincingly substantiated. Fourth, research should continue to model sequenced, non-linear strategies of transitional justice in an effort to analyse what mechanisms work in combination at different stages of the process. Also, it should focus more on the specifics of mechanisms across cases, for example, the publicity of truth commission reports, to discover whether variation in these institutional details has generalizable effects. One promising new volume from Leigh Payne and her associates could serve as a starting point for those interested in tackling these issues in an exhaustive and methodological rigorous fashion (see Payne et al. forthcoming). Fifth and finally, researchers should resist blanket statements about the quality of decisions by comparing them to an "ideal" (see Sikkink 2008). No state will catapult itself to fully realized social justice, fair institutions and commodious living on the back of incipient accountability mechanisms. It is likely that transitional justice, like all other political actions, will leave demands unsatisfied, but that does not mean it should be rejected or consigned to the realm of the unworthy.

ACKNOWLEDGEMENTS

Many thanks to Kathryn Sikkink, David Samuels, Bud Duvall, Eric Wiebelhaus-Brahm and Leigh Payne for thorough and productive comments on the manuscript, and to Hunjoon Kim, Moira Lynch and Eric Wiebelhaus-Brahm for sharing data from their own projects. I am also grateful to Catherine Guisan, David Forrest, Giovanni Mantilla, Dara McCracken, Ralitsa Donkova and other participants in the Minnesota International Relations Colloquium (MIRC) for their constructive feedback. Finally, I would like to extend special thanks to Menaka Philips, without whose editorial comments this chapter would never have found its current form.

NOTES

1. Catherine O'Rourke (2009, p.269) defines "transitional justice" as "the legal and quasi-legal mechanisms used by societies emerging from conflict and repression in order to address the human rights violations committed during the period of violence. For the UN definition of the term, see UN S/2004/616. "The rule of law and transitional justice in conflict and post-conflict societies," 23 August 2004.
2. This chapter will make use of a dataset that has been compiled by the author. This dataset borrows extensively from other quantitative and qualitative sources. These include Kathryn Sikkink and Hunjoon Kim's Transitional Rights Trials Database, Louise Mallinder's (2008) Amnesty Law Database, Dancy, Kim and Wiebelhaus-Braum (2010) truth commission database, and David Backer's (2009) list of transition cases. I also owe Moira Lynch for her compilation of vetting and lustration cases.
3. Ruti Teitel (2008) lays claim to this phrase in an editorial note within the *International Journal of Transitional Justice.*
4. For definitions of amnesty, see Mallinder (2008) and Bassiouni (2002); for trials, see Sikkink and Walling (2007); for truth commissions, see Hayner (2001) and Dancy et al. (2010); for lustration, Kaminski and Nalepa (2008); and for reparations, see de Greiff (2006).
5. On Iraq and Afghanistan, see Stover (2005) and Rubin (2003). On use of the term "conflicted democracy," see Ni Aolain and Campbell (2005). I borrow "pre-post-conflict" from Joanna Quinn, who used the term when presenting her extensive field research in Uganda at the 2009 International Studies Association Annual Conference.
6. Which have been exhaustively and usefully arranged by Andrew Reiter at the Wisconsin Transitional Justice Data Base Project, http://users.polisci.wisc.edu/tjdb/bib.htm.
7. Originally, functionalism had British anthropological and Marxist structural variants. I used "functionalist" in a slightly different way to mean the assumption that tools are created solely to perform a specific task, or that specific institutions arise when a particular function needs to be performed. For more on functionalism, see Elster (1982). For the relationship between institutions and functionalism, see Keohane (1984, Chapter 6).
8. These types of arguments also apply to the use of lustration, vetting and reparations. For the sake of brevity, I omit detailed claims about these mechanisms.
9. Judith Shklar (1986, p. 1) defines legalism as "the ethical attitude that holds that moral conduct is to be a matter of rule following, and moral relationships to consist of duties and rights determined by rules." For more on the legal precedent for punishment, see

Ruti Teitel (1995, p. 148), who counters that it requires "interpretive leaps" to make a case for punishment using international law (see also Scharf 1996). It is worth noting that Orentlicher has modified her arguments to some extent over time. See Orentlicher (2007).

10. "Reconciliation" was self-reflexively used by Desmond Tutu to justify the amnesty-for-testimony compromise that was built into truth and reconciliation (TRC) procedure. A capacious term, many scholars have attempted to discover its essence by equating it with a host of other reducible concepts. These include, negatively, tolerance, co-existence or reconstruction; and, positively, harmony, empathy and erasure of hatred, among others (Crocker 2000; Gutman and Thompson 2000; Fletcher and Weinstein 2002; Mendeloff 2004; Halpern and Weinstein 2004).

11. Critical reflection has also turned on the political ramifications of the discourses of "truth." Scholars have pondered the modernist roots of the belief that an apolitical, objective truth can be discovered, especially by those operating within the state, or if a gap exists between macro-level truth and micro-level truths (Norval 1999; Lundy 2009; cf. Chapman and Ball 2001).

12. In this respect, argues de Greiff, "reconciliation" is a term very similar to "happiness."

13. Zerilli (1998, p. 11), citing Ernesto Laclau on the topic of empty signifiers like the word "liberal," writes "The universal cannot be fixed because it 'does not have a concrete content of its own but is an always preceding horizon resulting from an indefinite expansion of equivalent demands.' Put slightly differently, universal is just another word for placeholder of the 'absent fullness of the community.' It can never actually *be* that fullness – not even as a regulative ideal."

14. On the concept of recognitional legitimacy, see Buchanan (2004).

15. I adopt the definition set forth by Cortell and Davis (2000, p. 68–9) in their comprehensive research note on the role of international norms in domestic politics: norms are "prescriptions for action in situations of choice."

16. There is a high degree of nuance in these theories. Huntington actually separates transitions into three types: transplacements, replacements and transformations. Linz (1978) uses rupture and reforma as categories.

17. See, in general, Rotberg and Thompson (2000).

18. Jon Elster (2004, p. 213) writes, "Funds, personnel, and political attention may be channeled into such forward-looking tasks as constitution making, economic reconstruction, or economic transformation, rather than into the backward tasks of trials and purges."

19. Here I make use of the dataset referenced in Endnote. 2 for the purpose of factual analysis.

20. This amounts to roughly 25 percent of all transitional justice regimes. On the confusions in mission this has created in places like Sierra Leone, see Schabas and Darcy (2004).

21. The maximum number of years between transition and trials was in Uruguay, while the maximum number of years between transition and truth commission was in Paraguay.

22. The Haitian Truth Commission cost around US$1 million, while the South African TRC cost US$35 million. See Chapman (2009).

23. This study argues that the normative environment is shaped by the actions of UN mediation and peacekeeping efforts, along with the regional diffusion of transitional justice mechanisms.

24. Kim (2009) uses two specifications of "neighbors." The first is those regional states which are culturally similar, and the other is those states that are geographically contiguous.

25. Or in the words of another group of scholars, "They [policymakers] faced many questions presented above, but most of them paid little attention to the experiences of other countries that had implemented transitional justice procedures" (Kaminski, Nalepa and O'Neil 2006, p. 298).

26. The exception here is Kim (2009), who, citing Anthony Giddens, models this process as one of structuration (see Chapter 1 for a discussion).

27. An important note is that civil society and negotiation processes can, and normally do, have both national and international dimensions. In this way, they combine exogenous and endogenous processes of institutional formation. However, it is mainly, with few exceptions, regime leaders who make transitional justice decisions.
28. See Article 5, Section 8, https://www.trcofliberia.org/about/trc-mandate.
29. "A Faulty Legislative Process to Combat Impunity", *Africa News*, 18 February 2009.
30. At the same time, large-scale efforts at justice might deplete human capital, which works against the functioning of the market economy, thereby creating heavy opportunity costs (Boettke and Coyne 2007).
31. Nor do I think that a game-theoretic approach is theoretically impervious to criticism. It is, of course, plausible to argue that actors in these situations do not have clear preferences, that decisions are not strategic and that there are multiple equilibria. I concede these arguments; however, thinking of transitional justice as strategy is, I think, accurate given that a great deal of thought goes into shaping these processes. To ignore this fact would be historically inaccurate.
32. This echoes observation within the field of transitional justice that transitional justice usually proceeds in a non-linear fashion.
33. There is a widespread debate in criminology over the potential deterrent effect of punishment. For a discussion of this in the context of transitional justice, see Mennecke (2007).
34. Louise Mallinder (2008) comes to a similar conclusion about the use of amnesties in particular. In a magisterial work, she carefully categorizes amnesty types while also arguing that they can be put to use in particular strategic contexts to facilitate demobilization and power-sharing arrangements.
35. On the "discovery of rule of law" concept, see Smulovitz (2002).
36. This should be distinguished from characteristics of the transition itself, like balance of power and so forth.
37. For a summary of the Polity IV data, see Marshall, Jaggers and Gurr (2006). To define "democratic transitions," I chose all of those cases which had a 3-score increase over the threshold of 0. If the 3-point change was incremental, I began coding in the year of the first signs of upward movement.
38. I define "major violent conflict termination" using the UCDP/PRIO Armed Conflict Dataset, version 4-2009 (see Gleditsch et al. 2002). These cases where generated using the following steps: (1) I selected out all years before 1970; (2) I chose those conflicts that were coded by the UCDP/PRIO Armed Conflict Dataset Codebook, version (available at www.ucdp.uu.se) as "internal" or "internationalized internal" wars using the "Type" variable; (3) I selected as major all of those conflicts which reached a historical threshold of 1000 deaths using the cumulative intensity ("CumInt") variable; (4) I coded as "one" every country-year that reached a threshold of 25 battle deaths within that major conflict (derived from "Startdate2"); 5) I then applied a three-year rule to determine the conflict's end, meaning that if the conflict did not resume in time (t) through time (t+3), it was considered to be terminated starting at time (t).
39. Karl (2005) refers to these as "double transitions." In these cases, I apply a three-year rule: if a major conflict transition and a democratic transition occur within three years of one another, I consider them to be concurrent events; otherwise, I coded them as separate. A few cases would seem double transitions but do not fall within this coding scheme. For example, Argentina is a major conflict termination in 1977, then a democratic transition seven years later in 1983. For this reason, it is coded as two separate transitional regimes.
40. I refer to these transitional justice regimes, or "TJ Regimes." I include international trials, hybrid trials, domestic trials, truth commissions and lustration in the category of accountability mechanism. In my aggregate measure, I make no distinction between retributive and restorative types, though the conventional wisdom is to suspect that these have different effects. In this summary, I am more interested in whether any form of accountability was sought. I do not consider amnesty to be a strategy of

accountability, so it is coded separately. I also do not include reparations because of limited data availability.

41. For this reason, the data I use are right-censored, meaning that they end with time period chosen. "Reversion" is defined as a loss of three points or more on the Polity II scale. "Recurrence" is defined building on my measure for "major conflict termination." After a major conflict termination, which lasts three years, if the regime again begins fighting an internal war where the cumulative intensity ("CumInt") is coded as 1, I code it as a recurrence. Doing so this way eliminates those cases where peace is held tenuously for only a year or two, then resumes in its previous form. Coding recurrences by each year without the three-year rule would artificially inflate the number in this period to 90 because many cases where the conflict did not actually end would be included; instead, by being more selective, I come to 15 clear cases of termination followed by resumption.

42. The number of "total transitions" is not a sum of the three above categories because that would count double transitions twice. This number is the total of democratic transitions and major violent conflict transitions summed.

43. These include Algeria (2004), the Central African Republic (1991), Haiti (1991), Haiti (1993–94), Indonesia (1999), Mali (1990–92), Nepal (1990), Niger (1991–92), Nigeria (1998–9), Philippines (1986), Sierra Leone (1996), Spain (1975), Thailand (1992), Turkey (1983), DRC (2001), Ethiopia (1991–93), Serbia/former Yugoslavia (1991), Rwanda (1994), Burundi (1993), Chad (1990), India (1977), Iraq (2003), Sri Lanka (1994) and Uganda (1986).

44. "Democratic transitions" include those cases where a country experienced a 3-point increase in its Polity IV (over a threshold of 0). It also includes cases of divorce that transited to democratic regime. See Endnote 38 for "violent conflict terminations." The outside "other" category includes cases of adverse regime change, onset of illiberal multi-party elections, divorce that transited to non-democratic regimes, international interventions and others listed in Backer (2009).

REFERENCES

Acemoglu, D. and J.A. Robinson (2006), *Economic Origins of Dictatorship and Democracy*, New York, NY: Cambridge University Press.

Addison, T. (2009), "The political economy of the transition from authoritarianism" in P. de Greif and R. Duthie (eds), *Transitional Justice and Development: Making Connection*, Advancing Transitional Justice Series, International Center for Transitional Justice, New York, NY: Social Science Research Council, pp. 110–41.

Akhavan, P. (2001), "Beyond impunity: can international criminal justice prevent future atrocities?", *The American Journal of International Law*, **95** (1), 7–31.

Amstutz, M.R. (2005), *The Healing of Nations: The Promise and Limits of Political Forgiveness*, Lanham, MD: Rowman & Littlefield Publishers.

Arbour, L. (2008) "Justice v. politics: international justice", *The International Herald Tribune*. 17 September 2008.

Arenhövel, M. (2008), "Democratization and transitional justice", *Democratization*, **15** (3), 570–87.

Arriaza, L. and N. Roht-Arriaza (2008), "Social reconstruction as a local process", *International Journal of Transitional Justice*, **2**, 152–72.

Arthur, P. (2009), "How 'transitions' reshaped human rights: a conceptual history of transitional justice", *Human Rights Quarterly*, **31**, 329–67.

Ash, T. G. (1997), "True confession", *New York Review of Books*, 17 July, 36–7.

Askin, K.D. (2003), "The quest for post-conflict gender justice", *Columbia Journal of Transnational Law*, **41** (3), 509–22.

Asmal, K., L. Asmal and R.S. Robert (1996), *Reconciliation through Truth: A Reckoning of Apartheid's Criminal Governance*. Cape Town, South Africa: David Philip Publishers.

Backer, D. (2009), "Cross-national comparative analysis", in H. van der Merwe, V. Baxter and A.R. Chapman (eds) *Assessing the Impact of Transitional Justice: Challenges for Empirical Research,* Washington DC: United States Institute of Peace Press, pp. 23–90.

Barahona de Brita, Alexandra (2003), "Passion, constraint, law and fortuna: the human rights challenge to Chilean democracy", in N. Biggar (ed.) *Burying the Past: Making Peace and Doing Justice After Civil Conflict,* Washington DC: Georgetown University Press, pp. 177–208.

Bassiouni, M.C. (ed) (2002), *Post-conflict Justice.* International and Comparative Criminal Law Series. Ardsley, NY: Transnational Publishers.

Bell, C., C. Campbell and F. Ni Aolain (2004), "Justice discourses in transition", *Social Legal Studies* **13** (3), 305.

Bell, C. (2008), *On the Law of Peace: Peace Agreements and the Lex Pacificatoria,* Oxford, UK: Oxford University Press.

Bell, C. and C. O'Rourke (2007), "Does feminism need a theory of transitional justice? An introductory essay." *International Journal of Transitional Justice,* **1** (1), 23–44.

Bermeo, N. (2003), *Ordinary People in Extraordinary Times: The Citizenry and the Breakdown of Democracy,* Princeton, NY: Princeton University Press.

Bhargava, R. (2000), "Restoring decency to barbaric societies", in R. Rotberg and D. Thompson (eds) *Truth v. Justice,* Princeton, NY: Princeton University Press, pp. 45–67.

Boettke, P.J. and C.J. Coyne (2007), "Political economy of forgiveness", *Society,* **44** (2), 53–9.

Boraine, A. (2000a), *A Country Unmasked: Inside South Africa's Truth and Reconciliation Commission,* Oxford, UK: Oxford University Press.

Boraine, A. (2000b), "Truth and reconciliation in South Africa: The Third Way" in R. Rotberg and D. Thompson (eds) *Truth v. Justice,* Princeton, NJ: Princeton University Press, pp. 141–57.

Boraine, A. (2006), Transitional justice: a holistic interpretation. *Journal of International Affairs,* **60** (1), 17–27.

Brahm, Eric (2006), Truth and consequences: the impact of truth commissions in transitional societies, Ph.D. Dissertation, University of Colorado at Boulder.

Brahm, E. (2007), "Uncovering the truth: examining truth commission success and impact", *International Studies Perspectives,* **8**, 16–35.

Buchanan, A. (2004), *Justice, Legitimacy, and Self-Determination: Moral Foundations for International Law,* Oxford, UK: Oxford University Press.

Call, C.T. (2004), "Is transitional justice really just", *Brown Journal of World Affairs,* **11** (1), 101–13.

Call, C.T. (ed) (2007), *Constructing Justice and Security after War,* Washington DC: United States Institute of Peace Press.

Campbell, K. (2007), "The gender of transitional justice: law, sexual violence and the International Criminal Tribunal for the Former Yugoslavia", *International Journal of Transitional Justice,* **1** (3), 411–32.

Carothers, T. (2002), "The end of the transition paradigm", *Journal of Democracy,* **13** (1), 5–21.

Chapman, A. (2009), "Truth finding in the transitional justice process" in H. van der Merwe, V. Baxter and A.R. Chapman (eds) *Assessing the Impact of Transitional Justice: Challenges for Empirical Research,* Washington DC: United States Institute of Peace Press, pp. 91–114.

Chapman, A.R. and P. Ball (2001), "The truth of truth commissions: comparative lessons from Haiti, South Africa, and Guatemala", *Human Rights Quarterly,* **23**, 1–43.

Chesterman, S. (2007), "East Timor" in M. Berdal and S. Economides (eds) *United Nations Interventionism: 1991–2004,* New York, NY: Cambridge University Press.

Cole, E.A. (2007), "Introduction: reconciliation and history education" in E.A. Cole (ed.) *Teaching the Violent Past: History Education and Reconciliation,* Carnegie Council for Ethics in International Affairs, p. 13.

Cortell, A.P. and J.W. Davis, Jr. (2000), "Understanding the domestic impact of international norms: a research agenda", *International Studies Review,* **2** (1), 65–87.

Crocker, D. (2000), "Truth commissions, transitional justice, and civil society", in R. Rotberg and D. Thompson (eds) *Truth v. Justice*, Princeton, NJ: Princeton University Press, pp. 99–121.

Daly, E. (2008), "Truth skepticism: an inquiry into the value of truth in times of transition", *International Journal of Transitional Justice* **2** (1), 23–41.

Dancy, G., H. Kim and E. Wiebelhaus-Braum (2010), "The turn to truth: trends in truth commission experimentation", *Journal of Human Rights*, **9** (1), 45–64.

Dancy, G. and S.C. Poe (2006), "What comes before truth? The political determinants of truth commission initiation", ISA 47th Annual Convention, March 22–25, San Diego, CA.

David, R. and I. Holliday (2006), "Set the junta free: pre-transitional justice in Myanmar's democratization", *Australian Journal of Political Science*, **41** (1), 91–105.

Diamond, L. (2008), *The Spirit of Democracy*. New York, NY: Times Books.

Duthie, R. (2008), "Toward a development-sensitive approach to transitional justice", *The International Journal of Transitional Justice,* **2**, 292–309.

Duthie, R. (2009), "Introduction" in P. de Greiff and R. Duthie (eds), *Transitional Justice and Development: Making Connections,* Advancing Transitional Justice Series, International Center for Transitional Justice, New York, NY: Social Science Research Council, pp.17–27.

Du Toit, Andre (2000), "The moral foundations of the South African TRC: truth as acknowledgement and justice as recognition", in R. Rotberg and D. Thompson (eds) *Truth v. Justice,* Princeton, NJ: Princeton University Press, pp. 122–40.

Dwyer, S. (1999), "Reconciliation for realists", *Ethics and International Affairs* **13**, 81–98.

Elster, J. (1982), "The case for methodological individualism", *Theory and Society,* **11** (4), 453–82.

Elster, J. (2004), *Closing the Books: Transitional Justice in Historical Perspective*, Cambridge, UK: Cambridge University Press.

Finnemore, M. and K. Sikkink (1998), "International norm dynamics and political change," *International Organization* **52** (4), 887–917.

Forsberg, T. (2003), "The philosophy and practice of dealing with the past: some conceptual and normative issues", in N. Biggar (ed.), *Burying the Past: Making Peace and Doing Justice After Civil Conflict* , Washington DC: Georgetown University Press, pp. 65–86.

Fletcher, L.E. and H. Weinstein (2002), "Violence and social repair: rethinking the contribution of justice to reconciliation", *Human Rights Quarterly,* **24**, 573–639.

Geddes, B. (1990), "How the cases you choose affect the answers you get: selection bias in comparative politics", *Political Analysis*, **2**, 131–150.

Gibson, J.L. (2002), "Truth, justice, and reconciliation: judging the fairness of amnesty in South Africa", *American Journal of Political Science,* **46** (3), 540–56.

Gibson, J.L. (2004), "Does truth lead to reconciliation? Testing the causal assumptions of the South African truth and reconciliation process", *American Journal of Political Science,* **48** (2), 201–17.

Gibson, J.L. and A. Gouws (1999), "Truth and reconciliation in South Africa: attributions of blame and the struggle over apartheid", *The American Political Science Review*, **93** (3), 501–517.

Gleditsch, N.P., P. Wallensteen, M. Eriksson, M. Sollenberg and H. Strand (2002), "Armed conflict 1946–2001: a new dataset", *Journal of Peace Research*, **39** (5), 615–37.

De Greiff, P. (ed.) (2006), *The Handbook of Reparations*, Oxford, UK: Oxford University Press.

De Grieff, P. (2008), "The role of apologies in national reconciliation processes: on making trustworthy institutions trusted" in M. Gibney, Mark (ed.), *The Age of Apology: Facing Up to the Past*, Pennsylvania Studies in Human Rights. Philadelphia, PA: University of Pennsylvania Press, pp 120–136.

De Grieff, P. (2009), "Articulating the links between transitional justice and development: justice and social integration", in P. de Greiff and R. Duthie (eds), *Transitional Justice and Development: Making Connections,* Advancing Transitional Justice Series, International

Center for Transitional Justice, New York, NY: Social Science Research Council, pp. 28–75.

De Greiff, P. and R. Duthie (eds) (2009), *Transitional Justice and Development: Making Connections,* Advancing Transitional Justice Series, International Center for Transitional Justice, New York, NY: Social Science Research Council.

Gutmann, A. and D. Thompson (2000), "The moral foundations of truth commissions", in R. Rotberg and D. Thompson (eds), *Truth v. Justice,* Princeton, NJ: Princeton University Press, pp. 22–44.

Halpern, J. and H.M. Weinstein (2004), "Rehumanizing the other: empathy and reconciliation", *Human Rights Quarterly*, **26**, 561–83.

Hamber, B. (2007), "Masculinity and transitional justice: an exploratory essay", *International Journal of Transitional Justice*, **1** (3), 375–90.

Hayner, P.B. (2001), *Unspeakable Truths: Confronting State terror and Atrocities*, New York, NY: Routledge.

Huntington, S.P. (1968), *Political Order in Changing Societies,* London: Yale University Press.

Huntington, S.P. (1991), *The Third Wave: Democratization in the Late Twentieth Century*, J.J. Rothbaum Distinguished Lecture Series Vol. 4, Norman, UK: University of Oklahoma Press.

Huyse, L. (1995). "Justice after transition: on the choices successor elites make in dealing with the past", *Law & Social Inquiry*, **20** (1), 51–78.

Jelin, E. (2007), "Public memorialization in perspective: truth, justice and memory of past repression in the Southern Cone of South America", *International Journal of Transitional Justice* **1** (1), 138–56.

Kaminski, M. and M. Nalepa (2008), "Suffer a scratch to avoid a blow? Why post-communist parties in Eastern Europe introduce lustration", *Center for the Study of Democracy,* paper 08/01, University of California Irvine.

Kaminski, M.M., M. Nalepa, and B. O'Neill (2006), "Normative and strategic aspects of transitional justice", *Journal of Conflict Resolution*, **50** (3), 295–302.

Karl, T.L. (2005), "From democracy to democratization and back: before transitions from authoritarian rule", Center on Democracy, Development, and the Rule of Law, Stanford Institute on International Studies, Number 45, September.

Keohane, R. (1984), *After Hegemony: Cooperation and Discord in the World Political Economy*, Princeton, NJ: Princeton University Press.

Kim, H. (2009), "Expansion of transitional justice measures: a comparative analysis of its causes", Ph.D. dissertation, University of Minnesota.

Kim, H. and K. Sikkink (2010), "Explaining the Deterrence of Human Rights Prosecution in Transitional Societies" *International Studies Quarterly*, in press.

Kiss, E. (2000), "Moral ambition with and beyond political constraints: reflections on restorative justice", in R. Rotberg and D. Thompson (eds), *Truth v. Justice.* Princeton, NJ: Princeton University Press, pp.68–98.

Kritz, N.J. (1995), *Transitional Justice*, Washington DC: U.S. Institute of Peace Press.

Kritz, N.J. (2009), "Policy implications of empirical research on transitional justice", in H. van der Merwe, V. Baxter and A.R. Chapman (eds) *Assessing the Impact of Transitional Justice: Challenges for Empirical Research*, Washington DC: United States Institute of Peace Press, pp. 13–22.

Lambourne, W. (2009), "Transitional justice and peacebuilding after mass violence", *International Journal of Transitional Justice* **3**, 28–48.

Leebaw, B.A. (2008), "The irreconcilable goals of transitional justice", *Human Rights Quarterly*, **30**, 95–118.

Lie, T.G., H.M. Binningsbø and S. Gates (2007), "Post-conflict justice and sustainable peace", Post-Conflict Transitions Working Paper No. 5, Centre for the Study of Civil War, PRIO.

Linz, J. (1978), "Crisis, breakdown and reequilibration", in J. Linz and A. Stepan (eds) *The Breakdown of Democratic Regimes,* Baltimore, MD: Johns Hopkins University Press.

Loden, A. (2007), "Civil Society and Security Sector Reform in Post-conflict Liberia: Painting a Moving Train without Brushes", *International Journal of Transitional Justice* **1** (2), 297–307.

Long, W.J. and P. Brecke (2003), *War and Reconciliation: Reason and Emotion in Conflict Resolution.* Cambridge, MA: MIT Press.

Lundy, P. (2009), "Can the past be policed? Lessons from the historical enquiries team Northern Ireland", Transitional Justice Institute Research Paper No. 09-06, Transitional Justice Institute, University of Ulster, Jordanstown.

Lutz, E.L. and K. Sikkink (2001), "The justice cascade: the evolution and impact of foreign human rights trials in Latin America", *Chicago Journal of International Law*, **2** (1), 1–34.

McAdams, A.J. (1997) *Transitional Justice and the Rule of Law in New Democracies*, Helen Kellogg Institute for International Studies, Notre Dame, IN: University of Notre Dame Press.

McEvoy, L., K. McEvoy and K. McConnachie (2006), "Reconciliation as a dirty word: conflict community relations and education in Northern Ireland", *Journal of International Affairs*, **60** (1), 81–106.

Mahoney, J. and R. Snyder (1999), "Rethinking agency and structure in the study of regime change", *Studies in Comparative International Development.* Summer, 1999.

Malamud-Goti, J. (1995), "Transitional governments in breach: why punish state criminals?" in N.J. Kritz (ed.) *Transitional Justice*, Washington DC: US Institute of Peace Press.

Mallinder, L. (2008), *Amnesty, Human Rights and Political Transition : Bridging the Peace and Justice Divide*, Studies in International Law, Vol. 21, Oxford, UK: Hart.

Mani, R. (2002), *Beyond Retribution: Seeking Justice in the Shadows of War*, Cambridge, UK and Malden, MA: Polity Oxford, Blackwell.

Marshall, M.G., K. Jaggers and T.R. Gurr (2006), *Polity IV Project: Political Regime Characteristics and Transitions, 1800–2004.* Maryland, MD: Center for International Development and Conflict Management.

Meierhenrich, J. (2008), "Varieties of reconciliation", *Law and Social Inquiry*, **33** (1), 195–231.

Mendeloff, D. (2004), "Truth-seeking, truth-telling, and postconflict peacebuilding: curb the enthusiasm?" *International Studies Review*, **6** (3), 355–80.

Mendez, J.E. (1997), "Accountability for past abuses", *Human Rights Quarterly*, **19** (2), 255–82.

Mennecke, M. (2007), "Punishing genocidaires: a deterrent effect or not?" *Human Rights Review*, July 2007.

Minow, M. (1998), *Between Vengeance and Forgiveness: Facing History after Genocide and Mass Violence*, Boston, MA: Beacon Press.

Minow, M. (2000) "The hope for healing: what can truth commissions do?" in *Truth v. Justice: The Morality of Truth Commissions*, R.I. Rotberg and D. Thompson (eds), Princeton, NJ: Princeton University Press, pp. 235–60.

Moore, B. (1966), *Social Origins of Dictatorship and Democracy,* Boston, MA: Beacon Publishers.

Moravcsik, A. (1997), "Taking preferences seriously: a liberal theory of international politics", *International Organization*, **51**, 513–53.

Neier, A. (1999), "Rethinking truth, justice and guilt after Bosnia and Rwanda", in C. Hesse and R. Post (eds) *Human Rights in Political Transitions: Gettysburg to Bosnia*, New York, NY: Zone Books, p. 39.

Ni Aolain, F. and C. Campbell (2005), "The paradox of transition in conflicted democracies", *Human Rights Quarterly*, **27**, 172–213.

Nino, C. (1996), *Radical Evil on Trial*, New Haven, CT: Yale University Press.

North, D. and B. Weingast (1989), "Constitutions and commitment: the evolution of institutions governing public choice in 17th-century England", *Journal of Economic History*, **49** (4), 803–32.

Norval, A. J. (1999), "Truth and reconciliation: the birth of the present and the reworking of history", *Journal of Southern African Studies*, **25** (3), 499–519.

O'Donnell, G.A., P.C. Schmitter and L. Whitehead (1986), *Transitions from Authoritarian Rule: Comparative Perspectives*, Baltimore, MD: Johns Hopkins University Press.

Olsen, T., L. Payne and A. Reiter (2007), "At what cost? A political economy approach to transitional justice", Responses to Atrocities Workshop, Madison, WI.

Orentlicher, D.F. (1991), "Settling accounts: the duty to prosecute human rights violations of a prior regime", *Yale Law Journal*, **100** (8), 2537–615.

Orentlicher, D.F. (2007), "Settling accounts' revisited: reconciling global norms with local agency", *The International Journal of Transitional Justice*, **1**, 10–22.

O'Rourke, C. (2009), "The shifting signifier of community in transitional justice: a feminist analysis", Transitional Justice Institute Research Paper No. 09-03, Transitioanl Justice Institute, University of Ulster, Jordanstown, Northern Ireland.

Osiel, M. (1997), *Mass Atrocity, Collective Memory, and the Law*, New Brunswick, NJ: Transaction Publishers.

Pham, P. and P. Vinck (2007), "Empirical research and the development and assessment of transitional justice mechanisms", *The International Journal of Transitional Justice*, **1**, 231–48.

Pion-Berlin, D. (1994), "To prosecute or to pardon? Human rights decisions in the Latin American Southern Cone", *Human Rights Quarterly*, **15** (1), 105–30.

Popkin, M. and N. Roht-Arriaza (1995), "Truth as justice: investigatory commissions in Latin America", *Law and Social Inquiry*, 20 (1), 79–116.

Putnam, T. (2002), "Human rights and sustainable peace" in S.J. Stedman, D. Rothchild and E.M. Cousens (eds), *Ending Civil Wars: The Implementation of Peace*, Boulder, CO: Lynne Rienner, pp. 237–72.

Quinn, J.R. (2004), "Constraints: the un-doing of the Ugandan Truth Commission" *Human Rights Quarterly*, **26**, 401–27.

Quinn, J., T.D. Mason and M. Gurses (2007), "Sustaining the peace: civil war recurrence", *International Interactions*, **33**, 167–93.

Reuschemeyer, D., J.D. Stephens and E.H. Stephens (1992), *Capitalist Development and Democracy*, Chicago, IL: University of Chicago Press.

Roeder, P.G. (2001), "The rejection of auhtoritariansm" in R. Anderson, M.S. Fish, S.E. Hanson and P.G. Roeder (eds) *Postcommunism and the Theory of Democracy*, Princeton, NJ: Princeton University Press, pp. 21–53.

Roht-Arriaza, N. (2002), "Civil society in processes of accountability" in M.C. Bassiouni (ed.) *Post-Conflict Justice*, Ardsley, New York: Transnational Publishers, Inc, pp. 97–114.

Roht-Arriaza, N. and J. Mariezcurrena (eds) (2006), *Transitional Justice in the Twenty-First Century: Beyond Truth Versus Justice*, Cambridge, UK and New York, NY: Cambridge University Press.

Rotberg, R.I. and D. Thompson (eds) (2000), *Truth v. Justice: The Morality of Truth Commissions*, University Center for Human Values Series, Princeton NJ: Princeton University Press.

Rubin, B.R. (2003), "Transitional justice and human rights in Afghanistan", *International Affairs*, **79** (3), 567–81.

Schabas, W. and S. Darcy (eds) (2004) *Truth Commissions and Courts: The Tension Between Criminal Justice and the Search for Truth*, Dordrecht, The Netherlands and Norwell, MA: Kluwer Academic.

Schedler, A. (2002), "The nested game of democratization by elections", *International Political Science Review*, **23** (1), 103–122.

Scharf, M.P. (1996), "Swapping amnesty for peace: was there a duty to prosecute international crimes in Haiti?" *Texas International Law Journal*, **31** (1), 1–41.

Scharf, M. and N. Rodley (2002), "International law principles on accountability", in M.C. Bassiouni (ed.), *Post-Conflict Justice*. Ardsley, NY: Transnational Publishers, Inc., pp. 89–96.

Schiff, B.N. (2008), *Building the International Criminal Court*, Cambridge, UK: Cambridge University Press.

Shaw, R. (2007), "Memory frictions: localizing the truth and reconciliation commission in Sierra Leone", *The International Journal of Transitional Justice*, **1**: 183–207.

Shklar, J. ([1964] 1986), *Legalism: Law, Morals, and Political Trials*, Cambridge, MA: Harvard University Press.
Sieff, M. and L. Vinjamuri (1999), "Reconciling order and justice? New institutional solutions in post-conflict states", *Journal of International Affairs*, **52** (2), 757–80.
Sikkink, K. (2008), "The role of consequences, comparison, and counterfactuals in constructivist ethical thought" in R.M. Price (ed.) *Moral Limit and Possibility in World Politics*, New York, NY: Cambridge University Press, pp. 83–111.
Sikkink, K. and C.B.Walling (2007), "The impact of human rights trials in Latin America", *Journal of Peace Research*, **44** (4), 427–45.
Simmons, B. (2009), *Mobilizing for Human Rights: International Law in Domestic Politics*, Cambridge, UK: Cambridge University Press.
Smulovitz, C. (2002), "The discovery of law: political consequences in the Argentine case", in Y. Dezalay and B.G. Garth (eds) *Global Prescriptions: The Production, Exportation, and Important of a New Legal Orthodoxy*, Ann Arbor, MI: University of Michigan Press, pp. 249–71.
Snyder, J.L. (2000), *From Voting to Violence: Democratization and Nationalist Conflict*, 1st edn, 1. New York, NY: W.W. Norton.
Snyder, J. and L. Vinjamuri, (2003/4), "Trials and errors: principle and pragmatism in strategies of international justice", *International Security*, **28** (3), pp. 5–44.
Stover, E. (2005), "Bremer's 'Guardian Knot': Transitional justice and the US occupation of Iraq", *Human Rights Quarterly*, **27** (3), 830–57.
Stromseth, J., D. Wippman and R. Brooks (eds) (2006), *Can Might Make Rights? Building the Rule of Law after Military Interventions*, New York, NY: Cambridge University Press.
Subotic, J. (2005), "Hijacked justice: domestic appropriation of international norms", Human Rights and Human Welfare, Working paper no. 28.
Subotic, J. (2009), "Hijacked justice: dealing with the past in the Balkans", Ithaca, NY: Cornell University Press.
Sutil, J.C. (1997) "No victorious army has ever been prosecuted. . .' The unsettled story of transitional justice in Chile" in A.J. McAdams (ed.), *Transitional Justice and the Rule of Law in New Democracies,* Notre Dame, IN: University of Notre Dame Press, pp.123–54.
Teitel, R.G. (1995), "How are the new democracies of the Southern Cone dealing with the legacy of past human rights abuses?" in N. Kriz (ed.), *Transitional Justice: How Emerging Democracies Reckon with Former Regimes,* Washington DC: United Institute of Peace Press, pp. 146–54.
Teitel, R.G. (2000), *Transitional Justice*, Oxford, UK: Oxford University Press.
Teitel, R.G. (2003), "Human rights in transition: transitional justice genealogy", *The Harvard Human Rights Journal*, **16**, 69–94.
Teitel, R.G. (2008), "Editorial note: transitional justice globalized", *International Journal of Transitional Justice*, **2**, 1–4.
Theidon, K. (2007), "Transitional subjects: the disarmament, demobilization and reintegration of former combatants in Colombia", *International Journal of Transitional Justice*, **1** (1), 66–90.
Thoms, O., J. Ron and R. Paris (2008), "The effects of transitional justice Mechanisms", Center for International Policy Studies Working Paper, University of Ottawa.
Tsebelis, G. (1991), *Nested Games: Rational Choice in Comparative Politics*, Berkeley, CA: University of California Press.
Tully, J. (2005), "On law, democracy and imperialism", Twenty-First Annual Public Lecture, Centre for Law and Society, University of Edinburgh, 10–11 March, pp. 2–48.
Turner, C. (2008), "Delivering lasting peace, democracy and human rights in times of transition: the role of international law", *International Journal of Transitional Justice*, **2**, 126–51.
Van der Merwe, H., V. Baxter and A.R. Chapman (eds) (2009), *Assessing the Impact of Transitional Justice: Challenges for Empirical Research*, Washington DC: United States Institute of Peace Press.
Van Zyl, P. (1999), "Dilemmas of transitional justice: the case of South Africa's truth and reconciliation commission" *Journal of International Affairs*, **52** (2), 647–68.

Vinjamuri, L. and A.P. Boesenecker (2007), "Accountability and peace agreements: mapping trends from 1980 to 2006", Geneva, Switzerland: Centre for Humanitarian Dialogue.

Vinjamuri, L. and J. Snyder (2004), "Advocacy and scholarship in the study of international war crime tribunals and transitional justice", *Annual Review of Political Science*, **7** (1), 345–62.

Weinstein, H.M. and E. Stover (2004), "Introduction: conflict, justice and reclamation" in E. Stover and H.M. Weinstein (eds), *My Neighbor, My Enemy: Justice and Community in the Aftermath of Mass Atrocity*, Cambridge, UK: Cambridge University Press, pp. 1–26.

Widner, J. A. (ed) (1994), *Economic Change and Political Liberalization in sub-Saharan Africa*, Baltimore, MD: Johns Hopkins University Press.

Wiebelhaus-Brahm, E. (2010), "Truth commissions" in W. Schabas and N. Bernaz (eds). *The Handbook of International Criminal Law*, New York, NY: Routledge.

Williams, P. R. (2002), "The role of justice in peace negotiations" in M.C. Bassiouni (ed.), *Post-Conflict Justice*, International and Comparative Criminal Law Series, Ardsley, NY: Transnational Publishers, pp. 115–134.

Wilson, R. (2001), *The Politics of Truth and Reconciliation in South Africa: Legitimizing the Post-Apartheid State*, Cambridge, UK: Cambridge University Press.

Zalaquett, J. (1991), *The Ethics of Responsibility: Human Rights, Truth and Reconciliation in Chile* Washington DC: Washington Office on Latin America.

Zalaquett, J. (1995), "The dilemma of new democracies confronting past human rights violations", in Kritz N.J. (ed), *Transitional Justice*. Washington DC: US Institute of Peace Press, pp. 203–206.

Zalaquett, J. (1998), "Moral reconstruction in the wake of human rights violations and war crimes", in J. Moore (ed.), *Hard Choices: Moral Dilemmas in Humanitarian Intervention*, Lanham, MD: Rowman and Littlefield, pp. 211–28.

Zehr, H. and H. Mika (2003), "Fundamental concepts of restorative justice" in E. MacLaughlin, R. Fergusson, G. Hughes and L. Westmarland (eds), *Restorative Justice: Critical Issues*, London: Sage Publications, pp. 40–3.

Zerilli, L. (1998), "This universalism which is not one", *Diacritics*, **28** (2), 3–20.

21 Dynamics of military occupation
Michael Hechter and Oriol Vidal-Aparicio

21.1 INTRODUCTION

The recent American invasion of Iraq and Afghanistan has revived interest in the outcomes of military occupation, which is the most extreme form of alien rule. In contrast to annexation and colonialism, in this chapter military occupation refers to a type of alien rule that is imposed on the native society by a foreign power, and that the international community refuses to recognize as constituting permanent sovereign[1] control.[2]

There is a pervasive consensus that alien rule, at least in modern times, is invariably malign, illegitimate and unsustainable (Hechter 2009a). This conclusion is far from wholly mistaken; there are many reasons why the histories of occupation in country after country have so often been unhappy. Occupation is generally disparaged because it entails major uncertainty and a high risk of loss for the bulk of those who are subjected to it.

Occupation ushers in great uncertainty – this is why people flee the impending arrival of an occupying army en masse. Whose justice will rule the land? The common expectation is that it will not be the native's justice. If alien soldiers confiscate or destroy native private property, will the alien rulers be motivated to seek justice? If occupying soldiers rape native women, will the occupying authorities step in to halt the practice?[3] If most people dislike uncertainty, they are also quite averse to the prospect of certain loss (Kahneman and Tversky 1979). Especially for native elites, occupation typically results in the certain loss of their authority.

At the same time, the official historiographies of countries that have undergone occupation often romanticize their resistance to it. This results in a tendency to exaggerate the selflessness and heroism of the native population and downplay its collaborationist proclivities (MacKenzie 1997, pp. 1–2; Kalyvas 2006, p. 37).[4] This bowdlerization ignores the inconvenient truth that some military occupations (like those in postwar Japan and Germany) evidently succeeded in fostering new legitimate and sustainable regimes, whereas many others (like the Soviet occupation of Afghanistan) indeed did inspire fierce resistance and ultimately failed.

This chapter attempts to account for these varying outcomes. Since there are surprisingly few systematic studies of the effects of military occupations, it proceeds by dipping into the large and heterogeneous case-study literature. For heuristic purposes, this literature can be divided into macro- and micro-level accounts of military occupation.

21.2 MACROANALYSIS

At the macro level, domestic reactions to occupation are the outcome of characteristics of the occupier's regime and the native society, as well as of mediating and exogenous factors.

21.2.1 Regime Characteristics

In the first place, not all occupation regimes are the same. One cause of this variation emanates from the characteristics of the occupying power itself. An occupation regime imposed by one state is likely to differ from one set up by another if only because the institutions of the states themselves are different. Even though both France and the United Kingdom are full-fledged democracies, their state structures and policies are far from identical. Since the characteristics of the occupied territories also differ, the same state may also adopt different institutions and policies in its multiple occupation regimes in different territories. Thus, due in part to ecological considerations, the British resorted to direct rule in some parts of the territory of a given colony and indirect rule in others (Boone 2003; Lammers 2003). The Nazis did likewise in their occupation of France: they ruled the north directly but relied on the Vichy government to rule the south. Finally, both institutions and policies of a given occupation regime may shift as circumstances – such as the occupying power's fortunes in war – change: it is less costly to produce goods that benefit the native population when the occupying power reckons victory is at hand than when it must devote greater resources to fighting an intractable enemy.

At a given time, however, several key dimensions of any occupation regime will exert influence on native resistance. Two of these dimensions – the effectiveness of the regime's production of public goods, and the degree to which it enacts fair governance – affect native resistance via their consequences for the regime's legitimacy.

To the degree that alien rulers are resented by native populations, their costs of control must be correspondingly higher than those of native rulers. How can these surplus costs ever be borne?

Indirect rule
The answer lies in granting some decision-making power to a native elite through some type of indirect rule (Hechter 2000, p. 51). Indirect rule

employs native intermediaries who are induced to collaborate with the alien power to govern the native population. Collaborators are essential because occupation regimes always aim to rule on the cheap (Robinson 1972).[5] Since they depend on collaborators to provide social order, which is the prerequisite for any of their aims in occupying the country in the first place, it is not in the interest of alien rulers to undermine their authority.

During the Nazi occupation of Europe, the Channel Islands stand out as the territories which had the least resistance (Bunting 1995). In contrast to much of Europe, the Germans made extensive use of indirect rule and did not change the islands' system of government. The island government took responsibility for food rationing and distribution, thereby shielding the Germans from criticism of these policies. By contrast, in Holland, the Germans reneged on their agreement to merely supervise Dutch authorities, and abolished local and provincial self-government, restructuring administration in line with that in Germany.

When devising the post-World War II occupation policy for Japan, American experts discussed whether the occupation should be run directly or indirectly, and Japan specialist Hugh Borton forcefully argued for indirect rule, as "the United States and her allies had insufficient trained men to administer Japan down to the smallest hamlet" and indirect rule, moreover, would minimize resentment toward the occupier (Daniels 1984, pp.161–2).

Likewise, the Nazi occupiers of Northern France delegated authority over the South to the (French) Vichy regime, which was anxious to maximize whatever limited control that it could. By 1942, its best hope in this regard depended increasingly upon its hold over the police. The secretary general of the police in the Vichy regime, René Bousquet, cooperated well beyond what he was asked for on the deportation of Jews so that he could preserve a higher degree of autonomy for his police. The reasoning seemed to be: we will accept subordination to the occupier, but whenever possible we will execute orders ourselves instead of letting the occupier's agents execute them directly; this way we will still maintain an appearance of control on the ground – since who patrols the streets seems to be the one in charge. Bousquet saw this as his only alternative to falling into "total subordination" (Mazower 2008, pp. 437–40). Even when indirect rule was not enacted, many foreign occupiers have striven to create the appearance of self government.[6]

Ideology and information control

Whereas all governments invest resources in persuading their citizens and subjects of their right to (and rightness for) rule (Lasswell 1927; Weber 1968), some invest more than others. If the occupier's ideology catches on in native society, then compliance with the regime will flow from internal sources rather than policing (Orwell [1949] 1984). Moreover, the longer-term the occupation will be, the more useful ideological investment (Carlton 1992). However, very little is known about how to successfully instill a new ideology in occupied populations.

Despite this difficulty, occupation regimes have a more readily available cognitive tool that can be used to mute resistance to their rule – information control. Two kinds of information are particularly critical to control in this regard. In the first place, if credible, information about the benefits deriving from the occupation can help reduce native opposition to it. In the second, due to bandwagon effects, information suggesting that the occupying power will be victorious in war will likewise mute resistance.

For this reason, the American occupiers of postwar Japan employed censorship – especially of information related to the atomic bomb – to advance their vision of "a Japan where everybody had free access to information . . . where everybody could say and write what they wanted, where there was *no censorship*" (Braw 1991, p. 145, emphasis added).[7] Thus at the same time that the United States was dismantling the information control apparatus of the Japanese state in the name of democratic freedoms, the occupation authorities secretly adopted their own means of censorship.

Consider the information control policies in the American occupations of Germany and Iraq (Goldstein 2008). During the occupation of Germany the US authorities rigorously controlled the media to block pro-Nazi and, later, pro-communist propaganda (Goldstein 2009). In contrast, during the American occupation of Iraq the occupying forces did not establish a monopoly of the media, which allowed the effective use of the press, radio, television and the Internet by the forces opposing the occupation, decisively contributing to the failure of the occupier's goals. One factor which contributed to success in media control during the German occupation was the use of officers (often émigré scholars) with extensive knowledge of the German language, culture, society and history. In contrast, in Iraq the US Government outsourced propaganda tasks to private corporations with no experience in the Middle East.

These characteristics of the occupation regime affect differential resistance via their effects on its legitimacy.

21.2.2 Legitimating Occupation Regimes

The concept of legitimacy was invented to help account for social order in large societies (Hechter 2009b). As such, it has an ancient lineage (Zelditch Jr. 2001). Since it is too costly to attain order in the long run on the basis of sanctions or naked coercion, it stands to reason that political stability must also rest, in part, on some normative basis. Rousseau understood that "The stronger is never strong enough to be forever master unless he transforms his force into right and obedience into duty" (Rousseau [1797] 1997, Book I, Chapter 3, p. 43). Legitimacy refers to this normative basis of the social order.

In general, a government is legitimate to the extent that its rules are considered rightful by both dominant and subordinate members of society. In this circumstance, compliance with these rules demonstrates consent with the regime. Note that this is an exceedingly demanding condition to meet, however. Among other things, it implies that the government's rules will be honored even when it is powerless to impose sanctions on the noncompliant. When an individual or group obeys rules because they anticipate that failure to do so will be met with sanctions, compliance owes more to the government's power than its legitimacy. The existence of a large public relations industry and of other agencies that spin reality to suit their clients' interests provides compelling indirect evidence of the importance of legitimacy in modern society.

Although compliance often is observable, it is difficult to discern legitimacy in the absence of reliable subjective evidence. As Max Weber famously noted, "the merely external fact of the order being obeyed is not sufficient to signify" that it is seen as legitimate (Weber 1978, p. 946). By the same token, anything less than fully compliant behavior does not necessarily reveal some shortfall of legitimacy. Since reliable evidence about the internal states of collectivities was impossible to come by before the advent of the sample survey in the 1930s – and even now such evidence often is tantalizingly elusive – the measurement of legitimacy poses a formidable challenge. On this account, most empirically oriented social scientists try to refrain from discussing it. But the concept is so fundamental to the attainment of social order that it is difficult to avoid.

What then are the determinants of legitimacy in the modern world? Recent research suggests that two factors are necessary if not sufficient causes of the legitimacy of *any* government. The first is the regime's *effectiveness* at producing an appropriate bundle of public goods. The second is its *fairness* in allocating these goods and in instituting policy most generally (Hechter 2009a). These two elements are part of any conception of good governance (Rothstein 2009). Like native rulers, occupiers can attain legitimacy to the degree that they govern well.[8]

In any modern society government is responsible for supplying a panoply of public goods, including social order, public services (clean water, sanitation, electricity and so forth), dispute resolution, education and economic growth. To the degree that any government fails in producing some or all of these public goods, its legitimacy is compromised.

This implies that the legitimacy of an occupation regime, and its ultimate viability, is heightened by the effectiveness of its provision of these public goods (see the American occupation of Iraq).[9]

The provision of social order – the most fundamental public good, since it is necessary for the provision of all others – is intimately bound up with legitimacy (Edelstein 2004). The attainment of social order enables individuals to go about their own business without fearing for physical injury or their very lives. If, at least after its onset, occupation disrupts expectations and invokes widespread uncertainty, the return of social life to normality, to the routine of everyday life, is a vital stabilizing factor. The Japanese understood this when they occupied parts of Central China (1937–1945). A document produced by Japanese Special Service officers advised: "To get the common people to return speedily to their rightful occupations, we have to guarantee their life and property. To first settle their minds, we have to restore order" (quoted in Brook 2005, p. 38). Ditto in Nazi-occupied France (Carlton 1992, p.143).

There is a certain irony to be found when the agent providing order had recently been responsible for its demise in the first place. This irony was often present during the first months of the Japanese occupation of the Chinese Yangtze Delta in 1937–38:

> The first concern of the pacification team had to be to project the appearance of stability and good government – ironically, the very social goods that the violence of their invasion had shattered – even and especially when they did not exist. The pacification process must cause the violence by which the occupation authority was imposed to disappear and make the new arrangement appear to be other than abruptly imposed. It must project the idea that a state structure exists where it does not; it must construe nominal submission as engaged support (Brook 2005, pp. 62–3).

Although no studies directly test the proposition linking the provision of public goods with successful occupations (but see Hechter 2009c), a comparison of seven cases of US-led nation-building efforts undertaken since World War II – Germany, Japan, Somalia, Haiti, Bosnia, Kosovo and Afghanistan – provides some supportive evidence (Dobbins 2003). What principally distinguishes the relatively successful outcomes from the least successful ones "is the level of effort the United States and the international community put into their democratic transformations. Nation-building . . . is a time- and resource-consuming effort. The United States and its allies have put 25 times more money and 50 times more troops, on a per capita basis, into postconflict Kosovo [a relatively successful occupation] than into postconflict Afghanistan [in 2003, an utter failure]" (Dobbins 2003, p. xix).[10]

Legitimation does not merely flow from the quantity of public goods provided by the occupation regime, however. The manner in which these goods are allocated also matters a great deal (Tyler 2006).[11] To the degree that some social groups are systematically excluded from regime-provided benefits, this will breed resentment and delegitimate the regime in their eyes. It will also create new social divisions or reinforce existing ones.

The occupation regime therefore has two quite different cost-effective means of inhibiting native resistance.[12] It can do so by increasing its legitimacy, but this is a highly costly strategy. Alternatively, as discussed further below, it can employ the much less costly strategy of fomenting social divisions in native society by systematically favoring one set of social groups as against others (*divide et impera*).

Alien rulers' choice of a governing strategy hinges on their incentives. Since *divide et impera* is a much less costly strategy than legitimation, this accounts for its greater prevalence. Yet given the appropriate incentives, alien rulers can be motivated to provide fair and effective governance – and, hence, to earn some measure of legitimacy. Alien rulers can be motivated to provide fair and effective governance when they impose rule on native territory in order to augment their own security (for which they are prepared to incur some cost), or when they share in the profits of increased trade and commercial activity (Hechter 2009a).

21.3   MICROANALYSIS

All forms of alien rule pose a serious governance dilemma. To adequately govern the territory, a state and civil apparatus of roughly similar size to the previous regime must be established. Police have to be hired, electricity and water must be provided, roads must be repaired, hospitals have to be administered, judges have to be appointed to resolve disputes. Even in the unlikely event that an adequate supply of labor existed in the occupying country, the costs of creating such an administration de novo are simply astronomical. Large numbers of officials and workers would have to be imported, and these new arrivals would also have to be bilingual. Small wonder, then, that alien rulers' first imperative is to minimize their control costs. In practical terms, this means that they must obtain the services of native collaborators.

To some degree, the supply of collaborators is a function of the characteristics of native society – particularly the nature and degree of its social divisions. The greater these are, the more difficult it is to create a resistance coalition and the easier it is for the occupier to employ *divide et impera*. Beyond their service, however, collaborators can help to legitimize the occupation, especially if they are influential in the native community. In this way, each influential collaborator has a multiplier effect on the process of legitimation – and, by implication, on diminishing resistance. Thus the larger the proportion of collaborators, the smaller the potential resistance.

What counts as collaboration? The question is tricky because it relies on motivational issues which are notoriously difficult to discern. Two broad types of collaboration have been distinguished: *collaborationism*, which is based on an ideological identification with the occupier, and *state collaboration*, a pragmatic decision to work with the occupier so as to maintain social order and a working economy (Hoffman 1968).[13] This dichotomy leaves out the third reason why individuals collaborate: because it is in their self-interest to do so. For the purposes of this chapter, collaboration can be loosely defined as any kind of help *willingly* provided by the local population to an occupying power, and is best understood in contrast to resistance to that same power.[14]

Recent research has pointed to a diverse mix of motivations for collaboration. The stronger the inducements the occupier offers, the greater its chances to recruit collaborators. Conversely, if a resistance movement can offer more compelling inducements, it will be able to outbid the occupier. Some of the conditions affecting the rate of collaboration are national in scope, whereas others are more purely local.

The first impression one has of military occupation is that it pits the alien ruler against the native society *tout court*. When a foreign ruler comes on the scene this will unite native society into a solidary brotherhood dedicated to resistance. Whereas this kind of scenario indeed may occur, it is far from universal. It depends, in good part, on characteristics of the native society.

21.3.1   Societal Characteristics

Social divisions

To the degree that the native society is rent with social divisions – by class, ethnicity, nationality, religion and language among others – this will blunt its capacity to engage in any kind of collective action, let alone resistance. On the one hand, bureaucrats may reckon (with some justification) that their patriotic duty lies with continuing to supply electricity, water, education, mass transit, sanitation, public health, dispute resolution and other public goods to their compatriots. On the other, the occupier may provide some groups with a counterbalance to an even more hateful internal enemy. Thus Protestants welcomed the Dutch *stadtholder* William of Orange to the English throne in 1688 to thwart the political ambitions of their Catholic rivals for power. This illustrates that the occupier–collaborator relationship may be between two principals (rather than between a principal and an agent) each having their own agendas (Kalyvas 2008b). Moreover, collaborators are not necessarily unpatriotic, nor do they necessarily support the occupier's agenda. Thus occupiers and – at least some – natives have certain common interests which make collaboration mutually beneficial. When one of the parties in this relationship ceases to benefit from it, collaboration will likely cease.[15]

An occupier who is aware of preexisting ideological, political, social or ethnic cleavages in native territory and takes advantage of them will be more likely to succeed. In Arab Palestine under the British Mandate, two leading camps had formed whose rivalry was rooted in social and political structures dating from the Ottoman period (Cohen 2008, p. 7). While the Palestinian nationalists (the Husseini camp) hoped to liberate the country from the British and Zionists, the Arab opposition (including the Nashashibi and the Abu-Gosh families) allied themselves with both of these alien forces. Needless to say, the Zionists took full advantage of this cleavage within Palestinian society.[16] Nazi Germany also profited from the social divisions of many of the countries it invaded (Mazower 2008, p. 8). Many of the countries in Central and Eastern Europe were newly established and characterized by deep social cleavages that inspired internecine clashes once war broke out. As the French case indicates, however, even relatively nationally integrated societies can be torn asunder in the face of occupation.[17]

Other sources of collaboration

Collaboration can also emanate from more idiosyncratic roots. At the ground level the alien ruler tends to be seen as one of the actors in a microcosm rather than as a key player in the national struggle (Kalyvas 2008a, p. 111). Most individuals live the conflict (and help to produce its outcomes) only from a local perspective, primarily taking into account survival considerations and opportunities for private benefit which mostly determine whether collaboration takes place (Kalyvas 2006, p. 12; Cohen 2008, p. 236).[18] Thus, many Chinese collaborators with the Japanese administration in Shanghai saw their recruitment by the new occupation administration as 'getting their job back' (Brook 2005, p. 170), while other examples – such as Belorussian collaboration with the Nazis to obtain confiscated Jewish property (Baranova 2008, p. 120) – are easier to classify as the consequence of economic opportunism. One of the leading collaborators in Japanese-occupied Nanjing, 'Jimmy' Wang, is reported to have said that the Japanese occupation was "such a good opportunity to make a fortune" (Brook 2005, p.155). Likewise, after World War II, Eastern Germans enjoyed the opportunity to materially advance in the

Soviet-occupied area: the Soviets staffed the zonal administration with German communists, but for less ideologically committed Germans "loyalty could be ensured by material inducements or by blackmail" (Seton-Watson 1984, p. 10).

Another example is provided by Palestinian collaboration with Zionism before the establishment of the Israeli state. In this period, Arabs had ample opportunity to reap private benefit by selling their lands to Jewish settlers. These purely material considerations often trumped ideology: the willingness of Arabs to sell land and arms to Jews increased in tandem with Jewish immigration to Palestine. This occurred despite the nationalist movement's strictures against such trafficking. In 1929, the Arab Executive Committee called on Arabs to boycott Jewish stores and products, but this prohibition was increasingly ignored by the Arab merchants, who needed Jewish-produced merchandise and who therefore violated the ban (Cohen 2008, pp. 40–1).

When the local population must decide whether to collaborate with the occupier, another factor that trumps ideology is actual control on the ground – that is, the degree to which a given group is able to establish exclusive rule on a territory (Kalyvas 2000, pp. 152–3; 2006, p. 111). Thus, the higher its control, the greater the extent of native collaboration. For instance, Brook (2005, pp. 7–8) found that as the Japanese army consolidated its control across the Chinese Yangtze Delta in the spring of 1938, "the incentives to cooperate with the new rulers increased."

One of the few quantitative analyses of collaboration concerns Greece in the later stages of World War II when Germany was already losing the war. From 20000 to 30000 men are estimated to have fought on the German side against fellow Greeks (Kalyvas 2008b). In the southern territory of the Argolid, standard economic, social and political variables had no capacity to predict levels of collaboration. Instead, the key determinants were violence that was perpetrated by the Communist-led National Liberation Front (EAM) in the period preceding recruitment of armed collaborators,[19] and the degree of German control over particular regions. These findings suggest that the principal motives for collaboration in the Argolid were the desire to wreak revenge for previous victimization at the hands of the resistance movement, and the opportunity to take advantage of incentives that the Germans could mete out in the territories in which they exercised full control.

The role of elites

As discussed above, native elites play a vital role in the reaction to occupation. Those who confer their allegiance on the occupiers can help to legitimate the regime, whereas rebellious elites are likely to mobilize popular resistance. This is revealed by a comparison of popular reactions to the Japanese occupation of Taiwan and Korea (Hechter, Matesan and Hale 2009). The Japanese occupied both Taiwan and Korea in the same period (from 1910 until 1945), but resistance was much greater in Korea. When they occupied Taiwan – then a province within Qing China – the Japanese permitted its Confucian elite to leave the island. Most returned to China, where they attempted to resume their careers. A new Taiwanese elite was recruited to fill the now-vacated positions. Since this elite owed its elevation to the occupation, it was dependent on the Japanese, and quite well-disposed to them. In consequence, the Taiwanese elite refrained from nationalist resistance and helped to reduce antagonism to the Japanese.[20] In contrast, after Japan occupied Korea it soon took measures to curtail the prerogatives of its elite (the *yangban*). Unlike the former Taiwanese elite, the *yangban* had no means of maintaining its privilege outside of Korea and so many remained in the country. Resentful of their reduced powers and status, they helped to foment resistance to the occupation. Hell hath no fury like a native authority scorned by an occupying regime (Petersen 2002; see also Ricks 2006 on the Sunni reaction to the American occupation of Iraq).

21.3.2   Exogenous Factors

The preceding analysis concentrated on determinants located within the boundaries of native society. However two exogenous factors, in particular, also contribute to the likelihood of resistance. The first has to do with the *occupiers' wartime prospects*. The idea here is simple. As an occupying power finds itself losing the war, it is compelled to extract more resources – including manpower – from the native society. When the Nazis' resources began to be sapped by their losses in a two-front war, they instituted forced labor even in the most favored occupied lands, like the Channel Islands (Bunting 1995). This increases the burden of the occupation, and therefore the prospects for resistance. Losses in war not only affect resources, but also attitudes. Postwar expectations regarding who will ultimately win and the political scenarios that this will bring are also important determinants of collaboration. After all, the Germans took control of Europe so swiftly and ruthlessly that it was easy for both sides to imagine that Nazi rule was there to stay. That sense of inevitability disappeared once the tides of war turned (Liberman 1996, p. 24).[21]

During the Arab Rebellion in Palestine of 1936–39, expectations of a final Jewish victory affected the willingness to collaborate: "[S]ome of [the collaborators] assumed that the Jews, with British assistance, would be able to subdue the [Arab Palestinian] rebellion and that it would be best to support the winning side from the start" (Cohen 2008, p. 115). Similarly, one of the main goals of the Japanese "pacification teams" when they were sent to newly conquered locations in the Yangtze Delta (China) in 1937 was to "convince collaborators and noncollaborators alike that Japan would succeed in its project to control China, and that this control was in China's long-term interests" (Brook 2005, p. 62). They expected to reassure those who had already been collaborating with the Japanese army during the armed conflict and hopefully to convert some non-collaborators as well.

The second exogenous determinant is *external support for the resistance.* To the degree that the resistance is afforded territory for sanctuary, or more directly funds and arms, its prospects improve. Successful insurgent movements tend to have access to such external support.[22] One of the most impressive examples was the United States' Central Intelligence Agency's covert support to the Islamic resistance against the Soviet-imposed government of Afghanistan in the 1980s. The CIA poured over US$1 billion to fund the *mujahedeen* – the largest covert action ever undertaken (Crile 2007). External support is often a critical factor in all types of insurgency. Most recently, a prominent New York hedge fund billionaire, Raj Rajaratnam, founder of Galleon Group, has been accused of being one of a number of wealthy Sri Lankans in the United States whose donations to a Maryland-based charity ended up with the Liberation Tigers of Tamil Eelam, the Tamil nationalist insurgency (Perez and Bellman 2009). Eight people pleaded guilty to attempting to provide material support to the organization, which was designated as terrorist by the United States. Ostensibly collecting money for the victims of the tsunami, the charity instead funneled support to the Tamil Tigers. Groups from the Irish Republican Army to Al Qaeda and the Taliban likewise have profited handsomely from external funding sources.

21.4   CONCLUSION

Resistance to failed occupations and collaboration in military occupations are social phenomena that are intrinsically difficult to study. Nationalist historians and journalists are apt to exaggerate the prevalence of the former and understate that of the latter. For this reason, if no other, evidence about resistance and collaboration is elusive. In spite of this, there is an impressive consistency of findings from a variety of historical case studies conducted in widely varying societies. This enables us to provide two tentative models, one of resistance and one of collaboration. The first concentrates on the macroscopic level (Figure 21.1) and proposes

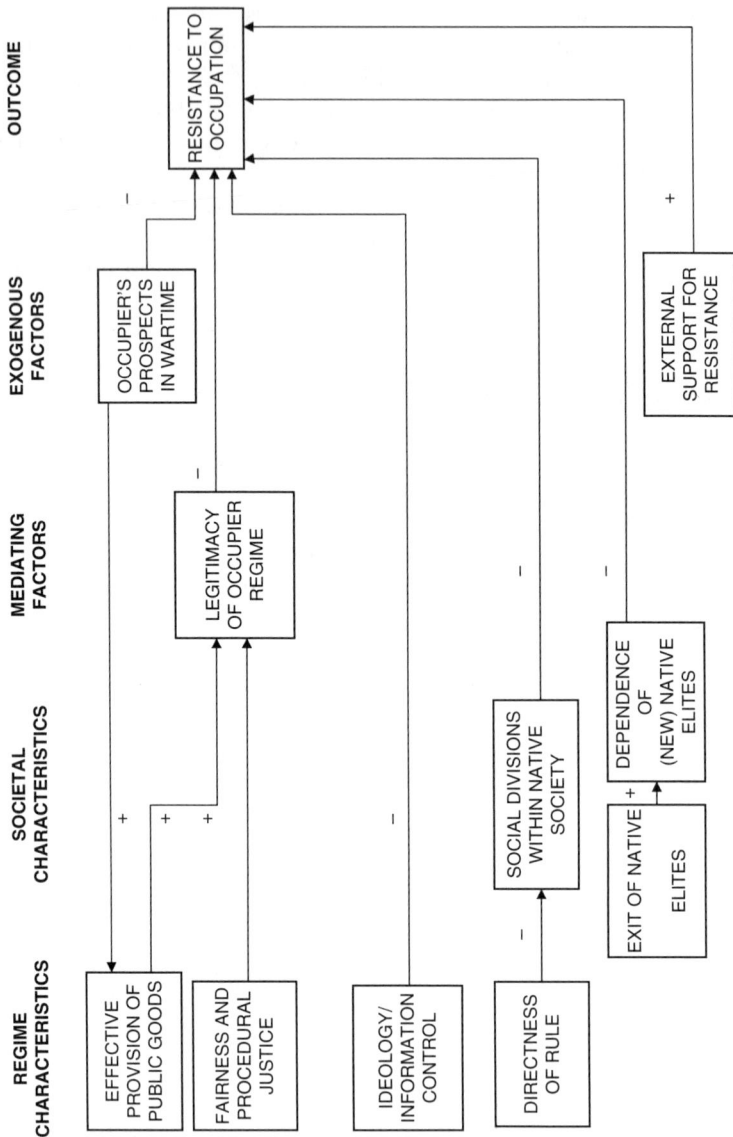

Figure 21.1   A macro-level model of resistance to occupation regimes

that resistance is a function of the characteristics of the regime, the native society, the mediating factor of legitimacy and exogenous factors (namely, the occupiers' wartime prospects and external support for the resistance). Since no quantitative studies exist providing indicators of all of these kinds of elements, the relative importance of these causes of resistance to occupation cannot be estimated at this time.

The second model concentrates on the microscopic level, and suggests that the rate of collaboration is a function of the natives' dependence on the occupier for access to private goods, relative to the native community (Figure 21.2). The greater the net benefits provided by the occupier to the native community, the greater the probability of collaboration.[23] Conversely, the greater the net benefits provided by native organizations, the less the probability of collaboration.

Some of the determinants of the occupier's capacity to provide private benefits include their understanding of the relationship of effective and fair governance to the attainment of legitimacy,[24] their fortunes in war and the degree of their internal political support (this hampered the American occupation of Vietnam). The determinants of dependence on the native community include its degree of solidarity (Hechter 1987), and the aforementioned external support.

These models are clearly incomplete and should be amended in subsequent research. Nevertheless they offer a starting point for more systematic analyses of military occupation to be carried out in the future.

NOTES

1. In reviewing and discussing the concept of sovereignty under military occupation, Stirk (2009, Chapter 6) clearly distinguishes between *sovereignty*, which in its modern sense is denied to the occupier and said to rest in the hands of the occupied population, and *authority*, which is possessed temporarily by the occupier. Sovereignty itself is never transferred to the occupier in military occupation, and therefore sovereignty cannot be qualified as permanent or temporary; it simply never ceases to be in the hands of its legitimate owners, the occupied population. This is consistent with the modern understanding of sovereignty as popular sovereignty. As Benvenisti (2004, p. 95) notes, the currently accepted "principle [is] that sovereignty lies in a people, not in a political elite" and therefore "the fall of a government has no effect whatsoever on the sovereign title over the occupied territory, which remains vested in the local population."

2. This definition excludes all cases in which occupation is elected and occurs at the behest of the native society, often in response to its perception of external threat (cf. Edelstein 2004, which includes such cases). Even though such elected occupations may also engender some native resistance, this resistance is likely to be much less vigorous than when occupation is imposed. It also excludes cases such as that of Iceland, which, despite its declaration of neutrality, was invaded by the British in 1940 and subsequently by the United States, but whose existing government cooperated with the Allied powers for the duration of the war.

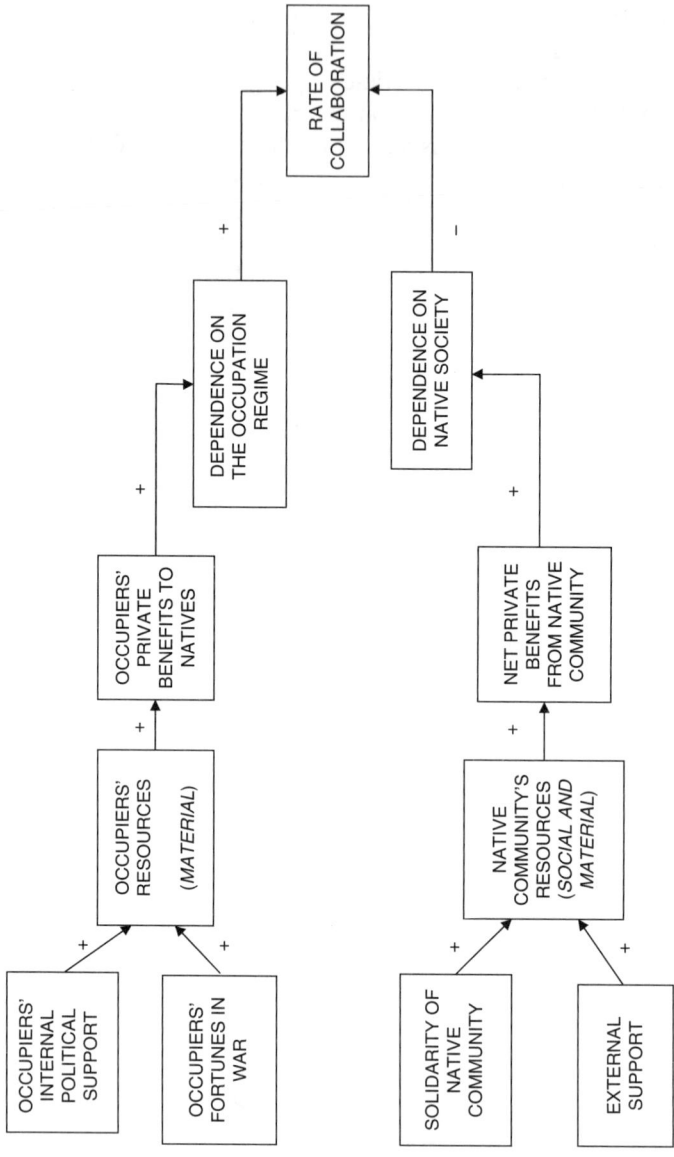

Figure 21.2   A micro-level model of collaboration

3. After a number of years when an occupation regime stabilizes and becomes routinized, much of this uncertainty will be resolved. Therefore, initial resistance to the occupation is likely to be relatively high.

4. World War II offers numerous examples of this tendency.

> [F]or much of the war . . . Europeans fell into line and contributed what [Nazi Germany] demanded anyway. After 1945, this was conveniently forgotten. Those who had endured the German occupation hailed the heroic *résistants* and passed in silence over the fact that German officials in most of Europe had not been overly troubled by resistance until late in the day. That the Germans had managed to divert the resources of the continent to the benefit of their own war economy was attributed to coercion [not to willing collaboration] (Mazower 2008, p. 6).

> Compared with many aspects of the history of the Second World War, the phenomenon of cooperation by Soviet citizens with the German occupation authorities has received less critical attention by scholars and has not been systematically examined for various reasons. Whilst doggedly prosecuting and punishing those suspected of 'collaboration' as traitors in the postwar period, the Soviet government was reluctant to acknowledge publicly that this wartime phenomenon took place on Soviet territories during the occupation or sought to diminish the significance of this phenomenon. Since the existence of collaboration could raise the question of the legitimacy of the Soviet regime and also could question the allegiance of the population to the Soviet state, the government refused to divulge the real scale of this movement and to openly analyse its origins and reasons (Baranova 2008, p. 114).

Likewise, Esdale (2003) challenges the historiographical myth created around the Spanish resistance to the Napoleonic occupier in the Peninsular War.

5. Indirect rule helps keep the costs of occupation down, both in terms of resources and knowledge, as it makes it possible to govern without erecting, financing and feeding a bulky administrative apparatus, as well as providing economies of information (Hechter 2000, 50–1). For instance, Napoleon ruled Habsburg Lombardy and mainland Naples indirectly because "the Habsburgs and Neapolitan Bourbons possessed administrative elites intellectually prepared for Napoleonic rule" and "assumed direct responsibility for exactly those parts of the [Italian] peninsula where [his] rule, and the culture it rested upon, would seem most alien, and where indigenous intermediaries would be hardest to find" (Broers 2003, p. 55).

6. For further discussion of the appearance of self government during military occupation, see Brook (2005, Chapter 3).

7. In September 1945, the Press, Pictorial and Broadcast Division (PPB) under the US Civil Censorship Detachment (CCD) issued the *Manual on Censorship in Japan* (Braw 1991, p. 62), and that same month the Supreme Commander of the Allied Powers (SCAP) in Japan issued a Press Code warning the Japanese press, among other things, that "no false or destructive criticism of the Allied Powers" would be allowed and that it should not "invite mistrust or resentment of [the Allied] troops" (ibid., p. 41). The Basic Initial Post-Surrender Directive issued by president Truman (which reached Japan on 8 November 1945) stated that censorship was to be established over mail, wireless, telephone, telegraph and cables, films, and the press "as may be necessary in the interests of the military security and the accomplishment of the purposes set forth in this directive" (ibid., p. 32).

8. In addition to these factors, legitimacy can be adversely affected by several disruptive effects that the occupying troops cause in the occupied society. Demographic effects can be troubling in small societies, especially in long occupations. Such was the case in Iceland, occupied by British forces in 1940 and by American forces in 1941 until 1947 – subsequently the Americans kept an air force base in Iceland between 1951 and 2006. The main problem of that occupation was that American troops (mostly unmarried males) outnumbered Icelandic marriageable females (Roehner 2009a). A high number of marriages between Icelandic women and American men would have been highly disruptive in a population of roughly 120 000, especially if many of these

women subsequently emigrated to America. Aware of the tensions this was causing, the American Command decided to prohibit American soldiers from marrying Icelandic women in March 1942 (ibid., pp. 10–11). A similar problem occurred during the post-war American occupation of Germany, sometimes with fatal consequences both to the occupying soldiers and their native girlfriends: "To German women, American soldiers appeared pretty attractive, if only because their income was between five to ten times higher than the income of an average German or Austrian. As this competitive advantage appeared unfair to many, it gave rise to an anti-fraternization movement . . . which brought about the murder of several military, sometimes together with their lovers" (Roehner 2009b, pp. 10). Another factor that could potentially breed hostility to the occupier, and therefore negatively affect the occupation, especially in a small society like Iceland, was the disruptive effects that the greater purchasing power of the foreign troops could cause in local economies. Often this could create (localized) high inflation and/or the appearance of black markets, which might benefit a minority but be detrimental to most (Roehner 2009a).

9. During the Nazi occupation of France, André Gide wrote in his journal on 9 July 1940, "If German rule were to bring us affluence, nine out of ten Frenchmen would accept it, three or four with a smile" (Gide 2000, p. 30).

10. Unfortunately, this study does not empirically disentangle the effects of public goods provision from coercion as the cause of successful occupation. It is also possible that alien rulers put more resources into nation building in countries where they expect to succeed.

11. Note that government policies are considered as public goods for the purposes of this discussion.

12. The key modifier in this statement is "cost–effective." Native resistance to occupation can always be tamped down by coercion, but this strategy is anything but cost effective.

13. When government bureaucrats and firms continue to serve the occupying regime, this is an example of state collaboration.

14. This definition excludes forms of passive collaboration such as sexual liaisons between native women and occupying troops. Between 1943 and 1946, 20 000 French women who were accused of such liaisons had their heads shaved and have been estimated to be subjected to public humiliation (Virgili 2002). The roughly 200 000 children that have been estimated to be the issue of such liaisons (*les enfants Boches*) were often treated badly by their neighbors. If, however, someone trades a piece of critical information to the occupier for food or lingerie, this constitutes active collaboration.

15. Other collaboration examples are more difficult to consider as a principal–principal relationship: General Nedić's collaborationist administration in Serbia (May 1941–October 1944) pursued its own goals: to have Serbia "become an equal member of the 'New European Order' dominated by the Nazis" (Ristović 2008, p. 186), and to more precisely reorganize Serbian society "on the basis of the long tradition of rural extended family communities, traditional values of rural life and preserved traditional morals" (ibid.). But Nedić so openly and thoroughly embraced Nazi principles and policies that he can perfectly be said to have been a Nazi agent in Serbia – Ristović (2008, p. 188) characterizes Nedić's administration as the German occupier's "product and instrument." Baranova (2008, p. 123) argues that both "collaboration and resistance are occupier-driven phenomena: the population of [Nazi-]occupied countries did not formulate its attitude and behaviour towards the Germans spontaneously but, rather, reacted to the comportment of the occupation authorities." This insight, says Baranova, is consistent with István Deák and Jan T. Gross's (Gross 2000). This does not contradict Kalyvas's argument about the principal–principal relationship. The fact that many occupied populations decided to collaborate reactively (as a *response* to a particular occupation) does not make them agents of the occupier; they can still have their own agenda.

16. Fast forwarding to the present day, the Israeli intelligence service, Shin Bet, is engaged in a comprehensive strategy to develop Palestinian collaborators within the Gaza Strip who will provide information about Hamas' military capacities (Barthe 2009).

17. "Had the country not been so bitterly divided when it was invaded, the occupation would probably have taken a very different course . . . In fact, many French welcomed the collapse of parliamentary democracy and saw occupation as the chance to settle scores with the left that went back decades" (Mazower 2008, p. 417); they saw "German domination as the price that had to be paid for restoring France to greatness" (ibid., p. 418; see also Ermakoff 2008).

18. One must
   go below the superstructure of ideology by which every state justifies its existence and look instead at what went on down at the most local level of the occupation state. It is plausible that collaboration there, in country towns on the Yangtze Delta, involved the considerations of national honor and personal integrity that haunted politicians of the new regime; but most of the time . . . collaboration dealt with more mundane problems – supplying food, organizing transportation, arranging security – the sorts of matters that local elites and local officials have to solve under any political dispensation to ensure social reproduction and to maintain themselves in power (Brook 2005, p. 12).

19. Presumably this violence stimulated resentment against the resistance. For similar conclusions about the sources of Palestinian collaboration with Zionists, see Cohen 2008, pp.151–2.

20. Likewise, in the late 1930s the collaborationist administration in Shanghai under Japanese occupation relied mainly on the city's "lesser elite, one that had been unsuccessful previously in gaining access to political office," as opposed to the previous ruling elite linked to the Nationalist administration. Collaboration was giving this lesser elite the opportunity to move into power it had been denied before (Brook 2005, p. 167). Thus, occupiers can take advantage of previously marginalized or unsuccessful elites who are willing, even anxious, to displace the previous ruling elite.

21. During the Franco-Belgian occupation of Germany's industrial Ruhr Valley after World War I, France denied any intentions of annexing the region. Hence the local population knew that eventually local sovereignty would be returned to Germany. "Potential collaborators . . . had more to fear from German prisons than French ones, and therefore German collaboration with the Franco-Belgian occupiers was low – at least until starvation became an issue in fall 1923" (Liberman 1996, p. 96). Likewise, "The wave of resistance that swept Nazi-occupied Europe on the eve of the Allied landings reflected the fact that the odds-on, imminent Allied campaign diminished the likelihood of German reprisals and increased the chances that resistance might have an impact" (ibid., p.149). The perception that the Nazis were losing ground in Belarus offers another example from World War II:
   During the spring and summer of 1942, the German advance came to a standstill and the Red Army managed to regain the initiative and returned to the attack. The population feared allying with the losing side and often sought to join the stronger one. German victory was no longer sure and previous experiences of Soviet rule suggested that there would be retributions for collaborating with the invaders. Therefore, by the end of 1942, to be seen as not compliant with the Germans became increasingly important for many civilians (Baranova 2008, p.124).

22. See, for instance, the *Secret Agent's Pocket Manual* that the Allies provided to members of the European resistance movements during the Nazi occupation (Bull 2009).

23. Louis Malle's superb movie *Lacombe Lucien* (1974) provides a graphic illustration of this point. Lucien Lacombe, a bored teenager living in a rural village in Vichy, France, attempts to join the resistance to provide some spice to his life, but they turn him down. He then turns right around and approaches the Vichy authorities, who welcome him with open arms.

24. The American experience in Iraq is especially instructive. After the invasion the US pursued a counterterrorism strategy aimed to defeat the resistance. Although this strategy was a spectacular failure, it was maintained for years. The relatively successful surge strategy was based on a different theory – namely, counterinsurgency theory – which

aimed to protect native society against the insurgents and to provide them with public goods (Ricks 2009).

REFERENCES

Baranova, O. (2008), "Nationalism, anti-Bolshevism or the will to survive? Collaboration in Belarus under the Nazi Occupation of 1941–1944", *European Review of History*, **15** (2), 113–28.

Barthe, B. (2009), "A Gaza, les 'collaborateurs', enjeu d'une guerre secrète entre Israël et le Hamas", *Le Monde*, 12 November 2009, p. 6.

Benvenisti, E. (2004), *The International Law of Occupation*, Princeton, NJ: Princeton University Press.

Boone, C. (2003), *Political Topographies of the African State: Territorial Authority and Institutional Choice*, Cambridge, UK: Cambridge University Press.

Braw, M. (1991), *The Atomic Bomb Suppressed. American Censorship in Occupied Japan*, Amonk, NY: East Gate.

Broers, M. (2003), "Centre and periphery in Napoleonic Italy: the nature of French rule in the *departments réunis, 1800–1814*", in M. Rowe (ed.), *Collaboration and Resistance in Napoleonic Europe. State-formation in an age of Upheaval, c. 1800–1815*. New York, NY: Palgrave Macmillan, pp. 55–73.

Brook, T. (2005), *Collaboration: Japanese Agents and Local Elites in Wartime China*, Cambridge, MA: Harvard University Press.

Bull, T. (2009), *The Secret Agent's Pocket Manual, 1939–1945*. London: Conway.

Bunting, M. (1995), *The Model Occupation: the Channel Islands under German Rule, 1940–1945*, London: HarperCollins.

Carlton, E. (1992), *Occupation. The Policies and Practices of Military Conquerors*, New York, NY: Routledge.

Cohen, H. (2008), *Army of Shadows. Palestinian Collaboration with Zionism, 1917–1948*, Berkeley and Los Angeles, CA: University of California Press.

Daniels, G. (1984), "The American Occupation of Japan, 1945–52", in R.A. Prete and A.H. Ion (eds), *Armies of Occupation*, Waterloo, Ontario: Wilfrid Laurier University Press, pp. 157–76.

Dobbins, J. (2003), *America's Role in Nation-building: From Germany to Iraq*. Santa Monica, CA: RAND.

Edelstein, D. (2004), "Occupational hazards: why military occupations succeed or fail", *International Security*, **29** (1), 49–91.

Ermakoff, I. (2008), *Ruling Oneself Out: A Theory of Collective Abdications*, Durham, NC: Duke University Press.

Esdale, C. (2003), "Popular mobilisation in Spain, 1808–1810", in M. Rowe (ed.), *Collaboration and Resistance in Napoleonic Europe. State-formation in an Age of Upheaval, c. 1800–1815*. New York, NY: Palgrave Macmillan, pp. 90–106.

Gide, A. (2000). *Journals. Volume 4: 1939–1949*, J. O'Brien (ed.), Champaign-Urbana, IL: University of Illinois Press.

Goldstein, C.S. (2008), "A strategic failure. American information control policy in Occupied Iraq", *Military Review* (March–April), 58–65.

Goldstein, C.S. (2009), *Capturing the German Eye: American Visual Propaganda in Occupied Germany*. Chicago, IL: University of Chicago Press.

Gross, J.T. (2000), "Themes for a social history of war experience and collaboration", in I. Deák, J. Gross and T. Judt (eds), *The Politics of Retribution in Europe. World War II and Its Aftermath*, pp. 15–36.

Hechter, M. (1987), *Principles of Group Solidarity*, Berkeley, CA: University of California Press.

Hechter, M. (2000), *Containing Nationalism*, Oxford, UK: Oxford University Press.

Hechter, M. (2009a), "Alien rule and its discontents", *American Behavioral Scientist*, **53** (3), 289–310.

Hechter, M. (2009b), "Introduction to 'Legitimacy in the modern world'", *American Behavioral Scientist*, **53** (3), 279–88.

Hechter, M. (2009c), "Special Issue: Legitimacy in the Modern World", *American Behavioral Scientist*, **53** (3), 279–481.

Hechter, M., I.E. Matesan and C. Hale (2009), "Resistance to Alien rule in Taiwan and Korea", *Nations and Nationalism*, **15** (1), 36–59.

Hoffmann, S. (1968), "Collaborationism in France during World War II", *Journal of Modern History*, **40** (3), 375–95.

Kahneman, D. and A. Tversky (1979), "Prospect theory: an analysis of decision under risk", *Econometrica*, **47** (2), 263–91.

Kalyvas, S.N. (2000), "Red terror: leftist violence during the occupation", in M. Mazower (ed.), *After the War Was Over: Reconstructing Family, State, and Nation in Greece, 1944–1960*, Princeton, NJ: Princeton University Press, pp. 142–83.

Kalyvas, S.N. (2006), *The Logic of Violence in Civil War*, New York, NY: Cambridge University Press.

Kalyvas, S.N. (2008a), "Collaboration in comparative perspective", *European Review of History*, **15** (2), 109–111.

Kalyvas, S.N. (2008b), "Armed collaboration in Greece, 1941–1944", *European Review of History*, **15** (2), 129–42.

Lammers, C.J. (2003), "Occupation regimes alike and unlike: British, Dutch and French patterns of inter-organizational control of foreign territories", *Organization Studies*, **24** (9), 379–403.

Lasswell, H. (1927), "The theory of political propaganda", *American Political Science Review*, **21** (3), 627–31.

Liberman, P. (1996), *Does Conquest Pay? The Exploitation of Occupied Industrial Societies*, Princeton, NJ: Princeton University Press.

MacKenzie, S.P. (1997), *Revolutionary Armies in the Modern Era. A Revisionist Approach*, London: Routledge.

Mazower, M. (2008), *Hitler's Empire: Nazi Rule in Occupied Europe*, London: Allen Lane.

Orwell, George ([1949] 1984), *Nineteen Eighty-four*. Oxford, UK: Clarendon Press.

Perez, E. and E. Bellman (2009), "Officials say investor's donations would wound up with Sri Lanka rebels", *The Wall Street Journal*, October 19, 2009, pp. A4.

Petersen, R.D. (2002), *Understanding Ethnic Violence: Fear, Hatred, and Resentment in Twentieth-century Eastern Europe*, Cambridge, UK: Cambridge University Press.

Ricks, T.E. (2006), *Fiasco: The American Military Adventure in Iraq*. New York, NY: Penguin Press.

Ricks, T.E. (2009). *The Gamble: General David Petraeus and the American Military Adventure in Iraq, 2006–2008*. New York, NY: Penguin Press.

Ristović, M. (2008), "Rural 'anti-utopia' in the ideology of Serbian collaborationists in the Second World War", *European Review of History*, **15** (2), 179–92.

Robinson, R.E. (1972), "Non-European foundations of European imperialism: a sketch for a theory of collaboration", in R. Owen and B. Sutcliffe (eds), *Studies in the Theory of Imperialism*, London: Longman, pp. 117–42.

Roehner, B.M. (2009a), "Relations between Allied Forces and the population of Iceland, 1940–2006", Version of 14 April 2009, available at http://www.lpthe.jussieu.fr/~roehner/occupation.html, accessed 1 September 2009.

Roehner, B.M (2009b), "Relations between Allied Forces and the populations of Germany and Austria, 1 May 1945–31 December 1958", Version of 14 April 2009, available at http://www.lpthe.jussieu.fr/~roehner/occupation.html, accessed 1 September 2009.

Rothstein, B. (2009), "Creating political legitimacy: electoral democracy versus quality of government", *American Behavioral Scientist*, **53** (3), 311–30.

Rousseau, J-J. ([1797] 1997), *The Social Contract and Other Later Political Writings*,

V. Gourevitch (ed.), Cambridge Texts in the History of Political Theory, Vol. 2. Cambridge, UK: Cambridge University Press.

Seton-Watson, H. (1984), "Military occupations: some reflections from recent and more distant history", in R.A. Prete and A.H. Ion (eds), *Armies of Occupation*, Waterloo, Ontario: Wilfrid Laurier University Press, pp. 1–15.

Stirk, P.M.R. (2009), *The Politics of Military Occupation*, Edinburgh: Edinburgh University Press.

Tyler, T.R. (2006), "Psychological perspectives on legitimacy and legitimation", *Annual Review of Psychology*, **57**, 375–400.

Virgili, F. (2002), *Shorn Women: Gender and Punishment in Liberation France*, New York, NY: Berg.

Weber, M. (1978), *Economy and Society*, G. Roth and C. Wittich (eds), Berkeley, CA: University of California Press.

Zelditch Jr., M. (2001), "Theories of Legitimacy", in J.T. Jost and B. Major (eds), *The Psychology of Legitimacy*, Cambridge, UK: Cambridge University Press, pp. 33–53.

22 Three's company? Towards an understanding of third-party intervention effectiveness

David Carment and Martin Fischer

22.1 INTRODUCTION

When we consider the word "effectiveness" we often think of "measurement" as an associated term to help us better understand the conditions under which a particular kind of action leads to a specific kind of outcome. The idea that effectiveness can be "isolated," "measured" and "assessed" comes from the understanding that there is a real-world, and proven way of achieving a specific outcome or achieving a precise effect. More specifically, effectiveness is something that is understood as existing in fact, having the power or ability, to create a specific end state and having a capability that has demonstrated itself to be appropriately matched to an objective, goal or end state. Using such an approach, authors such as Esman (1995), Licklider (1995), Diehl, Reifschneider and Hensel (1996), Lund (1996), Kleiboer (1996), Regan (1996) and Walter (1997) among others, have all provided extensive and varied definitions of the term effectiveness in order to understand third-party intervention success and failure.

Taken in the context of third-party intervention, for the purposes of this chapter, there are a number of important questions that arise when we consider the issue of effectiveness. For example, is the effectiveness of third-party intervention simply about achieving a specific end goal, or end state, or do other parameters and activities, such as process and context matter? If effectiveness is just about understanding what works in the real world, what then is the appropriate place of theory, either as a basis for establishing evaluative benchmarks or as a body of inductively derived empirical evidence that we might call law-like generalizations? And finally, if we are to seek a better understanding of third-party intervention effectiveness what might be the major impediments and opportunities for success in conducting such an enquiry?

In this chapter, we will examine the various debates surrounding the issue of third-party intervention effectiveness and in doing so will seek to answer these and related questions. Suffice to say that, research and findings on the effectiveness of third-party intervention are characterized by significant conceptual and theoretical uncertainties, and occasionally, misunderstandings that are rooted in multiple sources of tension, misinterpretations and ambiguities.

22.2   THEORETICAL AND PRACTICAL DILEMMAS

The political implications of getting intervention right are, of course, significant. As Walter (1999, p.3) argued ten years ago, "on the one hand it is unlikely that the international community will be able to ignore civil war since outside intervention appears to play a crucial role in the resolution of these conflicts . . . On the other hand, both the United States and the international community seem unsure when to intervene in these conflicts, how to intervene in them and which conflicts to target." In response, several major initiatives were undertaken to understand the theory and practice of intervention, in order to determine why some succeed and some fail (Diehl, Reifschneider and Hensel 1996; Walter 1997; Mason, Weingarten and Fett 1999; Walter and Snyder 1999; Regan 2000; Regan and Stam 2000). The results of these studies were twofold. First, what emerged is a better understanding of the use of force. Second, they clarified how a lack of resolve and credibility within coalitions and security organizations can induce escalation and prolonged conflict (Regan 1996; Harvey 1998; Walter and Snyder 1999; Dixon 2000).

Because third-party intervention is the subject of divergent, independent disciplines, including, but not limited to, political science, labor and industrial relations, psychology and management studies, the term itself is burdened with imprecision. Properly understood, in the domain of international relations, we can define third-party intervention as comprising three distinct components. First, there is the meaning of intervention itself, which, in the political science literature, is most often, but not always, construed as forceful and often violent direct action associated with military techniques and strategies in which consent is neither desired nor required.

However, not all coercive actions are necessarily interventions in the sense they do not involve the direct use of force coupled with territorial incursion. Nor do all interventions entail coercive action. For example, in the former case, sanctions and embargoes have a coercive component, as do deterrence and compellance, and various other and related threats to use to force. In the latter case, mediation and third-party assisted negotiation through diplomacy can be considered forms of intervention that have little or no coercive elements. Likewise, economic action, such as trade sanctions or the withholding of aid, imposed unilaterally or collectively, may be considered threatening if not coercive and they undoubtedly constitute interference in the affairs of states.

For our purposes we will consider intervention to have different, sometimes complementary, sometimes contradictory, meanings. In the purest sense, intervention is a form of direct coercive interference in the internal affairs of states which can, of course, change in both scope and intensity over time. The most basic definition of intervention taken in this narrow sense would be dictatorial interference in the affairs of states in situations where consent is absent. However, as we shall see below, consent is a complex issue and often difficult to interpret in the context of a hot war or in situations where no viable government is in place. Therefore, a broader understanding of the term, which places emphasis on the presence or absence of consent, rather than on the use of force is more generally tolerable.

Turning to the second component, we are primarily concerned with the actions or behaviors of another (or third) party which suggests that, that other "party" need not be a single state or any state for that matter. The party could be a collection of states in an "ad hoc" coalition, acting in unison within a formally recognized organization (or outside of it) or it could indeed be a single state, acting unilaterally on its own or with the support, legal sanction or tacit endorsement of other states and organizations. It may, under some circumstances, be a non-state actor who "intervenes" on behalf of or with the tacit or open support of a state, in return for which it receives sanctuary and resources. For our purposes, we are concerned primarily with state-to-state interactions and so the party in question would usually be a single state, or a collection of states acting unilaterally or on behalf of an organization or an organization, representing a collection of states.

This choice limits us considerably in terms of both the domain of what we might characterize as interactions between states and the behavior of those states within these interactions. For example, not all disputes between states necessarily advance to the stage at which intervention is a possibility or a necessity, nor for that matter do all hostile interactions such as international crises, possess the gravity of threat that might be understood as dictatorial interference. By the same token, intervention must be more than statements and words; a key component is the willingness to intervene or the allocation of resources by one state (or other entity) to physically affect or alter the behaviour of another.

Finally, we come to the last element of our definition and that is the meaning of "third" as in third party. Herein lie three difficulties. The first difficulty is the idea of a third party itself. It implies there are already two (or more) parties involved in what is most likely, but not necessarily, a dispute or conflict which may, or may not, exhibit open, overt armed violence. However, it is obviously not always the case that conflicts leading to intervention are necessarily initiated and driven by two (or more) parties. Failed states, coups and humanitarian disasters, where belligerents within or outside the state may be non-existent or difficult to discriminate and identity, are relatively common. Therefore, we would be hard pressed to conclude that the "third" party in all interventions are necessarily those involving themselves in an internal conflict in which groups within the state are at war with one another (such as a civil war).

Obviously, it is much simpler to identify a third party in a conflict between two or more states and that is where our slippage in terminology probably originates, in the sense of what is appropriate for understanding "conventional" interstate phenomena, such as crisis management, is not necessarily useful for understanding intrastate or internal phenomena where actors may lack legal personality, are difficult to identify and lack the tools and resources that states do.

A second and related difficulty is the legal and normative significance of a third party. A third party in the legal sense usually connotes an independent organization or representative of that organization acting with the sanction of an international governing body such as the United Nations. The "thirdness" in the legal and normative sense implies both impartiality and neutrality; terms that are often applied in the context of a peacekeeping or a diplomatic mission but which themselves are highly ambiguous.

The final and related issue is concern over what we mean by third in the sense that the third party is removed from, or distinctly disconnected from, the conflict. However, this "disconnectedness" is difficult to discern as the third party itself may be part of the conflict. More importantly, some may think of a third party as being free of bias in the sense that they have not chosen sides in a conflict or that they have no "interests" in the conflict. As we will show further on, both of these assumptions are misleading. In sum, we have a general understanding of third-party intervention which is broad in scale and all encompassing.

A complicating factor is that third-party intervention is evaluated by numerous but ultimately dissimilar research projects, theories and methodologies that cover everything from research on civil war, to peacekeeping (and peace enforcement), to mediation and coercive and non-coercive diplomacy. Compounding this issue is the fact that third-party intervention is operationalized and measured using distinct and sometimes idiosyncratic methodologies such that cross comparison and validation are difficult if not impossible.

These methods might include, but are not limited to, qualitative first-person narratives, historical process tracing, single case studies, case studies that are comparative and inductive in design, large-N or quantitative approaches that rely on statistical techniques to evaluate proposition and formal models with an emphasis on deducing law like generalizations. Finally, research on third-party intervention can be actor-centric, focusing on questions such as "who intervenes – why, how and on whose side?" or phenomenon-centric, seeking to address questions of the type of conflict, conflict duration, termination and sequencing.

22.3 DIMENSIONS OF EFFECTIVENESS

In order to alleviate some of these conceptual and methodological uncertainties, we focus our analysis on several distinct dimensions. First, we discuss different types of third-party interventions and interveners as they relate to bias and consent issues. We also consider issues of timing and expected outcomes, respectively. In simpler terms, we can make two distinctions within the literature: first, research that focuses on explaining the independent variable and, second, research that seeks to understand the dependent variable as noted in the final category, Section 22.5. While a great deal of research effort has been expended on understanding the first three categories of inputs and independent variables, significantly less has been devoted to understanding outcomes or more generally what constitutes intervention success and failure.

The implications of the lacuna in the latter category are fairly significant. On the one hand, we are confronted with a need to provide a precise and replicable definition of an outcome that has general acceptance in the field. Such a definition might include, for example, the cessation of violence, a formal agreement to end hostilities or even a peace accord. On the other hand, there is clearly a need to move beyond somewhat simplistic and binary interpretations that focus less on arbitrary end states and more on process and perceptions. For example, what difference does it make, if there is an end to open hostilities, if one party to the conflict believes that it has been treated unfairly or there remain deep-seated unresolved tensions? Such a distinction, while philosophical in nature, in fact goes to the heart of different schools of thought on the causes of conflict and has significant implications for policy.

22.4 TYPES OF INTERVENTION AND TYPES OF INTERVENER

Focusing on types of intervention is a good place to start our analysis since it is here that comparisons are usually made on the basis of different, but arguably complementary techniques and strategies. The idea of contingency is a good place to begin. The idea of contingency can be found in the work of Pat Regan, among others, who has produced a body of research on questions of third-party intervention. In his early studies, Reagan (1996) argued that third-party interventions seek to "alter the calculations by which the antagonists arrive at particular outcomes . . . The goal is to make it too costly for the combatants to continue fighting" (1996, p. 341). Using Regan's basic insight we can think of third-party intervention as a continuum or spectrum of techniques and strategies, rather than a simple distinction between force or no-force. And this is more or less how the literature considers it as well (Lund 1996; Druckman and Diehl 2006; Zartman 2007; Bercovitch and Gartner 2009).

Dixon (1996, p. 653) proposes a comprehensive list of third-party interveners that include single or coalitions of nation states; international, regional or subnational organizations; ad hoc commissions; NGOs; individuals; or any other actor with international standing. In their analysis of third-party intermediaries' behaviour in militarized disputes, Frazier and Dixon (2006) present a two-fold approach that distinguishes between broad types of third parties (state, coalition, inter-governmental organization, NGO) and specific types of third parties (head-of-state, minister, representatives, council, assembly, and/or ad-hoc committee or commission).

When considering their involvement in multilateral interventions, individual member states will undertake different cost–benefit calculations than for unilateral engagement. Regan (1998, p. 757) suggests that "because of the way costs and benefits from outside interventions are distributed when the policy is carried out under the auspices of a collective group, state-level decisions are less encumbered by the political costs related to the intervention and its possible failure." Specifically, the "ability to distribute the costs – at least the political costs – makes the decision criteria somewhat different from those associated with unilateral interventions."

At one end of the spectrum are less coercive diplomatic efforts such as pure mediation: the facilitation of a negotiated settlement through persuasion, control of information and identification of alternatives by a party who is perceived to be impartial. Half-way up the spectrum is "mediation with muscle" or the deliberate and strategic use of rewards and punishments to bring the belligerents to the negotiating table. At the opposite end of the spectrum lie economic and military measures (Regan 2000). Related ways to consider this spectrum are in terms of scale or intensity. For example, in an early study on the subject Hass (1983) makes a rather broad distinction between "small" (mediation) and "large" (peace operations) third-party interventions. A lot of empirical studies have focused on various types of third-party intervention. These include public appeals, communication, mediation, observation, physical intervention, humanitarian aid and adjudication. Fisher (2001) draws a line between those strategies which, in his view tend to diminish conflict (such as conventional peacekeeping, track two diplomacy and consultation) and those which do not (such as economic sanctions and peace enforcement).

Some years later, Fisher (2007) developed his arguments further into a six-item taxonomy that includes the following interventions. First, conciliation focuses on the provision of informal communication links between the parties. Second, in consultations, third parties facilitate creative problem-solving. Third, pure mediations attempt to facilitate negotiated settlements. Fourth, power mediation allows third parties to employ leverage and coercion. Fifth, through arbitration, third parties provide legally binding judgments. Sixth, through peacekeeping, third parties provide military personnel to perform traditional peacekeeping tasks such as monitoring of cease fires and trust-building activities.

Fisher's taxonomy makes no mention of economic measures or uses of military force outside peacekeeping. Similarly, Frazier and Dixon (2006) omit economic measures from their five categories of third-party intermediary interventions: verbal expressions; diplomatic approaches; legal/judicial processes; civil administration/assistance; military involvement.

Focusing on aspects of endogeneity in the context of intrastate conflict, Carment and Rowlands (1998, p. 579) "assume that the specific characteristics of an intrastate conflict heavily influence the matrix of trade-offs that a third-party force must consider before making decisions regarding a potential intervention." In addition to one endogenous factor, the intensity of the third party's intervention, they list "three exogenous factors: the salience of the conflict to the intervener, the strength of the combatants in the conflict, and the gains the combatants expect to achieve should the fighting continue." In sum, there is no one size fits all formula for success that can be applied universally across all conflicts.

Third-party interveners will generally begin with low-cost peaceful tactics such as mediation and condemnation. If those fail then the third party may choose to escalate. Thus, intervention "progresses" in the following way: reassurance and preventive diplomacy; verbal appeals to de-escalate; inducements; deterrence; compellance and pre-emption. Some actions can be considered positive strategies (persuasion and rewards). Others are more negative and more coercive in nature.

Two other important features help us distinguish between types of intervention. On the one hand, there is consent. Briefly, consent refers to the ability of a party to arrive at a decision independent of pressure. Consent implies autonomy and freedom of choice. Bias, on the other hand, is a characteristic of the third party and tells us something about how the third party is aligned with the interests of the parties in conflict (Rowlands and Carment 2006).

There is literature that examines bias and consent in pacific forms of intervention such as mediation, on the one hand, and research on peace-keeping and peace enforcement, on the other. For example, in his assessment of mediator pressure, Boskey (1994) argues that the first principle of mediation is that any agreement that results from the process should be voluntary and must not compromise the autonomy of either party. Matz (1994) challenges this claim, stressing that autonomy is preserved even if constraints are imposed.

Hence, pressure applied by the mediator is a legitimate tool; adversaries invite third-party intervention precisely because they seek pressure as a means of solving a dispute that they cannot solve themselves (Kydd 2000). Using experimental techniques, Carnevale and Arad (1996) examine the relationship between mediator pressure and autonomy. They argue that third-party bias does not significantly constrain the mediation process, especially if the bias is communicated so that both sides can adjust their positions prior to and during the negotiations. Research by Gibson, Thompson and Bazerman (1996) supports this conclusion. They ask how and why mediators often reach agreements that are less than ideal, and conclude that inappropriate agreements are frequently a result of mixed and poorly communicated signals and a preoccupation with mediator impartiality.

In brief, research on pure mediation shows that bias can act as a catalyst to move the settlement process forward because it allows the disputants to more readily develop a position that will maximize their own gains. It remains to be seen, however, if this basic finding on effectiveness can be extrapolated to incidences where third-party intervention consists of mediation, essentially a voluntary process, coupled with more forceful measures, as a way of preventing or managing violent conflict between groups of peoples. Traditional perspectives assume that a violation of impartiality goes against the underlying precepts of specific kinds of third-party involvement such as peacekeeping: to avoid escalation and to avoid taking sides. For example, James (1998) has consistently argued that favoritism in intrastate conflict is more likely to make peacekeepers targets rather than intermediaries. Citing evidence from the Congo, Lebanon and Bosnia, James suggests that outside forces should not intervene unless the three basic conditions, the use of force for self defense only, the interposition of troops after a ceasefire and the maintenance of tactical and strategic impartiality, can be reasonably met. This is somewhat supported by an assessment by the International Crisis Group (1999, p. 15): "the sad lesson from Bosnia is that reconciliation between former foes cannot be expected for years. The war produced no clear result, unlike in 1945, to allow for some form of de-nazification and a completely fresh start."

The type of diplomatic measures applied by third parties depends, to a large extent, on the parties' ability to come to an agreement on their own: "the less capable the disputants are of negotiating their own settlement, the more third parties should rely on heavy, controlling tactics" (Pruitt 2000, p. 245). Mediation is often referred to as the most prominent diplomatic third-party intervention. Fisher (2007, p. 312) suggests that "mediation involves the use of reasoning and persuasion, the suggestion of alternatives, and at times the application of leverage in order to facilitate a negotiated settlement on the substantive issues in the conflict."

Bercovitch (1992) provides a classification of mediation activities that distinguishes between strategies of facilitation/communication, formulation and manipulation. First, in situations where parties may not be that far apart and exhibit a willingness to settle, mediators will likely act as facilitator (Burton 1984; Bercovitch 1992; Bercovitch and Houston 1996) or communicator (Touval and Zartman 1985; Zartman and Touval 1996; Bercovitch 1997), limiting their role to opening communication channels through contacting relevant parties and delivering messages as well as ensuring that both parties continue their discussions and dialogue. Based on the assumption that incomplete information will lead actors to make sub-optimal decisions, facilitative mediators seek to "ensure that the actors have access to all necessary information to best estimate the range of mutually preferable outcomes" (Beardsley et al. 2006, p. 63).

Second, when mediators take the role of formulator, they actively enter into the negotiations (Touval and Zartman 1985; Hopman 1996). They involve themselves by providing innovative solutions and sometimes even persuade parties. The goal is to "help the actors to more easily select an existing mutually acceptable alternative" (Beardsley et al. 2006, p. 63). Third, in unfavourable conditions with hostile parties that distrust each other, mediators will take on the role of manipulators. They may use their muscle to bring conflict parties to agree to a settlement by using a combination of carrots and sticks, for example, publicly supporting one side or condemning another, pressing for solutions and attempting to manipulate parties' incentives. By offering carrots, manipulating mediators can reward or compensate cooperative parties. The use of sticks allows for the manipulation of non-compliant parties' costs for non-agreement. However, the mediator as manipulator needs to walk a fine line and avoid the inherent danger of exhibiting such a strong bias that would force one of the parties to abandon the negations because it regards any settlement as less attractive than continuing to fight (Svenson 2009).

Moving beyond mediation, we might consider peacekeeping as one step removed. According to Ruggie, peacekeeping is an attempt to overcome a coordination problem between belligerents by enhancing transparency and establishing clearly defined rules of the game. Highly intense operations are compared to a game of chicken; an escalatory ladder of means up to and including war is used to "force an aggressor off its track" (Ruggie 1994, p. 29). Further evidence supporting this argument is provided by Roberts (1996), who chronicles the experiences of the UN operation in Cambodia from 1991 to 1993 (UNTAC). He shows that UN impartiality promoted conflict there, and that it failed to maintain consent from the two core actors: the government in Phnom Penh and the Khmer Rouge. This loss of consent, argues Roberts, severely hampered UNTAC's ability to implement its broad and sophisticated mandate, which was the largest and most expensive peacekeeping operation at the time.

The UN experience shows that when third parties are faced with an intrastate conflict with regional consequences, they are likely to be extremely hesitant in engaging in costly strategies at the outset because they lack the sufficient "political will" and resources to fulfill their commitments. Slow escalation of violent conflict may evolve as a result of this unwillingness to "get involved." However, settlements also require the stamp of institutional legitimacy upon which long-term measures depend. As Haas (1983) and Diehl et al. (1996) have shown, in areas where state interests converge, states have generally provided strong support for the application of institutionalised forms of conflict management. In the absence of cooperation among states, institutions, especially the United Nations, have proved far less effective. The most notable aspect of Haas's analysis is UN ineffectiveness when "meta-issues" around which state interests coalesce (for example, post-war decolonisation and for example, self-determination in Asia and Africa) are absent.

Betts (1996) uses the examples of UN intervention in Bosnia, US intervention in Somalia and US and UN intervention in Haiti to underscore this argument. He argues that impartial intervention can work in more limited instances – such as the ceasefire mediation between Iran and Iraq and the political receivership of the UN Transitional Authority in Cambodia. However, these instances prove only that impartiality works best where intervention is needed least, where wars have "burned out" and the fighting factions need only the good offices of mediators to end the fighting formally.

Gent (2008, p. 715) suggest that the "main effect of a biased military intervention is to shift the balance of power in favor of one side or another." Regan and Aydin (2006, p. 743) argue that "solely military or economic interventions lack the explicit link to the notion of conflict management." If military measures take the form of military support to warring parties, they will "look for solutions to their disputes in fighting rather than the negotiation table." However, the provision of military aid can also contribute to reaching a "hurting stalemate" more quickly, thus potentially shortening the conflict.

Roberts (1996) sees the problematic nature of forceful interventions in terms of "loss of consent" rather than in terms of "loss of impartiality." He characterizes the downgrading of the consent of the parties to a conflict as a requirement for UN action to be at the heart of peacekeeping failures, citing case evidence from Iraq, the former Yugoslavia and Somalia. He further cites the incongruity between the UN's stated willingness to use force within the scope of its peacekeeping operations and a reluctance to perform this role in practice; instead, the UN contracts out the use of force to regional organizations or specific countries. Like James (1998), Roberts believes that the willingness to use force leaves lightly armed UN peacekeepers vulnerable to attack and exposes the UN to criticism for engaging in military activity that may have an adverse impact upon civilian populations.

Rothchild and Lake (1998) argue both for forceful intervention and impartiality. Like Krain (2005), they believe it alters the internal balance of power. This can be useful in equalizing forces and in creating a hurting stalemate in which neither side can be victorious, thereby encouraging a negotiated settlement. But it can also lead to situations wherein the intervention emboldens the weaker party to the conflict, encouraging it to increase its demands and thus prolong the conflict. Accordingly, Rothchild and Lake argue that pressure must be exerted on both sides to moderate their demands.

Similarly, Mason, Weingarten and Fett (1999, p. 252) suggest that because a biased intervention in intrastate conflict increases the resource base of the participant that is supported by the intervener, it should be expected that the intervener is "subsidizing the beneficiary's capacity to absorb the additional costs of conflict and to inflict damage on its rival." Since the subsidized party has a de facto veto over a settlement by refusing to stop fighting, the probability of a settlement should diminish if an intervening nation subsidizes one actor's effort. They go on to argue that because a biased intervention increases both the number of parties who can veto a settlement and the amount of time required to reach a settlement, it is likely to diminish the probability of a settlement ever being reached. Instead, they recommend mediation as the best approach to addressing intrastate conflict, a claim supported by Walter (1997), who shows that a neutral arbiter is a pre-requisite for a successful settlement of civil wars. For some observers, institutionalised forms of pure mediation do not exist in international politics (Zartman and Touval 1996). Others have suggested that any form of institutionalised mediation is likely to violate the principles of pure mediation. Pure mediation, they argue, is found only in informal, non-power-based situations involving non-state actors.

Finally, using a dynamic model of conflict duration, Elbadawi (1999) considers whether external intervention has positive or negative impacts. He argues that external intervention in favour of rebel groups may have the effect of reducing the cost of sustaining a rebellion by a small ethnic group, which otherwise might not materialize or may be quickly crushed by the government. In a related paper, Elbadawi and Sambanis (2000) found that external intervention was more likely to extend the duration of civil wars.

In contrast, others have argued that forceful and more biased interventions are merited under specific circumstances, especially when the outcome is otherwise likely to result in the significant defeat of one party. For example, Betts (1996) argues that only in instances where the outside power takes complete command of the situation and imposes a peace settlement will the intervention result in stability. More limited forms of intervention undertaken with the goal of impartiality may keep either belligerent from defeating the other, but will not stop the adversaries from waging war in an attempt to do so.

These arguments find resonance in Zartman and Touval (1996) and Watkins and Winter (1997), who argue that an intervener may be more effective in achieving short-term stability when it has a vested interest in a specific outcome that may favor one side over another. Using a game-theoretic model, Carment and Rowlands (1998) also suggest that forceful and biased measures directed at the ascendant force are appropriate under a pre-specified set of conditions, particularly when the conflict is salient to the outside party. Less forceful measures are likely to prevent continued fighting only when the belligerents' expected gains are low. Dixon (2000) suggests that if a quick end is desired, intervention with ground forces on behalf of the stronger side may be the most effective strategy. An intervener committed to a compromise outcome may instead find cost imposition to be a more productive solution than ground troops. Citing evidence from Bosnia, Ruggie (1994) argues that outside forces should gradually escalate in order to dissuade, deny and deter an ascendant force, a result supported by Stedman's (1997) analysis of spoilers in a peace process.

The dilemma for the third party, as Regan has demonstrated, is whether to quickly terminate a conflict by favoring the stronger side, or to protect the weaker side and thereby risk prolonging the conflict. Arguably, under certain circumstances, such as genocide, failed peace accords or prolonged conflict, can have very negative effects.

The problem is demonstrated by Licklider (1995), who found that instances of genocide towards a group generally increased after that group was defeated in an identity-based civil war. The problem, Licklider illustrates, is that intrastate conflicts that end with a military victory are generally more stable than those that have a negotiated settlement. But these are precisely the cases where third parties appear to have the most impact, according to the empirical analysis of 152 civil conflicts between 1820 and 1992 in Balch-Lindsay and Enterline (2000).

Regan (1996), Bercovitch (1996), Dixon (1996) and Haas (1983) conclude that, in any given conflict, third parties will generally employ as many different strategies as possible, pacific and forceful. Regan concludes that mixed strategies by powerful interveners on behalf of a government are more likely to lead to a cessation of hostilities. Similarly, Harvey (1998) suggests that the use of force is appropriate when coupled with the basic tenets of deterrence, credibility and commitment, thereby drawing attention not simply to the choice of strategy, but the tactical efficacy with which it is implemented. Finally, Luttwak (1999) argues that intervention, disallows for the possibility of a decisive conclusion, or the true exhaustion of the parties to the dispute, which would allow them to seek a sincere agreement.

Beyond mediation, peacekeeping and more forceful efforts, we must consider economic measures that provide opportunities for the imposition of non-military pressures that can still influence the balance of power. Siqueira (2003) considers the impact of third parties' military subsidies to allies. As subsidies increase, so will the recipients' ability to continue hostilities or maintain control of territory. Military subsidies can also be used as economic sticks as third parties have the ability to raise the cost of military goods or withholding assistance all together. Reagan and Aydin (2006, p. 754) find that the "independent effect of an economic intervention is to increase war duration, whereas its combined effect with diplomacy would lead to the conflict ending . . . earlier." Sanctions and embargoes are easily circumvented, which limits their effectiveness. The formalities of applying economic measures against recognized governments may be well established, however, impacting non-state actors through economic sanctions is more difficult.

22.5 TIMING AND OUTCOMES

Beyond understanding types of interveners and their interventions, related issues include timing and outcomes. With respect to timing, in general, third-party interventions occur only "after some period of development and escalation has elapsed" (Fisher 2001, p. 20). It is widely assumed that "as conflict continues, the parties become increasingly aware of their inability to achieve their goals through violence" (Greig and Regan 2008, p. 761). Conflicts reach a stage at which they impose "unacceptably painful costs upon both sides such that neither side can unilaterally impose a settlement [and] disputants become motivated to change the status quo by moving toward a compromise outcome" (Greig and Regan 2008, p. 761).

These assumptions are based on Zartman's (1985) concept of "ripeness" and a "hurting stalemate." Zartman suggests that the willingness of conflicting parties to consider outside intervention will increase over time as they approach a "hurting stalemate" at which both sides' costs outweigh the benefits and they see no way of exiting. If the parties see no further benefit from fighting and perceive it to be likely that their situation will deteriorate then a conflict has become "ripe" for third-party intervention. Zartman's assumptions have been criticized for the prolonged passiveness of third parties as they wait for the conflicting parties to reach a "hurting stalemate." In fact, Rubin (1991) has argued that third-parties should attempt to "ripen" the conflict at all stages of the conflict. However, empirical evidence supports Zartman's assumptions on ripeness. In a study of civil conflicts from 1945 to 1999, Regan and Aydin (2006, p. 753) find that if "diplomatic initiatives by third parties are undertaken at the sixtieth month, the evidence would suggest that the war would terminate within the next five months. However, the same intervention in the third month would to termination of the conflict in the twenty-sixth month."

Turning now to outcomes, on an abstract level, the objectives of third-party intervention are very complex, ranging from the strengthening of international norms reducing and eliminating armed violence to the pursuit of larger geostrategic goals. On the other hand, it is important to measure outcomes based on their contribution to resolving conflict, not just ending the violence. Stable and long lasting outcomes – as perceived through the eyes of the belligerent and the third party – are important for several reasons. Outcomes provide a reasonable indication of how "solid" a settlement is from the perspective of the belligerents. They tell us about the possibility of recurrence and the degree to which the conflict's underlying issues have been resolved. A decisive outcome is one in which the starting and end points are more autonomous. Stable outcomes are those with definitive end points. Victory and defeat may be more readily identifiable and accepted as such (Brecher and Wilkenfeld 1997).

It is also important to measure effectiveness by the form of outcome achieved. Was a formal settlement achieved? Did one party impose a unilateral solution? Did the third party impose a solution or did the crisis simply fade away only to recur again? Thus, outcomes also can be assessed objectively by their content. The form of the outcome refers to how the conflict was terminated ranging from formal negotiated agreements to tacit understandings that a crisis will fade until the next outbreak of the next crisis.

When evaluating the outcomes of third-party interventions, two inter-linked considerations need to be taken into account. First, different third-party interventions have different objectives. Gent (2008, p. 715) suggests that interveners' objectives "could be the sovereignty or autonomy of an ethnic group, the type of government or economic system of the country, the policy of the government concerning the distribution of resources or access to resources by external parties." Therefore, defining the dependent variable will vary from case to case. Second, these objectives will determine the way in which third parties evaluate to what extend expected outcomes have been successfully achieved. In general terms, Regan (1998, p. 760) argues that "a successful outcome is one in which the intervention contributes to the cessation of hostilities."

In general, empirical studies have come to diverging conclusions regarding the effect of third-party interventions on the duration of civil wars. For example, Balch-Lindsay and Enterline (2000, with Joyce 2008) study civil wars from 1820 to 1992 and find that third-party interventions contribute to shortening civil wars. Reagan (2002), however, finds that interventions tend to lengthen hostilities. Specifically, mediation has been show to have two broad effects. First, it creates conditions that allow opposing parties to reach a settlement (Dixon 1996; Bercovitch and Diehl 1997, Bercovitch and Regan 2003). Second, Regan and Stam (2000) have shown mediation to contribute to the shortening of conflicts.

Mason, Weingarten and Fett (1999) assess the impact of third-party intervention on three different outcomes of government versus rebel civil wars: government military victory, rebel military victory and negotiated settlement. Their findings suggest that, in the earlier stages of a conflict, the likelihood of arriving at a negotiated settlement is weakened by third-party intervention. If one side receives third-party support, its ability to achieve military victory increases. However, the longer a conflict lingers on, the more likely a settlement negotiated though a third party becomes. The likelihood further increases if third parties can provide the parties with security guarantees (Walter 2000).

An important aspect of third-party intervention in civil wars concerns itself with the impact of external support on the parties' willingness to cease hostilities and arrive at a negotiated settlement. If third parties support the government early on, this will strengthen its ability to continue hostilities and thus reduce its willingness to negotiate a settlement. If third parties support the opposition early on, this can contribute to levelling out the opposing parties' capabilities and therefore make a negotiated settlement more likely.

Using data from the International Crisis Behavior Project, Beardsley et al. (2006) test the impact of mediation on three outcomes: achievement of a formal agreement, a post-crisis reduction of tensions between conflicting parties and whether or not mediation influenced crisis abatement. First, in general, mediated crises are more likely to lead to formal agreements. Specifically, formulative and manipulative efforts contribute more effectively to formal agreements. Second, they find that mediated crises are more likely to lead to tension reduction.

Specifically, formulation is found to be most effective at reducing tensions while facilitation is found to be most effective at preventing a relapse into conflict. Third, mediation generally contributes to crisis abatement. Specifically, formulation is the most effective way to lead to crisis abatement. Regan and Aydin (2006, p. 742) maintain that "structural [military and economic] interventions often prolong a conflict." Their studies of civil wars from 1945 to 1999 suggest that "when controlling for instances of diplomatic interventions, the effect of economic intervention is to prolong the expected duration of a conflict, whereas military interventions bear no relationship to the outcome" (ibid. 2006, p. 750). Additionally, economic sanctions typically require a longer time period to become effective.

Others conclude that civil wars over political or economic issues are distinct from ethnic disputes by virtue of the ease by which they are terminated (Licklider 1995; Regan 1996; Brecher and Wilkenfeld 1997). It would also be anticipated that terminations are more ambiguous, in identity-based conflicts as well. Ambiguous terminations and resolutions are those resulting in indecisive results, like compromise or stalemate symbolizing an unresolved conflict. Subsequent crises and violence are anticipated by all adversaries. In addition, the substance of the outcome refers to the degree to which a political solution is perceived to be either ambiguous or definitive. For peace to be durable it must be accepted by the opposing leaders and their followers. Lund (1996) has found that a key impediment to terminating a conflict quickly is a process into which the belligerents cannot put their faith and trust. For a settlement to hold, the participants must perceive that a negotiated solution is capable of maintaining a stable and lasting peace into the unforeseeable future (Lake and Rothchild 1996).

22.6   CONCLUSION

We can conclude that there is little agreement within the discipline on the kinds of strategies necessary for the termination of intrastate ethnic conflicts. There remains, in the normative and empirical sense, one obvious dividing line that permeates the literature. Force is usually perceived as choice of last resort in the policy realm as well. It is therefore perceived as separate from other strategies, although here too there is a great deal of ambiguity in understanding its effectiveness since the threat to use force, which is a cornerstone of deterrence theory and policy, and the use of a pre-emptive force are fundamental aspects of modern statecraft.

Critics have suggested that coercive and unilateral forms of intervention serve only to erode international norms of mutual restraint among states. Others, more provocatively, have argued that the quickest way to terminate a conflict with fewest casualties is to favor the stronger side in any conflict, which is more often than not the state (Siquereia 2003). But such a simplistic dichotomy is not useful for several more important theoretical reasons. First, in considering different techniques or strategies most research lacks the methodological precision to isolate cause and effect such that we cannot conclude with a high degree of certainty that a specific technique is the cause of a specific outcome. This is particularly problematic in the international domain where different techniques or strategies, some of which may entail coercive strategies while others may not, are applied simultaneously rather than in sequence. In the simplest sense, we lack the methodological capability to conduct truly experimental research and must be satisfied with largely probabilistic and correlational research and findings. If we are to conclude, for example, that force is indeed an effective strategy for third-party interveners it might be best achieved on the basis of looking at both detailed case analysis and large samples so that we could be more confident that we have isolated cause and effect.

A second and related issue, rarely considered in the literature is the "selection effect." Simply put, the problem is one of reverse causality in which certain techniques or strategies are selected by conflicting parties as being conducive to their interests or more generally their "values" (such as that embedded in the democratic peace thesis). They are in a general sense "pre-conditioned" by habituation, norms and interests to be more open or responsive to certain techniques or strategies. The selection effect plays out in a number of different ways.

First, let us consider a situation where two countries involved in a territorial conflict seek resolution through a recognized international organization by legal means and the conflict is resolved peacefully without recourse to violence. Here we might conclude that a pacific, non-coercive technique was successful in resolving a territorial dispute. Indeed, that appears to be the case; but if we examine the situation more closely, we will recognize that the conflict involved two states with legal status and a large body of international law backed by formalized institutional mechanisms to support the process. Simply put, the choice of this particular strategy and the likelihood of its success was determined in part by who the conflicting parties are, their past history and the opportunities and constraints placed upon them by the third party.

Conversely, consider a complex intrastate conflict in which the belligerents lack any legal personality and are conditioned by a history of long, open violence between them. It seems likely that any strategy employed by a third party will be fundamentally different than those that apply to state-to state interactions. This not only pertains to the sense of whether to legitimize belligerent actions through recognition but in terms of how to interact with them.

Based on our analysis, we see that third parties select a type of intervention strategy that most likely will achieve desired outcomes with minimal costs. We can conclude that there is no single best type of third-party intervention. Intervention involves a range of techniques and strategies that may be employed sequentially or simultaneously. Finally, we can suggest that third-party intervention is strategic and contingent in the sense that the third parties adopt strategies that are capable of interacting with the strategies chosen by the belligerents.

REFERENCES

Balch-Lindsay, D. and A.J. Enterline (2000), "Killing time: the world politics of civil war duration, 1820–1992", *International Studies Quarterly*, **44** (4), 615–42.

Balch-Lindsay, D., and A.J. Enterline and K.A. Joyce (2008), "Third-party intervention and the civil war process", *Journal of Peace Research*, **45** (3), 119–142.

Beardsley, K.C., D. Quinn, B. Biswas and A. Wilkenfeld (2006), "Mediation style and crisis outcome", *Journal of Conflict Resolution*, **50** (1), 58–86.

Bercovitch, J. (1992), "The structure and diversity of mediation in international relations", J. Bercovitch and J.Z. Rubin (eds), *Multiple Approaches to Conflict Management*, New York, NY: St. Martin's, pp.1–29.

Bercovitch, J. (1996), *Resolving International Conflicts: Theory and Practice of Mediation*, Boulder, CO: Lynne Rienner.

Bercovitch, J. (1997), "Mediation in international conflict: an overview of theory, a review of practice", in I.W. Zartman and J.L. Rasmussen (eds), *Peacemaking in International Conflict*, Washington DC: US Institute of Peace Press, pp. 125–154.

Bercovitch, J. and P.F. Diehl (1997), "Conflict management of enduring rivalries: frequency, timing, and short-term impact of mediation", *International Interactions*, **22** (4), 299–320.

Bercovitch, J. and S.S. Gartner (eds) (2009), *International Conflict Mediation: New Approaches and Findings*, London, New York: Routledge.

Bercovitch, J. and A. Houston (1996), "The study of international mediation: theoretical issues and empirical evidence", in J. Bercovitch (ed.), *Resolving International Conflicts*, Boulder: Lynne Rienner, pp. 11–35.

Bercovitch, J. and P.M. Regan (2003), "Mediation and international conflict management: a review and analysis", in Z. Maoz (ed.), *Multiple Paths to Knowledge in International Relations*, Lexington, MA: Lexington Books, pp. 249–72.

Betts, R.K. (1996), "The delusion of impartial intervention", in C.A. Crocker, F.O. Hampson and P. Aal (eds), *Managing Global Chaos: Sources of and Responses to International Conflict*, Washington DC: United States Institute of Peace Press, pp. 333–43.

Boskey, J.B. (1994), "The proper role of the mediator: rational assessment, not pressure", *Negotiation Journal*, **10** (4), 367–72.

Brecher, M. and J. Wilkenfeld (1997), *A Study of Crisis*, Ann Arbor, MI: University of Michigan Press.

Burton, J.W. (1984), *Global Conflict: The Domestic Sources of International Crisis*, Brighton, UK: Wheatsheaf.

Carment, D. and D. Rowlands (1998), "Evaluating third-party intervention in intrastate conflict", *Journal of Conflict Resolution*, **42** (5), 572–99.

Carnevale, P.J. and S. Arad (1996), "Bias and impartiality in international mediation", in J. Bercovitch (ed.), *Resolving International Conflicts*, Boulder, Co: Lynne Rienner, 39–53.

Diehl, P.F., J. Reifschneider and P. Hensel (1996), "United Nations intervention and recurring conflict", *International Organization*, **50** (4), 683–700.

Dixon, W.J. (1996), "Third-party techniques for preventing conflict escalation and promoting peaceful settlement", *International Organization*, **50** (4), 653–81.

Dixon, W.J. (2000), "Curing the disease without killing the patient: effects of military intervention strategies on civil war outcomes, 1816–1997", Annual Conference of the American Political Science Association, Washington DC.

Druckman, D. and P.F. Diehl (eds) (2006), *Conflict Resolution*, Thousand Oaks, CA: Sage.

Elbadawi, I. (1999), *Civil Wars and Poverty: The Role of External Interventions, Political Rights and Economic Growth*, Washington DC: World Bank.

Elbadawi, I. and N. Sambanis (2000), *External Interventions and the Duration of Civil Wars*, Washington DC: World Bank.

Esman, M.J. (1995), "Ethnic actors and international politics", *Nationalism and Ethnic Politics*, **1** (1), 111–25.

Fisher, R.J. (2001), "Methods of third-party intervention", in N. Ropers, M. Fischer and E. Manton (eds), *Berghof Handbook for Conflict Transformation*, Berlin: Berghof Center for Conflict Management, pp. 1–25.

Fisher, R.J. (2007), "Assessing the contingency model of third-party intervention in successful cases of prenegotiation", *Journal of Peace Research*, **44** (3), 311–29.

Frazier, D.V. and W.J. Dixon (2006), "Third-party intermediaries and negotiated settlements, 1946–2000", *International Interactions*, **32** (4), 385–408.

Gent, S.E. (2008), "Going in when it counts: military intervention and the outcome of civil conflicts", *International Studies Quarterly*, **52** (4), 713–35.

Gibson, K., L. Thompson and M. Bazerman (1996), "Shortcomings of neutrality in mediation: solutions based on rationality", *Negotiation Journal*, **12** (1), 69–80.

Greig, M.J. and P.M. Regan (2008), "When do they say yes? An analysis of the willingness to offer and accept mediation in civil wars", *International Studies Quarterly*, **52** (4), 759–81.

Haas, E. (1983), "Regime decay: conflict management and international organizations, 1945–1981", *International Organization*, **30** (2), 189–256.

Harvey, F. (1998), "Deterrence failure and ethnic conflict: the case of Bosnia", in D. Carment and P. James (eds), *Peace in the Midst of Wars: Preventing and Managing International Ethnic Conflicts*, Columbus, SC: University of South Carolina Press, pp. 230–64.

Heraclides, A. (1991), *The Self-Determination of Minorities in International Politics*, Portland, OR: Frank Cass.

Hopman, T.P. (1996), *The Negotiation Process and the Resolution of International Conflicts*, Columbia, SC: University of South Carolina Press.

International Crisis Group (1999), *Kosovo: Let's Learn from Bosnia. Models and Methods of International Administration*. Brussels International Crisis Group.

James, A. (1998), "Peacekeeping and ethnic conflict: theory and evidence", in D. Carment and P. James (eds), *Peace in the Midst of Wars*, Columbia, SC: University of South Carolina Press, pp. 163–93.

Kleiboer, M. (1996), "Understanding success and failure of international mediation", *Journal of Conflict Resolution*, **40** (2), 360–89.

Krain, M. (2005), "International intervention and the severity of genocides and politicides", *International Studies Quarterly*, **49** (3), 363–88.

Kydd, A. (2000), *Whose Side Are You On? Mediation as Cheap Talk*, Cambridge, MA: Olin Center, Harvard University.

Lake, D.A. and D. Rothchild (1996), "Containing fear: the origins and management of ethnic conflict", *International Security*, **21** (2), 41–75.

Licklider, R. (1995), "The consequences of negotiated settlements in civil wars, 1945–1993", *American Political Science Review*, **89** (3), 681–90.

Lund, M. (1996), *Preventing Violent Conflicts: A Strategy for Preventive Diplomacy*, Washington DC: US Institute of Peace Press.

Luttwak, E.N. (1999), "Give war a chance", *Foreign Affairs*, **78** (4), 36–44.

Mason, D.T., Jr., J.P. Weingarten and P.J. Fett (1999), "Win, lose, or draw: predicting the outcome of civil war", *Political Research Quarterly*, **52** (2), 239–68.

Matz, D.E. (1994), "Mediator pressure and party autonomy: are they consistent with each other?," *Negotiation Journal*, **10** (4), 359–65.

Pruitt, D. (2000), "Ethnic conflicts: the tactics of third-party intervention", *Orbis*, **44**, 245–254.

Regan, P.M. (1996), "Conditions of successful third-party interventions in intrastate conflicts", *Journal of Conflict Resolution*, **40** (2), 336–58.

Regan, P.M. (1998), "Choosing to intervene: outside interventions in internal conflicts", *The Journal of Politics*, **60** (3), 754–79.

Regan, P.M. (2000), *Civil Wars and Foreign Powers, Outside Intervention in Intrastate Conflict*, Ann Arbor, MI: The University of Michigan Press.

Regan, P.M. (2002), "Third-party intervention and the duration of intrastate conflicts", *Journal of Conflict Resolution*, **46** (1), 55–73.

Regan, P.M. and A. Aydin (2006), "Diplomacy and other forms of intervention in civil wars", *Journal of Conflict Resolution*, **50** (5), 736–56.

Regan, P.M. and A.C. Stam (2000), "In the nick of time: conflict management, mediation timing and the duration of interstate disputes", *International Studies Quarterly*, **44** (2), 239–60.

Roberts, A. (1996), "The crisis in UN peacekeeping', in C.A. Crocker, F.O. Hampson and P. Aall (eds), *Managing Global Chaos: Sources of and Responses to International Conflict*, Washington DC: United States Institute of Peace Press, pp. 297–320.

Rowlands, D. and D. Carment (2006), "Force and bias: towards a predictive model of effective third party intervention", *Journal of Defence and Peace Economics*, **15** (5), 435–56.

Rothchild, D. and D.A. Lake (1998), "Containing the fear: the management of transnational ethnic conflict", in D.A. Lake and D. Rothchild (eds), *The International Spread of Ethnic Conflict: Fear, Diffusion, and Escalation*, Princeton, NJ: Princeton University Press, pp. 203–26.

Rubin, J.Z. (1991), "The timing of ripeness and the ripeness of timing", in L. Kriesberg and S.J. Thorson (eds), *Timing and De-Escalation in International Conflicts*, Syracuse, NY: Syracuse University Press, pp. 237–46.

Ruggie, J.G. (1994), "The new US peacekeepig doctrine", *The Washington Quarterly*, **17** (4), 175–84.

Ruggie, J.G. (1996), *Winning the Peace: America and World Order in the New Era*, New York, NY: Columbia University Press.

Siquereia, K. (2003), "Conflict and third-party intervention", *Defence and Peace Economics*, **14** (6), 389–400.

Stedman, S. (1997), "Spoiler problems in the peace processes", *International Security*, **22** (2), 5–53.

Svenson, I. (2009), "Who brings which peace? Neutral versus biased mediation and institutional peace arrangements in civil wars", *Journal of Conflict Resolution*, **53** (3), 446–69.

Touval, S. and I.W. Zartman (1985), "Introduction: mediation in theory", in S. Touval and I.W. Zartman (eds), *International Mediation in Theory and Practice*, Boulder, CO: Westview, pp. 7–17.

Walter, B.F. (1997), "The critical barrier to civil war settlement", *International Organization*, **51** (2), 335–64.

Walter, B.F. (1999), "Introduction", in B.F. Walter and J. Snyder (eds), *Civil War, Insecurity, and Intervention*, New York, NY: Columbia University Press, pp. 1–14.

Walter, B.F. (2000), *Committing to Peace: The Successful Settlement of Civil Wars*. Princeton, NJ: Princeton University Press.

Walter, B.F. and J. Snyder (eds) (1999), *Civil War, Insecurity, and Intervention*, New York, NY: Columbia University Press.

Watkins, M. and K. Winters (1997), "Intervenors with interests and power", *Negotiation Journal*, **13** (2), 119–42.

Zartman, I. W. (1985), *Ripe for Resolution: Conflict and Intervention in Africa*, New York, NY: Oxford University Press.

Zartman, I.W. (2007), *Peacemaking in International Conflict*, Washington DC: US Institute of Peace Press.

Zartman, I.W and S. Touval (1996), "International mediation in the post-Cold War era", in C.A. Crocker and F.O. Hampson (with P. Aall) (eds), *Managing Global Chaos*, Washington DC: US Institute of Peace Press, pp. 445–61.

23 Credible commitment in post-conflict recovery
Thomas Edward Flores and Irfan Nooruddin

23.1 INTRODUCTION

As the contributions in this volume attest, civil war is common and deadly. By one count, civil conflicts have killed nearly 20 million people since 1945 (World Bank 2006). Perversely, the social, political and economic damage inflicted during civil conflicts often persists or even worsens once hostilities end, in turn planting the seeds of future civil conflicts. Paul Collier and his co-authors (2003) describe this cycle as a "conflict trap" and urge international donors to assist post-conflict countries in their economic reconstruction or risk further war. That logic suggests two related questions for post-conflict countries. First, what factors favor the deepening of peace after civil conflicts? Second, what political steps are needed to speed economic reconstruction and provide opportunities to impoverished citizens? Research seeking to answer these questions not only furthers our understanding of civil conflicts, but also provides valuable guidance to politicians, aid agencies and non-governmental organizations (NGOs) working in the shadow of violent conflicts.

Indeed, the challenge of promoting post-conflict economic recovery while avoiding conflict recidivism is daunting. Collier et al. (2003, p. 83) show that the risk of further conflict for countries emerging from civil war (that is, in the first year of post-conflict peace) is almost twice as high as it was on the eve of that conflict. Our own data support a pernicious version of the "conflict trap" and dramatically emphasizes the importance of short-term economic recovery; if a country does not recover economically in its first post-conflict year, a relapse into violent conflict becomes dramatically more likely (Flores and Nooruddin 2009a, p. 10).

In this chapter, we contend that the central obstacle to post-conflict peace and recovery is the inability of former warring parties to commit credibly to peaceful contestation of political and economic power (see also Coyne and Boettke 2009). In the often-chaotic politics of post-conflict communities, erstwhile enemies cannot rely on a hegemonic authority to enforce peace agreements; in the language of international relations, anarchy is the central political condition. Professed commitments to peace are unenforceable and hence non-credible. In turn, economic actors – be they foreign companies contemplating direct investments or small farmers attempting to return to lands abandoned during the conflict – understand this dilemma and therefore put little stock in post-conflict promises of peace. Their reluctance to commit resources in this unstable post-conflict environment obstructs economic reconstruction, facilitating the conflict trap.

Overcoming the credible commitment problem is therefore the lynchpin for post-conflict peace and recovery. Specifically, two related yet distinct sets of steps are necessary to reinforce the peace and galvanize recovery. Internally, former enemies must take steps to reassure each other that they will forego future violence. Externally, those groups must jointly signal both domestic and international audiences that they may invest their labor and capital without fear of violence and predation. If they do not accomplish each of these goals, they risk further political violence and socioeconomic dislocation.

Yet how can groups that only recently sought each other's destruction pursue these goals? We argue that re-conceptualizing post-conflict reconstruction as a credible commitment problem not only furthers our theoretical understanding, but also allows a re-evaluation of post-conflict interventions designed to forestall the violence, thus serving as a guide to policymakers and practitioners in the field. In the broadest sense, former combatant groups must take three steps to signal their credibility: create mechanisms that raise the expected utility of cooperation relative to that of defection, send costly signals of their commitments and empower third-parties to police agreements. More specifically, we re-interpret five post-conflict interventions in terms of their ability to bolster the credibility of post-conflict actors and evaluate evidence regarding each of them. Two of these deal directly with the political structures governing the distribution of power in the post-conflict era. *Elections* have become an increasingly common means of allocating power and forming new governments in the immediate post-conflict period. Elections may reinforce the credibility of post-conflict commitments, since participating in elections may be seen as a credible signal of peaceful intentions. Furthermore, democracy's checks and balances bolster the credibility of executives' promises and constrain them from re-initiating violence. However, recent evidence suggests that elections' record is mixed. Sometimes this process is accompanied by explicit *power-sharing arrangements* between the former combatants as a way of assuaging the worst fears of the participants should the election results not favor them.

We then turn to three international interventions designed to galvanize economic reconstruction, focusing on how third-parties can use their interventions to overcome the credible commitment problem. *Peacekeeping operations* are designed to enforce the terms of peace agreements and thus build trust in former combatant groups that the peace will endure. Often, such operations include *disarmament, demobilization and reintegration (DDR)* programs, which offer a third-party-enforced credible signal that each party to the conflict is releasing its control over its soldiers. *Foreign aid*, whether provided bilaterally by regional and world powers or multilaterally through international financial institutions, also plays a critical role in helping rebuild state institutions devastated by war.

The remainder of this chapter is therefore divided into two sections. First, we describe more fully the logic of credible commitments in the post-conflict environment, focusing on how the credible commitment problem retards economic recovery. Second, we translate this more conceptual discussion of the importance of credible commitment into an analysis of mechanisms for conflict resolution in post-conflict environments.

23.2   CIVIL WAR AND CREDIBLE COMMITMENTS

The logic of the credible commitment problem permeates research on civil war's causes, duration and resolution. Much of this research finds its foundations in the study of interstate war. In that field, neo-realist scholars' focus on anarchy – the absence of a dominant authority regulating states' behavior – informed the rationalist analysis of the causes of interstate war (Fearon 1995; Powell 2006). Without a sovereign that can observe and punish violations of interstate agreements, rational leaders of states cannot be confident that such agreements can be enforced. Anarchy thus creates a self-help system resembling a prisoner's dilemma. If the leader of country A trusts the leader of country B's public declaration of her commitment to a peaceful resolution of some dispute, the former leaves the latter the opportunity to defect from the agreement – with potentially disastrous consequences for country A. When leaders perceive significant first-strike advantages and/or shifts in relative power, particularly when those shifts depend on the resolution of the current disagreement, the benefits from defection increase, exacerbating the credible commitment problem (Fearon 1995). Rational leaders will thus choose war over the peaceful resolution of disputes, even when mutually acceptable bargains exist, due to the lack of enforcement (Fearon 1995, p. 401). Incomplete information about relative power or the motivations of other actors, though it can reinforce the credible commitment problem, is not necessary for war to occur.

In applying this logic to countries emerging from civil conflicts, we must first consider how domestic conditions, particularly the condition of anarchy, differ from the international system described by Fearon (1995) and others. By the mid-1990s, the tragic breakup of the former Yugoslavia and genocide in Rwanda had convinced scholars that the concept of anarchy – and with it the fundamental premise of the credible commitment problem – applied within countries as well as between them. Posen (1993, pp. 27–8) argues that, for countries emerging from Soviet rule, anarchy largely replaced hierarchy; weak post-Soviet states subjected ethnic groups to a self-help system in which they were largely responsible for their own security. Scholars of "failed states" followed Huntington (1968) in describing the collapse of state authority (for example, Fund for Peace 2009).

In line with such thinking, Fearon (1998) formalizes the credible commitment problem in his analysis of domestic ethnic conflict. In discussing Eastern Europe in the immediate post-Cold War period, Fearon seeks to explain why some ethnic conflicts turn violent, whereas others do not. He argues that the credible commitment framework helps us understand these questions, since majority groups cannot credibly commit to fair treatment of minority groups. In the formal model he presents, a majority group and minority group bargain over some set of benefits (*B*). In the first round of the model, the minority group can choose to fight or accede to a political process that divides B, which he assumes amounts to a division of B by the majority group. Fighting is a costly lottery, with costs for each side and some probability that the majority wins. If the political process for dividing *B* leaves the minority group dissatisfied, it can again choose to fight in the second round, though with a lower probability of winning. The majority group, therefore, can offer a division of *B* that leaves the minority group indifferent between fighting and acquiescing. However, it cannot commit to implementing this offer, since once the minority group agrees, the majority group can defect and offer nothing; understanding this, the minority group will choose violence in the first round, when its chances of success are better.

Fearon (1998) contends five factors can weaken the intensity of the credible commitment problem. First, if the minority group is militarily weak or has relatively weak cultural preferences for secession, then the expected benefits from fighting will tend not to exceed even those from the worst compromise. Second, physical separation of the two groups weakens the credible commitment problem, since the minority can secede with little violence. Third, an external power could enforce the division of benefits. Fourth, the less stark the anticipated drop in power between first and second rounds, the less difficult the problem. Finally, when a large percentage of the members of the minority group has the option of "exiting" the game by emigrating, the minority group's will to fight decreases. Using this logic, Fearon (1998) suggests that, since rural dwellers have comparably less of an exit option, they tend to bear a larger percentage of the costs of fighting in "sons of the soil" wars.

Fearon (2004) also applies the logic of the credible commitment problem to the question of conflict resolution by asking why some civil wars last longer than others. In particular, he is interested in why "sons of the soil wars," which he defines as "land or natural resource conflicts between a peripheral ethnic minority and state-supported migrants of a dominant ethnic group" (Fearon 2004, p. 277), last longer than other types of wars. Fearon presents a formal model of civil conflict in which a central government bargains with regional elites over control of their region. If the regional elites initiate war in response to a negative shock to the central government's power, then the war ends only if one side prevails militarily or one side quits. Critically, Fearon finds that under certain conditions, the central government cannot credibly offer a division of power over the region to the regional elites. Since wars tend to occur when the government is weak, it would prefer to settle wars with the rebels. However, the rebels cannot trust wartime offers of political autonomy from the central government, since they will suspect that when the government regains its strength, it will renege on the offer and reassert control over the region (Fearon 2004, p. 294). Therefore, war continues even when there exists a bargain that both sides would prefer to war. The equilibrium holds as long as the government's benefits from controlling some breakaway region exceed its costs of fighting and the rebels value the expected returns to autonomy more than their costs of war (Fearon 2004, p. 293–94).

Walter (1997, 1999) also applies the logic of credible commitments to civil war settlement, beginning with a central puzzle – whereas 55 percent of international wars are settled through negotiations, only 20 percent of civil wars are, despite the fact that 42 percent of civil wars witness some kind of peace bargaining (Walter 1997, p. 335). She argues that in both international and civil wars, a credible commitment problem exists due to anarchy; in both, therefore, commitments to peace are inherently non-credible. Any party that disarms, therefore, risks punishment from its enemy. Nevertheless, the credible commitment problem is more pernicious in the domestic case. In international wars, adversaries may retreat to some agreed upon boundary and keep command of their respective armies, retaining a deterrent to defection by their enemies. In contrast, in domestic conflict, each side must relinquish its military capability as part of the peace process (Walter 1997, p. 337). Given this dilemma, even when a bargain exists that would satisfy each side in a civil war, the parties cannot credibly expect to respect its parameters; as a result, they do not complete agreements and civil wars last longer than interstate wars. Walter

(1997, p. 337) concludes, "the only way enemies in a civil war can prematurely end the bloodshed is to force themselves through a transition period during which they can neither encourage cooperation nor survive attack."

Walter (1999) extends this work on security guarantees to include political terms of peace agreements. Even if former adversaries are able to implement the immediate terms of a ceasefire, a second stage of the credible commitment presents itself – the challenge of re-establishing normal politics. Whether by democratic or non-democratic mechanisms, the selection of the first post-conflict government risks granting one party to the conflict unparalleled power, which it can subsequently use to cement its hold on power indefinitely, particularly if a former group leader now holds power while the other side must disband militarily (Walter 1999, p. 137–8). Even if adversaries choose to enter a period of extended vulnerability, the selection of new political leaders presents another credible commitment problem, as promises by a new government to respect the rights of former adversaries are not credible.

This research on civil conflicts suggests that anarchy before, during and after civil conflicts creates a credible commitment problem that escalates disputes and complicates conflict resolution. We fuse this argument from peace studies with political economy to contend that the credible commitment problem is the primary obstacle to post-conflict economic recovery (Flores and Nooruddin 2009a). A substantial literature in political economy offers strong theoretical and empirical support for the proposition that individuals will underinvest in physical and human capital when they fear for the security of their investments (Keefer and Knack 1997; Clague et al. 1999; Olson, Sarna, and Swamy 2000). Because many investments are irreversible, firms might choose not to invest for fear of expropriation or future policy changes that imperil their investments (Aizenman 1997, 1998, 2003; Aizenman and Marion 1999; Dixit and Pindyck 1993; Grabel 2000; Stasavage 2002). During the post-conflict period, we argue that this calculus shifts. During civil war, the capital stock declines, creating privately lucrative and socially beneficial rebuilding opportunities, which should attract investors, laborers and entrepreneurs to post-conflict countries.[1] However, we argue that rational, risk-averse economic actors will understand the non-credibility of former combatants' commitments to the peace and its implications for the returns to their investments. In such a volatile environment, the risk of war and its concomitant risks of destruction and predation will foment underinvestment and slower economic recovery. In turn, a lack of economic opportunities for both civilians and former combatants provides ideal circumstances for conflict recurrence.

Coyne and Boettke (2009) also place the credible commitment problem at the center of the post-conflict reconstruction challenge. The process of post-conflict reconstruction inevitably depends on the reformation of existing social, political and economic institutions, if not their creation from whole cloth. Without citizens' support for such reforms, they will fail. However, politicians' hold on power grants them the power to renege on commitments made in the past. The credible commitment problem therefore relegates citizens to using imperfect information to differentiate between "sincere" and "insincere" politicians. If they support "insincere" politicians, the latter will renege on their commitments, leaving citizens far worse off; however, if they fail to support "sincere" politicians, they will prevent necessary post-conflict reforms (Coyne and Boettke 2009, p. 7). The policy challenge, they argue, is to create commitments to reform that are credible, binding on politicians and culturally appropriate, in that the mechanisms for establishing "credibility" will differ across contexts.

We may therefore describe two components of the post-conflict credible commitment problem, one internal and one external. Former combatants must first create mechanisms by which they enforce peace agreements, bolstering each group's confidence in the others' commitments. Externally, former enemies must jointly, publicly and credibly signal these commitments to economic actors. Furthermore, we contend that such signals must also include more general commitments to improve the political economic environment for investment. In addition to the risk of conflict recurrence, economic actors must attend to the possibility that even peaceful post-conflict politics will yield an economic environment that will depress their income. If the new post-conflict government cannot commit credibly to protecting private property rights, potential investors will reduce their presence (Flores and Nooruddin 2009a, Table 3). Similar tasks include reducing corruption and regularizing tax collection. For example, a power-sharing agreement could conceivably join former enemies in rent-seeking efforts. Keefer (2009, p. 7) argues that "the inability of political actors to make broadly credible promises to citizens is . . . a disincentive to pursue growth-promoting policies." Successfully implementing a peace agreement in the short-term is therefore necessary for post-conflict recovery, though not sufficient. Parties to peace agreements must attend not only to their commitments to each other, but their joint commitments to private entrepreneurs.

Conceptualizing the credible commitment problem in this manner helps to explain how it shifts based on how the conflict ends. Civil conflicts end either through the outright victory of one side, the conclusion of a peace and/or ceasefire agreement or the slow ebbing of the violence. Peace scholars have focused on how the nature of the termination alters the credibility of the peace. Hartzell, Hoddie and Rothchild (2001) argue that negotiated settlements are inherently precarious. Similarly, Licklider (1995) and Atlas and Licklider (1999) contend that outright military victory of one side or the other in civil conflict greatly reduces the risk of recidivism. In short, an outright military victory ameliorates the credible-commitment problem; while one side is eliminated, the other presumably forms a government and is confident in its security. However, outright military victories do not eliminate the credible commitment problem, as leaders must still convince citizens that they will forego political retribution, allowing minority groups that formerly supported the defeated parties to participate in politics and live without fear of state-sponsored discrimination. The nature of the credible commitment problem therefore shifts away from forging credibility among former combatant groups (as in peace agreements) and towards making credible promises to citizens. Though the credible commitment problem may reduce in complexity, it does not disappear.

We may also define two temporal parts of the credible commitment problem. Former combatant groups must not only make credible commitments among themselves and towards citizens in the short run, but also in the long run. In the short term, credible commitments are necessary to end the fighting and initiate economic reconstruction. In the longer term, they are necessary for a peaceful transition to "normal" politics and economics, as winners of post-conflict political power make credible commitments to losers that they will forego using the power of the state to exact political revenge or engage in economic predation. Steps to solve the short-term credible commitment problem must not do so at the expense of long-term economic and political concerns.

The above discussion conceptually defines the nature of the credible commitment problem and its effect on reconstruction. However, we do not suggest mechanisms by which such commitments might be made. In Section 23.3, we turn to this question.

23.3 IMPLICATIONS FOR POLICY: MECHANISMS FOR STRENGTHENING CREDIBLE COMMITMENTS

A focus on the credible commitment problem in civil war reshapes policy priorities in post-conflict countries. If enforcement of agreements, and not their terms, is the central barrier to peace, then we should focus on how to overcome that hurdle. Broadly, doing so involves three steps. The first involves changing the parameters of the expected utility calculus of the parties involved, such that honoring the commitment becomes a dominant strategy. This is typically done by increasing the costs of defection or increasing the benefits of cooperation or, better still, both. Second, the parties to an agreement may send costly signals (for example, a tit-for-tat disarmament process) of their commitments to the peace, distinguishing them from insincere parties that will only engage in "cheap talk." Finally, third-parties can be empowered to enforce the agreement, essentially solving the problem of anarchy by ceding power to a third-party willing to observe and enforce the agreement (Walter 1999, p. 135). In the long term, these interventions must be followed by political economic institutions that enshrine commitments to peace. In particular, both time frames must effectively transform formerly violent contestation of political power, economic benefits and physical security into peaceful channels.

Here, we focus on five post-conflict interventions designed to accomplish these two steps: shift the expected utility of cooperation and provide third-party support of post-conflict political actors. Two of these focus on domestic political interventions that seek to constrain post-conflict politicians from breaking their commitments (democracy) and/or distribute power among erstwhile enemies to raise the benefits of cooperation (power-sharing). The last three interventions focus on military (third-party interventions; DDR) and economic (foreign aid) interventions that require the participation of external actors to enhance the credibility of post-conflict commitments to the peace.

23.3.1   Domestic Political Solutions

Internal war is a political problem, and requires a political solution. At their core, civil conflicts are fought because at least one group in society is unhappy about the status quo, and seeks violent redress of the situation. The resort to violence points to the weakness of existing political institutions, and, in particular, to the lack of faith the belligerents have in the political process as a means of resolving peacefully their grievances. In the period of peace that follows the resolution of the conflict, a primary task to be attended to is the reinstitution of a peacetime political process, ideally with reforms in place to assuage the concerns of the belligerents that led them to conflict in the first place. Two such reforms are most commonly emphasized in the post-conflict reconstruction literature: holding elections as a first step in establishing democratic rule and the adoption of power-sharing arrangements. We consider each below.

Democratic elections
Elections are not democracy, but they are arguably the latter's most visible indicator. And as democratic principles have gained ascendance in the aftermath of the Cold War, so has the emphasis on holding elections as

part of the post-conflict recovery process. Holding democratic elections, in addition to their normative attractiveness, is argued to yield benefits to post-conflict governments seeking to assert control domestically and signal the start of a new era to external audiences. Governments elected through democratic elections can claim legitimacy at home and signal a deeper commitment to their policy promises to external audiences upon whom they depend for investment and development.

Peace scholars have suggested that democratic political institutions – especially the power of public opinion and opposition parties – strengthen the credibility of leaders' promises due to the steeper audience costs (that is, sanctions from the public for breaking their word) incurred if they renege on a public commitment (Fearon 1994). Schultz (1998) makes a similar point by emphasizing the role played by opposition parties, arguing that they constrain the executive from bluffing during crisis bargaining; the leader will accept only agreements that the opposition will approve or it will call her bluff. Therefore, Schultz reasons, when the opposition backs the executive's position, it lends credibility to her commitment. However, since autocrats do not have a credible opposition to check them, they do not enjoy such a credibility boost. Political economists studying the dynamics of foreign investment and capital flows make similar arguments. Jensen (2003) argues that the larger number of veto actors in democracies facilitates commitments to protecting private property and foreign direct investment (FDI). Li (2006) extends this logic to explain that the greater credibility of democratic leaders' commitments to private property rights allows them to attract capital even though they offer fewer tax incentives to potential investors. And Nooruddin (2010) shows that domestic checks and balances enhance democracy's credible commitments to policy stability, encouraging investment and reducing capital flight and economic volatility.

The scholarship reviewed above implies that democratization should heighten post-conflict political leaders' ability to commit credibly to the peace by institutionalizing responsiveness to public opinion and creating a credible opposition that can at times veto violations of peace agreements. Indeed, at least one scholar has referred to a "democratic reconstruction-ism" paradigm, in which early elections are central to short-term economic recovery and implementation of peace agreements (Ottaway 2003). However, scholars studying post-conflict countries increasingly doubt the effectiveness of rapid democratization as a key to securing peace and recovery (Ball and Halevy 1996; Walter 1997, 1999; Reilly 2003, 2004; Paris 2004; Newman and Rich 2004; Coyne 2008; Flores and Nooruddin 2009a, 2009c). As Huntington (1968) argued 40 years ago, the coherent, flexible, adaptable, and cohesive institutions that are taken for granted in well-institutionalized democracies are a rarity in those states making an initial transition to democracy. Instead, these institutions must be created from whole cloth. In the post-conflict environment – where the baseline probability of reverting to violent political competition is already high – democratization confronts still more perils, including embryonic electoral institutions and political parties; weak civil society and media; and an unfamiliarity with ceding power peacefully (Paris 2004; Collier 2009). In line with these contentions, Flores and Nooruddin (2009a) find that rapid post-conflict democratization retards economic recovery and makes conflict recurrence more likely.

Elections in any setting introduce uncertainty: participants are uncertain about who will win, by how much, and how the opposition will fare. In post-conflict situations such uncertainty is heightened since the normal patterns of domestic politics have been disrupted significantly. In countries where the post-conflict election is the first such experience in their history, this uncertainty is exacerbated. Newly formed political parties have no basis by which to ascertain their relative strength, and so unfavorable electoral returns are viewed with suspicion and fear. In particular, potential losers worry that the winners might use their newfound (and internationally legitimated) political power to exclude them permanently from the political process. And there is little potential winners can say that can assuage these concerns. Indeed, on-going research by Flores and Nooruddin (2009c) finds that post-conflict elections in new democracies are highly correlated with conflict recidivism and slower economic recovery, though the precise causal mechanisms underpinning this dismal result are little understood at this point (see also Collier 2009).

In the aggregate, this body of research suggests that rapidly built democratic institutions lack the robustness necessary to constrain the executive, strengthen the opposition and withstand inflammatory rhetoric in the media. In short, democratic institutions do not lend credibility to the assurances of former armed groups that they will abide by peace agreements. Instead, post-conflict democratic institutions likely require a lengthy incubation period before they can provide an effective bulwark against civil conflict. If so, then other steps must fill the gap during the dangerous post-conflict period.

Power-sharing

The primary limitation of elections is the inability of winners to commit credibly to respecting the political rights of the losers. To tackle this problem, scholars increasingly advocate the adoption of explicit power-sharing provisions in peace agreements (for example, Sisk 1996; Hartzell, Hoddie and Rothchild 2001; Hartzell and Hoddie 2003, 2007). Such arrangements have the advantage of providing potential electoral losers

– principally ethnic or religious minorities – with guaranteed access to political power and means of checking the power of the new government.

Not all power-sharing arrangements are created equal. Four principal types of such arrangements can be identified: political, territorial, military and economic (Mattes and Savun 2009, p. 741). Political power-sharing arrangements allocate quotas of seats or cabinet positions to minority groups, or they might reserve a share of civil service positions for members of such groups. Territorial provisions provide minorities with autonomy over local politics in a given region, or institute decentralizing or federalizing reforms designed to dilute the power of the central government over the minority-dominated regions. Military arrangements allow members of the minority's armed forces to be integrated into the new military forces, ideally preserving their rank. Economic power-sharing could include commitments to redistributive policies or the allocation of economic decision-making roles to members of the minority group.

Interestingly, in spite of their popularity, the evidence as to whether such power-sharing arrangements are successful in preserving a negotiated peace is at best mixed. Hartzell and Hoddie (2003, 2007) use an aggregated index of power-sharing provisions since they argue there is little a priori reason to believe that any one type of arrangement is more effective than another. Their contention is that the major distinction in terms of peace agreements is not the *type* of power-sharing arrangement included, but the *number*. Their evidence appears to bear this aggregate notion out, though, as Mattes and Savun (2009, p. 741) note, Hartzell and Hoddie's own evidence suggests that territorial power-sharing arrangements are the most likely – indeed only – type of provision to have a statistically significant effect on post-conflict peace.

Mattes and Savun (2009) build on the work of Hartzell and Hoddie to offer a theoretical argument for why we should expect political power-sharing to be particularly useful. The Mattes-Savun framework distinguishes usefully between "fear-reducing" and "cost-increasing" provisions in peace agreements, and argues that political power-sharing is a prime example of a fear-reducing provision that should ameliorate the commitment problems that threaten to undermine a fragile peace. By providing both sides with control over policies, and by diluting the unilateral power of the majority, political power-sharing should reduce groups' insecurity and make upholding commitments easier. Their analysis, based on an original coding of a number of peace agreements, supports this hypothesis. We should note also that, contrary to Hartzell and Hoddie (2007), their results indicate that territorial power-sharing is not a significant predictor.

Our own research on post-conflict recovery offers mixed evidence about how external audiences (that is, non-belligerents) view power-sharing arrangements. We find that power-sharing arrangements have no effect on attracting foreign direct investment to a post-conflict situation, but that their presence is correlated highly with an increase in domestic savings rates (Flores and Nooruddin 2009a). Within the country at least this does suggest that economic actors value the signals sent by power-sharing arrangements, though it remains to be understood why international investors are less sanguine.

Research on the contributions of power-sharing arrangements to bolstering credible commitments in post-conflict situations represents a fecund and productive area for future work. Two concerns remain to be addressed satisfactorily at both the theoretical and empirical levels, however. The first, which scholars do address more frequently today than in the past, is the issue of endogeneity. The concern here is that power-sharing arrangements only emerge where peace was already more probable so that any correlation between the existence of such provisions and longer peace durations is spurious. Conventional practice in this literature is to see if the same factors that predict the existence of such provisions also predict conflict recurrence (see Mattes and Savun 2009 p. 746; also, Walter 2002; Fortna 2003, 2004, Hartzell and Hoddie 2007), and, to the extent that they do not, to conclude that power-sharing arrangements are not "epiphenomenal." This is at best a partial solution as it cannot address the problem of selection on unobservables. Given how well-established statistical techniques for dealing with unobservability and selection bias have become in economics and political science, future work would do well to address the endogeneity problem head on.[2]

The second concern is that the literature on power-sharing arrangements does not address adequately the mechanisms by which actors' commitments to such provisions are made credible. That is, what is to stop the majority group in the post-conflict period from either ignoring these provisions or demanding their renegotiation on terms less favorable to the minority? In essence, to claim that power-sharing is a solution to the credible commitment problem created by political reforms such as the holding of elections is to replace one such problem with another. This insight is at the core of Walter's (2002) argument that third-party guarantees are the only means by which negotiated settlements can be made credible and therefore successful. We consider this argument, and the broader literature on third-party and external interventions next.

23.3.2   External Interventions

The two political interventions discussed above both focus on the actions of domestic actors. Yet, as many have recognized, these actors have a difficult time making credible commitments to each other on account of their history of antagonism and recent violent conflict. Consequently scholars have considered how third-parties to the conflict might intervene to help these actors achieve peace. In this section, we first consider the key findings of third-party interventions in bolstering security arrangements, and then turn to how external actors can help rebuilding war-torn economies.

Third-party Security Interventions

Third-party interventions in civil conflicts are of two main types. The first, which falls beyond the scope of our survey here, is interventions to end a conflict (Regan 2000; Gent 2007, 2008). Peace scholars, often centered at Uppsala University's International Peace Research Institute (PRIO), have focused on the role of conflict mediation by third-parties and their role in overcoming the credible commitment problem to secure a peace agreement, particularly when considering their bias towards one or another side (Svensson 2007, 2009). The second is interventions to help preserve the peace once it is struck, of which three are of particular interest: security guarantees, peace-keeping operations and DDR programs.[3]

Barbara Walter uses the same commitment perspective employed fruitfully in much of the post-settlement literature surveyed here. She argues that commitment concerns make it impossible for erstwhile combatants to negotiate satisfactory peace agreements. A climate of poor information and high distrust threatens to undermine peace. Therefore, Walter argues, third-parties must participate in the peace process to guarantee that the terms of the negotiated settlements are upheld (1997, 2002). Such guarantees are essentially promises of military interventions should one side be found to be violating the terms of the peace agreement.

Increasingly such security guarantees are provided multilaterally in the form of peacekeeping operations organized and sponsored by international or regional organizations. United Nations peace-keeping operations in particular have been the focus of two path-breaking scholarly treatments by Michael Doyle and Nicholas Sambanis (2006), on the one hand, and Page Fortna (2008), on the other. How might such peace-keeping operations help preserve peace? And, do they?

Peace-keeping operations are fundamentally a third-party security guarantee. Peacekeepers are charged with monitoring and verifying that all participants in the peace treaty are honoring their obligations as specified by that treaty, particularly commitments to disarm and demobilize armed forces. One of the main concerns after internal conflict is that one side will preserve its military might and use this advantage to attack the other side; since neither side wishes to be caught unprepared, both sides have an incentive to renege on such provisions and to perpetuate conditions for war. Further, since neither side's proclamations of adherence to its obligations are thought credible by the other, the only way to build confidence is to have both sides' actions be subject to monitoring and verification by a legitimate third-party. In addition, because peacekeepers possess military expertise, they are well-suited to conduct the tasks involved in disarmament and demobilization, and certainly more so than their diplomatic and political counterparts who helped negotiate the peace they are charged with keeping. In addition, the use of force by peacekeepers to quell violence is less likely to be marred by allegations of bias than if the states' own armed forces, which are too often dominated by one group, did so. Peacekeepers can therefore preserve the peace by providing the internal security crucial to allowing actors to adjust their expectations about the durability of the peace and to begin a return to normalcy in their everyday lives.

Complementing the hands-on role they play in maintaining law and order, peacekeepers serve two additional functions. First, they open channels of communication between the principals to the recently concluded conflict (Fortna 2008, p. 95). Peacekeepers can serve as a neutral arbiter, to whom each side can take its concerns and complaints about the other, allowing for increased communication between the sides and a reduced risk of a pre-emptive return to arms. In short, they moderate anarchy by providing some neutral authority. Second, the mere presence of peacekeepers can serve as a credible signal of the intention of both sides to maintain the peace. Peacekeeping operations are an example of what Mattes and Savun (2009) term "cost-increasing provisions" because they increase the costs associated with conflict recidivism. The willingness of the combatants to invite peacekeepers thus serves as a credible signal of their intentions, and, conversely, helps identify potential spoilers whose intentions are murkier.

Research on peacekeeping has reached mixed conclusions about its efficacy, though Fortna's recent book is far more optimistic in its conclusions than prior analyses. Surveying UN peacekeeping operations between 1989 and 2000 that were conducted after civil wars, Fortna (2008, p. 17) concludes that, "peace lasts significantly longer, all else equal, when international personnel deploy to maintain peace than when they do not" even though "peacekeepers tend to go to the most difficult cases." In their comprehensive survey of UN peacekeeping, Doyle and Sambanis study all peace processes after civil wars that ended between 1945 and 1999 – 151 in total – and conclude that "while the UN is very poor at 'war,' imposing a settlement by force, it can be very good at 'peace,' mediating and implementing a comprehensively negotiated peace" (Doyle and Sambanis

2006, p. 5). Specifically, Doyle and Sambanis identify two factors common to successful peacekeeping operations: they are well designed to fit conditions on the ground and they prioritize economic recovery. While the first factor, as Fortna correctly points out, is difficult to translate into a policy recommendation since we only ever know if an operation was designed well post hoc, the emphasis on the economic dimension of peacekeeping is useful and worthy of further consideration.

DDR programs have generated increasing attention as part of the United Nations' package of post-conflict peacekeeping operations. DDR programs are designed to rehabilitate former combatants and reinsert them into society with a real chance to pursue non-violent means of economic and social support, as well as political expression. Third-party interveners thus take steps to disarm combatants, remove them from military structures and train them for productive jobs. In theory, DDR programs play a different role than the peacekeeping operations that nominally govern them. In the terminology of the credible commitment problem, DDR programs grant heads of combatant groups the opportunity to send a credible signal of their commitment to the peace. By submitting to a program administered by an unbiased third-party designed to demobilize and reintegrate their fighters, combatant groups will aid reconstruction by assuring their former enemies of the credibility of their commitments.

DDR programs are increasingly included in peace agreements and are an essential portion of UN peacekeeping operations, including ongoing operations in Sierra Leone and Liberia. We do not know of cross-national studies of DDR programs' efficacy in preventing conflict recurrence or speeding economic reconstruction. However, survey studies of ex-combatants have begun to investigate whether such programs indeed aid them in their reintegration. Humphreys and Weinstein (2004, 2007) report on surveys of ex-combatants in Sierra Leone, finding little evidence that non-participants in DDR programs suffered in comparison to participants.[4] In contrast, parallel survey research conducted in Liberia reports that DDR programs have improved ex-combatants' lives, particularly their ability to reintegrate into society (Pugel 2007). Future research, in particular through micro-level surveys and randomized trials, should continue to tackle these questions.

Economic interventions

While most students of civil wars focus understandably on violence, there has been an increasing recognition in recent years of the critical need to rebuild the domestic economy if the country is to sustain its hard-won peace. As mentioned above, Doyle and Sambanis find conclusive evidence that peacekeeping operations accompanied by extensive economic programs are most successful; likewise, Spear (2002) points out that demobilization efforts are more successful when former soldiers can find economically viable occupations in peace time. However, fostering broad-based economic recovery in post-conflict situations is difficult, even if individual groups or actors in society found war profitable. As Collier et al. (2003) put it, war is "development in reverse."

The often tragic costs of civil conflict have inspired large bilateral and multilateral aid transfers to post-conflict countries (Flores and Nooruddin 2009b; Keefer 2009). Developed countries provide large amounts of aid to countries recovering from conflict, and, more recently, the international financial institutions have gotten in the act as well. The World Bank, for example, allocates between 20 to 25 percent of its total lending portfolio to post-conflict countries, according to one estimate (Weiss 2004, p. 1). Such aid serves two related functions: by providing opportunities outside of violence, it makes committing to the peace process easier for former combatants, and it can serve as a signal to other actors of how credible donors view the commitment. In the latter sense, international aid can serve a catalytic function and help mobilize additional capital flows for the country.

Susan Woodward makes a persuasive case for the centrality of economic recovery efforts within the larger post-conflict reconstruction paradigm. She identifies three sets of economic tasks "necessary" for sustainable peace: "sufficiently rapid economic revival to buy confidence in the peace process; funding to implement specific commitments in the peace agreement; and the economic foundations necessary to sustain peace over the long term" (Woodward 2002, p. 185). Yet, the accumulated evidence is pessimistic about the usefulness of external donor efforts in post-conflict situations. Collier and Hoeffler (2000), for instance, find that donors suffer aid "amnesia" and that aid tapers out towards the end of the first decade after the cessation of violence, and, further, that donor efforts are often misguided, emphasizing macroeconomic policy reform over much more important social policies. Woodward's survey of the literature reaches a similar conclusion: external assistance is too often misguided, misappropriated and misallocated.

Aid's alleged ineffectiveness would be less troubling if it was not for the potentially critical role those resources could play in assuaging the credible commitment problem, and, further, that the misuse of these funds undermines the brittle peace in place. Allegations of corruption, or of biased allocation of aid resources, can fan concerns among groups that they are being ignored at the expense of their enemies, and that such discrimination will place them in a permanently inferior position. Donors must therefore design aid programs to encourage transparency as a confidence-building mechanism.

The logic of the credible commitment problem suggests that aid's effectiveness in post-conflict countries depends on whether or not it is a means to fostering credible commitments to the peace. Keefer (2009) argues that "political market dysfunctions" make it unlikely that aid will be used effectively in a post-conflict country, but that donors too often ignore this reality in their emphasis on the size of aid transfers. Rather Keefer argues for a greater focus on how aid is utilized through the use of "peace conditionality" in which aid is linked to specific steps taken to bolster peace and to enforce the provisions of the peace agreement (see also Frerks 2006 and Boyce 2008). Violations of these provisions, by contrast, could result in aid sanctions, increasing the expected benefits from peace.

A potential limitation of Keefer's advice is that it reinforces the temptation to give aid only where it is most likely to be successful. While understandable from the donor's perspective since aid funds are scarce and donors must account for their use (Dollar and Svensson 2000), it does mean that aid would flow away from the hardest-hit countries and towards those with the "easiest" problems. Such choices also make the evaluation of aid's effectiveness more complicated. For instance, Flores and Nooruddin (2009b) analyse the World Bank's efforts in post-conflict reconstruction. They argue that the World Bank, needing to provide evidence of success to its principals, picks countries where conditions are most propitious to success. Indeed, their empirical analysis indicates that once the World Bank's selection process is accounted for, there is no discernible effect of the World Bank on either conflict recidivism or economic recovery.

Concurrent research with considerable promise does suggest that aid can be "locally" effective if designed and allocated more wisely. Fearon, Humphreys and Weinstein (2009) use a randomized field experiment to evaluate the impact of "community-driven reconstruction" (CDR) programs in northern Liberia. Their results are extremely encouraging, and suggest that CDR had a positive impact on community cohesion, social inclusion for marginalized groups and democratic norms and values. Future work should identify the potential for "scaling" up these findings to the national level.

This discussion suggests that, while post-conflict aid from the international financial institutions has done little to aid economic recovery or prevent conflict recurrence, aid has the power to strengthen credible commitments to the peace if focused on grassroots social cohesion and/ or conditioned on continued respect for peace agreements. Coupled with findings of economic recovery's contributions to the peace in the Doyle and Sambanis work on peacekeeping, this finding is a siren call for peace researchers to pay as much attention to butter as they do to guns.

23.4   CONCLUSIONS

As the number and intensity of civil wars has increased in recent years, a new problem has become prominent for development and peace researchers: how best to rebuild war-torn societies? In this chapter, we have utilized a dominant framework for analysing the post-conflict environment to identify the strengths and weaknesses of the most commonly attempted interventions in these situations. We argue that the problems of post-conflict reconstruction stem from a double-edged credible commitment problem. First, erstwhile combatants must develop technologies enabling them to signal credibly to each other their intentions to honor the provisions of the negotiated settlement that brought fighting to a close. Second, these principals must find a way to signal credibly their mutual commitments to domestic and external audiences of economic investors and aid donors. Though the shape and intensity of the commitment problem shifts, its essential nature does not – credible commitments are simply difficult to make during the post-conflict period. Even when conflicts end in the outright military victory of one side over others, the victors must credibly commit to foreswearing vengeance against the communities formerly represented by armed groups. Failure to do so will likely slow short-term recovery and raise the long-term probability of further conflict.

A theory of post-conflict reconstruction that emphasizes credible commitments allows not only theoretical insight but also a guide to the politics of interventions intended to stave off further violence and galvanize reconstruction. In the broadest sense, successful interventions must raise the benefits from peaceful involvement in politics and/or the costs of defections and continued violence. We therefore re-evaluate five major post-conflict policy interventions that have dominated this literature. Politically, scholars typically advocate a rapid transition to democracy, particularly in the form of early elections, as a means of installing a government with some claim to domestic legitimacy. In addition to its obvious normative desirability, democracy could bolster the credibility of commitments to peace by constraining leaders from exacting retribution through its system of checks and balances; credibly signaling the commitment of former military commanders when they participate in democratic politics; and raise the expected benefits of cooperation, since former combatant groups will anticipate sharing power in future governments. However, the winner-takes-all – or at least takes-most – nature of elections makes potential losers insecure and embryonic democratic institutions likely cannot constrain a newly elected leader who has promised peace, but is bent on subverting all opposition. Indeed, on-going research suggests that such rapid transitions to democracy can be counterproductive.

An alternative to elections involves negotiated power-sharing arrangements written into the peace agreement. Power-sharing arrangements have the theoretical virtue of reducing the volatility of stakeholders' assessment of their post-conflict political power and reducing their fears that their former enemies will have access to unparalleled political or military power to reinitiate violence with a significant advantage. More realistically, however, power-sharing agreements seem to replicate the very enforcement difficulty that we describe here. The precise sharing of power itself is an element to bargain over in peace agreements and is not inherently self-enforcing. Furthermore, such arrangements reflect a static view of the power balance in society and, as previous statements of the credible commitment problem state, the anticipation of such changes in the future may drive violations of such agreements, exacerbating the credible commitment problem.

This discussion suggests the difficulty of solving the credible commitment problem without a third-party that is willing and able to enforce the agreement. One high-profile form of external intervention is a peace-keeping operation in which foreign governments contribute troops charged with maintaining domestic law and order, monitoring disarmament and demobilization efforts and maintaining a channel for communication between the two sides. In short, such interventions replace the anarchy that underlies the enforcement problem with hierarchy through the imposition of a third-party that can arbitrate and enforce the agreement. On the whole, such operations play an invaluable role in prolonging peace after conflict, though critics validly point out that they might undermine the building of domestic state capacity by providing the security services typically offered by governments. Therefore, they risk trading long-term capacity-building – perhaps the only means to post-conflict rehabilitation – for short-term security. Another aspect of such interventions is a DDR program, which limits the ability of combatant groups to reform through the rapid remobilization of soldiers and command structures. Such programs should bolster the credibility of the peace because they raise the costs of returning to violence, but there are few systematic evaluations of such programs.

The last noteworthy external action is the provision of bilateral or multilateral aid. Ideally such aid plays multiple roles, beginning with reviving the economy to providing jobs for former combatants and improving social services for marginalized groups to the longer-term goals of establishing the foundations of a robust economy. Unfortunately, too often aid has been squandered because of a lack of transparency over its spending or incentives to do otherwise in the absence of conditionality, or the advice offered by donors has focused too heavily on macroeconomic orthodoxies relative to practical peacekeeping tasks. However, in principal, post-conflict aid packages might be better designed if they included peace conditionality terms, which credibly withdraw aid if combatants pursue paths anathema to peace.

The credible commitment problem thus provides a window to understand the complicated political economy of post-conflict reconstruction, as well as a means to evaluate post-conflict interventions. Multiple sources of evidence point to the tragic track record of countries emerging from civil conflicts. If post-conflict interventions more carefully attend to these dynamics, involve third-parties dedicated to enforcement and allow for a longer period for the incubation of native institutions, there is hope for reversing that record.

NOTES

1. Collier (1999) argues that the capital stock rebounds quickly after longer civil wars, whereas it continues to decline after shorter civil wars.
2. Examples of the applications of such techniques in political science include Achen (1986), Reed (2000), Przeworski and Vreeland (2000), Lemke and Reed (2001), Nooruddin (2002), Vreeland (2003), Nooruddin and Simmons (2006), Savun (2008), Flores and Nooruddin (2009b).
3. DDR programs are formally part of peace-keeping operations. However, since they fulfill a different function than security guarantees or peace-keeping operations involving intervening soldiers, we consider their effects separate from their parent operations.
4. The authors rightfully point out that, without a randomized control trial in which combatants are randomly assigned to the DDR programs, it is impossible to conclude that DDR programs were unsuccessful.

REFERENCES

Achen, C.H. (1986), *The Statistical Analysis of Quasi-Experiments*, Berkeley, CA: University of California Press.
Aizenman, J. (1997), "Investment in new activities and the welfare cost of uncertainty", *Journal of Development Economics*, **52**, 259–77.
Aizenman, J. (1998), "Political uncertainty, the formation of new activities and growth", in S. Borner, M. Paldam and M. Paldam (eds), *The Political Dimension of Economic Growth*, New York, NY: Palgrave Macmillan, pp. 154–70.
Aizenman, J. (2003), "Volatility, employment, and the patterns of FDI in emerging markets", *Journal of Development Economics*, **72**, 585–601.
Aizenman, J. and N. Marion (1999), "Volatility and investment: interpreting evidence from developing countries", *Economica*, **66**, 157–79.
Atlas, P.M. and R. Licklider (1999), "Conflict among former allies after civil war settlement: Sudan, Zimbabwe, Chad, and Lebanon", *Journal of Peace Research*, **36** (1), 35–54.
Axelrod, R. (1984), *The Evolution of Cooperation,* New York, NY: Basic Books.
Ball, N. with T. Halevy (1996) *Making Peace Work: The Role of the International Development Community*, Washington DC: Overseas Development Council.
Boyce, J. (2008), "Post-conflict recovery: resource mobilization and peacebuilding", Political

Economy Research Institute Working Paper 159 (February), University of Massachusetts, Amherst.

Clague, C., P. Keefer, S. Knack and M. Olson (1999), Contract-intensive money: contract enforcement, property rights, and economic performance. *Journal of Economic Growth*, **4** (2), 185–211.

Collier, P. (1999), "On the Economic Consequences of Civil War". *Oxford Economic Papers*, **51** (1), 168–83.

Collier, P. (2009), *Wars, Guns, and Votes: Democracy in Dangerous Places*, New York, NY: Harper.

Collier, P., V.L. Elliott, H. Hegre, A. Hoeffler, M. Reynal-Querol and N. Sambanis (2003), *Breaking the Conflict Trap: Civil War and Development Policy*, Washington DC: World Bank and Oxford University Press.

Collier, P. and A. Hoeffler (2000), "Aid, policy and growth in post-conflict societies", *European Economic Review*, **48** (4), 1125–45.

Coyne, C.J. (2008), *After War: The Political Economy of Exporting Democracy*, Palo Alto, CA: Stanford University Press.

Coyne, C.J. and P.J. Boettke (2009), "The problem of credible commitment in reconstruction", *Journal of Institutional Economics*, **5** (1), 1–23.

Dixit, A. and R. Pindyck (1993), *Investment Under Uncertainty*, Princeton, NJ: Princeton University Press.

Dollar, D. and J. Svensson (2000), "What explains the success or failure of structural adjustment programmes?" *The Economic Journal*, **110**, 894–917.

Doyle, M.W. and N. Sambanis (2006), *Making War And Building Peace: United Nations Peace Operations*, Princeton, NJ: Princeton University Press.

Fearon, J.D. (1994), "Domestic political audiences and the escalation of international disputes", *American Political Science Review*, **88** (4), 577–92.

Fearon, J.D. (1995), "Rationalist explanations for war", *International Organization*, **49** (3), 379–414.

Fearon, J.D. (1998), "Commitment problems and the spread of ethnic conflict", in D. Lake and D. Rothchild (eds), *The International Spread of Ethnic Conflict*, Princeton, NJ: Princeton University Press, pp. 107–26.

Fearon, J.D. (2004), "Why do some civil wars last so much longer than others?", *Journal of Peace Research*, **41** (3), 275–301.

Flores, T.E. and I. Nooruddin (2009a), "Democracy under the gun: understanding post-conflict recovery", *Journal of Conflict Resolution*, **53** (1), 3–29.

Flores, T.E. and I. Nooruddin (2009b), "Financing the peace: evaluating World Bank post-conflict assistance programs", *Review of International Organizations*, **4** (1), 1–27.

Flores, T.E. and I. Nooruddin (2009c), "Voting for peace: do post-conflict elections help recovery?", George Mason University and Ohio State University.

Foreign Policy and The Fund for Peace (2009), "The Failed States Index 2009", available at: <http://www.foreignpolicy.com/articles/2009/06/22/2009_failed_states_index_interactive_map_and_rankings>, accessed September 10, 2009.

Fortna, V.P. (2003), "Inside and out: peacekeeping and the duration of peace after civil and interstate wars", *International Studies Review*, **5** (4), 97–114.

Fortna, V.P. (2004), *Peace Time: Cease-fire Agreements and the Durability of Peace*, Princeton, NJ: Princeton University Press.

Fortna, V.P. (2008), *Does Peacekeeping Work? Shaping Belligerents' Choices after Civil War*, Princeton, NJ: Princeton University Press.

Frerks, G. (2006), *The Use of Peace Conditionalities in Conflict and Post-conflict Settings: A Conceptual Framework and a Checklist*, The Hague: Clingendael Institute.

Gent, S. (2007), "Strange bedfellows: the strategic dynamics of major power military interventions", *Journal of Politics*, **69** (4), 1089–102.

Gent, S. (2008), "Going in when it counts: military intervention and the outcome of civil conflicts", *International Studies Quarterly*, **52** (4), 713–35.

Grabel, I. (2000), "The political economy of "policy credibility": the new-classical macroeconomics and the remaking of emerging economics", *Cambridge Journal of Economics*, **24**, 1–19.

Hartzell, C. and M. Hoddie (2003), "Institutionalizing peace: power sharing and post-civil war conflict management", *American Journal of Political Science*, **47** (2), 318–32.

Hartzell, C. and M. Hoddie (2007), *Crafting Peace: Power-sharing Institutions and the Negotiated Settlement of Civil Wars*, University Park, PA: The Pennsylvania State University Press.

Hartzell, C., M. Hoddie and D. Rothchild (2001), "Stabilizing the peace after civil war: an investigation of some key variables", *International Organization*, **55** (1), 183–208.

Humphreys, M. and J.M. Weinstein (2004), "What the fighters say: a survey of ex-combatants in Sierra Leone", Center on Globalization and Sustainable Development (CGSD) Working Paper No. 20, in conjunction with The Post-Conflict Reintegration Initiative for Development and Empowerment, July 2004.

Humphreys, M. and J.M. Weinstein (2007), "Demobilization and reintegration", *Journal of Conflict Resolution*, **51** (4), 531–67.

Huntington, S.P. (1968), *Political Order in Changing Societies*, New Haven, CT: Yale University Press.

Jensen, N.M (2003), "Democratic governance and multinational corporations: political regimes and inflows of foreign direct investment", *International Organization*, **57** (3), 587–616.

Keefer, P. (2009), "Foreign assistance and political market imperfections in post-conflict countries", *Foresight: Investigating Tomorrow's Development Challenges Today*, **2** (2), 1–14.

Keefer, P. and S. Knack (1997), "Why don't poor countries catch up?" *Economic Inquiry*, **35** (3), 590–602.

Li, Q. (2006), "Democracy, autocracy, and tax incentives to foreign direct investors: a cross-national analysis", *Journal of Politics*, **68** (1), 62–74.

Licklider, R. (1995), "The consequences of negotiated settlements in civil wars, 1945–1993", *American Political Science Review*, **89** (3), 681–90.

Mattes, M. and B. Savun (2009), "Fostering peace after civil war: commitment problems and agreement design", *International Studies Quarterly*, **53** (4), 737–59.

Newman, E. and R. Rich (eds) (2004), *The UN Role in Promoting Democracy: Between Ideals and Reality*, Tokyo: United Nations University Press.

Nooruddin, I. (2002), "Modeling selection bias in studies of sanctions efficacy", *International Interactions*, **28** (1), 57–74.

Nooruddin, I. (2010), *Coalition Politics and Economic Development*, Cambridge, UK: Cambridge University Press.

Nooruddin, I. and J.W. Simmons (2006), "The politics of hard choices: IMF programs and government spending", *International Organization*, **60** (4), 1001–1033.

Olson, Jr., M., N. Sarna and A.V. Swamy (2000), "Governance and growth: a simple hypothesis explaining cross-country differences in productivity growth", *Public Choice*, **102** (3), 341–64.

Ottaway, M. (2003), "Promoting democracy after conflict: the difficult choices", *International Studies Perspectives*, **4** (3), 314–22.

Paris, R. (2004), *At War's End: Building Peace After Civil Conflict*, New York, NY: Cambridge University Press.

Posen, B. (1993), "The security dilemma and ethnic conflict", *Survival*, **35** (1), 27–47.

Powell, R. (2006), "War as a commitment problem", *International Organization*, **60** (1), 169–203.

Przeworski, A. and J.R. Vreeland (2000), "The effects of IMF programs on economic growth", *Journal of Development Economics*, **62** (2), 385–421.

Pugel, J. (2007), "What the fighters say: a survey of ex-combatants in Liberia", Washington DC: UNDP Report.

Reed, W. (2000), "A unified statistical model of conflict onset and escalation", *American Journal of Political Science*, **44** (1), 84–3.

Regan, P. (2000), *Civil Wars and Foreign Powers: Interventions and Intrastate Conflict*, Ann Arbor, MI: University of Michigan Press.

Reilly, B. (2003), "Post-conflict elections: constraints and dangers", *International Peacekeeping*, **9** (2), 118–39.

Reilly, B. (2004), "Elections in post-conflict societies", in E. Newman and R. Rich (eds), *The UN Role in Promoting Democracy: Between Ideals and Reality*, Tokyo: United Nations University Press, pp. 113–34.

Savun, B. (2008), "Mediator types and the effectiveness of information-provision strategies in the resolution of international conflict", in J. Berkovitch and S. Gartner (eds), *International Conflict Mediation: New Approaches and Findings*, New York, NY: Routledge, pp. 96–114.

Schultz, K.A. (1998), "Domestic opposition and signaling in international crises", *American Political Science Review*, **92** (4), 829–44.

Sisk, T.D. (1996), *Power Sharing and International Mediation in Ethnic Conflicts*, Washington DC: United States Institute for Peace.

Spear, J. (2002), "Disarmament and demobilization", in S.J. Stedman, D. Rothchild and E.M. Cousens (eds), *Ending Civil Wars: The Implementation of Peace Agreements*, Boulder, CO: Lynne Reinner Publishers, pp. 141–82.

Stasavage, D. (2002), "Private investment and political institutions", *Economics and Politics*, **14**, 41–63.

Svensson, I. (2007), "Bargaining, bias, and peace brokers", *Journal of Peace Research*, **44** (2), 177–94.

Svensson, I. (2009), "Who brings which peace? Neutral versus biased mediation and institutional peace arrangements in civil wars", *Journal of Conflict Resolution*, **53** (3), 446–69.

Vreeland, J.R. (2003), *The IMF and Economic Development*, Cambridge, UK: Cambridge University Press.

Walter, B.F. (1997), "The critical barrier to civil war settlement", *International Organization*, **51** (3), 335–64.

Walter, B.F. (1999), "Designing transitions from civil war: demobilization, democratization, and commitments to peace", *International Security*, **24** (1), 127–55.

Walter, B.F. (2002), *Committing to Peace: The Successful Settlement of Civil Wars*, Princeton, NJ: Princeton University Press.

Weiss, M.A. (2004). *World Bank Post-conflict Aid: Oversight Issues for Congress*, Washington DC: Congressional Research Service, Library of Congress.

Woodward, S.L. (2002), "Economic priorities for successful peace implementation", in S.J. Stedman, D. Rothchild and E.M. Cousens (eds), *Ending Civil Wars: The Implementation of Peace Agreements*, Boulder, CO: Lynne Reinner Publishers, pp. 183–214.

World Bank (2006), "Postconflict Fund and LICUS Trust Fund: Annual Report, Fiscal Year 2005", Washington DC: World Bank.

24 Conflict, credibility and asset prices
Gregory M. Dempster and Justin P. Isaacs

"As I dare say you are aware, negotiations to end the war have been going on for some time: that is why my principal and I have been to Paris. They have succeeded. Peace will be signed in the next few days."

"Good Lord above!" cried Jack.

"Yes, indeed," said Palmer. "And of course there are an infinity of reflections to be made. But what is to my immediate purpose is that as soon as the news is made public, Government stock and a large variety of commercial shares will rise enormously, some of them cent per cent."

"Good Lord above," said Jack again.

"A man who bought now," said Palmer, "would make a great deal of money before next settling day; he might borrow or pledge his credit or make time bargains with great confidence."[1]

24.1 INTRODUCTION

No matter what the specific nature of the contract, a problem inherent in all types of conflict resolution is the uncertainty of whether the participants are legitimately committed to delivering on their part of the agreement. The absence of an effective enforcement mechanism often means that parties to peace agreements will have an incentive to defect from the contract in future periods. Furthermore, each party involved in the negotiation process will recognize that other parties have an incentive to change their behavior in future periods, and will thus be wary of making binding agreements in the interest of ending the conflict. Absent a solution to the problem of credible commitment, agreements to moderate or end long-running conflicts will often prove unsustainable.

The problem of credible commitment in developing effective policies and reform is well established. In a seminal paper, Kydland and Prescott (1977) highlighted the general problem of time inconsistency in public policy. They noted that policymakers face a commitment problem because the public will realize that future government policies will not necessarily coincide with policy announced in the current period. Building on this earlier work, a large literature recognizes the importance of credible commitment for political outcomes. For example, Boettke (1993, 2001) explores how the absence of credible commitments contributed to the failure of reforms in the former Soviet Union. Persson and Tabellini (2000) show that the effects of institutional changes vary from society to society depending on the ability to make credible political promises prior to elections. Keefer and Vlaciu (2005) explore how different policy choices across democracies can be explained by the ability of political competitors to make credible commitments to voters in the pre-election period. Keefer (2006) argues that the inability of political actors to make credible commitments to broad segments of society is a driving factor behind revolt and civil war. Coyne (2007) and Coyne and Boettke (2009) explore the problem of credible commitment as a consideration for foreign military occupiers engaged in reconstruction and nation-building efforts.

The problem of credible commitment is a major constraint on efforts by the international community to facilitate peace and help countries escape conflict. International policymakers must often decide the type and level of resources (for example, monetary and humanitarian aid, negotiators, troops and peacekeepers and so on) invested in conflict-torn states. Understanding the likelihood of continued peace or conflict is critical for making correct decisions over the allocation of resources. As such, a central issue in the effectiveness of the international community in helping countries escape the conflict trap is the identification of mechanisms which reveal the true intentions, and hence credibility, of the parties involved in the peace process.

24.2   EXPECTATIONS, ASSET PRICES AND REGIME CHANGES[2]

It is our contention that the true intentions of participants to peace agreements are accurately and quickly reflected in the behavior of long-term financial asset prices. As such, changes in asset prices are one means of gauging the credibility of parties to negotiations and potential agreements. Our central argument is that long-term financial asset prices accurately reflect the confidence of investors in the stability of institutions and can therefore be used an indicator of the perceived credibility of the participants in a negotiation process. If agreements are viewed as lacking credibility, meaning that they will likely prove unsustainable, investors will modify downward their expectations regarding institutional stability, leading to a fall in demand for fixed, long-term financial assets whose ability to provide future cash flows is dependent on the stability of those institutions. Thus, we should expect to see a drop in the prices of those assets in response to news or events that undermine the credibility of one or more parties to an agreement. Similarly, if agreements are viewed as being credible and enforceable, indicating sustained peace and institutional stability, we should expect to see an increase in the prices of those same long-term assets. This has important policy implications to the extent that long-term financial assets can be used to predict the sustainability of peace agreements in conflict-torn areas.

The idea that the long-run processes determining financial asset values are subject to sudden, permanent shifts based on the arrival of new, publicly available information is often referred to with the terms *structural change* and/or *change in regime*. The term "regime change" has undoubtedly acquired a very different meaning in some circles within the conflict resolution literature, due to recent use of the term by neo-conservative pundits to describe the goals of foreign policy with respect to rogue states, but we retain the older language here because it quite directly expresses the logic behind our thesis. The "regime" in this case is an expectations-driven, institutions-dependent process that produces – through bid and ask prices submitted to a marketplace – a series of prices that reflect those underlying expectations. One of the functions of a financial market, in this view, is to relate the expectations of market participants concerning future cash flow, risk, marketability and so forth, *within the perceived constraints of a particular expected institutional regime*, to the prices produced in the marketplace. Although these prices will be subject to much short-run volatility due to the day-to-day variance in these factors, the underlying process can be thought of as stable in the sense that the set of institutional constraints under which price discovery is taking place remains stable. A process of this sort can be thought to produce an ergodic probability distribution of returns with stable moments (means and variances) from which actual observations are drawn on a stochastic basis.[3]

A regime change is said to occur when important news, events or even changes in market psychology cause the perceived institutional constraints to realign with a new expected state of future affairs, including any expectations of changes to property rights, contract enforceability and the like. The transformation of the expected institutional environment in which prices are determined will cause changes in the entire subjective distribution of expected outcomes that informs the price discovery process itself. Thus, over time, the price discovery process is nonergodic, meaning that the underlying moments (mean, variance and so forth) are subject to alteration on the basis of developments that market participants interpret as indicating change in the underlying structure. It is precisely these types of developments that we believe characterize the discovery process in long-term financial asset markets where expected future outcomes are dependent upon the credibility and commitment of parties to peace agreements and other contracts negotiated between belligerents.

24.3   EARLY MODERN FINANCIAL MARKETS AND WARTIME FINANCE[4]

The origins of modern financial markets can be traced to the attempts by European governments to finance their wartime expenditures in an efficient manner, a process identified by Bordo and White (1991) as a form of "tax smoothing." The formation of the Dutch Republic in 1581 from the remnants of the Hapsburg Netherlands resulted in a small, highly vulnerable state at odds with its southern, Catholic neighbors. Most commentators trace the development of modern financial markets to this period in Dutch history. The Republic eventually became allied with protestant England in its continued conflict with Catholic Europe when William of Orange ascended to the English throne in 1688, by which time the center of international finance was shifting from Amsterdam to London. Since most of the major episodes of these long-running conflicts between European nations occurred in the continent's interior, it made sense for the Dutch and English, in particular, to make use of proxy armies – especially mercenaries recruited from Hesse and other provinces in northern Europe – rather than send their own troops at great expense and leave their respective countries undefended. The problem with such arrangements, of course, is that they require large amounts of convertible currency to be raised in short, discrete time periods, at a rate far in excess of the ability to acquire additional tax revenues for the purpose. The reasonable solution to such a problem is to borrow convertible funds against future tax revenues, thus "smoothing" the revenue stream and paying debts down with peacetime surpluses.[5]

From the late sixteenth century onward, the Dutch, English and other European nation-states systematically engaged in operations intended to ease their respective governments' ability to raise funds and fight wars. The formation of the international mercantile economy is a direct by-product of these attempts. For example, the Dutch East India Company, formed in 1602, was granted a monopoly on the Dutch spice trade in Asia in exchange for assistance in the republic's wars with Spain and others; the British followed suit early the following century with the establishment of the United East India Company in 1708, an even more explicit exchange of monopoly rents for funds.[6] The British company's charter granted exclusive trading privileges to the new company in exchange for a loan of 3.2 million pounds to the Treasury, and was modeled on the charter that had earlier (1694) created the Bank of England as the English government's exclusive bank in exchange for a loan of 1.2 million pounds (Neal 1990, pp. 44–61). As the mercantile period continued, the purpose of granting monopoly trading privileges shifted to the goal of allowing governments to borrow in the form of liquid liabilities that would attract large numbers of investors at reasonable rates of return. Thus, modern financial markets developed partially as a response to the colonial designs of nation-states.

Methods of signaling credibility and commitment in fulfilling financial promises also date to these early market developments. The Dutch *Wisselbank*, established in Amsterdam in 1609, was a means by which merchant bankers could transfer payments denominated in bank money between themselves and their international counterparts, thus moderating the uncertainties of exchange rate movement and coin debasement as well as providing a clearinghouse mechanism that enhanced the credibility of time contracts. Major innovations in governmental finance took place over the next two centuries as nation-states dealt with the credible commitment problem in fiscal policy. These innovations included the use of private joint stock companies to service the national debt, and the (ultimately) more successful creation of the perpetual government annuity pioneered by the British with the Three-percent Consol in 1753.

Thus, as illustrated in the fictitious conversation at the beginning of this article, financial market participants recognized the importance of credible commitments and their impact on financial asset prices even in the early years of financial market development. The question remains, however, as to how effectively financial asset markets transmit important information reflecting changes in the underlying structure of price discovery. In the next section, therefore, we turn our attention to the empirical aspects of identifying structural change in long-term financial asset markets.

24.4 EMPIRICAL APPLICATIONS OF FINANCIAL MARKET THEORY TO WAR AND PEACE

Empirical methods are increasingly employed to help identify relationships between political, economic, social and military events in conflict-torn areas and their corresponding effects on expectations and perceptions of credibility and commitment. These methods, typically called "event studies" or "intervention analyses," make use of some form of the theoretical framework provided in Section 24.2 of this chapter. The counterpart to a regime change is a structural shift in the parameters of an empirical model. In other words, one can model the time series process generating observations of a "credibility" variable and then test for changes in the parameters of that model as possible evidence of events that have changed the underlying process. A regime change is, thus, interpreted empirically as an occasional, discrete shift in the parameters regulating the time series behavior of an economic variable. The implementation of this approach is essentially one of determining the existence of regime changes in response to, or even in anticipation of, observable events.

The ability to determine the credibility of a threat or agreement using market prices and asset values rests on two important points. First, we must assume that at least some rational agents understand the true intentions of the various parties to a conflict and can act on this information, so that the market achieves an expectations-consistent equilibrium. This may seem controversial, but in reality equilibrium could be reached in a market in which only a few knowledgeable speculators act as monitors. We view these agents as insiders and others who are privy to the intentions of the government and who use this information to avoid capital losses and pursue capital gains. The second necessary element concerns the theoretical effects of pre-announced or anticipated changes in policy on variables, such as financial asset prices, that are sensitive to expectations. In the case of anticipated changes in fundamentals, we assume a discontinuity or "jump" in the level of the variable at the time of the announcement. When the anticipated change in policy actually does take place, the variable will nonetheless remain at the same value it had immediately before the correctly anticipated change. This is based on the so-called "asset price continuity principle" (see Auernheimer and Lozada 1990) that no unexploited capital gains or losses can occur at the time of a fully anticipated or pre-announced change. Gains or losses only take place in response to new information that is not foreseen by agents, as they are unable to plan their portfolios to take advantage of such events. It is this "news" that generates jumps in the level of asset prices.

In the following section, we present an example of this empirical methodology by making use of a financial data set from the national stock market of Sri Lanka, a South Asian nation that has experienced a long-running ethnic conflict between the government of the majority Sinhalese and a rebel group representing the Tamil minority. At issue, again, is the extent to which long-term financial asset prices give useful signals about the commitment of negotiating parties and the credibility of peace initiatives.

24.5   CREDIBLE COMMITMENT AND FINANCIAL ASSET MARKETS: THE CASE OF SRI LANKA[7]

24.5.1   Data and Methodology

One simple and flexible model that can be applied to determine the presence of a structural shift in the mean of a single time series is a two-step procedure like those employed by Banerjee, Lumsdaine and Stock (1992) and Willard, Guinnane and Rosen (1996). The first step is a systematic search for all possible break dates within the sample. This involves estimating an autoregression on a small portion of the sample referred to as the "window." The date "s" is determined by the midpoint in the window. The size of the window is somewhat arbitrary, but is in part a function of the frequency of observations on the variable. For example, using monthly data, a window of 15 months would identify regime changes that affected the behavior of the variable for 7.5 months or more.

The main concern in this first step is with the sign and significance of the parameter which indicates a possible break in the mean of the series. A significant F-statistic associated with this parameter would suggest that a regime change may have occurred on date "s." Next, the window is moved one observation closer to the end of the sample and the equation re-estimated, again testing for a significant F-statistic. In this way, one rolls through the entire sample and tests for possible breaks over the entire sample except for the first and last half-windows. The vector of F-statistics associated with each possible break date reveals information on the most likely dates of regime change.

The second stage regressions involve identifying local maximums in the series of F-statistics, isolating the window around those dates, and then searching for the "peak" within the isolated window. For each of the windows identified here, we estimate a sequence of equations like those above and test for a break at each date contained in the window (except, again, the first and last half sub-window). Within each window, we again identify the largest F-statistic as the most likely date of a change in regime. Matching these dates to recorded events from the conflict indicates how the public viewed various incidents as affecting the probability of war and peace.

As an example of this application, we employ this technique to test for structural changes in long-term financial asset markets in Sri Lanka during the extended conflict between government forces and the rebel Liberation Tigers of Tamil Eelam (LTTE). Our data consists of monthly closing index prices of Sri Lanka's only national stock market – the Colombo Stock Exchange (CSE) – from July 1997 to May 2008. The CSE keeps two main price indices, the All Share Price Index (ASPI) and the

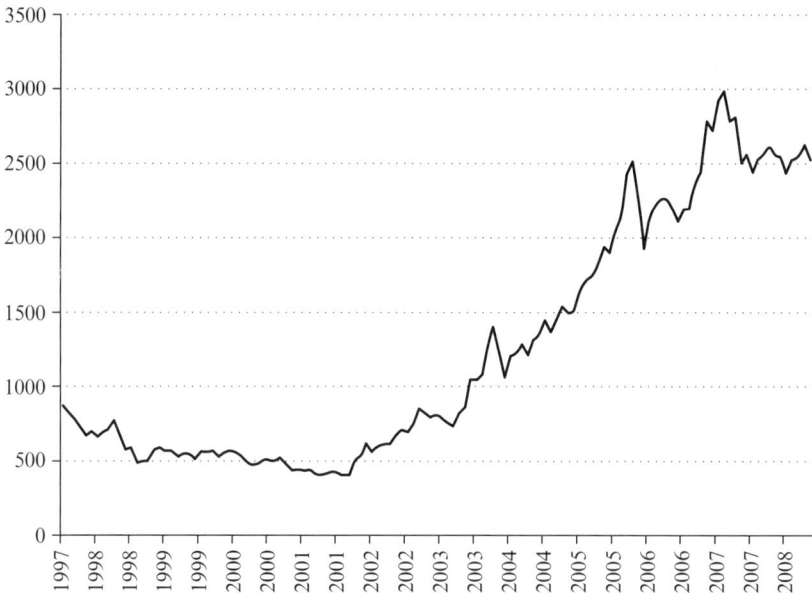

Figure 24.1   Monthly stock market index values, July 1997–May 2008

Milanka Price Index (MPI). Our analysis uses the ASPI data because it comprises all companies listed on the exchange.[8] The data is plotted above in Figure 24.1.

Rather than assume breaks exist a priori, we run the aforementioned tests for structural change in order to identify the precise locations and magnitudes of possible regime shifts, and to verify that they indeed qualify as significant changes in regime according to our pre-determined window length. Because Augmented Dickey-Fuller (ADF) tests suggest that the index series is non-stationary, we run all of our estimation procedures on the differenced index series rather than on its levels.[9] Furthermore, because of the presence of heteroskedasticity, we employ a Generalized Autoregressive Conditional Heteroskedasticity (GARCH) model in estimating the autoregressions. We employ a window length of two years throughout the analysis, so that our technique detects structural change only for innovations that affect the time-dependent mean for at least one year.

24.5.2   Empirical Results

Our rolling regression technique on the baseline window yields a number of possible break points in the series mean, illustrated in Figure 24.2 below:

F-value   20 ⌐

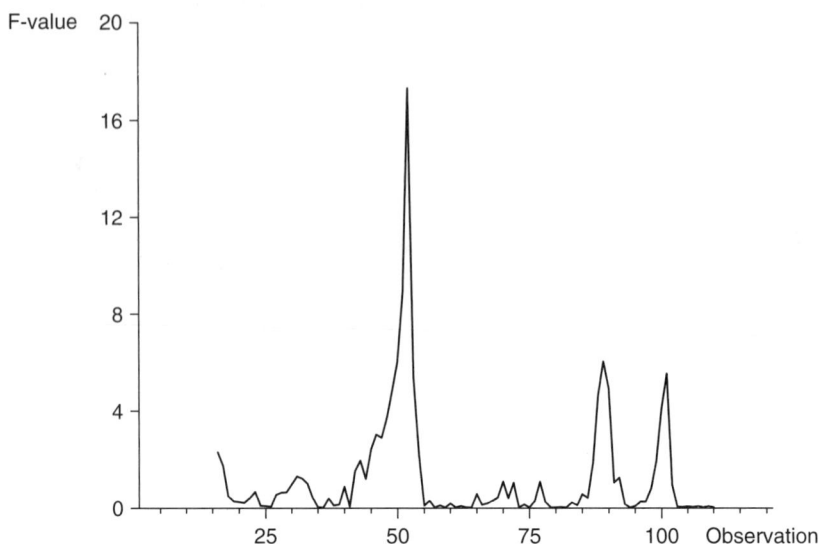

Figure 24.2   Rolling regression F-values for two-year windows

Among the series of F-values produced, there are 'spikes' at observations 52, 89 and 101.[10] These observations correspond to the months October 2001, November 2004 and November 2005. Further verification of the importance of these break dates is obtained by testing individually and jointly for statistical significance of regime shifts in both the intercept and slope of the differenced stock index series. Individual and joint tests of significance are run within the context of a GARCH model in order to account for the time-variant volatility that the series exhibits. The results indicate that all three potential break dates pass tests for significance both individually and when tested jointly with the other observations.[11] It is notable, also, that all three dates pass individual and joint tests of statistical significance for change in the variance. In sum, our empirical method produces evidence of three breaks with respect to the means and variance of the stock index series. The shifts in mean can be interpreted as regime changes that affected the time path of the Sri Lankan monthly stock index series, and the shifts in variance as changes that have affected the level of volatility around those time paths.

24.5.3   Analysis and Interpretation

Recall that we assume that rational agents can assign subjective probabilities to the distribution of possible returns based on their assessments of the commitment of the parties involved in a peace agreement. Our empirical analysis suggests a number of specific regime shifts in our asset price data. In this sub-section, we match the dates of the regime shifts identified in our empirical analysis to events that changed the relative probabilities assigned to conflict and resolution, and then determine the extent to which those changes in expectations reflected observable long-term changes in the prospects for peace.

There are three dates, in particular, that seem to indicate structural change: October 2001, November 2004 and November 2005. The first regime change represents a positive shift, indicating an increase in the probability of conflict resolution. The latter two, however, were negative shifts from the previous mean, suggesting an increase in expectations of continued conflict or, at the very least, a lack of credible commitment to negotiations. All three dates retain statistical significance even when the other break dates are taken into account. Our aim is to understand the context of events that resulted in changes in the perceived credibility of peace efforts, and to determine whether our index is a useful predictive (leading) indicator of actual changes in the relative probabilities of conflict and peace.

October 2001

As a result of the attacks on the United States by the terrorist organization Al Qaeda, the United Nations passed Resolution 1373 on 28 September, 2001. The resolution set a framework for the international community regarding terrorism. In particular, the resolution advocated freezing sources of funding, combining the resources of the international community and monitoring all organizations that used terror as part of their operations. Under this resolution the LTTE was named as a terrorist organization.

Soon after Resolution 1373 was passed, both Canada and the United Kingdom publicly named the LTTE as a terrorist organization. This increasing international pressure had the effect of raising the cost to the LTTE of using violence to achieve their desired end. In other words, the actions of the international community increased the net benefit to the LTTE of credibly committing to the peace process. On the other side, the Sri Lankan government realized the LTTE was now going to find it difficult to secure international funding, providing an incentive to negotiate to a peace agreement (Raman 2002). At the same time, however, the Sri Lankan government was in the midst of a recession and unable to advance any significant military objective. The regime shift that occurred in October 2001 seems to indicate a change in the credibility of peace initiatives in that the LTTE was "unlikely to carry out major attacks in view of the post September 11 global situation, [and that] the change in stance by the international community" presented a binding constraint on the actions of the LTTE (Chandrasekharan 2001a). In his Heroes' Day speech on 27 November, 2001, Prabhakaran, the political leader of the LTTE, indicated that his group was not "the run of the mill terrorist outfit" but was "fighting for a noble cause," and that one "has to distinguish the freedom fighters from those who commit blind terrorist acts based on fanaticism" (Chandrasekharan 2001b). Prabhakaran's speech can be seen as an attempt to signal the LTTE's credible commitment to peace, both to the Sri Lankan government and to the international community.

Within the context of an international community pushing to eradicate the funding of terrorism, and the perception by the government of an intractable stalemate, both sides agreed to Norway-brokered peace talks in November 2001. Three months later the Ceasefire Agreement (CFA) – the first such agreement since 1997 – was reached. Our analysis of the asset price data shows a change in expectations regarding the feasibility of sustainable peace four months before the CFA.

November 2004

Just over three years after the first regime shift is detected, a second shift occurs. Unlike the first one, however, our analysis shows agents perceiving a reduction in the commitment to the peace process by one or both of the parties. This change of expectations in late 2004 appears to be solely the result of domestic influences. Two interrelated incidents provided agents with information that changed the probabilities they assigned to the credibility of the parties' commitment to the ceasefire agreement.

First, the governing-coalition partner the United National Party (UNP) publicly stated that they would not support the peace process. Second, the LTTE's leader replied that if the Sri Lankan government did not come back to the peace talks, they would have "no alternative but to advance the freedom struggle. . ." (Marwan-Markar, 18 November, 2004). Importantly, the peace process had at this point already been stalled for 19 months, but it was the revelation that President Karamantanga could not form a consensus government without the UNP, in conjunction with the growing impatience of the Tamil leadership, that ultimately changed people's perceptions about the sustainability of the ceasefire agreement. Tamil National Alliance MP Jeyanandamoorty even proclaimed, "Sinhala parties will never come to a consensus on a political settlement to the ethnic conflict. It won't happen even if the Tamils wait patiently for another 50 years" (Marwan-Markar, 18 November, 2004).

This incident is unique, we believe, in that it shows the value of financial assets as a measure of peace agreement credibility. Due to the instability of the Sri Lankan government and the continued demands of the LTTE for

Interim Self-Governing Authority (ISGA), neither side was seen as demonstrating a credible commitment to the peace process – although neither had yet actively re-engaged in armed hostilities.

November 2005

On 22 September, 2005, the LTTE publicly announced that agreements signed by the Sri Lanka Freedom Party (SLFP) presidential candidate Mahinda Rajapakse with the People's Liberation Front (JVP) and the National Heritage Party (JHU) precluded the possibility of finding a negotiated solution to the "national question" of constitutional autonomy for the LTTE-controlled areas. On 19 November, Rajapakse was sworn in as the new President. He won the election, in part, because the Tamil minority – at the behest of the LTTE – boycotted the elections.

The JVP did not immediately join Rajapakse's government to form a coalition, despite earlier indications that they would. Specifically, the JVP stated that they "would wait and observe the way the new President performs" before they decided to join his government (Daily Mirror, 21 November, 2005). The lack of a broad-based coalition prevented the government from returning to the peace process, and this news resulted in a seven percent drop in the CSE's ASPI Index for the week following her victory. Agents perceived this as a sign that the Sinhalese government had little ability and/or willingness to make peace, and the LTTE boycott ensured that only the Sinhalese voice was revealed in the election.

24.6   SUMMARY AND CONCLUSIONS

The economic approach to conflict resolution suggests that the perceived credibility of participants in peace-making arrangements will be an important, perhaps defining, aspect of the success or failure of such arrangements to produce long-lasting change. The issue is of vital importance especially to less-developed countries (LDCs) who are caught in a conflict trap, whereby a nation is "stuck in a pattern of violent internal challenges to government" which impede its ability to deal with fundamental issues of poverty, development and sustainable growth (Collier 2007, p. 18). Without the appropriate tools to ensure verifiable commitments to credible policies, such nations are destined to remain in a vicious cycle of violent conflict which adds to existing problems of development and poverty by dislocating families, destroying infrastructure and exacerbating inequalities. This may, in turn, lead to even more violence as aggrieved, disenfranchised segments of the population are drawn to militant groups that promise changes in their societal status.

We have presented evidence that a promising solution to the problem of verifying credible commitments to negotiations, treaties, agreements and other aspects of the peace process lies in the use of long-term fixed financial asset market prices. These prices are, by their very nature, forward-looking and information-sensitive. As such, the markets generating these prices will tend to reflect the expectations of those market participants with the most pertinent and reliable information about the likelihood of events that will change their underlying time paths. Our historical evidence demonstrates that even participants in the earliest developing financial markets realized their power in quickly and accurately reflecting the impact of important events on the likelihood of war and peace. More recent evidence, from the protracted conflict in Sri Lanka, suggests that even relatively undeveloped (by modern standards) emerging long-term financial asset markets retain this power in the information age, often outperforming both survey-based confidence measures and short-term currency markets in this regard.[12]

The price discovery approach to credibility and commitment is a wide open field for future research. Economists have long recognized both the local information-discovery aspect of markets (Hayek 1945) and the general problem of time inconsistency (Kydland and Prescott 1977) in public policy, and many attempts have been made to combine the two strands of literature in the context of asymmetric information (adverse selection and moral hazard) where transactions costs are high. Our research represents an extension of these same concepts beyond their more familiar fields of monetary and regulatory policy and into the realm of international relations. As economists continue to reach beyond the standard neo-classical paradigm into a broader, more far-reaching program of political economy, we expect that future applications of this approach will multiply rapidly, increasing our understanding of the inter-relatedness of economic, political and social aspects of human action and exchange.

NOTES

1. Quoted from a conversation between protagonists in Patrick O'Brien's *The Reverse of the Medal* (1986, p. 135).
2. The material in this section is drawn substantially from Dempster and Isaacs (2008) and Coyne, Dempster and Isaacs (2010).
3. See Davidson (1996) for a discussion of ergodic versus. nonergodic environments and their importance for economic analysis.
4. This section summarizes literature drawn from Ashton (1955), Riley (1980), Neal (1990) and Dempster, Wells and Wills (2001).
5. Bordo and White (1991), p. 303–309. See also North and Weingast (1989).

6. The establishment of the first British East India Company actually preceded the Dutch version by a year.
7. The material in this section is drawn substantially from Coyne, Dempster and Isaacs (2010).
8. The All Share Price Index (ASPI) is based on the share movements of all companies on the stock market. Calculations for the ASPI use 1985 as a base year. The ASPI equals the total market capitalization times 100 divided by the base market capitalization, where market capitalization equals the number of shares issued times the market price, and base market capitalization is the number of issued shares at the base year times the base year market price.
9. Since ADF tests for non-stationarity are now standard in the literature, we do not outline the procedure or results here. Details of such procedures can be found in Enders (1995). It is not uncommon for stock prices and indexes to exhibit non-stationary behavior.
10. Regressions using three-year windows produced a similar series. Since the results do not seem overly sensitive to the window length, we are fairly confident as to the robustness of our procedures.
11. Coefficient values for each of the three respective breaks – Oct. 2001, Nov. 2004 and Nov. 2005 – are as follows (z-stats in parentheses): $B_{2001} = 73.5$ (2.76); $B_{2004} = -66.4$ (7.00); and $B_{2005} = -457.7$ (1.90). For further details of the empirical results, see Coyne, Dempster and Isaacs (2009).
12. See Coyne, Dempster and Isaacs (2010) for a comparative summary of these methods in the context of Sri Lanka's conflict.

REFERENCES

Ashton, T.S. (1955), *An Economic History of England: The 18th Century*, London: Oxford University Press.

Auernheimer, L. and G.A. Lozada (1990), "On the treatment of anticipated shocks in models of optimal control with rational expectations: an economic interpretation", *American Economic Review*, **80**, 157–69.

Banerjee, A., R.L. Lumsdaine and J.H. Stock (1992), "Recursive and sequential tests of the unit-root and trend-break hypotheses: theory and international evidence", *Journal of Business & Economic Statistics*, **10** (27), 1–87.

Boettke, P.J. (1993), *Why Perestroika Failed: The Politics and Economics of Socialist Transformation*, New York, NY: Routledge.

Boettke, P.J. (2001), "Credibility, commitment, and soviet economic reform," In P.J. Boettke (ed.), *Calculation and Coordination*, New York, NY: Routledge, 154–175.

Bordo, M.D. and E.N. White (1991), "A tale of two currencies: British and French finances during the Napoleonic Wars", *Journal of Economic History*, **51** (2), 303–16.

Chandrasekharan, S. (2001a), "Sri Lankan Update No. 28: amidst political crisis, tigers are waiting", South Asia Analysis Group, available at: http://www.saag.org/notes2/note138.html, accessed 10 May 2008.

Chandrasekharan, S. (2001b), "Sri Lankan Update No. 29: Heroes Day speech – an analysis", South Asia Analysis Group, available at: http://www.saag.org/notes2/note139.html, accessed 10 May 2008.

Collier, P. (2007), *The Bottom Billion: Why the Poorest Countries are Failing and What Can Be Done About It*, New York, NY: Oxford University Press.

Coyne, C.J. (2007), *After War: The Political Economy of Exporting Democracy*, Palo Alto, CA: Stanford University Press.

Coyne, C.J. and P. Boettke (2009), "The problem of credible commitment in reconstruction", *Journal of Institutional Economics*, **5** (1), 1–23.

Coyne, C.J., G. Dempster and J. Isaacs (2010), "Asset values and the sustainability of peace prospects", *Quarterly Review of Economics and Finance*, **50** (2), 146–56.

Davidson, P. (1996), "Some misunderstanding on uncertainty in modern classical economics", in C. Schmidt (ed.), *Uncertainty in Economic Thought*, Cheltenham, UK: Edward Elgar.

Dempster, G. and J. Isaacs (2008), "Economic implications of peace agreements: the case of Sri Lanka", *Virginia Economic Journal*, **36** (1), 1–27.

Dempster, G., J. Wells and D. Wills (2000), "A common features analysis of Amsterdam and London financial markets during the 18th century", *Economic Inquiry*, **38** (1), 19–33.

Enders, W. (1995), Applied Econometric Time Series, Hoboken, NJ: Wiley and Sons, Inc.

Government of Sri Lanka (2003), "Donors firm: no aid If peace process is stagnant", *Current Affairs*.

Hayek, F.A. (1945) "The use of knowledge in society," *American Economic Review*, **35** (4), 519–30.

Keefer, P. (2006), "Insurgency and credible commitment in autocracies and democracies", World Bank Working Paper 4185, Washington DC.

Keefer, P. and R. Vlaicu (2005), "Democracy, credibility and clientelism", World Bank Policy Research Working Paper 3472.

Kydland, F.E. and E. Prescott (1977), "Rules rather than discretion: the inconsistency of optimal plans", *Journal of Political Economy*, **85** (3), 473–91.

Neal, L. (1990), The Rise of Financial Capitalism: International Capital Markets in the Age of Reason, Cambridge, UK: Cambridge University Press.

North, D.C. and B.R. Weingast (1989), "Constitutions and commitment: the evolution of institutions governing public choice in seventeenth-century England", *Journal of Economic History*, **49** (4), 803–32.

O'Brien, P. (1986), *The Reverse of Metal*, New York, NY: William Collins and Co.

Persson, T. and G. Tabellini (2000), *Political Economics: Explaining Public Policy*, Cambridge, MA: The MIT Press.

Raman, B. (2002), "The LTTE – the metamorphsis", South Asia Analysis Group, available at: www.saag.org, accessed 6 April 2008.

Riley, J.C. (1980), *International Government Finance and the Amsterdam Capital Market, 1740–1815*, New York, NY: Cambridge University Press.

Willard, K.L., T.W. Guinnane and H.S. Rosen (1996), "Turning points in the civil war: views from the greenback market", *American Economic Review*, **86**, 1001–18.

PART VII

ALTERNATIVES TO WAR

25 Disaggregated trade flows and international conflict
Han Dorussen and Hugh Ward

25.1 INTRODUCTION

The proposition that trade promotes peace is one of the cornerstones of liberal thought. Commerce makes stable interstate relations more valuable, because producers derive benefits from exports and consumers from imports. It is also a source of revenue and possibly even more important political support for governments (Schumpeter 1951; Polachek 1980, 2002; Russett and Oneal 2001). Classical Liberals, like Codben and Mill, further emphasized that trade necessitates transnational communication. Traders can become valuable mediators with a clear interest in avoiding any escalation of conflict that may threaten their livelihood (Dorussen and Ward 2010). Proponents of the so-called Capitalist Peace argue that trade – among other valuable interstate connections such as investments – allows states to avoid conflict because it reduces the uncertainty in interstate relations and hence makes it more likely that states are able to resolve their conflict without having to resort to the use of force (Gartzke 2007).[1]

The significance of trade is challenged regularly on both theoretical and empirical grounds. A pertinent question is whether the effect of trade on conflict is uniform across commodities or heterogeneous; in other words, does it matter what goods are being traded? The liberal view is that trade always reduces the likelihood of conflict, even though trade in some goods may be particularly pacifying (Dorussen 2006). In contrast, critics emphasize that the security implications of trade in, for example, strategic or high-tech goods, are bound to shape trade policies, and that such trade is associated with conflict rather than peace (Hirschman [1945] 1980; Choucri and North 1975).[2] Any heterogeneous effects of trade on conflict are bound to bias the results of analyses using total trade, but only recently have scholars begun to disaggregate trade in large-N statistical analyses.

This chapter first surveys the main arguments suggesting that goods vary in their strategic importance; that is, in their relative importance for a state's (military) security, the difficulty in finding alternative sources and markets in case of conflict and the attractiveness of conquest to appropriate the gains from trade. Next, it evaluates the empirical support for the hypothesis that trade in certain goods actually increases the probability of interstate conflict. The motivating question is whether recent research using disaggregated trade flows has succeeded in undermining the liberal thesis; are there circumstances under which trade in particular goods increases the likelihood of conflict? The main conclusion is that, so far, the liberal thesis still stands. Even though it matters what goods are being traded, heterogeneity weakens but does not invalidate the result that trade reduces the probability of conflict. This general conclusion is placed within the context of the emerging literature on trade networks and conflict which emphasizes that both direct and indirect trade linkages matter. There is indeed evidence that as the global trade network has become denser over time the general embeddedness of state dyads in the trade network has become more relevant. Consequently, it matters less what precisely gets traded between any two countries.

25.2   HOW COULD TRADE LEAD TO CONFLICT?

There are a number of counterarguments against the liberal position that focus on the specific goods being traded. First we sketch the theoretical arguments linking trade in strategic goods to conflict and focus on the various attempts to specify "strategic" goods. A pertinent problem is to specify what goods are strategic with any precision. Next, we evaluate arguments suggesting asymmetric trade or dependency as a potential cause of interstate conflict.

25.2.1   Strategic Goods and the Gains from Conquest

Implicit in the linkage between trade and conflict are concerns about secure access to essential goods and markets. Gilpin (1977, pp. 41–42) argues that uncertainty about continued supply of strategic goods increases states' insecurity which would lead to a greater potential of conflict. Choucri and North (1975) suggest competition for resources as a direct cause for conflict. Similarly, Sen (1984) argues that international political competition encourages states to focus on "strategic" industries increasing national defense capabilities, particularly intermediate manufactured products, apart from the strategic importance of self-sufficiency in food and energy. Sen (1984, pp. 176–8) further suggests that the military origins of industrialization and uneven development result in economic rivalry and create a situation of potential conflict. However, he addresses neither why such potential conflict would escalate into war nor the significance of trade. Liberman (1996) argues explicitly that states can gain from direct occupation and plunder of goods from extractive industries. Instead of trade, states may prefer to control directly the sources of production in order to appropriate the gains from trade.

In order to establish the link between trade, conflict and the appropriation of resources, it is important to recognize the complexity of the calculus motivating a state's decision to use force. First of all, domestic politics is a complicating factor. States generally depend on economic actors, both domestic and foreign, to realize any gains from trade. Support for the use of force depends on a coalition of actors expecting to gain from conflict and whether it is able to overcome any opposition. Reuveny (2001, p. 404) argues accordingly: "When traders lobby governments for various interventions, their actions may affect bilateral relations. It is conceivable that the extent of these efforts will vary across sectors, depending on such factors as the economic importance of sectors, their political power, or the extent to which sectors depend on trade." Well-known is Schumpeter's (1951, pp. 83–130) argument that as capitalism develops more fully, the willingness of economic actors to support the use of force diminishes at the same time as their political influence increases. *Free* trade is particularly important because it erodes the privileges of aristocratic classes and pre-modern interests more supportive of the state's use of force (Schumpeter 1951; McDonald 2004, 2009). Since conflict can only be attractive if the gains from appropriation exceed the gains from trade, free trade in particular should reduce the probability of conflict, since it maximizes the possible gains from trade.

A further problem is that it has proven to be difficult to specify what goods are strategic with any precision, so it is not clear that these arguments give rise to testable hypotheses about conflict. One approach is to look at states' efforts to regulate trade. Trade in goods that are especially important for a state's (military) security is indeed commonly regulated. Trade in strategic goods in particular should thus be endogenous to any history or expectations of conflict, and we should observe more trade in strategic goods between two countries if the risks of future conflict are low. During the Cold War, the Coordinating Committee for Multilateral Export Controls (CoCom) was pivotal in the common efforts of the United States, Western Europe and Japan to limit their export of strategic goods to the Soviet bloc and its allies. Gasiorowski and Polachek (1982, p. 727) investigate the effect of increased US–Warsaw Pact trade on conflict and generally find trade to have a pacifying effect on both sides. The effect was notably larger for the Warsaw Pact countries, for which trade in general was more valuable, and for trade in industrial supplies, for which countries in Eastern Europe relied in particular on the West for their industrialization.

The history of CoCom does not clearly show that more heavily regulated trade necessarily increases the probability of conflict. CoCom occasionally contributed to East–West tensions, but the regulation and subsequent lack of trade in strategic goods was primarily a consequence of the Cold War. Even though there was persistent disagreement within CoCom about the content and aims of the strategic embargo, these "conflicts" were settled diplomatically and never militarized. The particular items covered under CoCom's strategic embargo generally included materials used principally for the production and deployment of arms, items that relied on advanced technological know-how and materials for which the Soviet bloc experienced persistent shortages. Førland (1991) and Mastanduno (1992) document how the definition of strategic goods within CoCom was the subject of extensive political disputes and varied over time both in content and detail.[3]

Following the Cold War and now including the former Warsaw Pact members, the Wassenaar Arrangement regulates trade in arms technology as well as any trade that could lead to proliferation of weapons of mass destruction. In addition, oil and high-technology industries are often considered to have the most obvious strategic importance. Ripsman and Blanchard (1996/7) identify separate lists of strategic commodities for World War I and World War II respectively. Marlin-Bennett, Rosenblatt and Wang (1992), Borrus and Zysman (1992) and Tyson (1992) discuss the commercial rivalry in high-technology industries and possible security implications.

An alternative approach is to consider what goods and trade provide economic opportunities that may cause war. Dorussen (2006, pp. 92–3) suggests that goods with a high concentration of production, such as mining, energy and heavy industry in chemicals and primary metal products, as well as the production of goods which relies on foreign capital, are significant for conflict. In contrast, it is more difficult to appropriate the gains from the production of advanced industrial societies with highly diversified and dispersed industrial production relying on specialized highly skilled labor (Liberman 1996). Goenner (2010) also argues that countries that specialize in the production of goods that have strategic importance are more likely to be the target of plunder. Using the Herfindahl-Hirschmann Index to measure export concentration, he concludes that export of energy, non-ferrous metals and nuclear materials increases the chances of conflict.

Ultimately it may be questioned whether any strict separation of strategic and nonstrategic goods is possible. Schelling (1958, pp. 498–504) argues that what really matters is the comparative cost of producing each type of goods at home and thus the impact of trade on the total military strength of a country attainable within its production possibility frontier. Ultimately, variations in the comparative costs of local production, or the opportunity costs, are more relevant than the military usefulness of particular goods. The impact of trade on the costs of conflict should vary across goods since the expectations about costs depend on the difficulties of substituting lost trade. Goods that are more difficult – and thus more costly – to substitute should have a stronger pacifying effect (Gasiorowski and Polachek 1982; Polachek and McDonald 1992; Reuveny and Kang 1998). What is noticeable, however, is that it is difficult to use this insight to help us understand the types of goods that are commonly listed as strategic. In part this is because of the difficulty with getting relevant data for such variables as supply and demand elasticities for particular types of goods.[4]

25.2.2 Dependency and Conflict

A trade relationship may display asymmetries or even dependency, which is used occasionally to link trade to conflict. In his seminal study, Hirschman ([1945] 1980, p. 36) discusses Germany's trade policy under National Socialism to illustrate power politics by means of trade. He argues that a central element of German policy was "to concentrate on exports of finished products, on the one hand, and on exports to agricultural countries, on the other." The policy was most clearly implemented in relation to states in Eastern Europe, and allowed Germany to exert influence because "agricultural countries have generally but little mobility of resources . . . and . . . manufactured products, being highly differentiated, are often difficult to replace immediately by similar products from other countries." In other words, the opportunity costs of exporting manufactured goods were considered low compared to those of exporting agricultural products. Conversely, the opportunity costs of importing manufactured goods were high compared to those of importing agricultural products. German trade policy created asymmetric dependence which entangled East European states and allowed Nazi Germany to pursue its aggressive foreign policy objectives.[5] However, asymmetric dependence also motivated East European states to appease Germany, leaving the ultimate implication of the pattern of trade on conflict indeterminate.

Hirschman's argument begins to suggest that the effects of trade on conflict will differ depending on the type of good traded. Building on Schelling's (1958) insights, Polachek (1980, 1992; see also Polachek and Seiglie 2006) develops a simple expected-utility framework which emphasizes changes in the relative costs of imports and exports. The model assumes that countries maximize utility functions with two elements: consumption of goods which can be produced either locally or abroad and the preferred political state of the world. The political state results from countries' decisions on the intensity of conflict (and cooperation) with others. Hostility requires the use of costly and limited resources. Conflict intensity also affects the prices of imported and exported goods, and the implicit cost of conflict is the lost gains from trade. Two main propositions follow directly from the model: (1) a country chooses less conflict (more cooperation) relative to a major trading partner, and (2) the more unfavorably conflict affects the relative prices of imports and exports, the smaller will be the degree of conflict initiated. Conflict affects the prices at which goods are traded differently depending on their specific opportunity costs and elasticity of demand and supply. When conflict actually increases the relative price of exports (for example, in the case of oil and other minerals), exporting countries may choose to become more hostile. Park, Abolfathi and Ward (1976) and Polachek (1980, pp. 70–71) demonstrate that oil-exporting countries become more hostile toward oil importers if the amount of trade increases, but de Soysa and Lie (2008) observe that although conflict is indeed more likely between oil-exporters and oil-importers, this does not necessarily mean that war is more likely.

The model analysed by Li and Reuveny (n.d.) is closely related to that of Polachek (1980). Their model assumes that conflict affects demand and supply within a dyad directly and prices indirectly. It examines the conditions under which trade affects the incentives for one country (the "actor") to initiate a conflict against another country (the "target"). Conflict requires these countries to look for alternative buyers and suppliers, and they may vary in their ability to locate alternative trading partners. Higher imports raise an actor's hostility if that actor's import demand for a particular good from the target is more sensitive to conflict than the target's export supply of the same good. In this case, conflict makes it cheaper to import the particular good from the target. Alternatively, the higher the level of exports of a particular good the greater the actor's hostility if the actor's export supply is more sensitive to conflict than the target's import demand for the same good. In this case, increased hostility increases the price of the exported goods. The distinguishing feature of Li and Reuveny's model is that hostility does not affect prices directly but the quantities of goods demanded and supplied. Interestingly, they show that in some cases, countries may gain from reduced demand or supply.

There remain a number of problems with Polachek and Li and Reuveny's argument about the effects of conflict on terms of trade. First, there are issues about causality. Even if conflict affects terms of trade favorably, it is an open question why countries would have to, and even more would want to, initiate conflict to get better terms. Common understandings of conflict take not only the initiation of hostility into consideration but also the response of any countries targeted. Because of this the effect of trade on conflict is indeterminate even if one country expects to gain from conflict while the other stands to lose, since increased hostility may be met with an increased willingness to acquiesce. Polachek (1980) finds indeed that increased trade in oil makes the foreign policy of oil exporters more hostile, but the policy of oil importers more cooperative.

Second, the effects of trade on conflict can go beyond the trading partners directly involved. For instance East European trade with Germany may have increased the probability of conflict between Germany and the Soviet Union, because of Communist Bloc dependence on the Soviet Union. However, the third-party effects may not always take this form. As we discuss further below, third parties may become involved as mediators or as communication channels, and these effects may depend on the patterns of third-party trade and the types of good traded.

25.3 WHAT, IF ANY, TRADE LEADS TO CONFLICT? EMPIRICAL ASSESSMENTS AND OUTSTANDING ISSUES

A small number of empirical studies use disaggregated trade flows to analyse the link between interdependence and conflict. To highlight the main empirical findings and outstanding issues, we focus on three recent studies, namely Dorussen (2006), Goenner (2010) and Li and Reuveny (n.d.).[6] Departing from previous studies on disaggregated trade, these studies all use large samples and examine the probability of militarized interstate disputes. Another similarity is that their model specifications broadly follow Russett and Oneal (2001) and include democracy, distance, capability-ratios or gross domestic products as controls, with peace years and cubic splines as temporal controls (Beck, Katz and Tucker 1998). Regardless, their main conclusions are partly contradictory. Dorussen finds that trade is generally pacifying although trade in manufactured products, in particular consumer goods, has stronger effects. The other studies argue that certain forms of trade actually increase the probability of conflict. Goenner finds that trade in energy, non-ferrous materials and electronics is associated with more conflict. Li and Reuveny find that exports of energy as well as a rise in manufactured imports and exports make countries more likely to initiate conflict. The results are also useful to draw attention to several thorny issues and open questions, namely, simultaneity bias, level of aggregation, appropriate unit of analysis and proper definition of conflict.

If the effect of trade on conflict is indeed heterogeneous, Polachek's

(1992, p. 97) suggestion that "ideally dyadic commodity by commodity trade flows are needed" follows naturally. At the same time, practical concerns force researchers to aggregate trade. Dorussen, Goenner and Li and Reuveny all aggregate trade differently making a direct comparison of their findings difficult. An intuitive solution is to focus on trade in goods that are deemed to be of strategic importance; for example, Park et al. (1976) and Polachek (1980) examine the effect of the oil trade on conflict. On the basis of the NBER-UN 4-digit SITC (revision 2) classification of commodity trade, Goenner identifies goods within the following categories to be of strategic importance: energy, non-ferrous metals, chemicals, electronics, nuclear and armaments, since these goods are generally considered to be essential to a country's economic and military strength. In line with our previous discussion, he also notes that there is no general agreement on a list of strategic commodities and that his list is hardly exhaustive. A further issue is whether an ideal list of strategic commodities would have to be country and time specific. Goenner, however, shows that the import and export elasticity estimated by Broda and Weinstein (2006) are strongly correlated across time periods and across countries. Using this additional information Goenner argues that among his list of strategic commodities energy and oil have more elastic import demand and export supply and are expected to have a less pacifying effect.

Dorussen and Li and Reuveny use more highly aggregated categories of trade data. Dorussen uses the classification of trade into 35 industry sectors as originally compiled by Statistics Canada (Feenstra 2000). As noted above, Hirschmann ([1945] 1980) compared the strategic strength and vulnerabilities of the production and trade of agricultural and mining products compared to manufacturing (see also Gasiorowski and Polachek 1982). Dorussen accordingly aggregates industry sectors further into food and kindred products and manufacturing, where the latter is disaggregated into chemicals, metal products, textiles, building supplies, machinery, electronics and low- and high-technology products. Based on earlier studies, he expects variation in opportunity costs across these industry sectors but does not specify the direction of any effects. An obvious problem with more highly aggregated data is that some categories are bound to encompass goods of very different strategic importance. The classification of industry sectors is based on product characteristics instead of military usefulness; for example, machinery encompasses lawn mowers and battleships. Li and Reuveny use the five sectors defined by Italianer (1986), namely, agriculture/fishery, chemical/mineral, energy, manufactured products and miscellaneous consumption. For the hypothesized effect of these five sectors on conflict initiation, Li and Reuveny rely on the estimates, including conflict effects, from Reuveny (2001) for their supply/demand coefficients. The five sectors aggregate SITC one-digit sectors and, as in Dorussen, are not based on strategic importance.[7]

Apart from the aggregation of trade, the analyses also differ in the exact specification of trade used in the various models. Most significantly, Dorussen and Goenner control for total trade, and analyse sector- or good-specific trade relative to total trade. Both find increased total trade to have a pacifying effect. They differ in whether a shift in trade port-folio, that is, the relative shares of trade of particular commodities, can offset this effect. Dorussen finds that it cannot, while Goenner finds that increased share of trade in energy, non-ferrous metals and electronics increases the probability of conflict *holding total trade constant*. Dorussen only considers trade shares, Goenner also includes trade asymmetries and Li and Reuveny analyse imports and exports separately. Li and Reuveny do not include total trade and consider increases of the volume of trade in particular sectors.

The models further differ in their approach to possible simultaneity bias. Trade is expected to suffer especially if countries find themselves embroiled in a militarized disputed. The expectation that conflict reduces trade is at least implicit in nearly all models linking trade to conflict. The risk of simultaneity bias thus exists for all trade and conflict studies,[8] but may be particularly severe for analyses of trade in strategic goods. It seems reasonable to assume that, particularly for strategic goods, "trade follows the flag." Dorussen and Li and Reuveny employ the common, albeit sub-optimal, solution to lag their independent variables. In earlier studies using events data and a limited number of dyads, Reuveny and Kang (1998) assess Granger causality to argue for simultaneous estima-tion of disaggregated trade and conflict. Goenner analyses both single-equation and simultaneous equations models. He finds that in the latter model, increased bilateral trade shares in energy, non-ferrous metals, electronics and nuclear materials increase conflict. Trade in chemicals and arms reduce conflict. These findings are similar to those found for the single-equation model. However, when trade in a strategic commodity is allowed to be endogenous, bilateral trade in general reduces conflict, while increased share of trade in non-ferrous materials significantly increases and trade in chemicals reduces the probability of conflict. Clearly, simul-taneity bias and proper specification of endogeneity remains an area for future research.

Even though Dorussen, Goenner, and Li and Reuveny all analyse militarized interstate disputes as defined by the Correlates of War project, there remain notable differences in the definitions of conflict.[9] Dorussen excludes minor conflicts and limits the analysis to disputes that involve the threat with or the actual use of force by at least one side. Goenner analyses all militarized interstate disputes, while Li and Reuveny analyse all militarized disputes and major conflicts separately. Li and Reuveny's findings are largely consistent between the two models with the exception of chemical/mineral and consumption exports with only statistically significant pacifying effect on the initiation of major conflicts. Potentially more relevant is that Dorussen and Goenner analyse undirected dyads, while Li and Reuveny analyse the initiation of conflict in directed dyads. Li and Reuveny formulate and test separate hypotheses for exports and imports on the *initiation* of conflict making the use of directed dyads essential. In practice, the difference between the directed and undirected dyads may be minor since conflict in an undirected dyad also only requires the threat (or use of force) by one side.

There remains, however, a gap between theoretical models and empirical analyses of conflict. Theoretically, conflict is generally modeled as escalation in which one side refuses to give in to demands made by another side. Even though the model of Li and Reuveny is most explicit, it still only considers the (dis)incentives to initiate conflict without reflecting on likely responses. Interestingly, Li and Reuveny find that the effects of energy imports and exports are opposite, which corresponds to earlier findings of small-N studies (Polachek 1980). Further they find that both increased imports and exports of agriculture, chemical/mineral and consumption goods make the initiation of conflict less likely, while increased exports and imports of manufactured goods make initiation of conflict more likely. The latter finding is the most surprising even though Li and Reuveny refer to conflict in the US–Japan dyad as a possible example (Marlin-Bennett et al., 1992). It is, however, important to interpret the finding of their empirical models with care. The multivariate nonlinear (logistic) models give the effect of, for example, increased actor imports from a particular target country on the actor's willingness to initiate conflict holding all other variables constant, including exports from the actor to the target. Since the baseline values for the actor and target may vary widely, the actual impact of actor imports and target exports on conflict initiation may differ considerably (even though exports equal imports).[10] Most importantly, the models tell us nothing about the target's responses to any increased probability of conflict initiation.

25.4   HETEROGENEOUS TRADE INTERESTS, TRADE NETWORKS AND CONFLICT

Dyadic models have become the dominant mode of analysis in quantitative studies of conflict, but are increasingly under scrutiny (Ward,

Siverson and Xun 2007; Kinne 2009; Maoz 2009). In our recent work, we have argued accordingly that not only direct but also indirect linkages matter for the interstate relations. Shared membership of intergovernmental organizations (Dorussen and Ward 2008) but also commercial ties (Dorussen and Ward 2010) embed states in networks of membership in intergovernmental organizations and trade links. These networks allow for direct and third-party transmission of information about interests, intentions and resolve. Indirect links also encourage third parties, either government representatives or actors with predominantly commercial interests, to mediate in latent crises. The global trade network, in particular, has become more dense over time, and the general "embeddedness" of state dyads has thus become crucial (Gartzke 2007; Dorussen and Ward 2010), suggesting that the period since World War II has seen progressive realization of the classical-liberal ideal of a security community of trading states.

The flow of goods between countries creates a network of ties and communication links. If two countries are more embedded in this network, their relations should be more peaceful, because there is greater possibility for direct and indirect communication between them. Consider a pair (or dyad) of countries A and B. The volume of direct trade between these two countries creates one set of connections, but trade also creates indirect linkages; for instance, if both countries trade with a third country C, trade connects country A also indirectly to B. This is already implicit in the notion of opportunity costs, since it assumes that countries can partly substitute lost trade by diverting to third countries. Since the trade channels information flows alongside the goods and services, the indirect linkages arguably matter. Moreover, from a network perspective, there is no obvious reason to stop at channels with only one intermediary: countries A and D can be connected, because of A's trade with B, B's trade with C and eventually C's trade with D. After all, goods and services have always passed through chains of intermediaries in different countries, from the Silk Road linking China to medieval Europe through electronic goods designed in the USA, manufactured in China and packaged and distributed in Europe. If goods flow along such chains, so does information.

"Maximum flow" (*maxflow*) is a relevant network measure of total connectedness between the members of a dyad, taking into account both direct and indirect connections and captures the "embeddedness" of a pair of countries via the global trade network.[11] There are two plausible arguments which suggest that the effect of *maxflow*, seen as the possible flow of communication, could differ across sectors. First of all, a similar amount of trade in value terms could involve more people (either as producers, traders or consumers). Trade in goods that are labor intensive should then be more pacifying than trade in capital-intensive goods. Unfortunately, we lack good indicators for the relative labor/capital intensiveness of goods produced in the various industry sectors. Alternatively, the connections should be more valuable if they are more enduring. If so, the various links in the chain provide a more reliable source of information and the information is more credible. The second argument is directly related to the notion of opportunity costs, since trade links will be more stable if the opportunity costs are higher. So, for instance, the opportunity costs in terms of loss of information should be lower for disruption in agricultural trade, because the easy availability of substitute sources should mean that the agricultural trade network is less stable. On the other hand, the difficulty of substituting for certain manufactured goods should mean that the trade networks are more stable and, therefore, more valuable in informational terms. Moreover, seen in this way, the opportunity costs of trade are not limited to trade partners and possible third parties, but extend to more indirect trade links as well. Accordingly, we distinguish between primary, agricultural and manufactured goods, and use maxflow based on trade in each type of commodity to analyse the embeddedness of countries in the various trade networks.

The possible heterogeneous effects of disaggregated trade linkages are analysed using the standard model of the Kantian peace (Russett and Oneal 2001; Dorussen 2006; Gartzke 2007; Dorussen and Ward 2008, 2010). The temporal domain of the analysis is limited to the period from 1970 to 1997 because of availability of sector-specific trade data. The dependent variable is militarized interstate disputes (*mid*) from the Correlates of War project in which the use of force is threatened or actually implemented. The dependent variable is actually *mid_y1*, which takes on the value of *mid* in the following year to the one in question. This helps with the problem of establishing causality as the analysis is equivalent to lagging all the variables one year. Since the dependent variable is binary, logistic regression is used. The models include both "realist" and "liberal" controls. "Realist" constraints include contiguity and distance, power ratios and alliance structures. The "liberal" controls are democracy and co-membership of international organizations. We follow the suggestion of Carter and Signorino (2007) to use peace-years variables in linear, squared and cubed functional form to correct for temporal dependence. The implementation of these variables was done using EUGene (Bennett and Stam 2000a).

The main source for the data on disaggregated trade is the United Nations Statistical Office as recoded by Feenstra (2000). Dorussen (2006, p. 96–97) contains further detail on the classification and the correspondence with BEA industry codes. Trade is classified on the basis of four industry sectors: non-manufacturing, food and kindred products, and manufacturing. Manufacturing is further separated between primary chemical and metal products (highly capital intensive) and consumer goods (relatively labor intensive). The trade data are indexed and given in constant value dollar.

To analyse the effects of trade on conflict, the models include total bilateral trade and GDP_{low} and GDP_{high}, the size of the smaller and of the larger economy, respectively. Since dependency is considered to reduce the likelihood of conflict, the expectations in the statistical models are a negative coefficient for dyadic trade and positive coefficients for GDP_{low} and GDP_{high}. The disaggregated trade data contain a large number of missing observations, and we assume that as long as there is any trade recorded between two countries, missing data are in effect zero or near-zero trade levels. Trade volume (in constant value dollars) is used to calculate *maxflow* for aggregate as well as disaggregate trade flows using UCINET, a standard network package (Borgatti, Everett and Freeman 2002). The models include the proportion of *maxflow* attributable to a particular industry sector relative to the *maxflow* achieved by total dyadic trade in a given year. The models exclude at least one industry sector since *maxflow* on total trade is the sum of the proportions of trade-*maxflow* in all sectors.

In all three models in Table 25.1, the coefficients for *maxflow* are negative and significant, indicating that conflict is less likely if countries are more "embedded" in the global trade network. In models 2 and 3, the composition of trade is included in the basic model. In model 2, trade is disaggregated into manufacturing, non-manufacturing, and food and kindred products, where the latter is the (excluded) baseline category. In model 3, manufacturing is further disaggregated into building and chemical products (capital intensive/bulk products) and consumer goods. It is noteworthy that the composition of trade flows is generally not significant. Compared to food and kindred products, only increasing the proportion of total *maxflow* based on consumer goods significantly reduces the probability of conflict. These findings largely agree with earlier findings on disaggregating trade based on bilateral trade flows, but suggest that heterogeneity effects of disaggregated trade become less significant when indirect effects are also considered. Gasiorowski and Polachek (1982), and Polachek and McDonald (1992) also find manufacturing to be more pacifying. Dorussen (2006), in particular, emphasizes the pacifying effect of trade in consumer goods. The findings contrast, however, with Reuveny (2003) and Li and Reuveny (n.d.) who find that trade in agricultural products is more pacifying.[12]

Table 25.1   Information flows, disaggregating trade and militarized interstate disputes, 1970–97

Mid_yl	(1)	(2)	(3)
Dyadic trade (ln)	0.05	0.05	0.06
	(0.05)	(0.05)	(0.05)
GDP (ln/low)	0.08	0.09	0.09
	(0.06)	(0.06)	(0.06)
GDP (ln/high)	0.13	0.14	0.15
	(0.07)+	(0.07)*	(0.07)*
Maxflow(all trade)	−0.06	−0.06	−0.05
	(0.02)**	(0.02)**	(0.02)**
Maxflow(non-manufact.) / maxflow(all)		−0.01	−0.16
		(0.76)	(0.72)
Maxflow(manufacturing) / maxflow(all)		−1.27	
		(0.79)	
Maxflow(build._chem.) / maxflow(all)			−0.88
			(1.09)
Maxflow(consumer) / maxflow(all)			−1.76
			(0.82)*
Democracy (low)	−0.04	−0.04	−0.04
	(0.02)**	(0.02)*	(0.02)*
Democracy (high)	0.02	0.03	0.02
	(0.01)*	(0.01)*	(0.01)*
IGO memberships	0.02	0.02	0.02
	(0.01)*	(0.01)*	(0.01)*
Contiguity	2.47	2.53	2.52
	(0.24)**	(0.24)**	(0.24)**
Distance (ln)	−0.36	−0.37	−0.38
	(0.09)**	(0.09)**	(0.09)**
Minor powers	−1.16	−1.18	−1.17
	(0.20)**	(0.20)**	(0.20)**
Allies	0.09	0.05	0.03
	(0.18)	(0.18)	(0.18)
Peace years	−0.17	−0.16	−0.16
	(0.03)**	(0.03)**	(0.03)**
(Peace years)^2	0.00	0.00	0.00
	(0.00)**	(0.00)**	(0.00)**
(Peace years)^3	−0.00	−0.00	−0.00
	(0.00)	(0.00)	(0.00)
Constant	−3.98	−3.42	−3.25
	(0.90)**	(1.04)**	(1.01)**

Table 25.1 (continued)

Mid_y1	(1)	(2)	(3)
Wald χ^2	1956.42**	1856.27**	1880.87**

Notes: Logistic Regression; Robust standard errors in parentheses; + sig. at 10%; * sig. at 5%; ** sig. at 1%; Pseudo $R^2 > .26$; N = 148515 (1) and 148497 (2/3).

25.5 CONCLUSIONS

The main finding of the literature on disaggregated trade on conflict is that the composition of trade matters. However, it remains disputed whether trade in particular goods can actually increase the likelihood of conflict. As we argued above, the disagreement partly stems from differences in model specification; in particular, the specific level of disaggregation of trade, the treatment of possible simultaneity bias, the definition of conflict, the baseline used to assess the effect of any changes in trade and also whether indirect links are taken into account. To some extent, the different research designs reflect more serious underlying issues. First of all, we lack a good theoretical foundation for the idea that particular types of trade are more likely to lead to conflict. The idea that certain types of trade are more easily appropriable by force (Dorussen 2006; Goenner 2010) is interesting but theoretically underdeveloped. The theoretical model of Li and Reuveny (n.d.) interestingly explores the notion that conflict has different effects on the demand and supply of imports and exports, and hence indirectly on the prices at which various types of goods will be traded. Their model, however, shares with earlier work of Polachek (1980) a rather basic model in which conflict results from choices about levels of hostility made largely independently by states.

A further issue is that in our opinion the research agenda has become overly dominated by the dyadic research design. The obvious advantage is that the findings from the various models are at least somewhat comparable. The problem is, however, that dyadic models may not always be appropriate to assess the effect of trade on conflict. The pattern of bilateral trade can often not be understood independently from latent conflict with third parties; for example, the USSR was the essential to understand the trade of Nazi Germany with Eastern Europe before World War II, as well as the trade between the USA and Western Europe during the Cold War. As we have shown above it is possible to include indirect trade linkage into dyadic models, but this only partly addresses more fundamental issues.

Our research still suggests that in a dense global trade network the general embeddedness of states matters most, and that, consequently, it matters less what precisely gets traded between any two countries.

NOTES

1. Weede in the current volume addresses the general relationship between trade and conflict. Further review articles are Schneider, Barbieri and Gleditsch (2003); Mansfield and Pollins (2003); and Polachek and Seiglie (2006). Martin, Mayer and Thoenig (2008) is a particularly important recent article.
2. Critics are commonly labelled as either Realists or (Neo-)Marxists (for example, by Barbieri 2002; Goenner 2010) but it is neither obvious that they would label themselves as such nor that their arguments about trade and conflict are always closely linked to these theoretical approaches.
3. Interestingly, the CoCom lists were not publicly available and traders who requested export permissions had to rely on executive discretion.
4. The various approaches suggested by Goenner (2010) and Li and Reuveny (n.d.) to deal with this issue are discussed below.
5. Hillmann (1940) is an earlier analysis of how Nazi German trade policies encouraged trade blocks. Both Hillman and Leitz (2004) note the inability and unwillingness of German industry to meet the demand for their products and that the success of the German policy thus partly depended on the lack of interest of the Allied states to exploit these opportunities.
6. In the remainder, we will simply refer to these studies as Dorussen, Goenner and Li and Reuveny.
7. Goenner further observes that in Dorussen "other manufacturing" contains toys but also nuclear reactors, questioning their general classification as low-tech consumer goods. The finding of Li and Reuveny that "miscellaneous-consumption" exports reduce conflict becomes less intuitive if one realizes that the category includes armoured vehicles, arms and ammunition (SITC 9510).
8. There is, however, disagreement about the seriousness of the problem. Keshk, Pollins and Reuveny (2004) and Kim and Rousseau (2005) argue that, with proper controls for simultaneity, trade is no longer pacifying; a finding which is contested by Hegre, Oneal and Russett (2010). Using instruments, Martin, Mayer and Thoenig (2008) find that bilateral trade is pacifying while trade openness increases the probability of conflict; the latter finding is at odds with nearly every other study on the topic. Finally, Pollins (1989) argues that "trade follows the flag," while Barbieri and Levy (1999) find that, at least historically, conflict did not always affect commerce even for goods of military significance – see also Anderton and Carter (2001, 2003).
9. Earlier quantitative analyses of heterogeneous effects of trade on conflict relied on COPDAB and WEIS events data (Polachek 1980; Gasiorowski and Polachek 1982; Polachek and McDonald 1992; Reuveny and Kang 1998). Reuveny (2003) compares the pros and cons of using militarized interstate disputes rather than event data.
10. Bennett and Stam (2000b) discuss the implications of using directed versus undirected dyads in greater detail.
11. Ford and Fulkerson (1956) and Dorussen and Ward (2008, 2010) provide exact definitions of *maxflow* as well as illustrative examples. The maximum flow network measure is also conceptually and empirically distinct from openness.
12. There is nothing particularly surprising in the coefficients for the control variables in the models presented so far. Capability matters, in that minor powers and countries supporting a smaller economy are less likely to engage in conflict (Hegre 2005). Opportunity is also important as shown by the highly significant impact of contiguity

and distance. The alliance variable, however, is insignificant. The model further confirms the relevance of the major "liberal" variable, namely democracy. If the least democratic country in the dyad becomes more democratic, conflict becomes less likely. Contrary to liberal expectations, IGO co-membership appears to lead to more (instead of the expected less) conflict (cf., Boehmer, Gartzke and Nordstrom 2004; Dorussen and Ward 2008).

REFERENCES

Anderton, C.H. and J.R. Carter (2001), "The impact of war on trade: an interrupted time-series study", *Journal of Peace Research*, **38** (4), 445–57.

Anderton, C.H. and J.R. Carter (2003), "Does War Disrupt Trade?", in G. Schneider, K. Barbier and N-P. Gleditsch (eds), *Globalization and Armed Conflict*, Lanham, MD: Rowman and Littlefield, pp. 299–310.

Barbieri, K. (2002), *The Liberal Illusion: Does Trade Promote Peace*, Ann Arbor, MI: University of Michigan Press.

Barbieri, K. and J.S. Levy (1999), "Sleeping with the enemy: the impact of war on trade", *Journal of Peace Research*, **36** (4), 463–79.

Beck, N., J.N. Katz and R. Tucker (1998), "Taking time seriously: time-series-cross-section analysis with a binary dependent variable", *American Journal of Political Science*, **42** (4), 1260–88.

Bennett, D.S. and A.C. Stam (2000a), "EUGene: a conceptual manual", *International Interactions*, **26**, 179–204. (Eugene data: http://eugenesoftware.org, accessed 16 July 2008).

Bennett, D.S. and A.C. Stam (2000b), "Research design and estimator choices in the analysis of interstate dyads: when decisions matter", *Journal of Conflict Resolution*, **44** (5), 653–85.

Boehmer, C., E. Gartzke and T. Nordstrom (2004), "Do intergovernmental organizations promote peace", *World Politics*, **57** (October 2004): 1–38.

Borgatti, S.P., M.G. Everett and L.C. Freeman, 2002. "Ucinet for Windows 6: software for social network analysis", Harvard, MA: Analytic Technologies.

Borrus, M. and J. Zysman (1992), "Industrial competitiveness and American national security", in W. Sandholtz, M. Borrus, J. Zysman, K. Conca, J. Stowksy, S. Vogel and S. Weber (eds), *The Highests Stakes: The Economic Foundations of the Next Security System*, New York, NY: Oxford University Press, pp. 7–52.

Broda, C. and D.E. Weinstein (2006), "Globalization and the gains from variety", *Quarterly Journal of Economics*, **121** (2), 541–85.

Carter, D.B. and C.S. Signorino (2007), "Back to the future: modelling time dependence in binary data", paper presented at the 24th Annual Society for Political Methodology Summary Conference.

Choucri, N. and R.C. North (1975), *Nations in Conflict: National Growth and International Violence*, San Francisco, CA: W.H. Freeman.

Dorussen, H. (2006), "Heterogeneous trade interests and conflict: what you trade matters", *Journal of Conflict Resolution*, **50** (1), 87–107.

Dorussen, H. and H. Ward (2008), "International organizations and the Kantian peace. A network perspective", *Journal of Conflict Resolution*, **52** (2), 189–212.

Dorussen, H. and H. Ward (2010), "Trade networks and the Kantian peace", *Journal of Peace Research*, **47** (1), 29–42.

Feenstra, R.C. (2000), "World trade flows, 1980–1997", University of California, Davis.

Ford, L.R. and D.R. Fulkerson (1956), "Maximal flow through a network", *Canadian Journal of Mathematics*, **9**, 210–18.

Førland, T.E. (1991), "'Economic warfare' and 'strategic goods': a conceptual framework for analysing COCOM", *Journal of Peace Research*, **28** (2), 191–204.

Gartzke, E. (2007), "The capitalist peace", *American Journal of Political Science*, **51** (1), 166–91.

Gasiorowski, M. and S.W. Polachek (1982), "East-West trade and linkages in the era of détente", *Journal of Conflict Resolution*, **26** (4), 709–29.

Gilpin, R. (1977), "Economic interdependence and national security in historical perspective", in K. Knorr and F.N. Trager (eds), *Economic Issues and National Security*, Lawrence, KS: Regents Press of Kansas: pp.19–66.

Goenner, C.F. (2010), "From toys to warships: interdependence and the effects of disaggregated trade on militarized disputes", *Journal of Peace Research*, **47** (5), 547–59.

Hegre, H. (2005), "Identifying how trade matters in empirical studies of interstate conflict", *Conflict Management and Peace Science*, **22** (3), 217–24.

Hegre, H., J.R. Oneal and B. Russett (2010), "Trade does promote peace: new simultaneous estimates of the reciprocal effects of trade and conflict", *Journal of Peace Research*, **47** (6), forthcoming.

Hillmann, H.C. (1940), "Analysis of Germany's foreign trade and the war", *Economica*, **7** (25), 66–88.

Hirschman, A.O. ([1945] 1980), *National Power and the Structure of Foreign Trade*, Berkeley, CA: University of California Press.

Italianer, A. (1986), *Theory and Practice of International Trade Linkage Models*, Dordrecht, The Netherlands: Martinus Nijhoff.

Keshk, O.M.G., B. Pollins and R. Reuveny (2004), "Trade still follows the flag: the primacy of politics in a simultaneous model of interdependence and armed conflict", *Journal of Politics*, **66** (4), 1155–79.

Kim, H.M. and D.L. Rousseau (2005), "The classical liberals were half right (or half wrong): new tests of the 'liberal peace,' 1960–88", *Journal of Peace Research*, **42** (5), 523–43.

Kinne, B. (2009), "Beyond the dyad: how networks of economic interdependence and political integration reduce interstate conflict", Ph.D. Dissertation, Yale University, New Haven, CT.

Leitz, C. (2004), *Nazi Foreign Policy, 1933–1941: The Road to Global War*, Oxford, UK: Routledge.

Li, Q. and R. Reuveny (n.d.), "Trading for peace? Disaggregated bilateral trade and interstate military conflict initiation", *Journal of Peace Research*, forthcoming.

Liberman, P. (1996), *Does Conquest Pay? The Exploitation of Occupied Industrial Societies*, Princeton, NJ: Princeton University Press.

Mansfield, E.D. and B.M. Pollins (2003), "Interdependence and conflict: an introduction", in E.D. Mansfield and B.M. Pollins (eds), *Economic Interdependence and International Conflict: New Perspectives on an Enduring Debate*, Ann Arbor, MI: University of Michigan Press, pp. 1–30.

Maoz, Z. (2009), "The effects of strategic and economic interdepedence on international conflict across levels of analysis", *American Journal of Political Science*, **53** (1), 223–40.

Marlin-Bennett, R., A. Rosenblatt and J. Wang (1992), "The visible hand: the United States, Japan, and the management of trade disputes", *International Interactions*, **17** (3), 191–213.

Martin, P., T. Mayer and M. Thoenig (2008) "Make trade not war?", *Review of Economic Studies*, **75** (3), 865–900.

Mastanduno, M. (1992), *Economic Containment: CoCom and the Politics of East–West Trade*. Ithaca, NY: Cornell University Press.

McDonald P.J. (2004), "Peace through trade or free trade", *Journal of Conflict Resolution*, **48** (4), 547–72.

McDonald, P.J. (2009), *The Invisible Hand of Peace. Capitalism, The War Machine, and International Relations Theory*, New York, NY: Cambridge University Press.

Park, T., F. Abolfathi and M. Ward (1976), "Resource nationalism in foreign policy behavior of oil exporting countries", *International Interactions*, **2**, 247–63.

Polachek, S.W. (1980), "Conflict and trade", *Journal of Conflict Resolution*, **24** (1), 57–78.

Polachek, S.W. (1992), "Conflict and trade: an economics approach to political international interactions", in W. Isard and C. Anderton (eds), *Economics of Arms Reduction and the Peace Process*, Amsterdam: Elsevier Science, pp. 89–120.

Polachek, S.W. (2002), "Trade-based interactions: an interdisciplinary perspective", *Conflict Management and Peace Science*, **19** (1), 1–21.

Polachek, S.W. and J.A. McDonald (1992), "Strategic trade and the incentive for cooperation", in M. Chatterji and L.R. Forcey (eds), *Disarmament, Economic Conversion, and Management of Peace*, Westport, CT: Praeger, pp. 273–84.

Polachek, S.W. and C. Seiglie (2006), "Trade peace and democracy: an analysis of dyadic dispute", IZA Discussion Paper Series, No. 2170.

Pollins, B.M. (1989), "Does trade still follow the flag?", *American Political Science Review*, **83** (2), 465–80.

Reuveny, R. (2001), "Disaggregated bilateral trade and conflict: exploring propositions in a simultaneous framework", *International Politics*, **38** (3), 401–28.

Reuveny, R. (2003), "Measuring conflict and cooperation: an assessment", in E.D. Mansfield and B.M. Pollins (eds), *Economic Interdependence and International Conflict. New Perspectives on an Enduring Debate*, Ann Arbor, MI: Michigan University Press, pp. 254–72.

Reuveny, R. and H. Kang (1998), "Bilateral trade and political conflict/cooperation: do goods matter?", *Journal of Peace Research*, **35** (5), 581–602.

Reuveny, R. and Q. Li (2003), "The joint democracy-dyadic conflict nexus: a simultaneous equations model", *International Studies Quarterly*, **47**, 325–46.

Ripsman, N. and J.-M. Blanchard (1996/7), "Commercial liberalism under fire: evidence from 1914 and 1936", *Security Studies*, **6** (2), 4–50.

Russett, B.M. and J.R. Oneal (2001), *Triangulating Peace. Democracy, Interdependence, and International Organization*, New York, NY: Norton.

Schelling, T.C. (1958), *International Economics*, Boston, MA: Ally & Bacon.

Schneider, G., K. Barbieri and N.P. Geditsch (2003), "Does globalization contribute to peace? a critical survey of the literature", in G. Schneider, K. Barbieri and N.P. Gleditsch (eds), *Globalization and Armed Conflict*, Lanham, MD: Rowman and Littlefield, pp. 3–30.

Schumpeter, J.A. (1951), *Imperialism and Social Classes*, New York, NY: Augustus M. Kelley.

Sen, G. (1984), *The Military Origins of Industrialisation and International Trade Rivalry*, London, UK: Pinter.

De Soysa, I. and T.G. Lie (2008), "If oil flows, blood flows. Petroleum and militarized interstate disputes and strategic rivalries, 1946–1990", Peace Research Institute Oslo, CSCW working paper.

Tyson, L. D'A. (1992), *Who's Bashing Whom? Trade Conflict in High-technology Industries*, Washington DC: Institute for International Economics.

Ward, M.D., R.M. Siverson and C. Xun (2007), "Disputes, democracies, and dependencies: a reexamination of the Kantian peace", *American Journal of Political Science*, **51** (3), 583–601.

26 Sanctions as alternatives to war
David Cortright and George A. Lopez

26.1 INTRODUCTION

Manipulating trade relations and offering or withholding economic assistance, private investment and favorable trade conditions have been tools by which regimes have long been able to influence each other's policies. Authors such as Albert Hirschman, David Baldwin and Richard Rosecrance have described the important role that such economic incentives and sanctions have played in international affairs. (Hirschman 1980; Baldwin 1985; Rosecrance 1987).

In recent decades, the use of economic sanctions and incentives has become quite frequent. Since World War II, the United States has employed sanctions and other tools of economic influence frequently in the conduct of foreign affairs. In the post-Cold War era the UN Security Council has become increasingly active in imposing multilateral sanctions. In the 1990s, the European Union and the British Commonwealth utilized economic sanctions and incentives as primary means of influencing other states. In recent years, the Organization of American States and the African Union have also utilized multilateral sanctions against their own members.

Sanctions are imposed for a wide range of foreign policy purposes that in earlier days would have drawn states into war. In recent decades, nations have adopted sanctions to promote democracy and human rights, to enforce international law and resolutions of the UN Security Council, to prevent military aggression and armed conflict, to encourage military demobilization and post-conflict reconstruction and to counter terrorism and prevent the proliferation of nuclear weapons. They are means of applying pressure against wrongdoers without incurring the costs and risks of war. They offer a middle course "between words and wars" (Wallensteen and Staibano, eds. 2005). When combined with economic incentives, they form the very essence of diplomacy.

In this chapter, we examine the role of economic sanctions and incentives as tools of international political economy that provide decision-makers with viable alternatives to war or military intervention. In some circumstances sanctions have been used to curtail or end war, and have contributed to postwar peacebuilding (Cortright and Lopez 2009). We provide an overview of the different types of sanctions and evaluate their overall effectiveness. We focus on multilateral sanctions imposed by the UN Security Council and examine the significant historical shift that has occurred since the 1990s toward the use of selective and targeted measures. We discuss two of the most important previous episodes of UN sanctions – Iraq and Libya – and review the most important current cases – counterterrorism sanctions against Al Qaeda and the Taliban, and sanctions against weapons proliferation in Iran and North Korea. We conclude with observations on the challenges that now complicate the imposition and implementation of sanctions and incentives.

26.2   THE SANCTIONS ERA

Sanctions can be imposed by a single state, a regional organization, or the United Nations. In an increasingly globalized world unilateral sanctions generally are less effective than multilateral measures, since a sanctioned regime can find substitute trade options, as Cuba has done for decades in surviving the US trade embargo. Multilateral measures imposed through the United Nations are more likely to be effective, provided there is broad international compliance and enforcement. The legal authority for UN sanctions is contained in Chapter VII of the UN Charter, which provides in Article 41 that the Security Council may call upon states to impose nonmilitary measures such as interruptions of economic and diplomatic relations to protect international peace and security (United Nations 1945, Article 41). This authority was not effectively used by the Council until 1990, as Cold War political differences prevented agreement among the permanent five members of the Council on international peace and security issues. In its first 45 years of operation the Council was able to impose only limited sanctions measures in just two cases, Southern Rhodesia in 1966 and South Africa in 1977 (United Nations Security Council, S/RES/232, 16 December 1966; United Nations Security Council, S/RES/418, 4 November 1977). The end of the Cold War removed the political roadblocks preventing collective action. The dynamics of economic globalization have meant that nations gain little benefit from trying to cheat on sanctions enforcement. Instead, nongovernmental actors and criminal networks have tended to be the major sanctions busters (Andreas 2005, pp. 35–60).

The sanctions era of multilateral measures commenced with the UN sanctions against Iraq in 1990 when the Council used its Chapter VII authority with increasing frequency. Over the next two decades the Security Council imposed mandatory measures against specific regimes and nonstate actors in 18 separate episodes (Cortright and Lopez, eds. 1995; Cortright and Lopez 2000; Cortright, Lopez and Gerber-Stellingwerf 2007, pp. 349–69). The list of the sanctions imposed by the Security Council from 1990 to 2009 reveals a substantial set of cases where sanctions are not imposed against a government but rather against nonstate actors or militia forces operating within a particular country or nearby. Examples of this trend include the cases of UN sanctions against actors in Somalia, Angola, Rwanda, Sierra Leone, Democratic Republic of the Congo Sudan, and Côte d'Ivoire. In the cases of Afghanistan and Iraq, sanctions initially were imposed against governments, but after the US–led overthrow of these governments Security Council measures were redirected against individuals and entities associated with the former regime and/or insurgent/terrorist groups. Sanctions imposed in Iraq, Somalia, Liberia and Afghanistan have changed significantly over the years, in line with changing political conditions within the targeted regime, but because the sanctions have been continuous they can be considered a single episode. In two cases, Sudan and the former Yugoslavia, initial Security Council sanctions were discontinued and new measures were imposed subsequently, so we view these as separate episodes.

Evaluating the effectiveness of UN sanctions is an uncertain endeavor subject to a wide range of interpretations which vary among scholars and policymakers. The most authoritative empirical study is that of Hufbauer et al., which appeared in a third edition in 2007 (Hufbauer et al. [1983] 2007). The authors examine 204 cases covering the period 1914 to the present. Their dataset includes a large number of cases of unilateral sanctions, mostly imposed by the United States. They define success according to the degree of intended policy change, and the extent to which sanctions contributed to that change. They measure success according to several distinct factors, including military impairment and the disruption of military adventures. Their conclusion is that sanctions contributed to policy change in 70 of the cases studied, for an overall success rate of 34 percent (Hufbauer et al. [1983] 2007, p. 159). Hufbauer et al. and other scholars have found that sanctions are most effective when economic costs are high for the target but low for the sender, when the gross domestic product of the sender is much larger than that of the target and when the target and the sender have extensive trade relations. Drezner has described what he terms the paradox of sanctions. Economic sanctions are most likely to be effective when the sender and the target are interdependent economically and have cooperative political relations, yet coercive measures are rarely necessary under such conditions and, in fact, are often imposed when political relations and interdependence are low (Drezner 1999).

In our own comparative assessment of the effectiveness of sanctions

Table 26.1 United Nations Security Council sanctions episodes, 1990–2009

Sanctioned Country	Authorizing Resolutions	Type of Sanction	Security Council's Stated Reasons for Authorizing/Extending Sanctions	Impact of Sanctions
Iraq	SC Res. 661 of 6 Aug. 1990 SC Res. 1483 of 22 May 2003	Comprehensive sanctions.* Sanctions lifted, but arms embargo continued. Assets freeze imposed on former regime members.	Originally authorized to achieve immediate and unconditional withdrawal of occupying troops from Kuwait and restore legitimate government of Kuwait. Following the liberation of Kuwait, sanctions were upheld until Iraq would unconditionally accept obligation to disarm, and accept long-term monitoring of its weapons program; recognize newly demarcated border with Kuwait (SC Res. 687 of 3 April 1991).	Significant impact. Aided the success of the UN disarmament mission; helped convince the regime to accept redrawn border with Kuwait; contributed to military containment of the Baghdad government. Associated with severe humanitarian problems.

Table 26.1 (continued)

Sanctioned Country	Authorizing Resolutions	Type of Sanction	Security Council's Stated Reasons for Authorizing/Extending Sanctions	Impact of Sanctions
Yugoslavia				
	SC Res. 713 of 25 Sep. 1991	Arms embargo on all of Yugoslavia.	To end the fighting in Yugoslavia; secure compliance with cease-fire agreements; achieve a peaceful solution of the conflicts.	Significant impact, though the arms embargo was widely ignored. May have contributed to the pressure on the Belgrade government to accept the Dayton Accords.
	SC Res. 757 of 30 May 1992	Comprehensive sanctions on Federal Republic of Yugoslavia.		
	SC Res. 1021 of 22 Nov. 1995	Arms embargo lifted.		
	SC Res. 1022 of 22 Nov. 1995	Sanctions suspended indefinitely, though suspension did not apply to Bosnian Serbs.		
	SC Res. 1074 of 1 Oct. 1996	Sanctions on Bosnian Serbs lifted.		
Somalia				
	SC Res. 733 of 23 Jan. 1992	Arms embargo.	To end the conflict in Somalia and to provide conditions for increased humanitarian assistance.	No impact. Poorly enforced.
	SC Res. 1725 of 6 Dec. 2006	Arms embargo partly suspended—does not apply to protection and training mission in Somalia.		

Libya	SC Res. 748 of 31 Mar. 1992	Aviation, arms embargo, travel, diplomatic sanctions.	To commit the Libyan government to cease all forms of terrorist action and all assistance to terrorist groups. Requested that the government promptly, by concrete action, demonstrates its renunciation of terrorism, and fulfils demands made in SC Res. 731 of 21 Jan. 1991, in particular extraditing the two suspects of the Lockerbie bombing to the UK.	Significant impact. Helped to convince regime to extradite terrorist suspects and to reduce support for international terrorism.
	SC Res. 883 of 11 Nov. 1993	Assets freeze, ban on provision of petroleum equipment to Libya.		
	SC Res. 1506 of 12 Sep. 2003	Sanctions lifted.		
Liberia	SC Res. 788 of 19 Nov. 1992	Arms embargo.	To end the fighting in Liberia; secure compliance with the ceasefire agreement and achieve implementation of the Yamoussoukro IV Accords.	Some impact. Helped to weaken and isolate Charles Taylor regime.
	SC Res. 1343 of 7 Mar. 2001	Arms embargo under SC Res. 788 lifted. Imposed new arms embargo, assets freeze, travel/aviation ban, diamond embargo, called for establishment of Certificate of Origin scheme for diamonds.	To end financial and military support for RUF rebels in Sierra Leone by the Liberian government, expel Revolutionary United Front (RUF) rebels from Liberian territory, cease import of non-certified Sierra Leonean diamonds; and cease support by the government for other armed rebel groups in the region.	

539

Table 26.1 (continued)

Sanctioned Country	Authorizing Resolutions	Type of Sanction	Security Council's Stated Reasons for Authorizing/Extending Sanctions	Impact of Sanctions
	SC Res. 1478 of 6 May 2003	Timber embargo.	To ensure that the ceasefire in Liberia is being fully respected and maintained, disarmament, demobilization, reintegration, repatriation and restructuring of the security sector have been completed, the provisions of the Comprehensive Peace Agreement are being fully implemented and significant progress has been made in establishing and maintaining stability in Liberia and the sub-region.	
	SC Res. 1521 of 22 Dec. 2003	Terminated SC Res. 1343 and 1478 sanctions. Imposed arms embargo, travel ban, ban on diamond and timber exports from Liberia, called for establishment of Certificate of Origin scheme for diamonds.		
	SC Res. 1532 of 12 Mar. 2004	Assets freeze on Charles Taylor and other designated individuals.		
	SC Res. 1689 of 20 June 2006	Timber embargo suspended.		

Country	Resolutions	Sanctions	Objective	Impact
Haiti	SC Res. 841 of 16 June 1993 SC Res. 917 of 6 May 1994 SC Res. 944 of 29 Sep. 1994	Fuel and arms embargo, funds freeze. Comprehensive sanctions.* Sanctions terminated upon Aristide's return to power.	To bring about the restoration of the legitimate government of Haiti and the return of the elected President Aristide.	Considerable impact. Effective in convincing military junta to negotiate the return of civilian power, but the resulting Governors Island accord was not enforced and gave way to military intervention.
Angola (Unita Rebel Movement)	SC Res. 864 of 15 Sep. 1993 SC Res. 1127 of 28 Aug. 1997 SC Res. 1173 of 12 June 1998 SC Res. 1448 of 9 Dec. 2002	Arms embargo, petroleum embargo. Travel, aviation, diplomatic sanctions. Assets freeze, financial, diamond imports not certified by Angolan government, travel. Lifted all sanctions.	To establish a cease-fire; full implementation by UNITA of the Acordos de Paz and provisions of the relevant Security Council resolutions.	Considerable impact. Initial limited sanctions replaced by more comprehensive and better-enforced measures, which contributed to the isolation and weakening of UNITA.

541

Table 26.1 (continued)

Sanctioned Country	Authorizing Resolutions	Type of Sanction	Security Council's Stated Reasons for Authorizing/Extending Sanctions	Impact of Sanctions
Rwanda				
	SC Res. 918 of 17 May 1994	Arms embargo.	To end violence and violations of human rights and international humanitarian law.	No impact.
	SC Res. 1011 of 16 Aug. 1995	Arms embargo terminated in relation to Rwandan government.	Arms embargo against non-governmental forces in Rwanda was maintained, to end the uncontrolled circulation of arms, including to civilians and refugees, which the Security Council considered the major cause of destabilization in the Great Lakes subregion.	
Sudan				
	SC Res. 1054 of 26 Apr. 1996 SC Res. 1070 of 16 Aug. 1996	Diplomatic, travel restrictions. Travel, aviation (never went into effect), terminated in September 2001.	To bring about the extradition from Sudan of terrorist suspects for attempted assassination of Egyptian President; and to end Sudan supporting terrorist activities and sheltering terrorist elements.	Little direct impact, although Osama bin Laden was expelled from the country soon after sanctions were imposed, and the regime subsequently took steps to improve counterterrorism cooperation with the West.
	SC Res. 1372 of 28 Sep. 2001	Terminated all 1054 and 1070 measures.		

542

Sierra Leone			
SC Res. 1132 of 8 Oct. 1997	Oil embargo, arms embargo, travel restrictions.	To end violence by the military junta and its interference with the delivery of humanitarian aid, and to bring about relinquishing of power by the junta and the restoration of the democratically elected government.	Moderate impact in helping to isolate the RUF.
SC Res. 1171 of 5 June 1998 SC Res. 1306 of 5 July 2000	Arms embargo and travel ban reinforced. Diamond exports prohibited (except under Certificate of Origin scheme).	Sanctions against former junta and RUF rebels to bring about end of their resistance to the legitimate government.	
Yugoslavia			
SC Res. 1160 of 31 Mar. 1998 SC Res. 1199 of 23 Sept. 1998	Arms embargo.	To end violence by Kosovo Liberation Army and Serb police and paramilitary forces in Kosovo, bring about political settlement, and to prevent the use of funds in violation of the arms embargo.	Limited impact, but in combination with US and EU measures contributed to regime's isolation.
SC Res. 1367 of 10 Sep. 2001	Sanctions terminated.		

Table 26.1 (continued)

Sanctioned Country	Authorizing Resolutions	Type of Sanction	Security Council's Stated Reasons for Authorizing/Extending Sanctions	Impact of Sanctions
Afghanistan, Al Qaeda and the Taliban				
	SC Res. 1267 of 15 Oct. 1999	Aviation, financial.	To suppress international terrorism; required Taliban to turn over Osama bin Laden and cease training and harbouring terrorists.	Little impact.
	SC Res. 1333 of 19 Dec. 2000	Arms embargo, travel, assets freeze, diplomatic, aviation.		
	SC Res. 1390 of 16 Jan. 2002	Aviation ban lifted. Financial, travel, arms measures imposed against designated individuals.		
	SC Res. 1526 of 30 Jan. 2004	Assets, travel, arms embargo.		
Ethiopia and Eritrea				
	SC Res. 1298 of 17 May 2000 UN doc. S/ PRST/2001/14 of 15 May 2001	Arms embargo (sunset clause of one year). Arms embargo expired.	Ethiopia and Eritrea to cease military action and conclude peaceful definitive settlement of the conflict.	Little impact.

544

Democratic Republic of the Congo

SC Res. 1493 of 28 July 2003	Arms embargo.	To end the violence in North and South Kivu and Ituri, to achieve significant progress in the peace process, in particular an end to support for armed groups, an effective ceasefire and progress in the disarmament of foreign and Congolese non-government armed groups.	Little impact. Arms embargo poorly enforced.
SC Res. 1596 of 18 April 2005	Travel, assets freeze, aviation.		

Sudanese Rebel Groups (including Janjaweed)

SC Res. 1556 of 30 July 2004	Arms embargo on Janjaweed.	To bring about disarming of the Janjaweed by the Sudanese government, and bring to justice those who have carried out human rights and humanitarian law violations.	Little impact.
SC Res. 1591 of 29 Mar. 2005	Travel restrictions, assets freeze on designated. Sudanese and Janjaweed leaders.	To end offensive military flights by the Sudanese government, to bring about implementation of the ceasefire agreement, and disarmament of Janjaweed.	

Table 26.1 (continued)

Sanctioned Country	Authorizing Resolutions	Type of Sanction	Security Council's Stated Reasons for Authorizing/Extending Sanctions	Impact of Sanctions
Côte D'ivoire				
	SC Res. 1572 of 15 Nov. 2004 SC Res. 1643 of 15 Dec. 2005	Arms embargo, travel, assets freeze. Diamond embargo.	To implement all commitments under the Accra III Agreement, requiring full implementation of Linas-Marcoussis Agreement.	Moderate impact.
North Korea				
	SC Res. 1718 of 14 Oct. 2006 SC Res. 1874 of 12 June 2009	Arms embargo, embargo on luxury goods, travel. Authorized weapons inspections of vessels sailing to/from North Korea; extended financial sanctions.	North Korea to desist from further nuclear tests, abandon weapons of Mass Destruction and programs and retract its announcement of withdrawal from Non-Proliferation Treaty.	Potential impact. February 2007 denuclearization agreement.

Iran

SC Res. 1737 of 23 Dec. 2006	Trade embargo on all items, materials, equipment, goods and technology which could contribute to Iranian uranium enrichment program, assets freeze on selected Iranian individuals and entities. Urged states to monitor the travel of individuals associated with nuclear activities.	Iran to suspend all enrichment-related and reprocessing activities, including research and development, as verified by the IAEA, to allow for negotiations; and meet requirements of IAEA Board of Governors.
SC Res. 1747 of 24 March 2007	Broadened financial restrictions; arms embargo.	Iran to comply with the Non-Proliferation Treaty, suspend enrichment activities, and take steps to comply with the IAEA Board of Governors.
SC Res. 1803 of 3 March 2008	Broadened further financial restrictions; imposed travel restrictions on designated individuals; technology freeze on weapons-related materiel; authorized inspection of cargo and vessels bound to/from Iran.	Iran to suspend all enrichment related and reprocessing activities and heavy water related projects.

Notes: * In the cases of Iraq, Yugoslavia and Haiti comprehensive sanctions included a broad range of measures including trade, financial, assets, travel/aviation, arms embargos, diplomatic and commodity restrictions.

(Cortright and Lopez 2002) we consider three pragmatic, rather modest criteria. Did sanctions help to convince a targeted regime to comply at least partially with Security Council demands? Did sanctions contribute to an enduring, successful bargaining process leading to a settlement of conflict? Did sanctions help to isolate or weaken the military and political power of an abusive regime? These are subjective criteria, admittedly (Cortright and Lopez 2002, pp. 1–22). Analysts will disagree about the degree of partial compliance or political isolation and containment occurring in a particular case. The definition of what constitutes partial compliance or successful bargaining does not lend itself to precise measurement or quantification. Nonetheless, these criteria reflect the objectives policymakers articulate as the purposes of sanctions, and we believe that they provide a basis for making judgments about political effectiveness.

In examining 18 cases of Security Council sanctions between 1990 and 2009, we find clear evidence of partial success in six episodes, for an effectiveness rate of 33 percent, equivalent to the findings of Hufbauer et al. The cases of partial success included Iraq, where the pressure of sanctions helped to produce political concessions in 1993 (the acceptance of UN weapons monitoring and dismantlement) and 1994 (the acceptance of the redrawn border with Kuwait). Sanctions also prevented the regime from rebuilding its military machine and impeded the development of weapons of mass destruction. In Yugoslavia during the Bosnian War, sanctions exerted bargaining leverage on the Milošević regime that helped to produce the Dayton Peace Accords. In Libya, sanctions were a central factor in negotiations that eventually brought suspected terrorists to trial and convinced the regime to end its support for international terrorism. In Sierra Leone, sanctions combined with military pressures to isolate and weaken the Revolutionary United Front (RUF) military rebels. In Angola, sanctions that were initially ineffective became stronger over the years and combined with military pressures to weaken the National Union for the Total Independence of Angola (UNITA) rebel movement. In Liberia more vigorous sanctions imposed in 2001 helped to isolate and weaken the Charles Taylor regime and, starting in 2006, helped to facilitate the transition to a new democratically elected government. In none of these cases did sanctions achieve full and immediate compliance, but in six of the episodes – Iraq, Yugoslavia, Libya, Sierra Leone, Angola and Liberia – sanctions achieved modest to considerable success in attaining UN objectives. In two other cases, sanctions may have had some impacts; in Côte d'Ivoire as a form of pressure on armed rebels and in North Korea as means of preventing further weapons proliferation, although as of this writing it is too early to make a definitive judgment on this latter case.

Measuring effectiveness depends upon the purposes for which sanctions are imposed and how the imposers may judge success (Brzoska and Lopez 2009). O'Sullivan identified three broad categories of goals: policy change, containment and regime change. Sanctions can be effective in changing the policy preferences and political behavior of a regime, or in constraining its military potential and political ambitions, but sanctions by themselves are not capable of achieving regime change (O'Sullivan 2003). Giumelli differentiated sanctions according to whether they are intended to coerce, constrain behavior or send a political signal (Giumelli 2009). At times, sanctions are ineffective in compelling or coercing policy change because the targeted regime resists pressure and calculates that the costs of compliance are higher than the pain imposed by the sanctions (Hufbauer et al. [1983] 2007, pp. 159–60). Often sanctions are ineffective in policy terms because they are meant merely to send a political signal. They are imposed as a response to domestic political pressures to "do something" about a particular international issue. Crosscutting political agendas also may weaken political will and lead to lackluster implementation. In fact, if there is a single factor that best explains sanctions failure across a large number of cases, it is weak and inconsistent implementation (Wallensteen and Staibano 2005).

Because we can posit conditions for sanctions success, it is not surprising that we also know when UN multilaterial sanctions are destined for failure. In addition to not meeting the conditions consistent with sanctions' success noted above, failure of UN sanctions occurs when:

- sanctions are so excessively punitive that they isolate a target from continued bargaining with either the Council or member states;
- sanctions provide leaders in the target state with a classic "rally around the flag" situation whereby they can successfully portray the Council and its members as the offending party and deflect the focus from their own behavior;
- the Council or its members fail to recognize and engage/reward a target manifesting partial compliance with sanctions;
- certain member states overtake the voice and role of the Council as leader of the sanctions process;
- successful application of economic coercion on the target has the desired economic impact but produces no change in the political behavior or compliance of the target (Lopez 2006, pp. 147–58).

26.3   TARGETED SANCTIONS

Controversies over the humanitarian impact of sanctions in Iraq during the 1990s led to a reevaluation of the appropriateness of general trade embargoes and prompted the adoption of more selective and targeted measures, so called smart sanctions. Sanctions against Iraq included a prohibition on trade and investment and an embargo on all oil exports (which accounted for more that 90 percent of the country's earnings). The result was an acute social and humanitarian crisis that led to hundreds of thousands of preventable deaths. In response, the Security Council altered the design of sanctions in Iraq and in subsequent cases. General trade embargoes were abandoned in favor of targeted measures. The Security Council adopted general trade sanctions against Iraq in 1990 and the former Yugoslavia in 1992 and then again in Haiti in 1994, but in all other cases it imposed targeted or selective measures.

Sanctions are now imposed exclusively against specific decision-making elites and the entities they control, and/or applied on specific products, such as arms or commodities that are necessary for the supply and financing of armed conflict. Imposing targeted or selective sanctions is a way of reducing unintended humanitarian consequences while focusing coercive pressure on those responsible for wrongdoing and cutting off their sources of weapons and money. By exerting pressure against those responsible for objectionable policies, while avoiding harm to innocent bystanders, the Security Council has sought to enhance international peace and security without jeopardizing its parallel mission of defending human rights.

Targeted sanctions including the following:

- arms embargoes, which ban the supply of weapons, military-related technology and other forms of military assistance;
- financial sanctions, which freeze the assets (including property) of and block financial transactions with designated individuals and entities, and which also include restrictions on specific banks;
- travel sanctions, which deny visas and ban the travel of designated individuals or prohibit travel on designated airlines or to targeted regimes;
- commodity sanctions, which prohibit imports or exports of commodities such as diamonds, oil, timber and selected stones and metals;
- diplomatic sanctions, which deny participation in international events or organizations or withdraw the diplomatic privileges of designated individuals or regimes (Cortright and Lopez 2002b).

Targeted financial sanctions have the potential to be highly selective measures, affecting only the assets of the most wealthy and powerful who are responsible for developing and implementing the policies that the UN Security Council condemns. At the same time, they are meant to avoid harm to vulnerable populations. Banks and major financial institutions in the United States, Europe, Japan and other countries have established protections against money laundering and forms of financial crime and are required by law to implement financial sanctions. Most international hard currency transactions are screened through name detection software, which provides an effective means of interdicting illicit transfers and enforcing financial sanctions. Many nations also have financial intelligence units that assist law enforcement officials in detecting and thwarting financial crime and sanctions violations.

UN financial sanctions are intended to block the financial lifeblood that sustains armed violence and repression. In the early 1990s financial sanctions were imposed against government assets. Beginning with the sanctions against the military junta in Haiti in 1993, and continuing through the cases of Angola, Afghanistan, and all other sanctions cases since, financial sanctions have been applied exclusively against the assets of designated individuals and entities. To implement these measures the Council has created sanctions committees and authorized the committees to establish lists of designated individuals and entities whose assets are to be frozen. In most cases those listed are also subject to travel and visa restrictions. The Al-Qaida and Taliban Sanctions Committee has the largest list, with approximately 500 names, but designation lists also exist for the sanctions in Liberia, Côte d'Ivoire, Democratic Republic of the Congo and Sudan, and for the sanctions against insurgents and supporters of the former regime in Iraq. As of 2009, the total number of individuals and entities on UN sanctions committees lists was over 900. The procedures for designating and removing names from these lists have proven to be highly controversial, especially for the Security Council's Consolidated List of alleged supporters of Al Qaeda and the Taliban. As noted below, court challenges and political criticisms within governments and among human rights advocates have focused on the need for improved due process rights in listing and delisting.

Arms embargoes are the most frequently employed forms of sanctions. In the 18 cases of Security Council sanctions listed here, arms embargoes were imposed in all but two cases. Arms embargoes are ideal forms of targeted or selective pressure. They deny aggressors and human rights abusers the tools of war and repression, while avoiding harm to vulnerable and innocent populations. The enforcement of arms embargoes requires a high degree of international cooperation. Arms smuggling networks are highly sophisticated and pervasive and are often able to circumvent international weapons embargoes. Certain nations may have a political interest in supporting and supplying arms to rebel movements or insurgencies in rival countries. These and other factors frequently impede the potential effectiveness of arms embargoes. Only in a few instances – Iraq in the 1990s, North Korea today – has international cooperation been sufficiently strong to make Security Council restrictions on the supply of arms and advanced weapons technologies relatively effective. On the other hand, recent studies have shown that arms embargoes are successful in accomplishing other war-ending goals of sanctions (Brzoska and Lopez 2009) and for strengthening the impact of UN peacekeeping efforts (Wallensteen et al. 2007).

Over the years the Security Council has adopted a number of policy improvements and innovations to strengthen the implementation of arms embargoes. The language and technical terms employed in Council resolutions have become more precise, covering a much wider range of materials and arms-related activities, including training and various support services. Political reforms and capacity building efforts have encouraged UN member states to criminalize violations of Security Council arms embargoes and strengthen export control laws and regulations. The European Union has made the enforcement of vigorous export control laws a condition of membership for newly applying states from Central and Eastern Europe, a region that was rife with illicit arms trafficking in the immediate post-Cold War years. These and other initiatives have helped to create a stronger legal and regulatory foundation in many states for penalizing violations of UN arms embargoes (Alexander 2009, pp. 138–49). As we address more directly below, monitoring efforts have also become more vigorous. Beginning in 2004, the Security Council directed its peacekeeping forces in Africa to assist with the monitoring of arms embargoes. The peacekeeping forces in the Democratic Republic of Congo and Côte d'Ivoire have been assigned these new responsibilities in monitoring arms embargoes.

Commodity sanctions are means of preventing rebel movements from exploiting natural resources to finance and sustain armed conflict. Commodity sanctions have also helped to facilitate more effective governance by newly emerging post-conflict regimes in the wake of United Nations-approved peace settlements. The Security Council imposed oil embargoes as part of the sanctions against Iraq, former Yugoslavia and the other countries in the 1990s. An embargo on the export of logs was imposed in Liberia in 2003. Beginning in 2006, following the election of President Johnson-Sirleaf, the Security Council worked with the new democratic government to establish proper forest management systems to facilitate more sustainable and stable governance in Liberia. The most significant and successful effort to impose commodity sanctions involved embargoes against so-called blood diamonds, used to finance armed conflict. Beginning in 1998 with the case of Angola, and continuing with the sanctions in Sierra Leone and Liberia, the Security Council prohibited the import of diamonds from territory controlled by rebel groups. This effort to ban the sale of conflict diamonds was spurred by the research reports and advocacy campaigns of human rights groups and nongovernmental organizations, including Global Witness, Action Aid and Human Rights Watch. Alarmed by the possibility of consumer backlash, the diamond industry joined with governments and the Security Council in establishing the Kimberley Process, an agreement among dozens of countries to prevent trade in conflict diamonds. A certificate-of-origin system is now in place to protect the legitimate diamond trade by screening out conflict-related diamonds. The creation of the Kimberley certification system was a significant success that benefited the diamond industry and has helped to shrink the financial base of armed conflict in diamond producing regions (Cortright, Lopez and Gerber 2002, pp. 181–99; *Interlaken Declaration* 2002; Kimberley Process Secretariat 2002).

26.4 MONITORING SANCTIONS IMPLEMENTATION

Beginning in the late 1990s, the Security Council developed a number of mechanisms for monitoring and improving sanctions implementation. As the situations in which sanctions were imposed – such as long-standing civil wars, or in failed economies characterized by extensive criminalization – increased in complexity, the Security Council recognized the need for expert analysis of the prospects for sanctions compliance in the various cases. To address these concerns, the Council began to appoint independent expert panels and monitoring mechanisms to provide support for sanctions implementation. The first panel was established in conjunction with the arms embargo against Rwandan Hutu rebels (United Nations Security Council 1995, S/RES/1013). The panel, known as the United Nations International Commission of Inquiry (UNICOI), issued six reports from 1996 through 1998 documenting the illegal supply of arms to the rebel groups in eastern Zaire. UNICOI reports provided voluminous evidence of wholesale violations of the arms embargo and contained numerous recommendations for cracking down on arms smuggling in the region. A breakthrough toward more effective monitoring came in the case of Angola. In 1999, the Angola Sanctions Committee became more active in monitoring sanctions violations and encouraging greater implementation efforts. The Security Council also appointed a Panel of Experts and a subsequent monitoring mechanism to improve compliance with the Angola sanctions (United Nations Security Council 1999, S/RES/1237). The Panel of Experts and monitoring mechanism issued a series of reports that focused continuing attention on sanctions implementation efforts (United Nations Security Council 2000, S/2000/203; United Nations Security Council 2000, S/2000/1026; United Nations Security Council 2000, S/2000/1225; United Nations Security Council 2001, S/2001/363; United Nations Security Council 2001, S/2001/966; United Nations Security Council 2002, S/2002/486; and United Nations Security Council 2002, S/2002/1119).

The Angola Panel of Experts and the monitoring mechanism were followed by similar investigative panels for Sierra Leone and Liberia. The Security Council also created a monitoring group for the Afghanistan sanctions in 2001 (United Nations Security Council 2001, S/RES/1363), which was later transformed into the Analytical Support and Sanctions Monitoring Team to provide support for the restructured financial, travel and arms sanctions on former Taliban leaders and members of Al Qaeda. In 2000, an investigative panel was created to examine the exploitation of mineral wealth and natural resources in the Democratic Republic of the Congo. The mandate of the panel was renewed and expanded in 2003 and several times since (United Nations Security Council 2003, S/RES/1457; Levitte, United Nations Security Council 2000, S/PRST/2000/20). An expert panel was created to monitor the arms embargo in Somalia in 2002. Panel reports were also commissioned in 2004 in the case of Sudan and in 2005 for the sanctions in Côte d'Ivoire. In 2009, the Security Council created an expert panel to monitor the nonproliferation sanctions against North Korea. In each of these cases, the investigative panels produced detailed reports on sanctions violations and smuggling activities. The Sierra Leone Panel of Experts focused on the link between arms trafficking and diamond smuggling and found a pattern of widespread violations of UN sanctions. The Panel issued numerous policy recommendations, the most important of which was that sanctions be imposed on the government of Liberia for its role in undermining sanctions implementation and providing support for the rebels in Sierra Leone (United Nations Security Council 2000, S/2000/1195). Sanctions on the Charles Taylor regime soon followed (United Nations Security Council 2001, S/RES/1343). The Liberia Panel of Experts report confirmed allegations of the Monrovian government's extensive involvement with and support for the armed rebellion of the Revolutionary United Front (RuF) in Sierra Leone. The Panel recommended a series of measures for strengthening the enforcement of the arms embargo diamond embargo, and travel sanctions against Liberia (United Nations Security Council 2001, S/2001/1015).

26.5   SANCTIONING IRAQ

No case of UN Security Council sanctions has generated more debate and controversy than the measures imposed on Iraq from 1990 until 2003. The sanctions caused severe humanitarian and social hardships (Gordon 1999, p. 123–42, pp. 43–52; Weiss et al., 1997), but they were largely successful in achieving Iraq's disarmament by pressuring the regime to accept (however grudgingly) the UN weapons monitoring mandate (Cortright and Lopez 2004, pp. 90–103). The embargo on oil exports drastically reduced the revenues available to the Baghdad regime, prevented the rebuilding of Iraqi defenses after the Gulf War and blocked the import of vital materials and technologies for producing weapons of mass destruction (Gellman 2004, p. A01). Sanctions were less successful in encouraging greater Iraqi cooperation with the international community. In part, this was due to the truculent nature of the Iraqi regime, but it also resulted from the unwillingness of the US government to consider any lifting of UN sanctions in exchange for Iraqi concessions. As early as May 1991, President George H.W. Bush stated, "my view is we don't want to lift these sanctions as long as Saddam Hussein is in power" (Woolley and Peters 1991). This policy continued under President Bill Clinton, who remarked in November 1997 that "sanctions will be there until the end of time, or as long as he [Hussein] lasts" (Crossette 1997, p. 4). This position was contrary to Resolution 687, passed at the end of the 1991 Gulf War (United Nations Security Council 1991, S/RES/687), which stated that sanctions were to be lifted when Iraq complied with UN disarmament obligations. This moving of the "political goalposts" became an obstacle in diplomatic relations between Iraq and the United Nations.

According to the first head of the UN Monitoring, Verification and Inspection Commission, Rolf Ekéus, sanctions were crucial to the success of UN weapons inspection and dismantlement efforts in Iraq (Ekéus 1996). On several occasions, UN officials used the leverage of sanctions, and the hope that the embargo might be lifted, to persuade the Baghdad government to cooperate. According to Ekéus:

> Sanctions were the way to convince Iraq to cooperate with inspectors . . . In this case it was a combined carrot-and-stick approach. Keeping the sanctions was the stick, and the carrot was that if Iraq cooperated with the elimination of its weapons of mass destruction, the Security Council would lift the sanctions. Sanctions were the backing for the inspections, and they were what sustained my operation almost for the whole time (Rice and Scoblic 2000, p. 6).

Beyond helping to drive the disarmament process, sanctions undermined Iraqi military capabilities by cutting off the regime's financial lifeblood.

Sanctions kept the revenues from Iraq's vast oil wealth out of the hands of Saddam Hussein. Estimates of the total amount of oil revenue denied to the Iraqi government range as high as US$250 billion (O'Sullivan 2003, p. 139). For the first six years of sanctions, Iraq sold no oil whatsoever, except for small allowances to Jordan and Turkey. After the oil-for-food program began in 1996, oil sales were permitted and eventually generated a total of US$64.2 billion in revenue (United Nations Office of the Iraq Programme 2003). The proceeds were deposited in a UN escrow account, not the Central Bank of Iraq. While the Iraqi government used smuggling and kickback schemes to siphon hard currency out of the oil-for-food program, these funds were only a fraction of the total oil revenues being generated. The Independent Inquiry Committee into the United Nations Oil-for-Food Program (Volcker Commission), investigating corruption in the oil-for-food program reported Iraqi earnings from oil smuggling outside the sanctions regime for the period 1991 to 2003 at about US$11 billion. Total illicit income within the oil-for-food program from illegal surcharges and fees was approximately US$1.8 billion (Independent Inquiry Committee into the United Nations Oil-for-Food Programme, *Management* 2005, p. 95; Independent Inquiry Committee into the United Nations Oil-for-Food Programme, *Manipulation* 2005, p. 1). These were enormous sums, but they represented less than 20 percent of total oil revenues generated through the UN program. Dozens of companies and their executives in several countries were convicted of accepting kickbacks in the oil-for-food program, but no UN officials faced legal charges.

By denying financial resources to the Iraqi government, the sanctions prevented the regime from rebuilding its military capabilities. US government figures showed a precipitous drop in Iraqi military spending and arms imports after 1990. Iraqi military expenditures dropped from over US$15 billion in 1989 to an average of approximately US$1.4 billion per year through the 1990s (O'Sullivan 2003, p. 139). Estimated Iraqi arms imports showed a similar steep decline, dropping from more than US$3.5 billion in 1989 to minimal levels through the 1990s (United States Department of State, Bureau of Verification and Compliance 2002, pp. 77, 129; United States Department of State, Bureau of Verification and Compliance 2000, p. 87). The realization of military containment goals did not produce changes in Iraqi political behavior, however, as Saddam Hussein continued to impede the inspection process (Lopez and Cortright 1998, pp. 39–43; Cortright and Lopez 2004, pp. 90–103; Bures and Lopez 2009, pp. 29–53).

In the late 1990s, political support for continued sanctions against Iraq began to erode. In response, the Security Council sought to reform the sanctions system by easing restrictions on civilian imports, while tightening pressure on weapons and military-related goods. The strategy became known as "smart sanctions" and was a major impetus in shifting the emphasis in sanctions policymaking toward targeted measures. The goal in Iraq was to enable the rehabilitation of the civilian economy while maintaining restrictions on military goods and dual-use imports (Megally 2000). The Security Council came close to approving this approach a number of times in 2000 and 2001, and finally adopted the smart sanctions package unanimously in Resolution 1409 of 14 May 2002 (United Nations Security Council 2002, S/RES/1409). The new plan restored political consensus on the sanctions regime in the Security Council and created an effective and sustainable arms-denial system.

The US government was unwilling to settle for a revived military containment system, however. A year later, Washington rejected the renewed weapons monitoring program and launched its ill-fated invasion. As analysts weigh the costs and consequences of the Iraq War, it will be important to remember that viable alternative means were available, and were functioning effectively, to contain the threat from Saddam Hussein without the use of military force (Cortright and Lopez 2004, pp. 90–103).

26.6   TAMING TERRORISM IN LIBYA

The UN Security Council entered the fight against international terrorism nearly a decade before September 2001 when it imposed sanctions against Libya in March 1992. This was the first use of Security Council sanctions to combat international terrorism (Cortright et al. 2000, pp. 107–21). The Council demanded the extradition for trial of suspects wanted for the bombing of Pan Am flight 103 over Lockerbie in 1988 and Union des Transports Aériens (UTA) flight 772 over Niger in 1989. The Council also demanded that the Libyan regime end its support for and harboring of international terrorist organizations. To back up its demand, the Council banned all flights to and from Libya. In November 1993, in the face of Libyan defiance of UN demands, the Council broadened UN sanctions to include a ban on imports of oil equipment and included an assets freeze (United Nations Security Council 1993, S/RES/883).

The sanctions against Libya did not lock down the entire economy. Selective measures were imposed to isolate Libya from the rest of the world community, reduce its ability to support terrorism and impose modest but targeted economic hardships on the country. The aviation sanctions were appropriate to the crime of aviation terrorism and were effective in halting nearly all international flights to the country. The sanctions caused some economic losses, but their primary impact was diplomatic and symbolic, isolating Libya from the global community and branding it an international pariah.

The sting of the sanctions proved more painful to Libya than some would have estimated. When sanctions were initially imposed, the Qaddafi regime offered to turn over the terrorist suspects to an international tribunal, but this offer was unacceptable to the Security Council and was rejected. A diplomatic stalemate ensued, which was not broken until August 1998, when the United States and Great Britain responded to demands from Arab and African states to negotiate a compromise settlement. Washington and London agreed to hold the trial of the two Libyan suspects under Scottish law in a court in the Netherlands. Libya accepted the deal, although it took months of additional diplomatic wrangling before the suspects were finally delivered to The Hague for trial in April 1999. The Security Council subsequently suspended the sanctions against Libya (United Nations Security Council 1998, S/RES/1192; Dejammet, United Nations Security Council 1999, S/PRST/1999/10).

The UN sanctions on Libya were a partial success. Although the economic impact of the measures was limited, they were sufficiently burdensome to motivate the Libyan leadership to search for a negotiated settlement of the dispute. The sanctions provided bargaining leverage that eventually led to an agreement (Conroy 2002, pp. 145–69). When UN Secretary-General Kofi Annan was asked if the imposition of sanctions on Libya was effective, he responded:

> I prefer to think it played a role . . . No country likes to be treated as an outcast and outside the society of nations . . . I think Libya wanted to get back to the international community. Libya wanted to get on with its economic and social development. And Libya wanted to be able to deal freely with its neighbours and with the rest of the world (United Nations, Department of Public Information 1999, SG/SM/6944, pp. 3–4).

In addition to helping to resolve the dispute over the trial of suspects wanted in the airline bombings, the imposition of sanctions helped to persuade the Libyan government to end its support for international terrorism. The US State Department's 1996 report on global terrorism stated: "Terrorism by Libya has been sharply reduced by UN sanctions" (United States Department of State 1996). In the context of the global struggle against terrorism, this was a significant result. UN sanctions helped to deter state support of terrorist activities. After the imposition of UN sanctions in 1992, Libya gave up its role as a state sponsor of terrorism and by the end of the decade began to cooperate with the United States and other governments in disrupting the operations of Al Qaeda (McNamara 2007, pp. 83–122).

26.7   COUNTERTERRORISM SANCTIONS AND DUE PROCESS RIGHTS

After the 1998 bombings of US embassies in Africa, the Security Council imposed sanctions against Al Qaeda and the Taliban regime in Afghanistan for harboring the terrorist network. Resolution 1267 (adopted in October 1999) applied aviation and financial sanctions against the Taliban government, demanding that it cease its support for Al Qaeda and turn over Osama bin Laden to "proper authorities" for his role in the bombing of US embassies in Africa in August 1998 (United Nations Security Council 1999, S/RES/1267, para. 2). An arms embargo and other measures were added in 2000 (United Nations Security Council 2000, S/RES/1333). After the overthrow of the Taliban regime in the fall of 2001 the Security Council restructured the sanctions. Resolution 1390 (adopted in January 2002) lifted the aviation sanctions but continued the financial sanctions and travel ban on designated Taliban and Al Qaeda leaders (United Nations Security Council 2002, S/RES/1390). The Al-Qaida and Taliban Sanctions Committee developed a list of hundreds of individuals and entities subject to targeted sanctions. Among the measures imposed against those on this Consolidated List were a freeze on financial assets, a travel ban and a prohibition on the supply of arms and related military goods and services. The measures imposed in Resolution 1390 were similar to and adopted some of the language of the sweeping counterterrorism provisions contained in resolution 1373, passed shortly after the attacks of 9/11 (United Nations Security Council 2001, S/RES/1373). The Council also created the Analytic Support and Sanctions Monitoring Team (the Monitoring Team) to report on member state compliance and make recommendations for improved implementation (United Nations Security Council 2004, S/RES/1526).

The Al-Qaida and Taliban Sanctions Committee hastily designated hundreds of additional names of alleged terrorist supporters in the aftermath of 9/11, mostly at the behest of the US government (Wayne 2003), as the Consolidated List quickly grew to approximately 500 names. Many of the names added to the list during this period were designated with little supporting documentation. In addition to the UN list, the European Union (EU) and individual states established their own lists, often choosing to designate names on the basis of joint intelligence operations with powerful Western states, especially the United States and Great Britain.

Legal scholars and human rights experts questioned the legality of the procedures used to list individuals and entities. Critics noted that names were often added on the basis of political rather than judicial considerations. The US government and other states driving the process described the sanctions as temporary administrative measures not requiring full judicial legal protections. Legal experts countered that placing a name on a terrorist blacklist was an act that denied basic liberties and restricted the right to property. Since these were punitive measures usually reserved for criminal violations, according to legal scholars, the individuals or entities subjected to such action should have been afforded judicial rights (Lopez et al. 2009).

As controversy and debate over these due process issues mounted, political support for UN counterterrorism sanctions began to erode. The December 2004 report of the Secretary-General's High-level Panel on Threats, Challenges and Change observed that "[t]he way entities and individuals are added to the terrorist list maintained by the Council and the absence of review or appeal for those listed raise serious accountability issues and possibly violate fundamental rights, norms and conventions" (United Nations, Secretary-General's High-level Panel on Threats, Challenges and Change 2004, A/59/565, para. 152). In response to such concerns the UN General Assembly declared in the 2005 World Summit Outcome document that the Security Council and the Secretary-General should "ensure that fair and clear procedures exist for placing individuals and entities on sanctions lists and for removing them, as well as for granting humanitarian exemptions" (United Nations General Assembly 2005, A/RES/60/1, para. 109). The Eminent Jurists Panel of the International Commission of Jurists described Security Council listing and delisting procedures as "arbitrary" and discriminatory. It is a system, said the Panel, "unworthy" of international institutions such as the United Nations and the European Union (International Commission of Jurists 2009, pp. 116–17). A May 2008 report from the 1267 Committee Monitoring Team stated that problems associated with the lack of due process rights were creating problems that could "seriously undermine implementation" (United Nations Security Council, Analytical Support and Sanctions Monitoring Team 2008, S/2008/324, para. 2). Unless these "defects" are remedied, said the report, "the sanctions regime will continue to fade" (United Nations Security Council, Analytical Support and Sanctions Monitoring Team 2008, S/2008/324, para. 23).

In response to mounting public criticisms and concerted lobbying by a group of European like-minded states, the Security Council began to take steps to reform its listing and delisting procedures. In 2006 (Resolution 1730), the Council established a Focal Point within the UN Secretariat to process delisting requests (United Nations Security Council 2006, S/RES/1730). The same year the Council adopted Resolution 1735 mandating that more detailed information be provided when a name is added to the Consolidated List and also requiring notification to individuals and entities so listed (United Nations Security Council 2006, S/RES/1735). In 2008, the Council adopted Resolution 1822, further improving listing and delisting procedures and mandating regular review of all names on the Consolidated List (United Nations Security Council 2008, S/RES/1822). Despite these modest improvements, Security Council procedures still do not meet fundamental human rights standards, which include the right to judicial review, the right to procedural fairness, the right to be heard and the right to judicial remedy. These rights form the very basis of due process of law and are guaranteed by leading international legal agreements, including the Universal Declaration on Human Rights, the International Covenant on Civil and Political Rights, the European Court of Human Rights, the Inter-American Commission on Human Rights and the African Charter on Human and Peoples' Rights. The debate over these issues has continued, posing serious political and legal challenges to the viability of UN counterterrorism sanctions (Lopez et al. 2009).

26.8 BOMBS, CARROTS AND STICKS

Sanctions have been used frequently over the years to prevent weapons proliferation, but the results have been varied, if not meager. The United States applied a wide range of coercive unilateral measures for two decades but was unable to dissuade India and Pakistan from developing nuclear weapons. US sanctions have been equally unsuccessful so far in convincing Iran to abandon its nuclear program. The Security Council has imposed multilateral sanctions for nonproliferation purposes in three cases – Iraq, North Korea and Iran. UN multilateral measures were effective in the Iraq case (Cortright and Lopez 2004, pp. 90–103), but have yet to produce successful results in the North Korea and Iran cases.

The problem is not with the use of economic statecraft per se, but rather with the excessive emphasis on punitive and coercive measures. Effective nonproliferation diplomacy requires a combination of carrots and sticks, incentives and sanctions. Case studies of nonproliferation efforts in other countries show that successful diplomacy to prevent weapons proliferation depends upon the skillful combination of positive inducements and coercive sanctions (Cortright 1997).

A significant problem for the credibility of UN sanctions has been (and remains) the perception by many countries that the United Nations tolerates a double standard, avoiding criticism of the nuclear weapons states that retain their nuclear arsenals (who also happen to be the five permanent members of the Security Council), while imposing sanctions on those countries that attempt to develop nuclear capability. The Nuclear

Non-Proliferation Treaty (NPT) is based on a bargain in which nations agree not to develop nuclear weapons in exchange for a commitment by the nuclear weapons states to negotiate for disarmament. The credibility of the NPT regime depends upon fulfillment of that bargain and continued progress toward disarmament.

In Iraq, UN sanctions and weapons inspections were successful in achieving disarmament. The intrusive weapons monitoring efforts of the UN Special Commission (1991–98) and the UN Monitoring, Verification and Inspection Commission (2002–03) were able to eliminate both Iraq's existing weapons arsenal and the infrastructure for redeveloping such weapons. The inspection system often seemed futile and ineffective at the time, but the disarmament program ultimately succeeded in destroying Iraq's nuclear, chemical and biological weapons and the ballistic missiles that would be used for their delivery. As former chief weapons inspector Hans Blix wrote in his book, *Disarming Iraq*, "the UN and the world had succeeded in disarming Iraq without knowing it" (Blix 2004, p. 259).

The Security Council has been less successful in using sanctions to dissuade current nuclear aspirants. A review of the North Korea case illustrates the futility of punitive sanctions that are accompanied by political hostility and security tensions, in contrast to the benefits of diplomatic engagement and incentives-based bargaining. The first nuclear crisis on the Korean peninsula emerged in 1993–94, when the Pyongyang regime threw out international inspectors and threatened to withdraw from the NPT. The United States and North Korea negotiated the Agreed Framework, which halted nuclear production and reprocessing and permitted on-site inspection. The United States and its partners agreed to provide North Korea with fuel oil, new nuclear reactors less prone to proliferation and the beginnings of diplomatic recognition. The agreement was constructed as a sequence of conciliatory steps and consequent reciprocal actions that, it was hoped, would create a pattern of sustained cooperation between the two sides. North Korea was "punctilious in observing the letter of the agreement," according to Leon Sigal, but the United States fell behind in its deliveries of fuel oil and failed to fulfill its incentive offers (Sigal 2005, pp. 19–24). As the diplomatic agreement unraveled, North Korea resumed production of weapons-grade nuclear material.

The Bush administration created the Six Party Talks as a venue for multilateral negotiations and convinced North Korea to enter the talks. The diplomatic process sputtered, however, and collapsed altogether when North Korea conducted a nuclear test in October 2006. In response to that test the Security Council adopted Resolution 1718 demanding that the North refrain from further weapons tests and return to the Six Party Talks (United Nations Security Council 2006, S/RES/1718, p. 2, para. 1–6; p. 5, para. 14). The sanctions included a ban on weapons transfers to and from North Korea and a prohibition on the delivery of materials and technologies related to the production of weapons of mass destruction. Resolution 1718 also prohibited states from selling luxury goods to the North and imposed an assets freeze and travel ban on designated individuals and entities associated with North Korea's weapons program.

In 2007 it appeared that the sanctions pressures were having the desired effect, as Pyongyang returned to the Six Party Talks and US negotiators indicated a new willingness to offer incentives. The result was an agreement in which the United Nations and the US pledged to lift most of the sanctions, and North Korea promised full disclosure of its nuclear activities and dismantlement of its nuclear facilities. The 2007 agreement stalled in 2008 as the two sides sparred over continuing disagreements. North Korea demanded that the United States lift the freeze on its financial assets and remove the country from the American list of state sponsors of terrorism. Washington agreed to these demands, but Pyongyang provided only a partial disclosure of its nuclear activities and rejected US inspection demands. Once again the diplomatic process collapsed.

In May 2009, North Korea conducted another nuclear test, and the Security Council responded by imposing more draconian sanctions. Resolution 1874 reiterated the ban on weapons and technology transfers and the assets freeze and travel ban. The resolution went further in authorizing states to conduct inspections on the high seas of ships sailing to or from North Korea suspected of transporting prohibited weapons (United Nations Security Council 2009, S/RES/1874, p. 3, para. 11–12). The new resolution extended the financial sanctions by calling upon "all Member States and international financial and credit institutions not to enter into new commitments for grants, financial assistance, or concessional loans to the DPRK [Democratic People's Republic of Korea], except for humanitarian and developmental purposes directly addressing the needs of the civilian population, or the promotion of denuclearization" (United Nations Security Council 2009, S/RES/1874, p. 4, para. 19). The resolution created a panel of experts to monitor and report on international implementation of the sanctions.

Resolution 1874 was one of the toughest and most far-reaching sanctions measures ever adopted by the Security Council. The sanctions resolution was described as a breakthrough in part because China and Russia, previously reluctant to apply stronger pressure on Pyongyang, were fully supportive of the measures and willing to assist in their implementation (McFarquhar 2009). US Ambassador Philip S. Goldberg reported in August 2009 that states were cooperating in the enforcement of the sanctions. He highlighted the example of a North Korean ship, the *Kang*

Nam 1, which was heading toward Southeast Asia with a suspected cargo of weapons and was interdicted and tracked for weeks before eventually turning back to North Korean ports (United States Department of State 2009). In early August, the Indian Coast Guard intercepted another North Korean ship, the *MV Mu San*, charging it with entering Indian waters illegally. The ship was inspected but no weapons-related materials were found. In the same month, the United Arab Emirates seized a Bahamas-flagged cargo ship carrying North Korean weapons bound for Iran (Heilprin 2009). The maritime inspections were a significant form of pressure that further isolated the Pyongyang regime. The UN Sanctions Committee also designated for targeted measures an expanded list of persons and entities associated with DPRK weapons production and identified as collaborators in the proliferation of prohibited materials.

The United States began imposing sanctions on Iran soon after the 1979 Islamic revolution and has maintained a policy of hostility ever since. The focus of Washington's ire has been Tehran's support of terrorist organizations and its steadily expanding nuclear program. In 1996 the US Congress passed the Iran and Libya Sanctions Act, intensifying sanctions pressures and imposing secondary sanctions on non-US companies, mostly European, that invest in Iran. These and other US unilateral measures had little impact in weakening the Iranian economy, however, with the possible exception of US-imposed banking restrictions established in 2007, and they did not alter the regime's policies of supporting terrorist groups and building nuclear capability. Sanctions have been counterproductive, strengthening national and conservative forces within the country. Iranian officials point out, correctly, that they have the right under the NPT to develop a nuclear industry, and that the US and other nuclear states have not fulfilled their responsibilities to achieve nuclear disarmament. They have vowed to resist coercive pressures.

The UN Security Council first applied sanctions on Iran in 2006. In response to the regime's violation of its safeguards agreement with the International Atomic Energy Agency (IAEA), the Security Council adopted Resolution 1737 in December of that year, demanding that Iran cooperate fully with the IAEA and suspend all uranium enrichment-related and reprocessing activities, including research and development (United Nations Security Council 2006, S/RES/1696, p. 2, para. 2). The sanctions resolution directed states to prevent the transfer to Iran of all goods and technology and financial resources that could contribute to enrichment-related activities or the development of nuclear weapons delivery systems (United Nations Security Council 2006, S/RES/1737, p. 2, para. 3). In March 2007, in the face of continued Iranian defiance of its demands, the Council adopted additional sanctions. Resolution 1747 prohibited Iran from selling or transferring arms and urged states "to exercise vigilance and restraint" in supplying arms to Iran (United Nations Security Council 2007, S/RES/1747, p. 2, para. 5). Resolution 1747 broadened the financial restrictions, directing "all States and international financial institutions not to enter into new commitments for grants, financial assistance, and concessional loans, to the Government of the Islamic Republic of Iran, except for humanitarian and developmental purposes" (United Nations Security Council 2007, S/RES/1747, p. 3, para. 7). Resolutions 1737 and 1747 imposed an assets freeze and travel monitoring on individuals associated with Iran's nuclear activities or nuclear weapon delivery systems (United Nations Security Council 2006, S/RES/ 1737, p. 4, para. 10). In March 2008, the Council adopted a third sanctions resolution, adding further restrictions on the regime (United Nations Security Council 2008, S/RES/1803).

Recent history shows that sanctions against Iran and North Korea are unlikely to be effective in the absence of positive inducements and a commitment by the United States and other major powers to normalize diplomatic and commercial relations. For the Iran case, this will require international acceptance of Iran's right to enrich uranium. It will also require the opening of direct and unconditional talks between Washington and Tehran, and the progressive lifting of coercive sanctions. The Security Council has few incentives to offer, other than the lifting of sanctions. The United States is the major player in this case and it must be willing to open the door to dialogue and compromise if progress is to be achieved. In the North Korea case as well, US leadership will be necessary. Past failures will make renewed agreement more difficult, but the basic formula from previous negotiations remains valid: a willingness in Washington to offer and sustain incentive offers, in exchange for verified North Korean steps toward full nuclear dismantlement.

26.9 THE FUTURE OF MULTILATERAL ECONOMIC SANCTIONS

The development of sanctions policymaking has reached a crossroads. On the one hand, the diversity of global economic relations, especially in financial transactions, has made it more possible for nations to avoid war by resolving their grievances through the employment of multilateral economic sanctions. In the last two decades, the UN Security Council has instituted many refinements in the design and implementation of targeted economic sanctions. The record of success for multilateral sanctions is mixed but no less so than for the use of military force. On the other hand, concerns about the lack of due process rights in listing and delisting procedures for targeted sanctions have created a political backlash against UN sanctions. A number of European states, long-time supporters of sanctions, have both criticized Security Council procedures and redrawn some of the boundaries of sanctions imposition as a result of court rulings and administrative decisions. Multilateral sanctions have been used as means of controlling nuclear proliferation, but the success of these efforts will depend upon the intelligent integration of incentives, sanctions and security assurances as part of a diplomatic bargaining process. Sanctions can be imposed and implemented by the UN Security Council but security assurances and inducements are the purview of individual nations, particularly the United States and other major powers, acting on their own or in concert beyond the UN framework. Resolving current proliferation concerns with both Iran and North Korea will require a more holistic approach that incorporates, but goes beyond, economic sanctions.

REFERENCES

Alexander, K. (2009), *Economic Sanctions: Law and Public Policy,* London: Palgrave Macmillan.

Andreas, P. (2005), "Criminalizing consequences of sanctions: embargo busting and its legacy", *International Studies Quarterly,* **49** (2), 35–60.

Baldwin, D.A. (1985), *Economic Statecraft,* Princeton, NJ: Princeton University Press.

Blix, H. (2004), *Disarming Iraq,* New York, NJ: Pantheon Books.

Brzoska, M. and G.A. Lopez (eds.) (2009), *Putting Teeth in the Tiger: Improving the Effectiveness of Arms Embargoes,* Bingley, UK: Emerald Group Publishing, Ltd.

Bures, O. and G.A. Lopez (2009), "The unprecedented embargo: the UN arms sanctions against Iraq, 1990–2004", in M. Brozska and G.A. Lopez (eds), *Putting Teeth in the Tiger: Improving the Effectiveness of Arms Embargoes,* Bingley, UK: Emerald Group Publishing, Ltd., pp. 29–53.

Conroy, R.W. (2002), "The UN experience with travel sanctions: selected cases and conclusions", in D. Cortright and G.A. Lopez (eds), *Smart Sanctions, Targeting Economic Statecraft,* Lanham, MD: Rowman & Littlefield, pp. 145–69.

Cortright, D. (ed.) (1997), *The Price of Peace: Incentives and International Conflict Prevention,* Lanham, MD: Rowman & Littlefield.

Cortright, D. and G.A. Lopez (eds) (1995), *Economic Sanctions: Panacea or Peacebuilding in a Post–Cold War World?* Boulder, CO: Westview Press.

Cortright, D. and G.A. Lopez (2000), *The Sanctions Decade: Assessing UN Strategies in the 1990s,* Boulder, CO: Lynne Rienner Publishers.

Cortright, D. and G.A. Lopez (eds) (2002), *Smart Sanctions: Targeting Economic Statecraft,* Lanham, MD: Rowman & Littlefield.

Cortright, D. and G.A. Lopez (2004), "Containing Iraq: sanctions worked", *Foreign Affairs,* **83** (4), 90–103.

Cortright, D. and G.A. Lopez (2009), "Targeted sanctions, counter-terrorism and strategic peace-building", in D. Philpott and G.F. Powers (eds), *Strategies of Peace,* Oxford, UK: Oxford University Press.

Cortright, D., G.A. Lopez and L. Gerber (2002), "The viability of commodity sanctions: the case of diamonds", in D. Cortright and G.A. Lopez (eds), *Sanctions and the Search for Security: Challenges to UN Action,* Boulder, CO: Lynne Rienner Publishers, pp. 181–99.

Cortright, D., G.A. Lopez and L. Gerber-Stellingwerf (2007), "Sanctions", in T.G. Weiss and S. Daws (eds), *The Oxford Handbook on the United Nations*, Oxford, UK: Oxford University Press, pp. 349–69.

Cortright, D. et al. (2000), "Taming terrorism: sanctions against Libya, Sudan, and Afghanistan", in D. Cortright and G.A. Lopez (2000), *The Sanctions Decade: Assessing UN Strategies in the 1990s,* Boulder, CO: Lynne Rienner Publishers, pp. 107–21.

Crossette, B. (1997), "For Iraq: a dog house with many rooms", *New York Times*, 23 November 1997, p. 4.

Dejammet, A., President, United Nations Security Council (1999), Statement by the President of the Security Council, S/PRST/1999/10, New York, 8 April 1999.

Drezner, D.W. (1999), *The Sanctions Paradox: Economic Statecraft and International Relations,* Cambridge, UK: Cambridge University Press.

Ekéus, R. (1996), Speech to the Carnegie Endowment for International Peace, Conference on Nuclear Non-Proliferation and the Millennium: Prospects and Initiatives, Washington DC, 13 February 1996.

Gellman, B. (2004), "Iraq's arsenal was only on paper; since Gulf War, nonconventional weapons never got past the planning stage", *Washington Post*, 7 January 2004, p. A01.

Gordon, J. (1999), "A peaceful, silent, deadly remedy: the ethics of economic sanctions", *Ethics and International Affairs* **13** (1), 123–42.

Gordon, J. (2002), "Cool war: economic sanctions as a weapon of mass destruction", *Harper's Magazine*, November 2002, pp. 43–52.

Giumelli, F. (2009), "Coercing, constraining, and signaling: explaining UN and EU sanctions after the Cold War", Paper presented at the annual convention of the International Studies Association, New York, 14–18 February 2009.

Heilprin, J. (2009), "UAE reports ship seizure with North Korea arms for Iran", Associated Press, 28 August 2009, available at http://i.abcnews.com/US/WireStory ?id=8439023&page=1, accessed 8 September 2009.

Hirschman, A. (1980), *National Power and the Structure of Foreign Trade*, expanded edn, Berkeley, CA: University of California Press.

Hufbauer, G.C. et al. ([1983] 2007), *Economic Sanctions Reconsidered*, 3rd edn, Washington DC: Peterson Institute for International Economics.

Independent Inquiry Committee into the United Nations Oil-for-Food Programme (2005), "The Management of the United Nations Oil-for-Food Programme", New York, 7 September 2005, available at www.iic-offp.org/, accessed 20 August 2009.

Independent Inquiry Committee into the United Nations Oil-for-Food Programme (2005), "Manipulation of the Oil-for-Food Programme by the Iraqi Regime", New York, 27 October 2005, p. 1, available at www.iic-offp.org/, accessed 20 August 2009.

Interlaken Declaration of 5 November 2002 on the Kimberley Process Certification Scheme for Rough Diamonds (2002), Interlaken, Switzerland, 5 November 2002.

International Commission of Jurists (2009), *Assessing Damage, Urging Action: Report of the Eminent Jurists Panel on Terrorism, Counter-Terrorism and Human Rights,* Geneva: International Commission of Jurists.

Kimberley Process Secretariat, Ministry of Mines and Energy, Namibia (2002), "Kimberley Process Certification Scheme", 5 November 2002, available at http://www.kimberleyprocess.com, accessed 2 September 2009.

Levitte, J-D, President, United Nations Security Council (2000), *Statement by the President of the Security Council,* S/PRST/2000/20, New York, 2, June 2000.

Lopez, G.A. (2006), "UN sanctions after oil-for-food: still a viable diplomatic tool?", Hearing on the Sub-committee on National Security, Emerging Threats, and International Relations of the Committee on Government Reform, House of Representative, 109th Congress, 2nd session, 2 May 2006, pp. 147–58.

Lopez, G.A. and D. Cortright (1998), "Trouble in the Gulf: pain and promise", *The Bulletin of the Atomic Scientists*, **54** (3), 39–43.

Lopez, G.A. et al. (2009), "Overdue process: protecting human rights while sanctioning alleged terrorists", A report to Cordaid from the Fourth Freedom Forum and Kroc

Institute for International Peace Studies at the University of Notre Dame, Notre Dame, Indiana, April 2009.

McFarquhar, N. (2009), "UN security council pushes North Korea by passing sanctions", *The New York Times*, 13 June 2009, available at http://www.nytimes.com/2009/06/13/world/asia/13nations.html, accessed 17 August 2009.

McNamara, T.E. (2007), "Unilateral and multilateral strategies against state sponsors of terror: a case study of Libya, 1979–2003", in D. Cortright and G.A. Lopez (eds), *Uniting Against Terror: Cooperative Nonmilitary Responses to the Global Terrorist Threat*, Cambridge, MA: The MIT Press, pp. 83–122.

Megally, H. (2000), "Letter to United Nations Security Council", Letter written to Amb. Richard Holbrooke, president of the UN Security Council, New York, 4 January 2000, available at http://www.temple.edu/lawschool/drwiltext/docs/Human%20Rights%20Watch%20Ltr%20to%20UN.pdf, accessed 22 August 2009.

O'Sullivan, M.L. (2003), *Shrewd Sanctions: Statecraft and State Sponsors of Terrorism*, Washington DC: Brookings Institution Press.

Rice, M. and J.P. Scoblic (2000), "Shifting priorities: UNMOVIC and the future of inspections in iraq: an interview with Ambassador Rolf Ekéus", *Arms Control Today*, **30** (2), 6.

Rosecrance, R. (1987), *The Rise of the Trading State*, New York, NY: Basic Books.

Sigal, L. (2005), "Averting a Train Wreck with North Korea", *Arms Control Today*, **35** (2), 19–24.

United Nations (1945), "Chapter VII: action with respect to threats to the peace, breaches of the peace, and acts of aggression", *Charter of the United Nations*, San Francisco, 26 June 1945, Article 41.

United Nations, Department of Public Information (1999), "Transcript of press conference by Secretary-General Kofi Annan at Headquarters, 5 April", Press release, SG/SM/6944, New York, 5 April 1999.

United Nations General Assembly (2005), *Resolution Adopted by the General Assembly 60/1: 2005 World Summit Outcome*, A/RES/60/1, New York, 24 October 2005.

United Nations Office of the Iraq Programme (2009), "Oil Exports (By Phase)", updated 21 March 2003, available at www.un.org/Depts/oip/background/basicfigures.html, accessed 20 August 2009.

United Nations, Secretary-General's High-level Panel on Threats, Challenges, and Change (2004), *A More Secure World: Our Shared Responsibility, Report of the High-level Panel on Threats, Challenges and Change*, A/59/565, New York, 2 December 2004.

United Nations Security Council (2009), *Security Council Resolution 1874*, S/RES/1874, New York, 12 June 2009.

United Nations Security Council (2008), *Security Council Resolution 1822*, S/RES/1822, New York, 30 June 2008.

United Nations Security Council (2008), *Security Council Resolution 1803*, S/RES/1803, New York, 3 March 2008.

United Nations Security Council (2007), *Security Council Resolution 1747*, S/RES/1747, New York, 24 March 2007.

United Nations Security Council (2006), *Security Council Resolution 1737*, S/RES/1737, New York, 27 December 2006.

United Nations Security Council (2006), *Security Council Resolution 1735*, S/RES/1735, New York, 22 December 2006.

United Nations Security Council (2006), *Security Council Resolution 1730*, S/RES/1730, New York, 19 December 2006.

United Nations Security Council (2006), *Security Council Resolution 1718*, S/RES/1718, New York, 14 October 2006.

United Nations Security Council (2006), *Security Council Resolution 1696*, S/RES/1696, New York, 31 July 2006.

United Nations Security Council (2004), *Security Council Resolution 1526*, S/RES/1526, New York, 30 January 2004.

United Nations Security Council (2003), *Security Council Resolution 1457,* S/RES/1457, New York, 24 January 2003.

United Nations Security Council (2002), *Security Council Resolution 1409*, S/RES/1409, New York, 14 May 2002.

United Nations Security Council (2002), *Security Council Resolution 1390*, S/RES/1390, New York, 28 January 2002.

United Nations Security Council (2001), *Security Council Resolution 1373,* S/RES/1373, New York, 28 September 2001.

United Nations Security Council (2001), *Security Council Resolution 1363,* S/RES/1363, New York, 30 July 2001.

United Nations Security Council (2001), *Security Council Resolution 1343,* S/RES/1343, New York, 7 March 2001.

United Nations Security Council (2000), *Security Council Resolution 1333,* S/RES/1333, New York, 19 December 2000.

United Nations Security Council (1999), *Security Council Resolution 1267,* S/RES/1267, New York, 15 October 1999, para. 2.

United Nations Security Council (1999), *Security Council Resolution 1237,* S/RES/1237, New York, 7 May 1999.

United Nations Security Council (1998), *Security Council Resolution 1192*, S/RES/1192, New York, 27 August 1998.

United Nations Security Council (1995), *Security Council Resolution 1013,* S/RES/1013, New York, 7 September 1995.

United Nations Security Council (1993), *Security Council Resolution 883*, S/RES/883, New York, 11 November 1993.

United Nations Security Council (1991), *Security Council Resolution 687,* S/RES/687, New York, 3 April 1991.

United Nations Security Council (1977), *Security Council Resolution 418*, S/RES/418, New York, 4 November 1977.

United Nations Security Council (1966), *Security Council Resolution 232*, S/RES/232, New York, 16 December 1966.

United Nations Security Council, Analytical Support and Sanctions Monitoring Team (2008), *[Eighth] Report of the Analytical Support and Sanctions Monitoring Team pursuant to resolution 1735 (2006) concerning Al-Qaida and the Taliban and associated individuals and entities,* S/2008/324, New York, 14 May 2008.

United Nations Security Council, Monitoring Mechanism on Sanctions Against Angola (2000), *Interim Report of the Monitoring Mechanism on Angola Sanctions Established by the Security Council in Resolution 1295 (2000) of April 2000*, S/2000/1026, New York, 25 October 2000.

United Nations Security Council, Monitoring Mechanism on Sanctions Against Angola (2000), *Final Report of the Monitoring Mechanism on Angola Sanctions*, S/2000/1225, New York, 21 December 2000.

United Nations Security Council, Monitoring Mechanism on Sanctions Against UNITA (2001), *Addendum to the Final Report of the Monitoring Mechanism on Sanctions Against UNITA*, S/2001/363, New York, 11 April 2001.

United Nations Security Council, Monitoring Mechanism on Sanctions Against UNITA (2001), *Supplementary Report of the Monitoring Mechanism on Sanctions Against UNITA*, S/2001/966, New York, 12 October 2001.

United Nations Security Council, Monitoring Mechanism on Sanctions Against UNITA (2002), *Additional Report of the Monitoring Mechanism on Sanctions Against UNITA*, S/2002/486, New York, 26 April 2002.

United Nations Security Council, Monitoring Mechanism on Sanctions Against UNITA (2002), *Additional Report of the Monitoring Mechanism on Sanctions Against UNITA*, S/2002/1119, New York, 16 October 2002.

United Nations Security Council, Panel of Experts on Liberia, Appointed Pursuant to Security Council Resolution 1343 (2001), *Report of the Panel of Experts Pursuant to*

Security Council Resolution 1342 (2001), Paragraph 19, Concerning Liberia, S/2001/1015, New York, 26 October 2001.

United Nations Security Council, Panel of Experts on Sierra Leone Diamonds and Arms, appointed pursuant to Security Council Resolution 1306 (2000), *Report of the Panel of Experts Appointed Pursuant to Security Council Resolution 1306 (2006), paragraph 19, in Relation to Sierra Leone*, S/2000/1195, New York, 20 December 2000.

United Nations Security Council, Panel of Experts on Violations of Security Council Sanctions Against UNITA (2000), *Report of the Panel of Experts on Violations of Security Council Sanctions Against UNITA*, S/2000/203, New York, 10 March 2000.

United States, Department of State (1996), *Patterns of Global Terrorism 1996*, publication 10535, Washington DC: US Government Printing Office.

United States Department of State (2009), "Implementation of UN Security Council Resolution 1874 on North Korea", available at http://www.state.gov/r/pa/prs/ps/2009/aug/127860.htm, accessed 17 August 2009.

United States Department of State, Bureau of Verification and Compliance (2002), *World Military Expenditures and Arms Transfers 1999–2000*, Washington DC: US Government Printing Office.

United States Department of State, Bureau of Verification and Compliance (2000), *World Military Expenditures and Arms Transfers 1998*, Washington DC: US Government Printing Office.

Wallensteen, P. and C. Staibano (eds) (2005), *International Sanctions: Between Words and Wars in the Global System*, New York, NY: Frank Cass.

Wallensteen, P. et al. (2007), "United Nations arms embargoes: their impact on arms flows and target behaviour", report by the SIPRI Arms Transfers Project, Stockholm International Peace Research Institute, and the Special Program on the Implementation of Targeted Sanctions, Department of Peace and Conflict Research, Uppsala University, Stockholm.

Wayne, E.A. (2003), "International dimension of combating the financing of terrorism", testimony to the House Committee on International Relations, Subcommittee on International Terrorism, Nonproliferation and Human Rights, 108th Cong., 1st session, Washington DC, 26 March 2003.

Weiss, T.G. et al. (eds.) (1997), *Political Gain and Civilian Pain: Humanitarian Impacts of Economic Sanctions*, Lanham, MD: Rowman & Littlefield.

Woolley, J.T. and G. Peters (1991), "The President's News Conference", news conference with Hon. President George H.W. Bush and Chancellor Helmut Kohl of Germany, 20 May 1991, The American Presidency Project, University of California, Santa Barbara, CA, available at http://www.presidency.ucsb.edu/ws/index.php?pid=19601, accessed 20 August 2009.

27 International negotiation and conflict prevention

I. William Zartman

27.1 INTRODUCTION

Literally innumerable violent interstate conflicts have been prevented and non-violent conflicts handled by the practice of normal diplomacy, with negotiation as the prime means of dealing with them. In fact, given the number of pairs of states with relations with each other (interstate dyads), violent conflict is extremely rare, which is what makes the event so striking. Because it is a costly distraction from productive peaceful relations, violent conflict is a prime target for prevention; however, it is also an occasional pursuit of states, either by mistake, by entrapment or because it is seen to involve goals that are important or attainable to one of the parties.

Prevention depends on early warning, and early warnings abound (Verstegen 1999; Dorn 2004). Academic analyses and government files are filled with indications of the causes and signs of war, even if the exact dates of the crash are not predictable. Less prolific is early awareness and early action, that is, the ability to listen, hear and act on the early warnings. The real need is to overcome such problems as scenario unreliability ("the tropical storm problem"), bureaucratic inertia ("the three-monkeys' problem"), current crisis' overshadowing of future dangers ("the smoke-and-fire problem"), repeated false warnings ("the cry-wolf problem") and other impediments to policymakers' hearing and responding to the many visible signs of impending conflict (Zartman and Faure 2005). Surprises in this business are rare, but deafness is widespread. Awareness and action require a conscious decision to give attention and credit for proactive efforts at prevention, instead of simply reactive policymaking. USAID has its conflict assessment, UNDP its early warning assessment, CIA its state failure task force, the Fund for Peace its analytical model and the UN its article 99, where the Secretary-General may serve as the agent of early warning (although it has never been used before the outbreak of hostilities). However, the real problem remains: the analytical inability to distinguish storm warnings that precede hurricanes from those that do not ("the tropical storm problem"), and to act upon them (Zartman 2005).

Three categories of strategies can be used to reduce the danger of violent interstate conflict through the use of international negotiation: "early," generic negotiations to establish and enforce standards for non-conflictual structural prevention corresponding to types of situations likely to cause escalation and violent conflict; "early late," pre-crisis negotiations for operational prevention to halt the violent escalation of the conflict and restore harmony responding to warnings of specific, impending war; and "late" or post-crisis negotiations to heal wounds, prevent a repetition of conflict and respond to residual warnings of left-over hostilities (Zartman 2010). This chapter will present a summary of what works and why, and why not when it does not, in these three stages, to prevent interstate war; internal or intrastate conflict is not addressed here except as it relates to interstate conflict.

27.2   CONFLICT AND NEGOTIATION

Conflict, defined simply as an incompatibility of positions, is a normal, natural and even beneficial occurrence. Since perfect harmony is an angelic, not a human, condition, the absence of conflict can be obtained only in a perfectly authoritarian system, which does not exist either, at least on the interstate level. Mere incompatibility is passive or static conflict; it is when one side seeks to prevail in that situation of incompatibility of positions by escalating its efforts that one can talk of active conflict (Rothchild et al. 1996; UCDP 2010). Such activity begins by being political or non-violent; further escalation leads to violent conflict. Prevention therefore seeks to keep active conflicts in the political stage so as to be able to resolve them ("early"), to block the escalation of violence ("early late") and to create conditions for handling further conflict ("post") (Boutros Ghali 1992).

Relations among states are carried out by a process that can be referred to in its ideal type as "normal diplomacy," that is, ongoing communication between formally equal parties for the purpose of maintaining relations, doing business and handling conflicts as they may arise and preventing them from becoming violent, using negotiation as its prime means (Zartman 2009). In a mercantilist formulation, "If you want it and can't take it, you must buy it," with negotiation the process of setting the price. Negotiation is a process of combining divergent positions into a jointly agreed outcome (Kissinger 1965). It seeks a positive-sum outcome, "giving something to get something" and thus providing something for both parties, not for goodness' sake, but in order to give an incentive to keep the agreement from which each party also benefits.

Conflict occurs primarily under one of two different perspectives, seen

PDG

I

	give in	hold out
give in	3/3***	1/4*
hold out	4/1*	2/2****

Notes: 4 is high. The games differ in that the worst outcome for both parties is stalemate in CDG but surrender to the other party in PDG. Single asterisks mark zero-sum outcomes, double asterisks negative sum outcomes, triple asterisks positive-sum outcomes, four asterisks mark salient solutions

Figure 27.1   The prisoner's dilemma game

as zero sum and positive sum encounters. Zero sum perspectives focus on winning the conflict at the other party's expense or making relative gains. In the classical Prisoner's Dilemma Game (PDG) (Figure 27.1), zero-sum outcomes are found in the northeast and southwest corners, where one party holds out (wins) and the other gives in (Pillar 1983; Brams 1985; Snyder and Diesing 1969). As a result, assuming equal power, the parties end up in deadlock – the Nash Equilibrium (1950), the determinate outcome – and are unable to attain the second best, cooperative outcome. The Cold War itself or the Arab–Israeli and Indian–Pakistani conflicts are good examples of a PDG situation, where the absence of trust between the parties has long prevented them from negotiating mutually beneficial outcomes of cooperation. The only two ways for the parties to get out of the determinate outcome in a PDG perception of conflict is to establish a joint willingness to seek some outcome between their hold-out positions or to repeat the game alternating between southwest and northeast outcomes (Axelrod 1970). If negotiation does take place, the type that relates to a zero-sum situation is *concession* bargaining, either to converge toward the middle between their positions or to agree to alternate outcomes, one party's gain still being the other's loss.

In the Chicken Dilemma Game (CDG) perception (Figure 27.2), there is no determinate outcome, and the worst outcome is stalemate, not one of giving in to the other party. In principle, this forces the parties to think and try to negotiate a positive sum cooperative solution to the northwest in order to avoid the worst (Goldstein 2010). A CDG situation, as shown, has two salient or Nash Equilibria where neither party can improve its position unilaterally, whereas the PDG has only the one: stalemate. The conflict here is not seen as (despite the technical term) a cooperation problem as in

CDG

I

	give in	hold out
give in	3/3***	2/4****
hold out	4/2****	1/1**

Notes: 4 is high. The games differ in that the worst outcome for both parties is stalemate in CDG but surrender to the other party in PDG. Single asterisks mark zero-sum outcomes, double asterisks negative sum outcomes, triple asterisks positive-sum outcomes, four asterisks mark salient solutions

Figure 27.2   The chicken dilemma game

PDG, where the preferred outcome of both parties is noncooperation even though higher payoffs could be achieved through mutual cooperation, but a coordination problem shown as in CDG, where non-cooperation is unattractive, a number of mutually exclusive conflicting solutions for cooperation are presented, and deadlock is avoidable only by combining or redefining a jointly agreeable outcome, as discussed. A CDG obtained in the early 1990s in South Africa, where the perception of a mutually hurting stalemate (MHS) in the southeast corner enabled the parties to negotiate a new and beneficial conflict resolution outcome (Zartman 1989, 2000) or in Nagorno-Kakabakh in 1994, where the same perception, with a mediator's help, led the parties into a conflict management ceasefire that has lasted at least a decade and a half (Mooradian and Druckman 1999).

Positive sum perspectives are those where both sides gain something, even if not equally; the allocation of the gains is another matter. Positive sum outcomes are found in the northwest corner of both the PDG and CDG; the challenge of negotiation is to define this outcome to the parties' joint satisfaction. Parties can achieve positive sums either through compensation or through construction (reframing) (or by adding the satisfaction of avoiding the worst to a zero-sum *concession* outcome). *Compensation* refers to an exchange of concessions on different matters, with one party "paying for" a favorable outcome in one matter by granting the other party a favorable outcome on another matter. By Homans' Maxim (1961, p 60), the key to successful negotiation (and also the basis of the Nash Point, the optimal solution) is "the more the items at stake can be divided into goods valued more by one party than they cost to the other and goods valued more by the other party than they cost to the first, the greater the chances of a successful outcome." Agreement to prevent further escalation in Namibia and Angola in 1988 and to end the conflict was reached by "purchasing" a withdrawal of South African troops from Namibia (and its consequent achievement of independence) with the withdrawal of Cuban troops from Angola, and vice versa, thus achieving a full realization of both parties' goals. Of course, not all stakes are Homansdivisible, still leaving a distribution problem in many cases. In such cases, compensations can be made only out of items external to the original stakes, as side payments.

Construction or reframing refers to a redefinition of the stakes in such a way that both parties can find an interest in the outcome, instead of defining it distributively (Walton and McKersie 1965). It is unlikely that reframing can totally recast the stakes to the elimination of all distributive concerns, but it can provide superordinate goals and a cooperative atmosphere, in addition to redefined stakes, so that distribution becomes less contentious. Another wear in the "last territorial conflict in Latin America" was prevented in 1999 when Peru and Ecuador reached settlement by beginning to focus on the development of the poor and isolated region in contest rather than on the legalisms of their incompatible border claims.

Parties turn to negotiations when their efforts to escalate a conflict lead them into an impasse. When, in addition, that impasse is perceived and felt to be painful to both parties, they turn to a search for a jointly agreeable solution, although they may still need the help of a third party mediator to see the situation correctly and to work toward that solution. This situation, termed a mutually hurting stalemate (MHS), is merely the necessary but not sufficient condition for the beginning of negotiations (Zartman 1989, 2000). For the negotiations to arrive at a successful conclusion, the parties must devise a way out (WO) or mutually enticing outcome (MEO) out of their discussions, a pull factor that complements the push factor that impelled them into diplomatic discussions. Although the notion of a MHS is most readily understandable in matters of violent conflict, where rising costs of conflict and falling chances of a favorable unilateral outcome impel the parties to seek a negotiated solution, it also applies to non-violent conflicts impelling two or more states to pool their efforts in cooperation to prevent further damage when unilateral efforts to handle the problem fail and the costs of that failure rise.

Mediation is the process of negotiation with a third-party catalyst, and hence also the means of helping other states resolve their problems and conflicts as a third party. States pursue mediation in their own interest (Zartman and Touval 2007). Sometimes they seek to achieve an outcome favorable to themselves out of other states' conflicts, but much more frequently they are motivated by a desire to end a conflict that is disturbing to them too, or to improve relations with one or both of the conflicting parties. Thus, the international mediator does not have to be neutral and unbiased (as it may in labor relations or domestic counseling) but simply to be trustworthy as a message carrier and supportive of the parties' efforts to find a stable solution preventing further conflict. If the mediator does have favorable ties with a party in the conflict, however, the assumption is that it will deliver that party's assent to the evolving outcome.

Since parties begin negotiations under the pressure of a (perceived) mutually hurting stalemate, the mediator's first challenge is to help the parties develop that perception. Ripening, or heightening the parties' realization that they cannot escalate their way out of the conflict and that staying in it imposes increasingly burdensome costs, is the ticket to mediation (Zartman and de Soto 2010). If this is not possible and the mediator's interests make resolution important to it, then *positioning* is the best policy in order to be available when the parties have developed a greater awareness of their need for mediation

Once mediation has begun, the mediating state's job varies according to the type of obstacle that prevents the parties from seeking an agreement (Zartman and Touval 2007). If the parties are unable to hear and get messages to and from each other, they need a *communicator* as a mediator, serving only as a clear telephone line between the parties, as did the Vatican in the Beagle Channel dispute between Argentina and Chile (Prinzen 1992). If the parties are so engrossed in their conflict that they cannot think of collaborative solution to it, they need a *formulator* as a mediator, injecting ideas of its own and persuading the parties of the need and opportunity of a positive outcome, as the US has done in its successive mediations in the Middle East Peace Process and by the various mediators – Zaire, the US, the UN – in the Angolan conflict. But if the obstacle to an agreement is the absence of sufficient payoffs to attract the parties away from their conflict, or the absence of sufficient equality of strength between the parties for them to come to a balanced and stable agreement, then the need is for a *manipulator* as a mediator, as with the US huge foreign aid promise to Egypt and Israel in 1975, making the second Sinai disengagement attractive to them. The manipulator's role contains the greatest degree of involvement and is also the most dangerous.

27.3   PREVENTION

The notion of prevention is by no means new, it was emphasized after World War II in the work of Ralph Bunche, by Secretary-General Dag Hammarskjöld, and then by his distant successor, Boutros Boutros Ghali (1992), who brought it back into prominence after a Cold War interlude, focusing on peacemaking, peacekeeping and peacebuilding. During the 1990s, preventive diplomacy was also addressed by academic analysis within nongovernmental research organizations, such as the Council on Foreign Relations, the US Institute of Peace (Lund 1996) and the Carnegie Corporation (Holl 1997; Jentleson 2000; Zartman 2001; Hamburg 2008). The 2000 meeting of the G-8 foreign ministers in Japan (Miyakazi 2000) and the Swedish presidency of the European Union (EU) (Swedish Ministry of Foreign Affairs 1997, 1999) led to the Canadian-sponsored International Commission on Intervention and State Sovereignty (Evans and Sahnoun 2001, Evans 2008), whose report examined the "responsibility to protect [R2P], to prevent, to react and to rebuild." These concerns then found their place in the Secretary-General's High Level Panel that was unanimously adopted by the General Assembly at the 2005 World Summit (United Nations 2004). The elements of prevention, reaction and rebuilding, like Boutros Ghali's peacemaking, peacekeeping and peacebuilding, can be presented as early, generic measures of structural prevention that establish and enforce standards for non-conflictual behavior; "early late," pre-crisis measures of operational prevention to halt the violent escalation of the conflict; and post-crisis measures to heal wounds and prevent a repetition of conflict.

27.3.1   Early or Structural Prevention

The best way to accomplish early prevention is to remove the structural or root causes that activate conflict. Accepted standards of behavior can be established, to be used as guidelines for states to deal healthily with their own challenges and problems, and also for third parties to assist them in achieving appropriate responses. It is here where early prevention can begin, with the construction of international regimes – "principles, norms, rules, procedures and programs that govern the interactions of actors in specific issue areas" – for dealing with situations likely to lead to conflict escalation (Krasner 1983; Hasenclever, Mayer and Rittberger 1997; Spector and Zartman 2003). Such regimes for handling interstate conflict exist in regard to *boundaries, territory, arms races and proliferation*, and *population displacement*, among others (other regimes for sources of intrastate conflict relate to ethnic relations, democratization, human rights, good governance, responsibility to protect and genocide [Zartman 2010]).

Boundary disputes have been a major source of interstate conflict, as recently seen between Ethiopia and Eritrea, India and Pakistan, Israel and Palestine, and Ecuador and Peru, among others. The norms for handling boundary conflicts include the advisability of delimitation and demarcation (negotiating a mutually agreed line and providing hard markers on the ground), permeability (measures for allowing normal civilian traffic, especially by borderland habitants), control (routine customs and immigration measures) and rectification (review to take into account local geographic changes) (Nordquist 2001). It is better to negotiate and observe such requirements for a peaceful border while the border is indeed peaceful, rather than awaiting escalation over points left undecided. Boundary disputes also include maritime boundaries, where norms concern projections from land boundaries, also open to negotiation, as in the case of the Caspian Sea regime.

Territorial conflicts extend beyond a simple disagreement on the borderline and concern pieces of land, often endowed with sacred value (Ayissi 2001; Hopmann 2001; Toft 2003; Vasquez and Valeriano 2009). In addition to those boundary disputes mentioned above, such conflicts include Serbia and Kosovo, Greece and Macedonia, Morocco and Algeria, China and Taiwan, Russia and Georgia, Moldova and Dniestria, and Armenia and Azerbaijan, among others. International norms do not help decide the disposition of the territory; that is a prime candidate for creative negotiation, as happened in the Peru–Ecuador case. But they do set standards that help frame that allocation, such as unacceptability of conquest, absence of settlement and population displacement and requirement of self-determination in a number of forms. These norms are powerful deterrents to irresponsible claims and serve as the basis for negotiation.

Arms races and proliferation of Weapons of Mass Destruction (WMD) are the subject of a number of stringent regimes that have been negotiated in order to limit the path to violent conflict (Goodby and Kremenyuk 2001; Meerts, Melamud and Hampson 2010). Negotiation comes in the creation of such regimes, on chemical weapons, land mines, nuclear acquisition, nuclear weapons testing and acquisition of fissible materials, among others. It also is involved in their application, in regard to the entry of the "intermediate states" of Israel, India and Pakistan and the rogue states of Iran and North Korea into the Nuclear Club, where the challenges and the dangers of irresponsible use and war are much greater. Thus negotiation prepares the background for prevention and the base for further negotiation in application.

Population displacement, either between states as refugees or within states as internally displaced persons (IDPs), is the subject of two complementary regimes (Deng and Cohen 1998). Although these norms and standards are not universally applied and have no mechanism of accountability, they are broadly accepted and form the basis for dealing, however imperfectly, with the repercussions of violence and persecution of identity groups, as seen in the handling of boat people in Vietnam in the 1970s and Haiti in the early 1990s and 2010s, Rwandans into Congo in the 1990s, Kurds in Turkey in 1988, and the Fur, Zaghawa and other groups into

Chad and Central Africa in the 2000s, among others. Negotiations based on the international refugee and IDP regimes dealt with these and other conflicts, often inconclusively,

The matter of regimes might seem to be toothless and idealistic compared with the brutal and dirty processes of war. But without negotiation among states to establish such standards, management of the causes of war is left ad hoc and contradictory, lacking justification and coordination. As consensual methods of problem-solving, regimes coordinate and facilitate the generic prevention of escalation and violent conflict. Their universal standards and coverage are applicable to specific situations in need of diagnosis, prescription and further preventive negotiation.

27.3.2 Early–Late or Crisis Prevention

Early prevention is often insufficient. On occasion, more direct and immediate measures in the early part of the overt phase of conflict are necessary to make a final effort at prevention, lest the conflict move to violence or already occurring violence escalate further. Crisis prevention measures are needed when the crisis looms ahead, before it actually breaks out and crisis management is required as a "late" late measure (Brecher 1993). Direct negotiation between conflicting parties is always the best preventive policy, but if the parties themselves do not take such action, third party measures to facilitate negotiation become necessary. These include *dialog*, *ripening*, *mediation*, and *preemptive accountability*. *Dialog* can be considered to be prenegotiation or negotiation without an outcome, for purposes of better understanding and deescalation. The conflicting states may not easily agree to sit down together, so a firm and helpful conciliator is often needed. Both sides have been deeply committed before their publics by this point, making it hard to climb down from established perceptions and positions. Such an effort is also particularly difficult because it is not a brief one-shot activity; it needs sustained attention to overcome the hardened perceptions and reverse the sharpened policies, and that requires repeated, not too far spaced meetings, a suspension of actions that might be interpreted as hostile, and an effort to use external events positively, as an occasion to meet, explain and work out common responses. Measures to be accomplished include a cooling-off period, a disengagement of forces, joint study and cooperative measures, and a hard look at grievances and images, as accomplished by the various Pugwash and Dartmouth Conferences of the Kettering Foundation between the US and the USSR (Vorhees 2002), and more recently in the Inter-Tajik Dialog and the Israeli-Palestinian dialog initiatives (Saunders 1999).

Three challenges mark this effort. The first is for the external party to achieve welcome entry into the impending conflict. International organizations, friendly states and nongovernmental organizations (NGOs) need to develop the sense among the parties that current policy is heading to costly deadlock and that problems and perceptions are better handled positively. The second challenge concerns the amount of pressure, including sanctions, to apply. Third parties arranging confrontation to head off violence cannot be limited to good counsel; advice needs to be accompanied by incentives against defection from the path of reconciliation. Too little pressure leaves the course of conflict costless, but too much pressure arouses a defensive reaction and closes the door to external attentions. A third challenge lies in the search for appropriate ways for the parties to back down, to explain to their publics that they are sitting down with and then assuaging the very parties that they claimed were posing a security threat.

Ripening is required if the parties do not feel themselves to be caught in a mutually hurting stalemate that pushes them to begin lowering tensions (Crocker 1992; Zartman 2000, 2010). Conflicting parties do not look for a way out of a conflict if they think they can win and if the conflict is not hurting them. Therefore to open their minds to pre-crisis prevention, whether before the conflict has turned violent or after, they must be made aware that winning is rare and attempts to win costly; in other words, the conflict must be ripened for prevention in their perceptions. This is a primary challenge for external parties.

The perception of stalemate is enhanced by measures to show that victory is rarely possible and if possible, is rarely stable and costless – for example, that coveted territory cannot be seized and even if it is, the conquest will not be recognized, as in the case of Israeli occupation of the West Bank and the Golan Heights, or that cleansing an ethnic group will be prevented and even if it is not, the resulting political arrangement will not be recognized, as in the case of the Serbian attempted absorption of Kosovo. The perception of cost is enhanced by measures to make the parties realize that the conflict entails penalties larger than expected benefits, that the opponent can offer a more costly resistance than expected and that continued conflict will be met by sanctions and withheld recognition, as in the 1988 Iran–Iraq ceasefire. In sum, negotiators seeking to ripen identity conflicts for prevention need to muster enormous skills of persuasion, but they may also need to create objective facts on the ground to enhance the subjective perception of ripeness.

Mediation is appropriate when there is a limited number of clear sides and when the interests of all need to be incorporated in ending violence and remaking a functioning political system (Stenlo 1972; Rubin 1981; Touval and Zartman 1985; Kressel and Pruitt 1989; Berccovitch and Rubin 1992; Bercovitch 1996, 2006). Mediated negotiations require authorized spokesmen for the various sides and a small number of parties, as seen in the Dayton mediation over Bosnia in 1995 (Holbrooke 1998; O'Brien 2005) or the Oslo negotiation between Israel and the PLO in 1993 (Corbin 1994). Mediation, like any negotiation, implies legitimacy of the parties and their interests, equality of the parties in standing (even if not in power), a mutual sense of stalemate in unilateral attempts to win the conflict and a recognition that none of the parties is seeking suicide.

The purpose of mediation is to help the parties overcome obstacles to their own direct negotiation of conflict reduction. Obstacles can come in three forms, each requiring a particular type of mediation. If the conflicting parties simply cannot talk to each other, for physical or political reasons, a mediator as a communicator – sometimes termed a facilitator – is needed to carry messages but not to be substantively involved in the negotiations, much as the Norwegians did in most of the Oslo talks in 1993. If the communicating but conflicting parties have no ideas on how to prevent further escalation and violence, then a mediator as a formulator is needed to help find formulas for agreement; more than just procedurally, the mediator is now substantively involved, supplying ideas for solutions, as did Ambassador Richard Holbrooke in Bosnia in 1995. But if the stakes are not large enough to attract agreement or the parties not strong enough to stay in the negotiations, then a mediator as a manipulator is needed; here the mediator is deeply engaged in the process, not directly as a party to the conflict but as a party in the solution, as was the US under Secretaries Kissinger and Baker in the Middle East.

Pre-emptive accountability is not negotiation and it may actually impede negotiation, but it is necessary to consider in order to prevent the implantation of a culture of impunity that facilitates further conflict. The national heroic status in interstate conflicts, whether victorious or – curiously – defeated, tends to encourage emulation and, if necessary, another try. International judicial enforcement of the ban on crimes against humanity and genocide works best as a threat to counter this tendency, although like any threat, it works best when not used often. But it must be used on occasion to make its threat credible. On the other hand, judicial accountability can operate as a strong impediment to peaceful conclusion of interstate conflict, since leaders who know they will be indicted while the war is going on are unlikely to consider measures to end the war to be attractive. As a result, indictments should be issued only once the subject is already captured. It is difficult to assess the use of judgment preventively, since it is hard to find instances where the threat of indictment kept a war from arising, but a few successful uses can be surmised to make rulers think before engaging on violent conflict.

27.3.3   Late Post-Crisis Prevention

It may seem odd to talk of prevention after conflict, but to do so recognizes the need to take steps to close the current conflict and to prevent it from recurring, in the same way as Boutros Ghali (1992) spoke of peace-building as both healing and preventing. Additional measures used beyond those discussed above include *separation and power-sharing, monitoring and reconstruction*, and *reconciliation and remediation*, once violence has been brought under control.

Separation and power-sharing are formulas for negotiation to prevent conflicts, giving space and time for more harmonious relations to develop. They can be used in negotiations in pre-crisis mode, during a crisis, and emerging from a crisis. Separation pulls the conflicting parties apart, giving them space to breathe and room to reflect; it reduces the danger of a security dilemma that occurs when countries take measures to improve their security and in so doing threaten the security of their neighbors, who react in the same way, threatening the others' security and so on. Separation must be accomplished by negotiation with the parties; forced separation of intermingled populations, particularly under harsh conditions, is ethnic cleansing, a form of identity conflict and a low-level form of genocide, depending on the number of deaths the forced migration brings.

Separation may take the form of a pause or delay in impending pre-crisis developments, a truce, ceasefire, safe havens, buffer zones or disengagement in the midst of conflict that threatens to escalate, or withdrawal and cantonments as conflict ends. It can be the outcome of negotiation arising from a sense of stalemate and loss on both sides in the conflict. Separation can be carried out by the original instigators of the conflict having come to their senses, or by a moderate faction that has taken over and led the conflicting party or government into a more constructive direction. Separation is particularly useful as a longer-term solution to prevent future conflict in interstate conflicts that concern national minorities across the border, either before or after crisis, in the form of autonomy or some other form of regional self-government (Hannum 1990; Lapidoth 1997; Ghai 2000) or, less frequently, through consociational power-sharing (Lijphart 1977). Transnational minorities, such as the Basques, Kurds, Tyroleans and Serbs, among others, were given autonomous self-government (under whatever name) to prevent conflict between the host and home states in Spain, Iraq, Italy and Kosovo. It has sometimes been objected that autonomy merely leads to secession, but the record shows that it is annulled autonomy that leads to demands for secession, as in Eritrea, Sudan, Nigeria and Kosovo.

Sharing power, on the other hand, brings the parties together as separate groups, assuring them a role in government. Power can be shared legislatively or executively, through separate reserved seats, quotas and assigned roles in legislative bodies, or through an executive coalition of identity-group representatives, in a consociational form of government, respectively. As noted, power-sharing is actually a form of separation in that it freezes the identity group divisions in society and accords them participation in governance only through their representatives, precluding the possibility of gradually erasing the salience of separate identities in politics.

Despite extensive academic discussions, power-sharing is less utilized than recommended, at any stage of conflict, although there are a few examples. Preventive power-sharing among identity groups brought decades of peace to Lebanon before it fell apart due to demographic and generational changes among the groups; it was the key to a durable regional settlement in South Tyrol/Alto Adige in Italy in 1969, a fragile federalized system in Belgium after 1970 and a shaky conflict management in the Good Friday Agreement of 1998 in Northern Ireland. To work effectively to prevent interstate conflict, the "home" state must accept that its protector role of the transborder community is satisfied by the separate or sharing status in the host state.

Peace-keeping forces (PKFs) can be used preventively to separate the parties, either before, during or after violent conflict (Diehl 2009). Peacekeeping as "early late" prevention can help defuse a situation nearing violence by introducing a tripwire, removing from either party the excuse that they are merely responding to the other's provocation. Less recognized is a moment within violent conflict when the parties pause, temporarily exhausted, leaving an opportunity for the introduction of separating PKFs before they can regroup, rearm and pick up the offensive. After hostilities, PKFs monitor and, with a proper mandate, enforce the ceasefire. PKFs provided an unusual example of pre-crisis interposition in Macedonia in 1992–98 as UNPREDEP and in 2001 as a NATO preventive deployment. A crucial occasion for a PKF in a mid-conflict calm in inter-group/inter-partisan conflict in Congo-Brazzaville in 1997 was turned down by the Security Council, which ordered a study of African conflicts instead (Zartman 1998)!

Monitoring and reconstruction constitute crucial and neglected links between successful pre-crisis prevention and "normal politics." The natural human tendency is to declare victory, with self-congratulations, and to go on to other conflicts, leaving the averted conflict to disappear or resume on its own. Conflict relations cause damages that need repairs and contain unresolved details that can bring the conflict back again;

preventive negotiation requires provision for an intense surge of material help and attention, requiring sustained international support for their implementation over a substantial period of time. This is particularly true when the conflict has been managed, as with a ceasefire, rather than resolved, with a comprehensive agreement, as in the cases of Nagorno Karabakh or Morocco–Algeria, for example. For these reasons, preventive agreements need to contain not only scheduled implementation commitments but also scheduled monitoring commitments from third parties – states, international organizations and/or NGOs, such as UNMEE and the boundary commission in Ethiopian–Eritrean post-conflict relations. Monitoring requires sufficient numbers of observers with appropriate mandates and rules of engagement, operating on sufficient budgets, with continuing diplomatic and civilian attention to the problems of carrying out the initial agreement; the monitoring of the 1999 Lusaka Agreement among the Democratic Republic of the Congo and its neighbors by the UN Mission to the Congo (MONUC) was deficient on every count – mandate, rules of engagement, money, troops.

Reconciliation and remediation are necessary to prevent further interstate conflicts. Both are long processes but need attention, lest it be thought that violent conflicts are contained incidents with neither antecedents nor consequences, neither causes nor impacts (Hayner 2000, 2001). Interdependent projects and cooperation need to be negotiated and relations and histories need to be reexamined. Atonement and forgiveness are key elements in burying the conflict, and they require specific gestures, not simply passive page turning. Wounds untreated fester rather than becoming scars; since scars never disappear, they cannot be ignored and need gentle treatment. Efforts at reconciliation must come from within the society, but they can be encouraged from the outside, notably by NGOs as well as external official actions. Interstate truth and reconciliation commissions (TRCs) are an applicable institution to be set up by negotiation in many cases; internal and external NGOs can also hold sessions conducive to reconciliation. Joint learning experiences for youth, either within integrated educational institutions or in special programs abroad, can also be helpful, but they must be accompanied by organized follow-up exercises; revision of school texts, as undertaken by Europeans and by Israelis (not yet Arabs), is important. The key to effective reconciliation is a common project that engages the formerly conflicting parties in cooperative efforts and focuses their attention on a common goal of joint benefit; of this the joint efforts of France and Germany in building Europe, leading to the European Union (EUI), provide the best example.

27.4   PROBLEMS

It is hard to document prevention. The fact that something did not happen is prima facie evidence that it was not going to happen anyhow. For that reason, prevention is often hard to justify until it is too late (and so not longer prevention), since, in early late and post conflict cases at least, it means interference in policies a state believes are required for its security. Preventing conflicts not yet violent from becoming so amounts to telling sovereign states not to pursue their conflict with external enemies (Zartman 2010; Anstey, Meerts and Zartman 2010). The UN doctrine on peacekeeping, as constituted in "Article VI 1/2" not written in the Charter, is that PKFs are rigorously held to keeping a peace already agreed to rather than intervening in situations of violence; the Mission of the UN in Congo (MONUC) has stretched this doctrine toward intervention when it learned that no peace had been agreed to in Eastern Congo, but possible UN prevention was dodged in 1997 in Congo-Brazzaville on the grounds that peace had not taken hold. Governments carrying out a policy of violent conflict against an identified – and, almost necessarily, demonized – external enemy are not likely to take kindly to external attempts to interfere with their efforts for the defense of the country or regime.

"What to prevent when" is a major operative as well as conceptual question. Early prevention is the most difficult to justify, for the chances of the foreseen event's taking place are highly uncertain and, if prevented, can never be proven. Commentators call for early action to validate early warning, but the guarantee that a tropical storm warning will turn into a tropical storm is elusive (Zartman and Faure 2005). Warnings and intervention to prevent Israel from carrying out expansionist policies that arguably will take it to Masada, or Egypt from carrying out repressive policies that predictably will introduce a Muslim Brotherhood takeover, or Iran from carrying out nuclear policies that will assuredly feed their persecution complex inevitably complicate attempts to cultivate better relations with respective countries. On the other hand, "early late" prevention efforts, before the conflict has reached the crisis or "too late" stage, have major obstacles of overcommitment to overcome, that earlier action would have avoided. Yet so much conflict has been prevented that it is inexcusable not to learn its lessons and mechanisms to apply them to the instances that continue to appear.

REFERENCES

Anstey, M., P. Meerts and I.W. Zartman (eds) (2010), *Reducing Identity Conflicts and Preventing Genocide*, Oxford, UK: Oxford University Press.

Axelrod, R. (1970), *Conflict of Interest*, Chicago, IL: Markham.

Ayissi, A. (2001), "Territorial conflicts: claiming the land', in I.W. Zartman, (ed.), *Preventive Negotiation: Avoiding Conflict Escalation*, Lanham, MD: Rowman & Littlefield Publishers, Inc., pp. 41–66.

Bercovitch, J. (2006), "Mediation in international conflicts: theory, practice, and developments", in I.W. Zartman (ed.), *Peacemaking in International Conflict*, Washington DC: USIP, pp. 163–94.

Bercovitch, J. (ed.) (1996), *Resolving International Conflicts*, Boulder, CO: Lynne Rienner.

Bercovitch, J. and J.Z. Rubin (eds) (1992), *Mediation in International Relations*, New York, NY: Palgrave Macmillan.

Boutros Ghali, B. (1992), *Agenda for Peace*, New York, NY: United Nations.

Brams, S. (1985), *Superpower Games*, New Haven, CT: Yale University Press.

Brecher, M. (1993), *Crises in World Politics*, Oxford, UK: Pergamon.

Corbin, J. (1994), *The Norway Channel*, New York, NY: Atlantic Monthly Press.

Crocker, C.A. (1992), *High Noon in Southern Africa*, New York, NY: Norton.

Deng, F. and R. Cohen (1998), *Guiding Principles on Internal Displacement*, New York, NY: United Nations.

Diehl, P. (2009), "Peacekeeping and beyond", in J. Bercovitch, V. Kremenyuk and I.W. Zartman (eds), *Handbook of Conflict Resolution*, London: Sage Publications, pp. 525–42.

Dorn, W. (2004), "Early and late warning by the UN Secretary-General", in D. Carment and A. Schnable (eds), *Conflict Prevention from Rhetoric to Reality*, Lanham, MD: Lexington Books, pp. 305–44.

Evans, G. (2008), *The Responsibility to Protect*, Washington DC: Brookings Institution Press.

Evans, G. and M. Sahnoun (eds) (2001), *The Responsibility to Protect*, Ottawa, Canada: International Committee on Intervention and State Sovereignty.

Ghai, Y. (2000), "Autonomy as a strategy for diffusing conflict", in P.C. Stern and D. Druckman (eds), *International Conflict Resolution After the Cold War*, Washington DC: The National Academic Press, pp. 483–530.

Goodby, J. and V. Kremenyuk (2001), "Global security conflicts I: controlling arms races", in I.W. Zartman (ed.), *Preventive Negotiation: Avoiding Conflict Escalation*, Lanham, MD: Rowman & Littlefield Publishers, Inc., pp. 243–62.

Goldstein, J.A. (2010), "Chicken dilemmas: crossing the road to cooperation", in I.W. Zartman and S. Touval (eds), *International Cooperation: The Extents and Limits of Multilateralism*, Cambridge, MA: Cambridge University Press, pp. 135–60.

Hamburg, D. (2008), *Preventing Genocide*, Boulder, CO: Paradigm Publishers.

Hannum, H. (1990), *Autonomy, Sovereignty and Self-Determination*, Philadelphia, PA: University of Pennsylvania Press.

Hasenclever, A., P. Mayer and V. Rittberger (1997), *Theories of International Regimes*, New York, NY: Cambridge University Press.

Hayner, P. (2000), "Past truths, past dangers: the role of official truth seeking in conflict resolution and prevention", in P. Stern and D. Druckman (eds), *International Conflict Resolution after the Cold War*, Washington DC: National Academy Press.

Hayner, P. (2001), *Unspeakable Truths: Confronting State Terror and Atrocity*, New York, NY: Routledge.

Holbrooke, R. (1998), *To End a War*, New York, NY: Random House.

Holl, J.E. (ed.) (1997), *Preventing Deadly Conflict*, Washington DC: Carnegie Commission.

Homans, C. (1961), *Social Behavior*, New York, NY: Harcourt, Brace & World.

Hopmann, P.T. (2001), "Disintegrating states: separating without violence", in I.W. Zartman (ed.), *Preventive Negotiation: Avoiding Conflict Escalation*, Lanham: Rowman & Littlefield Publishers, Inc., pp. 113–64.

Jentleson, B. (ed.) (2000), *Opportunities Missed, Opportunities Seized*, New York, NY: Rowman & Littlefield Publishers, Inc.

Kissinger, H.A. (1965), *The Troubled Partnership: A Re-Appraisal of the Atlantic Alliance*, New York, NY: McGraw Hill.

Krasner, S. (ed.) (1983), *International Regimes*, Ithaca, NY: Cornell University Press.

Kressel, K. and D.G. Pruitt (eds) (1989), *Mediation Research*, New York, NY: Jossey-Bass.

Lapidoth, R. (1997), *Autonomy*, Washington DC: USIP.

Lijphart, A. (1977), *Democracy in Plural Societies*, New Haven, CT: Yale University Press.

Lund, M. (1996), *Preventing Violent Conflicts*, Washington DC: USIP.

Meerts, P., M. Melamud and F.O. Hampson (2010), *Negotiating the Comprehensive Test Ban*, Austria: IIASA.

Miyakazi (2000), *Miyakazi Initiative for Conflict Prevention*, Miyakazi, Japan: G-8.

Mooradian, M. and D. Druckman (1999), "Hurting stalemate or mediation?", *Journal of Peace Research*, **36** (6), 709–27.

Nordquist, K.Å. (2000). "Boundary disputes: drawing the line", in I.W. Zartman (ed.), *Preventive Diplomacy: Avoiding Conflict Escalation*, Lanham, MD: Rowman and Littlefield Publishers, Inc., pp. 19–40.

O'Brien, J. (2005), "The Dayton Agreement in Bosnia", in I.W. Zartman and V. Kremenyuk (eds), *Peace Versus Justice*, Lanham, MD: Rowman & Littlefield, pp. 89–112.

Pillar, P. (1983), *Negotiating Peace*, Princeton, NJ: Princeton University Press.

Prinzen, Thomas (1992), *Intermediaries in International Conflict*, Princeton, NJ: Princeton University Press.

Rubin, J.Z. (ed.) (1981), *The Dynamics of Third Party Intervention*, New York, NY: Praeger.

Rothchild, D., F.M. Deng, I.W. Zartman, S. Kimaro and T. Lyons (1996), *Sovereignty as Responsibility*, Washington DC: Brookings Institution Press.

Saunders, H. (1999), *A Public Peace Process*, New York, NY: St Martin's Press.

Snyder, G. and Paul Diesing (1969), *Conflict Among Nations*, Princeton, NJ: Princeton University Press.

Spector, B.I. and I.W. Zartman (eds) (2003), *Getting It Done: Post-Agreement Negotiations and International Regimes*, Washington DC: USIP.

Stenelo, L. (1972), *Mediation in International Negotiations*, Malmö, Sweden: Nordens Boktryckeri.

Swedish Ministry of Foreign Affairs (1997), *Conflict Prevention*, Stockholm, Sweden: Swedish Ministry of Foreign Affairs.

Swedish Ministry of Foreign Affairs (1999), *Preventing Violent Conflict*, Stockholm, Sweden: Swedish Ministry of Foreign Affairs.

Toft, M. (2003), *The Geography of Ethnic Violence*, Princeton, NJ: Princeton University Press.

Touval, S. and I.W. Zartman (eds) (1985), *International Mediation in Theory and Practice*, Nashville, TN: Westview Publishing Co.

UCDP (2010), "Conflict Trends", Uppsala Conflict Data Project, University of Uppsala.

United Nations (2004), "A more secure world: Our shared responsibility", Report of the Secretary-General's High-level Panel; on Threats, Challenges and Change, New York: United Nations.

Vasquez, J. and B. Valeriano (2009), "Territory as a source of conflict and a road to peace", in J. Bercovitch, V. Kremenyuk and I.W. Zartman (eds), *Handbook of Conflict Resolution*, London: Sage Publication, pp. 193–209.

Verstegen, S. (1999), "Conflict prognostication: toward a tentative framework for conflict assessment, Mimeo, The Hague.

Vorhees, J. (2002), *Dialog Sustained: The Multilevel Peace Process and the Dartmouth Conference*, Washington DC: USIP.

Walton, R.E. and R.B. McKersie (1965), *A Behavioral Theory of Labor Negotiations*, New York, NY: McGraw Hill.

Zartman, I.W. (1989), *Ripe for Resolution*, Oxford, UK: Oxford University Press.

Zartman, I.W. (1998) "An apology needs a pledge", *New York Times*, 2 April 1998.

Zartman, I.W. (2000), "Beyond the hurting stalemate", in P.C. Stern and D. Druckman (eds.), *International Conflict Resolution after the Cold War*, Washington DC: National Academy Press, pp. 225–50.

Zartman, I.W. (ed.) (2001), *Preventive Negotiation: Avoiding Conflict Escalation*, Lanham, MD: Rowman & Littlefield Publishers, Inc.

Zartman, I.W. (2005), *Cowardly Lions: Missed Opportunities to Prevent Deadly Conflict and State Collapse*, Boulder, CO: Lynne Rienner Publishers.

Zartman, I.W. (ed.) (2009), *Imbalance of Power: US Hegemony and International Order*, Boulder, CO: Lynne Rienner Publishers.

Zartman, I.W. (2010), *Preventing Identity Conflicts leading to Genocide and Mass Killings*, New York, NY: International Peace Institute.

Zartman, I.W. and G.O. Faure (eds) (2004), *The Dynamics of Escalation and Negotiation*, Ann Arbour, MI: University of Michigan Press.

Zartman, I.W. and A. de Soto (2010), *The Timing of Peace Initiatives: Hurting Stalemates and Ripe Moments*, Washington DC: USIP.

Zartman, I.W and S. Touval (2007), "International mediation", in C.A. Crocker, F.O. Hampson, P.R. Aall (eds), *Leasing the Dogs of War: Conflict Management in a Divided World*, Washington DC: United States Institute of Peace Press, pp. 437–54.

28 The economics of peacekeeping
Lloyd J. Dumas

28.1 INTRODUCTION

There is a certain ambiguity to the term "peacekeeping," and therefore to the meaning of the "economics of peacekeeping." On the one hand, there is the idea of peacekeeping as preventing the eruption (or more frequently, the re-eruption) of violent conflict in areas where the cessation of hostilities is tenuous and the peace is fragile. In these circumstances, peacekeeping typically means operations in which armed third party military forces, such as the famous "Blue Helmets" of the United Nations, are interposed between the armed forces of two groups recently engaged in war or threatening to war with each other. The support of such peacekeeping forces involves a variety of issues that have economic implications, including financing the forces and their logistical requirements, as well as the impact the presence of these forces may have on the local economy where they are deployed. The economics of peacekeeping in this sense is not all that different from the economics of supporting comparable military forces with a more conventional military mission.

On the other hand, there is the deeper and much more compelling issue of "peacekeeping" that is the sense of generalized war prevention. In this context, the "economics of peacekeeping" takes the form of the intriguing political economic question of whether economic relationships are capable of creating positive incentives to avoid war, and if so how these incentives might be made stronger and more effective. It is on this latter, more promising and consequential issue that we focus here.

28.2 BACKGROUND LITERATURE

The role of economic relationships has long been an important area of disagreement about the causes of war between the so-called realist-neorealist school and the liberal-neoliberal school, contained largely within the literature of political science. Realists believe that the nation state is the principle actor in an international system that, lacking any overarching global political authority, is largely anarchic. Because nation states are inherently conflictual, in such an anarchic world a nation that is powerful and thus dominant has a great advantage. Therefore, even if trade produces benefits for all trading partners, realists believe that trade will weaken the position (and therefore the security) of those states that gain relatively less. Liberals, however, focus more on the individual than the state. They believe that ongoing stable cooperation among the people and governments of different nations is not only possible but also desirable. Like the realists, they recognize that the gains from international trade are, for the most part, not equally distributed. But they believe that if the gains are large enough, trade will still be a binding force in the international system as long as all the trading partners experience some absolute gain. Keohane [1990, p. 185] points out that liberals so often stress institution building not because they are naïve about "harmony among people," but because they fundamentally agree with realists that a world without rules or institutions would be "a jungle in which governments seek to weaken one another economically and militarily, leading to continual strife and frequent warfare."

Old school realists such as Morgenthau (1973) argue that it is rational for a nation to accumulate national power for its own sake, while neorealists such as Waltz (1988) do not so much see national power as an end in itself but rather as a means for achieving security and other less crucial national goals. But realists and neorealists both agree that the distribution of power is the key issue in keeping the peace. They see economic relationships as either irrelevant to the question of war and peace or they believe that the differential gains these relationships generate are more likely to provoke war than prevent it. Jean Jacques Rousseau long ago argued that the inequality fostered by the unequal gains of trade was dangerous, so that "interdependence breeds not accommodation and harmony, but suspicion and incompatibility" (Hoffman 1963, p. 319).

In the realist view, because economic interdependence gives other nations the ability to coerce a state by threatening to reduce or cut off trade, it creates weakness, vulnerability and hence insecurity – especially if the advantage in the trade lies with the nation's trading partners. Gilpin (1977) argues that realists find economic interdependence particularly threatening when it involves reliance on other states for key strategic goods such as military equipment, or for resources such as oil on which both the military sector and the economy as a whole are dependent. The security-reducing effects of unbalanced dependence in the trade of strategic goods make the outbreak of war more likely.

Both realists and liberals agree that cooperation is more desirable than conflict; the difference between them lies in the issue of whether cooperation is likely to occur. Although liberals recognize that there is no overarching international political authority, they see the international arena as more stable and the actors within it more prone to self-interested cooperation than do realists. Liberals believe that the state is not a unitary entity with a well-defined national interest, as the realists contend, but argue that the interaction of individual and organizational actors within nations, engaging in behaviors that cut across nations, constitutes a form of "transnational" relations that undercuts the centrality of the state (for example, see Keohane and Martin 1995). International business and economic relationships can be considered among the most important transnational behaviors.

Liberals are clearly not as convinced as realists that the combination of anarchy and unequal distribution of the gains from international trade is a recipe for ongoing interstate conflict. Keohane and Martin (1995) lay heavy emphasis on building institutions, which are defined as formal or informal organizations to which nations voluntarily belong because of the benefits of cooperation. Of course, many international organizations and arrangements have already been created, a substantial fraction of which are intimately concerned with the support of international economic relationships – perhaps most notably including the World Trade Organization and the European Union, along with international agreements on airlines, the mails and the environment.

Perhaps the best illustration of how independent units, uncoordinated by any central authority, can and do find ways of cooperating to their mutual advantage is the market system itself. After all, markets amount to a network of ongoing, voluntary cooperative interactions that take place among economic units. The glue that holds the market system together is an incentive structure that plays on self-interest. There is no sovereign to compel cooperation, but there is a system of norms of behavior, which can be usefully reinforced by agreed institutions, such as contract law and systems of adjudication of contract disputes. The meaningful enforcement of some of these supporting institutions (such as contract law) on subnational actors (such as firms) can be accomplished by national institutions, even in the absence of international government or institutions. It is certainly possible that states operating under the right set of incentives can also find creative ways of cooperating and enforcing key economic and peacekeeping agreements without establishing anything remotely resembling world government.

Keohane [1990] points out that early economic liberals (for example, Baron de Montesquieu) argued that "the natural effect of commerce is to lead to peace," but were not all that specific as to how that connection operated. In the twentieth century, liberalism focused on the idea that international trade would inhibit war because widening trade made war a more costly and less effective means of pursuing the self-interest of states.

Perhaps the best and most comprehensive version of this argument was made in Rosecrance (1986, p. 24–5):

> While trading states try to improve their condition and their own domestic allocation of resources, they do so within a context of accepted interdependence. They recognize that the attempt to provide every service and fulfill every function of statehood on an independent and autonomous basis is extremely inefficient, and they prefer a situation which provides for specialization and a division of labor among nations. One nation's attempt to improve its own access to products and resources, therefore does not conflict with another state's attempt to do the same. The incentive to wage war is absent in such a system for war disrupts trade and the interdependence on which trade is based.

A reinforcing set of ideas that McMillan (1997) calls "sociological liberalism" emphasizes the importance of the connections among people that form in the course of commercial relationships. The idea is that the communication and cooperation that continuing economic relationships require will increase people's knowledge and appreciation of each other, their customs and culture, undoing stereotypes and reducing violent confrontations. Of course, frequent close contacts among people could lead to more rather than fewer conflicts among them if their interests or behaviors were not compatible. Even so, Deutsch (1968) argues that "conflicts can still be reduced by increasing the salience and weight of parallel or interlocking interests among the countries concerned," making collaboration so rewarding that it has the potential to overcome tendencies toward conflict.

After reviewing a diverse group of 20 empirical studies bearing on the realist/liberal debate, McMillan (1997) reports that only four were consistent with the realist contention that greater international interdependence either had no effect on military conflict or actually made it more likely, while ten supported the liberal hypothesis that increased economic interdependence was associated with less military conflict. The other six studies produced either mixed results or results that were conditional. Empirical analyses supporting the realist-neorealist view include Russett (1967), Uchitel (1993), and Barbieri (1996); those supporting the liberal-neoliberal view include Azar (1980), Polachek (1980) and Oneal et al. (1996).

Up to this point, we have focused primarily on the connection between economic relationships and international war. Although it has become commonplace to think of civil wars, at least in modern times, as being caused by deep-seated social grievances, ideological rivalries and ethnic hatreds, the fact is economic agendas can and do play an important role here as well. Collier [2000, p. 91] writes, "I have investigated statistically the global pattern of large-scale civil conflict since 1965, expecting to find a close relationship between measures of . . . [intergroup] hatreds and grievances and the incidence of conflict. Instead, I found that economic agendas appear to be central to understanding why civil wars start." Based on his analysis of a sample of twentieth century civil wars, Reno (2000, p. 64) goes farther arguing that "Experiences in Sierra Leone, Liberia, Sudan, Somalia, El Salvador, Chechnya and Cambodia show that the economic interests of belligerents may be a powerful barrier to the termination of conflict. They may use war to control land and commerce, exploit labor, milk charitable agencies, and ensure the continuity of assets and privileges to a group."

28.3   THE PRINCIPLES OF PEACEKEEPING ECONOMICS

The realist-neorealist and liberal-neoliberal schools of thought are not entirely incompatible. They illuminate different key aspects of the real connection between economic relationships and war. From liberals comes the importance of interdependent economic relationships in creating positive incentives to avoid conflict; the possibility that the personal interactions involved in ongoing economic relationships can help to strengthen those incentives; and the importance of seeing international relations as consisting of relationships between individuals and organizations reaching across national boundaries, as well as relationships between nation states. From realists comes the importance of paying attention to how equally the gains of trade are distributed; the strategic risk involved in depending too heavily on foreign sources of supply of goods vital to the nation; the importance of power, and the value of a certain healthy skepticism about the assumption that nations will always act in a purely economically self-interested way.

Based on this understanding, it is possible to formulate a series of sensible economic principles of peacekeeping from the apparently conflicting perspectives of the two-sides of this longstanding intellectual debate. Economic relationships based on these principles should be useful in helping to prevent the outbreak of both international and civil war.

28.3.1   Principle I: Create Balanced, Mutually Beneficial Economic Relationships

Economic relationships are capable of helping to prevent or provoke war. Which they actually do depends more on their nature than their extent. Exploitative relationships, those in which one party benefits much more than the other, tend to provoke hostility and conflict because they are inherently unfair. Even if those being exploited gain something, the fact that the flow of benefit is overwhelmingly in the other direction is bound to create or aggravate antagonisms. That is even more obvious if those being exploited are suffering a net loss. The Age of Empire offers many examples of lop-sided colonial relationships that eventually built up hostilities to the point of war. The revolution that gave birth to the United States is one clear example of the power of economic exploitation (or even the perception of such exploitation) to build up tensions that can lead to war.

Because those who are the targets of exploitative relationships are gaining little if anything from them, they have an incentive to try to disrupt, destroy or at least fundamentally restructure them. They might also feel compelled to strike back for purposes of revenge. Since they have little to lose and may actually gain if the relationship collapses, the exploited are often ready to raise the intensity of whatever economic or other conflicts might occur to the breaking point. If those dominating them come under stress from external sources, the exploited have a strong incentive to take advantage of the pre-occupation of their exploiters to try to balance their relationship or tear it apart. The exploiters, of course know this, and it is a great source of insecurity for them, especially if their economy has become reliant on the relationship. As a result, those who have the upper hand feel compelled to put an extraordinary amount of effort into maintaining control, often at much greater expense than they expected. This can turn what initially looked to them like a beneficial economic relationship into a serious net drain on their nation as a whole, economically and otherwise.

In contrast, the flow of benefit in balanced relationships is more or less equal in both directions. Because balanced relationships are fair and mutually beneficial, they do not tend to provoke antagonism. On the contrary, as each party begins to realize how much they are actually gaining, they start to see the welfare of the other party as in their own best interests. The mutual flow of benefits ties the parties together. Because they all benefit more or less equally, they will all be more likely to look for ways of maintaining or strengthening the relationship, out of simple self-interest. When serious disagreements do occur, they will have a strong incentive to try to avoid disruption by settling them amicably. If their partners come under stress from external sources, they will have an incentive to help relieve, rather than aggravate, the pressure. Everyone in the relationship will feel more secure; no one will feel the need to expend a great deal of extra effort and expense just to keep it going. Put simply, *a balanced relationship is a more efficient relationship: the benefits are achieved at a much lower cost.*

Though he was not particularly focused on the implications of balanced versus exploitative relationships for war and peace, Adam Smith saw this clearly more than 230 years ago. In the founding book of capitalism, *The*

Wealth of Nations (published in 1776), Smith ([1776] 1937, pp. 581–2) wrote of the British colonial empire:

> 'Under the present system of management . . . Great Britain derives nothing but loss from the dominion which she assumes over her colonies.
> . . . Great Britain should voluntarily give up all authority over her colonies . . . [She] would not only be immediately freed from the whole annual expense of the peace establishment of the colonies, but might settle with them such a treaty of commerce as would effectually secure to her a free trade, more advantageous to the great body of the people [of Britain] . . . than the monopoly which she at present enjoys.'

Balanced gain is not the only important dimension of balanced relationships. There also need to be a balance of decision-making power. If the decision-making process in the relationship is unbalanced, those with less influence and control may feel that they are unduly dependent on the good graces of the others. Even if gain is balanced now, feeling that the terms of the relationship can be changed arbitrarily and unilaterally in the future creates insecurity and reduces commitment. When there is a more equitable decision-making structure, everyone involved has more of a feeling of ownership in the relationship. It belongs to them; it is not simply a gift someone has granted them and can just as easily withdraw. As a result, every participant will feel a greater sense of responsibility for taking care of the relationship, for insuring its continuation and success. This will also strengthen the incentives of all participants to find peaceful ways of settling the conflicts they will inevitably have with each other from time to time.

It is a fundamental tenet of capitalism that ownership of a wealth-generating asset promotes responsible and efficient use. There is no reason why that should be any less true of a valuable wealth-generating relationship than it is for a piece of tangible property. On the other hand, a lack of fairness and balance in the power to make decisions over economic relationships can contribute to building up political and economic tensions that can eventually lead to war. The alienating power of not having a say over the terms of an economic relationship is, for example, illustrated by one of the most famous American pre-revolutionary war slogans: "Taxation *without representation* is tyranny" (emphasis added).

The effectiveness of mutually beneficial, balanced economic relationships in keeping the peace is illustrated by the development and growth of the European Economic Community (EEC), forerunner of today's European Union (EU). The EEC began as the European Coal and Steel Community (ECSC) formed by six nations in 1952, only a few years after World War II had destroyed much of Europe. Having suffered through two devastating wars in only three decades, the Europeans' explicit goal in creating the ECSC was to build economic bonds (especially between France and Germany) to make the outbreak of another war among them less likely (Rittberger 2001). Within 30 years, the dozen nations that belonged to the EEC included Belgium, France, Germany, Great Britain, Italy, the Netherlands, Portugal and Spain. These nations not only had gone to war with each other repeatedly over the centuries (including World Wars I and II), they were also major colonial powers that militarily dominated and exploited much of the rest of the world. Yet because of the web of balanced mutually beneficial economic relationships in which they are enmeshed today, the odds of any of these countries fighting a war *with each other* over the next 50 years have become vanishingly small.

It is important to note that this is not because the EU nations have lost their interest in military matters or their willingness to fight. France has intervened militarily in Africa more than once since the 1970s (for example, in Ivory Coast). Britain fought a war with Argentina over the Falkland (Malvinas) Islands in the early 1980s. As members of the NATO military alliance, all of these nations were directly or indirectly involved in NATO's bombing of Kosovo in the late 1990s and it subsequent occupation. Troops from Britain, Italy, the Netherlands and Spain were part of the US-led invasion and occupation of Iraq that began in 2003; and seven years later, the NATO nations continue to be engaged in an ongoing war in Afghanistan.

It is also not as though these countries no longer have conflicts with each other. They have quite a few, economic and otherwise, some of them serious. In the last few years alone, there was the controversy about the banning of British beef by other EU member states because of "mad cow" disease in Britain; continuing disputes over the adoption of the single European currency (the euro); a sharp split over the 2003 war in Iraq (with the governments of Britain, the Netherlands and Spain strongly in support and those of France, Germany and Belgium strongly opposed); and ongoing arguments over immigration policy. Yet the EU nations understand that the web of balanced, mutually beneficial economic relationships they have created with each other gives them a strong reason to find ways to manage, and if possible resolve the conflicts they have with each other. They have too much to lose to let their disagreements get out of control. So they debate and they argue, but they no longer threaten – or even think about threatening – each other with war.

28.3.2   Principle II: Seek Independence in Critical Goods

The liberal strategy of maximizing economic interdependence seems like an effective approach to preventing war as long as relationships are balanced. But as the realist's argue, high interdependence can also create fear-inducing vulnerabilities. Potential opponents within the network of economic relationships might use a nation's dependence on foreign sources of supply as a lever to gain advantage. A high degree of dependence also increases the chance of suffering unintentional harm as a result of the actions of other nations that are simply pursuing their own interests. Or the mere fact of vulnerability engendered by high dependence may be read as a sign of weakness, increasing the likelihood that rivals will feel free to engage in provocative and threatening behavior. Whether these fears are exaggerated or justified, the insecurity they generate is real. It can precipitate defensive, belligerent behavior offsetting at least some of the benefits that economic interdependence produces.

This dilemma could potentially be resolved by reducing interdependence in those areas of economic interaction in which vulnerability to disruption is most disturbing, while increasing it in all other areas that have real potential for balanced mutual gain. High dependence on outside sources of supply is more troubling the more critical the good or service in question is to the nation's wellbeing: the population is more exposed and vulnerable if it must rely on foreign suppliers for critical elements of its food supply than if it is a large net importer of television programs.

Such "critical goods" are similar to the realists' concept of "strategic goods," except that realists emphasize that strategic goods are those important to applying coercive military power, rather than to economic health. In other words, strategic goods are those on which the nation's offensive and defensive military capabilities depend, while critical goods are primarily those that are key to the population's material well-being. Which goods and services are vital to economic well-being depends in part on the nature and level of development of the nation's economy. But some categories of goods are critical everywhere.

Potable water is crucial to the health of every human being. Foods that are central to the population's diet (and cannot be easily substituted) are also critical goods. Energy is a key resource for every economy, although the amount and type of energy on which the economy depends differs. Dependence on mined and otherwise artificially produced (as opposed to naturally available) energy resources is generally larger the bigger the size of the economy. Finally, virtually every economy requires continuing supplies of certain key raw materials.

A nation that was entirely independent of foreign suppliers for all critical goods would certainly be less vulnerable to other nations sending shockwaves through its economy – or maybe even precipitating an economic collapse – by disrupting access to crucial supplies. Practically speaking, it is unlikely that highly developed nations could ever be so completely self-sufficient in critical goods – at least not unless the public is willing to forego the considerable benefits of international specialization and trade. But most nations could certainly be much less dependent on foreign suppliers of critical goods than they currently are without seriously compromising the economic fortunes of their people. A substantial reduction in critical goods dependence should significantly reduce the stresses that can lead to war.

There are essentially three pragmatic strategies for substantially reducing critical goods dependence that can be pursued alone or, better still, in combination with each other: (1) increase domestic production, (2) diversify the network of foreign suppliers, and (3) work toward "contingent independence." Increasing domestic production involves working out ways of trying to supply as much of the country's requirement for critical goods as possible from sources within its own political boundaries. Diversification means relying on a larger and more varied network of alternative foreign suppliers in order to avoid overdependence on suppliers from any one nation or closely-knit group of nations. "Contingent independence" involves relying on interdependent trade patterns for critical goods in normal times, while doing what is necessary (for example, creating critical goods stockpiles) to make independence possible if and when a key trading partner tries to exert pressure by cutting off vital supplies.

28.3.3   Principle III: Emphasize Development

Economic deprivation and the frustration it generates create a fertile breeding ground for violent conflict. Nearly all of the more than 150 wars that have been fought since the end of World War II have been fought in the less developed world. People in desperate straits are more likely to reach for extreme solutions and are therefore more easily manipulated by demagogues. Keohane [1990, p. 192] admits that liberalism may be appealing "To satisfied modern elites and middle classes . . . but it is not likely to be as appealing to the oppressed or disgruntled." The peacekeeping benefits that balanced economic interdependence promises to deliver are more difficult to achieve under conditions of deprivation and marginalization.

Nye (2002, p. 549) argues that in "postindustrial societies" (that is, countries at higher levels of development), "the foundations of power have been moving away from the emphasis on military force and conquest." He contends that there is an inverse relationship between the level of a nation's development and its readiness to tolerate the use of force: "Roughly speaking there are three types of countries in the world today: poor, weak pre-industrial states, which are often the remnants of collapsed empires; modern industrializing states such as India or China; and the post-industrial societies that prevail in Europe, North America and Japan. The use of force is common in the first type of country, still accepted in the second, but less tolerated in the third" (Nye 2002, pp. 549–50).

Emphasizing economic development is important to keeping the peace because people in good economic condition are much less likely to support violent revolutionary change. They have a strong vested interest in avoiding serious disturbances in, let alone risking destruction of, the economic system under which they are doing well. Whether domestic or international, violence and the disruption it brings is more threatening to them; they have so much more to lose.

Because there are many reasons why violence erupts, both domestically and internationally, there are few grounds for believing that, by itself, even a vast improvement in everyone's material wellbeing would put an end to war. But encouraging inclusive and widespread development is important to giving the largest possible part of the world's population a direct, obvious and personal stake in avoiding disruptive explosions of violent mass conflict, making war that much less likely. Furthermore, development can bring the more powerful and politically influential economic elites within a nation considerable long-term benefit (excluding, of course, those whose livelihoods depend on the prospects for military conflict). It may benefit them directly by diversifying and strengthening the overall economy, thus reducing risk and increasing returns to domestic investment; and it may benefit them indirectly by reducing internal tensions and thus stabilizing the society. Thus development creates a stronger vested interest in preventing disruptive war. Moreover, because real development improves the economic condition of the broad mass of the population, it causes the number and size of economically influential groups that have a strong interest in avoiding war to grow over time.

Economic development is useful for discouraging civil, as well as international war. According to the global, cross-national statistical analysis in Collier (2000, p. 91), "economic agendas appear to be central to understanding why civil wars start." This conclusion is strengthened by the fact that "rapid economic decline" is the sole category of "grievance" that his analysis shows to be a statistically significant cause of civil war (Collier 2000, p. 97). Development is also the key to establishing "positive peace," a broad concept that incorporates both the prevention of war and the elimination of socially systemic causes of debilitation and death, such as inadequate access to healthful food and water. Positive peace is at least as important as war avoidance in much of the less developed world. As Renner (2005, p. 5) points out, "Whereas about 300 000 people were killed in armed conflicts in 2000, for example, as many people die each and every month because of contaminated water or lack of adequate sanitation."

Emphasizing development will also make it easier to establish balanced mutually beneficial relationships, as called for by Principle I. If the main exports of countries at low levels of development are natural resources that are useful mainly as raw materials (such as metal ores and crude oil), they will have little to trade with each other, since they are not likely to have manufacturing sectors that require such inputs. But they will also have little reason to trade if their main exports are similar agricultural products: why would they be interested in importing the same products from other nations that they already produce for themselves and for export? Real development requires a deepening and broadening of diversified economic activity, which would certainly mitigate both these problems.

It is also difficult to build balanced and mutually beneficial economic relationships among countries that are at radically different levels of development. Among other things, it takes greater effort and commitment because of the very different economic bargaining power they bring to the market. Countries at higher and more equal levels of development not only come to the bargaining table with more equal economic power, they also have more to offer each other in variety, quantity and quality of goods, services and profitable investment opportunities.

28.3.4   Principle IV: Minimize Ecological Stress

There is no question that competition for depletable energy and mineral resources can generate conflict. The compulsion to gain (and if possible monopolize) access to natural resources was one of the reasons why the more economically and militarily advanced nations set out to conquer and colonize much of the world in times past. This same competition for energy and material resources continues to bring nations, and sometimes sub-national groups, into conflicts in which at least one party believes that their own continued economic well-being (and perhaps, political sovereignty) are at stake. While it has been less important as a source of interstate war, competition for critical *renewable* resources, especially water, has certainly heightened tensions in the past and could conceivably trigger more violent conflicts in the future.

There is little doubt, for example, that the major powers would be much less concerned about and therefore much less politically and militarily involved in Middle East conflicts if it were not for the region's vast supplies of easily extractible oil. For centuries, when the economically viable deposits of non-renewable resources to which they had ready access became depleted enough, major powers have used force outside their borders to assure continued access to abundant supplies elsewhere. During the colonial era, this took the form of outright and often brutal conquest and subjugation of peoples. In more modern times, this direct approach has largely been replaced by various forms of economic and political pressure up to and including forceful military coercion aimed at bringing about a change in policy or in regime. But the central purpose has remained the same.

That is easy enough to understand – though not necessarily to justify – when key depletable resources are involved. Yet competition for renewable resources, which by definition can be indefinitely available if properly managed, can also play a significant role in generating conflict. Homer-Dixon (1994, p. 6) reported on the results of a three-year research project on environmental scarcity and violent conflict sponsored by the American Academy of Arts and Sciences, involving 30 researchers from ten countries: "Our research showed that environmental scarcities are already contributing to violent conflicts in many parts of the developing world. These conflicts are probably the early signs of an upsurge in violence in the coming decades that will be induced or aggravated by scarcity." If there were going to be conflict, violence and even war over a renewable resource, it would most likely be over water, the resource most vital to life. While Wolf et al. [2005, pp. 83–4] contend that "no states have gone to war specifically over water resources since . . . 2500 BC," they point out that since the 1950s, in the wars and other violent confrontations between Israel and various Arab nations, "water was an underlying source of political stress and one of the most difficult topics in subsequent negotiations . . . [E]ven though the wars were not fought over water, allocation disagreements were an impediment to peace." From the point of view of Principle II (critical goods independence), it is worth noting that more than half of Israel's water supply comes from aquifers, and two of the three major aquifers on which that nation is dependent – although they drain into Israel – lie mainly beneath the West Bank (Homer-Dixon 1994, p. 14).

Pollution can also be an important source of conflict. Environmental damage does not recognize or respect political borders. That is clearly illustrated both by acute environmental disasters such as the nuclear power accident at Chernobyl in 1986, and chronic environmental problems such as acid rain and global warming. Trans-border pollution might not by itself precipitate war, but it has already generated considerable conflict and has the prospect of generating a great deal more. Every additional source of tension strains our ability to keep the peace: the higher the level of tension, the easier it is for the added stress of other sources of conflict to push us over the threshold and trigger the eruption of violence.

As a result of the eighteenth century industrial revolution, economic growth increased, population grew and the environment became more and more polluted. In the first few decades of the twentieth century, technology-driven change in the kinds of materials and products we produced, and the techniques we used to produce them, resulted in a sharp increase in the rate of environmental pollution (as well as resource depletion). More and more, synthetic detergents, fibers, fertilizers, pesticides and the like displaced their natural counterparts, adding substances to the environment that did not fit into any of the many natural recycling mechanisms that had evolved slowly over millions of years. The combustion of ever-larger quantities of fossil fuels, along with rampant deforestation and other ecologically damaging practices helped to unbalance the earth's oxygen–carbon dioxide cycle, leading to a build-up of atmospheric carbon dioxide. Combined with other so-called "greenhouse gases" (GHGs), such as methane, nitrous oxide and water vapor, the build-up of carbon dioxide began to raise the average temperature of the earth. The climate change that is resulting from this human-induced global warming is a classic example of trans-boundary pollution with transnational environmental impacts. It is widely acknowledged today as a globally chronic problem capable of periodically setting off acute disasters.

Though it is unlikely that war will break out over greenhouse gas emissions or the destruction of forests and other natural greenhouse gas sinks, all of the stresses generated by trying to cope with the negative effects of global warming add to the strain on the international system. Still more tension and stress are created when nations who are known to be major contributors to global environmental threats refuse to join others in taking serious action to mitigate them. There was, for example, widespread international hostility to the US as a result of the Bush administration's unilateral decision to abandon the Kyoto accords, which the US had signed and helped to negotiate. There is no doubt that this hostility was largely due to the dramatic effect that continued trans-boundary pollution by greenhouse gases is projected to have on climate change, with the potential of imposing enormous long run costs on the economies of all nations, as well as directly threatening the physical well-being of their people.

Some argue that modern production techniques and consumption activities generate an unavoidable degree of ecological stress, so we must abandon the expansion of economic activity if we are to maintain, let alone improve environmental quality. While there is clearly a tradeoff here, it is nevertheless possible to maintain the levels of economic well-being to which the people of the more developed countries have become accustomed and extend them to the people of the less developed nations without even generating current levels of environmental damage if we commit ourselves to: (1) paying a great deal more attention than is currently being paid to the efficient use of natural resources; (2) developing and extensively using pollution-abating technologies and procedures; and finally (3) shifting the focus of economic growth from the mainly quantitative to the qualitative, particularly on the part of the more developed countries.

It is particularly important to shift our way of thinking about economic growth. To continue to conceive of economic growth in primarily quantitative terms – as is implicit in the emphasis given to the growth of GDP, a measure that captures only quantitative economic size – is foolish and unnecessary. Standards of living are also raised by improvements in the quality of goods and services. Shifting attention to qualitative growth will allow the more developed nations to restrain their insatiable appetite for nonrenewable resources, reduce environmental pollution and create space for the quantitative expansion of goods and services still required in many less developed nations.

To the extent that we follow these ecological stress-reducing strategies, we will not only substantially improve the quality of the environment, but also reduce what is likely to be an increasingly important source of international conflict and strain on our ability to keep the peace.

28.4 CONCLUSION

The four basic principles of economic peacekeeping are key elements of an ideologically eclectic yet consistent attempt to harness a number of seemingly disparate forces that can be integrated and made to work together to help keep the peace. Trade and investment relationships that are balanced in benefit and decision power maximize the extent to which self-interests become compatible and mutually reinforcing. This turns the pursuit of self-interest that drives free market capitalism into a potentially powerful binding force among nations, creating strong positive incentives to manage conflict so as to prevent war. Establishing independence in critical goods while expanding interdependence everywhere else helps to overcome the conflict-generating fear of the vulnerability that excessive dependence can create, while permitting the considerable benefits of competition, specialization and trade to flow freely.

By increasing the economic well-being of those in the less developed world, emphasizing development strengthens their stake in peace. Development is a powerful force for reducing persistently high levels of inequality and the political economic marginalization that can so easily give rise to violent conflict. With a better, more prosperous material life comes a stronger reluctance to reach for or accept extreme solutions. Development also facilitates the kind of balanced, mutually beneficial economic relationships that help keep the peace, since it is much easier to achieve balance among economic partners at higher and more equal levels of development.

Despite the large and impressive technological progress we have made in the past 300 years or so, the natural environment still provides many of the basic resources and services on which our lives and our economic well-being depend. From filtering, renewing and recirculating the air we breathe and the water we drink, to serving as a source of raw materials and energy, to carrying away or recycling the wastes we generate, the environment is the critical context within which all economic activity must operate. The damage that any one of us does to the environment becomes a cost for everyone else. Those of us who continue to add substantially to the problem while standing apart from the cooperative efforts to solve it, will generate understandable hostility, and that hostility will make it that much more difficult to keep the peace. Furthermore, to the extent that our economic activities put us in competition with each other for nonrenewable natural resources, that competition can, as it has all too often in the past, lead to violence and even war. Carrying on our economic lives while minimizing the pollution we generate and our reliance on virgin depletable resources are therefore not just proper things to do, they are essential if we are to have both economic progress and peace.

The economics of peacekeeping in the deepest most profound sense involves far more than supporting the efforts of the international community to deploy military forces to help keep opposing armies at bay, as important as those efforts may be. It is about structuring the economic relationships on which we depend for material well-being in such a way as to imbed in the economic system itself powerful incentives to manage or resolve the conflicts that inevitably develop, and to persist in finding ways to maintain peace.

REFERENCES

Azar, E.E. (1980), "The Conflict and Peace Data Bank (COPDAB) project", *Journal of Conflict Resolution*, **24** (1), 143–52.
Barbieri, K. (1996), "Economic interdependence: a path to peace or a source of interstate conflict", *Journal of Peace Research*, **33** (1), 29–49.
Collier, P. (2000), "Doing well out of war: an economic perspective", in M. Berdal and D.M. Malone (eds), *Greed and Grievance: Economic Agendas in Civil Wars*, Boulder, CO: Lynne Rienner Publishers, pp. 91–112.
Deutsch, K.W. (1968), *The Analysis of International Relations*, Englewood Cliffs, NJ: Prentice Hall.
Gilpin, R. (1977), "Economic interdependence and national security in historical perspective", in K. Knorr and F. Trager (eds), *Economic Issues and National Security*, Lawrence, KS: Regents Press of Kansas, pp. 19–67.

Hoffman, S. (1963), "Rousseau on war and peace", *American Political Science Review*, **57** (2), 317–33.

Homer-Dixon, T.F. (1994), "Environmental scarcities and violent conflict: evidence from cases", *International Security*, **19** (1), 5–40.

Keohane, R.O. (1990), "International liberalism reconsidered" in J. Dunn (ed.), *The Economic Limits to Modern Politics*, Cambridge, UK: Cambridge University Press, pp. 165–94.

Keohane, R.O. and L.L. Martin (1995), "The promise of institutionalist theory", *International Security*, **20** (1), 39–51.

McMillan, S.M. (1997), "Interdependence and conflict", *Mershon International Studies Review*, **41** (1), 33–58.

Morgenthau, H.J. (1973), *Politics Among Nations*, New York, NY: Alfred Knopf.

Nye, J.S. (2002), "Limits of American power", *Political Science Quarterly*, **117** (4), 545–59.

Oneal, J.R., F.H. Oneal, Z. Maoz and B. Russett (1996), "The liberal peace: interdependence, democracy, and international conflict, 1950–85", *Journal of Peace Research*, **33** (1), 11–28.

Polachek, S.W. (1980), "Conflict and trade", *Journal of Conflict Resolution*, **24** (1), 55–78.

Renner, M. (2005), "Security redefined", in the Worldwatch Institute, *State of the World, 2005*, New York, NY: W.W. Norton, pp. 3–19.

Reno, W. (2000), "Shadow states and the political economy of civil wars", in M. Berdal and D.M. Malone (eds), *Greed and Grievance: Economic Agendas in Civil Wars*, Boulder, CO: Lynne Rienner Publishers, pp. 43–68.

Rittberger, B. (2001) "Which institutions for post-war europe? Explaining the institutional design of Europe's first community", *Journal of European Public Policy,* **8** (5), 673–708.

Rosecrance, R. (1986), *The Rise of the Trading State: Commerce and Conquest in the Modern World*, New York, NY: Basic Books.

Russett, B. (1967), *International Regions and the International System*, Chicago, IL: Rand McNally.

Smith, A. ([1776] 1937), *The Wealth of Nations*, New York: The Modern Library, Random House.

Uchitel, A. (1993), "Interdependence and instability" in J. Snyder and R. Jervis (eds), *Coping with Complexity in the International System*, Boulder, CO: Westview Press, pp. 243–64.

Waltz, K.N. (1988), "The origins of war in neorealist theory", *Journal of Interdisciplinary History*, **18** (4), 615–28.

Wolf, A.T., A. Kramer, A. Carius and G.D. Dabelko (2005), "Managing Water Conflict and Cooperation" in the Worldwatch Institute, *State of the World, 2005*, New York, NY: W.W. Norton, pp. 80–99.

Index

Abadie, A. 135
Abdolali, N. 283
Abolfathi, F. 520
accountability, pre-emptive 581
accountability mechanisms 397, 398, 402
Acemoglu, D. 3, 52, 188, 189, 420
Achen, C.H. 494
Achenbach, J. 329
Addison, T. 405
Adler, E. 238
Afghanistan 97, 276, 379, 381, 382, 386, 391, 398, 421, 443
  impact of UN sanctions 544, 551, 554
  sanctions 536, 559
Africa 65–6
  colonization 67–8
  ethnic fractionalization 136
  illicit arms trade 235, 236
  interstate conflicts 227
After Hegemony 363
agency problems 46–7
Aghion, P. 62
agrarian revolutions 3
agreements 42, 43, 44, 46, 178, 373, 479, 480
  and asset prices 499–500
agricultural sector 203
aid 490–91, 493–4
Aizenman, J. 479
Akerlof, G.A. 72, 86, 87, 113
Akhavan, P. 402
Alesina, A. 59, 60, 61, 62, 63
Alexander, K. 552
Alexandrova, A. 301
Algeria 101, 103, 105, 110
  terrorism 129
alien rule 432
Allan, P. 86
Allee, T.L. 317
alliance defense, as a collective good 343

alliance ties 293
alliances 343
  armament cartel hypothesis 347–50
  centralization of decision-making 346
  demand for security 344–6
  domestic premium 347
  economics of 343–4
  share of spending and share of costs 344
Allouche, J. 393
Alter, K.J. 83
Amazon jungle 187–8
American Civil War 287, 288
amnesties 104, 400, 413, 421, 423
Amnesty International 109
Amstutz, M.R. 402
anarchy 16, 114, 357, 358, 370, 476, 477, 479
Anderson, G.M. 165, 168
Anderson, M.B. 3
Anderton, C.H. 146, 530
Andreas, P. 535
Andreas, P. 535
Angola 536, 575
  impact of UN sanctions 541, 548, 551, 552–3, 553–4
Angrist, J.D. 159, 164
Annett, A. 59
Anstey, M. 585
Anthony, I. 223
appropriation 178
Arad, S. 460
Arbour, L. 419
Arce, D.G. 131
Arenhövel, M. 397, 408
Argentina 256, 260, 261, 414, 596
armament cartel hypothesis 347–50, 353
armament decisions 50–51, 55
Armaments, Disarmament and International Security 224
armed conflict models 3
armed peace, versus war 182–5

arms embargoes 551–2
arms race 251, 340, 578
arms trade 217–19
  Africa 235, 236
  data collections 223–5
  and ethnic uprisings 229–30
  future research direction 231–8
  hegemonic supply pattern 220
  hierarchies in supply 220–23
  illicit arms transfers to Liberia 231–4
  industrial supply pattern 220
  and instability 228
  and internal conflict 229–31
  and interstate conflict 226–9
  major weapon systems 219
  models 225–6
  and repression 230–31
  restrictive supply pattern 220
  small arms and light weapons
    (SALW) 219, 220, 231, 237–8
    data collections 225
    structural features of trade 222–3
  and social network analysis 231–7
  strategic interaction in the arms
    market 225–6
  supplies during and after World
    War II 221
  trade in finished systems 219
arms trade offsets 243
  agreements 245–6
  and arms globalization 262–3
  and arms industries 262
  cost reduction 251–4
  countries' objectives and strategies
    246–7
  data, access and audits 260
  definition 244
  and economic development 254–5
  future of 263
  magnitude 244–6
  Military Malthusianism 261–2
  minimum offset-contract values
    249–50
  motivation 244
  multipliers 250
  and new and sustainable work
    256–7
  offset characteristics 247–8
  offset mandates 248–9
  penalties 250–51

  and small and medium-sized
    enterprises 254
  and technology transfer 257–9
  US 245–6
  vulnerabilities 260–61
Armstrong, D.A. 116
Arreguin-Toft, I. 75
Arriaza, L. 413
Arthur, P. 397
Asch, B.J. 157, 159, 171
Ash, T.G. 404
Ashton, T.S. 510
Ashworth, S. 145
Askin, K.D. 413
Asmal, K. 402
Asmal, L. 402
"asset price continuity principle" 503
asset prices 499–501
  asset markets and credible
    commitment, Sri Lanka case
    study 504–509
  and regime chance 500–501
asymmetric information 3
  and bargaining failures 40–43
  and democratic peace 49
Aten, B. 117
Atlantic Charter 129, 145
Atlas, P.M. 481
"audience costs" 49, 319–21, 330
Auernheimer, L. 503
Aumann, R.J. 54
Aust, S. 146
Australia 248, 251, 264
  Strategic Industry Development
    Activities 253
Austria 110
autocracies 303–304, 318, 319
Auvinen, J. 114
Axelrod, R. 573
Aya, R. 206
Aydin, A. 462, 465, 466, 468
Ayissi, A. 578
Ayoob, M. 226
Azam, J.P. 142
Azar, E.E. 592

Backer, D. 414, 416, 424
Bai, C.-E. 159
Baker, P.H. 382
Baker, W.D. 352

balance of power 17–18, 361, 462, 463
Balch-Lindsay, D. 465, 467
Baldwin, D.A. 534
Baliga, S. 42, 43
Ball, N. 483
Banerjee, A. 504
Baquir, R. 60
Barahona de Brita, A. 409
Baranova, O. 440, 447, 448, 449
Barber, B.M. 79
Barbieri, K. 26, 30, 272, 278, 309, 530, 592
Bardos, G.N. 227
bargaining failures 34
  and asymmetric information 40–43
  and commitment problems 43–6
  multilateral 47–8
  reasons for 35
  and war 39–48
  war as part of bargaining process 45–6
bargaining model of war 3, 19–21
Barkow, J.H. 86
Barnett, M. 357, 368, 369, 370, 371
Barr, A. 61
Barro, R.J. 117
Barthe, B. 448
Barton, J.H. 371
Baskaran 249, 252, 258
Bassiouni, M.C. 412, 414, 421
Basuchoudhary, A. 137, 144
Baugh, W.H. 239
Baumann, R.A. 227
Baumeister, R.F. 78
Baxter, V. 412
Bazerman, M. 460
Beardsley, K.C. 461, 468
Beck, N. 286, 309, 521
Beckett, I.F.W. 106
Beevor, A. 111
Bélanger, G. 337
Belgium 252
beliefs, inconsistency 42
Bell, C. 404 399, 410, 413, 420
Bellman, E. 443
Bennett, A. 281
Bennett, D.S. 30, 78, 286, 317, 318, 328, 526, 530
Benoit, K. 272
Benvenisti, E. 445

Berbaum, M.L. 272
Bercovitch, J. 458, 461, 465, 467, 580, 581
Berdal, M. 3
Berger, S.R. 379
Berman, E.B. 131, 142
Bermeo, N. 410
Besley, T. 189, 352
Bester, H. 183
Betts, R.K. 462, 464
Bevia, C. 44, 54
Bhargava, R. 402
Bickers, K.N. 321
Biddle, S. 115
Bienen, H. 324
Bilmes, L. 80, 180
Bishop, D.T. 52
Bitzinger 249, 252, 255, 257, 258
Blainey, G.A. 19, 20, 25, 26, 30, 42, 78, 79
Blanchard, J.-M. 518
Blanton, S.L. 230
Blattman, C. 3, 4, 179, 192
Blimes, R.J. 62
Blix, H. 562
Bloch, F. 54
Blomberg, S.B. 134, 135, 147, 180, 182, 192
Boden, J.M. 78
Bodin, J. 358, 372
Boehmer, C.R. 272, 274, 324, 531
Boer War 287, 288
Boesenecker, A.P. 410
Boettke, P.J. 409, 423, 474, 479, 480, 486, 499
Bohara, A.K. 115
Boone, C. 433
Boraine, A. 400, 402, 406
Bordo, M.D. 501, 510
Borgatti, S.P. 527
Borrus, M. 518
Boskey, J.B. 460
Bosnia 461, 464, 581
Bossert, W. 59
Boswell, T. 196, 212
boundary disputes 577–8
Bourne, M. 222, 223, 238, 239
Boutros Ghali, B. 572, 576, 582
Boyce, J. 491
Brahm, E. 411, 413

Brams, S. 572
Brandeis, L.D. 371
Brauer, J. 226, 243, 245, 254, 256, 260,
    261, 262
Braumoeller, B.F. 317
Braw, M. 435
Brazil 298
    arms trade offsets 246, 249, 252, 255,
        256, 258, 260
Brecher, M. 466, 468, 579
Brecke, P. 410
Bremer, S.A. 19, 117, 270, 283
British Guyana 298
Brito, D.L. 42
Britton, R.L. 81
Broda, C. 522
Brodie, B. 97
Broers, M. 447
Brook, T. 437, 440, 441, 443, 447, 449
Brooks, R. 413
Brooks, S.G. 18
Brown, C.V. 324, 351
Brown, J.D. 79
Brown, M.E. 78, 86
Browne, E.C. 324
Brzoska, M. 227, 238, 247, 248, 249,
        250, 251, 254, 256, 257, 258, 264,
        549, 552
Buccola, S. 135
Buchanan, A. 422
Bueno de Mesquita, B. 23, 24, 47, 55,
        145, 296, 297, 300, 310, 319, 324,
        325
Bull, H. 358, 371
Bull, T. 449
Bunting, M. 434, 442
Buonanno, P. 160
bureaucracy 369
Bures, O. 556
Burnham, T. 74
Burton, J.W. 461
Bush, G.W. 381, 388
Buzan, B. 222

Caldwell, W.B. 389
Call, C.T. 381, 408, 411
Callwell, C.E. 96
Cambodia 462
Camerer, C. 31, 79
Campbell, C. 416, 421

Campbell, K. 413
Canning, D. 58
Cannings, C. 52
Cao, X. 309
capital accumulation 201, 202, 203
capitalism 276
    compared to democracy 269
capitalist peace 25–6, 293
    compared to Kantian or liberal
        peace 273–4
    concept and context 269
    econometric studies 270–74
        dyadic design 270
    historical arguments 274–5
    and trade 275, 515
    and World War II 274
Caplan, B. 143
Carbonnier, G. 4
Card, D. 159
Carey, S.C. 116
Carilli, A.M. 66
Carlton, E. 435, 437
Carment, D. 459, 460, 464
Carnevale, P.J. 460
Carothers, T. 414
Carter, D.B. 526
Carter, J.R. 146, 530
Carus, W.S. 222
Case, A. 352
Cashdan, E. 147
Caucasus 188
Cauley, J. 145, 147, 148
causes of war 13, 78–9
    dyadic-level theories 15, 19–21
    individual-level theories 27–9
    levels-of-analysis framework 15
    overconfidence 78–9
    state and societal-level theories 22–6
    system-level theories 16–19
Central African Republic 381
Cerra, V. 180
Chad 381
Chan, S. 32, 319, 330
Chandrasekharan, R. 390
Chandrasekharan, S. 508
Channel Islands 434
Chapman, A.R. 412, 422
Chassang, S. 45, 51, 54
Chauvert, L. 179
Chechnya 188

Chehabi, H. 205
Chesterman, S. 409
Chicken Dilemma Game (CDG) 573–4
Chile 298, 411
China 18, 76, 101, 443, 449
  and Japan 101–102
  and US 275
Chinworth 248, 249, 250, 252, 255,
  258
Chiozza, G. 55, 301, 319, 321, 323,
  325, 330
Choi, J.K. 74
Choi, S.-W. 167
Choucri, N. 515, 516
Chwe, M. 183
CIA World Factbook 59
Cingranelli, D.L. 117
Cipollone, P. 160
civil war 13–14, 62, 177, 474, 593
  budgetary cost 179
  and capital flight 179–80
  and commitment problems 185–91
  cost of 179–82
  and credible commitments 476–81
    implications for policy 481–91
  deaths caused by 180–81
  definitions of 178
  direct costs 177
  and disease 181
  domestic political solutions 482–6
  duration 42–3
  and economic growth 180, 599
  and elections 482–4
  external interventions 486–91
  indirect costs 177
  infrastructure 179
  and interstate war 309
  and per capita income 177
  and population displacement 181
  and poverty 182
  and power-sharing 484–6
  private capital 179
  and property rights 177–8
  role of outsiders 189–91
  and third-party intervention 467–8
Clague, C. 479
Clare, J. 286
Clark, D.K. 317
Clarke, R.A. 325
class conflict 196

Clausewitz, C. von 13, 131
  on guerilla war 98–9
Clayton, M. 116
Clovic, P. 86
Cloward, R.A. 208
Coats, R.M. 146
cognitive dissonance 80
Cohen, B.J. 359
Cohen, E. 390
Cohen, H. 440, 441, 443, 449
Cohen, R. 289, 578
Colaresi, M. 19, 319, 325
Cold War 45, 182, 189, 218, 228, 229,
  290, 292, 294, 298, 310, 517–18
  and arms trade 230, 238
  and defense spending 339
Cole, E.A. 398
Coll, R.S. 128
collaboration 432, 434, 438–43,
  440–41, 445, 446, 447, 448, 449,
  592
Collier, P. 4, 6, 60, 62, 63, 135, 146,
  177, 178, 179, 181, 182, 192, 385,
  474, 484, 490, 494, 509, 592, 599
Colombia 101, 189
colonial wars 297, 298
commitment *see* credible commitment
commitment problems 21, 49, 178,
  184–5
  and bargaining failures 43–6
  and civil war 185–91
  commitment not to attack 44
common knowledge 183
communism 269, 298
compensation 574
compromise 3
Conconi, P. 48
conflict
  definition of 472
  positive sum outcomes 574
  welfare costs of 182
*Conflict Management and Peace
  Science* 4
conflict prevention, and international
  negotiation 571–85
"conflict trap" 474
Conroy, R.W. 558
conscription 154
  and democracy 164–5, 168, 170
  dynamic effects 159–60

equity issues 163–4
intergenerational issues 160
military record of 167–8
opportunity costs and excess burden
    158–9
origins of 154
public choice perspective 160–63
public support for 162
social cohesion and national identity
    164
social and political record 163–5
and special interests 165–7
specialization and production
    efficiency 157–8
as a tax 155–60, 171
throughout the world 155
construction 574
constructivism 356, 357, 367
and Weber, M. 356, 370
contest model 3
*Conventional Arms Transfers to
    Developing Nations* 224
conventional wars 80–81
Cooper, H.H.A. 132
Cooper, J. 75, 80
cooperation 590–91
Coordinating Committee for
    Multilateral Export Controls
    (CoCom) 517–18
Corbin, J. 581
Corchon, L. 44, 54
Correlates of War (COW) dataset 300,
    309, 523
corruption 61, 490
Cortell, A.P. 409
Cortright, D. 534, 536, 548, 550, 553,
    555, 556, 557, 561
cost plus contracts 340
costs of war 4, 300, 301–302, 317
Côte d'Ivoire 379, 536
    impact of UN sanctions 546, 548,
        551, 554
Council on Foreign Relations Task
    Force (CFR) 382
counterinsurgency 103–106, 382, 388,
    389–90
counterterrorism 559–61
Cowden, J. 87
Coyne, C.J. 4, 66, 144, 343, 352, 409,
    423, 479, 480, 483, 499, 510, 511

Craft, C. 227, 228
Crain, N.V. 134
Crain, W.M. 134, 346
Crantz, C. 227
Crawford, V. 54
credible commitment 498–9
    and civil war 476–81, 481–91
    and financial asset markets, Sri
        Lanka 504–509
    verification 510
Crenshaw, M. 133, 145
Crocker, C.A. 580
Crocker, D. 422
Cronberg, T. 162
Crossette, B. 555
Crusades 37, 46
Cuba 101, 102, 535
cultural factors 5
Curwen, P.A. 231, 232, 233, 234
Cyprus 132, 277

Daly, E. 398
DALYs (disability-adjusted life years),
    and wars 181
D'Ambrosio, C. 59
Dancy, G. 408, 421
Daniels, G. 434
Danilovic, V. 286
Darcy, S. 422
Darley, J.M. 75
Dassel, K. 321
Davenport, C. 115, 116
David, R. 400
Davidson, P. 510
Davis, D.R. 321
Davis, J.W. Jr. 409
Dawkins, R. 142
de Greiff, P. 402, 404, 410, 420
de Soto, A. 576
De Soysa, I. 520
de Vattel, E. 372
decision-making 14, 75
    and psychological biases 78–9, 84–5,
        86
defense and alliance policy
    and defense lobbyists 337
    and information 335, 336
    median voters 335–6
    and politicians 336–7
    public choice analysis 335

and public servants 337
voter's optimization calculus 338–9
defense budget
    allocation of resources 340
    and voters' demand for security 338
defense bureaucracy 346
defense goods, import or domestic
    production 341
defense lobbyists, and defense and
    alliance policy 337
defense policy, conflicts in 337–40
Dejammet, A. 558
democracies, risk of war between 271
democracy 82, 83, 137
    compared to capitalism 269
    and conscription 164–5, 168, 170
    definitions of 290–91
    and ethnic fractionalization 63
    and peace 270
democratic culture and norms model
    22
democratic peace 22–5, 48–9, 271–2,
    273, 281–3, 318–19
    and accountability 295, 300–301
    and alliance ties 293
    causal mechanisms 294–306
    and democratic wars 287–8
    durability of 306–308
    dyadic 318–19
    and economic factors 293
    evidence for
        between 1870 and 1945 292
        during the Cold War 292
    and group constraint 296, 302–304
    and information 296, 305
    and institutions 295–7, 300
    and militarized disputes 285–6,
        290–94
    and norms 294–5, 297–8
    and preference affinity 293
    and public constraint 296, 301–302
    and slow mobilization 296, 304
    and stable borders 293–4
    and surprise attack 296, 304
    and trust and respect 298–300
    and victory 296, 305–306
    and war 283–5, 287
    weak link model 291
"democratic reconstructionism"
    paradigm 483

Democratic Republic of the Congo
    177, 180, 187, 190, 379, 381,
    536
    impact of UN sanctions 545, 551
democratic wars 287–8
democratization 276, 298, 397, 483–4,
    492
Dempster, G. 510, 511
Demsetz, H. 148
Deng, F. 578
Denmark, arms trade offsets 248, 249,
    250, 252, 254
Department for International
    Development (DFID) 380
DeRouen, K.R. 321
Desch, M.C. 83, 301, 306, 308
Deutsch, K.W. 592
diamond industry, sanctions 553
Diamond, J. 76
Diamond, L. 410
Diehl, P.F. 19, 453, 454, 458, 462, 467,
    583
Diermeir, D. 324
Diesing, P. 572
Dincer, O.C. 61
diplomacy 572
disaggregated trade flows *see* trade
disarmament, demobilization and
    reintegration programs (DDR)
    476, 482, 489, 493, 494
diversionary war theory 23, 321–2
Dixit, A. 479
Dixon, W.J. 196, 212, 294, 454, 458,
    459, 464, 465, 467
Djankov, S. 189
Dobbins, J. 385, 388, 437
Dollar, D. 491
domestic order, theories of 358–60
Dorn, W. 571
Dorussen, H. 272, 278, 330, 515, 518,
    521, 525, 526, 527, 529, 530,
    531
Dostoevsky, F. 126
Downes, A.B. 277, 305, 306
Downs, A. 137, 336, 337
Downs, G.W. 55
Doyle, M.W. 22, 30, 48, 283, 287, 294,
    295, 309, 487, 488
Drakos, K. 135
Drazen, A. 61

Dreher, A. 116, 346
Drezner, D.W. 536
Druckman, D. 458, 574
du Toit, A. 403
Dube, O. 189
Dubner, S.J. 132
Dudley, L. 339
Duffield, M. 4
Dumas, L.J. 259
Dunne, J.P. 160, 243, 255, 257, 259
duration of wars 52–3
Durch, W.J. 228
Dutch East India Company 501
Duthie, R. 402, 407, 411, 420
Dwyer, S. 404
dyadic democratic peace 318–19
dyadic models 529–30
dyadic-level theories 15, 19–21

Easterly, B. 4
Easterly, W. 58, 59, 61, 63, 116, 135,
    147, 186
Eckstein, S. 212
Eckstein, Z. 135
economic growth, and ethnicity 187
economic incentives 4
economic interdependence 25–6, 590
economic interventions 489–91
economic liberalism 591
economic shocks 188–9
economic stagnation 5–6, 25
Economics of Alliances 342, 343, 344
Economie des Guerres Civiles 3
Economist 110, 379
Ecuador 575, 578
Edelstein, D. 437, 445
Egypt 129
Ekéus, R. 555
Elbadawi, I. 464
elections 23, 137, 144, 287, 492
    and civil war 482–4
    and post-conflict recovery 475
    and uncertainty 484
    voters 335–6
electoral cycles 341–2
    and leadership tenure 322–3
Ellingsen, T. 54, 62
Elms, D.K. 86, 87
Elster, J. 404, 407, 409, 421, 422
Encyclopedia Britannica 59

Enders, W. 127, 128, 130, 133, 134,
    135, 138, 139, 140, 141, 142, 143,
    146, 147, 148, 511
endogenous power 49–51
enemies 77–8
Engelbrecht, H.C. 217
Enterline, A.J. 321, 465, 467
equality 360–64
    Locke on 360–61
Ermakoff, I. 449
Esdale, C. 447
Esman, M.J. 453
Esteban, J. 39, 45, 69, 136, 147, 186
Ethiopia
    impact of UN sanctions 544
    and Somalia 229
ethnic cleansing 39
ethnic conflict 61–2, 186–7, 477
ethnic fractionalization 62
    and democracy 63
ethnic uprisings, and arms trade 229–30
ethnicity 3–4
    and economic growth 187
Eubank, W.L. 134, 146, 147
Europe, emergence of states 387
European Arms Procurement Agency
    262
European Economic Community
    (ECE) 595–6
European Security and Defence Policy
    (ESDP) 345, 346
Evans, G. 577
Evans, M.D. 109, 110
Evans, P. 196, 202
Everett, M.G. 527
export controls 225
external interventions 486–91
Eyerman, J. 320

failed states 6, 379
    costs of reconstruction 388
    and counterinsurgency 389–90
    definitions of 380–81
    response of US government agencies
        390–91
    as a security threat 379, 381
    and state building 389–90
    targeting and repairing 384–5
Failed States Index (FSI) 379, 380,
    381, 383, 384, 393

Failing to Win 326
Fallows, J. 79, 80, 83
Farber, H.S. 292, 293, 309, 310
Faria, J.R. 131
Faure, G.O. 571, 585
Fay, M. 58
Fearon, J.D. 3, 4, 19, 20, 21, 30, 34, 40,
    45, 46, 49, 53, 59, 62, 64, 78, 114,
    117, 178, 180, 187, 192, 319, 330,
    379, 385, 476, 477, 478, 483, 491
Feaver, P.D. 320, 330
federalism 371, 372
Feenstra, R. 522, 526
Fein, H. 116
Fenton-O'Creevy, M. 74, 79
Ferguson, N. 144
Festinger, L. 80
Fett, P.J. 454, 463, 467
Fielding, D. 135
Filson, D. 114
financial market theory 502–503
financial markets, and wartime finance
    501–502
Finel, B.M. 305
Finland, arms trade offsets 248, 250,
    252, 254
Finnemore, M. 238, 357, 368, 369, 370,
    371, 409
first strike advantages 44–5
Fischel, W.A. 171
Fisher, L. 83
Fisher, M. 37
Fisher, R.J. 459, 461, 466
Fiske, S.T. 72, 77
Fitzgerald, V. 4, 179
Fleischer, A. 135
Fletcher, L.E. 412, 422
Flores, T.E. 474, 479, 480, 483, 484,
    486, 490, 491
Flynn, G.Q. 162, 163
Foran, J. 198, 199–200, 204, 212
force, use of 517
Ford, L.R. 530
Fordham, B. 321
foreign direct investment 277, 483, 486
foreign investment 273
foreign policy, and variation in
    domestic institutions 315
Førland, T.E. 518
Forsberg, T. 399, 404

Fortna, V.P. 486, 487, 488
fractionalization 58, 136, 147
    and centralized political regimes 62
    and economic outcomes 59–62
    ethnic 62, 63, 186
    and institutions 62–8
    measurement 58–9
framing 28
France 434, 449
    mercenaries 169
    and World War I 275
Frank, O. 239
Frazier, D.V. 459
free riding 343
    and peacekeeping 342
free trade 276–7
Freeman, L.C. 527
Frendreis, J.P. 324
Frerks, G. 491
Freshtman, C. 55
Frevert, U. 171
Frey, B.S. 131, 134, 146, 352
Friedman, M. 159
Fromkin, D. 146
Fujiwara, A. 110
Fukuyana, F. 379, 382, 386, 388
Fulkerson, D.R. 530
functionalism 401, 402, 421
Fundamental Attribution Error (FAE)
    75, 76, 78

Gabel, K. 145
Gallup, J.L. 117
Galston, W.A. 164
Gambetta, D. 145
game theory 2, 114
Ganguly, S. 79, 83
Garcia, D. 238
Garcia-Alonso, M.D.C. 225
Gardeazabal, J. 135
Garfinkel, M.R. 3, 55, 114, 184, 192
Garg, A. 60
Gartner, S.S. 317, 328, 458
Gartzke, E. 25, 26, 42, 272, 273, 277,
    278, 293, 301, 310, 515, 525, 526,
    530
Gasiorowski, M. 517, 519, 522, 527,
    530
Gassebner, M. 116
Gates, S. 114

Gates, T. 171
Gatti, R. 116
Gaubatz, K. 322
GDP 527
Geddes, B. 415
Gelleny, R.D. 115
Gellman, B. 555
Gelpi, C.F. 278, 317, 320, 321, 322, 323, 330
Geneva Convention 110, 111
genocide 465
Gent, S.E. 462, 467, 487
geography 187–8
geopolitics 190
George, A.L. 27, 73, 84
George, J.L. 84
Gerber, L. 553
Gerber, T.P. 162
Gerber-Stellingwerf, L. 536
Germany 121, 140, 449
    arms trade offsets 248, 249, 251, 254, 258–9
    and the Geneva Convention 111
    occupation of 435
    trade policy under National Socialism 519
Gerner, D.J. 239
Ghai, Y. 582
Ghana 61
Ghani, A. 379
Ghobarah, H. 181
Gibler, D.M. 271, 293
Gibson, J.L. 403, 412
Gibson, K. 460
Gide, A. 448
Gil, R. 115
Gilovich, T. 72, 73, 86
Gilpin, R. 30, 365, 516, 590
Giumelli, F. 549
Gladwell, M. 79
Glaser, J. 135
Gleditsch, K.S. 321, 330
Gleditsch, N.P. 26, 278, 283, 284, 423, 530
Gleiber, D.W. 324
globalization 86, 276, 535
    and terrorism 97
Gochman, C.S. 283
Goemans, H.E. 20, 55, 301, 310, 317, 319, 321, 323, 325, 326, 330

Goenner, C.F. 518, 521, 522, 529, 530
Goertz, G. 19, 30
Goff, B.L. 352
Goldfrank, W. 196, 206
Goldsmith, B.E. 115
Goldstein, C.S. 435
Goldstein, J. 366
Goldstein, J.A. 573
Goldstone, J. 195, 196
Goldstone, J.A. 381
Goleman, D.J. 79
Gonzalez, R.A. 339, 343
Goodby, J. 578
Goodwin, J. 205
Gordon, J. 555
Gordon, R.H. 159
Goundinoff, P. 352
Gourevitch, A. 383
Gourevitch, P. 110
Gouws, A. 403
Gowa, J. 26, 271, 292, 293, 321, 323, 366
Grabel, I. 479
Granovetter, M. 186
Gray, C.S. 106
"Great Game" 190
Greece 441
Green, D.P. 135, 309
Greig, M.J. 466
Grieco, J.M. 278, 323, 363, 364
Griesdorf, M. 317, 320
Griffin, D.W. 72, 79
Grigsby, A. 179
Grillot, S.R. 237
Grimmett, R.F. 224
Grofman, B. 324
Gross, J.T. 448
Grossman, H.I. 147, 192
groups 3–4
"groupthink" 79, 83
Guatemala 298
guerrilla war 96–7
    and amnesties 104
    causes of 95–6
    and civilian population 105
    Clausewitz on 98–9
    early conflicts 97–8
    failures 101–102
    and firearm supplies 104
    and food supplies 104–105

and Mao Tse-Tung 99–100
outside aid 100–101
and rectitude 106
successful counterinsurgency
103–106
tactics 98
urban 103
guerrillas, compared to terrorists 95
Guevara, E. 100
Guinea 381
Guinnane, T.W. 504
Gulf War 328–9
Gunnemark, E.V. 58
Gurr, T.R. 14, 61, 116, 423
Gurses, M. 410
Gutmann, A. 402, 422
Gutmann, M.P. 38
Gwartney, J. 117

Haas, E. 462, 465
Haavelmo, T. 3
Hafner-Burton, E.M. 111, 234
Hagelin 248, 249, 250, 252, 254, 258
Haggard, S. 207
Hague Convention 110
Haines 250, 253, 255
Haiti 379, 422
impact of UN sanctions 541, 551
Halcoussis, D. 168
Hale, C. 442
Halevy, T. 483
Hall, P. 248, 249, 250, 251, 252, 253,
255, 259, 264
Halpern, J. 412, 422
Haltiner, K.W. 154, 157, 162
Hamas 140
Hamber, B. 413
Hamburg, D. 577
Hampson, F.O. 578
*Handbook on the Political Economy of
War* 1
Hanighen, F.C. 217
Hanna, M.E. 237
Hannum, H. 582
Hardin, R. 130
Harkavy, R.E. 221, 223, 238
Harmon, C.C. 106
Harris, V.A. 75
Hart, O. 178
Hart, R.A. Jr. 320

Hartley, K. 2, 156, 251, 252, 256, 260,
261, 335, 336, 337, 339, 340, 343,
344, 346, 351, 352, 353
Hartz, L. 307
Hartzell, C. 480, 484, 485, 486
Harvey, F. 454, 465
Hasenclever, A. 577
Hass 458
Hathaway, A.O. 111
Hayek, F.A. von 269, 510
Hayner, P.B. 400, 421, 584
hazard rate 324
Healy, A. 118, 122
Hechter, M. 432, 434, 435, 436, 437,
438, 442, 445, 447
Heckelman, J.C. 171
hegemonic stability theory 356
"hegemonic wars" 17
Hegre, H. 114, 179, 271, 284, 530
Heilprin, J. 564
Heinlein, J. 132
Helman, G.B. 379
Henderson, C.W. 115, 116
Henderson, E.A. 116, 281, 286, 289,
291, 292, 293, 309, 310
Hensel, P. 453, 454
Herfindahl–Hirschman index 147, 518
Hermann, R.K. 74
Herring, E. 222
Hess, G.D. 49, 134, 135, 147, 180, 182,
192, 321, 341, 342, 352
Heston, A. 117
Hewitt, J.J. 14
Hewstone, M. 77
hierarchy, in international politics 372
Hillman, H.C. 530
Hirschman, A.O. 26, 515, 519, 522, 534
Hirshleifer, J. 3, 50, 114, 132, 138, 148,
192
history education reforms 398
Hitler, A. 39, 44
Hobbes, T. 43, 357, 364, 367, 371
and hegemonic stability theory 356
Hoddie, M. 480, 484, 485, 486
Hoeffler, A. 4, 62, 135, 146, 490
Hoff, P.D. 234
Hoffman, B. 127, 132, 133, 145
Hoffmann, S. 439, 590
Holbrooke, R. 581
Holcombe, R.G. 337, 338

Holl, J.E. 577
Holliday, I. 400
Holmes, S.A. 370
Holsti, O.R. 27
Holtom, P. 239
Homans, C. 574, 575
Homer-Dixon, T.F. 601
homogenization policies 67
Hooks, G. 116
Hopman, T.P. 461
Hopmann, P.T. 578
Horne, A. 129, 146
Horowitz, D.L. 4, 136, 137, 147
Horowitz, M. 324
Houston, A. 461
Howard, M. 79
Huang, C. 180
Huddy, L. 72
Hufbauer, G.C. 536, 548, 549
human rights 397, 416, 561
human rights violations 397–8
humanitarian intervention 369, 370
Humphreys, M. 489, 491
Huntington, S.P. 30, 397, 405, 406,
    410, 477, 483
"hurting stalemates" 230, 463, 466,
    573, 574, 576
Huth, P.R. 181, 317
Huyse, L. 406

Iannaccone, L.B. 142
Iceland 447–8
ideology 197–8, 209–11
Ikenberry, G.J. 281, 360, 366
Iliad 39, 53
Illicit Arms Transfers Database 239
Imbens, G. 159
IMF 371
imperial wars 297
in-group/out-group bias 77–8
inadvertent wars 17, 30
incomplete contracting 178, 184–5
incomplete information 42–3, 183
inconsistency, in beliefs 42
India
    arms trade offsets 246, 249, 252,
        258
    and Pakistan 229
individual-level theories 14, 15, 27–9
indivisibilities 21, 35, 46, 54

Indonesia 298
    arms trade offsets 246, 252–3, 255,
        256–7, 261
Industrial revolution 221
inequality 3, 203, 364–6
information 296
    and defense and alliance policy 335,
        336
    incomplete 42–3
information flows, disaggregating
    trade and militarized interstate
    disputes 1970–97 528–9
Infratest 171
institutional constraints model 23
institutions 185, 187
    and fractionalization 62–8
insurgency 97
inter-democratic wars 287
inter-group conflict 66–7
interethnic cooperation 64–5
intergovernmental organizations
    (IGOs) 273–4
internal conflict, and arms trade
    229–31
internal violence, and economic
    stagnation 5–6
International Action Network on
    Small Arms (IANSA) 237
International Campaign to Ban
    Landmines (ICBL) 237
international conflict
    and disaggregated trade flows
        515–31
    and leadership tenure 315
International Criminal Court 398
International Crisis Behavior (ICB)
    285–6, 468
International Crisis Group 460
international hierarchies 359–60
*International Journal of Conflict, and
    Violence* 4
*International Journal of Transitional
    Justice* 399, 421
    Bell 399
international mercantile economy 501
international negotiation, and conflict
    prevention 571–88
international order, theories of
    358–60
International Organization 4

International Peace Research Institute 487
international regimes
  and material circumstances 370
  and post war settlements 366
  and war 356–72
International Rescue Committee 180, 192
international security, as a rival good 362
international system 14
interstate disputes 1970–97,
    information flows and
    disaggregating trade 528–9
interstate war 476
  Africa 227
  and arms trade 226–9
  causes 13–14
  and civil war 309
Intriligator, M.D. 42
invisibilities 46
Iran 298
  impact of UN sanctions 547
  and Iraq 229
  sanctions 564–5
Iranian Revolution 130, 197–8, 211
Iraq 276, 379, 381, 388, 390, 391, 398, 421
  disarmament 562
  impact of UN sanctions 537, 548, 549–50, 551, 552
  and Iran 229
  occupation 435, 449–50
  and oil 555–6
  sanctions 536, 555–7
Iraq War 80, 83, 110, 340
Isaacs, J. 510, 511
Islam 130, 146
Israel 38, 110, 129, 135, 142, 147, 327–8, 441, 581
Italianer, A. 522
Italy 110
  conscription 160
Ito, H. 135

Jackson, M.O. 47, 48, 50, 53, 54
Jackson, P.M. 351
Jaggers, K. 423
James, A. 460, 463
James, P. 23, 168, 309, 310, 321

Janis, I.L. 79, 82, 83
Japan 249, 254, 434, 435, 437, 440, 441, 442, 443, 447
  and China 101–102
Jean, F. 3
Jelin, E. 398
Jenkins, J.C. 208
Jensen, N.M. 330, 483
Jentleson, B.W. 81, 577
Jervis, R. 14, 17, 27, 30, 72, 75, 86, 88, 361, 362, 372
Job, B.L. 321
Joes, A.J. 95, 105
Johnson, D.D.P. 75, 79, 81, 84, 87
Johnson, D.P. 326
Johnson, L.C. 146
Johnson, S. 189
Joll, J. 183
Jones, E.E. 75
Jones, P.R. 344, 351
Jones, S. 55
Jones, S.G. 382
Journal of Conflict Resolution 4
Journal of International Affairs 4
Journal of Peace Research 4
Joyce, K.A. 467
Judd, K.L. 55
Justesen, M.K. 136
Justino, P. 182

Kagel, J.H. 73
Kahl, C.H. 389
Kahler, M. 75, 234
Kahn, D. 83
Kahneman, D. 27, 72, 76, 79, 86, 132, 432
Kalyvas, S.N. 389, 432, 440, 441
Kaminski, M. 421, 422
Kang, H. 519, 523, 530
Kant, I. 22, 48
Kantian or liberal peace, compared to
    capitalist peace 273–4
Kaplan, R.D. 391
Karahan, G. 146
Karl, T.L. 397, 405, 416, 423
Katz, J.N. 309, 521
Katzenstein, P. 368
Kaufman, R. 207
Kaufmann, C. 82, 83, 310
Keck, M. 237

Keefer, P. 137, 147, 479, 480, 490, 491, 499
Keegan, J. 154
Keen, D. 3
Keith, L.C.. 115
Kellen, K. 126, 130
Keller, K. 160
Keltner, D. 77
Kennan, G.F. 310, 361
Kenya 411
Keohane, R. 363, 373, 421, 590, 591, 598
Kerstens, K. 158
Keshk, O.M.G. 278, 530
Kessler, G. 391
Keteku, G. 272
Khanna, J. 342
Kiker, B.F. 167
Kilcullen, D. 87, 382, 386, 388
Kim, H. 408, 413, 420, 422
Kim, H.M. 530
Kim, Q.-Y. 206
Kim, S.Y. 309
Kimmel, M. 206
Kindleberger, C. 365
Kinne, B. 525
Kinsella, D. 229, 231, 238, 239
Kirshner, J. 54
Kiss, E. 397
Kissinger, H.A. 572
Kleiboer, M. 453
Klemmensen, R. 136
Klingen, B. 344, 345, 352
Knack, S. 147, 479
Knapp, C.B. 167
Koch, M.T. 296
Koppl, R. 113, 114
Korea, and US 303
Kowert, P.A. 82, 84
Krain, M. 116, 463
Krasner, S.D. 54, 357, 359, 365, 379, 382, 385, 577
Krause, K. 221–2, 223, 238, 239
Krebs, R. 164
Kremenyuk, V. 578
Kressel, K. 581
Kritz, N.J. 408, 414, 415
Krueger, A.B. 135, 136
Kuhn-Tucker multiplier 120
Kuran, T. 186

Kurlat, S. 116
Kurrild-Klitgaard, P. 136
Kutan, A.M. 135
Kydd, A.H. 42, 460
Kydland, F.E. 498, 510

La Ferrara, E. 59
La Porta, R. 59, 61
Lacey, J. 84
Laitin, D.D. 4, 62, 64, 117, 131, 136, 180, 187, 192, 379, 385
Lake, D.A. 54, 295, 297, 308, 310, 359, 360, 366, 463, 468
Lalman, D. 296, 297
Lamb, G. 255, 257, 259
Lambourne, W. 403
Lammers, C.J. 433
Landes, W.M. 138
landmines 181–2
Langer, E. 393
language differences 58–9
Lapidoth, R. 582
Laqueur, W. 126, 128, 143
Lasswell, H. 434
Latin America 398, 406
Lau, M.I. 160
Lawson, R. 117
Layne, C. 287, 288, 289, 299, 310
Le Carré, J. 148
Leader, S. 352
leadership, turnover 328
leadership tenure
   and audience costs 319–21
   as a cause of international conflict 315–16
      public opinion constraints 317–19
   and conditions for war 329–30
   direct effect of international conflict on 323–9
   and diversionary war 321–2
   and domestic political institutions 324
   and dyadic democratic peace 318
   and election cycles 322–3
   formation of expectations 326–7
   methods of removal of leaders 326
Leander, A. 163
Lebanon 143
Lebow, R.N. 30, 79
Lee, D.R. 135, 140, 159

Lee, J-W. 117
Leebaw, B.A. 402, 414
Leeds, B.A. 321
Leeson, P.T. 64, 65, 66, 69, 145
legalism 403, 404, 421
Leitz, C. 530
Lemieux, T. 159
Lemke, D. 494
Lenin, V.I. 22
Levenotoglu, B. 45, 330
Levi, M. 155, 165
Leviathan 43
Levine, P. 225, 226
Levine, R. 4, 58, 59, 61, 147, 186
Levitt, S.D. 132
Levitte, J-D. 554
Levy, J.S. 13, 17, 18, 28, 29, 30, 31, 45,
    76, 79, 277, 282, 326
Li, D.D. 159
Li, Q. 134, 146, 272, 310, 483, 520, 521,
    527, 529, 530
liberal institutionalism 363
liberal states, and terrorism 134
liberalism 318, 589–90, 591
    sociological 592
Liberia 410, 489, 491
    illicit arms transfers 231–4
    impact of UN sanctions 539–40,
        551, 552, 554
Liberman, P. 442, 449, 516, 518
Libya
    impact of UN sanctions 539, 548
    sanctions 557–8
Licklider, R. 453, 465, 468, 481
Lie, T.G. 413, 520
Lieven, A. 188
Lijphart, A. 582
Lindsey, B. 274
Linz, J. 205, 405, 406, 409, 422
Lipson, C. 270, 271, 282, 330
Llussá, F. 147
Loayza, N. 137
Lobell, S.E. 30
Locke, J. 362, 363, 373
    on equality 360–61
    and neoliberal institutionalism 356
Lockhart, C. 379
Loden, A. 398
Logan, J. 379, 391
The Logic of Political Survival 324

Lokshin, M. 158
Long, A. 97
Long, S. 115
Long, W.J. 410
Lopez, G.A. 534, 536, 548, 549, 550,
    552, 553, 555, 556, 557, 560, 561
Lord, K.M. 305
Lovallo, D. 79
Lozada, G.A. 503
Ludwig, A.M. 73
Luechinger, S. 131, 134, 146
Lumsdaine, R.L. 504
Lund, M. 453, 468, 577
Lundy, P. 422
lustration 398, 421
Luttwak, E.N. 465
Lutz, E.L. 398, 409

MacDonald, P.K. 308
Machiavelli, N. 107, 169
Mack, A.J.R. 75
MacKenzie, S.P. 432
Macmillan, J. 310
Macmillan, M. 145
Mahoney, J. 405
Malamud-Goti, J. 403
Malaya 101, 103, 104, 105
Maleckov á, A. 136
Maleckov á, J. 135
Malinowski, B. 13
Mallinder, L. 400, 410, 421, 423
Malmendier, U. 79
Mandel, R. 75, 86
Mandelbaum, M. 271, 275
Mani, R. 403, 408
Manigart, P. 162
Mann, K. 67
Mansfield, E.D. 271, 309, 530
Mao Tse-tung 99–100, 101–102, 106,
    107
Maoz, Z. 22, 234, 283, 284, 285, 290,
    292, 309, 525
Mariezcurrena, J. 407, 414
Marinov, N. 324
Marion, N. 479
market system 591
marketplace of ideas 82, 83
Markowski, S. 248, 249, 250, 251, 252,
    253, 255, 259, 264
Markusen, J.R. 251, 264

Marlin-Bennett, R. 518, 523
Marsh, N. 239
Marshall, M.G. 423
Martel, W.C. 75
Martin, L.L. 330, 591
Martin, P. 530
Marx, K. 196
Marxist–Leninist theories 22
Mason, D.T. 454, 463, 467
Mason, T.D. 410
Mastanduno, M. 518
Matesan, I.E. 442
Mattes, M. 485, 486, 488
Matthews, R. 264
Matz, D.E. 460
Maurin, E. 158
Mauro, P. 58, 61
Mawdsley, J.L. 247, 248, 249, 250, 251,
    254, 256, 257, 258, 264
Mayer, P. 577
Mayer, T. 530
Mazower, M. 189, 434, 440, 447, 449
McAdam, D. 208
McAdams, A.J. 398, 400
McBride, M. 3, 184
McConnachie, K. 404
McCormick, G. 133, 145
McCormick, J.M. 116
McCormick, R.E. 346
McCoy, K.E. 109, 112
McDaniel, T. 205
McDermott, R. 29, 73, 75, 76, 85, 87,
    324
McDonald, J.A. 519, 527, 530
McDonald, P. 272, 273, 274, 275
McDonald, P.J. 517
McEvoy, K. 404
McEvoy, L. 404
McFarquhar, N. 563
McGillivray, F. 330
McKenzie, R.B. 159
McKersie, R.B. 575
McMillan, S.M. 592
McNamara, T.E. 558
McNeill, W.H. 155
McPherson, J.M. 128, 145
Mearsheimer, J.J. 18, 282, 289, 307,
    329, 363, 364, 372
mediation 487, 575–6, 581–2
Meernik, J. 321

Meerts, P. 578, 585
Megally, H. 557
Mehay, S.L. 339, 343
Meierhenrich, J. 404
Meirowitz, A.H. 51, 53
Melamud, M. 578
Melian Dialogue 16
Mellinger, A. 117
Mendeloff, D. 402, 422
Mendelson, S.E. 162
Mendez, J.E. 403
Mennecke, M. 423
mercenaries 168–9, 172
Mercer, J. 75
Merchants of Death 217
Merrouche, O. 181
Meyermans, E. 158
Mickolus, E.F. 146
Midlarsky, M. 205
Miettinen, T. 54
Migúe, J-L. 337
Miguel, E. 3, 4, 177, 179, 180, 189, 192
Mika, H. 403
Militarized Interstate Dispute (MID)
    286
military expenditure, demand for 339
military occupation 432
    and collaboration 432, 434, 438–9,
        448
        micro-level model 446
        sources of 440–41
    domestic reactions to 432–3
    and elites 441–2
    external support for resistance 443
    ideology and information control
        434–5, 447
    indirect rule 433–4, 447
    legitimating occupation regimes
        435–8, 445, 447
    model of resistance to occupation
        regimes 444–5
    occupiers' wartime prospects 442–3
    regime characteristics 433
    and social divisions 439–40
    and social order 437
    in World War II 447
military recruitment, forms of 157
Military Revolution, fifteenth century
    221
Miller, J. 113, 122

Miller, R. 321
Minehan, P.B. 189
minimal group paradigms 77
Minow, M. 400, 402, 403
Mintz, A. 74, 238
Mitchell, G.E. II 23
Mitchell, N.J. 115, 116
Mitchell, S.M. 114, 321
Miyakazi 577
Mjoset, L. 159
Mo, J. 330
monadic-level theory 16
monitoring 583–4
Montalvo, J.G. 62, 136, 147
Montgomery, A.H. 234
Montmarquette, C. 339
Moon, B.E. 276, 277
Mooradian, M. 574
Moore, B. 405
Moore, B. Jr. 196
Moore, W.H. 61, 321
Moravscik 410
Morelli, M. 39, 47, 48, 50, 53, 54
Morgan, R. 109, 110
Morgan, T.C. 21, 321
Morgenthau, H.J. 17, 590
Morris, E. 110
Morrow, J.D. 26, 325
motivation of war 75
Mousseau, M. 269, 271, 277, 285, 293
Mouzakis, F. 226
Mueller, J.E. 81, 83, 336, 341
Muller, H. 310
Muller, S.H. 59
Mulligan, C.B. 115, 164, 165
multilateral bargaining failures 47–8
Munich Agreement 39, 44
Munich Conference (1938) 15
Murdoch, J.C. 339, 343, 352
Murdock, J.M. 146
Murray, W. 84
Myerson, R.B. 40

Nafziger, E.W. 114
Nagl, J. 382
Nagorno-Kakabakh 574
Nalepa, M. 421, 422
Namibia 575
Napoleon 96, 97
Narang, V. 271

Narizny, K. 30
Nash Equilibrium 573
Nash, J. 54
Nathan, J.A. 84
"nation building" 80–81, 387
national level 14, 15
National Public Radio (NPR) 381
national security 338
nationalism 301
NATO 346, 353, 373
    explanations of support for 345
    strategic crisis management 343
Naylor, R.T. 239
Neal, J. 502, 510
Neary, H. 192
negotiation
    and conflict 572–6
    dialog 579–80
    international 572
    ripening 580
    separation and power sharing 582
Negrusa, S. 159
Neier, A. 400
Nelson, H.T. 77
Nelson, R. 271
neoliberal institutionalism 356
    and Locke, J. 356
neorealism 590
Nepal, M. 115
nested games 409
Netherlands 246, 434, 439
    formation of the Dutch Republic
        501
    Wisselbank 502
Nettle, D. 79
Neuman, S.G. 238
Neumayer, E. 109, 111
Neutrality Acts (1935–39) 217
New State Ice Co. v. Liebmann 371
New Zealand 248, 250, 251
Newman, E. 483
NGOs (non-governmental
    organizations) 190
Ni Aolain, F. 416, 421
Nicaragua 179, 198, 211, 298
Nicholson, M. 85
Nincic, M. 81
Nino, C. 406
Niou, E.M.S. 55
Niskanen, W.A. 337

Nitsch, V. 135
Nooruddin, I. 479, 480, 483, 484, 490, 491, 494
Nordhaus, W.D. 353
Nordquist, K.A. 578
Nordstrom, T. 274, 530
norms 366–70
North, D.C. 363, 410, 510
North, J. 110
North Korea, impact of UN sanctions 546, 548, 552, 554, 562–3
North, R.C. 515, 516
Northern Ireland 110, 398, 404
Norval, A.J. 405, 422
Norway, arms trade offsets 248, 250
Norwegian Initiative on Small Arms Transfers (NISAT) 225
Nuclear Non-Proliferation Treaty (NPT) 562
Nye, J.S. 598, 599

O'Ballance, E. 105
Obama, B. 381, 393
O'Brien, J. 581
O'Brien, P. 510
OCCAR 251
Odean, T. 79
O'Donnell, G.A. 397
Oduro, A. 61
Office of the Coordinator of Counterterrorism 127
Office of the Director of National Intelligence (ODNI) 381
Ohlson, T. 238
Oi, W.Y. 161
oil 520, 522
    and Iraq 555–6
Olsen, T. 407
Olson, M. 2, 130, 140, 337, 343, 352
Olson, M. Jr. 479
Oneal, J.R. 15, 22, 23, 25, 26, 117, 171, 270, 271, 272, 273, 274, 277, 285, 286, 290, 291, 292, 293, 309, 310, 321, 352, 515, 521, 526, 530, 592
O'Neill, B. 95, 100, 422
Ordeshook, P.C. 55, 336
Oren, I. 288, 299
Orentlicher, D.F. 403, 422
Organski, A.F.K. 18
O'Rourke, C. 413, 421

Orphanides, A. 49, 135, 321, 341, 342, 352
Orwell, G. 435
Osiel, M. 400
Ostrom, C.W. Jr. 321
O'Sullivan, M.L. 549, 556
Ottaway, M. 483
overconfidence 78–9
Owen, J. IV 22
Owen, J.M. 295, 299, 303, 318

Padró i Miquel, G. 45, 51, 54
paid-rider option 140, 148
Paige, J. 195, 196, 212
Pakistan 381
    and India 229
Palestine 443–4, 448
Palmer, G. 320
Pape, R.A. 128, 133, 142, 145
paradox of power 132
Paris, R. 409, 483, 484
Parise, G.F. 135
Park, T. 520, 522
Parsa, M. 195, 196, 197, 202, 207
Partell, P.J. 320
Pascual, C. 379, 382
Patrick, S. 379, 392
patriotism 302, 336, 339, 351, 352
Paul, T.V. 75
Pax Britannica 361
Payne, L. 407, 420
peace, and trade 272–3
peace agreements 498
peacekeeping 583, 585
    background literature 589–93
    and ecological stress 600–603
    economics of 589
        creation of economic relationships 593–6
    emphasis on development 598–600
    and free riding 343
    independence in critical goods 596–7
    and post-conflict recovery 476
    principles of 593–603
peacekeeping missions 342–3, 487–9, 493
Pearson, F.S. 226, 227, 229, 230
Peck, M.J. 2
Peled, A. 172

Percy, S. 169
Perez, E. 443
Perlo-Freeman 249, 252, 255, 256
Persson, T. 61, 115, 189, 499
Peru 105, 575, 578
Peters, G. 555
Petersen, R.D. 442
Pham, P. 412
philanthropy 392
Philippines 103, 104, 105, 197, 211
Piazza, J.A. 383
Pillar, P.R. 133, 143, 572
Pindyck, R. 479
Pinker, S. 86
Pion-Berlin, D. 409
Piven, F.F. 208
Poe, S.C. 115, 116, 408
Polachek, S.W. 25, 293, 515, 517, 519,
    520, 521, 522, 523, 527, 529, 530,
    592
Poland, arms trade offsets 247, 248,
    249, 250–51, 252, 255, 260
politically relevant dyads 283–4, 285,
    289, 309
politicians, and defense and alliance
    policy 336–7
Politics of Bureaucracy 343
Pollins, B.M. 278, 530
Popkin, M. 402
Popular Front for the Liberation of
    Palestine (PFLP) 129
population displacement 181, 578–9
Posen, B.R. 392, 477
Posner, D.N. 60
Posner, R.A. 161
Post, J.M. 73
post-conflict reconstruction 6, 343,
    583–4
    community driven reconstruction
        (CDR) 491
    and the credible commitment
        problem 480
post-conflict recovery 474
    civil war and credible commitments
        476–81
    commitment problem 475
    disarmament, demobilization and
        reintegration programs (DDR)
        476
    and elections 475

external interventions 486–91
and peacekeeping 476
and power-sharing arrangements
    475, 484–6
Poutvaara, P. 157, 160, 171
Powell, R. 3, 21, 43, 45, 50, 54, 55, 86,
    184, 364, 476
power
    distribution of 17, 21, 360
    endogenous 49–51
power transition theory 18
power-sharing 475, 484–6, 493, 582–3
    endogeneity 486
    types of 485
Preble, C. 379, 391
preemptive accountability 581
preemptive war 44
Prescott, E. 498, 510
prevention 576–84
    early or structural 577–9
    early–late or crisis 579–81
    late post-crisis 582–4
    problems 585
    and warning 571
preventive logic 18
preventive war 45
price discovery approach 510
principal-agent models 322
Prins, B.C. 272, 273, 320
Prinzen, T. 576
Prisoner's Dilemma Game 573–4
private information path 20
private property rights 63–4, 137, 144
property rights 363
    and civil war 177–8, 191
prosecution of war 80
prospect theory 27–9, 76
proxy war 1
Pruit, D.G. 581
Pruitt, D. 461
Prunier, G. 177, 190, 192
Przeworski, A. 373, 494
psychological biases 72, 73–4
    and decision-making 78–9, 84–6
    enemies 77–8
    in-group/out-group bias 77–8
    regime type 82–4
    risk-taking 76–7
    sources of variation 82–5
    threat assessment 75–6

urgency 85
and war 74–81
psychological variables 20
Public Choice 4
public choice analysis, on defense and
alliance policy 335–50
public debt 2
public goods, and social diversity
60–61
public opinion constraints 317–19
public servants 337, 351
Pugel, J. 489
Putnam, R.D. 117
Putnam, T. 398

Querou 54, 55
Quinn, J. 410, 420, 421

Rabbie, J.M. 78
Raknerud, A. 284
Raman, B. 507
Rapoport, D.C. 129, 132, 133, 134,
145, 146, 147
Rasler, K.A. 19, 30, 116
Rathbone, A. 130
rational choice, and terrorism 126
rationality 35–9, 72
Ratner, S.R. 379
Ray, D. 39, 55, 69, 136, 147, 186
Ray, J.L. 22, 75, 270, 271, 281, 282,
284, 287, 288, 290, 309
Reagan 467
realism 363–4, 589, 590, 591
realist theories 16–17, 19
reasons for war 34
recognitional legitmacy 404, 422
reconciliation 403, 404, 410, 412, 422,
548
reconstruction *see* post-conflict
reconstruction
Record, J.107 100
Redd, S.B. 74
Reed, W. 317, 494
reference dependence 28
Regan, P.M. 116, 351, 453, 454, 458,
462, 465, 466, 467, 468, 487
regime change
and asset prices 500, 503
and sanctions 549
and transitional justice 405, 420

regime type 82–4
regression analysis 4, 5
regulative effect 369–70
Reich, W. 128
Reid, P. 110
Reifsneider, J. 453, 454
Reilly, B. 483
Reinhardt, E. 321
Reiter, A. 407, 421
Reiter, D. 23, 82, 277, 298, 310
Rejali, D. 109, 113, 116
religion 36–8, 186–7
remediation 584
Renner, M. 599
Reno, W. 593
Renshon, J. 79
rent seeking 61
reparations 398, 411, 421
repression 205–12
and arms trade 230–31
resource competition 3, 478, 516
resources 499
Reuschemeyer, D. 405
Reuveny, R. 310, 517, 519, 520, 521,
522, 523, 527, 529, 530
revenge 38–9
revolutions
alternative theoretical model 200
and the capitalist class 204
and class conflict 196
consolidation and coalition
formation 206–208
defined 195
in developing countries 195–6, 198–9
and ideology 197–8, 209–211
political outcomes 211
social 195–6
and social conflicts 201–204
and the state 196–206
state intervention 201–205
structural models 196–7
working class mobilization 203–204
Reynal-Querol, M. 62, 136, 147, 189
Rice, C. 281
Rice, M. 555
Rich, A. 135
Rich, R. 483
Richards, D. 322
Richards, D.L. 115, 116, 117
Richardson, L.F. 351

Ricks, T.E. 442, 450
Riker, W.H. 336, 344
Riley, J.C. 510
Rioux, J. 317
Ripsman, N. 518
risk-taking 76–7
Risse-Kappen, T. 23
Ristovic, M. 448
Rittberger, B. 596
Rittberger, V. 577
Robberts, R. 67
Robert, R.S. 402
Roberts, A. 84, 205, 462, 463
Roberts, J. 59
Roberts, K. 205
Robinson, J. 3, 188, 189
Robinson, J.A. 420
Robinson, R.E. 434
Robinson, R.J. 77
Rock, S.R. 299
Rocke, D.M. 55
Rodley, N. 400
Rodrik, D. 60
Roeder, P.G. 405
Roehner, B.M. 447, 448
Rogerson, W.P. 340
Rogowski, R. 25
Rohner, D. 39
Roht-Arriaza, N. 402, 407, 410, 413, 414
Roland, G. 61, 180
Rolf, D. 110
Ron, J. 409
Rosato, S. 308, 310, 319
Rose, G.F. 55
Rosen, H.S. 504
Rosen, S.P. 74, 85
Rosenblatt, A. 518
Rosenrance, R. 534, 592
Rosolia, A. 160
Ross, A.L. 226
Rotberg, R.I. 379, 422
Roth, A.E. 73
Rothchild, D.S. 463, 468, 480, 484, 572
Rothenberg, R.B. 239
Rothstein, B. 436
Rousseau, D.L. 285, 286, 530
Rousseau, J-J. 373, 436
Rowlands, D. 459, 460, 464
Rowley, C.K. 130, 146

Royko, M. 329
Rrejali 116
Rubin, B.R. 421
Rubin, J.Z. 466, 580, 581
Rubin, M. 77
Rueschemeyer, D. 196, 202
Rueveny 529
Rufin, J.-C. 3
Ruggie, J.G. 368, 462, 464
rule of law paradox 398
Rummel, R.J. 116, 272
Runciman, S. 37
Russett, B.M. 15, 22, 23, 25, 26, 48, 81, 117, 181, 201, 270, 271, 272, 273, 274, 277, 278, 282, 283, 284, 285, 286, 287, 288, 290, 291, 292, 293, 294, 295, 296, 297, 308, 309, 310, 321, 351, 515, 521, 526, 592
Russett, N.M. 285, 530
Russia 110, 235
conscription 158, 167
Rwanda 187, 190–91, 192, 398, 536
impact of UN sanctions 542, 553

Sachs, J.D. 117
Sacko, D.H. 115
Safran, W. 319
Sagan, S.D. 373
Sahnoun, M. 577
Sahuguet, N. 48
Sala-i-Martin, X. 115
Sambanis, H. 147
Sambanis, N. 464, 487, 488
Sanchez-Pages, S. 54
sanctions
arms embargoes 551–2
commodity 552
and containment 549
counterterrorism and due process rights 559–61, 566
diamond industry 553
Iraq 536, 555–7
Libya 557–8
monitoring implementation 553–4
multilateral 535–6
multilateral economic 565–6
and policy change 549
and regime change 549
role of 534
targeted 549–53

targeted financial sanctions 550–51
UN 535–6
    evaluation 536
    failure of 549
    impact of 537–47
    USA 534
    and weapons proliferation 561–5
Sandel, M.J. 163, 169
Sandler, T. 2, 127, 128, 130, 132, 133,
    134, 135, 138, 139, 140, 141, 142,
    143, 145, 146, 147, 148, 156, 226,
    339, 340, 342, 343, 346, 351, 352,
    353
Sanjian, G.S. 228–9, 238
Sarna, N. 479
Satori, A.E. 51, 53
Satterthwaite, M.A. 40
Satyanath, S. 177
Saudi Arabia 264
Saunders, H. 579
Savun, B. 485, 486, 488, 494
Saxena, S.C. 180
Schabas, W. 422
Scharf, M.P. 400, 402, 422
Schedler, A. 409
Schelling, T.C. 2, 31, 42, 54, 113, 518,
    519
Scherer, F.M. 2
Schiff, B.N. 398
Schleifer, A. 164, 165
Schmidt, C. 86
Schmitter, P.C. 397
Schneider, G. 26, 530
Schneider, T. 164
Schrodt, P.A. 239
Schultz, K.A. 24, 295, 296, 305, 317,
    320, 321, 330, 372, 483
Schumacher, D. 135
Schumpeter, J.A. 515, 517
Schwartz, M. 208
Schwarz, M. 54
Schweller, R.L. 308
Scoblic, J.P. 555
Scowcroft, B. 379
Sears, D.O. 72, 73, 75, 86
security guarantees 487
security sector reforms 398
Segura, G.M. 317, 328
Seiglie, C. 519, 530
Selbin, E. 206

selectorate theory 47, 324–5
self-enforcement 43–4
self-interest 126, 130
Sen, G. 516
Sen, S. 225
Senese, P.D. 19
Serafino, N.M. 390, 391
Serbia 448
Sergenti, E. 177
Seton-Watson, H. 441
shared sovereignty 385
Shaw, G.B. 217–18
Shaw, R. 413
Sherborne, L. 116
Sherwin, R. 239
Shiller, R.J. 72, 86, 87
Shimko, K.L. 307
Shklar, J. 421
Shleifer, A. 61
Short, A. 105
Shue, H. 109, 112
Shughart, W.F. 129, 131, 137, 140, 144
Sieff, M. 406
Siemers, L.R. 116
Sierra Leone 489, 536
    impact of UN sanctions 543, 548,
        553, 554
Sigal, L. 562
Signorino, C.S. 526
Sikkink, K. 237, 238, 398, 407, 409,
        411, 413, 414, 420, 421
Silberner, E. 25
Silverstone, S.A. 45
Simmons, B. 410
Simmons, J.W. 494
Simpson, E. 115
Singapore 246, 249, 258
Singer, J.D. 14, 78, 117
Singer, P.W. 169, 190
Siquereia, K. 465, 469
Sisk, T.D. 484
Sislin, J. 229, 230
Siverson, R.M. 55, 296, 310, 317, 325,
    525
Six-Day War 129
Sjöström, T. 42, 43
Skaperdas, S. 3, 50, 55, 114, 177, 184,
    192
Skocpol, T. 195, 196–7, 198
Sköns 249, 252, 256, 258

Slantchev, B.L. 20, 45, 54, 301, 307, 308, 317, 320, 328
slavery 188
Small Arms Survey 224–5
Small, M. 78
Smith, A. 2, 42, 146, 157, 320, 322, 325, 330, 594–5
Smith, J.M. 52
Smith, N. 146
Smith, R. 225, 226, 393
Smith, R.P. 160
Smulovitz, C. 423
Snidal, D. 364, 365
Snyder, G. 572
Snyder, J. 30, 82, 271, 303, 308, 309, 400, 409, 410, 412, 413, 414, 454
Snyder, R. 205, 405
social chance 188–9
social differences 58
social distance 58–9
social diversity, and public goods 60–61
social identity theory 77
social network analysis, and arms trade 231–7
Solberg, E. 309
Solomon, B. 342
Somalia 81, 329, 381, 536, 554
and Ethiopia 229
Sonin, K. 54
Soubeyran, R. 54
South Africa 535
arms trade offsets 247, 248, 250, 252, 255, 257, 259
Truth and Reconciliation Commission 398, 405, 406, 412, 422
South Korea, arms trade offsets 247, 249, 250, 252, 254
Souva, M. 272, 273, 291
sovereignty 358–9, 371–2, 432, 445
dual 410
shared 385
Soviet Union 110, 189
Soylu, U. 346
Spain 135
Spanish–American War 287, 288
Spear, J. 490
Spector, B.I. 577
Spencer, D.L. 167

spiral theory of war 39, 42–3
Spiro, D.E. 309
Spolaore, E. 60
Squires, M.J. 239
Sri Lanka 443
credible commitment and financial asset markets, case study 504–9
stability 47, 51, 55
Staibano, C. 534, 549
Stam, A.C. 23, 30, 42, 78, 82, 115, 277, 286, 298, 310, 317, 318, 324, 328, 454, 467, 526, 530
Stapley, C.S. 237
Stasavage, D. 479
state capacity paradox 398
state failure *see* failed states
"State Failure Task Force Report" 380
states 589–90
administrative 201
bargaining 387
definition of 367
in developing countries 203
exclusive 205–206
formation of 287
homogenization 387
hyperactive 201, 202, 203, 204
regulative 201, 202
Stedman, S. 464
Stein, A. 86
Stenelo, L. 581
Stephens, E.H. 405
Stephens, J.D. 405
"steps to war" model 19
Stevenson, R.T. 324
Stewart, F. 4, 179, 180
Stewart, R. 386
Stiglitz, J.E. 80, 180
Stirk, P.M.R. 445
Stock, J.H. 504
Stockholm International Peace Research Institute (SIRPI) 220, 224
Stoessinger, J.G. 79
Stoll, R.J. 321
Stone, R. 325
Stover, E. 413, 421
Strange, S. 365
Straubhaar, T. 167
Streich, P. 31
Stromseth, J. 413

Stroup, M.D. 171
Struys 252
Stuckey, J. 117
Stutzer, A. 134
Subotic, J. 420
Sudan 381, 536
    impact of UN sanctions 542, 545,
        551, 554
Summers, R. 117
Sutil, J.C. 406
Svenson, I. 461
Svensson, I. 487
Svensson, J. 491
Swamy, A.V. 479
Sweden, arms trade offsets 246, 248,
    250, 252, 254, 258
Swedish Ministry of Foreign Affairs
    577
Syropoulos, C. 184
system-level theories 16–19
Szvircsev Tresch, T. 162

Tabarrok, A. 112, 122
Tabellini, G. 60, 61, 499
Taiwan 442
    arms trade offsets 246, 249, 254, 255,
        258
Tajfel, H. 77
Taliaferro, J.W. 76
Tamil Tigers 131
Tammen, R.L. 15, 18, 19
Tarar, A. 55, 322, 330
Tate, C.N. 115, 116
Tate, G. 79
Tavares, J. 135, 147
Taylor, A.J.P. 45
Taylor, S.E. 72, 73, 79
technology gap 261
technology transfer 257–9
Teitel, R.G. 397, 398, 400, 421, 422
territorial conflicts 578
terrorism
    and airport security 138–9, 147
    Algeria 129
    costs of 131, 134–5
    defined 95, 127–37
    economic model of 128–37
    and liberal states 134
    macro terrorism 134–5
    micro terrorism 129–33

paid-rider option 140, 148
and personality 128
political economy of 135–7
psychology and sociology of 128
in a rational choice perspective 126
rational terrorists 138–41
suicide attacks 128, 133, 141–3
target selection 131–3
transnational 133, 146
terrorist attacks of 9/11 379, 380
terrorists, compared to guerrillas 95
Tetlock, P.E. 73, 74, 82, 86
Thacker, S. 135
t'Hart, P. 79, 82, 83
Theidon 398
third-party intervention
    arbitration 459
    and balance of power 462, 463
    and civil wars 467–8
    conciliation 459
    and consent 459–60
    consultations 459
    and contingency 458
    definition of 454–6
    economic measures 465
    effectiveness 453–70
        dimensions of 457
    endogeneity 459
    evaluation 456–7, 467
    force 469
    legal and normative significance of
        third party 456
    loss of consent 463
    mediation 458, 459, 460, 461, 463–4,
        467, 468
    outcomes 466–7
    peacekeeping 459, 460, 462
    political implications 454
    selection effect 469
    timing 465–6
    types of intervention 457–65
third-party security interventions
    487–9
Thirty Years War 37–8
Thoenig, M. 530
Thomas, H. 102
Thompson, D. 402, 422
Thompson, L. 460
Thompson, W.R. 17, 18, 19, 30, 310
Thoms, O. 409, 415

threat assessment 75–6
Thucydides 16
Thuenen, J.H. von 167
Ticchi, D. 52
Tierney, D.R. 75, 81, 87, 326
Tillema, H.K. 229
Tilly, C. 195, 387
Tinbergen, N. 86
Tobias, S. 352
Toft, M. 578
Toft, M.D. 75
Tollison, R.D. 146, 161, 168, 352
Tomz, M. 320
torture 397
    as an enforcement mechanism 113
    in conflict literature 113–14
    and conventions 111–12
    defined 109
    and democracies 114–15
    determinants of 114–17
    and economic development 116
    history of 109–10
    for information gathering 118
    optimal choice under different
        probabilities 121
    positive arguments on 112–13
    prisoner's dilemma applied to
        119–20
    selected pair-wise correlates for 117
Touval, S. 461, 464, 575, 576, 581
trade 25, 26, 65, 66, 270, 272, 590
    and bilateral cooperation 293
    and capitalist peace 275, 515
    composition of 529
    and conflict 516–21
    dependency and conflict 519–21
    disaggregated trade linkages 521,
        526–7
        data on 526–7
        heterogeneous effect of 526
        information flows, and militarized
            interstate disputes 1970–97
            528–9
    effects on conflict 527
    free trade 517
    heterogeneous trade interests 524–9
    "maximum flow" 525–6, 527, 530
    models linking trade to conflict
        522–4
    and peace 272–3, 515

simultaneity bias 523
strategic or critical goods 596–8
strategic goods and gains from
    conquest 516–19
strategic importance of goods
    515–16
    and World War I 274
trade networks 525
transaction costs 178
transitional justice
    in the 1990s 398
    accountability mechanisms 397, 398,
        402, 410
    amnesties 400, 413
    causal theories of 405–415
    and choice 406–409
    classifying type of transition 415–16
    consequences 412–15
    criminal trials 400, 402, 407, 413,
        421
    definition of 421
    field of 399–405
    history 404–405
    justice, truth and reconciliation
        402–404
    justice-as-social-restoration model
        403
    lustration 398, 421
    mechanism and function 400–402
    negativity bias 415
    as nested 409–12
    reassessment of 415–19
    and reconciliation 404
    and regime change 405
    reparations 398, 411, 421
    restorative model 403
    retributive models 403
    success and failure 416–19
    truth commissions 400, 407, 413, 421
    universe of transition regions
        1970–2007 417
Trebbi, F. 62
trend indicator values (TIVs) 224
Trojan war 39
"tropical storm problem" 571
truth commissions 400, 421, 584
Tschirhart, J.T. 145
Tsebelis, G. 409, 411
Tsiddon, D. 135
Tsui, K.K. 115

Tsutsui, K. 111
Tuchman, B. 75, 79, 85
Tucker, R. 309, 310, 521
Tullock, G. 131, 144, 343
Tully, J. 404
Turk, A.T. 128
Turkey 142
Turner, C. 404
Turner, J.C. 77
Tversky, A. 27, 76, 79, 86, 132, 432
Tyler, T.R. 438
Tyson, L.D. 418

Uchitel, A. 592
Uganda 398
uncertainty 16
United Arab Emirates 257
United East India Company 501–502
United Kingdom
    arms trade offsets 247, 248, 249, 250,
        251–2, 254, 256, 257–8
    colonial empire 595
    Imperialism 303
    and the US 299
    War with United States (1812) 288
United Nations High Commission for
        Refugees (UNHCR) 181
United Nations (UN) 219, 371, 462,
        463, 577
    and Bosnia 462
    Convention Against Torture (CAT)
        111, 122
    Department of Disarmament Affairs
        239
    impact of sanctions 537–47
    sanctions 535–6, 537–47, 549
United States 17–18, 162, 189, 250,
        251, 263, 298–9, 304
    Bureau of Industry and Security
        (BIS) 245, 259, 263
    and China 275
    climate change policy 76–7
    Congressional Research Service
        (CRS) 224
    decision-making 84
    defense industry 344
    Department of Defense (USDOD)
        390
    Department of State 223
    foreign policy 281

Government Accountability Office
        (USGAO) 391
Government Interagency
        Counterinsurgency Initiative
        (COIN) 382
Interagency Counter Insurgency
        Initiative (USICI) 381
    and Iraq 27
    and Korea 303
    Lend-Lease Act 217
    National Security Strategy 381
    Office of the Coordinator
        for Reconstruction and
        Stabilization (S/CRS) 390–91
    Pearl Harbor 83
    probability of presidents going to
        war (1953–88) 342
    Provincial Reconstruction Teams
        391
    sanctions 534
    Statistical Office 526
    and the United Kingdom 299
    and Vietnam 303
    War Powers Resolution (1972) 304
    War with the United Kingdom
        (1812) 288
Unspeakable Truths 400
urban guerrilla war 103
urgency 85
US–Warsaw Pact 517

Valeriano, B. 578
Van Creveld, M. 172
Van de Walle, N. 324
Van den Steen, E. 79
van der Klaauw, W. 159
Van der Merwe, H. 412
Van Evera, S. 78, 79, 330
van Holde, S. 159
Van Roozendaal, P. 324
van Zyl, P. 400
Vargas, J.F. 189
Vasquez, J. 578
Vasquez, J.A. 13, 19, 30, 78
Vasquez, J.P. 168
Vaubel, R. 346, 353
Vedlitz, A. 74
Verstegen, S. 571
victory 296
Vidal, G. 132

Vietnam 81, 105, 164, 171, 180, 303
Vinck, P. 412
Vindigni, A. 52
Viner, J. 353
Vinjamuri, L. 400, 409, 410, 412, 413, 414
Virgili, F. 448
Vishny, R. 61
Vlaicu, R. 499
volunteers 156, 158, 171
Vorhees, J. 579
voters 335–6
  demand for security 338
  optimization calculus 338–9
  preference for security 339–40
Vreeland, J.R. 111, 494

Wagener, A. 157, 160, 171
Wagner, R.H. 19, 21, 42
Wall Street Journal 80, 277
Wallensteen, P. 534, 549, 552
Walling, C.B. 407, 411, 414, 421
Walt, S.M. 18, 30
Walter, B.F. 75, 453, 454, 463, 467, 478, 479, 482, 483, 486, 487
Walton, J. 204, 206, 212
Walton, R.E. 575
Waltz, K.N. 14, 17, 42, 86, 272, 282, 358, 359, 361, 371, 372, 373, 392, 590
Wang, J. 518
Wang, K. 75
Wang, M. 180
Wantchekon, L. 118, 122
war
  concept of 1
  definitions of 13, 283
  duration of 52–3
  as part of bargaining process 45–6
  as a political instrument 13
  probability of US presidents going to war 342
  types of 80–81, 87
  versus armed peace 182–5
war of attrition 52, 61
war games 87
War Resister's International (WRI) 164
"war on terror" 382, 383
Ward, H. 515, 525, 526, 530, 531

Ward, M.D. 234, 321, 520, 525
Warner, J.T. 157, 159
Warner, L.A. 98
Warneryd, K. 183
warning, and prevention 571
wartime finance, and financial markets 501–502
Warwick, P.V. 324
Wassenaar Agreement 518
Waterman, P. 321
Watkins, M. 464
Wayne, E.A. 559
Wealth of Nations 2, 595
The Weapons Acquisition Process 2
weapons of mass destruction (WMD) 578
weapons proliferation 561–5
Weart, S.R. 284, 294
Weber, M. 367, 368, 369, 434, 436
  and constructivism 356
Weede, E. 25, 269, 276
Weeks, J.L. 301, 320
Weerapana, A. 135, 147, 180
Weinberg, L.B. 134, 146, 147
Weingarten, J.P. 454, 463, 467
Weingast, B.R. 117, 188, 410, 510
Weingast, R. 372
Weinstein, D.E. 522
Weinstein, H.M. 412, 413, 422
Weinstein, J.M. 489, 491
Weisberg, J. 329
Weiss, M.A. 390, 490
Weiss, T.G. 555
Welch, D.A. 75
welfare costs of conflict 182
Wells, J. 510
Wendt, A. 357, 360, 368, 371, 372, 373
Werner, S. 114, 317
White, E.N. 501, 510
White, R.K. 79
Whitehead, L. 397
Widmaier, U. 321
Widner, J.A. 411
Wiebelhaus-Brahm, E. 403
Wilkenfeld, J. 14, 466, 468
Wilkinson, P. 134, 147
Willard, K.L. 504
Willenbockel, D. 160
Williams, P.R. 410
Willis, H. 77

Wills, D. 510
Wilson, M.L. 78
Wilson, R. 404
Wilson, T.D. 74
Wilson, W. 370
Winters, K. 464
Wintrobe, R. 142
Wippman, D. 413
Wohlforth, W.C. 18
Wolf, A.T. 601
Wolf, E. 212
Wolff, J. 310
Wolford, S. 323
Wolfson, M. 309
Woller, G. 310
Woods, K. 84
Woodward, B. 79, 80, 83
Woodward, S.L. 490
Woolley, J.T. 555
World Bank 474, 490, 491
World Military Expenditures and Arms Transfers (WMEAT) 223
World Trade Organization (WTO) 371
World War I 183, 274, 288–9
  and France 275
  and trade 274
World War II
  arms supplies during and after 221
  and capitalist peace 274
  treatment of POWs 110, 121

Woroniak, A. 167
Wrangham, R.W. 78, 79

Xenogiani, T. 158
Xiang, J. 272
Xu, X. 272
Xun, C. 525

Yakovlev, P.A. 115
Yared, P. 54
Yemtsov, R. 158
Yom Kippur War 327–8
Yoon, D.H. 309
Yugoslavia 398, 536
  impact of UN sanctions 538, 543, 548, 552

Zakaria, F. 130, 142
Zalaquett, J. 402, 405, 406
Zanardi, M. 48
Zanger, S.C. 116
Zartman, I.W. 230, 458, 461, 464, 466, 571, 572, 574, 575, 576, 577, 580, 581, 583, 585
Zarzecki, T.W. 222
Zeckhauser, R. 2, 343, 352
Zehr, H. 403
Zelditch, M. Jr. 435
Zerilli, L. 404, 422
Zimbabwe 381
Zysman, J. 211, 518